READINGS IN
THE PSYCHOLOGY
OF ADJUSTMENT

READINGS IN
THE PSYCHOLOGY
OF ADJUSTMENT SECOND EDITION

Edited by

LEON GORLOW   Pennsylvania State University

WALTER KATKOVSKY   Fordham University

McGRAW-HILL BOOK COMPANY

New York   St. Louis   San Francisco   Toronto
London   Sydney

**READINGS IN
THE PSYCHOLOGY
OF ADJUSTMENT**

Library of Congress Catalog Card Number 67–22956

1 2 3 4 5 6 7 8 9 0 MPMM 7 4 3 2 1 0 6 9 8 7

PREFACE

One of the heavy demands upon departments of psychology is to provide instruction in the area of personal adjustment and mental hygiene. The demand comes from a variety of sources: students who require a general introduction to the study of human behavior, students who seek a better understanding of their own problems, and students who seek an orientation to the area of adjustment as a basis for advanced training in psychology. The first group includes persons who are entering fields which necessitate an understanding of personal relationships, such as teaching, school administration, guidance and counseling, business and personnel work, and nursing. The second group includes students having difficulty adjusting to college work, students seeking aid with personal problems, and those who need guides to more effective living. The third group consists of undergraduate students who wish to pursue advanced training in the behavioral sciences.

The content of the psychology of adjustment is vast. It includes material from many other disciplines and overlaps other areas of psychological inquiry. Consequently the courses of instruction and textbooks variously labeled "mental hygiene" or "adjustment" generally are limited in the amount of material they are able to encompass. There is a need for a more comprehensive presentation of material relating to human adjustment than is provided by most texts. We believe the student's interests are served by a presentation of varied issues and controversies in the field. Our hope is that we have produced a book of readings which will serve this purpose.

This volume introduces the reader to the main currents of thought in the psychology of adjustment and may be used in several ways. It may be used as a supplementary text which contains source material for discussion. In addition, since the readings have been structured in orderly fashion, the book may be used as a basic text in courses on mental hygiene, the psychology of adjustment, personal adjustment, mental health and education, etc. Finally, the general reader who is interested in the contributions of psychology to the pressing social problems related to psychological health and illness will find it rewarding.

An introduction to each section alerts the reader to the highlights of the papers in that section and indicates some of the relationships among the papers. In several instances, the introductory sections contain comments on the ideas of a particular author or make additional points concerning the issues which he raised. The student may wish to read the introduction to a section before turning to the papers in that section, or he may find that the opening statements serve as a brief review after he has completed a given section.

We should like to acknowledge the kindness of the authors, editors, and publishers whose permission to reproduce the reading selections made this volume possible. Specific permission citations are noted at the bottom of the first page of each selection. We hope that the organization, editing, and introductory materials, which have been prepared jointly by the editors, facilitate the understanding of the ideas presented by the authors of the papers.

Leon Gorlow

Walter Katkovsky

CONTENTS

INTRODUCTION

The span of eight years since the first edition of this book is not a long interval in terms of dramatic changes in scientific knowledge. No one expects major revisions in theories or the abandonment of traditional ideas and practices without extensive checking and cross-checking over an extended period. In fact, the tendency for individual scientists to identify with specific theories and to resist ideas which differ from their theoretical orientations is not uncommon, and for this reason, changes are likely to occur across, rather than within, generations. At the same time, many forces in present-day society are encouraging scientific inquiry and research—more than at any other time in our history—and while the social sciences fall far behind the natural sciences in the support they have received, it is likely that such fields as psychology, psychiatry, sociology, and anthropology have benefited and have advanced as a result of the current emphasis on science.

In any field, the impact of new ideas, methods, and findings is slow and unsystematic. Science, as well as less disciplined activities, tends to have its fads, and a particular theory or technique may become extremely popular and then quietly fade from the scene after having failed to fulfill its initial promise. On the other hand, ideas which attract little attention initially sometimes grow into important contributions. When a field of study takes its content from many other subjects, as does the study of psychological adjustment, the changes over time are even more difficult to evaluate and predict.

In reviewing the literature on adjustment, we have asked ourselves, What have been the significant changes and dominant trends in the field since 1958? Our major conclusions are that controversies have become even more apparent, that positions taken by different theorists are more diverse, and that the problems associated with the field are more prominent and demanding. Do these conclusions mean there has been no progress? Should we be pessimistic about future developments? We think not. We believe that the increase in argument and the heightened awareness of problems in the field are signs of growth and that future contributions must build on these. In the first edition of this book, we intentionally emphasized the numerous questions, problems, and controversies in the area of adjustment because we felt that the controversial issues and unsolved problems defined the field as it then existed and would determine its development. We have adhered to this position in the revision and hope that by bringing together varied and opposing points of view, the book will make the study of adjustment stimulating and challenging to the student.

Although the basic organization of the first edition has been retained, some changes have been introduced to correspond with changes in the field and in the way psychology is taught at most universities. Less space has been devoted to the section on scientific method since this topic has been given increased attention in introductory courses in psychology, and we therefore assume that the student has been exposed to it prior to his enrollment in courses on adjustment. Rather than present a separate group of readings to illustrate methods of scientific inquiry, we have integrated a number of research papers and case reports into the other major sections of the volume. For example, several research articles deal with empirical efforts to define adjustment and mental health and to delineate factors which characterize psychopathology. Another change is that the present edition has no separate section on adjustment and development; articles dealing with development have been included as determinants of adjustment. This change does not mean to imply that developmental psychology has become any less important in contributing to our understanding of adjustment. Rather, growth in developmental psychology and work in this field pertinent to adjustment have become too varied and extensive to attempt to cover in a few articles. We have, therefore, limited the readings from developmental psychology to two of the most stimulating reports in recent years, one on the work in Harlow's laboratory on rearing practices and one on Erikson's theoretical ideas concerning stages of psychosocial development.

Our primary aim has been to bring to the reader a survey of the most recent trends and ideas in the study of adjustment. All of the theories and issues presented are of topical interest and concern to persons working in the field. The new topics which have been introduced in this edition include reports of research on creativity and conformity, the importance of self-disclosure to mental health, investigations of suicide, family psychotherapy, and behavior therapy. While the three theories which have made the major contribution to the study of adjustment remain psychoanalysis, phenomenology, and learning theory, several additional theoretical orientations and developments have gained widespread attention. The contributions of existentialism to psychology and psychotherapy are described, and summaries of George Kelly's personal construct theory and Julian Rotter's social learning theory are presented. In addition, one paper reports on some of the latest developments in psychoanalytic theory or, as these developments are often called, ego psychology. The final section of the book draws the reader's attention to several current issues which warrant the concern of both scientist and layman. These pertain to methods of obtaining scientific knowledge on adjustment as well as to problems in the application of such knowledge. Included are papers on deception in research, the relationship between abnormal psychology and criminal law, and difficulties associated with the prevention of emotional disturbances.

ONE

SECTION ONE

THE PHILOSOPHY OF SCIENCE AND METHODS OF INQUIRY

The psychology of adjustment is concerned with the total range of psychological adjustments involved in human experience. It seeks to give an understanding of a person's mode of dealing with both internal and external sources of stimulation. It inquires into basic sources of motivation; it studies the transformation of motives by learning; it studies the variability of response to experience; and it seeks to define the conditions under which people alter their behavior. The scope of inquiry is extremely broad, and consequently, the method of inquiry must be a disciplined one.

In its attempt to study human experience, psychology, in common with many other disciplines, shares a fundamental commitment to the method of science. It is important to acknowledge that science is not a set of facts, a set of laws, or a set of relationships. These are rather the fruits of science; they are the consequences of *behaving* scientifically. Science is controlled operations and procedures designed to answer questions pertaining to a specific area of inquiry. Since investigators in the psychology of adjustment for the most part adhere to the scientific method, the readings in this section are devoted to an elaboration of the meaning of science.

The first selection is taken from Churchman and Ackoff's *Methods of Inquiry*. Their book is a work in the philosophy of science, and its title suggests appropriately that science is foremost a way of behaving, a method. The selection provides a general definition of science as *controlled inquiry*, and it is this element of control which distinguishes scientific work from work of a nonscientific nature. Intuition, for example, does not constitute scientific inquiry inasmuch as it lacks conscious efforts at control. The selection is extremely pointed in defining the behavior of scientists. The distinction which the authors draw between scientific inquiry and commonsense inquiry is worth noting. Rather than being completely antithetical, the two methods are viewed as different in degree only. The scientist is more aware of the possibility of error and strives for increased precision in his operations.

A section from a paper by Feigl on the scientific outlook is presented next. It may be approached as an elaboration in some detail of the view presented by Churchman and Ackoff. Feigl leads us through a carefully stated discussion of the general criteria of the scientific method, indicating that scientific inquiry may be formulated as ideals to be approximated but never fully attained. In order to approximate an ideal, the scientist pursues the successive elimination of error. Thus we again see that precision is one of the key attributes of the scientific method. Such concepts as testability, reliability, and comprehensiveness are used to further define the field of inquiry, and the paper closes with an extremely valuable and well-considered critique of some common misconceptions about science.

It may be useful at this point to note some of the specific methods which are employed in research in the study of adjustment. Psychology would prefer to seek answers to its questions through experimentation. With this method, we can have the greatest amount of confidence in the conclusions our research yields. Experiments, by definition, involve the controlled manipulation of human behavior, and sometimes the systematic manipulation of human behavior is impractical and repugnant to us. For example, in order to test experimentally a hypothesis about the effects of punishment upon a certain aspect of child behavior, the investigator would need to instruct a group of mothers to follow a controlled regimen in punishing their children. The consequences for children subjected to this planned punishment would be sought in comparison with children of a group of mothers who were instructed in not providing such pain. Such an experiment might well violate our ethical standards. It is for reasons such as this that psychologists, in studying adjustment, resort to a variety of methods in addition to direct experimentation.

A method which continues to be useful and in many ways productive of generalizations about adjustment is the *case report*. This method involves an effort to account for the behavior of *an individual* by describing the history of his experience which presumably operated to cause the behavior under study. The disadvantages of this method reside in the serious lack of control. The observer can, in fact, discover any historical antecedents he wishes to discover. Freud will discover psychosexual difficulty; Adler will discover the early experiencing of inferiority; and Sullivan will almost certainly discover anxiety experienced in an empathic relationship with the mothering one. In other words, the method is open to serious bias on the part of the observer. In addition, the case study is based on a single individual and limits the degree of generality of the findings. It is, however, a fruitful method for generating hypotheses about behavior which may become amenable to more controlled investigation.

Another relatively common procedure for investigating human adjustment is the *field study*. Essentially this method consists in the investigator's immersion in a given context and his subsequent narrative account of the phenomena under study. This approach is fruitful in widening our view of human behavior to include the effects of sociocultural institutions upon human actions. For example, Margaret Mead has studied the cultures of the South Pacific; the Lynds have studied Middletown. The field-study method, however, relies heavily on the interpretations of the observer, and his presence may influence or alter the phenomena he is studying. We must ask: Has he been biased in his observations? Has his presence as an observer led to a change in what would have occurred otherwise? Has his selection of data to report affected the accuracy of his portrayal? All observations are necessarily selective and the field-study approach maximizes subjective impressions about what is important. On the other hand, we feel some confidence in an observer's analysis when similar accounts are provided by other independent observers. And the method again is fruitful in suggesting hypotheses for more controlled study.

In some studies, investigators have tried to control observer bias by recording everything that took place within a given context and in a defined and limited time span. *One Boy's Day* by Barker and Wright (Harper & Row, New York, 1951) represents such an effort. It is a straightforward account of the experience of one boy from the moment his mother wakes him in the morning to the moment he goes to bed that night. In this approach, a vast amount of material is collected for the relatively simple experiences of one boy's day. The reader is soon lost in a mass of data over which he has difficulty achieving some meaningful integration.

Owing to our reluctance to perform controlled experiments with human beings where there is some danger of harm, psychologists often prefer to analyze the consequences of events which occur naturally. This method of study has been called the *natural experiment*. In lieu of administering a *planned* regimen of pain to children in some systematic fashion, psychological researchers have simply identified children whose day-to-day experience has involved pain. That is, children with known histories involving pain are compared with children whose known histories involve little or no pain. Note, however, that in this procedure the experimenter, or we may better call him the researcher, has not been able to control the conditions of pain. This lack of control points to the need for caution in forming conclusions and for cross validation of results. The method of natural experimentation is widely used wherever it is impractical or hurtful to conduct a controlled experiment.

The reader may want to consider that, as one moves from case reports to field studies to natural experiments to controlled experimentation, one encounters fewer and fewer possible sources of error in both the conduct of inquiry and the conclusions which stem from it. Many examples of varied approaches to research in adjustment are presented in the readings in this book.

C. West Churchman and R. L. Ackoff

THE MEANING OF SCIENCE *

Science has come to play such an important part in our lives that it is often difficult for us to realize that its pursuit and products have only become major factors in society in the last few hundred years. It has become so important that one could not hope today to understand our culture without understanding the role science plays in it. Science has come to mean "efficient inquiry" to us. It has a fundamental role to play in the basic activities of the people who make decisions and try to solve problems. Many of our critical social problems today hinge on the nature and role of science. We often hear such questions asked as, Can and should science investigate such and such an area? Can and should science tell us how to live? Can science save us? We are all anxious to know what science can do now, what it will eventually be able to do, and what it ought to do. Consequently, an understanding of science is no longer the exclusive concern of the scientist, though it may be his primary concern.

What do we mean by "science"? It is usually defined as "an organized body of knowledge." But this is too "passive" a definition to lead to an understanding of it. Science is not a mere state or accumulation; it is an activity as well as the products of that activity. Science is inquiry; but not all inquiry is scientific. This fact gives us a clue to how we may go about defining it. Science as a kind of inquiry must differ from other types of inquiry either by virtue of *what* it inquires into, or *how* it inquires; that is, on the basis of either its content, or its method—or perhaps both.

* From C. West Churchman and R. L. Ackoff, *Methods of Inquiry,* 1st ed., Educational Publishers, Inc., St. Louis, 1950. Pages 9–11 reprinted by permission of the authors and the publisher.

Let us call "common sense" inquiry the kind of inquiry we indulge in as laymen in our everyday lives. First we want to ask whether scientific and common sense inquiry differ with respect to subject matter, that is, content. It is sometimes said that common sense deals only with immediate and practical problems, whereas science is restricted to long-run, and not immediately practical problems. It is easy to see the inadequacy of this assertion on the basis of the types of inquiry with which we commonly observe common sense and science to be concerned. Science certainly inquires into immediately practical problems: applied sciences like engineering are no less scientific for their applications. Nor is common sense restricted to the immediate, for such general inquiries as have produced the wisdom contained in proverbs have been performed on a common sense basis.

No, it seems more fruitful to look for difference between scientific and common sense inquiry in terms of their method. Common sense itself immediately suggests a distinction: science is *controlled* inquiry, and common sense is not. This suggestion is not, of course, a solution for at best it only gives the problem a name. What is meant by control? Before seeking an answer, however, it is worth noting the conformity of the suggestions with normal usage. We are inclined to say, among other things, not so much that science is an organized body of knowledge, as an organized way of obtaining knowledge. To be sure, science organizes its results, but so does philosophy. Scientists create systems, but so do poets. But science uses an organized and systematic method of inquiry, in some sense a *controlled* method, which makes it unique.

Now again to the question: What is control? We say a man has his automobile under control if he can use it efficiently as an instrument for the pursuit of his objective, say, safe and rapid transportation. In effect, he controls his car when he leads it; but he loses control when it leads him. By analogy we would say that a method of inquiry is under control if the inquirer can use it efficiently in solving the problems that force him into the inquiry in the first place. The *degree* of that efficiency will be a measure of the degree of his control. But we still have to find out what is involved in saying that the inquirer can "use his method efficiently," or that he can lead it rather than have it lead him.

Suppose a scientist is forced to take a certain step in his inquiry for which he has no alternative. Then this step "leads him," he does not lead it—or analogously, he does not have it under control. Practically in science, this means that he cannot investigate the advisability of his step. In so far as the scientist can examine the adequacy of his steps and make an efficient selection, then he leads or controls his steps, and they do not lead him.

We often say that common sense takes a lot for granted; science is more sceptical since it wants to examine everything. This contains in simple language the essence of the notion of control. Common sense inquiry is led by habits of inquiry, by things and methods it takes for granted. Science seeks to test every aspect of its procedure and its assumptions. It is this that differentiates between common sense and science. A method of inquiry, then, is under complete control when every aspect of the activity is itself subject to inquiry with respect to its adequacy for the problematic purpose.

Of course, complete control is something we do not have, or ever expect to have. It represents, however, something we seek. Nor do we ever completely lack control. Complete lack or presence of control are the extreme values of a continuous scale. Science and common sense represent the upper and lower portions of the scale, respectively.

To say a method of inquiry is not under control is not to say that the conclusion it reaches must be wrong. On the contrary, we know that common sense, or the most primitive kind of inquiry, might give us a correct answer to a question. But in the long run we are not confident about the solutions of common sense. Here is the critical point in our high evaluation of science: we believe a controlled method of inquiry is *more apt* to produce correct answers than uncontrolled methods.

We can see now why an understanding of scientific *method* is so critical to an understanding of science. It is its method which provides the essential difference between science and common sense. To know what science can, will, and ought to do, we must know what the method of science is, i.e., the nature of its controls, and what is controlled by it.

Herbert Feigl   **THE SCIENTIFIC OUTLOOK ***

Criteria of the scientific method

What . . . are the basic characteristics of the scientific method? The often alleged difficulties of an adequate definition of science seem to me mainly a matter of terminology. We must first distinguish be-

* From Herbert Feigl, "The Scientific Outlook: Naturalism and Humanism," *Amer. Quart.*, 1949, *1*, 135–148. Pages 138–148 reprinted by permission of the author and the Editor, *American Quarterly*.

tween pure mathematics as an exclusively formal-conceptual discipline, and the factual (or empirical, that is, the natural and the social-cultural) sciences.   The certainty, complete exactitude, and necessity of pure mathematics depends precisely on its detachment from empirical fact.   Mathematics as applied in the factual sciences merely lends its forms and deductive structures to the contents furnished by experience.   But no matter how predominant mathematics may be in the formulations and derivations of empirical facts, factual knowledge cannot attain either the absolute precision or necessity of pure mathematics.   The knowledge claimed in the natural and the social sciences is a matter of successive approximations and of increasing degrees of confirmation.   Warranted assertibility or probability is all that we can conceivably secure in the sciences that deal with the facts of experience.   It is empirical science, thus conceived as an unending quest (its truths claim to be held only "until further notice"), which is under consideration here.   Science in this sense differs only in degree from the knowledge accumulated throughout the ages by sound and common sense.

The aims of science are description, explanation, and prediction. The first aim is basic and indispensable, the second and third (closely related to each other) arise as the most desirable fruits of scientific labors whenever inquiry rises beyond the mere fact-gathering stage. History, often and nowadays quite fashionably declared an art, is scientific to the extent that it ascertains its facts concerning past events by a meticulous scrutiny of present evidence.   Causal interpretation of these facts (in history, but similarly also in psychology, sociology, cultural anthropology, and economics) is usually much more difficult than, but in principle not logically different from, causal interpretation (that is, explanation) in the natural sciences.   The aims of the pure (empirical) sciences are then essentially the same throughout the whole field.   What the scientists are seeking are descriptions, explanations, and predictions which are as adequate and accurate as possible in the given context of research.

The quest for scientific knowledge is therefore regulated by cer in standards or criteria which may best be formulated in the form of ideals to be approximated, but perhaps never fully attained.   The most important of these regulative ideals are:

1   Intersubjective testability.   This is only a more adequate formulation of what is generally meant by the "objectivity" of science. What is here involved is not only the freedom from personal or cultural bias or partiality, but—even more fundamentally—the requirement that the knowledge claims of science be in principle capable of test (confirmation or disconfirmation, at the least indirectly and to some degree) on the part of any person properly equipped with intelligence

and the technical devices of observation or experimentation. The term *intersubjective* stresses the social nature of the scientific enterprise. If there be any "truths" that are accessible only to privileged individuals, such as mystics or visionaries—that is, knowledge-claims which by their very nature cannot independently be checked by anyone else—then such "truths" are not of the kind that we seek in the sciences. The criterion of intersubjective testability thus delimits the scientific from the nonscientific activities of man.

Religious ecstasy, the elations of love, the inspiration of the artist, yes, even the flash of insight on the part of a scientific genius are not in themselves scientific activities. All these processes may eventually become subject matter for scientific study. But in themselves they do not validate knowledge-claims. They may, as in the case of the scientific intuition (or empathy in the psychological-cultural field) be instrumental in the generation of knowledge-claims. But it is these knowledge-claims which have to be, first, formulated in an intersubjectively intelligible (or communicable) manner, and, second, subjected to the appropriate kind of tests in order to ascertain their validity. Beliefs transcending all possible tests by observation, self-observation, experiment, measurement, or statistical analysis are recognized as theological or metaphysical and therefore devoid of the type of meaning that we all associate with the knowledge-claims of common sense or factual science. From the point of view of the scientific outlook in philosophy it may be suggested that the sort of significance with which the in-principle-unconfirmable assertions of transcendent theology and metaphysics impress so many people is largely emotive. The pictorial, emotional, and motivational appeals of language, no matter how indispensable or valuable in the contexts of practical life, art, education, persuasion, and propaganda, must, however, not be confused with the cognitive meanings (purely formal-and/or factual-empirical) that are of the essence of science. Each type of significance has its function, and in most uses of language both are combined or even fused. The only point stressed here is that they must not be *con*fused, that is, mistaken for one another, if we wish to be clear as to what we are about.

2   Reliability, or a sufficient degree of confirmation.   This second criterion of scientific knowledge enables us to distinguish what is generally called "mere opinion" (or worse still, "superstition") from knowledge (well-substantiated belief). It may be considered as the delimitation of the scientific from the unscientific knowledge-claims. Clearly, in contrast to the first criterion, we face here a distinction of degree. There is no sharp line of demarcation between the well-confirmed laws, theories, or hypotheses of science, and the only poorly substantiated hunches and ideas-on-trial which may ultimately either

be included in the corpus of scientific knowledge or else rejected as unconfirmed.   Truth-claims which we repudiate as "superstition," and, quite generally, as judgments based upon hasty generalization or weak analogy (if they fulfill the criterion of testability), differ from what we accept as "scientific truth" in the extremely low degree of probability to which they are supported by the available evidence.   Astrology or alchemy, for example, are not factually meaningless, but they are considered false to fact in that all available evidence speaks overwhelmingly against them.   Modern techniques of experimentation and of statistical analysis are the most powerful tools we have in the discernment between chance and law and hence the best means of enhancing the reliability of knowledge.

3   Definiteness and precision.   This obvious standard of scientific method requires that the concepts used in the formulation of scientific knowledge-claims be as definitely delimited as possible.   On the level of the qualitative-classificatory sciences this amounts to the attempt to reduce all border-zone vagueness to a minimum.   On the level of quantitative science the exactitude of the concepts is enormously enhanced through the application of the techniques of measurement.   The mensurational devices usually also increase the degree of objectivity.   This is especially clear when they are contrasted with purely impressionistic ways of estimating magnitudes.   Of course, there is no point in sharpening precision to a higher degree than the problem in hand requires.   (You need no razor to cut butter.)

4   Coherence or systematic structure.   This is what T. H. Huxley had in mind when he defined science as "organized common-sense." Not a mere collection of miscellaneous items of information, but a well-connected account of the facts is what we seek in science.   On the descriptive level this results, for example, in systems of classification or division, in diagrams, statistical charts, and the like.   On the explanatory levels of science sets of laws, or theoretical assumptions, are utilized.   Explanation in science consists in the hypothetico-deductive procedure.   The laws, theories, or hypotheses form the premises from which we derive logically, or logico-mathematically, the observed or observable facts.   These facts, often belonging to heterogeneous domains, thus become integrated into a coherent, unifying structure.   (Theological and metaphysical systems have, frequently enough, ambitiously tried to imitate this feature of science; but even if they succeeded in proceeding *more geometrico,* the important difference from science remains: they either lack testability or else reliability in the senses specified in our previous points.)

5   Comprehensiveness or scope of knowledge.   This final point in our enumeration of criteria of science also characterizes scientific knowledge as different in degree (often enormously) from common-sense knowledge.   Not only through bold and sweeping hypotheses, but especially through the ingenious devices by means of which they are tested, science acquires a reach far beyond the limits of our un-aided senses.   With telescopes, microscopes, spectroscopes, Geiger counters, lie detectors, and the thousands of other contrivances of modern science we manage to amplify our senses and thus open up avenues of at least indirect access to the worlds of the very distant, the very large, the extremely small, or the disguised and concealed. The resulting increase in the completeness of our knowledge is, of course, popularly the most impressive feature of science.   It must be kept in mind, however, that the scope thus achieved is a product of hard labor, and not to be confused with the sham completeness metaphysicians procure for their world pictures by verbal magic.   In-stead of presenting a finished account of the world, the genuine scien-tist keeps his unifying hypotheses open to revision and is always ready to modify or abandon them if evidence should render them doubtful. This self-corrective aspect of science has rightly been stressed as its most important characteristic and must always be kept in mind when we refer to the comprehensiveness or the unification achieved by the scientific account of the universe.   It is a sign of one's maturity to be able to live with an unfinished world view.

The foregoing outline of the criteria of science has been set down in a somewhat dogmatic tone.   But this was done only for the sake of brevity.[1]   The spirit behind it is that of a humble account of what, I think, an impartial and elaborate study of the history of thought from magic to science would reveal.   In any case, these criteria seem un-questionably the guiding ideals of present-day empirical science. They may therefore be used in a definition of science as we under-stand this term today.   It seems rather useless to speculate about just what this term, by a change of meaning, might come to connote in the future.

It should be remembered that the criteria listed characterize the *pure* factual (empirical) sciences.   The aims of the *applied* sciences —the technologies, medicine, social and economic planning, and others—are practical control, production, guidance, therapy, reform, and so forth.   Responsible activity in the application of science clearly presupposes information which is fairly well substantiated by the methods of the pure sciences.   (These remarks intend to draw merely a logically important distinction.   The obvious practical in-

---

[1] A thorough discussion of the logical, epistemological, methodological, and histori-cal issues connected with the criteria would require a whole book, not just another essay.

terpenetration and important mutual fertilization of the pure and the applied disciplines is of course not denied here.)

Critique of misconceptions

Having indicated at least in broad outline the nature of scientific method we may now turn to the critique of some of the misconceptions to which it is all too commonly exposed. In what follows, a dozen typical charges against science are stated and answered consecutively.[2]

Science arises exclusively out of practical and social needs and has its only value in serving them in turn. (*Dialectical Materialism and Vocationalism*)

While this is important it does not tell the whole story. Science has always also been the pursuit of knowledge, the satisfaction of a deep-rooted curiosity. It should be recognized as one of the cultural values along with art, literature, and music. Better teaching of the sciences and their history can redress the balance. Fuller utilization of results and suggestions from the history and the philosophy of science would give the student a deeper appreciation of the evolution of scientific knowledge and of the scientific point of view. Through proper instruction, the student could be led to rediscover some of the important results of science. The intellectual gratification that comes with a grasp of the order of nature, with the understanding of its processes by means of laws and theories, is one of the most powerful incentives in the pursuit of pure knowledge.

Science cannot furnish a secure basis for human affairs since it is unstable. It changes its views continually. (*Traditionalism*)

While there is constant evolution, and occasionally a revolution, in the scientific outlook, the charge is a superficial (usually journalistic) exaggeration. The typical progress of science reveals that later views often contain much of the earlier views (to the extent that these have stood the test of repeated examination). The more radical or revolutionary changes usually amount to a revision of the conceptual frame of a scientific discipline. The criticism often also presupposes other sources of certainty which will simply not bear critical scrutiny. The quest for absolute certainty is an immature, if not infantile, trait of thinking. The best knowledge we have can be established only by the method of trial and error. It is of the essence of science to make such knowledge as reliable as is humanly and technically possible.

---

[2] These charges are not straw men. In more than twenty years of reading, listening, teaching, and argument I have encountered them again and again in Europe and just as frequently in this country. If space permitted and time were less valuable, I could quote many well-known writers in connection with each charge.

Science rests on uncritical and uncriticized presuppositions. It validates its outlook by its own standards. It therefore begs the question as regards alternative approaches for settling problems of knowledge and action.

Science has been clarifying and revising its basic assumptions throughout its development. Particularly since the beginning of the modern age and still more intensively since the beginning of our century, an increasing awareness of, and critical attitude toward, the fundamental presuppositions has been most fruitfully applied in the repudiation of dogmatic prejudices and in the articulation of the conceptual frame of scientific method. It can be shown (through logical analysis) that the procedure of science is the only one we are *certain* will yield the results (reliable knowledge, that is, valid explanation and predictions) *if* such results can at all be achieved. Any alleged rival method—theology, metaphysics, mysticism, intuition, dialectics—if it made any contributions at all could not be examined and appraised on any basis other than the usual inductive criteria of science. Generally, it seems that these alleged alternatives do not even aim primarily at knowledge but, like the arts, at the enrichment of experience. They may therefore more properly be said to be *non*scientific, rather than *un*scientific.

Science distorts the facts of reality. In its Procrustean manner it introduces discontinuities where there is continuity (and vice versa). The abstractions and idealizations used in science can never do justice to the richness and complexities of experience.

Since the task of science is to discover as reliable and precise a knowledge of what happens under what conditions, it always tries to approximate the facts as closely as the problem on hand requires and permits. Both continuity and discontinuity can be formulated mathematically and be given an adequate formulation only with the help of modern mathematics.

Science can deal only with the measurable and therefore tends to "explain away" that which it cannot measure.

While measurement is eminently desirable in order to enhance the precision and objectivity of knowledge, it is not indispensable in many branches of science or, at least, on their more qualitative levels of analysis. Science does not explain away the qualities of experience. It aims at, and often succeeds in, making these qualities more predictable.

Science never explains, it merely describes the phenomena of experience. The reality beyond the appearances is also beyond the reach of science.

This is partly a terminological issue and partly a result of the (traditional but most misleading and useless) metaphysical distinction between appearance and reality. In the sense in which the word *explaining* is used in common life, science *does* explain facts—it deduces them from laws or theoretical assumptions. Questions which are in principle incapable of being answered by the scientific method turn out, on closer analysis, not to be questions of knowledge. They are expressions of emotional tensions or of the wish for soothing (or exciting) experience.

Science and the scientific attitude are incompatible with religion and the religious attitude.

If by religion one refers to an explanation of the universe and a derivation of moral norms from theological premises, then indeed there is logical incompatibility with the results, methods, and general outlook of science. But if religion means an attitude of sincere devotion to human values, such as justice, peace, relief from suffering, there is not only no conflict between religion and science but rather a need for mutual supplementation.

Science is responsible for the evils and maladjustments of our civilization. It is creating ever more powerful weapons of destruction. The employment of scientific techniques in the machine age has contributed to the misery, physical and mental, of the multitudes. Moreover, the biological facts of evolution imply the negation of all morality: the law of the jungle.

These are particularly superficial charges. It is the social-political-economic structure of a society that is responsible for these various evils. Scientific knowledge itself is socially and morally neutral. But the manner in which it is applied, whether for the benefit or to the detriment of humanity, depends entirely on ourselves. Scientists are becoming increasingly aware that they, even more than the average citizen, have to work for enlightenment toward the proper use of knowledge. The facts and theories of evolution have been construed in many ways as regards their implications for ethics. Julian Huxley reads them very differently from the way his grandfather Thomas Henry did.[3] It should be easy to see that the forces active on the level of human civilization and intelligent communal life are not completely reducible to those involved in the ruthless struggle for survival.

The ethical neutrality of scientific truth and the ivory tower situation of the pure researcher is apt to generate an attitude of indifference toward the pressing problems of humanity.

[3] Compare Julian Huxley, *Touchstone for Ethics* (Harper, 1947); but see also C. D. Broad, "Review of Julian S. Huxley's Evolutionary Ethics" (*Mind 53*, 1949), reprinted in H. Feigl and W. Sellars, *Readings in Philosophical Analysis* (New York, 1949).

Only maladjusted individuals are unable to combine the detachment necessary for the pursuit of truth with an ardent interest in the improvement of the condition of humanity.

Scientific method, while eminently successful in the explanation, prediction, and control of physical phenomena, is distinctly less successful in regard to the facts of organic life and almost altogether hopeless in the mental and social realm. The methods of the physical sciences are essentially mechanistic (if not materialistic) and therefore reductionistic; they cannot do justice to the complex organismic, teleological, and emergent features of life and mind.

"Scientism" as a slogan of criticism and reproach is very fashionable these days. It is true that some scientists and especially some of the popularizers of science have indulged in reductive fallacies of various sorts. But the true scientific spirit as exemplified in some of the foremost researchers is free from that impatience and simple-mindedness that tries to finish the unfinished business of science by hasty speculation. Admittedly, there are tremendous problems yet to be solved. On the other hand what method is there but the method of science to solve them? Explanations of the mechanistic type (in *one* sense of the term) have been abandoned even in physics. But mechanistic explanation in a wider sense of a search for law (deterministic or statistical) is still the indispensable procedure of all sciences that have gone beyond the purely classificatory level. Organic wholeness, teleology, and emergence can be understood, if at all, only by causal analysis on the usual empirical basis. Purposiveness and freedom of choice, far from being incompatible with causality, presuppose causal order.

The methods of science can never replace the intuitive insight or empathic understanding of the practical psychologist, psychiatrist, cultural anthropologist, or historian. This claim is made particularly wherever the object of knowledge is the individual, the unique and unrepeatable.

It is only through the scientific method that the validity and reliability of the intuitive approach can be gauged. There is, on this ground, some doubt as to its more exaggerated claims. However, there is nothing in the principles of scientific method that would deny the occasional, or even frequent, efficacy of intuitive judgments based, as they must be, on a rich (but often not articulated) background of experience in the given field. Aside from the mere artistic contemplation of the unique and individual, knowledge, in the proper sense of the word, always means the subsumption of the specific case under general concepts or laws. This holds in the social sciences just as much as in the natural sciences.

Science cannot determine values. *Since scientific knowledge can (at best) find out only what is the case, it can, by its very nature, never tell what ought to be.*

This final challenge often comes from theology or metaphysics. It usually maintains that questions of aims, goals, and ideals cannot be settled by the methods of science but rather require recourse either to divine revelation, the voice of conscience, or some metaphysical a priori truths. The answer to this in a scientific age would seem to be that a mature mankind should be able to determine its own value standards on the basis of its needs, wants, and the facts of the social condition of man. But it is true that science cannot dictate value standards. It can, as in social psychology, ascertain the actual evaluations of groups and individuals, study their compatibilities and incompatibilities, and recommend (that is *applied* science!) ways and means of harmonizing conflicting evaluations. True enough, in many of the urgent issues that confront us, we do not possess enough scientific knowledge to warrant a course of action. This means that we have to act, as so often in life, on the highest probabilities available even if these probabilities be low in themselves. But such estimates of probabilities will still be made most reliable by the scientific method. Common life experience and wisdom, when freed from its adherence to prescientific thought patterns, is not fundamentally different from scientific knowledge. In both we find the procedure of self-correction, so essentially needed if knowledge is to be a guide for action. There is an important common element in mature thinking (as we find it in science) and mature social action (as we find it in democracy): progress arises out of the peaceful competition of ideas as they are put to intersubjective test. Cooperative planning on the basis of the best and fullest knowledge available is the only path left to an awakened humanity that has embarked on the adventure of science and civilization.

The scientific view of the world that we have characterized and defended against criticisms from various quarters may with historical and terminological justice be called Naturalism.[4] It differs from mechanistic materialism (too often a mere straw man put up by theologians or idealistic metaphysicians) in that it steers clear of reductive fallacies. If uninformed persons insist on viewing science as essentially materialistic and the humanities as essentially idealistic (not to say

[4] It should scarcely need mentioning that this meaning of naturalism has only a distant and tenuous relation to the other meaning in which it is applied to a certain type of literature.

spiritualistic) the hopes of fruitful collaboration of both fields in education are slim indeed.   But science, properly interpreted, is not dependent on any sort of metaphysics.   It merely attempts to cover a maximum of facts by a minimum of laws.   On the other side, a mature humanism requires no longer a theological or metaphysical frame either.   Human nature and human history become progressively understood in the light of advancing science.   It is therefore no longer justifiable to speak of science *versus* the humanities.   Naturalism *and* humanism should be our maxim in philosophy and in education.   A Scientific Humanism emerges as a philosophy holding considerable promise for mankind—*if* mankind will at all succeed in growing up.

TWO

THE CONCEPT OF ADJUSTMENT

Perhaps no psychological concept in our everyday language is so popular as the term *adjustment.* Whether one happens to be discussing the state of mind of a given individual, the repairing or resetting of a watch, or the balancing of a financial ledger, the concept of adjustment is likely to creep into the conversation. In everyday discourse the term may be used to convey a variety of different ideas. Yet we seldom find it necessary to stop and question the precise meaning of the word; rather, we hopefully rely on the context in which it is used to make the meaning clear. For example, we may speak of the need to adjust to something that is inevitable in order to express the idea that we must *accept* things over which we have no control. Or we may refer to adjusting as *growing accustomed* to a particular condition, such as adjusting to the seasonal changes in the weather. We may debate the importance of adjusting our behavior and opinions to those of others, or in other words, *conforming* to the ways of the majority. Still other examples occur: We speak of adjusting our differences of opinion (*settling* them), adjusting our ideas to fit the facts (*making them more accurate*), adjusting our daily schedules (*regulating* them), and adjusting our wishes to those of others (*harmonizing* or *compromising*).

The variety of meanings to which the concept of adjustment applies constitutes both an advantage and a limitation. On the one hand, the multiple meaning may stimulate us to think more carefully and more broadly about a particular issue. Various word associations may compel us to qualify and elaborate the idea we wish to express. In this way the generality of the concept may enhance clarity of thought and expression. On the other hand, we may find ourselves using the term in an unclear and imprecise fashion. We may speak of someone's poor adjustment to a given set of circumstances, meaning no more than that we are dissatisfied with his behavior. When we speak of adjustment in a general way, without specifying our particular meaning, the idea communicated to our listener may be quite different from the one we intended.

Although the concept of adjustment in a psychological sense is less broad than in its everyday usage, it is nonetheless beset by many of the same complexities and difficulties.   When we speak of psychological adjustment and refer to some aspect of an individual's behavior, difficulties in communication are still present.   Varied meanings and criteria have been associated with the dimension *adjustment-maladjustment,* and these have promoted discussion and debate in the psychological literature.   One investigator may use as his criterion of adjustment the individual's ability to harmonize his own needs with those of his environment, while another may stress the extent to which the individual's behavior conforms to the dictates of his society, and still another may define adjustment in terms of the individual's subjective state of well-being and happiness.   Each of these criteria or emphases will often lead to different decisions as to the kinds of problems and psychological characteristics which will be labeled as maladjustment.

A further complexity in the meaning of adjustment and maladjustment concerns the relationship of these concepts to other terms, such as normal-abnormal, psychopathology, and mental health and mental illness.   In some instances these concepts are used interchangeably; in others, different and independent criteria are cited for each; and some psychologists may think of normality and adjustment and abnormality and maladjustment as overlapping, but not synonymous. One example of overlap is where the dimension *normal-abnormal* is used as the more general and inclusive variable to describe the degree to which a person deviates from culturally approved ways of behaving and where *adjustment-maladjustment* is used to refer to the more specific idea of the extent to which a person is able to *adapt* to the demands of a situation.   In this limited sense, failure to adapt or adjust may or may not constitute abnormality depending on how seriously that maladjustment departs from what is culturally approved. Failure to adapt to the demands of a chemistry course may then be regarded as maladjusted behavior, but not abnormal, whereas failure to adapt to society's requirement that each person must refrain from inflicting bodily injury on others may be regarded as both maladjusted and abnormal.   In contrast, some investigators may define abnormality in terms of the presence of specific deviant behaviors, such as anxiety, phobias, delusions, or depression, but regard these behaviors as independent of the individual's adjustment.   According to this view, the repeated occurrence of deviant acts means that the individual is abnormal or mentally ill; yet he may be able to deal satisfactorily with his everyday activities and the demands of his environment and thus not be considered maladjusted.

For the purpose of understanding the problems associated with definitions of the concept of adjustment-maladjustment, the student might initially consider this dimension synonymous with such terms as normality-abnormality and mental health-mental illness, since the varied criteria which have been applied to one of these variables have also been applied to the others. In the first selection in this section, Scott discusses the diverse meanings associated with adjustment or mental health. After summarizing many of the definitions and methods of measuring mental health and the limitations associated with each definition, he raises a number of questions concerning the potential overlap and disagreements of different definitions.

Historically the initial focus of investigators of the psychology of adjustment, mental health, or abnormal psychology has been on the pathological. For many years, investigators tended to concentrate on the identification of signs of abnormal behavior and maladjustment and to define normality and adjustment in terms of the absence of such signs. In addition, many scientists applied the medical profession's disease-entity model to pathological or maladjusted behavior and reasoned that the presence of specific signs or symptoms was indicative of a disease process which could be identified in any society or culture in which it occurred. These scientists hoped to discover symptom-criteria for mental illness which would be culture-free and universally valid. Thus, such terms as normality, adjustment, and mental health could be defined explicitly by the absence of pathological signs. The paper by Honigmann represents this point of view. Deviance, he says, occurs when in someone's judgment behavior exceeds the culturally determined limits of permitted variation. This definition therefore places great weight on the source of the judgment, and it is Honigmann's contention that in the case of psychiatric abnormality, the judgment is made by an authoritative and powerful specialist who applies successfully an objective and operational definition across cultures. In the case of nonpsychiatric deviance, no clear-cut specialist or procedure exists. Herein lies the major distinction Honigmann makes between psychiatric and nonpsychiatric judgments of abnormality.

One of the major criticisms of the disease-entity model is that the conceptualization of good adjustment or mental health is ignored and is described solely in a negative way as the absence of deleterious characteristics. Many theorists prefer to enumerate positive characteristics and to postulate that certain ways of acting and thinking are healthier psychologically than others. During the past ten years increasing attention and effort have been given to formulating a positive definition of adjustment and mental health. The paper by Shoben presents a theoretical discussion of "the normal personality" and lists a number of characteristics which he regards as possible universal criteria for good adjustment. Underlying Shoben's thinking is the assumption that man by nature (regardless of the culture, society, or group to which he belongs) has certain "unique potentialities." The development of these potentialities is regarded as the broad criterion for mental health, and the more an individual actualizes his potentialities, the better adjusted he is considered. Shoben's position may be termed an *idealistic* conception of adjustment since it stresses what man *could* be. If we were able to agree that all mankind has the same direction or goal, we would be able to evaluate individuals or groups with respect to that goal. The task then, according to this reasoning, is to determine the goal or the specific unique potentialities or ideals of mankind. As Shoben indicates, psychology's efforts along these lines must be considered quite tentative.

The positions of both Honigmann and Shoben, while they differ in their emphasis on illness or health, seek culture-free, absolute criteria. In contrast with the conceptualization of normal-abnormal behavior in absolute terms, there is also the view that, since most of man's behavior is learned within a given cultural context, pathological behavior must be influenced strongly by the particular standards and demands of the culture in which the learning occurs. Behavior which is considered pathological or maladjusted in one culture may be quite acceptable or even desirable in another. To the extent that a theorist attaches importance to the interdependence between specific environmental-cultural norms and demands and the criteria of psychopathology, his position is a *relativistic* one and he discounts the possibility of establishing a culture-free definition of mental health or mental illness. Some theorists have taken an extreme position on this score and have argued that pathology by necessity must be relativistic since it represents an evaluative judgment made about an individual's behavior for which no absolute standard exists. To call the hostile, aggressive behavior of the jungle inhabitant pathological in an environment where survival itself demands physical domination and assertion over other forms of life would be misleading. Similarly, to establish inner-directed achievement striving as an ideal goal for all mankind because this behavior is deemed appropriate and desirable in our culture may constitute no more than an imposition of our values on others. The paper by Freides adopts a relativistic position and raises criticisms of the idealistic conception of psychological normality. Freides argues that efforts to designate ideal characteristics inevitably become associated with value judgments concerning the desirability or undesirability of certain characteristics or what constitutes a good or bad way of life. He proposes that a choice of values cannot be determined by science and, instead, feels that psychologists can more profitably address themselves to questions about the potential achievements and limitations of specific behavioral characteristics in specific circumstances of life than to attempts to generalize about what might best be considered normal or adjusted behavior.

Freides' proposal that the concept of normality should be dropped completely, and by implication such concepts as adjustment and mental health, represents a strong position with which many psychologists would disagree.   Other psychologists would argue that despite the relativity of cultural values and demands, similarities between cultures may promote similarities in the forms of pathology and the ideal characteristics of normality.   Some theorists attempt to compromise the differences between the search for absolute universal criteria of mental health and the belief that all criteria are culture-bound. Many psychiatrists in particular seek basic personality characteristics which they associate with abnormality, but concede that the specific ways in which these characteristics will be expressed depends on the cultural context.   For example, a suspicious, paranoid attitude toward others is often regarded as an indicator of pathology, but the content of the individual's suspicions and the ways in which he makes his suspicions known will vary depending on the environment in which they occur.

The other articles in this section present empirical efforts to define and study criteria of adjustment.   Tindall's research represents an effort to investigate the relationships among various criteria of mental health in institutionalized adolescent boys.   The author selected measures of adjustment which sample those commonly used for diagnostic and research purposes, comparing each with the other.   While many of the intercorrelations are beyond what might be expected by chance, the overall findings indicate that it is reasonable both to question the usefulness of the concept of adjustment as one global personality characteristic and to seek more than one measure for diagnostic and predictive purposes.   Veroff, Feld, and Gurin in the next reading also obtain data which support the need for a multiple-criterion approach to the study of adjustment and mental health.   They obtained interview data concerning subjects' general feelings of distress, self-attitudes, marital adjustment, adjustment as a parent, job adjustment, and psychological and psychosomatic complaints.   Through factor analysis, five distinct factors were found which indicate that even when mental health is defined in terms of a subjective state of happiness or distress, an individual's feelings vary considerably about different aspects of his life.

The final article in this section describes still another empirical approach to the study of mental health.   One way of defining mental health is to ask experts what they mean when they use the term.   Solley and Munden arrived at a set of behavioral characteristics of mental health by having experienced clinicians describe personal acquaintances they regarded as mentally healthy.   Later, undergraduate college students were requested to do the same.   A high degree of consistency was found in the qualities of mentally healthy people cited by the two groups. Thus, despite the different definitions of mental health, normality, and adjustment, some agreement exists when individuals are asked to describe mentally healthy persons.

William Abbott Scott

DEFINITIONS OF MENTAL HEALTH AND ILLNESS *

A serious obstacle to research in the area of mental illness lies in the lack of a clear definition of the phenomenon to be studied. The term "mental ill health" has been used by different researchers to refer to such diverse manifestations as schizophrenia, suicide, unhappiness, juvenile delinquency, and passive acceptance of an intolerable environment. Whether some or all of these various reactions should be included in a single category of "mental illness" is not clear from a survey of the current literature. Theories describing the nature and antecedents of one sort of disturbance rarely relate it to another, and there is a paucity of research evidence indicating the extent to which such manifestations are empirically intercorrelated.

In the face of such ambiguity it would appear useful to attempt an organized review of the various definitions of mental illness which are explicit or implicit in recent research, with a view toward highlighting their commonalities and discrepancies on both a theoretical and an empirical level. Such a presentation might help students concerned with causative factors to assess the comparability of previous research findings on correlates of "mental illness," and also point toward some next steps in research to discover the degree to which these diverse phenomena represent either unitary, or multifold, psychological processes.

* From William Abbott Scott, "Research Definitions in Mental Health and Mental Illness," Psychol. Bull., 1958, 55, 29–45. Reprinted by permission of the author and the Managing Editor, the American Psychological Association.

This review was prepared for the Survey Research Center, University of Michigan, as background material for that organization's national survey of mental health, sponsored by the Joint Commission on Mental Illness and Health. The writer is indebted to Dr. Gerald Gurin of the Survey Research Center, and to Dr. Fillmore Sanford, formerly of the Joint Commission, for their contributions to the ideas presented here. Also appreciation is due the following researchers for their suggestions and for data from current studies which they provided: Harry Beilin, John Clausen, Benjamin Darsky, John Glidewell, Marie Jahoda, Morton Kramer, Thomas Langner, Charles Metzner, M. Brewster Smith, and Shirley Star.

The research criteria for mental illness to be reviewed here are subsumed under the following categories: (1) exposure to psychiatric treatment; (2) social maladjustment; (3) psychiatric diagnosis; (4) subjective unhappiness; (5) objective psychological symptoms; and (6) failure of positive adaptation. For each category we shall review studies which appear to have employed the definition, either explicitly or implicitly. This will be accompanied by a critical discussion of the adequacy of each definition, together with an assessment, based on empirical data where possible, of the relation between this and other definitions. Finally, we shall attempt to summarize the differences among the definitions, by indicating their divergent approaches to certain basic problems in the conceptualization of mental illness and health.

Mental illness as exposure to psychiatric treatment

The most frequently used operational definition of mental illness, at least in terms of the number of studies employing it, is simply the fact of a person's being under psychiatric treatment. And this definition is usually restricted to hospital treatment, rather than outpatient service. Nearly all the ecological studies (e.g., 3, 16, 22, 30, 35, 50) and most of the studies correlating mental illness with demographic characteristics (e.g., 5, 19, 29, 41, 47) use this as a criterion. They obtain their information from hospital records or, in unusual instances (e.g., 28), from psychiatrists in the area who furnish information about persons treated on an outpatient basis.

Such a definition of mental illness is operational rather than conceptual, but its implicit meaning for the interpretation of research results is that anyone who is regarded by someone (hospital authorities, relatives, neighbors, or himself) as disturbed enough to require hospitalization or outpatient treatment is mentally ill, and people who do not fit into such diagnoses are mentally healthy. Use of hospital records, moreover, requires that the criterion of the nature of the mental illness be the diagnosis which appears on the record.

Shortcomings of such an operational definition are recognized by no one better than its users. The reliability of psychiatric diagnosis is of course open to question, and any attempt to determine correlates of particular kinds of mental disturbance must take into account the large error inherent in the measuring process. (One study of the association between diagnosis at Boston Psychopathic Hospital and previous diagnoses of the patients at other hospitals showed only 51 per cent above-chance agreement between the two [cf. 15, pp. 42–43].)

If "under the care of a psychiatrist" is to be regarded as the criterion of mental illness, one must realize the automatic limitation on the size of the mentally ill population that such a definition imposes. Kramer

(34, p. 124) has estimated that the maximum possible number of mentally ill, under such a definition, would be less than 7,000,000, given the present number of available psychiatrists.

It has been suggested by both sociologists (7, 10) and physicians (17) that different rates of hospital admissions for different geographical areas may indicate more than anything else about the areas the relative degree to which the communities tolerate or reject persons with deviant behavior (11). Or as the Chief of the National Institute of Mental Health puts it: researchers using hospital records are dependent on the public's rather uneven willingness to give up its mentally ill members and to support them in institutions (17); this in addition to the admittedly unstandardized and often substandard methods of record-keeping used by the various hospitals is likely to render incomparable prevalence and incidence data from various geographical areas.

The effects of such differential thresholds for admission in various communities are difficult to estimate, since they cannot be uniform from study to study. In 1938 a house-to-house survey in Williamson County, Tennessee, yielded nearly one person diagnosed as psychotic, but never having been in a mental hospital, for every hospitalized psychotic from the county (48). By contrast, Eaton found in his study of the Hutterites (14) that more intensive canvassing by psychiatrists did not yield a larger number of persons deemed psychotic than did a more superficial count based on community reports.

Eaton's study *did* yield higher proportions of neurotic diagnoses the more intensive the case finding procedure became, and this observation relates to the finding in New Haven that neurotics under outpatient treatment came disproportionately from the upper socioeconomic strata (28). At first consideration, such differential rates seem readily attributable to the cost of psychiatric treatment, but Hollingshead and Redlich prefer to seek an explanation in the greater social distance between lower-class neurotics and the psychiatrists than in the case of middle- and upper-class neurotics. Whatever the sources of rate differences, it is clear that such correlations as have been reported make one wary of the hospital admissions or outpatient figures as indicative of the "true" incidence of psychiatric disorders. Thus the criterion of exposure to psychiatric treatment is at best a rough indicator of any underlying conceptual definition of mental illness.

Maladjustment as mental illness

Adjustment is necessarily determined with reference to norms of the total society or of some more restricted community within the society. Accordingly, one may conceptually define adjustment as adherence to social norms.   Such a definition of mental health has an advantage over the preceding in encompassing a range of more-or-less healthy, more-or-less ill behavior, rather than posing a forced dichotomy.   The operation for assessing mental health by this criterion might ideally be a community (or other relevant group) consensus concerning a given subject's degree of adjustment.   This has been approximated by at least one set of studies (1, 2).

Rather than assess consensus by pooling many divergent individual opinions, it is possible to assume that a law or other visible sign of social norms constitutes the criterion against which adjustment is determined.   Such reference is employed in studies of suicide (12, 26) or juvenile delinquency (25) or divorce (39, 53) as indicants of maladjustment.   While the operational criterion may become dichotomous in such cases (whether or not the person comes in contact with the law), this is not necessarily so.   Gordon (21) has suggested considering the "biologic gradient" of suicide, extending from contemplation of the act to its actual accomplishment.

Finally, it would be possible to assess degree of adjustment with reference to some externally defined set of requirements for a given social system.   Thus a work situation might be seen as demanding a high level of productivity from all its members, and the degree of adherence to this standard becomes the criterion of adjustment, without reference to the individual opinions of the group members or to the manifest norms of the group.   This criterion of conformity to the requirements of a given social structure has not been explicitly employed by any of the researchers covered in the present review, but it has been hinted at (37) and remains a possibility, provided that the structural requirements of a social system can be determined independently of the members' behaviors.

Theory of social structure suggests that these three criteria of adjustment would tend toward congruence: The demands of a particular social system lead to the development of social norms, which are expressed in laws or customs and also in the individual participants' notions of what is acceptable behavior.   Lack of congruence may be taken as evidence of cultural lag, of poor correspondence between manifest and latent function within the social structure, or of defensive psychological processes within the participating individuals.   Since all of these factors supporting discrepancy do occur within most social systems, the criteria may be expected to yield somewhat different results.

When maladjustment is assessed by community consensus, one finds considerable divergence of opinion among various segments of the public regarding what constitutes good and poor adjustment. The Minnesota Child Welfare studies (1) showed differences in criteria for assessing adjustment among different occupational groups in the community. Teachers tended to emphasize standards different from those emphasized by ministers, who in turn displayed some differences from a more heterogeneous group of community adults. Beilin concludes that it is meaningless to discuss "adjustment" in the abstract or to contemplate the prediction of "adjustment" in general. One must specify *adjustment to what, adjustment to whose standards* (2). Lindemann reflects this relativistic conception of mental health when he states: "We find it preferable not to talk about a 'case' in psychiatry —rather we try to assess functional impairment in specific situations as viewed by different professional groups in the community. So a case' is really a relationship of possibly pathogenic situation and appropriate or inappropriate behavior to that situation. It is often a matter of arbitrary choice whether such a person becomes an object of psychiatric care" (38, p. 130).

Thus, though adjustment appears a more conceptually adequate criterion of mental health than does exposure to treatment, the necessity for considering different personal frames of reference and the demands of different social structures poses seemingly insurmountable obstacles to the establishment of mutually consistent operational definitions. All such difficulties which lie "hidden," as it were, under the psychiatric treatment criterion, come to the fore to plague the researcher trying to establish a criterion for adjustment which applies to the treated and nontreated alike.

Psychiatric diagnosis as criterion for mental illness

There have been a few studies in which entire communities or samples of them have been systematically screened, either by direct examination (44, 48) or by evidence from community records or hearsay (13, 14, 54). Here the criterion for mental illness or health need not be dichotomous, but can be divided into several gradations. Such intensive case-finding can be expected to increase the yield of persons classified as neurotic (34, p. 124) over that provided by the criterion of exposure to treatment, but whether the psychotic group is thereby increased will depend on the community (34, p. 124; 48) and, of course, on the standards for diagnosis employed by the particular investigator.

The lack of standardization of diagnostic procedures and criteria contributes to the incomparability of mental illness rates derived from such studies (34, p. 139; 55). So long as the criterion of assessment is largely dependent on the psychiatrist's subjective integration of a different set of facts for each subject, nonuniform results can be anticipated. Expensive and unreliable though the method may be, it at least places the judgment regarding mental illness or health in the hands of professionals, which is not the case when adjustment is the criterion.   And though hospitalization is in part determined by the judgment of professionals, *who* is sent to the hospitals for psychiatric diagnosis is, for the most part, out of the hands of the psychiatrists. As Felix and Bowers (17) have observed, it is the community rather than the clinician that operates the case-finding process today, and this will continue to be so until diagnostic examinations are given regularly to all people.

Mental illness defined subjectively

It has been maintained by some that a major indication of need for psychotherapy is the person's own feeling of unhappiness or inadequacy.   Conversely, the degree of mental health may be assessed by manifestations of subjective happiness, self-confidence, and morale. Lewis (36) quotes Ernest Jones to the effect that the main criterion for effect of therapy is the patient's subjective sense of strength, confidence, and well-being.   Terman (52, 53) has used a "marriage happiness" test, composed largely of subjective items, and Pollak (43) has suggested that old-age adjustment be assessed in terms of the person's degree of happiness or well-being in various areas of his life.

That such criteria of mental health correlate somewhat with independent diagnoses by physicians has been indicated in two sorts of studies.   In the Baltimore Eastern Health District (9), cases diagnosed psychoneurotic were found to express complaints about their own physical health; it is suggested that persons who report chronic nervousness can be classified as suffering from a psychiatric condition. Rogers has maintained that a marked discrepancy between one's "perceived self" and "ideal self" constitutes evidence of psychiatric disturbance (45), and some empirical studies lend support to this position. When Q sorts of subjects' self concepts are compared with Q sorts of their ideal selves, it is possible to distinguish psychiatric groups from nonpsychiatric groups on the basis of the degree of discrepancy between these two measures (4).   Furthermore, progress in therapy (as judged by the therapist) tends to be associated with increasing similarity between the patient's self concept and ideal self (46).

Though subjective well-being is an appealing criterion for mental health in ordinary daily living, it might be presumed that under some circumstances psychological defense mechanisms could operate to prevent the person's reporting, or becoming aware of, his own underlying unhappiness and disturbance.   Jahoda (33) has rejected happiness as a criterion for mental health on somewhat different grounds: Happiness, she says, is a function not only of the person's behavior patterns, but of the environment in which he moves.   If one wants to relate mental health to characteristics of the environment, then one must not take as a criterion of mental health something that already presupposes a benign environment. "There are certain circumstances in which to be happy would make it necessary first to be completely sick" (33, p. 105).

Such objections to this criteria imply that it is possible to find persons who are mentally ill by some other criterion, yet who nevertheless report themselves as happy or self-satisfied. Empirical demonstration of this implication is not available at present. In fact, while one study predicted defensively high Q sorts for the self concept of paranoid psychotics, they were found to have a greater discrepancy between self- and ideal-sorts than normals, and no less discrepancy between these measures than psychoneurotics (4).

Mental illness defined by objective psychological symptoms

It is generally accepted almost by definition that mental illness entails both a disordering of psychological processes and a deviation of behavior from social norms (6). The latter aspect of disturbance may be assessed as maladjustment to one's social environment (discussed above); the former aspect can presumably be assessed by psychological inventories aimed at the assumedly critical processes. The distinction between the psychological inventory approach and the subjective assessment procedure discussed above is not really a clear one. Subjective well-being may be regarded as one of the psychological processes which becomes disordered. Yet more "objective" measures of psychological process, which do not require the subject's verbal report of his degree of happiness, are frequently preferred, both to guard against purposeful distortion and to tap areas of disorder which may not be accompanied by subjective counterparts.

Such "objective" psychological inventories may represent various degrees of manifest purpose. For some, the objective of assessment is transparent, and the only reason they are not classed as devices for subjective report is that they stop just short of requiring the subject to report his over-all level of well-being. Such a manifest-level inventory is Halmos' questionnaire concerning the respondent's difficulties in social relations (24).

At a somewhat less obvious level are such inventories as the MMPI, the War Department Neuropsychiatric Screening Battery, and the Cornell Medical Index, which require subjects to check the presence of various subjective and objective symptoms (e.g., "I smoke too much."). Once validated against an accepted criterion, such as psychiatric diagnosis, these are frequently used as criteria themselves. Rennie constructed a composite instrument of this type to assess his respondents' levels of mental health in the Yorkville study (44); at the

same time, a validity analysis of the index was undertaken, by correlating each item with independent psychiatric diagnosis on a subsample of the respondents. On the basis of their experience with
such a composite instrument, one of Rennie's colleagues (Langner,
personal communication, August 1956) suggests caution in abstract-
ing parts of previously validated batteries, since the item validities
are sometimes not maintained when they are used out of context of
the total instrument.

An adaptation of the psychiatric screening battery approach for
use with children is suggested in the work of the St. Louis County
Public Health Department (20). It involves obtaining information
about symptoms from the children's mothers rather than from the
children themselves. Naturally, the symptoms covered must be of
the "objective" type ("Does Johnny wet the bed?") rather than the
"subjective" type ("Does Johnny worry a lot?"). As validated by an
outside criterion (teachers' and psychiatric social workers' ratings of
the child's level of adjustment), the number of symptoms reported by
the mothers appears to be a promising index of the child's mental
health.

A general characteristic of the types of psychological inventories
reviewed so far is that each item in the battery is assumed, a priori,
to involve a "directional" quality, such that one type of answer (e.g.,
"yes" to "Are you troubled with nightmares?") may be taken as indicative of psychological disorder, and the opposite answer is indicative
of normal functioning. Thus the index of disturbance is computed
by adding all the positive indicators, weighted equally. That alternative methods of test construction may yield equally, or more, valid
indices of mental illness is indicated by the extensive investigations
of McQuitty (40).

McQuitty proposes several different methods of diagnostic test scoring, each based on explicit assumptions about the diagnostic procedure which the test is supposed to represent. One of the simplest
assumptions, for example, is that an individual is mentally ill to the
extent that his psychological processes deviate from the culturally
modal processes. Thus, any type of multiple-alternative test may be
administered to a group of subjects representing a "normal" population. Each alternative of each item is then scored for its "popularity."
The score for a subject is then computed by adding the popularity
scores of the items he checks (McQuitty calls this the T method of
scoring); a high popularity score is taken as evidence of mental health
(by this "typicality" criterion).

An alternative assumption proposed by McQuitty as underlying the
diagnostic procedure might be that mental health is manifest to the
degree that the subject's responses conform to *any* pattern of answers
represented by a significant number of community people, regardless

of whether that pattern is the most popular one. Such an assumption leads to a scoring procedure (H method) whereby a subject's index of "cultural harmony" is based on the degree to which his responses to different questions "go together" in the same manner as do the responses of all people in the sample who check the same alternatives he does.

Elaborations on these basic procedures provide for differential weighting of responses depending on their degree of deviance (WH method), and correction for "linkage" between successive pairs of items (WHc method).

The Bernreuter Personality Test and the Strong Vocational Interest Inventory were administered by McQuitty to a group of mental patients and to a group of university students; they were scored by different methods, the scores for the two tests were correlated, and the mean scores of the two groups compared. Results of the comparisons indicate that: (1) when appropriately scored, the Strong can discriminate mental patients from normals, though not so well as the Bernreuter; (2) better results are obtained if, instead of treating each answer as a separate, independent measure, it is evaluated in terms of the pattern of other answers with which it occurs (WHc scoring method); (3) within the Bernreuter, those items which correlated best with the total score (McQuitty's WHc method of scoring) and provided the best discrimination between patients and normals tended to be of the "subjective" type (i.e., they depended on the subject's introspection, as in "Do you often have disturbing thoughts?") rather than the "objective" (items which an observer could report, such as "Do you talk very much?"); (4) different scoring procedures appeared differentially appropriate for the "subjective" and "objective" items; (5) when the "subjective" items were scored by the method most appropriate to them (i.e., the method which best discriminated patients from normals), and the "objective" items by their most appropriate method, the correlation between the two scores on the same group of subjects was about zero, indicating that two independent dimensions of mental health were being tapped by these two sets of items.

A separate study reported by McQuitty (40) indicated that the simple T method of scoring (based on the popularity of the subject's responses) both subjective and objective items significantly discriminated groups of school children classified on the basis of independent criteria of mental health. There is considerable evidence from these studies that, especially with respect to those traits measured by the "objective" items, the person may be regarded as mentally ill to the extent that he deviates from the dominant community pattern.

The foregoing studies provide a certain amount of evidence that measures of mental illness according to psychometric criteria relate to two of the criteria discussed earlier—maladjustment and psychiatric diagnosis.   That such concurrent validation may yield somewhat different results from studies of predictive validity is indicated in Beilin's report of the Nobles County study (2).   Two indices of student adjustment predictors were constructed, one (the "pupil index") based on students' responses to five different instruments, and the other (the "teacher index") based on teacher ratings.   Both were concurrently validated against juvenile court judges' nominations of delinquent youngsters and against teachers' descriptions of the youngsters.   Four years later the mental health of the youth was assessed by a number of different criteria—community reputation, interviewers' ratings, self-assessment, and an adaptation of the Rundquist-Sletto morale scale. The predictors correlated significantly with only some of the subsequent criteria, and all of the correlations were at best moderate.   The "pupil index" correlated better with the interviewer's rating than with the community reputation criterion; while the "teacher index" correlated better with the subject's subsequent community reputation than with the interviewer's rating.   Or, stated more generally, the psychologist's predictor predicted better to a psychologist's criterion, and a community predictor predicted better to a community criterion. Though the time span (four years) between the predictor and criterion measures may have been such as to allow for considerable change in the subjects, one is nevertheless reminded by these results that various criteria for mental health are not necessarily highly correlated.

In summarizing the various studies of mental health and illness defined by psychological testing batteries, we may note that many of them lack an underlying conception of the nature of mental illness from which to derive items and scoring procedures (a notable exception being McQuitty's measures), that some of them challenge the notion of the unidimensional nature of mental health, and that their degree of correlation with other criteria, such as adjustment or psychiatric diagnosis, depends on the nature of the criterion.

Mental health as positive striving

A radically different approach to the assessment of mental health is indicated in the definitions proposed by some writers with a mental hygiene orientation.   Gruenberg suggests that, though failure to live up to the expectations of those around him may constitute mental illness, one should also consider the person's failure to live up to his own potentialities (23, p. 131).   Frank speaks of the "positive" aspect of mental health—healthy personalities are those who "continue to grow, develop, and mature through life, accepting responsibilities, finding fulfillments, without paying too high a cost personally or socially, as they participate in maintaining the social order and carrying on our culture" (18).   In a less exhortative tone, Henry (27) discusses successful adaptation of the person in the "normal stress-ful situation." He sees many normal situations as situations of in-herent stress. Some individuals in them develop mental disease, while others may develop out of them a more complex, but more successful, personality. It is this successful coping with the "normal stressful situation" that Henry regards as indicative of mental health.

Jahoda has translated this kind of emphasis on the positive, striv-ing aspects of behavior into a set of criteria amenable to empirical research. She proposes three basic features of mental health (31): (1) The person displays active adjustment, or attempts at mastery of his environment, in contrast to lack of adjustment or indiscriminate adjustment through passive acceptance of social conditions. (2) The person manifests unity of personality—the maintenance of a stable integration which remains intact in spite of the flexibility of behavior which derives from active adjustment. (3) The person perceives the world and himself correctly, independent of his personal needs.

Active mastery of the environment, according to Jahoda, presup-poses a deliberate choice of what one does and does not conform to, and consists of the deliberate modification of environmental condi-tions. "In a society in which regimentation prevails, active adjust-ment will hardly be possible; in a society where overt regimentation is replaced by the invisible compulsiveness of conformity pressures, active adjustment will be equally rare. Only where there exists social recognition of alternative forms of behavior is there a chance for the individual to master his surroundings and attain mental health" (31, p. 563).

Such an approach is quite at odds with the subjective criterion of personal happiness, and with the conformity criterion referred to above as "adjustment." Attempted adjustment does not necessarily result in success, for success is dependent on the environment. The best mode of adjustment only maximizes the chances of success. It is mentally healthy behavior even if the environment does not permit a solution of the problem (33). Jahoda proposes that the criterion of happiness be replaced with some more "objective" definition of mental health, based on an explicit set of values.

In an unpublished community study, Jahoda apparently attempted to assess only two of the aspects of mental health incorporated in her definition. Veridicality of perception (actually, of judgment) was de-termined by asking respondents to estimate certain characteristics of their communities concerning which objective data were available (e.g., proportion of people with only grade-school education), and at the same time inferring needs to distort reality from the respondent's evaluative statements about the problem (e.g., how important R be-lieved education to be). This method of assessing need-free percep-tion was regarded as something less than satisfactory (Jahoda, personal communication, August 1956), since the need was so difficult to determine, and it was difficult to establish unambiguously that distortion of judgment was due to the operation of a need rather than simply to lack of valid information.

The degree of attempted active adjustment was assessed by first asking a respondent to mention a particular problem in the community, then determining what he had done, or tried to do, about it, and how he felt about the problem at the time of interview (33).   Three aspects of respondents' reactions were coded from their replies (32): (1) the stage of problem solution—mere consideration of the problem, consideration of solutions, or actual implementation; (2) the feeling tone associated with the problem—continued worry or improvement in feeling (either through partial solution or through passive acceptance); (3) the directness or indirectness of the approach—i.e., whether *R* went to the heart of the problem in his attempted solution or merely dealt temporarily with recurrent nuisances.

In her analysis Jahoda relates her measures of problem-solving and need-free perception to various characteristics of the respondents and of the communities in which they live.   The relationships are interesting (e.g., in one of the communities the level of problem-solving was related to the degree of community participation of the respondent), but they appear to leave unanswered a basic question about the appropriateness of the criteria.   If one accepts Jahoda's definition of mental health as involving the two components assessed in the study, then the results can be interpreted as showing what patterns of social interaction are associated with mental health.   But if one is skeptical about the meaningfulness of the definition, then he is impelled to search for correlations between her two measures and other, more commonly accepted, criteria of mental health.   These are not reported, although it would appear to be a fair question to ask about the relation of her concepts to those employed by other researchers.

If one is wedded to the happiness criterion of mental health, for example, one may speculate about the possibility of a negative relation between it and those provided by Jahoda.   Unhappiness could conceivably lead to excessive coping behavior (attempted adjustment), or excessive coping behavior might elicit negative reactions from others which, in turn, would increase one's unhappiness.   In like fashion, it could be that need-free perception would lead to increased unhappiness, since psychological defenses are not available to bolster one's self image.   Though Jahoda might reject the suggestion that happiness is even relevant to her criteria, it would appear useful to explore, both conceptually and empirically, the interrelations among other measures of mental health and the novel one proposed by her.

Clausen (6) has maintained that researchers must ultimately face the task of relating mental health defined in positive terms to the individual's ability to resist mental illness under stress.   At present it is not known whether they represent a common factor or are independent characteristics.   Jahoda (personal communication, August 1956) suspects that positive mental health, as she defines it, may indeed represent a dimension orthogonal to that represented by the conventional psychological symptoms of mental illness.   Thus, from a different approach than that employed by McQuitty comes the suggestion that mental health and illness may be a multidimensional phenomenon.

In employing these particular criteria, especially that of active adaptation, Jahoda seems willing to defend the evaluative standards implicit in it.   And it may well be that values relating to attempted mastery of problems are every bit as defensible as the values of conformity implied in the adjustment criteria discussed above.   Nevertheless, the former appear to exemplify the application of the Protestant ethic to the mental health movement in a manner which might introduce culture and class biases into one's conclusions.   Miller and Swanson (42) have hypothesized that lower-class children will show more defeatism than middle-class children, as a result of different interpersonal and environmental experiences.   Would they thereby be less mentally healthy by any standards besides those of the middle class?   Truly, the problems posed in setting up absolute values from which to judge mental health and illness are perplexing.

Basic problems in the definition of mental health and illness

Underlying the diversities in definition of mental illness one can discern certain basic differences of viewpoint concerning how the phenomena should be conceptualized.   We may abstract certain foci of disagreement by posing the following four points of contention: (1) Does mental illness refer to a unitary concept or to an artificial grouping of basically different specific disorders?   (2) Is mental illness an acute or chronic state of the organism?   (3) Is maladjustment (or deviance from social norms) an essential concomitant of mental illness?   (4) Should mental illness be explicitly defined according to values other than social conformity?

Each of the proposed definitions takes a stand, either explicitly or implicitly, on one or more of these issues.   It is likely that resolution of disagreements will depend in part on the outcome of future empirical research.   But at least some of the divergence inheres in the theoretical formulation of the problem, and is more a matter of conceptual predilection than of empirical fact.   In either case, if one is to arrive at consistent theoretical and operational definitions of mental illness, it would be well to make explicit one's bias concerning each of these issues, and attempt to rationalize it in terms of his conception of the causes of disturbance.

The unitary or specific nature of mental illness

The position that mental illness is manifest in some rather general form, regardless of the specific diagnostic category in which the patient is placed, would appear to be implicit in the subjective definition of the phenomenon. If the person's feeling of happiness or adequacy is regarded as the crucial indicator of his mental state, this would appear to imply that over-all health or illness can be assessed for a particular person, regardless of the area of functioning referred to. Likewise, the definition of mental health in terms of purposeful striving or active adjustment tends to ignore differences in the underlying bases for such striving or lack thereof. Such a position has been stated explicitly by Stieglitz: "The mensuration of health . . . closely parallels the measurement of biological age as contrasted to chronological age. . . . We are no longer seeking to discover specific disease entities, or even clinical syndromes, but attempting to measure biological effectiveness in adaptation" (51, p. 79). And such a unitary view of the phenomenon is implied in Schneider's comment: "The major 'cause' of mental disease is seen as some form of disorientation between the personality and society" (49, p. 31).

By contrast, the specific view of mental illness is taken by Gordon: "What we choose to call mental disease is an artificial grouping of many morbid processes. The first essential, in my opinion, is to separate the various entities, and in the approach to an epidemiology of mental diseases, to center attention on some one condition, or a few selected conditions, which have functions in common with other mass diseases well understood in their group relationships" (15, p. 107). McQuitty offers empirical evidence in favor of a specific view, in his isolation of two quite independent measures of mental illness (by psychological testing), both of which correlate with external diagnostic criteria. And he further speculates that the number of areas in which the degree of personality integration varies rather independently is probably greater than the two which he has isolated. "One might expect that mental illness might develop within any one of more patterns. In order to understand the mental illness of a particular subject, we must isolate the pattern, or patterns, of characteristics to which his mental illness pertains" (40, p. 22).

While the weight of opinion and evidence appears to favor the multidimensional view, this may simply be a function of the operational definitions employed (e.g., mental health defined by responses to a battery of tests is bound to turn out multidimensional to the extent that intercorrelations among the test items are low). But there are yet insufficient empirical data collected from the unitary point of view to test whether its assumption is correct. Indeed, it seems quite plausible that both happiness and active adaptation may be partially a function of the situation; hence the concept of mental health implied by them must become multidimensional to the extent that they allow for intersituational variability.

The acute or chronic nature of mental illness

The psychologist's testing approach to assessing mental illness inclines him toward a view of the condition as chronic. That is, the predisposing conditions within the organism are generally presumed to be relatively enduring, though perhaps triggered off into an actual psychotic break by excessively stressful situations. The epidemiological approach, on the other hand, is usually concerned with the counting of actual hospitalized cases, and this may incline one toward a view of mental illness as predominantly acute. Felix has espoused this position explicitly: "Unless the kinds of mental illness are specified, I can't conceive that mental illness is a chronic disease. More mental illnesses by far are acute and even short term than there are mental illnesses which are chronic and long term" (15, p. 163). Of course, the epidemiological approach traditionally considers characteristics of the host, as well as characteristics of the agent and the environment. But the predisposing factors within the organism seem to be regarded, like "low resistance," not as a subliminal state of the disease, but rather as a general susceptibility to any acute attack precipitated by external factors.

It is easier to regard a psychosis as acute than it is similarly to regard a neurosis, since in the former disorder the break with normal behavior appears more precipitate. However, such a judgment, based on easily observable external behaviors, may be unduly superficial. Even in the case of such a discrete disturbance as suicide, at least one writer (21) recommends considering the biologic gradient of the disorder. He distinguishes varying degrees of suicide, with successful accomplishment as merely a possible end product. Where such continuity between morbid and nonmorbid states can be discerned, the possibility of chronic disturbance might well be considered.

The problem of mental health as conformity to social norms

The criterion of mental health based on adjustment clearly implies that conformity to the social situation in which the individual is permanently imbedded is a healthy response. And such an assumption would appear to be lurking, in various shapes, behind nearly all of the other definitions considered (with the possible exception of some of the "positive striving" criteria, which stress conformity to a set of standards independent of the person's immediate social group).   In fact, McQuitty's methods of scoring psychological inventories are all explicitly based on the assumption that conformity (either to the total community or to a significant subgroup) is healthy.

If the stability of the larger social system be regarded as the final good, or if human development be seen as demanding harmony in relation to that social system, then such an assumption would appear basic and defensible.   But one is still impelled to consider the possibility that the social system, or even an entire society, may be sick, and conformity to its norms would constitute mental illness, in some more absolute sense.   If any particular behavior pattern is considered both from the standpoint of its adaptability within the social structure to which the individual maintains primary allegiance and from the standpoint of its relation to certain external ideal standards imposed by the observer, perhaps a comparison of the two discrepancy measures would yield information about the degree to which the social system approaches the ideal.   On the other hand, such a comparison might be interpreted as merely indicating the degree to which the researcher who sets the external standards is himself adapted to the social system which he is studying.   The dilemma appears insoluble.

The problem of values in criteria for mental health

The mental hygiene movement has traditionally been identified with one or another set of values—ideal standards from which behavior could be assessed as appropriate or inappropriate.   The particular set of values adopted probably depends to a considerable degree on who is doing the judging.   Such a diversity of evaluative judgments leads to chaos in the popular literature and to considerable confusion in the usage of the term "mental health" in scientific research.   Kingsley Davis (8) presented a rather strong case for the proposition that mental hygiene, being a social movement and source of advice concerning personal conduct, has inevitably been influenced by the Protestant ethic inherent in our culture.   The main features of this Protestant ethic, as seen by him, are its democratic, worldly, ascetic, individualistic, rationalistic, and utilitarian orientations.

To the extent that research on mental health is based on criteria devolved from such an ideology, it is middle-class-Protestant biased. To the extent that it is based on some other set of "absolute" norms for behavior, it is probably biased toward some other cultural configuration.   At least one researcher, Jahoda (33), has clearly taken the position that mental health criteria must be based on an explicit set of values.   There is some advantage in allowing the assumptions to come into full view, but in this case the resulting criteria appear to be rather specialized and not comparable with those used by other researchers. Perhaps the difficulty lies not so much in the existence of explicit assumptions as in their level of generality. If a more basic set of assumptions could be found, from which the diverse criteria for mental health and illness can be derived, then comparability among researches might better be achieved. One would be in a better position to state when mental illness, as defined by psychological tests or by absence of active adjustment, is likely to be displayed in mental illness defined by psychiatric diagnosis or deviance from community standards.

Summary

The various categories of definitions of mental illness discussed here have been distinguished primarily on the basis of their differing operational definitions: the dependent variables employed in empirical research on the phenomena are clearly different. Moreover the conceptualizations of mental illness explicit or implicit in the empirical criteria are often quite divergent—viz., the radically different viewpoints underlying the "maladjustment," "subjective unhappiness," and "lack of positive striving" definitions.

Certain conceptual and methodological difficulties in each of these types of definition have been noted: "Exposure to treatment" is deficient in that only a limited proportion of those diagnosable as mentally ill ever reach psychiatric treatment. "Social maladjustment" is open to question because of the varying requirements of different social systems and the diversity of criteria for adjustment employed by community members. "Psychiatric diagnosis" provides an expensive, and often unreliable, method of assessing the state of mental health. "Subjective unhappiness" can be criticized as a criterion since it may be a function of intolerable environmental conditions as well as the psychological state of the person, and is subject to distortion by defense mechanisms. The validity of "objective testing procedures" appears to depend considerably on the method by which they are scored, and there is strong evidence that a major component of their score may simply be the degree of conformity of the person to the community average. Finally, criteria included under the heading of "positive striving" are subject to question in that they are inevitably based on disputable value systems of their proponents.

While many of these difficulties would not be considered damaging from the point of view of certain of the definitions of mental illness, they run into conflict with others. Also they suggest certain basic incompatibilities among the various approaches to conceptualization of mental illness. Whether these incompatibilities should be reconciled by further theoretical and empirical exploration, or whether they should be regarded as valid indicators that mental health and illness constitute multidimensional phenomena is still a moot question. We can only note that various studies employing two or more of these different categories of criteria have tended to yield moderate, but not impressive, interrelations.

The criterion of "exposure to psychiatric treatment" has been related to "maladjustment," "psychiatric diagnosis," "subjective unhappiness," and "objective psychometrics." Also "maladjustment" has been related to "psychiatric diagnosis" and to certain "objective" measures; and "psychiatric diagnosis" has been related to both "subjective" and "objective" measures of mental illness. The areas of interrelationship for which no empirical studies have been found are between "subjective" measures and both "maladjustment" and "objective" assessment; also between the "positive striving" criteria and all of the other types of measures.

Two directions for future theory and research are indicated by these results. First, more investigations are needed of the extent of relationship among the various criteria, and of the conditions under which the magnitudes of the intercorrelations vary. Second, assuming absence of high intercorrelations under many conditions, it would be worthwhile to explore the implications of poor congruence between one measure and another—implications both for the person and for the social system in which he lives.

References

1. Beilin, H. The effects of social (occupational) role and age upon the criteria of mental health. *J. soc. Psychol.*, in press.

2. Beilin, H. The prediction of adjustment over a four year interval. *J. clin. Psychol.*, 1957, *13*, 270–274.

3. Belknap, I. V., & Jaco, E. G. The epidemiology of mental disorders in a political-type city, 1946–1952. In *Interrelations between the social environment and psychiatric disorders*. N.Y.: Milbank Memorial Fund, 1953.

4. Chase, P. Concepts of self and concepts of others in adjusted and maladjusted hospital patients. Unpublished doctor's dissertation, Univer. of Colorado, 1956.

5. Clark, R. E. Psychoses, income and occupational prestige. *Amer. J. Sociol.*, 1949, *54*, 433–440.

6. Clausen, J. A. *Sociology and the field of mental health*. N.Y.: Russell Sage Foundation, 1956.

7. Clausen, J. A., & Kohn, M. L. The ecological approach in social psychiatry. *Amer. J. Sociol.*, 1954, *60*, 140–151.

8. Davis, K. Mental hygiene and the class structure. *Psychiatry*, 1938, *1*, 55–65.

9. Downes, Jean, & Simon, Katherine. Characteristics of psychoneurotic patients and their families as revealed in a general morbidity study. *Milbank Memorial Fund Quarterly*, 1954, *32*, 42–64.

10. Dunham, H. W. Current status of ecological research in mental disorder. *Social Forces*, 1947, *25*, 321–326.

11. Dunham, H. W. Some persistent problems in the epidemiology of mental disorders. *Amer. J. Psychiat.*, 1953, *109*, 567–575.

12. Durkheim, E. *Le suicide*. Paris: F. Alcan, 1897. (English translation, Glencoe, Ill.: Free Press, 1951.)

13. Eaton, J. W. *Culture and mental disorders*. Glencoe, Ill.: Free Press, 1955.

14. Eaton, J. W., & Weil, R. J. The mental health of the Hutterites. In A. M. Rose (Ed.), *Mental health and mental disorder*. N.Y.: Norton, 1955.

15. *Epidemiology of mental disorder*. N.Y.: Milbank Memorial Fund, 1950.

16. Faris, R. E. L., & Dunham, H. W. *Mental disorders in urban areas*. Chicago: Chicago Univer. Press, 1939.

17. Felix, R. H., & Bowers, R. V. Mental hygiene and socio-environmental factors. *Milbank Memorial Fund Quarterly*, 1948, *26*, 125–147.

18. Frank, L. K. The promotion of mental health. *Ann. Amer. Acad. of Pol. Soc. Sci.*, 1953, *286*, 167–174.

19. Frumkin, R. M. Occupation and major mental disorders. In A. M. Rose (Ed.), *Mental health and mental disorder*. N.Y.: Norton, 1955.

20. Glidewell, J. C., et al. Behavior symptoms in children and degree of sickness. *Amer. J. Psychiat.*, 1957, *114*, 47–53.

21. Gordon, J. E., et al. An epidemiologic analysis of suicide. In *Epidemiology of mental disorder*. N.Y.: Milbank Memorial Fund, 1950.

22. Gruenberg, E. M. Community conditions and psychoses of the elderly. *Amer. J. Psychiat.* 1954, *110*, 888–896.

23. Gruenberg, E. M. Comment in *Interrelations between the social environment and psychiatric disorders*. N.Y.: Milbank Memorial Fund, 1953.

24. Halmos, P. *Solitude and privacy*. London: Routledge and Kegan Paul, 1952.

25. Hathaway, S. R., & Monachesi, E. D. The Minnesota Multiphasic Personality Inventory in the study of juvenile delinquents. In A. M. Rose (Ed.), *Mental health and mental disorder*. N.Y.: Norton, 1955.

26. Henry, A. F., & Short, J. *Suicide and homicide*. Glencoe, Ill.: Free Press, 1954.

27. Henry, W. E. Psychology. In *Interrelations between the social environment and psychiatric disorders*. N.Y.: Milbank Memorial Fund, 1953.

28. Hollingshead, A. B., & Redlich, F. C. Social stratification and psychiatric disorders. *Amer. sociol. Rev.*, 1953, *18*, 163–169.

29. Hyde, P. W., & Kingsley, L. V. Studies in medical sociology. I: The relation of mental disorders to the community socio-economic level. *New England J. Med.*, 1944, *231*, 543–548.

30. Jaco, E. G. The social isolation hypothesis and schizophrenia. *Amer. sociol. Rev.*, 1954, *19*, 567–577.

31. Jahoda, Marie. Toward a social psychology of mental health. In A. M. Rose (Ed.), *Mental health and mental disorder.* N.Y.: Norton, 1955.

32. Jahoda, Marie. The meaning of psychological health. *Soc. Casewk*, 1953, *34*, 349–354.

33. Jahoda, Marie. Social psychology. In *Interrelations between the social environment and psychiatric disorders.* N.Y.: Milbank Memorial Fund, 1953.

34. Kramer, M. Comment in *Interrelations between the social environment and psychiatric disorders.* N.Y.: Milbank Memorial Fund, 1953.

35. Lemert, E. M. An exploratory study of mental disorders in a rural problem area. *Rural Sociol.*, 1948, *13*, 48–64.

36. Lewis, A. Social aspects of psychiatry. *Edinburgh med. J.*, 1951, *58*, 241–247.

37. Lindemann, E., et al. Minor disorders. In *Epidemiology of mental disorders.* N.Y.: Milbank Memorial Fund, 1950.

38. Lindemann, E. Comment in *Interrelations between the social environment and psychiatric disorders.* N.Y.: Milbank Memorial Fund, 1953.

39. Locke, H. *Predicting adjustment in marriage: a comparison of a divorced and a happily married group.* N.Y.: Holt, 1951.

40. McQuitty, L. L. Theories and methods in some objective assessments of psychological well-being. *Psychol. Monogr.*, 1954, *68*, No. 14.

41. Malzberg, B. *Social and biological aspects of mental disease.* Utica: State Hosp. Press, 1940.

42. Miller, D. R., & Swanson, G. E. A proposed study of the learning of techniques for resolving conflicts of impulses. In *Interrelations between the social environment and psychiatric disorders.* N.Y.: Milbank Memorial Fund, 1953.

43. Pollak, O. Social adjustment in old age. *Soc. Sci. Res. Council Bull.* No. 59, 1948.

44. Rennie, T. A. C. The Yorkville community mental health research study. In *Interrelations between the social environment and psychiatric disorders.* N.Y.: Milbank Memorial Fund, 1953.

45. Rogers, C. *Client-centered therapy.* Boston: Houghton Mifflin, 1951.

46. Rogers, C., & Dymond, Rosalind. *Psychotherapy and personality change.* Chicago: Univer. of Chicago Press, 1954.

47. Rose, A. M., & Stub, H. R. Summary of studies on the incidence of mental disorders. In A. M. Rose (Ed.), *Mental health and mental disorder.* N.Y.: Norton, 1955.

48. Roth, W. F., & Luton, F. H.   The mental health program in Tennessee. *Amer. J. Psychiat.*, 1943, *99*, 662–675.

49. Schneider, E. V.   Sociological concepts and psychiatric research.   In *Interrelations between the social environment and psychiatric disorders.* N.Y.: Milbank Memorial Fund, 1953.

50. Schroeder, C. W.   Mental disorders in cities.   *Amer. J. Sociol.*, 1942, *48*, 40–47.

51. Stieglitz, E. J.   The integration of clinical and social medicine.   In I. Galdston (Ed.), *Social medicine—its derivations and objectives.* N.Y. Acad. of Med., 1947.   N.Y.: Commonwealth Fund, 1949.

52. Terman, L. M., et al.   *Psychological factors in marital happiness.* N.Y.: McGraw-Hill, 1938.

53. Terman, L. M., & Wallin, P.   The validity of marriage prediction and marital adjustment tests.   *Amer. sociol. Rev.*, 1949, *14*, 497–505.

54. Tietze, C., et al.   Personal disorder and spatial mobility.   *Amer. J. Sociol.*, 1942, *48*, 29–39.

55. Tietze, C., et al.   A survey of statistical studies on the prevalence and incidence of mental disorders in sample populations.   *Publ. Hlth. Rep.*, 1943, *58*, 1909–1927.

John J. Honigmann

TOWARD A DISTINCTION BETWEEN PSYCHIATRIC AND NONPSYCHIATRIC JUDGMENTS OF ABNORMALITY *

Deviance

Abnormality implies deviation from some kind of ideal, or normal, condition.   Yet, it is a fact that the norm from which abnormal human behavior departs is often not explicitly defined and, in the case of human well-being, notoriously difficult to define positively, that is, as other than the absence of symptoms.   The difficulty encountered in defining behavioral normalcy positively undoubtedly stems partly from the extraordinary flexibility and adaptability of the human

* This paper, written especially for *Readings in the Psychology of Adjustment*, 2d ed., represents a substantial revision of an essay bearing a similar title, "Toward a Distinction between Psychiatric and Social Abnormality," *Social Forces*, 1953, *31*, 274–277.

being together with the vast range of situations in which human beings are required to participate according to some standard of adequacy. From time to time, age to age, place to place, and problem to problem, different and even mutually exclusive demands are made on human beings.

What is normal for one person in one social setting becomes abnormal for another in a different situation. Consequently, the more closely one stays with a particular situation or system of situations— which is what the culture of a community represents—the easier it is to specify what is normal or abnormal for that system. However, the positive definition of behavioral normalcy is only incidentally my problem for, as the title of this paper suggests, I am primarily concerned with various conceptions of abnormality or deviance.

Every society recognizes a range of behavior in which it accepts or permits people to engage.[1] Sometimes those limits apply to a very small segment of society indeed, perhaps only to a small group, a neighborhood, or a culturally distinct community such as the Hopi Indians. Occasionally the range of permitted behavior covers all mankind in a way that ignores cultural boundaries, as when theologians judge what it is for man to be in a state of grace and psychiatrists fix what it means to be psychiatrically disturbed. The society in which such arbiters presume to operate is a truly universal one. When individuals exceed the range of permitted variation, their behavior or resultant condition is no longer fully condoned by others. If they internalize the relevant standards, they may themselves experience qualms of conscience, worry about their health, fear their poor chance at salvation, or whatnot. These remarks allow me to define deviance conveniently for present purposes by saying that it occurs when, in somebody's judgment, behavior—either observable acts or inferred behavioral states—exceeds the culturally determined limits of permitted variation. Abnormal behavior is abnormal because it passes beyond somebody's bounds of acceptability. Who devises the limits of acceptability or helps bring about agreement on them is a question of fundamental importance, both for determining what is going to be judged deviant as well as for distinguishing between psychiatric and nonpsychiatric judgments of abnormality, the topic to which this paper is addressed. To this matter I will return, as well as to the special problems posed when several arbiters of the same or different cultures disagree in their evaluation of what is unacceptable.

One can, of course, also use the term abnormal to refer to permitted deviance, that is, to behavior that exceeds the usual level but is welcome or that, although abnormal, strikingly exemplifies cultural ideals and therefore merits social approval rather than disapproval.

[1] J. J. Honigmann, *Understanding Culture*. New York, Harper and Row, 1963; Ch. 12.

Social science has given little thought to this type of abnormality which, however, is not directly related to my problem.

I said that both observable and inferred behavior may be found deviant.   Usually social control tries to halt or correct manifest acts that arouse concern or that offend, but it is not unknown for groups and social systems also to venture to regulate thoughts and feelings. I am reminded of the Hopi Indians advising one another to keep a good heart, Catholics enjoined to avoid bad thoughts, Chinese Communists exploring one another's political philosophies, or for that matter, a psychiatrist who having been made aware of a patient's disturbed feelings seeks to restore the feeling tone to proper limits.

Psychiatric abnormality

Mental illness or psychiatric abnormality conforms to the general definition of deviance to the extent that it designates behavior exceeding limits of acceptability.   The process for establishing psychiatric abnormality is clear-cut, especially if we ignore professionally debated points of nomenclature and disregard rival theories that purport to explain how certain forms of mental illness arise.   Basically, the process depends on a judgment made by an authoritative specialist, a psychiatrist (armed, perhaps, with the *Diagnostic and Statistical Manual for Mental Disorder* published by the American Psychiatric Association), who is able to recognize symptoms in a patient's behavior.   From those clues, together with additional information provided by the patient's history, the psychiatrist infers a disturbed psychic state wherein the symptoms originate.   The identification of mental illness may primarily be nosological or existential, but in any event it constitutes a ruling concerning the acceptability of the behavior in question.   The psychiatrist has authority to say validly that the behavior exceeds desirable or healthy limits or, to put it the other way, he determines what is abnormal.   That the Church once played a similar role testifies to the importance of authority in the determination of abnormality and indicates the ease with which such authority may be lost.

It is not necessary that the stricken individual or members of his community themselves recognize that the person's behavior has passed beyond the bounds of acceptability in order for the psychiatrist's diagnosis to be valid.   The validity of his judgment depends on the accuracy of the observations he makes and on the logic of the reasoning by which he reaches his conclusion.   Exotic communities may expect, tolerate, or even reward behavior corresponding, say, to psychosomatic disorder, paranoid suspicion, hallucination, and a high level of anxiety, or they may ignore the underlying psychodynamic source of such symptoms—the chronically upset essential psychical condition, as Alexander Leighton so succinctly designates the motivating source of mental disorder.[2] In those cases such behavior would not be identified as abnormal by anybody in that community. However, regardless of local acceptability, the behavior would still be abnormal if a foreign psychiatrist using a professional theory and standards evaluated it as falling outside desirable limits of mental health.

No one can any longer deny that there is an objective or operational definition of psychiatric abnormality that has been successfully applied cross-culturally. Nor can anyone affirm that mental illness must be solely defined in relation to cultural context.[3] Though psychiatry as we know it represents a cultural specialty that has developed in European and American culture, its theory provides anyone qualified to use it with a yardstick for recognizing and explaining mental illness anywhere in the world, to a large extent independently of local cultural standards, and regardless of whether the people concerned share that yardstick. The theory will continue to be applied universally as long as experience in using it turns up no great inconsistency or other difficulty, or as long as it works successfully.[4] Psychiatry is far from being the only system of concepts which, though culture-bound in their inception, can be applied successfully cross-culturally. Once the Church could do this with sin, grace, and other ideas pertaining to related states of spiritual being. But its authority has declined in a changing intellectual climate wherein, for many people, those concepts have lost both their compelling emotional significance and their former truth value. When social science rose in authority, it saw little validity or, what is more to the point, use in evaluating people by such ideas as sin or grace. The new, powerful arbiters, interested in function, dysfunction, development, and lag, wouldn't acknowledge the claim of theological concepts to universality, a claim that has ceased to be taken seriously in our society by even some theologians. Practically all the valuable concepts of cultural anthropology are culture-bound in their origin, even though a number have benefited from their authors' cross-cultural experience, and like psychiatric notions of mental illness, work with considerable precision when used cross-culturally.

Since psychiatric judgments are necessarily culture-bound, the arbiter who makes them must be constantly and carefully alert lest they absorb too great a degree of cultural bias from his own, limited social milieu. Unless he is on guard, a psychiatrist may be too ready to evaluate behavior as psychiatrically abnormal that, regardless of its

2 A. H. Leighton, *My Name Is Legion*. New York, Basic Books, 1959; Ch. 5.

3 For an instance of extreme cultural relativism see M. J. Herskovits, *Man and His Works*. New York, Knopf, 1948; pp. 66–67.

4 For a neat demonstration of such applicability see A. H. Leighton et al., *Psychiatric Disorder among the Yoruba*. Ithaca, Cornell University Press, 1963.

psychodynamic source, is untenable in his own culture. His identification of symptoms may be unduly influenced by what his own community currently regards as social problems. The point I am making is that although psychiatric judgments are always value judgments, the degree to which they betray culture-bound, moral, or other values can be controlled. Recent epidemiological reports indicate a need for such control. I suspect that lower-class metropolitan people come through a psychiatric screening with worse average mental health than middle- and upper-class people not because their psychical condition is more grievously upset but because lower-class symptoms, like the lower-class culture in which those symptoms are learned, depart so outrageously from the psychiatrist's own class-bound values.[5]

Psychiatric and nonpsychiatric deviance compared

For several reasons nonpsychiatric deviance cannot be so neatly defined operationally as the psychiatric variety. In the first place, the specialists who are regarded as having power confidently to recognize it seldom possess so clear-cut a status as psychiatrists. Second, procedures for identifying it are both less explicit and less standardized. Finally, we lack sufficient faith in a base line comparable to positive mental health, a base line which, even though it is hard to define, like a myth justifies what psychiatrists are doing. A variety of persons evaluate behavior nonpsychiatrically to judge deviance. Fellow workers in a factory do so when they reprimand the rate-buster and so do teachers who spot abnormal study habits or unacceptable forms of spelling. In the same fashion neighbors complain about a minority group's religious services, thereby rendering them deviant according to segmental criteria of propriety, and the police halt acts that run afoul of legal codes. Everyone in society possesses some power to sanction behavior departing from social standards that he endorses or tries to enforce and extend.[6] A person's area of social power may be extremely circumscribed, perhaps being limited only to his family or peer group. But even very authoritative persons who hold considerable power in a community to say what is wrong and to make their evaluation stick are varied, especially in a large-scale community. Nonpsychiatric abnormality is a considerably less universal concept than psychiatric abnormality. That is, unlike psychiatrists, social scientists lack an explicit theory or even a simple list of criteria specifying deviant behavior across cultural boundaries.

[5] The point is documented in T. S. Langner and S. T. Michael, *Life Stress and Mental Health*, The Free Press of Glencoe, 1963; esp. Ch. 16. That source speaks of socioeconomic strata rather than classes. I discuss the question in J. Honigmann, *Personality in Culture*, New York, Harper and Row, 1967; Ch. 13.
[6] In large part I follow the theory of social pressure and power advanced by Godfrey and Monica Wilson in *The Analysis of Social Change*. Cambridge, England, University Press, 1945; pp. 28, 49–58.

With the possible exception of a few types of behavior—defiant homicide is one that comes most quickly to mind—it is practically impossible to say what behavior is deviant in some nonpsychiatric sense from one culture to another.   Our lack of concepts powerful enough authoritatively to identify deviance cross-culturally is only partially due to cultural variability, to the fact that the limits of what is acceptable differ greatly from one social system and one time to another.   Basically, as I have suggested, our difficulty lies in the lack of persons in our culture possessing authority to enforce one or more theoretical yardsticks that are well-nigh independent of other cultures, that inspire confidence, and that therefore reliably can be applied cross-culturally to determine behavior departing from some hypothetical base line.   I do not speak now of the acceptability of the yardstick abroad; what I emphasize is that there is not even agreement on universal criteria of deviance among European-American social scientists.   To be sure, from time to time attempts have been made to devise lists and theories pointing out how nonpsychiatric forms of abnormality arise in society, but instead of predicting such behavior specifically and explaining it theoretically, the best such attempts turn out to define social eufunctioning.   For example, we have functional prerequisites for continuing social life [7] and universal values that nearly every community is said to try to implement.[8]   Such lists are usually brief and for the most part usually very general or obvious. They provide little help in deducing particular forms of behavior that, because they conflict with functional prerequisites or violate basic values, are consequently abnormal.   Prescriptions of social eufunctioning and universal values also illustrate the problem I referred to earlier, namely, the difficulty of trying to define in positive and universal terms those norms in terms of which human behavior may be judged as normal or abnormal.[9]   The popular sociological theory which views deviance as the product of a hiatus between desired ends and available, legitimate means for attaining those ends can't reliably identify deviance as I define it.[10]   Not only is it also too general in what it predicts, but it is actually a theory of innovation.   Only when one of the innovative modes of individual adaptation that it

[7] J. W. Bennett and M. M. Tumin, *Social Life*.   New York, Knopf, 1948; pp. 41–44 and Ch. 4.

[8] C. Kluckhohn, "Universal Categories of Culture." In A. L. Kroeber, ed., *Anthropology Today*.   Chicago, University of Chicago Press, 1953; p. 520; C. Kluckhohn, "Universal Values and Anthropological Relativism." In *Modern Education and Human Values*. Pittsburgh, University of Pittsburgh Press, 1952.

[9] Alexander Leighton's criteria of social disintegration avoid starting with positive standards of social functioning.   However, useful as they may become for identifying "deviant" social systems, they offer slight help when it comes to evaluating nonpsychiatrically the normalcy of individual behavior. See Alexander Leighton, *My Name is Legion*, New York, Basic Books, 1959; Ch. 6.

[10] Robert K. Merton, *Social Theory and Social Structure*.   Revised and enlarged edition.   Glencoe, the Free Press, 1957; Ch. 4.

accounts for happens to be regarded as illegitimate in a community does it correspond to abnormality in the present sense of the term.

As though to fill in the void left by the lack of criteria capable of being used to evaluate nonpsychiatric abnormality universally, there has arisen a tendency to expand the concept of mental illness to cover troublesome behaviors that may in fact not always be symptomatic of psychological difficulty. I refer to such behaviors as homosexuality and promiscuity and to conduct that psychiatric textbooks list under the rubrics of "personality disorder" and "sociopathic disturbance." The latter category includes the "antisocial reactions" of persons who are always in trouble and maintain no real interpersonal loyalties and "dyssocial reactions" of individuals who, while they may be capable of strong loyalties, manifest a pervasive disregard for the usual social codes. Addiction to alcohol and drugs also comes under the heading of sociopathy. It is quite possible for a type of behavior deemed to be deviant by nonpsychiatric criteria sometimes to be psychiatrically abnormal. For example, an adolescent's reckless mischief may reveal the strain under which he labors. On the other hand, it may express his new-found strength and maturity. It has been suggested that delinquents from stable lower-class families residing in an area where delinquency rates are high who adopt the values of their peers are less likely to be psychiatrically disturbed than delinquents from middle-class homes marked by hostility and lack of love.[11] I don't question the possibility that morally or socially inappropriate acts may sometimes be symptomatic of an underlying psychological disturbance. But I fear the tendency too readily to regard such conduct as psychiatric abnormality. To diagnose homosexuality in general as "sick," the way some psychiatrists have done in print, impresses me as entirely gratuitous and a shocking confusion of moral and professional standards.[12] When the psychiatrist's social system embraces alternative, class-linked forms of behavior, some of which are morally, logically, and aesthetically opposed to others, the temptation may be great to use powerful psychiatric concepts and the prestige attached to his office to evaluate as psychiatrically abnormal alternatives which he and his class find unacceptable. He may experience subtle pressure and see good reasons to employ his authority in this manner, especially when his evaluations are in line with the direction in which one socially powerful class or group desires to alter, educate, or reform another. Professional persons neither oppose change nor embrace unlimited moral relativity if, under such conditions, they recog-

[11] A. J. Reiss, "Social Correlates of Psychological Types of Delinquency." *American Sociological Review*, 1952, 17, pp. 710–718. But see J. J. Conger and W. C. Miller, *Personality, Social Class, and Delinquency*, New York, John Wiley and Sons, 1966, who, in data obtained in Denver, find little empirical support for the distinction.
[12] O. Herbert Mowrer and Thomas S. Szasz offer a far more general criticism of psychiatry than I do.

nize that they must proceed warily.   Caution is especially warranted if we work in a climate of democratic values and recognize the importance of keeping the limits of tolerance as wide as possible in order to make life congenial for as many people as possible.

Edward Joseph Shoben, Jr.   **TOWARD A CONCEPT OF THE NORMAL PERSONALITY ***

Clinical practice and the behavioral sciences alike have typically focused on the pathological in their studies of personality and behavior dynamics.   While much of crucial importance remains to be learned, there is an abundant empirical knowledge and an impressive body of theory concerning the deviant and the diseased, the anxious and the neurotic, the disturbed and the maladjusted.   In contrast, there is little information and even less conceptual clarity about the nature of psychological normality.   Indeed, there are even those (5, 13) who argue that there is no such thing as a normal man; there are only those who manage their interpersonal relationships in such a way that others are strongly motivated to avoid them, even by committing them to a mental hospital or a prison, as opposed to those who do not incite such degrees of social ostracism.

This argument has two characteristics.   First, it appears to dispose of the problem by simply distributing people among a dimension of pathology.   All men are a little queer, but some are much more so than others.   Second, it has affinities with the two major ideas that have been brought to bear on the question of what constitutes normal or abnormal behavior: the statistical conception of the usual or the average and the notion of cultural relativism.   If pathology is conceived as the extent to which one is tolerated by one's fellows, then any individual can theoretically be described in terms of some index number that reflects the degree of acceptability accorded him.   The resulting distribution would effectively amount to an ordering of people from the least to the most pathological.   Similarly, if the positions on this continuum are thought of as functions of one's acceptance or avoidance by others, then they can only be defined by reference to some group.   The implications here are twofold.   First, the concep-

* From Edward Joseph Shoben, Jr. "Toward a Concept of the Normal Personality," *Amer. Psychologist*, 1957, *12*, 183–189.   Reprinted by permission of the author and the Managing Editor, the American Psychological Association.

tion of pathology is necessarily relativistic, varying from group to group or culture to culture. Second, the degree of pathology is defined as the obverse of the degree of conformity to group norms. The more one's behavior conforms to the standards of the group, the less he is likely to be subject to social avoidance; whereas the more one's behavior deviates from the rules, the greater is the probability of ostracism to the point of institutional commitment.

Statistical and relativistic concepts of normality

Yet the issues are fully clarified by these statistical or culturally relativistic ideas. Is it most fruitful to regard normality or integrative behavior as merely reflecting a minimal degree of pathology, or may there be a certain merit in considering the asset side of personality, the positive aspects of human development? This question becomes particularly relevant when one is concerned with the socialization process or with the goals and outcomes of psychotherapy or various rehabilitative efforts.

It seems most improbable that the family, the church, and the school, the main agents of socialization, exist for the minimizing of inevitable pathological traits in the developing members of the community. Rather, parents, priests, and educators are likely to insist that their function is that of facilitating some sort of positive growth, the progressive acquisition of those characteristics, including skills, knowledge, and attitudes, which permit more productive, contributory, and satisfying ways of life. Similarly, while psychotherapists may sometimes accept the limited goals of simply trying to inhibit pathological processes, there are certainly those (11, 16) who take the position that therapy is to be judged more in terms of how much it contributes to a patient's ability to achieve adult gratifications rather than its sheer efficiency in reducing symptoms or shoring up pathological defenses.

A general concern for such a point of view seems to be emerging in the field of public mental health (26). Beginning with an emphasis on treatment, the concept of community mental health swung to a preventive phase with the main interest focused on identifying the antecedents of mental disease and on reducing morbidity rates by attacking their determinants. The vogue of eugenics was one illustrative feature of this stage. More recently, there has been a considerable dissatisfaction with the whole notion of interpreting psychological states in terms of disease analogues (15, 23). Maladjustive behavior patterns, the neuroses, and—perhaps to a lesser extent—the psychoses may possibly be better understood as disordered, ineffective, and defensive styles of life than as forms of sickness. In consequence, there seems to be a growing tendency to conceive of the public mental health enterprise as emphasizing positive development with the prevention and treatment of pathology regarded as vital but secondary.

But in what does positive development consist? The statistical concept of the average is not very helpful. Tiegs and Katz (27), for example, reported a study of college students who had been rated for fourteen different evidences of "nervousness." By and large, these traits were normally distributed, suggesting that those subjects rated low must be considered just as "abnormal" (unusual) as those rated high. This conception seems to provide a superficial quantitative model only at the expense of hopeless self contradiction and violence to the ordinary categories of communication. Even in a case that at first blush seems to cause no difficulty, the problem remains. Criminal behavior, for example, is distributed in a J-shaped fashion with most cases concentrated at the point of zero offenses, ranging to a relatively few instances of many-time offenders. Few would argue that the usual behavior here is not also the most "positive." But one suspects that the sheer frequency of law-abiding behavior has little to do with its acknowledged integrative character. If conformity to social rules is generally considered more desirable than criminality, it is not because of its rate of occurrence but because of its consequences for both society and the individual.

Thus, a statistical emphasis on the usual as the criterion of positive adjustment or normality shades into a socially relativistic concept with an implied criterion of conformity. The terms "usual" or "most frequent" or "average" are meaningless without reference to some group, and this state of affairs poses two problems. First, conformity in itself, as history abundantly demonstrates, is a dubious guide to conduct. Innovation is as necessary to a culture's survival as are tradition and conservation, and conformity has frequently meant acquiescence in conditions undermining the maturity and positive development of human beings rather than their enhancement. On more personal levels, conformity sometimes seems related in some degree to personality processes that can quite properly be called pathological (2, 24). Second, relativistic conceptions of normality pose serious questions as to the reference group against which any individual is to be assessed. Benedict (3), for example, has made it quite clear that behavior which is considered abnormal in one culture is quite acceptable in others, that certain forms of abnormalities which occur in some societies are absent in others, and that conduct which is thought completely normal in one group may be regarded as intensely pathological in another. Such observations, while descriptively sound, can lead readily to two troublesome inferences. One is that the storm trooper must be considered as the prototype of integrative adjustment in Nazi culture, the members of the Politburo as best representing human normality Soviet style, and the cruelest adolescent in a delinquent gang as its most positively developed member. The other is that any evaluative judgment of cultures and societies must be regarded as inappropriate. Since normality is conceived only in terms of conformity to group standards, the group itself must be beyond appraisal. Thus, the suspicion and mistrust of Dobu (10), the sense of resigned futility that permeates Alor (6), and the regimentation that characterizes totalitarian nations can logically only be taken as norms in terms of which individual behavior may be interpreted, not as indications of abnormal tendencies in the cultures themselves.

Wegrocki (28), in criticizing such relativistic notions, argues that it is not the form of behavior, the actual acts themselves, that defines its normal or pathological character. Rather, it is its function. What he calls the "quintessence of abnormality" lies in reactions which represent an escape from conflicts and problems rather than a facing of them. This formulation, implying that integrative adjustments are those which most directly confront conflicts and problems, seems essentially free of the difficulties inherent in statistical conceptions and the idea of cultural relativism. But it presents troubles of its own. For instance, what does it mean to "face" a problem or conflict? On what ground, other than the most arbitrarily moralistic one, can such confrontations be defended as more positive than escape? Finally, does this facing of one's problems have any relationship to the matter of conformity in the sense of helping to clarify decisions regarding the acceptance or rejection of group standards?

To deal with such questions requires coming to grips with certain problems of value. It is at this point that the behavioral sciences and ethics meet and merge, and it seems unlikely that any conception of normality can be developed apart from some general considerations that are fundamentally moral. Once the purely relativistic ideas of normality are swept away, it becomes difficult to avoid some concern for the issues of happiness and right conduct, *i.e.*, conduct leading to the greatest degree of human satisfaction, that are the traditional province of the literary interpreter of human experience, the theologian, and the moral philosopher. A primary challenge here is that of providing a rational and naturalistic basis for a concept of integrative adjustment that is at once consistent with the stance and contributions of empirical science and in harmony with whatever wisdom mankind has accumulated through its history.

Symbolic and social aspects of human nature

One way to meet this challenge is by frankly postulating a basic principle of value. The fundamental contention advanced here is that behavior is "positive" or "integrative" to the extent that it reflects the unique attributes of the human animal. There are undoubtedly other ways of approaching a fruitful concept of normality. Nevertheless, this assertion is consistent with the implications of organic evolution, escapes the fallacy of the survival-of-the-fittest doctrine in its various forms, and permits a derivation of more specific criteria of positive adjustment from the distinctive characteristics of man. No discontinuity within the phylogenetic scale need be assumed. It seems clear, however, that man, while certainly an animal, can hardly be described as "nothing but" an animal; and his normality or integration seems much more likely to consist in the fulfillment of his unique potentialities than in the development of those he shares with infrahuman organisms.

Foremost among these uniquely human potentialities, as Cassirer (4) and Langer (14) make clear, is the enormous capacity for symbolization. What is most characteristic of men is their pervasive employment of *propositional* language. While other organisms, especially dogs (22) and the higher apes (29), react to symbols, their faculty for doing so indicates only an ability to respond to mediate or representative as well as direct stimuli. Man, on the other hand, uses symbols designatively, as a vehicle for recollecting past events, for dealing with things which are not physically present, and for projecting experience into the future. Goldstein (12) makes the same point in his discussion of the "attitude toward the merely possible," the ability to deal with things that are only imagined or which are not part of an immediate, concrete situation. In patients whose speech has been impaired because of brain damage, this attitude toward the possible is disrupted. Thus, aphasics are typically unable to say such things as, "The snow is black" or "The moon shines in the daytime"; similarly, they are incapable of *pretending* to comb their hair or to take a drink of water although they can actually *perform* these acts. Such patients appear to have lost the uniquely human capacity for thinking *about* things as well as directly "thinking things."

It is his symbolic ability, then, that makes man the only creature who can "look before and after and pine for what is not." Propositional speech makes it possible for him to learn from not only his own personal experience but from that of other men in other times and places, to forecast the consequences of his own behavior, and to have ideals. These three symbol-given attributes—the aptitude for capitalizing on experience, including the experience of others over time, the capacity for foresight and the self-imposed control of behavior through the anticipation of its outcomes, and the ability to envision worlds closer than the present one to the heart's desire—constitute a basic set of distinctively human potentialities.

A second set of such potentialities seems related to the long period of helpless dependence that characterizes infancy and childhood. Made mandatory by the relative biological incompleteness of the human body, this phase of development is likely to be lengthened as cultures become more complex. Thus, in such simpler societies as the Samoan (18), children can achieve a higher degree of independence at an earlier age than in the civilizations of the West, for example, where the necessity for learning complicated and specialized economic skills extends the period of dependence through adolescence and even into chronological young adulthood. The central point, however, is that unlike the young of any other species, human children in *all* cultural settings must spend a long time during which the gratification of their most basic needs is mediated by somebody else and is dependent on their relationship to somebody else.

This state of affairs exposes youngsters during their earliest and most formative stages of development to two fundamental conditions of human life. The first is that one's survival, contentment, and need fulfillment involve an inevitable element of reliance on other people. The second is that the relative autonomy, authority, and power that characterize the parent figures and others on whom one relies in childhood are always perceived to a greater or lesser extent in association with responsibility and a kind of altruism. This is, the enjoyment of adult privileges and status tends to occur in conjunction with the acceptance in some degree of the task of in some way mediating the need-gratifications of others. Mowrer and Kluckhohn (20) seem to be speaking of a similar pattern when they describe the socialization process as progressing from childhood *dependency* through *independence* to adult *dependability*.

Moreover, this reciprocal relationship between reliance and responsibility seems to obtain on adult levels as well as between children and parents, with the degree of reciprocity a partial function of the complexity of the culture. In simpler societies, a relatively small number of persons may assume primary responsibility for virtually all of the needs of the group in excess of its bare subsistence demands. Under civilized conditions, however, the specialization made necessary by technology and the pattern of urban living means that each adult is dependent on some other adult in some way and that, conversely, he is responsible in some fashion for the welfare of some other adult. The difference between the simpler and the more complex cultures, however, is only one of degree. The crucial point is that throughout human society, men are in one way or another dependent on each other both in the familiar situation of parents and children and in the course of adult living. This pattern of interdependency gives to human life a social character to be found nowhere else in the animal kingdom. Even among the remarkable social insects, the patterns of symbiosis found there seem to be a result of a genetically determined division of labor rather than the fulfillment of a potentiality for the mutual sharing of responsibilities for each other.

It is in this notion of the fulfillment of distinctively human potentialities that a fruitful conception of positive adjustment may have its roots. From the symbolic and peculiarly social character of human life, it may be possible to derive a set of potential attributes the cultivation of which results in something different from the mere absence of pathology and which forms a standard against which to assess the degree of integration in individual persons.   To accept this task is to attempt the construction of a normative or ideal model of a normal, positively developed, or integratively adjusted human being.

A model of integrative adjustment

In the first place, it would seem that as the symbolic capacity that endows man with foresight develops in an individual, there is a concomitant increase in his ability to control his own behavior by anticipating its probable long-range consequences.   The normal person is, first of all, one who has learned that in many situations his greatest satisfaction is gained by foregoing the immediate opportunities for comfort and pleasure in the interest of more remote rewards.   He lives according to what Paul Elmer More, the Anglican theologian, calls "the law of costingness":

. . . the simple and tyrannical fact that, whether in the world physical, or in the world intellectual, or in the world spiritual, we can get nothing without paying an exacted price.   The fool is he who ignores, and the villain is he who thinks he can outwit, the vigilance of the nemesis guarding this law of costingness . . . all (one's) progress is dependent on surrendering one interest or value for a higher interest or value.   (19, p. 158).

Mowrer and Ullman (21) have made the same point in arguing, from the results of an ingenious experiment, that normality results in large part from the acquired ability to subject impulses to control through the symbolic cues one presents to oneself in the course of estimating the consequences of one's own behavior.   Through symbolization, the future outcomes of one's actions are drawn into the psychological present; the strength of more remote rewards or punishments is consequently increased; and a long-range inhibitory or facilitating effect on incipient conduct is thereby exercised.

This increase in self-control means a lessened need for control by external authority, and conformity consequently becomes a relatively unimportant issue.   The integratively adjusted person either conforms to the standards of his group because their acceptance leads to the most rewarding long-range consequences for him, or he rebels against authority, whether of persons or of law or custom, on *considered* grounds. This considered form of revolt implies two things. The first is an honest conviction that rules or the ruler are somehow unjust and that the implementation of his own values is likely to lead to a more broadly satisfying state of affairs. Such an attack on authority is very different from revolts that occur out of sheer needs for self-assertion or desires for power or as expressions of displaced hostility. The main dimension of difference is that of honesty as opposed to deception. The normal person is relatively well aware of his motives in either conforming or rebelling. The pathological rebel, on the other hand, tends to deceive himself and others about his goals. His reasons for nonconformity amount to rationalizations, and his justifications are typically projections. This kind of self-defeating and socially disruptive deceptiveness is seen daily in clinical practice.

The second characteristic of nonconformity in the normal person is that it is undertaken with an essential acceptance of the possible consequences. Having considered the risks beforehand, he is inclined neither to whine nor to ask that his rebellious conduct be overlooked if he runs afoul of trouble. In keeping with the "law of costingness," he is willing to pay the price for behaving in accordance with his own idiosyncratic values. "We have the right to lead our own lives," John Erskine (8) makes Helen of Troy say to her daughter Hermione, "but that right implies another—to suffer the consequences. . . . Do your best, and if it's a mistake, hide nothing and be glad to suffer for it. That's morality." A psychological paraphrase of this bit of belletristic wisdom is not inappropriate: The assumption of responsibility [1] for one's actions is one of the attributes of personal integration.

But if personal responsibility and self-control through foresight can be derived as aspects of integrative adjustment from man's symbolic capacity, a third characteristic of interpersonal responsibility can be deduced from his social nature. If interdependency is an essential part of human social life, then the normal person becomes one who can act dependably in relation to others and at the same time acknowledge his need for others. The roots of the former probably lie, as McClelland (17) has pointed out, in the role perceptions which developing children form of parent figures and other agents of the socialization process. By conceiving of such people as at least in some degree the nurturant guides of others and through identification with them, the integratively adjusted individual "wants to be" himself trustworthy and altruistic in the sense of being dependable and acting out of a genuine

---

[1] This conception of responsibility is by no means antideterministic. As Fingarette (8) points out, one can *understand* his own or another's behavior, in the sense of accounting for it or rationally explaining it, by the retrospective process of examining the past. Responsibility, on the other hand, is neither retrospective in orientation nor explanatory in function. It is future oriented and refers to the *act* of proclaiming oneself as answerable for one's own conduct and its consequences. Thus, "responsibility," in this context, is not a logical term, implying causation, but a behavioral and attitudinal one, descriptive of a class of human actions.

concern for the welfare of others as he can best conceive it. Altruism in this context, therefore, means nothing sentimental. It certainly includes the making and enforcement of disciplinary rules and the imposition of behavioral limits, but only if these steps are motivated by an interest in helping others and express concern and affection rather than mere personal annoyance or the power conferred by a superior status.

Similarly, the acknowledgment of one's needs for others implies a learned capacity for forming and maintaining intimate interpersonal relationships. Erikson (7) refers to this aspect of the normal personality as the attitude of "basic trust," and it is not far from what can be meaningfully styled in plain language as the ability to love. One suspects that the origins of this ability lie in the long experience during childhood of having need gratifications frequently associated with the presence of another person, typically a parent figure. By this association and the process of generalization, one comes to attach a positive affect to others. But as the youngster develops, he gradually learns that the need-mediating behavior of others is maintained only by his reciprocating, by his entering into a relationship of mutuality with others. If this kind of mutuality is not required of him, he is likely to perpetuate his dependency beyond the period his biological level of development and the complexity of his culture define as appropriate; whereas if he is required to demonstrate this mutuality too soon, he is likely to form the schema that interpersonal relationships are essentially matters of traded favors and that instead of basic trust, the proper attitude is one of getting as much as possible while giving no more than necessary. The pursuit in research and thought of such hypotheses as these might shed a good deal of light on the determinants of friendship, marital happiness, and effective parenthood, the relational expressions of effective personal integration.

But there is still another interpersonal attitude relevant to a positive conception of adjustment that is somewhat different from that bound up with relationships of an intimate and personal kind. There is a sense in which each individual, even if he regards himself as unfortunate and unhappy, owes his essential humanity to the group which enabled him to survive his helpless infancy. As studies of feral children (25) have shown, even the humanly distinctive and enormously adaptive trait of propositional speech does not become usable without the stimulation and nurture of other people. A kind of obligation is therefore created for the person to be an asset rather than a burden to society. It is partly to the discharging of this obligation that Adler (1) referred in developing his concept of social interest as a mark of normality. While the notion certainly implies the learning of local loyalties and personal affections, it also transcends the provincial limits of group and era. Because man's symbolic capacity enables him to benefit from the record of human history and to anticipate the future, and because his pattern of social interdependency, especially in civilized societies, reaches across the boundaries of political units and parochial affiliations, it seems reasonable to expect the positively developed person to behave in such a fashion as to contribute, according to his own particular lights, to the general welfare of humanity, to take as his frame of reference mankind at large as best he understands it rather than his own group or clan.

Ideologies are at issue here, but there need be neither embarrassment nor a lack of room for debate regarding the specifics of policy and values in the hypothesis that democratic attitudes are closely bound up with personality integration. After all, democracy in psychological terms implies only a concern about others, a valuing of persons above things, and a willingness to participate in mutually gratifying relationships with many categories of persons, including those of which one has only vicarious knowledge. Departures from democratic attitudes in this psychological sense mean a restriction on the potentiality for friendship and imply both a fear of others and a valuation of such things as power over people, thus endangering the interpersonal rewards that come from acting on the attitude of basic trust. Democratic social interest, then, means simply the most direct route to the fulfillment of a distinctively human capacity derived from man's symbolic character and the inevitability of his social life.

Finally, man's ability to assume an attitude toward the "merely possible" suggests that the normal person has ideals and standards that he tries to live up to even though they often exceed his grasp. For an integrative adjustment does not consist in the attainment of perfection but in a striving to act in accordance with the best principles of conduct that one can conceive. Operationally, this notion implies that there is an optimum discrepancy between one's self-concept and one's ego-ideal. Those for whom this discrepancy is too large (in favor, of course, of the ideal) are likely to condemn themselves to the frustration of never approximating their goals and to an almost perpetually low self-esteem. Those whose discrepancies are too low, on the other hand, are probably less than integratively adjusted either because they are failing to fulfill their human capacity to envision themselves as they could be or because they are self-deceptively overestimating themselves.

This model of integrative adjustment as characterized by self-control, personal responsibility, social responsibility, democratic social interest, and ideals must be regarded only in the most tentative fashion. Nevertheless, it does seem to take into account some realistic considerations. It avoids the impossible conception of the normal person as one who is always happy, free from conflict, and without problems. Rather, it suggests that he may often fall short of his ideals; and because of ignorance, the limitations under which an individual lives in a complex world, or the strength of immediate pressures, he may sometimes behave in ways that prove to be shortsighted or self-defeating. Consequently, he knows something of the experience of guilt at times, and because he tries to be fully aware of the risks he takes, he can hardly be entirely free from fear and worry. On the other hand, a person who is congruent to the model is likely to be one who enjoys a relatively consistent and high degree of self-respect and who elicits a predominantly positive and warm reaction from others. Moreover, it is such a person who seems to learn wisdom rather than hostile bitterness or pathologically frightened withdrawal from whatever disappointments or suffering may be his lot. Guilt, for example, becomes a challenge to his honesty, especially with himself but also with others; and it signalizes for him the desirability of modifying his behavior, or greater effort to live up to his ideals, rather than the need to defend himself by such mechanisms as rationalization or projection. Finally, the model permits a wide variation in the actual behaviors in which normal people may engage and even makes allowance for a wide range of disagreements among them. Integrative adjustment does not consist in the individual's fitting a preconceived behavioral mold. It may well consist in the degree to which his efforts fulfill the symbolic and social potentialities that are distinctively human.

References

1. Adler, A. *Social interest: A challenge to mankind.* London: Faber & Faber, 1938.

2. Adorno, T. W., Frenkel-Brunswik, Else, Levinson, D. J., & Sanford, R. N. *The authoritarian personality.* New York: Harper, 1950.

3. Benedict, Ruth. Anthropology and the abnormal. *J. gen. Psychol.,* 1934, *10,* 59–82.

4. Cassirer, E. *An essay on man.* New Haven: Yale Univer. Press, 1944.

5. Darrah, L. W. The difficulty of being normal. *J. nerv. ment. Dis.,* 1939, *90,* 730–739.

6. DuBois, Cora. *The people of Alor.* Minneapolis: Univer. Minnesota Press, 1944.

7. Erikson, E. H. *Childhood and society.* New York: Norton, 1950.

8. Erskine, J. *The private life of Helen of Troy.* New York: Bobbs-Merrill Co., 1925.

9. Fingarette, H. Psychoanalytic perspectives on moral guilt and responsibility: A re-evaluation. *Phil. phenomenol. Res.,* 1955, *16,* 18–36.

10. Fortune, R. F. *Sorcerers of Dobu.* London: Routledge, 1932.

11. Fromm, E. *The sane society.* New York: Rinehart, 1955.

12. Goldstein, K. *Human nature in the light of psychopathology.* Cambridge, Mass.: Harvard Univer. Press, 1940.

13. Hacker, F. H. The concept of normality and its practical significance. *Amer. J. Orthopsychiat.*, 1945, *15*, 47–64.

14. Langer, Susanne K. *Philosophy in a new key.* Cambridge, Mass.: Harvard Univer. Press, 1942.

15. Marzolf, S. S. The disease concept in psychology. *Psychol. Rev.*, 1947, *54*, 211–221.

16. May, R. *Man's search for himself.* New York: Norton, 1953.

17. McClelland, D. *Personality.* New York: William Sloane Associates, 1951.

18. Mead, Margaret. *Coming of age in Samoa.* New York: William Morrow, 1928.

19. More, P. E. *The Catholic faith.* Princeton: Princeton Univer. Press, 1931.

20. Mowrer, O. H., & Kluckhohn, C. A dynamic theory of personality. In Hunt, J. McV. (Ed.), *Personality and the behavior disorders.* New York: Ronald Press, 1944. Pp. 69–135.

21. Mowrer, O. H., & Ullman, A. D. Time as a determinant in integrative learning. *Psychol. Rev.*, 1945, *52*, 61–90.

22. Pavlov, I. P. *Conditioned reflexes.* London: Oxford Univer. Press, 1927.

23. Riese, W. *The conception of disease.* New York: Philosophical Library, 1953.

24. Riesman, D. *The lonely crowd.* New Haven: Yale Univer. Press, 1950.

25. Singh, J. A. L., & Zingg, R. M. *Wolf-children and feral man.* New York: Harper, 1942.

26. Subcommittee on Evaluation of Mental Health Activities. *Evaluation in mental health.* Bethesda, Md.: Public Health Service, 1955.

27. Tiegs, E. W., & Katz, B. *Mental hygiene in education.* New York: Ronald Press, 1941.

28. Wegrocki, H. J. A critique of cultural and statistical concepts of abnormality. *J. abnorm. soc. Psychol.*, 1939, *34*, 166–178.

29. Yerkes, R. M. *Chimpanzees: A laboratory colony.* New Haven: Yale Univer. Press, 1943.

David Freides

**TOWARD THE ELIMINATION
OF THE CONCEPT OF
NORMALITY ***

In recent years, the literature concerning the nature of normality in human personality has shown increasing support for an "idealist" conception of psychological normality. Normality is viewed as an approximation to an ideal or combination of ideals, such as health, rationality, honesty, integration, maturity, or morality. This literature has justifiably criticized the traditional approaches to this problem, i.e., a "symptom-free" conception, specified as absence of pathological stigmata, or a "centrist" conception, specified either as the statistical average of normally distributed characteristics or as the balance between tendencies, which, in their extremes, are considered pathological, like introversion and extroversion. This paper will present a critique of normative perspectives in personality theory, focusing on the "idealist" position (criticism of traditional approaches may be found in works by Hartman, 1939; Maslow, 1954; Mowrer, 1954; Shoben, 1957, and others), and propose an alternative to these approaches.

A common starting point among authors proposing an idealist conception of normality is the recognition of the enormous extrabiological potential for variation inherent in human beings as evidenced by complex cultural activity, symbolization, and altruism. They stress that these inherently human qualities deserve more serious attention than they are getting from students of personality and should be embodied in the concept of normality. Shoben (1957, p. 185), for example, states, "the fundamental contention advanced here is that behavior is 'positive' or 'integrative' to the extent that it reflects the unique attributes of the human animal." As the "unique attributes" of humans are extremely varied and frequently repugnant, the writers go on to specify what they mean. Maslow (1954, Ch. 12) lists 17 characteristics of self-actualizing people including acceptance of self, others, and nature; spontaneity; problem centering; the quality of detachment; autonomy; democratic character structure; creativeness; and resistance to enculturation. Bond (1952) mentions freedom to focus energy on main purposes, ability to work and love with ease, and to achieve happiness and efficiency somewhat in proportion to circumstances. Shoben (1957) writes of self-control, personal responsibility, social responsibility, democratic social interests, and

* From David Freides, "Toward the Elimination of the Concept of Normality," *J. consult. Psychol.*, 1960, 24, 128–133. By permission of the author and the Managing Editor, the American Psychological Association.

ideals. McLaughlin (1950) enumerates emotional independence and self-reliance; balance between giving and getting; relative freedom from egotism, inferiority feelings, and excessive competitiveness; conscience; genital sexuality; constructive aggressiveness; solid sense of reality; flexibility; and adaptability.

Several major difficulties and limitations are inherent in this approach. First, it establishes as absolute desiderata patterns of behavior and values that grow out of a particular cultural context during a particular period of its history. It assumes that what is good for us is good for everybody everywhere. Several authors explicitly recognize that these criteria of normality involve assumptions in the nature of value judgments. Other writers do not, but cultural anthropology and history provide evidence that freedom from inferiority feelings or genital sexuality or constructive aggressiveness, for example, are not and have not been universally considered desirable goals for human behavior.

Second, this approach generally does not take into account the circumstances under which the personality is to function. It implies that variations in circumstances do not determine or even influence the functioning of the personality and precludes the study of how behavior and circumstance covary. Third, it largely assumes that postulated criteria of normality are positively correlated, or can be positively correlated. As to whether they are correlated, reference can be made to several attempts to study "normal, healthy individuals." Maslow (1954) and Bond (1952), for example, went to great efforts to obtain suitable examples. Bond guarded against his own selection biases by studying almost complete populations of student council members and concluded nonetheless that 57% could benefit from ideal mental health services. Maslow grudgingly devotes two pages to the imperfections of self-actualizing people. Roe's (1950) studies of eminent scientists (to be sure, using criteria of success and not of normality) amply indicate that nonnormal characteristics regularly accompany achievement, creativity, and success. Redlich (1952) reviews several studies of "normal" populations in which "rich pathological" material was found.

Perhaps even more significant is the question of whether it is reasonable to anticipate that characteristics of normality such as those under discussion can be positively correlated. Consider, for example, such positively valued attributes as love and independence. Ideal patterns of loving devotion and enduring commitment to one's beloved, coupled with independence, assertiveness, and freedom from infantile demands of succorance, are generally accepted as positive characteristics of the normal; but the conflictual nature of multiple human needs and aspirations is obscured by an approach which does not recognize that love and commitment *necessarily* and inevitably restrict independence.

Finally, a value based conception of normality tends arbitrarily to slant research so as to preclude investigations of the relationships between devalued patterns of behavior and ideal patterns of behavior.

These criticisms are not to be construed as arguments for banning values from consideration in personality theory. The question is where and how to deal with them in a way that is scientifically appropriate. Values and value systems may be studied objectively as variables, and the task of psychology is to assess their relationships with other variables and with behavior. Such an approach does not imply that every moral and ethical system is as good or as workable as any other nor that the search for the "good" in either individual or culture should be minimized, but it does indicate a way in which such problems may be considered at levels of discourse which are germane to science. In this manner science is not faced with questions it cannot answer.

It is significant that the proponents of the point of view under discussion seem to be all for the good life but are rather vague as to what they mean by it, while theologists and ethicians are quite explicit and vigorous defenders of the positions they take. The apparent proclivity for tolerance, understanding, and minimization of differences, characteristic of this school of thought (with few exceptions), conceals and overrides hard differences in the approach to life embodied in different value systems.[1] Yet, to consider values as variables seems definitely uncongenial to those who hold that the values they profess are the only values worthy of consideration and study. For example, Shoben (1957), while arguing that a normative approach based on a statistical average precludes the criticism of a culture, confuses a conflict of values with a scientific controversy when he disdains the possibility that the storm trooper would be considered the prototype of integrative adjustment in the Nazi culture. Disapproval of Nazi culture has nothing to do with understanding how a man raised in Nazi Germany might be expected to become a storm trooper. Science can do no more than predict the consequences of a value system. Political, religious, or cultural conflicts are fundamentally not resolved in the laboratory or on the couch.

Writers adopting an idealist approach concerning psychological normality take a position that is steeped in contradiction. On the one hand, their conception of normality has an absolutist quality that is laced with culture-bound value assumptions. On the other hand,

---

[1] See Herberg (1957) for a critical discussion of the ethical inadequacies of theoretical orientations in psychology which minimize differences in value alternatives and preclude the conceptualization of the realities of moral conflict in the individual.

they show marked reservations concerning a conception of normality based on social conformity and they abhor any taint of absolutism. Maslow (1954), for example, specifies autonomy, independence of culture and environment, and resistance to enculturation as characteristics of the self-actualizing (normal) person. In doing so, Maslow evidently means to divorce himself from purely statistical conceptions of social conformity. Certainly he does not mean compulsive autonomy, or compulsive resistance to enculturation, yet his whole perspective, shared with many others, including Fromm (1941), Mowrer (1954), and Shoben (1957), is one of meeting a specified ideal, and this inevitably involves some form of cultural bias, some form of limitation, some constriction of freedom.

In a discussion of this contradiction, Knight (1946) deals with the problem by (a) specifying that freedom is largely a subjective matter; (b) showing that many subjective feelings of freedom are spurious, and (c) concluding that genuine freedom and mental health involve the sense of inner compulsion and conformity based on a rational appreciation by the individual of the assumptions, conditions, motives, and values in his life. It is this bedrock of rationality to which all of these writers ultimately arrive.

Kubie (1954) takes perhaps the extreme position and asserts that the sole criterion for normality is the predominance of conscious and preconscious over unconscious factors in the determination of an act. Since Kubie rules out consciousness, per se, as a criterion (a delusion is conscious but not normal), he can only be interpreted to mean that rational, reasonable, reality-oriented behavior is normal. On the surface, this seems to be a satisfactory solution to the problem. It posits a criterion which is neutral as far as value is concerned and can conceivably lead to objective assessment procedures. However, such a point of view seemingly would label all nonrational behavior and motivation as abnormal and in doing so would devalue and implicitly condemn any manifestation of emotional spontaneity. Arguing, as Kubie does, that it is the origin of the act and not its subsequent automatic execution that must be assessed, would nonetheless require, at some point, meticulous evaluation of matters of taste, preferences in art, religious values and beliefs, and love objects in order to fulfill this criterion. Kubie's disclaimer (1954, p. 187), "Here is no unreal fantasy of a 'normal' individual out of whom all the salty seasoning of secondary unconscious motivations has been dissolved," when followed in the next paragraph by "What was unconscious . . . must become accessible enough to self-inspection to become conscious when needed," suggests that his conception of "salty seasoning" is not so spicy after all.

When the search for the normal leads to the elevation of the rational, a host of problems concerning the nature of reason, logic, and rationality may be overlooked. These include the distinctions between a rational process and rational content (Hartman, 1956; Reider, 1950), the illogical and prelogical factors which contribute to the development of intelligence and reason (Piaget, 1953), the role of unconscious and regressive factors in creativity (Kris, 1952), and the process of change in form and content of knowledge and logic through a history which has not ended and whose future course is unpredictable by any reliable means.

Finally, and this criticism is germane to practically every attempt to define normality, it assumes that rational, conscious, and preconscious processes, once established, carry on of their own accord without environmental support and stimulation. Recent studies on the effects of sensory deprivation (Hebb, 1955), the classic studies of perception under distorted conditions (Lawrence, 1949), and many studies of behavior under stress (Lazarus, Deese, & Osler, 1952) indicate that this is simply not the case. To specify consciousness or rationality as the essence of normality merely begs the question.

A truly objective, scientific solution to the problem of defining normality when one is concerned with something more than averaging existing traits and behaviors, when one seeks to embody in this definition a particular conception of what man may be, is impossible to attain. As soon as values, symbols, altruism, and the like are specified in the definition of normality, objectivity yields to time-bound and culture-bound assumptions which are not subject to scientific verification and which are of limited generality. That each person deliberately or unconsciously has a scheme of values, beliefs, and ethics which imparts to him his uniquely human character, that, indeed, to be a human requires such a scheme, is a proposition that does not establish a *particular* system of values or logic as an absolute criterion of normality.

Psychology should stop asking the question "What is normal?" Personality theory requires another orientation. It seems to me that, for purposes of scientific theory construction and also for practical clinical purposes, a rather different and potentially more fruitful approach can be taken. This would entail the viewpoint that human beings have a variety of potentialities, and that the achievement of certain potentialities may entail certain limitations and that achievement and limitation vary with conditions.

Consider it is the distant, withdrawn personality who is unable to form close relationships who, it has been said, stands the best chance of enduring the stress of a prolonged flight into space. The suspicious mistrusting individual, difficult to get along with, may, because of these very characteristics, be an excellent tax inspector, research scientist, or counterintelligence agent. The vain narcissistic personality can become a great entertainer. Reverse the point. Is great acting possible without narcissism? Is creative research possible without mistrust? Is prolonged isolation tolerable for a gregarious individual? The legitimate task of science is not to stand back smugly and label the various distributions of energy and effort as abnormal or normal. The task of theoretical psychology is to provide the concepts and principles which would enable us to comprehend achievements and failings *and their interrelationships.*

Such an approach focuses on man's behavior as the data available for scientific study. Existing terms and concepts such as repression, motive, conformity, defense mechanism, and habit need not be discarded as conceptual tools, but with this perspective the scientist does not imply damnation or praise when he uses them to characterize a psychological process. This approach sets no limits on the sophistication of the theories developed to encompass the facts of behavior, but it lessens the likelihood of confounding facts and theories and value assumptions. It avoids positing criterion value systems but freely admits the incorporation of value systems as variables contributing to or limiting different potentialities. It sets the stage for research into the development and exercise of man's potentialities for what, on other grounds, may be considered good or evil, but does not prejudge or condemn. It permits the description and understanding of man as he was, is, and can be.

Several features of the present position have been elaborated in the literature. Marmor and Pumpian-Mindlin (1950) and Jahoda (1953), for example, have stressed the interaction of personality and situational variables in the determination of behavior. Hartman (1951) points out that conflicts are inherent to human existence and (1939) that rationality and freedom do not necessarily imply health, while regression and defense are not necessarily maladaptive. Schafer (1954, p. 172) writes, "The growth and organization of personality appears to require that certain of each individual's potentialities be cultivated and others neglected or even plowed under." Marzolf (1947) concludes, "In fact there is no need for the term 'mental disease.'" Several writers (Darrah, 1939; Jones, 1942; Wile, 1940) are doubtful about the existence of "normal" personalities. But in one way or another, they all (with the exception of Wile, 1940) cling to the traditional perspective and express or reflect some concept of normality.

If the framework proposed is theoretically acceptable, objections may nevertheless be raised on practical grounds. If no valid conception of normality is possible, is treatment ever indicated and, if so, toward what goals is treatment directed? At present, certain personality patterns can be labeled abnormal and treatment is presumably directed toward changing abnormal personalities or patterns of behavior into normal ones. The definition of what is normal is considered critical to clinical practice and its elimination apparently leaves an enormous conceptual void.

Actually, there are several unwarranted assumptions implicit in the view that a conception of normality is central to clinical practice. First is the assumption that treatment is initiated with the finding of abnormality, however defined. Operationally, treatment is initiated when motivation from some source exists for treatment and when therapists are motivated and prepared to undertake treatment. There is a reciprocal relationship between professional personnel and patient pool in that the professional proffers the expectation of relief from distress and contributes to the development of this anticipation in potential clients. Absence of some relevant form of this expectation seems to be one of the factors underlying failure in the treatment of lower-class patients by predominantly middle- and upper-class professionals (Hollingshead & Redlich, 1958). The point is that the initiation of treatment results less from a finding of abnormality than from the meshing of reciprocally intertwined (more or less) motivations.

Second, the notion that the aim of treatment consists of changing the patient from abnormal to normal is unjustified. In many cases, in those perhaps most amenable to current forms of treatment, therapy consists largely of helping the patient to resolve conflicting trends within his personality rather than making him or helping him to become normal. The patient who has successfully completed this type of treament (in which the therapist can remain relatively neutral with regard to values) does not by any flight of the imagination meet the usual criteria of normality. (The individual who speaks of his having been analyzed or treated psychotherapeutically and implies that he is "normal" is usually labeled a prig.) Furthermore, as already noted, if the patient has been enabled to deal more successfully with certain kinds of problems and conflicts, this may be at the expense of other potentialities.

A third questionable point is the assumption that the goals of treatment are determined by scientific criteria. In many types of cases the resolution of conflict is only a minor part of therapy. Much more than the bolstering or the elimination of defensive patterns within the personality seems indicated in certain types of schizophrenia, in severely schizoid personalities or in antisocial personalities. Very many of these cases require that a way of life be taught. In other words, certain cases require far more than reorganization of the personality; they require education itself and the inculcation of values. Once again, it seems to me that science can contribute to an understanding of the educative process but that the content of this education is largely a matter that must be decided on other grounds. Here, the articulation and specification of the values under which or toward which the therapist operates is of great importance, *but these choices are not scientific matters.* We do the best we can much like any parent living at a particular time and in a particular place.

This point, that values, symbols, and the like *are* involved in psychotherapy (Hacker, 1945), brings the discussion full circle. Davis (1938, p. 65) in a little cited analysis of the mental hygiene movement has argued that the social function of the mental hygienist "is not that of a scientist but that of a practising moralist in a scientific, mobile world." It seems to me that what Davis is saying is that professionals dealing with "ways of life" inevitably have to rely on *some* consistent framework to fill gaps and resolve conflicts where they exist and that this framework willy-nilly will be that prevalent in the cultural group to which the professionals belong. If this issue may be obscured in the treatment of adults, it is blatantly apparent and quite inevitable in the treatment of children and in the advice given to parents about techniques of child rearing (Erikson, 1950). As a consequence, it seems likely that psychological treatment is a conservative force in any society no matter how radical the theories about psychotherapy sometimes appear to be. But the implicit or explicit commitment to values involved in the practice of psychotherapy is an issue separate and distinct from a scientifically useful specification of the concept of normality. The future development of a scientific understanding of personality depends on a less restrictive perspective which, ironically, should benefit clinical practice as well.

A shift in perspective in personality theory from one which looks upon man as normal or abnormal or somewhere in between to one which views him as having varying potentialities and limitations under varying conditions, seems to offer an orientation more viable, secure, and fruitful than that prevailing at present. The viable aspect of this position comes out of its capacity to conceive of man in different times and different circumstances. The security features result from the elimination of the necessity for the clinician to rationalize about his own normality (Reider, 1950), permitting his work to be evaluated objectively in terms of its results. Finally, the fruitfulness of this approach rests on its reluctance to condemn, to label abnormal, and its emphasis on the potentialities of every person under the proper conditions. It sets the stage for more extensive investigations into the nature of these potentialities and the conditions of their achievement, all the while keeping before us the pitfalls and limitations that such achievement may involve.

References

Bond, E. D. The student council study: An approach to the normal. *Amer. J. Psychiat.*, 1952, *109*, 11–16.

Darrah, L. W.   The difficulty of being normal.   *J. nerv. ment. Dis.*, 1939, *90*, 730–739.

Davis, K.   Mental hygiene and the class structure.   *Psychiatry*, 1938, *1*, 55–65.

Erikson, E. H.   *Childhood and society.*   New York: Norton, 1950.

Fromm, E.   *Escape from freedom.*   New York: Rinehart, 1941.

Hacker, F. J.   The concept of normality and its practical significance. *Amer. J. Orthopsychiat.*, 1945, *15*, 47–64.

Hartman, H.   Psychoanalysis and the concept of health.   *Int. J. Psycho-Anal.*, 1939, *20*, 308–321.

Hartman, H.   Ego psychology and the problem of adaptation.   In D. Rapaport (Ed.), *Organization and pathology of thought.*   New York: Columbia Univer. Press, 1951.

Hartman, H.   Notes on the reality principle.   *Psychoanal. Stud. Child,* 1956, *11*, 31–53.

Hebb, D. O.   The mammal and his environment.   *Amer. J. Psychiat.*, 1955, *111*, 826–831.

Herberg, W.   Freud, religion and social reality.   *Commentary*, 1957, *23*, 277–284.

Hollingshead, A. B., & Redlich, F. C.   *Social class and mental illness.* New York: Wiley, 1958.

Jahoda, Marie.   The meaning of psychological health.   *Soc. Casewk.*, 1953, *34*, 349–354.

Jones, E.   The concept of the normal mind.   *Int. J. Psycho-Anal.*, 1942, *23*, 1–8.

Knight, R. P.   Determinism, "freedom" and psychotherapy.   *Psychiatry*, 1946, *9*, 251–262.

Kris, E.   *Psychoanalytic explorations in art.*   New York: International Univer. Press, 1952.

Kubie, S.   The fundamental nature of the distinction between normality and neurosis.   *Psychoanal. Quart.*, 1954, *23*, 167–204.

Lawrence, M.   *Studies in human behavior.*   Princeton: Princeton Univer. Press, 1949.

Lazarus, R. S., Deese, J., & Osler, S. F.   The effects of psychological stress upon performance.   *Psychol. Bull.*, 1952, *49*, 293–317.

McLaughlin, J. T.   Normality and psychosomatic illness.   *Ment. Hyg., N. Y.*, 1950, *34*, 19–33.

Marmor, J., & Pumpian-Mindlin, E.   Toward an integrative conception of mental disorder.   *J. nerv. ment. Dis.*, 1950, *111*, 19–29.

Marzolf, S. S.   The disease concept in psychology.   *Psychol. Rev.*, 1947, *54*, 211–221.

Maslow, A. H.   *Motivation and personality.*   New York: Harper, 1954.

Mowrer, O. H.   What is normal behavior?   In L. A. Pennington & I. A. Berg (Eds.), *An introduction to clinical psychology.* (2nd ed.) New York: Ronald Press, 1954.   Pp. 58–88.

Piaget, J. *The origin of intelligence in the child.* London: Routledge & Kegan Paul, 1953.

Redlich, F. C. The concept of normality. *Amer. J. Psychother.*, 1952, 6, 551–569.

Reider, N. The concept of normality. *Psychoanal. Quart.*, 1950, 19, 43–51.

Roe, Anne. The use of clinical diagnostic techniques in research with normals. In M. Reymert (Ed.), *Feelings and emotions.* New York: McGraw-Hill, 1950. Pp. 336–342.

Schafer, R. *Psychoanalytic interpretation in Rorschach testing.* New York: Grune & Stratton, 1954.

Shoben, E. J. Toward a concept of the normal personality. *Amer. Psychologist*, 1957, 12, 183–189.

Wile, I. S. What constitutes abnormality? *Amer. J. Orthopsychiat.*, 1940, 10, 216–228.

Ralph H. Tindall

RELATIONSHIPS AMONG MEASURES OF ADJUSTMENT *

Many specific tests and devices have been used to establish overall adjustment indices. They imply that there is an entity labeled adjustment which can be legitimately assessed (1). A review of psychological literature dealing with diagnostic or therapeutic efforts shows that groups or individuals have been labeled relatively well adjusted on the basis of a single, or, at the best, a few indices purporting to measure adjustment status. This has occurred and continues to occur in spite of summaries, such as that of Ellis (4), which point out the weaknesses of using certain of these indices as independent criteria. Claims for the validity of various personality appraisal devices have usually been based upon their agreement with results obtained from using some other established technique. Frequently this comparison has been only with a test of similar type, e.g., comparing a self inventory with another self inventory; few studies have attempted to compare representative measures from all of the modes

* From Ralph H. Tindall, "Relationships among Indices of Adjustment Status," *Educ. Psychol. Measmt.*, 1955, 15, 152–162. Reprinted by permission of the author and the Editor, *Educational and Psychological Measurement.*

of measuring so-called adjustment. Such a study would indicate the extent to which these various types of measures are getting at something in common which might be labeled "adjustment"; an analysis of subareas of agreement and disagreement should help point up next possible steps in this measurement area. In brief, it is proposed to categorize existing techniques which purport to measure adjustment, select representative devices under each category, administer these carefully to a select population, and then analyze the nature of their interrelationships.

Methods

As a basis both for selecting and for constructing adequate measures of adjustment, it seemed an important first step to study definitions of adjustment commonly used in order to find aspects covered and areas of agreement. A review of representative writings dealing with the concept of adjustment disclosed that while there were differences in expression and terminology there was general agreement as to the general nature of adjustment (3, 6, 7, 8, 9). In brief, adjustment is usually described as a process that covers the individual life span, operating within a complex environmental field. The process is goal directed behavior instituted by a need which may arise at any level within a hierarchy of needs ranging from elementary physiological tissue needs through the most complicated psychological symbolizations. The process is sustained when this goal directed behavior meets, in a complex environmental setting, thwarting circumstances which serve to heighten tensions producing varied responses in the organism. One, or a combination of these varied responses, eventually leads to a solution response which enables the organism to attain a transitory goal that results in the reduction of that particular tension (2, p. 35). The very process of obtaining the transitory goal, against a complex environmental setting, frequently establishes the circumstances for the arousal of new tensions, thus perpetuating the process.

Seven characteristics or facets of adjustment were generally described as desirable by the majority of writers in the field. There was no implication in their writings, nor is there such implication here, that these facets are independent or mutually exclusive. Rather, these descriptive terms frequently coexist and complement each other in the behavior of individuals judged well adjusted. These seven facets briefly reviewed are:

1   *Maintaining an integrated personality.* This involves the coordination of one's needs and goal seeking behavior into smoothly functioning interaction with the environment.

2   *Conforming to social demands.*   Emphasis here is upon harmony with the standards of the cultural group without surrendering individual spontaneity.

3   *Adapting to reality conditions.*   This facet is characteristic of the ability to expose oneself to present hardship conditions in order to make gains toward long range goals.

4   *Maintaining consistency.*   A qualitative facet which makes possible prediction for behavior and permits hopes for the assessment of adjustment.

5   *Maturing with age.*   Allowance is made for maturation and development of the individual with concomitant growth of more complex adjustment processes.

6   *Maintaining an optimal emotional tone.*   In the face of emotionally loaded situations the well adjusted person is neither constricted in emotional involvement nor overwhelmed by his reactions.

7   *Contributing optimally to society through an increasing efficiency.* Here is an insurance that adjustive behavior reaches beyond self-centered goals.

In the course of developing a concept of adjustment, various commonly used mechanisms of adjustment were recognized.   It was found that while the mechanisms themselves were well recognized (i.e., withdrawal, projection, introjection, direct attack, sublimation, etc.), there was disagreement as to a mechanism's classification *per se* along the adjustment continuum.   Establishing the existence of a particular mechanism in operation would not automatically label the behavior as maladjustment or good adjustment.   It was necessary to take into consideration the complex environmental circumstances in which the behavior occurred.   Since the process of adjustment is a continuous one, since it exhibits itself against a complicated environmental background, and since it may occur at any level of a complex physiological-psychological hierarchy, the inherent difficulties of measurement were recognized.   Despite these difficulties, techniques purporting to measure adjustment exist and enjoy relatively wide usage.   It is these very attempts to appraise adjustment that make this study a legitimate project.

Into what categories of approach can commonly used measures of adjustment be placed?   What actual measurement devices were considered representative of these categories and used in this study?   It is believed that present day measures are of five major types: (1) questionnaires and inventories; (2) ratings by adult judges; (3) ratings by peers using sociometric techniques; (4) adjustment indices secured by means of projective techniques; and (5) systematized direct observation.   Representative techniques were chosen in each category in accordance with criteria that took into account suitability of use with the age group selected, systems of scoring resulting in a numerical index of adjustment, practicability of application, and differences of approach within the major type.

The type (1) approach, i.e., questionnaires and inventories, was represented by the *California Test of Personality*, which gave two indices of adjustment, self adjustment and social adjustment. The *Heston Personal Adjustment Inventory* was also selected under type (1) as representing an inventory built through the process of factor analysis. This inventory gave six indices of adjustment: analytical thinking, sociability, emotional stability, confidence, personal relations, and home satisfaction.

Three indices were used for the type (2) approach, ratings by adult judges. One was the average global rating of adjustment, made independently by two teachers and one cottage supervisor who had had experience with each boy in the selected population, in which variation in each of the seven facets of adjustment was taken into account. The second index under type (2) was secured by using the average rating of the two men in the Dean of Boys' office, secured by independent rating of each boy on the *Haggerty-Olson-Wickman Behavior Rating Schedule B*. The third index in type (2) was secured by having the psychologist make an overall adjustment rating of each boy on the basis of case history material, close acquaintanceship, and a semi-structured interview.

Type (3), sociometric techniques, was represented by a "Guess Who" index and a "Companionship Choice" index. The "Guess Who" index was secured by presenting an opportunity for nominating boys for characteristics shown by Tryon (10) to be most and least admired in adolescent societies. The "Companionship Choice" index was determined through opportunity to choose and to reject companions for desirable activities.

Type (4), projective techniques, was represented by an index secured through the use of the *Rotter Incomplete Sentence Test* and through the use of *Munroe's Rorschach Check List.*

Type (5), systematized direct observation, was exemplified by a Time Sample of behavior. Three well defined categories of generally considered maladaptive behavior were checked for occurrence in ten five minute periods. These periods were selected so as to sample representative daily activity.

Since the study was designed to examine the relationships among various techniques purporting to measure adjustment, it was necessary to select a relatively stable and well known population upon which to apply the various techniques. The writer was serving as resident psychologist at the Ohio Soldiers' and Sailors' Orphans' Home at the time. Within the larger population at the Home (over four hundred children), a population consisting of all the white boys who had reached their fourteenth birthday as of April 1, 1950, who had been in residence for at least six months, and who were not being immediately discharged, appeared to be the most appropriate. The resulting population consisted of sixty-six adolescent boys, who were known to vary in their adjustment status. They were found to be within the average range of ability, but to be retarded slightly by school placement standards. They would have rated low on a scale of family stability. Approximately five per cent of these boys were orphans, while the majority were children whose homes had been broken by reason of divorce, desertion of a parent, etc. The cultural background was somewhat below that usually considered middle class. The boys had lived in the orphanage an average of approximately six years. While an atypical group in some respects, the immediate environmental field was similar; they were well known, and they were available for study and follow-up. Since the emphasis of the study was on techniques, this population lent itself well to the study.

In addition to the sixteen indices of adjustment used, it was felt necessary to measure the effect of three extraneous variables on adjustment status. These were: chronological age, mental age, and months of residence in the institution.

In order to secure these various arrays of indices, each technique was applied to the population with utmost care taken to prevent bias in scoring. All protocols were identified by code numbers during the application and scoring process. Where published techniques were used, there was strict adherence to administrative directions. All techniques were applied in the time between April, 1950, and September, 1950. Raw scores were transmuted so that high scores indicated relatively good adjustment while low scores indicated maladjustment.

Results

Characteristics of the data.   The nineteen resulting arrays were inspected for normalcy of distribution and other characteristics. Means, standard deviations, and reliabilities for each technique were computed. One of the outstanding characteristics of the data secured from the chosen population was that on several measures, e.g., the *California Test of Personality,* the *Heston Personal Adjustment Inventory,* the *Haggerty-Olson-Wickman Behavior Rating Schedule B,* and the *Munroe Rorschach Check List,* the mean score of this population was considerably below the mean score of the standardization group. This implies that, while the scores of the population chosen were normally distributed as a group, they gave evidence of more maladjustment than was found in the standardization populations. This is the situation we would expect to exist with such an institutional group.   It was also found that the reliability coefficient of the average teacher-supervisor rating (T and S Rating), .58, was too low to assure confidence in this particular index.   The data showed that the Time Sample technique supplied a range of scores too narrow to be considered very discriminating.

Relationships of adjustment indices with extraneous variables. Correlations were found between each of the sixteen arrays of adjustment indices and each of the three arrays secured from measuring the extraneous variables of chronological age, mental age, and length of residence.   In general it was found that very few of these relationships were at a statistically significant level and there were logical explanations for the few instances found.   Thus, the index of adjustment established through the use of the *Haggerty-Olson-Wickman Behavior Schedule B* was significantly related to mental age, i.e., .26, but the former rating technique devotes one area to scales concerning ability status.   In fact it offers validating evidence for that particular area of the scale.   The "Guess Who" index was found to be significantly related to months in residence at the orphanage, i.e., .26, but with continued group living one would expect behavior modification in accordance with group standards.   The Time Sample index was related to both chronological age and months in residence at a significant level, i.e., .47 and .30, respectively.   This may be partially accounted for by a tendency for the behavior observed to become more covert with age.   Since the Time Sample index was also discovered to be rather poor in discriminating between persons in the population, little significance should be attached to relationships found with this measure.

Intercorrelations among adjustment indices.   The resulting intercorrelations are reported in Table 1.   In general, there is a positive but low correlation among the various arrays of adjustment indices. The median intercorrelation coefficient is .228.   This is sufficient to indicate just a thread of relationship among these common approaches to measurement of adjustment.   The results are insufficient to support strongly a global concept of adjustment.

An examination of Table 1 reveals that forty-one of the one hundred and twenty intercorrelations were significant at the .01 level or better, or about one-third of the possible correlations found (5, p. 209).   In addition, seventeen more of these intercorrelations were significant at the .05 level.   Thus, a number of the techniques used were tapping related processes; this lends some support to a global concept of adjustment.   However, the lowness of these relationships and the infrequency of their occurrence detract from the usefulness of this global concept.

Table 1
Intercorrelations of adjustment indices
r < .24 below .05 level; r > .32 above .01 level; N = 66

Indices	Self adjustment	Social adjustment	Analytical thinking	Confidence	Sociability	Personal relations	Emotional stability	Home satis.	"T. & S" rating	Deans' rating	Psych. rating	Guess who	Companion choice	Rorschach	Incomplete sentences	Time sample
Self-adjustment		.66	.24	.53	.20	.62	.48	.33	.71	.26	.40	.50	.32	.26	.32	.27
Soc. adjustment			.11	.35	.15	.46	.33	.38	.42	.27	.47	.28	.27	.35	.32	.12
Anal. th'k'g				.33	.31	.17	.30	-.13	-.04	.13	.07	.20	.07	.11	-.04	-.09
Confidence					.50	.76	.81	.33	.03	.17	.21	.30	.22	.14	.15	.01
Sociability						.29	.32	.02	-.09	-.06	.04	.33	-.04	.11	.08	.03
Pers. relations							.79	.38	.16	.25	.31	.27	.37	.18	.21	.12
Emot. stability								.43	.01	.07	.16	.22	.24	.18	.09	.07
Home satis.									.21	-.02	.20	-.05	.13	.20	.03	.10
"T. & S" rating										.55	.49	.53	.60	.29	.10	.46
Deans' rating											.58	.37	.63	.19	.10	.17
Psych. rating												.30	.49	.11	.36	.19
Guess who													.63	.25	.13	.29
Comp. choice														.32	.11	.22
Rorschach															.09	-.09
Inc. sentences																-.10
Mean	57.0	66.2	20.8	24.9	22.1	21.6	26.4	37.2	97.5	82.6	93.8	.8	.1	15.6	125.5	6.5
S.D.	11.3	11.9	4.5	7.0	6.8	6.1	7.6	7.6	33.1	18.5	16.2	25.8	27.6	4.8	16.3	2.9

80

Certain factors appeared present which could account for some of the relationships found. These factors may have influenced the amount of relationship found above and beyond that contributed by adjustment. Relationships among techniques within each of these major groupings were at a higher level than most of those relationships found among the various types. For example, the median r between self ratings was .33, and between peer ratings was .30. Thus, the bias of a particular rater affects the results irrespective of the device used. There was also more relationship among three of the major groupings of techniques than among the others. Questionnaires and inventories, ratings by adults, and ratings by peers using sociometric techniques had a median r of .30 with each other; all are established by some form of personal report, based perhaps on character reputation, which could plausibly account for some of the relationship found. Several of the tests provide ratings of self adjustment and social adjustment. Conceivably, these two aspects are inextricably bound together in a particular individual, and when attempts are made to measure them separately related results are obtained. In brief, then, while some generality of relationship was obtained, some of this is attributable to factors other than adjustment of the individual.

It will be noted that the two projective techniques are unrelated to each other and to other indices established by other techniques. On the other hand, in the intensive case studies these projective techniques were found useful in constructing hypotheses in regard to individual behavior dynamics.

It is interesting at this point to note that the rating of the psychologist, which is frequently used as the criterion measure when validation studies are made of an adjustment assessing technique, was related at a significant level to eight of the fifteen other indices, six of them at the one per cent level. These correlations were not high, the highest being .58 with the index established by averaging the ratings of the two deans.

In addition to studying the relationships among arrays of various adjustment indices, a detailed study of five individual cases was made. These cases were selected according to several criteria, the most important being that two of them evidence relatively high scores in the self adjustment area as measured by the *California Test of Personality,* and in the social adjustment area as measured by the *Companionship Choice Test.* Similarly, two were to evidence low scores in these areas while the fifth was to show discrepancy between scores in these areas. By using standard scores it was possible to compare all indices with behavioral, psychological, and historical data. This individual case study supported the hypothesis that reported self adjustment and social acceptance reported by peers were fruitful screening devices. Individual discrepancy among the various techniques for measuring adjustment could, in the majority of cases, be explained on the basis of the detailed case history. It was clearly indicated in these five cases that no one score taken alone could be depended upon to assess adjustment adequately in an individual case.

While such a correlation matrix as this would permit a factor analysis study, the very low relationships would not make such a study fruitful. The area known as adjustment apparently needs more careful definition. If meaningful concepts could be delineated, then more valid measuring devices might be constructed. More refined statistical techniques might then be applied.

Conclusions

1   The data secured in this study indicate that techniques purporting to appraise adjustment status when applied to the same population do not produce results that are closely related. This would imply that a global concept of adjustment, based on present day tests, is limited in usefulness. Assessment of adjustment by one technique has little predictive value in terms of results which might be secured by using another technique.

2   Evaluative studies, where claims are made in regard to change in adjustment status, should report several indices of adjustment. If it can be shown that there has been a significant change brought about in adjustment as measured by various techniques, more confidence can be placed in those results.

3   There is a need for clearer definitions within the concept of adjustment. We suggest that in our culture there should be certain common situations that should lend themselves to definition in terms of behavior that could be agreed upon as to position on an adjustment-maladjustment continuum.

4   Differences among techniques, within the same general type of adjustment assessing measures, point out the need for refinement of present techniques. The addition of more and more varieties of adjustment assessing techniques, validated through comparison of results established by existing techniques, serves to complicate rather than clarify the existing situation.

5   For the best use of existing techniques, the results of this study appear to indicate using many instead of one or a few indices before general conclusions in regard to adjustment status are drawn. Results secured should be checked with actual behavior manifestations as well as historical data. If it is desired to screen out those whose adjustment status is questionable in groups such as the one used in this study, a score indicating the subject's feelings in regard to self adjustment and a score based upon peer acceptance indicating social adjustment are useful.

Finally, one further caution may be added. After over two years of follow up on the individual cases making up this population, where fairly complete biographical, psychological, and educational data exist, there is yet to be in evidence any one clear-cut measure which would predict in more than a general way the course of individual adjustment.

References

1. Buros, O. K. *The Third Mental Measurements Yearbook.* New Brunswick, N.J.: Rutgers Press, 1949.

2. Dashiell, J. F. *Fundamentals of General Psychology.* Chicago: Houghton Mifflin, 1937.

3. Dysinger, D. W. "Signs of Personality Disintegration." In Pennington, L. A., and Berg, I. A. *An Introduction to Clinical Psychology.* New York: Ronald Press, 1948.

4. Ellis, Albert. "The Validity of Personality Questionnaires." *Psychological Bulletin,* XLII (1946), 385–440.

5. Fisher, R. A. *Statistical Methods for Research Workers.* New York: Hafner Publishing Company, 1950.

6. Krech, David, and Crutchfield, R. S. *Theory and Problems of Social Psychology.* New York: McGraw-Hill, 1948.

7. Shaffer, L. F. *The Psychology of Adjustment.* Chicago: Houghton Mifflin, 1936.

8. Symonds, P. M. *The Dynamics of Human Adjustment.* New York: Appleton-Century-Crofts, 1946.

9. Traxler, A. E. *Techniques of Guidance.* New York: Harper & Brothers, 1945.

10. Tryon, C. M. *Evaluation of Adolescent Personality by Adolescents.* Monograph of the Society for Research in Child Development, No. 4, 1939.

Joseph Veroff, Sheila Feld, and Gerald Gurin   # DIMENSIONS OF SUBJECTIVE ADJUSTMENT *

Research programs assessing mental health have a broad range of problems that are possible of exploration.   The criteria used to eval-

* From Joseph Veroff, Sheila Feld, and Gerald Gurin, "Dimensions of Subjective Adjustment," *J. abnorm. soc. Psychol.*, 1962, 64, 192–205.   Reprinted by permission of the authors and the Managing Editor, the American Psychological Association.

The investigations reported in this paper are based on data obtained within a national sample survey supported by the Joint Commission on Mental Illness and Health. Analysis of these data was supported by a grant from the National Institute of Mental Health, United States Public Health Service, Project M2280.

uate health or illness are diverse.   Problems of social adjustment, aspects of self-esteem, psychosomatic complications, creativity all can be investigated.   Or one can simply identify disturbance pragmatically by isolating those admitted to mental hospitals or those who have been exposed to some sort of psychiatric treatment.   Recent thinking about this confusing diversity of criteria for evaluating mental health and illness has converged on the reasonable viewpoint that different criteria for such evaluations are not only equally possible and equally valid but are required for a complete appraisal of mental functioning (Eaton, 1951; Fiedler, Dodge, Jones, & Hutchins, 1958; Jahoda, 1950, 1953, 1958; Scott, 1958; Smith, 1950, 1959).

In the present study, a factorial classification of various self-descriptions of adjustment and distress, the data for inferences about mental health were limited to self-reports, thereby ruling out considerations of criteria for mental health that are based on other sources of inference, such as the assessment of actual behaviors or the diagnoses of an "objective" clinical observer or the judgments of peers.   But even within this focus on self-evaluations of psychic distress, there exists the possibility of using several different kinds of dimensions for evaluating "good" and "poor" mental health.   Self-descriptions are often assumed to be a single criterion to be compared with criteria based on evaluations from psychiatrists, friends, etc.   (Eaton, 1951; Fiedler et al., 1958).   But there are many facets to self-descriptions. And many ways of defining felt distress appear in the research literature on mental health.   Different indices of dysfunctioning focus on different aspects of psychic adjustments: psychosomatic complaints (MacMillan, 1957), ways of perceiving the self (Rogers, 1951), life satisfactions in marriage (Terman & Wallin, 1949), in work (Herzberg, Mausner, & Snyderman, 1959; Morse, 1953), life happiness in general (Inkeles, 1960).   Each of these approaches is by itself inadequate for fully identifying distress.   Usually, the investigator concentrates on one aspect of these subjective evaluations.   In so doing he may be trapped into identifying this aspect of mental health as the most important criterion for defining mental health.   In the present study, rather than choosing among these various criteria of distress, a multiple criterion approach was adopted.   The research to be reported suggests that multiple criteria are needed in a description of subjective adjustment, and further suggests what these criteria might be psychologically.

The present paper is a further report on a nationwide sample survey recently reported on by the present authors (Gurin, Veroff, & Feld, 1960).   A total of 2,460 adult respondents were selected by area sampling probability methods to constitute a representative cross-section of adults, 21 years of age or older, living in private households in the United States (Kish, 1953).   This sample omits the hospitalized population.   They were interviewed about their lives, their experiences of distress or satisfaction in many *different* kinds of ways.   In utilizing a multiple criterion approach to the measurement of feelings of adjustment, each index was considered separately, on its own terms. No one measure was weighted more heavily than the other as a "better" measure of psychic distress.   Rather, we assumed that unhappiness, the sense of inadequacy, tension in a marriage or with children, problems at work, constant worries, feelings of an impending nervous breakdown, all reflect different areas of potential distress.   In the analyses already reported, the information in the survey was examined to see how *each* index varied from social group to group, and how *each* was related to patterns of seeking professional help for personal problems.

A major question remains from these analyses: How are the various indices covering different aspects of life adjustments related one to another—especially for groups for whom all indices were relevant— married women with children and employed married men with children who fall into our noninstitutionalized United States population?   This is the problem for this paper.   In this study, factor analytic techniques were used to assess the communalities in response to the diverse questions asked of the national sample.   The emerging factor structure may be indicative of basic psychological factors underlying the determination of self-descriptions of adjustment, and as such it represents an empirical basis for theorizing about the significance of these disparate measures.

The factor analytic technique allows the researcher to look at clusters of responses in different ways.   It may very well be in our analysis that certain clusters will reflect accommodations to strong cultural pressures to perceive the self in a prescribed manner.   Or it may be that the clusters reflect deeply felt reactions to the common psychological problems faced by most people in American society.   In general we will be following the latter interpretation of the significance of the analyses.   We recognize that the other interpretation is possible and will highlight the alternate view where it appears appropriate.

We have approached the problem of investigating self-descriptions with the assumption that separate components to self-evaluations were more than likely.   Orthogonal factors generating intercorrelations of responses are part of the assumptive framework used in procedures for this study in factor extraction and rotation.   This assumption will not guarantee multiple dimensions of self-descriptions, but it favors such a possibility of data analysis.

All the indices of adjustment are based on self-descriptions.   As such they raise the question of honesty of response.   Some distortion in self-report is inevitable in a study of subjective adjustment.   However, we would expect such distortion to be mainly reflected in a generalized tendency to admit or deny distress in the different life-areas investigated in this study, rather than in systematic distortions on certain of the measures. Since a factor analytic study would be mainly affected by systematic rather than generalized distortions, we might expect the error springing from such distortions to be less critical for the analyses reported here than in other analyses—for example, those which would involve interpretations of the absolute values of the responses to the different questions on which the adjustment measures are based. However, some systematic distortion may exist, and as such would add a source of error to the results.

Error springing from the problem of honesty of response may also be introduced when factor structures are compared for different subgroups of the population. For example, in the comparison between men and women that will be discussed in this paper, the question may arise as to whether the sex differences were affected by differences in either the prescribed stereotypes of responding for men or for women or in how willing men and women are to talk to an interviewer (usually a woman) in an interview situation. However, as will be noted in the later discussions, the similarities in the factor structures of men and women are more striking than the differences, and the differences that do exist do not seem relevant to the question of differences in honesty of response.

In the present study we have considered only a portion of the total sample of 2,460 subjects. Three interview forms were used in the study, each assigned randomly to one-third of the subjects. One-third of the total sample of men and two-thirds of the sample of women were asked all the questions dealt with in the present paper; certain questions were applicable only to currently married subjects with children or, among the men, to working subjects. The final Ns are 542 women and 255 employed men who are currently married and have children.

Procedure

The expression of distress was measured in six areas: general feelings of distress, attitudes towards the self, marital adjustment, adjustment as a parent, job adjustment (men only), and psychological and psychosomatic symptom complaints. The separate indices are listed in Table 1 under these headings together with the questions on which each index was based. For a full description of the coding procedures for each index and the complete interview schedule the reader is referred to *Americans View Their Mental Health* (Gurin et al., 1960).

For purposes of intercorrelation, the responses to the questions constituting each index were ranked—with a rank of 1 indicative of highest distress.   As can be seen in Table 1, the number of rank positions varied from index to index, with seven of the indices having only two rank positions.

Separate matrices of intercorrelations of these indices were obtained for men and women.   Since the sex differences in response to some of the separate indices were very great, it was felt that the possibility of distinctive factor structures emerging for men and women warranted consideration.   (Separate factor analyses for different age and educational groups may also be necessary; we anticipate following through these possibilities in future analyses.)

Kendall's tau beta was computed for each pair of indices.   This particular statistic was used for two reasons.   It avoids the necessity of collapsing categories of coding, as would have to be done if we employed tetrachoric correlations or phi coefficients; it also avoids the necessity of making unwarranted assumptions about units of measurement, as would be required if Pearsonian product-moment correlations were used.   The logic of factor analysis is applicable to tau beta's since the statistic has been found to operate similarly to Pearsonian product-moment correlations usually used in factor analyses; the sampling errors and distributions of the two statistics are similar.[1]

The centroid method of factor extraction and IBM 650 Principle Axis Varimax program for rotation were used to obtain the final factor structures for men and women.

Results and discussion

Tables 2 and 3 present the matrices of intercorrelations for men and women, respectively.   The significance of tau beta can be estimated: for the men ($N = 255$), tau's needed for significance at the .05 and .01 levels of confidence are .082 and .108, respectively; for the women ($N = 542$), the comparable figures are tau's of .054 and .091, respectively (cf. Kendall, 1948).   Since the size of the samples involved here is large, and the size of the correlations required for significant deviations from zero is therefore relatively small, our major interest in these data is in the communalities of responses shown in the factor analysis.

In Table 4, the rotated factor loadings for both men and women are presented.   The order in which the factors were extracted for men was 1,2,4,5,3; for women it was 1,3,2,4,5.   In attempting to interpret the factor structures for men and women, we limited our consideration to those items which had factor loadings of .30 or higher.

In the main, the factor structures for men and women are similar;

[1] The authors would like to express their appreciation to William L. Hays and to John A. Sonquist for their help with these statistical problems and procedures.

Table 1
Indices used in factor analyses of self-descriptions of distress

Questions	Indices
General feelings of distress	
Everybody has some things he worries about more or less. What kinds of things do you worry about most?	Worrying All the time Sometimes Never
Do you worry about such things a lot, or not very much?	
Taking things all together, how would you say things are these days—would you say you're *very happy, pretty happy,* or *not too happy* these days?	Unhappiness Not too happy Pretty happy Very happy
Compared to your life today, how do you think things will be 5 or 10 years from now—do you think things will be happier for you than they are now, not quite as happy, or what?	Future unhappiness Not as happy About the same Happier
Have you ever felt that you were going to have a nervous breakdown?	Nervous breakdown Yes No
Attitudes toward self	
People are the same in many ways, but no two people are exactly alike. What are some of the ways in which you're different from most other people?	Lack of uniqueness of self Sees no differences from others Mentions differences
Same as above.	Lack of self-acceptance (degree to which subject gives negative evaluation of the self in describing differences from others) Negative Ambivalent Neutral Positive Very positive
Many people when they think about their children, would like them to be different from themselves in some ways. If you had a son (daughter) how would you like him (her) to be different from you?	Shortcomings in the self Wants child to be different Does not want child to be different
How about your good points? What would you say were your strongest points?	Lack of strong points in the self Sees no strong points Mentions strong points
Marital adjustment	
Many men (women) feel that they're not as good husbands (wives) as they would like to be. Have you ever felt this way?	Feelings of marital inadequacy A lot of times Once in a while Never
What kinds of things make you feel this way? Do you feel this way a lot of times, or only once in a while?	

Table 1 (Continued)

Questions	Indices
Taking things all together, how would you describe your marriage—would you say your marriage was very happy, a little happier than average, just about average, or not too happy?	Marital unhappiness Not too happy Average A little happier than average Very happy
Even in cases where married people are happy there have often been times in the past when they weren't too happy—when they had problems getting along with each other. Has this been true for you?	Experience of problems in marriage Mentions problems Never had problems

Adjustment as a parent

First, thinking about a man's (woman's) life, how is a man's (woman's) life changed by having children?	Negative orientation to children: Coder rating of change seen as accompanying children Negative Neutral Positive
Most parents have had some problems in raising their children. What are the main problems you've had in raising your children?	Experience of problems in raising children Mentions problems Never had problems
Many men (women) feel that they're not as good fathers (mothers) as they would like to be. Have you ever felt this way? (If yes) What kinds of things have made you feel this way? Have you felt this way a lot of times, or only once in a while?	Feelings of inadequacy as a parent A lot of times Once in a while Never

Psychological and psychosomatic symptom complaints

Do you ever have any trouble getting to sleep or staying asleep? Check one: Nearly all the time (1)[b]; Pretty often (2); Not very much (3); Never (4).	Symptom factor 1: Psychological anxiety [a]
Have you ever been bothered by nervousness, feeling fidgety and tense? Check one: as above. Do you feel you are bothered by all sorts of pains and ailments of different parts of your body? Yes (2); No (4).	Six ranks ranging from very high to very low scores Symptom factor 2: Physical ill health [a]
For the most part, do you feel healthy enough to carry out the things you would like to do? Yes (4); No (2).	Three ranks
Do you find it difficult to get up in the morning? Check one: Nearly all the time (1); Pretty often (2); Not very much (3); Never (4).	Symptom factor 3: Immobilization [a] Six ranks
Are you troubled by your hands sweating so that you feel damp and clammy? Check one: Many times (1); Sometimes (2); Hardly ever (3); Never (4).	

Table 1 (Continued)

Questions	Indices
Have you ever been bothered by shortness of breath when you were not exercising or working hard? Check one: Many times (1); Sometimes (2); Hardly ever (3); Never (4). Have you ever been bothered by your heart beating hard? Check one: as above.	Symptom factor 4: Physical anxiety [a] Six ranks
Summation of 16 symptom questions used in Stirling County study (MacMillan, 1957).	Summary Symptom Score [c] Ten ranks
Job adjustment	
Taking into consideration all the things about your job, how satisfied or dissatisfied are you with it?	Job dissatisfaction Dissatisfied Ambivalent Satisfied Very satisfied
Have you ever had any problems with your work—times when you couldn't work or weren't getting along on the job, or didn't know what kind of work you wanted to do?	Experience of problems with job Mentions problems Never had problems
How good would you say you are at doing this kind of work—would you say you were *very good, a little better than average, just average,* or *not very good?*	Feelings of inadequacy on job Not very good Average Little better than average Very good

[a] These symptom factor indices are based on prior factor analyses of a symptom list of 20 items which were taken with slight changes, from the Health Opinion Survey (MacMillan, 1957. Each index represents the two items most clearly typifying the factor; these items are ones having not only high loadings on the factors they are assumed to represent, but also minimal loadings on other factors.
[b] Scores on the symptom factors are the sum of the values in parentheses.
[c] For a list of these items see Gurin, Veroff, and Feld (1960, Table 7).

four parallel factors emerge and one additional factor appears for men. The similarity in these factor structures for men and women is an important finding; unexplained sex differences in obtained relationships are often the bane of the psychological researcher. However, the differences between men and women in the factor loadings of the various items on each factor are provocative. We highlight these in the discussion to follow.

Factor structure for men

Factor 1　　Felt psychological disturbance.　　The variables that load highly on this factor are derived from the symptom checklist and questions concerning psychological and psychosomatic complaints (*psychological anxiety, immobilization, physical anxiety,* and *summary symptom score*). This factor represents an admission to symp-

Table 2

Intercorrelations (tau beta) of 22 indices of subjective adjustment

$N = 255$ employed married men with children [a]

Variable key:

01	Worrying
02	Unhappiness
03	Future unhappiness
04	Nervous breakdown
05	Lack of uniqueness of self
06	Lack of self-acceptance
07	Shortcomings
08	Lack of strong points
09	Marital inadequacy
10	Marital unhappiness
11	Marriage problems
12	Negative orientation to children
13	Problems with children
14	Inadequacy as parent
15	Psychological anxiety
16	Physical ill health
17	Immobilization
18	Physical anxiety
19	Summary symptom score
20	Job dissatisfaction
21	Job problems
22	Job inadequacy

	01	02	03	04	05	06	07	08	09	10	11	12	13	14	15	16	17	18	19	20	21	22
01		+19 [b]	−03	13	−04	13	18	−01	10	13	05	01	03	07	28	01	06	09	16	−01	08	−04
02			04	10	07	−01	10	04	15	38	14	04	20	08	16	14	12	12	24	13	03	−09
03				06	07	09	−01	08	−08	10	−10	−06	01	−02	07	17	−02	08	07	−08	−03	−16
04					−07	07	09	01	10	03	14	−11	−01	27	29	14	16	29	33	03	23	08
05						−12	−07	11	02	05	−05	−04	−07	−08	−04	−02	−11	05	00	00	02	04
06							01	−08	06	−09	−06	02	03	00	28	−02	12	06	13	05	−03	−01
07								06	15	14	07	00	10	18	06	03	07	05	09	14	13	06
08									11	18	13	−04	03	09	02	−01	01	06	03	08	06	16
09										04	19	04	02	30	20	12	24	10	15	03	26	07
10											23	−01	06	00	13	−01	04	11	17	11	01	00
11												02	09	15	21	−17	19	05	00	08	13	06
12													06	−01	01	02	09	−07	09	−01	00	−02
13														17	13	06	−01	12	23	09	10	05
14															15	16	14	17		10	25	18
15																	34	32	57	12	12	05
16																	11	32	36	06	11	−11
17																		27	41	14	16	03
18																			58	06	15	−04
19																				14	22	−04
20																					04	14
21																						−06
22																						

[a] Includes only men responding to the one form of the interview on which all 22 items were asked. Ns for specific correlations vary slightly due to incomplete data for some subjects.

[b] Plus sign is omitted from all other figures in table. All correlations are positive unless otherwise noted.

Table 3
Intercorrelations (tau beta) of 19 indices of subjective adjustment
$N = 542$ married women with children [a]

	01 Worrying	02 Unhappiness	03 Future unhappiness	04 Nervous breakdown	05 Lack of uniqueness of self	06 Lack of self-acceptance	07 Shortcomings	08 Lack of strong points	09 Marital inadequacy	10 Marital unhappiness	11 Marriage problems	12 Negative orientation to children	13 Problems with children	14 Inadequacy as parent	15 Psychological anxiety	16 Physical ill health	17 Immobilization	18 Physical anxiety	19 Summary symptom score
01		+18 [b]	−05	16	−04	10	05	−01	08	05	02	01	06	04	19	06	06	08	14
02			−04	11	02	02	00	04	−01	44	24	06	05	03	19	10	02	15	18
03				−01	05	−03	00	08	−12	01	−02	−03	−09	−02	−06	01	−10	05	01
04					−07	13	08	01	14	16	18	−01	20	12	32	21	20	31	45
05						−04	−05	13	−01	02	−04	−06	−05	04	−06	00	−01	−04	−03
06							07	07	14	02	01	−00	08	12	11	03	07	10	08
07								−03	20	04	10	03	07	16	08	−03	14	07	08
08									01	04	00	−03	−06	−01	01	07	−04	03	−01
09										01	14	03	15	37	15	−00	16	14	16
10											28	07	07	04	15	06	01	18	20
11												08	13	18	15	−06	08	14	19
12													04	−01	01	−04	07	08	07
13														17	14	−01	03	06	10
14															16	00	15	13	16
15																24	23	32	58
16																	07	25	38
17																		22	33
18																			58
19																			

a Includes only women responding to the two forms of the interviews on which all 19 items were asked. Ns for specific correlations vary slightly due to incomplete data for some subjects.
b Plus sign is omitted from all other figures in table. All correlations are positive unless otherwise noted.

Table 4
Factor loadings from normalized varimax rotations [a]

Indices of subjective adjustment	Factor 1		Factor 2		Factor 3		Factor 4		Factor 5		h^2 [b]	
	Men	Women	Men	Women	Men	Women	Men	Women	Men	Women	Men	Women
Worrying	+18[c]	13	28	-10	-08	-02	-26	-07	07	-27	19	11
Unhappiness	14	11	56	-66	04	07	09	01	-08	-14	35	47
Future unhappiness	00	02	08	00	13	08	-11	28	-32	07	14	09
Nervous breakdown	29	41	02	-13	-39	-16	-12	-06	-19	-35	29	34
Lack of uniqueness of self	-02	-03	04	-02	10	-02	31	33	-04	09	11	12
Lack of self-acceptance	26	08	03	02	07	-18	-40	03	00	-22	23	09
Shortcomings	00	05	31	-03	-28	-34	-07	-06	08	-02	19	12
Lack of strong points	06	02	18	-02	-05	-01	31	34	-02	-06	13	12
Marital inadequacy	28	10	12	01	-37	-58	09	-05	21	-11	28	36
Marital unhappiness	10	11	54	-64	07	-01	19	06	-09	-05	35	43
Marriage problems	21	07	20	-42	-22	-26	21	-06	14	00	20	25
Negative orientation to children	04	05	06	-14	12	-05	-05	-19	23	15	08	08
Problems with children	-03	02	31	-08	-16	-22	-06	-18	-05	-27	13	16
Inadequacy as parent	13	08	11	-06	-59	-56	05	05	-02	-09	38	33
Psychological anxiety	70	57	24	-14	-09	-11	-19	-10	-05	-28	59	44
Physical ill health	18	46	08	02	-05	14	06	12	-55	-15	35	27
Immobilization	53	36	04	01	-17	-26	02	-14	02	06	31	23
Physical anxiety	42	62	07	-19	-17	-15	07	03	-49	01	45	44
Summary symptom score	66	85	14	-14	-19	-12	00	00	-37	-06	64	76
Job dissatisfaction	15		20		-09		14		02		09	
Work problems	11		01		-44		01		-10		22	
Job inadequacy	08		-02		-15		28		20		15	

[a] Based on samples of 255 men and 542 women.
[b] h^2 is equal to the communality of the item.
[c] Plus sign is omitted from all other figures in table. All factor loadings are positive unless otherwise noted.

93

toms that have particular implications for potential psychological dysfunctioning.

Since the variables that load highly on this factor all derive from a symptom checklist, filled out by the respondent himself, the question may arise as to what extent this factor represents a response set. It may be noted, in this connection, that the physical ill health symptom index, which also derives from this symptom checklist, is *not* highly loaded on this factor, which argues against a general "response set" interpretation.

It is noteworthy that this factor, entirely composed of symptom factor indices, does not have high loadings from other measures and further, that the symptom factor indices do not have high loadings on other factors, except on Factor 5. This, as we shall see, raises certain questions about the diagnostic use that has been made of symptom checklists.

Factor 2   Unhappiness.   The general evaluations of *unhappiness* and *marital unhappiness* are the most highly loaded indices on this factor. In addition, the *problems with children* and *shortcomings* indices are also loaded on this factor. Thus "unhappiness" among men appears to be a general factor, tied to distress in several central life-areas—marriage, children, and the self-concept. While the loading of these different indices on an unhappiness factor is not surprising, it is interesting to note that a quite different pattern appears for women where, as we will see, only the marital indices are loaded on the unhappiness factor.

Factor 3   Social inadequacy.   This factor seems to represent the self-questioning that goes on when a man considers himself in relationship to his social world. Some men entertain considerable self-doubt in their role relationships with others; others are self-confident or refuse to admit to doubt. Items loaded on this factor seem to be measuring the extent to which a man asks himself: Am I doing a good job at the things I am doing—worker, husband, father? Such feelings are objectified into *job problems* (.44), *inadequacy as a parent* (.59), and *marital inadequacy* (.37).

If this factor is viewed as measuring general social inadequacy, the relative weights of the factor loadings of these indices suggest that feelings of inadequacy as a father may be the best indications of a man's general feelings of inadequacy, or at least may be better measures of this factor than feelings of inadequacy as a husband or as a worker. The difference between the loadings of the parental and marital indices is particularly interesting. It suggests that admission to inadequacy may involve minor rather than major deviance from ideal role behavior more often when one is thinking of one's behavior as a husband than when one is thinking of one's behavior as a father. In marriage—perhaps because of the greater complexity of the role—we find built-in allowances permitting deviance for men. This is rather graphically illustrated in the almost jocular sanction given to minor inattentiveness on the part of the husband to his wife—forgetting anniversaries, not helping with the dishes, going out with the boys. Being a father does not seem to provide such culturally approved safety valves, perhaps because the demands of the role are less complex—supporting the child being such an all important feature of the role. Consequently admission to inadequacy as a father may be diagnostic of more serious feelings of social inadequacy than admission to inadequacy as a husband.

Also loaded on this factor is the experience, some time in one's life of having had or been close to a "nervous breakdown." For a man, a nervous breakdown may be a crucial indication of collapse in the face of pressures in the outside world, an extreme disruption in his ability to face his life obligations.

In this factor, as in the others, the investigation of mental health through the layman's self-perceptions has yielded a cluster of indices that has a parallel in the "experts' " attempts to establish criteria for mental health. One of the six major criteria for mental health that Jahoda (1958) describes is that of "environmental mastery." Included in this category is the person's adequacy in a variety of life situations—love, work, play, interpersonal relations. While this criterion is usually evaluated from the "objective" observer's point of view, the present results indicate it is an important aspect of self-evaluations as well.

Factor 4   Lack of identity (versus heightened self-awareness). In the two factor analyses this is the only factor which emerges in a bipolar fashion (that is, with high loadings in both the negative and positive direction). On the one pole are found *lack of uniqueness of self,* together with *lack of strong points in the self;* on the other pole we find *lack of self-acceptance.* This at first seems like a perplexing factor, but results stemming from our previous analysis of self-perception in the national survey, suggest a possible explanation of the factor (Gurin et al., 1960, Ch. 3). As we noted in that study, responses to questioning about the self are influenced both by how introspective a person is and by how positively or negatively he evaluates himself. Furthermore, there was some evidence that these two determinants are interrelated, that tendencies toward introspection and self-awareness are related to feeling negative about the self. Being able to see negative traits in the self implies a certain degree of introspection.

In the light of these previous findings, we interpret one pole of this factor to be this heightened self-awareness, negatively loaded primarily with the lack of self-acceptance index.   Lack of self-acceptance was coded when the respondent reported any negative aspects of the self, something which, as we have indicated, we interpreted as a particular indication of self-awareness.   On the other pole we have an opposite reaction—a rejection of looking into the self, a rejection of considering the self as an object of appraisal, what we might call a lack of identity. The indices positively loaded on this pole of the factor are lack of strong points in the self and lack of uniqueness of self (for example, "There is nothing good about me," "I'm not different from anyone else").   Lack of strong points, in short, at least in its loading on this factor, is not so much a "negative" perception of the self as it is an indication of an inability to introspect.

This factor is of particular interest because theoretical discussions of positive mental health have tended to link self-awareness and positive feelings about the self: "a healthy person knows who he is and does not feel basic doubts about his inner identity" (Jahoda, 1958, p. 29).   Without denying this, it is also true (as Jahoda has also pointed out) that these "healthy" self-attitudes at the same time include the ability to see and realistically accept the negative aspects of the self.   And it is difficult at times to determine when the "healthy" relationship between self-awareness and realistic self-appraisal turns into a relationship between self-awareness and a negative view of the self.   This was illustrated in the previous analyses of the data in this study, where, in comparing the responses to the self-percept questions among the different demographic subgroups of the population, it was noted that ". . . the social and cultural conditions that lead to introspection and a heightened self-awareness may also lead not only to realistic self-criticism, but to a generally negative self-percept" (Gurin et al., 1960, p. 83).

Factor 5   Physical distress.   Some of the indices based on the symptom checklist again stand out in this factor—*physical ill health,* physical anxiety, and summary symptom score.   This factor thus seems to be defined by physical dysfunctioning.   An important side-light here is that the highest loading that the *future unhappiness* index has is on this factor (.32).   A man's optimism or pessimism about his future is tied in large measure to his potential as a worker and economic provider.   Physical disability in a man is a major condition interfering with this capacity.   Thus it is reasonable that anticipation of future happiness or unhappiness might draw its heaviest loading on this factor for men.

A comparison between Factors 1 and 5 is of interest because of the considerable overlap in the indices loaded on them.   These two factors account for the major portion of the variance of the indices based on the symptom checklist.   Physical anxiety and summary symptom score are highly loaded on both factors.   In contrast, the two most psychological symptom indices—psychological anxiety and immobilization—appear only on Factor 1, and the most physical symptom index —physical ill health—appears only on Factor 5. This points to a general as well as two specific components of the symptom checklist for men. Some implications of this distinction may be clarified when we examine the factor structure for women, where we will see quite a different structure for these symptoms.

Factor structure for women

Five factors were also extracted for women. Except for one of them, there seem to be some direct parallels between the two factor structures. Although there are differences which suggest ways of conceptualizing male and female differences in psychological functioning, the most striking over-all impression is that the two sets of data are very much alike. The four similar factors in the factor structure of both men and women are: felt psychological disturbance, unhappiness, social inadequacy, and lack of identity. There is no factor in the structure for women comparable to the physical distress factor found in the data from men's responses, and the fifth factor for women is difficult to interpret; only one index loads highly on it—*nervous breakdown.*

In what ways do the factors for females seem to differ from males? Let us consider each in order. There are many different theoretically important dimensions underlying sex as an analytic variable and each might have implications in the present analysis. However, we will select interpretations of differences that seem most plausible but recognize that other interpretations are possible.

Factor 1   Felt psychological disturbance.   This factor is both similar and dissimilar to Factor 1 for men. Four indices are highly loaded on this factor for both men and women: psychological anxiety, immobilization, physical anxiety, and summary symptom score. But the physical ill health index is highly loaded on this factor for females, whereas for males it was part of a physical distress factor (Factor 5), which we do not find in the factor structure for the females. Furthermore, for men physical anxiety and summary symptom score are not uniquely loaded on Factor 1, as they are for women. Thus it seems that women do not separate admission to bodily complaints from admission to complaints about their general psychological condition; men evidently make this distinction. Perhaps these results are tied to the greater tendencies among women to introspect and to see their problems in psychological terms, in contrast to men's greater tendencies to externalize their problems.

Factor 2   Unhappiness.   As was observed in the discussion of this factor for men, general unhappiness and marital unhappiness seem to go together, both being highly loaded on this "unhappiness" factor.

However, certain differences between men and women also appear. Among women this factor does not have high loadings on two indices —shortcomings and problems with children—that were highly loaded on this factor for men.   And among women this factor does have a high loading on one index—*marital problems*—which did not appear among the indices with high loadings on this factor for men.

Among women, then, the unhappiness factor, with high loadings on general unhappiness, marital unhappiness, and marriage problems, seems more exclusively tied to marriage than it was for men.   This may be taken as some support for the hypothesis that marriage is more central to a woman's life, and hence plays a more significant role in her general happiness.

But why are not the shortcomings and problems with children indices also included in this factor?   With respect to the shortcomings index particularly, one might have expected that marriage, being more central in a woman's life, would be more rather than less tied to self-evaluation and self-criticism, and that for women a factor heavily loaded on marital unhappiness would show higher rather than lower loadings on a shortcomings index.   But one of the findings reported in the larger study may suggest why this is not so.   In the analysis of adjustment to the marital role, it was noted that women blame their husbands for marital difficulties more often than men blame their wives (Gurin et al., 1960).   This difference in attribution of blame seemed to relate to the male-female role distinctions in marriage.   The fact that the woman's role in marriage is more passive and receptive than the man's apparently more often enables her to separate marital failure from failure in the self.

The activity-passivity dimension in role behavior may also help explain why marital unhappiness in women also seems to be separate from distress over the children.   Only in this case it is the active role that a woman plays as a mother and the contrast with the more receptive and passive role as a wife that might explain why problems in both areas are not loaded on the same factor, why a woman can apparently separate her reactions to marriage from her response to her children.   Unhappiness in the more passive role as wife may actually lead to an overly positive involvement in the more active role as mother—a phenomenon which has often been observed in women who, unhappy and feeling helpless in a frustrating unfulfilling marriage, attempt to compensate by an overinvestment in their children.

Factor 3   Social inadequacy.   The hypothesis that the marriage is more important for the feelings of adjustment for women than for men is given further support in a sex difference obtained in the social inadequacy factor.   The loading on this factor for marital inadequacy is .58 for women and .37 for men.   Both men and women have very high loadings on the inadequacy as parent index.   One further kind of self-questioning, the shortcomings index, is also highly loaded (.31) on this factor for women; this is again similar to the finding for men, where this index falls just short (.28) of our criterion for consideration.

Being a mother and being a wife are both central to a married woman's identity; feeling inadequate in either role is equally important in a woman's feelings of inadequacy and failure.   Neither role apparently provides the culturally allowed safety valves for deviance that were noted earlier in relation to the husband's role.

Factor 4   Lack of identity.   Only one pole of the comparable factor for men emerged for women: Lack of uniqueness of self and lack of strong points in the self again emerged together in this factor, but lack of self-acceptance does not load on the other pole of the factor for women.   What might be suggested is that women generally tend to be more introspective, so that a heightened self-awareness is not a special factor for them.

Implications of the factor analysis

The multiple criterion approach to the delineation of a person's adjustment that has received increasing support in recent writings is supported by these factor analyses.   Even in that limited evaluation of mental health that is available from what a person tells us as he describes his own adjustment, whether a person gives an "adjusted" response or a "maladjusted" response depends on what the question is.   Evidently people do not respond to a series of questions covering life adjustment with one general evaluative framework which one could call the person's subjective adjustment.   Rather, a person seems to respond to these series of questions from a number of different frameworks, perhaps represented by the factors that emerged from the factor analysis.   There are undoubtedly some people who approach all of the questions about adjustment in a general "distressed" way, for whom being high in one of these factors implies being high in all.   In his work with people who seek psychological help the clinician perhaps most often encounters this general discontent that transcends all dimensions of self-description—but this pattern of self-evaluation may be less common among the general population.

It is particularly interesting to observe that the distinctiveness of the factors applies to the symptom checklist as well as to the other adjustment measures that were studied.   Since symptom checklists such as the one on which the present symptom indices are based, are often used as a quick psychiatric screening technique, one might have expected the symptom indices to represent a general factor, highly loaded on all the factors.   But this is not so.   For both men and women one factor (Factor 1) is composed entirely of symptom indices. And although these symptom items do have some loadings on the other factors, these loadings are not high for women, and for men are high only on Factor 5, which is itself largely composed of the physically loaded symptom indices. Apparently, the major aspects of distress included in a symptom checklist, although partial components of other kinds of psychological distress experiences, are fairly distinct from them. Implicitly, then, the judgments that are based on utilizing such symptom batteries as a diagnostic tool seem to be minimizing the importance of other aspects of feelings of maladjustment. Essentially, they single out one from a number of possible mental health criteria.

This reliance upon one single criterion—whether of symptoms or other factors—has special significance when attempts are made to compare different subgroups of the population in mental illness or health. Such a comparison is questionable if these subgroups vary in their tendencies to experience distress as symptoms or in other ways. If subgroups do vary in the ways in which they experience distress, then the "mental health" evaluation of the different groups would vary according to the particular component of mental health that was chosen as the basis for evaluation; for example, a "symptom" criterion would provide a different ranking of groups than would be obtained from a "felt inadequacy" criterion.

That this does occur has been demonstrated in prior results reported by Gurin et al. (1960). Those results were based on the separate questions used in the present factor analysis. The general point can be illustrated better now that the results of the factor analyses are available. A systematic investigation of subgroup differences in responses to the indices based on the several factors is contemplated. For the present, we can illustrate this problem by considering the responses of groups differing in education.

In order to facilitate these comparisons, factor scores were computed for each of the factors for men and women. The factor scores were based on summations of those indices that were both highly loaded (.30 or more) on the factor in question *and* were not highly loaded on any other factor. These criteria were established in order to yield factor scores that would both be clearly representative of the respective factors and would be as independent of one another as possible.[2] In the summations, each index was given equal weighting.

The indices comprising each factor score are listed below:

2 Since no indices were loaded exclusively on only one factor, complete independence of factor scores was not obtained. But among the 16 possible intercorrelations (10 among the five factors for men and 6 among the four factors for women) 12 yielded tau's of .10 or less. The four exceptions were tau's of .13 between Factors 1 and 2 for men, .24 between Factors 1 and 3 for men, .25 between Factors 1 and 2 for women, and .20 between Factors 1 and 3 for women.

Factor 1   For men: psychological anxiety and immobilization; for women: summary symptom score.[3]

Factor 2   For men: unhappiness, shortcomings, marital unhappiness, and problems with children; for women: unhappiness, marital unhappiness, and marriage problems.

Factor 3   For men: nervous breakdown, marital inadequacy, inadequacy as parent, and job problems; for women: shortcomings, marital inadequacy, and inadequacy as parent.

Factor 4   For men: lack of uniqueness, lack of self-acceptance,[4] and lack of strong points; for women: lack of uniqueness and lack of strong points.

Factor 5   For men: future unhappiness and physical ill health.

The relationships between education and these factor scores are presented in Table 5.   The expectation, based on previous results, that the relationship between education and the experience of distress would vary for the several factor scores is clearly confirmed by the data presented in this table.   The less educated men would be judged as indicating *less* distress than the more educated ones if the felt psychological disturbance (Factor 1) and particularly the social inadequacy (Factor 3) scores were considered.   But, they would be judged as *more* distressed if the unhappiness (Factor 2), lack of identity (Factor 3), or physical distress (Factor 5) scores were considered.   It is interesting to note that some of these findings—specifically those relating to psychological disturbance, social inadequacy, and physical distress—support much of the thinking that has been done with respect to social class differences in the expression of psychological distress.   Using education as an index of social status, the findings conform to hypotheses that have been offered about psychological symptoms and intrapunitiveness being more common to the middle class, and bodily symptoms being a more characteristic working class mode of expression.

Women with differing levels of education also respond differentially to the several categories of self-evaluations of distress represented by the factor scores.   The less educated women indicate *more* felt psychological disturbance (Factor 1) and unhappiness (Factor 2), but *less* social inadequacy (Factor 3) than the more educated women. Education is unrelated to Factor 4—lack of identity—for women.

As can be seen, these relationships differ in some ways from those for men.   Particularly, they point up a difference between the symptom factors for men and women.   The computation of factor scores

---

[3] The summary symptom score was used as the sole basis for computing the Factor 1 score for women both because of its extremely high loading on the factor (.85) and because most of the items comprising the other symptom indices loaded on this factor are also included in the summary symptom score.

[4] Because of the bipolar nature of this factor, the rankings for the lack of self-acceptance index presented in Table 1 were reversed in computing the factor score.

Table 5
Education and factor scores based on self-evaluations of distress within-sex

Factor	Score [a]	Men Grade school [b]	Men High school	Men College	Women Grade school	Women High school	Women College
1. Felt psychological disturbance	H	18%	16%	23%	35%	21%	13%
	MH	21	19	25	25	23	30
	ML	22	24	19	18	28	23
	L	39	41	33	22	28	34
N [c]		85	112	57	139	315	82
2. Unhappiness	H	35%	29%	28%	32%	17%	17%
	MH	33	24	20	32	27	22
	ML	13	19	28	22	29	33
	L	19	28	24	14	27	28
N		70	97	50	139	317	82
3. Social inadequacy	H	19%	22%	38%	13%	21%	24%
	MH	19	25	30	19	26	35
	ML	35	24	18	24	25	26
	L	26	29	14	44	28	15
N		68	96	50	109	263	74
4. Lack of identity	H	15%	6%	2%	7%	5%	7%
	MH	41	34	32	{36	{31	{34
	ML	27	45	40	57	64	59
	L	17	15	26			
N		84	111	57	138	312	83
5. Physical distress	H	38%	11%	10%			
	M	35	31	39			
	L	27	58	51			
N		63	101	49			

[a] The scores represent the closest approximation into quartiles that was possible except for Factor 4 for women and Factor 5 for men where only thirds were possible. The abbreviations H, M, L stand for high, medium, and low, respectively.
[b] Categorization based on highest educational level begun.
[c] *N*s vary due to incomplete data on items comprising the several factor scores.

in a manner that accentuated the uniqueness of each factor had the effect of emphasizing the different determinants of the responses to symptom checklists for men and women. For men, there appear to be somewhat distinct psychological and physical components involved in the responses, as reflected both in the emergence of Factor 5 and in the differential relationships of Factors 1 and 5 with education; for women, only one symptom factor emerged. The use of a symptom checklist with women, like the summary symptom score which is the basis for their Factor 1 scores, clearly leads to the conclusion that the less educated groups are more distressed. For men this negative relationship is obtained only for the Factor 5 scores, where only the physical components of the symptom checklist (physical ill health) are included in the factor score. When the factor score is based on the more psychological components of a symptom checklist (Factor 1), a clear relationship with education is not obtained; the relationship is slightly positive, with college educated men scoring somewhat higher than grade school educated men. The multiple criterion point, however, remains true for both men and women: the selection of a symptom checklist as the more significant indicator of mental health means that certain groups will be selected as "sick" or "healthy"; a different selection would be made if other criteria for mental health were stressed.

We have highlighted the fact that *different distinctive factors* emerge in this factor analysis of self-evaluations of distress, and have used the analysis of educational subgroup differences to support the need for a multiple criterion approach to subjective adjustment. It is still possible, however, that one might find one factor or perhaps a pattern of the separate factors of self-evaluation which, through a method of external validation, might be chosen as *the* best indicator of mental illness or health. But the problem in such an attempt lies in determining what the external criterion should be. It is difficult to choose such an external validation criterion given the considerable conceptual disagreement as to what the definitions and criteria of mental illness and health should be. Some of these difficulties are illustrated in the attempt to single out symptom lists as the diagnostic tool, with psychiatrists' judgments being the external validating criterion. As we have seen, this seems to minimize certain aspects of psychic dysfunctioning which many would agree should be included in any psychiatric judgment of healthy or neurotic functioning.

Although the problem is partly a function of the imperfections of our knowledge in this area, it is likely that the many different relevant criteria of disturbance can never be encompassed within a single all-embracing criterion. In attempting to predict to some external criterion from the kinds of factors differentiated in this study, it is probably more appropriate to think of different factors being relevant for different predictions than to think in terms of a single criterion and prediction. For example, if we wish to predict the type of disturbance that seems to be implicit in psychiatrists' diagnoses, subjective evaluations that involve a heavy component of psychophysical symptomatology would be the best predictors. On the other hand, for predicting the kind of impairment that leads to immobilization, breakdown, and the self-diagnosis involved in going for help with one's problems we would look to a quite different set of subjective adjustment measures —for example, those heavily loaded on the inadequacy factor. And for a prediction of "positive" mental health still other factors might be most relevant.

In comparing the factor structures of the men and women in our study, both the similarities in the structures and the differences can have important implications. The communality between the two factor structures points to the important psychological dimensions of subjective distress that can transcend social roles and cultural subgroups. If one were looking for the basic underlying psychological parameters of distress, this focus on the communality would be of greatest importance. A logical step in such a focus would involve factor analyses on specific social groups—different age groupings, different educational statuses, different income levels—to pinpoint even further those communalities that exist in all groups.

What are the implications of finding differences in factors for men and women? Although both sexes may encounter similar problems in growing up and in current living, they undoubtedly have learned to deal with these problems in different ways. Differences in factors for men and women may reflect critical ways in which the sexes differ in handling or expressing psychic difficulties. For example, since the physical ill health symptom index appears as part of the felt psychological disturbance factor for women but is separate for men, one perhaps has support for the view that the externalization of psychic disturbance into somatic distress is more common for men than for women. Analyses which focus on such differences in factors can pave the way to a better delineation of the critical differential experiences of men and women, or of any other groups so compared.

Summary

A representative sample of the resident population of adults in the United States was interviewed about their feelings of distress in different life areas: perceptions of the self; symptoms of distress; adjustment in marriage, parenthood, and work. Nineteen indices were constructed for special subpopulations—married women with children and employed married men with children. In addition, three indices related to aspects of work adjustment were used only for these men.

The indices were intercorrelated and the intercorrelations were factor analyzed separately for men and women.

Five distinctive factors emerged for men and four for women.   There was considerable apparent overlap between the two factor structures. For both men and women the factors were identified as: felt psychological disturbance (Factor 1); unhappiness (Factor 2); social inadequacy (Factor 3); lack of identity (Factor 4).   For men the fifth factor was labeled physical distress.

The emergence of several distinct factors underlying self-evaluations of distress was discussed as reflecting the need for a multiple criterion approach to the definition of mental health.   In particular it was noted that findings about differential distress in population subgroups depend upon the particular syndrome of distress that is used as the criterion of mental health; this point was illustrated for educational subgroupings.

The overlapping factor structures of men and women point to basic dimensions of distress applicable to all people.   The differences in the factor structures for men and women point to major sex differences in the experience of distress.   In particular, physical distress seems to be a distinctive factor for men while it is tied to psychological symptoms for women.

References

Eaton, J. W.   The assessment of mental health.   *Amer. J. Psychiat.*, 1951, *108*, 81–90.

Fiedler, F. E., Dodge, Joan S., Jones, R. E., & Hutchins, E. B.   Interrelations among measures of personality adjustment in nonclinical populations.   *J. abnorm. soc. Psychol.*, 1958, *56*, 345–351.

Gurin, G., Veroff, J., & Feld, Sheila.   *Americans view their mental health.* New York: Basic Books, 1960.

Herzberg, F., Mausner, B., & Snyderman, Barbara.   *The motivation to work.* New York: Wiley, 1959.

Inkeles, A.   Industrial man: The relation of status to experience, perception, and value.   *Amer. J. Sociol.*, 1960, *66*, 1–31.

Jahoda, Marie.   Toward a social psychology of mental health.   In J. M. E. Senn (Ed.), *Symposium on the healthy personality.*   New York: Josiah Macy, Jr. Foundation, 1950.   Pp. 211–230.

Jahoda, Marie.   The meaning of psychological health.   *Soc. Casewk.*, 1953, *34*, 349–354.

Jahoda, Marie.   *Current concepts of positive mental health.*   New York: Basic Books, 1958.

Kendall, M. G.   *Rank correlation methods.*   London: Griffin, 1948.

Kish, L.   Selection of the sample.   In L. Festinger & D. Katz (Eds.), *Research methods in the behavioral sciences.*   New York: Dryden, 1953. Pp. 175–240.

MacMillan, A. M. The health opinion survey: Technique for estimating prevalence of psychoneurotic and related types of disorder in communities. *Psychol. Rep.,* 1957, 3, 325–329.

Morse, Nancy C. *Satisfactions in the white-collar job.* Ann Arbor: Survey Research Center, 1953.

Rogers, C. *Client-centered therapy.* Boston: Houghton Mifflin, 1951.

Scott, W. A. Research definitions of mental health and mental illness. *Psychol. Bull.,* 1958, 55, 67–87.

Smith, M. B. Optima of mental health: A general frame of reference. *Psychiatry,* 1950, 13, 503–510.

Smith, M. B. Research strategies toward a conception of positive mental health. *Amer. Psychologist,* 1959, 14, 673–681.

Terman, L. M., & Wallin, P. The validity of marriage prediction and marital adjustment tests. *Amer. sociol. Rev.,* 1949, 14, 497–505.

Charles M. Solley and
Kenneth Munden

TOWARD A DESCRIPTION OF MENTAL HEALTH *

As part of a research program on preventive psychiatry in industry, it became necessary to develop a concept of mental health—a task as complicated as the Gordian Knot. Our conception had to meet two basic criteria. It had to be linked to observable behavioral characteristics and it had to have the potentiality of being integrated with personality theory, in our case psychoanalytic theory.

From a survey of the literature (1), we concluded it was necessary to develop a behavioral concept of mental health. The present research represents the first step toward this goal.

Method

The procedure was a modification of Flanagan's critical incident technique (2), which is to ask experienced people to think of the best example they can recall of a specific incident, *e.g.,* the best troubleshooting by a mechanic, and then to record the described incident. From a set of such reports, common characteristics are abstracted

* From Charles M. Solley and Kenneth Munden, "Toward a Description of Mental Health," *Bull. Menninger Clinic,* 1962, 26, 178–188. Reprinted by permission of the authors and Editor, *Bulletin of the Menninger Clinic.*

that are used as multiple criteria for describing a concept, *e.g.*, good troubleshooting.

In our research, each interviewee was asked to describe a personal acquaintance who was "mentally healthy." The interviewer spoke only to encourage the interviewee to continue. When the interviewee had described one person, he was asked to describe a second "mentally healthy" person. After each description, the interviewee was asked the reasons for his choice. The interviewer recorded the interview as nearly verbatim as possible and the source was kept confidential.

Fourteen senior psychoanalysts, psychiatrists and clinical psychologists at The Menninger Foundation were interviewed and asked not to discuss the interview. None knew the nature of the research although each was informed that it was part of a project which required information based upon clinical experience. Of the 14 interviewees, eleven were men and three were women. Their ages ranged from 37 to 61 years; their years in clinical practice, from 13 to 36. Seven were born and reared abroad; seven in the United States. Their educational and professional training backgrounds were varied in European and American social and cultural settings.

All interviewees were extremely helpful and cooperative in the interviews. Since they did know what the researchers sought from them, some anxiety was aroused. This was relieved when they learned we were soliciting concrete *descriptions of real persons* rather than *abstractions*. Several were curious about their choices. Some did not believe mental health existed although they did describe some person (or persons) of their choice.

Results

The extreme variety of "healthy" persons described was both interesting and surprising. Altogether 41 persons were described. Twenty-five were males and 16 females. Their ages ranged from the early twenties to the late eighties. Their occupations varied from farming to teaching and from housekeeping to business. Twenty-six were American and 15 foreign.

Little clinical jargon was used describing the "healthy" persons. In general, simple English was used, with an occasional interjection of technical interpretation. As we suspected, the clinicians had some common, positive signs which they used in diagnosing "mental health." The data were analyzed in two ways. The first three interviews (or descriptions of six people) were read by the two researchers and major abstractions of characteristics were made from each description. The two sets of abstractions were compared and a common, agreed upon set was chosen. All of the protocols were then judged, using this set of characteristics.

To check the reliability of categorizing the behaviors described by the interviewees, three statisticians were told to check each of the 41 categories that "fitted" the person being described. There was a minimum of 95 per cent agreement among the three judges, indicating a high reliability in categorizing the described behaviors.

Such an all-or-none tally shows only the presence or absence of mention of a particular characteristic. Within each interview a single characteristic was often mentioned repeatedly. For example, the four most frequently mentioned attributes were in order: (a) the person is able to adjust and remain flexible under stress; (b) the person accepts himself and does not compete neurotically with others; (c) the person has inner peace as if he were satisfied that he had done in his life what was necessary; (d) the person is able to tolerate tragedy (he may have sorrow but not melancholia).

To examine the interrelationships among the characteristics, a 41 by 41 contingency table was used to tally the co-occurrences of the behavioral descriptions.[1] A high co-occurrence was found among six of the behavioral descriptions. They were: (1) Treats others as individuals; (2) Invests self in others; (3) Understands the needs of others; (4) Gets things done; (5) Is flexible under stress; and (6) Obtains pleasure from many sources. To check further on co-occurrence, protocols in which ten or less behaviors were described were similarly analyzed, thus allowing more variability and less restriction on the data. This analysis revealed that these six did co-occur highly and also they co-occurred with (7) being active and productive and (8) having capacity to see and accept self-limitations. These eight behavioral characteristics seemed to form a nucleus of mentally healthy behaviors.

Although our evidence seemed clear enough, there was a loophole. Our interviewees were psychoanalytically oriented and nonanalytically oriented people might give radically different descriptions of people whom they considered to be "mentally healthy." To check this possibility, at the beginning of a semester we asked the students of two undergraduate classes in introductory psychology at Wayne State University to write descriptions of the "most mentally healthy person they had ever known." Ninety-three students were given 15 minutes to write their descriptions. Eighty-five turned in their papers. They did not have to sign their names or give the name of the described persons unless they wished to do so.

These protocols were scored the same way as those for interviews at The Menninger Foundation. A behavioral characteristic *mentioned at least once* was tallied as "present"; otherwise it was tallied as

[1] A copy of the table is available upon request.

"absent." A high, positive correlation between the Menninger staff and the Wayne State University students was disclosed, indicating reliability of repetition of the mentally healthy characteristics. From these results we conclude that our original data from the Menninger staff were not due to any particular theoretical orientation.

The mere listing of the abstract characteristics does not convey the subtle complexity of the person described as mentally healthy. Such was not the immediate purpose of this present study. It is conveyed, however, in the actual words used by those interviewed. Here, for example, are two descriptions from the Menninger staff.

Protocol 1

"One person comes to my mind immediately. He was a boy I knew at medical school. He was disgustingly healthy (laughing). I envied him because he was so healthy. I used to wonder why. I didn't know him too well, although I did room with him for about six months. There are certain things that I would not have swapped. However, there was something about him, his aplomb, the way he was responsive to stimuli, unflustered, gracious, in spite of the fact that he had difficulties like anybody else. He made a good country practitioner. He was not brilliant, but just average. He was not a good athlete. He had none of the outstanding qualities one might associate with more successful men. He was quite attached to me. But there was something almost annoying about the way he did things so easily. He had a girl friend for many years whom he married after graduating from medical school. He had a family, mother, dad, sisters and brothers. He was always in the middle of the class and never became a president, in fact, he was just medium in most things he did.

"Another point is that he was not competitive. It just didn't distress him or upset him in any way that he was 35th in a class of 50. He was quite capable of doing the things he wanted to do without aspiring for things that he couldn't get. It was quite a thing the way he did his work, managed things and so forth. He was not all busy and tied up with ambition as was the case with most of us other medical students. The fact is, though, that he was not passive. His father was a country doctor and this boy strongly identified himself with his father. But he certainly wasn't the, you know, kind of ne'er-do-well. I know many much more ambitious, stronger people than he. I would evaluate them as certainly more ambitious and successful, but I certainly wouldn't consider them as healthy psychologically as this boy. I think that these ambitions and need for success come from additional conflicts which he did not have.

"Psychologically he was above average except in the medical group where he was just an average student. He knew what he wanted and he went about it without any difficulties.   I was president of the fraternity and of the students at the medical school, and yet he had a much better time than the rest of us.   I was ahead of him scholastically, but there was no question that he was happier.   You don't meet many people like him.   People like him are those with normal expectancies, few conflicts, and very little need of over-compensation. I think that I am defining him possibly in negative terms, in terms of absence of symptoms."

(Interviewer: "I should point out to you that in conjunction with his emotional health you have just mentioned several positive values.")

"Yes, he was a positive personality.   Oh, at times I felt that he was childish, but I believe that he had a greater freedom of expression. For example, I remember once there were a bunch of us in a car and we had trouble with the battery.   We went into a service station.   The man there looked at the battery and said that the cells and plates in the battery had gotten together.   He made a private sexual joke out of their 'getting together.'   Well, he was delighted and tremendously aroused by this remark.   He got a real childish pleasure out of it, and yet this is the whole point, he seemed to be able to regress without difficulty for the sheer pleasure of it.   I think this indicates a great deal of strength in doing this as part of his emotional health.   We others were sort of grim about our competing and getting status.

"There is no question but that we were less healthy than he was. But, I want to make clear that he was in no sense a clown.   Also, I know that he had to study and work harder than I did.   And yet, he had an ability to apply what he had.   We knew for instance at medical school that about half of the class would be busted at the end of the year.   This made for a tremendous amount of competition.   He was a good looking boy and I would say the most healthy that I can think of.   He may have had many unhappinesses, but it certainly didn't show on him.   On the other hand, it showed in many of the fellows there."

(Interviewer: "I wonder if you could concentrate now and think of some of the reasons why you selected him as the most healthy person, emotionally, that comes to your mind?")

"I think part of it is that I observed him in special situations, such as with his family and his girl friend, and it was the way he handled things.   His relationship with his father was much more mature than those of the other fellows.   Father was no longer someone to resent and fear and hand out the money.   It was a man-to-man relationship. He would write home saying 'Dad, I overspent my allowance and I drank too many beers.   I wonder if I could have another allowance?' His adolescent problems seem to have come to a pretty good solution. I think this was exemplified in his real lack of concern about competing.   Another thing, I approved of his girl friend that he later married. He seemed to have a very easy, comfortable relationship with women. He was not demanding or overbearing with them.

"I don't know how he got along with children, but he got along with older men and women and contemporaries. He was certainly better than just well adjusted, he was well rounded, not outstanding and yet not mediocre. He was so flexible. Most people that you see show so many things that indicate ill health. Before I entered medical school I had been in psychology some years and so was in a better position to elaborate and describe this particular person. I have known much more successful people and people that I would rather associate with, but none as much at ease with themselves as this particular person."

Protocol 2

"I am thinking of a married woman of thirty-five with a large family. I am struck by the amazing peace that she has. She presents a high degree of maturity and adjustment, that is to say, she is quite at ease with herself as a mother and a wife. How shall I put it? She is sterling in nature. She is quite untutored psychologically, yet has a psychological intuitiveness, which I envy, that is truly spectacular in meeting the needs of her children. This is what strikes me most about her, the degree of peace with her basic femininity, particularly in her way of dealing with her children.

"There is also a truly amazing lack of competition with her husband. She has no ambition for a career other than being a mother and a wife. However, she is quite active and enjoys social activities a great deal. She likes music, and, whenever she can, she enjoys reading. She has a special ability, peculiar to herself, to arrange her own time. So there is time for her children, time for her husband and time for herself. Another thing is the way she enters into anything whole-heartedly and yet is capable of turning to something else without any difficulty. For instance, she will put the children to bed when there are visitors and that is that. She will then give her entire attention to other matters at hand, such as entertaining socially, without any continued fussing or concern about the children.

"She has a generous sprinkling of compulsive traits, but these traits certainly are not crippling. She also strikes me as being quite free from abnormal anxiety. At least, it does not show up in any patho- logical symptoms. For instance, if the floor is not swept, that is that. She will get around to it in due and proper time. The amount of psychic energy she has to get things done is striking. (Laughing) I think I am getting religious now. But seriously, I believe that she lives a life in which she loses her identity in others. I think that she has found herself by losing herself in life. I don't mean that she is a will'o'-the-wisp. It is a quality of expanding herself into her environment. In fact, I would say that her narcissistic needs are operating at a level where she does things for others. This is an aspect of her maturity that appears to be of primary importance.

"Let me see if I can make this more clear. Recently I asked one of my patients the question about the three wishes. Her first wish was, 'I would wish to enjoy myself with the things I do always.' Well, she was quite unable to answer the other two wishes. This is what I'm trying to get at. This patient did not mention her husband, her children, or anybody else. The questions were entirely narcissistically oriented. Now, if I questioned the woman I have in mind, who to me represents the most emotionally healthy person that I can think of, I am sure that in none of the three wishes would she mention herself.

"I have thought a great deal about this subject of emotional health. In the case of this woman, I do not think that it is a matter of feminine masochism, but something well beyond that, in that she does not ask for payment. I assume that her sexual life with her husband is satisfactory.

"As I think of her, the quality that comes to my mind over and over again is that of being at peace with herself. To her, pregnancy is not a traumatic experience, it is a biological one, she has her child asymptomatically. I feel that she has come out of her developmental experience with very few scars, with a minimum residue of conflict over her femininity. She is charming, warm, affectionate, physically attractive, a loyal person, thoughtful, generous. Now, I come back to this 'religious area.' That is to say, how does one cope with the 'me' needs? I think that it has partly to do with the ability to delay gratification. She has an inner sense of security which permits her to give to the children, a relationship where the children receive love, without implying an emotional use of them. For instance, if one of her children were not too compulsive, she does not have to make him more compulsive. It's simply a question of difference between mothering and motherliness. It's the special ability to treat the child as an object, not as a narcissistic extension of the self. I would definitely feel that she can treat a child as an object, while narcissistic gratification is quite secondary in this relationship."

(Interviewer: "Although I realize that in the description above and in your explanation of this emotionally healthy person you have, of course, incorporated the why of your choice, I would like you to center your attention on this point. Namely, could you give me some of your reasons for selecting her?")

"Yes. At first, I observed the children more than the mother. The children seemed so happy and free from significant childhood symptoms of maladjustment; they were so comfortable with themselves. I began to wonder what made this possible, and, as a matter of fact as a clinician I was quite intrigued. Yes, the reason that she came to my attention was because of the children, who then led me to consider the relationship, and then I began to think of her."

In addition to these descriptions of mentally healthy people, descriptions of people regarded as unhealthy were incidentally obtained from the Menninger staff. Occasionally some persons were selected and a description began, but after some thought was given, they were rejected as "not as healthy" or "unhealthy." Reasons such as the following were given spontaneously for the rejection:

"He is ambitious, strong and successful. He is grim about competing and getting status. He is unhappy, much more successful, uneasy with himself. He goofs off, uses excuses, has an 'unconscious missing.' He gets involved in unhealthy, easily-rationalized situations where the self comes before others. He has strong narcissistic traits, distinguishing obvious success from narcissistic enjoyment. He is overbearing, has a drive for success, he struggles for success and he gives up certain vital things for success.

"He is influenced by other people's opinions. He is successful at the price of poor social relationships. He is brilliant, outstanding, but with neurotic quirks or deficiencies. He remains single, prudish, devoted to his parents until they die. He has strong biases and is remarkably rigid in some ways. He is distant and aloof. He is narcissistically arrogant. He is eccentric, admired for great achievements, but he has to do it, he is so compulsive. He has a give-receive quality. He is a martyr. He is unable to say no and is negative. He pursues wealth and prestige. He cannot be a happy man because he can only be happy through success."

Discussion

Our analyses led us to condense the eight behavioral characteristics to five, all of which tend to occur together. This, then, was to be our behavioral description of mental health. Operationally we could use this conception in the study of people in their work environment. We now need to discuss these five more fully.

1   *Treats others as individuals, by identifying himself with, accepting and understanding them.*

This major characteristic was frequently described in conjunction with two others: "invests self in others" and "understands the needs of others." In the description of the character of the interpersonal relationship and the behavior of the healthy person, definite qualifications were made: the treatment of others as human beings was defined in terms of identifying the object as a human being, accepting this being as a human one, and understanding this being as a person with individual needs and rights.

This does not mean an indiscriminate resulting relationship. The relationship may range from development of close, affectionate ties (love object), to rejection in the best interests of the other, determined not only by the trait of acceptance of self-limitations (below), but also by the demands, needs and capabilities of the other human being. There is no need to develop demanding relationships.

The recognition and acceptance of human beings is not qualified by age, sex, or ties of any type. The mentally healthy person is tolerant of people, whether he likes them or not. He gives the other a sense of security with a capacity of giving and responding when so required. His relationships are notable for the duration of his friendships which do not depend on any requirements or conditions. Therein lies his acceptance and esteem by others.

2   *Is flexible under both internal and external stress.*

The nature of stresses and the situations in which they were reported were varied. They occurred frequently and involved conflict over loss of love objects (relatives, possessions, friends), physical pain and illness, demanding pressures from figures in authority and suffering. The healthy person responds to such stresses with control of the critical, conflict-arousing situation, without emotional disturbance, but with freedom to express his feelings. The mentally healthy person arrives at a satisfactory solution for the stress (for example, getting another job or replacing a lost love-object). There is further a "quality of sameness" in that the individual may change his reactions to and methods of handling stresses, but preserves his own character.

3   *Obtains pleasure from many sources.*

The description of the sources in terms of objects, which can be of any type, underlines the *variety* (productivity, work completion, people, animals, etc.) and the *number*. The behavior denotes *interest in many things*, in particular a curiosity about what is new and about the world in general, both in terms of immediate and more remote environments. It is not simply intellectual curiosity, but a "native" curiosity to *find out* and know. A source of pleasure may be anything at all. There is a lack of emphasis on a particular area or object to the exclusion of others. *Interpersonal relationships* play a very particular role for the healthy person. Friendships are established when the opportunity arises, with an "acceptance of a sexual role congruent with the individual's sex." The friendship is not necessarily compulsively sought and the opportunity for friendship may at times be rejected.

4   *Sees and accepts self-limitations.*

This characteristic is descriptively separated from flexibility under stress, but the two are almost inseparable.   Flexibility under stress implies the recognition of self-limitations and assets.   The behavioral manifestations of this trait are conspicuous in what appears to be "a lack of success" [2] according to cultural and social standards, although there is a sense of personal contentment and satisfaction through the attainment of limited goals.   This is variously described in the protocols and is linked to the characteristics of "self-assurance with independence of thought," "lack of (neurotically driven) competitiveness" and "inner peace and serenity."

5   *Uses capacities to fulfill personal needs in carrying out productive tasks.*

Although "gets things done," "active and productive," and "capacity to terminate and complete work" are mentioned repeatedly in the protocols, in nearly every instance these phrases were qualified by the interviewee, *e.g.*, ". . . gets things done without being driven to get things done, without being driven either by anxiety or a need to prove oneself;" ". . . active and productive and obtains genuine pleasure in the activity and productivity, a noncompulsive activity, an ability to produce without strain;" ". . . capacity to terminate and complete work although without anxiety occurring if circumstances prevent termination or completion of work."   Activity and termination of activity, rather than being products of compulsivity, are important ways in which the mentally healthy person uses his available capacities to fulfill personal needs in productive tasks.   This tells us that productivity and work-completion are behaviors characteristic of mental health under certain conditions.   The surplus reservoir of energy at the ego's disposal is utilized in productive activities, from which the individual derives a sense of satisfaction.   The healthy person utilizes his strengths or capacities in work; and, in turn, work provides a focus in the environment from which satisfactions stem.

Conclusion

Five behavioral characteristics of mental health were abstracted from descriptions by experienced clinicians of people whom they regarded to be mentally healthy.   Similar criteria of mental health were drawn from written descriptions by university freshmen.   These behavioral characteristics comprise a tentative operational definition of mental health for research purposes.

These criteria do not solve the problem of definition.   Indeed, we have merely opened the way to new studies.   We need more research on the specific forms of behavior which reflect mental health as well as tools, such as interview schedules, designed to assess degrees of mental health.   We also need to know if we are really dealing with an

[2] Compulsive investment in and use of power.

inseparable constellation of behavior and, if not, to determine the dimensions of mental health.

References

1. Scott, W. A.: Research Definitions of Mental Health and Mental Illness. *Psychol. Bull.* 55:29–45, 1958.

2. Flanagan, J. C.: The Critical Incident Technique. *Psychol. Bull. 51:* 327–358, 1954.

THREE

SECTION THREE   **THEORIES OF PERSONALITY**

When we observe the behavior of human beings, the complexity of behavior and the differences among individuals are apparent. Individual A loves his children while individual B does not; individual C seems to us to defeat himself while D achieves his goals; E appears to live in a world of fantasy, unfamiliar to most of us; F is happy while G is depressed. How are we to comprehend the differences? Most of us entertain some set of implicit or explicit notions which define, somewhat to our satisfaction, human behavior. Most of us feel, more or less in a vague way, that we can account for the behavior of the persons who interact with us. Our private systems, however, are incomplete and do not share widespread acknowledgment.

There have been many formal attempts to comprehend man. The history of thought in philosophy and religion, literature and art, biology, economics, and psychology is replete with more or less fundamental analyses of human behavior and man's ultimate nature. The concern has been with stating basic considerations about the fundamental characteristics of man.

In this section of readings, we have illustrated a variety of ways in which contemporary psychology approaches the problem of the nature of man. How does the clinical psychologist understand the individual who is in distress? What does the research psychologist investigate? To pursue answers to these questions is to be made aware that there is a variety of systematic ways of understanding people and that these separate conceptualizations lead to differences in both clinical practice and research. We shall see that there is disagreement rather than fundamentally shared views. We shall see that psychology, in common with the other physical and behavioral sciences, argues and speculates in diverse ways.

The papers in this section belong to the domain of *personality theory*. We are here concerned with providing accounts of some of the major theories or sets of speculative hypotheses which guide psychologists in their search for explanation and control.

If we are to consider speculations about the nature of *personality*, we need to come to some more or less convenient definition of the term. Since different theories define the word differently, it is no easy task to find a definition acceptable to all psychologists.   In 1937, Gordon W. Allport published *Personality: A Psychological Interpretation,* (New York: Holt, Rinehart and Winston), which is extremely valuable for its report of his scholarly search for definitions of personality in a variety of settings.   Allport discovered forty-eight definitions or meanings which the term had acquired in sociology, law, philosophy, theology, psychology, and literature.   It became clear to Allport that there were two fundamentally opposed meanings.   One meaning defined personality in terms of outward appearance while the other defined personality in terms of inner experience.   Allport proposed a forty-ninth definition for psychology, what a man really is, which he elaborated in the following formal statement: "Personality is the dynamic organization within the individual of those psychophysical systems that determine his unique adjustment to his environment."   For Allport, this definition was sufficiently broad to represent a "synthesis of contemporary psychological usage."   While its generality involves limitations, it serves as a useful and convenient orientation to this section.   All the personality theories to be considered involve postulating an *organization of systems* (habits, traits, attitudes, needs, self-concepts, etc.) which determine adjustment.

Before we turn to the specific personality theories, we need to give some consideration to theories in a formal sense.   When can we say that we have a theory?   Neal E. Miller [in Krech, D., and Klein, G. S. (eds.), *Theoretical Models and Personality Theory.*   Durham, N.C.: Duke University Press, 1952], in commenting upon theoretical models, gives an unequivocal reply.   He writes that "a system can properly be called a model or theory if, and only if, one can use it to make rigorous deductions about some of the consequences of different sets of conditions.   High school geometry is a familiar example."   We have a theory here because we can deduce the consequences of a *great* number of different conditions from a *limited* set of definitions and axioms.   In addition, we can turn to recent analyses in the philosophy of science for the formal properties of theories. The consideration of philosophers of science has led to the view that a formal theory should contain *basic terms, defined terms, formation rules, transformation rules, postulates, and theorems.*

According to the criteria given above, a good many psychological theories are properly not theories at all but points of view or isolated hypotheses.   Miller calls them "articles of faith or intuition."   We shall, however, not utilize any formal definition of theory to preclude a point of view from consideration.   Still it is worth noting that most personality theories do not share in the properties which Miller and various philosophers of science have called to our attention.

It is important to indicate that the theories vary in many respects. Some will appear to be more scientifically rigorous than others, the scope of inquiry will differ, and the evidence available to support each will vary in its character. Freud's work, for example, will appear to be more rigorous than Jung's; Jung will surely appear to be more ambitious in his undertaking than Kelly; the evidence adduced in support of a learning-theory approach will be different from the evidence in support of psychoanalysis.

The section opens with selections relating to the theories of Freud, Adler, and Jung grouped together because they all belong to the psychoanalytic tradition. Both Adler and Jung, however, came to reject Freudian theory and founded what came to be known as individual and analytic psychology, respectively.

The selection from Freud provides the reader with many of the fundamental aspects of his total scheme. There is an account of his theory of unconscious determinism and his theory of infantile sexuality. The paper is unusually noteworthy in that it provides a historical view of the development of Freud's major concepts concerning human behavior. It summarizes a large share of his total contribution, which has had a significant impact on our view of the nature of man. His influence has been felt strongly not only in psychology and psychiatry, but in other disciplines as well. Literature, anthropology, sociology, education, art, law, theology, philosophy, political science, economics, etc., have all felt his persuasive force.

Freud's attempt to account for human behavior is the most ambitious theory of those considered. His concern is with the totality of human experience. While the scope of psychoanalytic theory enables us to speculate about a wide range of human behavior, the method of validating hypotheses, which consists of the careful examination in a treatment situation of the life history of the individual, leaves a good deal to be desired in rigor. Contemporary psychology, however, is continuing to find ways of subjecting Freudian hypotheses to controlled investigation and experimentation.

In contrast with Freud, Adler did not write a coherent and systematic account of his position. However, his position has been summarized by many of his followers. The paper by Ansbacher presents a concise statement of Adler's theory by one of his foremost interpreters. Adler analyzes the adjustment process in terms of an individual's relationships and methods of coping with his environment. Especially important in Adler's thinking is the individual's view of his own adequacy and his particular methods of attempting to exert his influence over others. Maladjustment results from the person's efforts to overcompensate for strong feelings of inadequacy by attempting to dominate and to control others. On the other hand, Adler's position equates adjustment with the ability to evaluate oneself realistically and to develop social relations which are beneficial to others and not merely designed for purposes of self-aggrandizement.

Jung's basic unit of investigation is the *psyche*. With this concept he refers to the psychological structure of the human being. He thinks of the psyche as a kind of nonphysical space wherein psychic phenomena occur. In order to describe these phenomena, Jung has found it necessary to develop a vocabulary which is not widely shared and which includes such concepts as *persona, personal unconscious, collective unconscious, anima, animus,* and *archetypes.* The paper by Storr, in giving a historical account of the development of Jung's theory, summarizes and integrates a number of Jung's difficult concepts and ideas with commendable clarity.

The article by Merton Gill is included in order to call attention to the viability of psychoanalytic theory. As Gill points out, the theory is often viewed by critics as a set of rigid constructions. The truth of the matter is that the propositions of the theory are under constant modification and addition.

Papers reflecting the positions of Karen Horney and Harry Stack Sullivan are given next. Again they are represented by interpreters, Norman Levy in the case of Horney and Patrick Mullahy in the case of Sullivan. Levy offers a synthesis of Horney's work derived from a review of her books. The reader will want to attend to Horney's insistence on the role of the environment in the production of maladjustment. In marked contrast to the biological position of Freud, Horney draws attention to the variety of adverse influences to which children are subjected. These engender *basic anxiety,* and this is the condition which promotes maladjusted ways of interacting with others. According to Sullivan's theory, which has become known as the *interpersonal theory of psychiatry,* personality is "the relatively enduring pattern of recurrent interpersonal situations which characterize a human life." The proper field of investigation is the interpersonal situation; the individual does not and cannot exist apart from his transactions with other people. Sullivan's fundamental hypothesis, therefore, led him away from preoccupation with biological drives and Freudian instinctual urges to the study of social interactions, mother and child, doctor and patient, etc. Mullahy's selection gives an account of Sullivan's view with respect to the goals of behavior, the modes of human experience, and the evolving of the self through interaction with others.

The next selection deals with a self-theory conception of the nature of man. The essential point is that behavior is a function, in some significant part, of one's self-concept, one's self-regarding attitudes. The self-concept refers to the totality of attitudes the individual holds with reference to himself. It is learned in evaluational transactions with others (notably, important others such as mother and father), and it influences behavior whether or not it is in accord with reality.   The selection from C. H. Patterson consists of a summary of the personality theory of Carl Rogers whose self-theory was developed concurrently with his client-centered or nondirective psychotherapy.

The next two papers, one by Bannister and the other by Pervin, represent ways of conceptualizing human behavior phenomenologically. Bannister's paper gives an account of the personality theory of George Kelly which views man as a "scientist" developing cognitive constructs by which he structures his world and the people in it.   An individual's behavior is a function of his *personal construct system* whose elements can be determined.   Pervin's paper, on the other hand, consists of a presentation of the *existential* position on the nature of man. Here, man is described as concerned with "the meaning of life."   In recent years, a great deal of interest has been generated for this position which, congruent with the views of some of the great existential writers and philosophers such as Camus and Sartre, declares that "man is free" and that man becomes what *he chooses*.   While both personal construct theory and existential psychology adopt a phenomenological point of view, they contrast sharply in that the former anticipates the possibility of giving an objective account of behavior, while the latter reflects a tradition that calls into question the whole possibility of objectifying the important aspects of human conduct.

The last selection defines the nature of man from the point of view of learning theory.   While there are important variations in the personality theories which different theorists have formulated based on learning concepts, the distinctive aspect of a learning approach is that complex human behavior is viewed as explainable and predictable from basic principles of learning.   The paper which is presented describes the social-learning theory of Julian B. Rotter which is referred to as an expectancy-reinforcement theory since the major formulation holds that behavior is a function of the individual's expectations concerning the reinforcements which occur as a consequence of his behavior.   This position indicates the possibility of viewing complex human behavior and problems meaningfully with the theoretical concepts which have been developed to explain relatively simple learning tasks.

Sigmund Freud   **PSYCHOANALYTIC THEORY ***

Psycho-analysis is the name (1) of a procedure for the investigation of mental processes which are almost inaccessible in any other way, (2) of a method (based upon that investigation) for the treatment of neurotic disorders and (3) of a collection of psychological information obtained along those lines, which is gradually being accumulated into a new scientific discipline.

History.   The best way of understanding psycho-analysis is still by tracing its origin and development.   In 1880 and 1881 Dr. Josef Breuer of Vienna, a well-known physician and experimental physiologist, was occupied in the treatment of a girl who had fallen ill of a severe hysteria while she was nursing her sick father.   The clinical picture was made up of motor paralyses, inhibitions, and disturbances of consciousness.   Following a hint given him by the patient herself, who was a person of great intelligence, he put her into a state of hypnosis and contrived that, by describing to him the moods and thoughts that were uppermost in her mind, she returned on each particular occasion to a normal mental condition.   By consistently repeating the same laborious process, he succeeded in freeing her from all her inhibitions and paralyses, so that in the end he found his trouble rewarded by a great therapeutic success as well as by an unexpected insight into the nature of the puzzling neurosis.   Nevertheless, Breuer refrained from following up his discovery or from publishing anything about the case until some ten years later, when the personal influence of the present writer (Freud, who had returned to Vienna in 1886 after studying in the school of Charcot) prevailed on him to take up the subject afresh and embark upon a joint study of it.   These two, Breuer and Freud, published a preliminary paper 'On the Psychical Mechanism of Hysterical Phenomena' in 1893, and in 1895 a volume entitled *Studies on Hysteria* (which reached its fourth edition in 1922), in which they described their therapeutic procedure as *'cathartic'*.

Catharsis.   The investigations which lay at the root of Breuer and Freud's studies led to two chief results, and these have not been shaken by subsequent experience: first, that hysterical symptoms have sense and meaning, being substitutes for normal mental acts; and secondly, that the uncovering of this unknown meaning is accom-

* From Vol. V of the *Collected Papers of Sigmund Freud*, edited by Ernest Jones, M.D., Basic Books, Inc., Publishers, New York, 1959.

Acknowledgment also to Sigmund Freud Copyrights Ltd., Mr. James Strachey, The Hogarth Press Ltd. for permission to quote from Vol. 18 of the Standard Edition of *The Complete Psychological Works of Sigmund Freud.*

panied by the removal of the symptoms—so that in this case scientific research and therapeutic effort coincide.   The observations were carried out upon a series of patients who were treated in the same manner as Breuer's first patient, that is to say, put into a state of deep hypnosis; and the results seemed brilliant, until later their weak side became evident.   The theoretical ideas put forward at that time by Breuer and Freud were influenced by Charcot's theories on traumatic hysteria and could find support in the findings of his pupil Pierre Janet, which, though they were published earlier than the *Studies*, were in fact subsequent to Breuer's first case.   From the very beginning the factor of *affect* was brought into the foreground: hysterical symptoms, the authors maintained, came into existence when a mental process with a heavy charge of affect was in any way prevented from being levelled out along the normal path leading to consciousness and movement (i.e. was prevented from being '*abreacted*'); as a result of this the affect, which was in a sense '*strangulated*', was diverted along wrong paths and flowed off into the somatic innervation (a process named '*conversion*').   The occasions upon which 'pathogenic ideas' of this kind arose were described by Breuer and Freud as '*psychical traumas*', and, since these often dated back to the very remote past, it was possible for the authors to say that hysterics suffered mainly from reminiscences (which had not been dealt with).   Under the treatment, therefore, '*catharsis*' came about when the path to consciousness was opened and there was a normal discharge of affect.   It will be seen that an essential part of this theory was the assumption of the existence of *unconscious* mental processes.   Janet too had made use of unconscious acts in mental life; but, as he insisted in his later polemics against psycho-analysis, to him the phrase was no more than a make-shift expression, a '*manière de parler*', and he intended to suggest no new point of view by it.

In a theoretical section of the *Studies* Breuer brought forward some speculative ideas about the processes of excitation in the mind. These ideas determined the direction of future lines of thought and even to-day have not received sufficient appreciation.   But they brought his contributions to this branch of science to an end, and soon afterwards he withdrew from the common work.

The transition to psycho-analysis.   Contrasts between the views of the two authors had been visible even in the *Studies*.   Breuer supposed that the pathogenic ideas produced their traumatic effect because they arose during '*hypnoid states*', in which mental functioning was subject to special limitations.   The present writer rejected this explanation and inclined to the belief that an idea became pathogenic if its content was in opposition to the predominant trend of the subject's mental life so that it provoked him into '*defence*'.   (Janet had attributed to hysterical patients a constitutional incapacity for holding together the contents of their minds; and it was at this point that his path diverged from that of Breuer and Freud.) Moreover, the two innovations which led the present writer to move away from the cathartic method had already been mentioned in the *Studies*. After Breuer's withdrawal they became the starting-point of fresh developments.

Abandonment of hypnosis. The first of these innovations was based on practical experience and led to a change in technique. The second consisted in an advance in the clinical understanding of neuroses. It soon appeared that the therapeutic hopes which had been placed upon cathartic treatment in hypnosis were to some extent unfulfilled. It was true that the disappearance of the symptoms went hand-in-hand with the catharsis, but total success turned out to be entirely dependent upon the patient's relation to the physician and thus resembled the effect of 'suggestion'. If that relation was disturbed, all the symptoms reappeared, just as though they had never been cleared up. In addition to this, the small number of people who could be put into a deep state of hypnosis involved a very considerable limitation, from the medical standpoint, of the applicability of the cathartic procedure. For these reasons the present writer decided to give up the use of hypnosis. But at the same time the impressions he had derived from hypnosis afforded him the means of replacing it.

Free association. The effect of the hypnotic condition upon the patient had been so greatly to increase his ability to make associations that he was able straight away to find the path—inaccessible to his conscious reflection—which led from the symptom to the thoughts and memories connected with it. The abandonment of hypnosis seemed to make the situation hopeless, until the writer recalled a remark of Bernheim's to the effect that things that had been experienced in a state of somnambulism were only *apparently* forgotten and that they could be brought into recollection at any time if the physician insisted forcibly enough that the patient knew them. The writer therefore endeavoured to insist on his *unhypnotized* patients giving him their associations, so that from the material thus provided he might find the path leading to what had been forgotten or fended off. He noticed later that the insistence was unnecessary and that copious ideas almost always arose in the patient's mind, but that they were held back from being communicated and even from becoming conscious by certain objections put by the patient in his own way. It was to be expected—though this was still unproved and not until later confirmed by wide experience—that everything that occurred to a patient setting out from a particular starting-point must also stand in an internal connection with that starting-point; hence arose the technique of educating the patient to give up the whole of his critical attitude and of making use of the material which was thus brought to light for the purpose of uncovering the connections that were being sought.   A strong belief in the strict determination of mental events certainly played a part in the choice of this technique as a substitute for hypnosis.

The 'Fundamental Technical Rule' of this procedure of 'free association' has from that time on been maintained in psychoanalytic work.   The treatment is begun by the patient being required to put himself in the position of an attentive and dispassionate self-observer, merely to read off all the time the surface of his consciousness, and on the one hand to make a duty of the most complete honesty while on the other not to hold back any idea from communication, even if (1) he feels that it is too disagreeable or if (2) he judges that it is nonsensical or (3) too unimportant or (4) irrelevant to what is being looked for. It is uniformly found that precisely those ideas which provoke these last-mentioned reactions are of particular value in discovering the forgotten material.

Psycho-analysis as an interpretative art.   The new technique altered the picture of the treatment so greatly, brought the physician into such a new relation to the patient and produced so many surprising results that it seemed justifiable to distinguish the procedure from the cathartic method by giving it a new name.   The present writer gave this method of treatment, which could now be extended to many other forms of neurotic disorder, the name of *psycho-analysis*.   Now, in the first resort, this psycho-analysis was an art of *interpretation* and it set itself the task of carrying deeper the first of Breuer's great discoveries—namely, that neurotic symptoms are significant substitutes for other mental acts which have been omitted.   It was now a question of regarding the material produced by the patients' associations as though it hinted at a hidden meaning and of discovering that meaning from it.   Experience soon showed that the attitude which the analytic physician could most advantageously adopt was to surrender himself to his own unconscious mental activity, in a state of *evenly suspended attention*, to avoid so far as possible reflection and the construction of conscious expectations, not to try to fix anything that he heard particularly in his memory, and by these means to catch the drift of the patient's unconscious with his own unconscious.   It was then found that, except under conditions that were too unfavourable, the patient's associations emerged like allusions, as it were, to one particular theme and that it was only necessary for the physician to go a step further in order to guess the material which was concealed from the patient himself and to be able to communicate it to him.   It is true that this work of interpretation was not to be brought under strict rules and left a great deal of play to the physician's tact and skill; but, with impartiality and practice, it was usually possible to obtain trustworthy results—that is to say, results which were confirmed by being repeated in similar cases. At a time when so little was as yet known of the unconscious, the structure of the neuroses and the pathological processes underlying them, it was a matter for satisfaction that a technique of this kind should be available, even if it had no better theoretical basis. Moreover it is still employed in analyses at the present day in the same manner, though with a sense of greater assurance and with a better understanding of its limitations.

The interpretation of parapraxes and haphazard acts. It was a triumph for the interpretative art of psycho-analysis when it succeeded in demonstrating that certain common mental acts of normal people, for which no one had hitherto attempted to put forward a psychological explanation, were to be regarded in the same light as the symptoms of neurotics: that is to say, they had a *meaning*, which was unknown to the subject but which could easily be discovered by analytic means. The phenomena in question were such events as the temporary forgetting of familiar words and names, forgetting to carry out prescribed tasks, everyday slips of the tongue and of the pen, misreadings, losses and mislayings of objects, certain errors, instances of apparently accidental self-injury, and finally habitual movements carried out seemingly without intention or in play, tunes hummed 'thoughtlessly', and so on. All of these were shorn of their physiological explanation, if any such had ever been attempted, were shown to be strictly determined and were revealed as an expression of the subject's suppressed intentions or as a result of a clash between two intentions one of which was permanently or temporarily unconscious. The importance of this contribution to psychology was of many kinds. The range of mental determinism was extended by it in an unforeseen manner; the supposed gulf between normal and pathological mental events was narrowed; in many cases a useful insight was afforded into the play of mental forces that must be suspected to lie behind the phenomena. Finally, a class of material was brought to light which is calculated better than any other to stimulate a belief in the existence of unconscious mental acts even in people to whom the hypothesis of something at once mental and unconscious seems strange and even absurd. The study of one's own parapraxes and haphazard acts, for which most people have ample opportunities, is even to-day the best preparation for an approach to psycho-analysis. In analytic treatment, the interpretation of parapraxes retains a place as a means of uncovering the unconscious, alongside the immeasurably more important interpretation of associations.

The interpretation of dreams.   A new approach to the depths of mental life was opened when the technique of free association was applied to dreams, whether one's own or those of patients in analysis. In fact, the greater and better part of what we know of the processes in the unconscious levels of the mind is derived from the interpretation of dreams.   Psycho-analysis has restored to dreams the importance which was generally ascribed to them in ancient times, but it treats them differently.   It does not rely upon the cleverness of the dream-interpreter but for the most part hands the task over to the dreamer himself by asking him for his associations to the separate elements of the dream.   By pursuing these associations further we obtain knowledge of thoughts which coincide entirely with the dream but which can be recognized—up to a certain point—as genuine and completely intelligible portions of waking mental activity.   Thus the recollected dream emerges as the *manifest dream-content,* in contrast to the *latent dream-thoughts* discovered by interpretation.   The process which has transformed the latter into the former, that is to say into 'the dream', and which is undone by the work of interpretation, may be called the *'dream-work'*.

We also describe the latent dream-thoughts, on account of their connection with waking life, as *'residues of the [previous] day'.*   By the operation of the dream-work (to which it would be quite incorrect to ascribe any 'creative' character) the latent dream-thoughts are *condensed* in a remarkable way, are *distorted* by the *displacement* of psychical intensities and are arranged with a view to being *represented in visual pictures;* and, besides all this, before the manifest dream is arrived at, they are submitted to a process of *secondary revision* which seeks to give the new product something in the nature of sense and coherence.   Strictly speaking, this last process does not form a part of the dream-work.[1]

The dynamic theory of dream-formation.   An understanding of the dynamics of dream-formation did not involve any very great difficulties. The motive power for the formation of dreams is not provided by the latent dream-thoughts or day's residues, but by an unconscious impulse, repressed during the day, with which the day's residues have been able to establish contact and which contrives to make a *wish-fulfilment* for itself out of the material of the latent thoughts.   Thus every dream is on the one hand the fulfilment of a wish on the part of the unconscious and on the other hand (in so far as it succeeds in guarding the state of sleep against being disturbed) the fulfilment of the normal wish to sleep which set the sleep going.   If we disregard the unconscious contribution to the formation of the dream and limit

[1] [In *The Interpretation of Dreams, Standard Ed.,* 5, 490, secondary revision is regarded as part of the dream-work.]

the dream to its latent thoughts, it can represent anything with which waking life has been concerned—a reflection, a warning, an intention, a preparation for the immediate future or, once again, the satisfaction of an unfulfilled wish. The unrecognizability, strangeness and absurdity of the manifest dream are partly the result of the translation of the thoughts into a different, so to say *archaic*, method of expression, but partly the effect of a restrictive, critically disapproving agency in the mind, which does not entirely cease to function during sleep. It is plausible to suppose that the '*dream-censorship*', which we regard as being responsible in the first instance for the distortion of the dream-thoughts into the manifest dream, is an expression of the same mental forces which during the day-time had held back or *repressed* the unconscious wishful impulse.

It has been worth while to enter in some detail into the explanation of dreams, since analytic work has shown that the dynamics of the formation of dreams are the same as those of the formation of symptoms. In both cases we find a struggle between two trends, of which one is unconscious and ordinarily repressed and strives towards satisfaction—that is, wish-fulfilment—while the other, belonging probably to the conscious ego, is disapproving and repressive. The outcome of this conflict is a *compromise-formation* (the dream or the symptom) in which both trends have found an incomplete expression. The theoretical importance of this conformity between dreams and symptoms is illuminating. Since dreams are not pathological phenomena, the fact shows that the mental mechanisms which produce the symptoms of illness are equally present in normal mental life, that the same uniform law embraces both the normal and the abnormal and that the findings of research into neurotics or psychotics cannot be without significance for our understanding of the healthy mind.

Symbolism.   In the course of investigating the form of expression brought about by the dream-work, the surprising fact emerged that certain objects, arrangements and relations are represented, in a sense indirectly, by 'symbols', which are used by the dreamer without his understanding them and to which as a rule he offers no associations. Their translation has to be provided by the analyst, who can himself only discover it empirically by experimentally fitting it into the context. It was later found that linguistic usage, mythology and folklore afford the most ample analogies to dream-symbols. Symbols, which raise the most interesting and hitherto unsolved problems, seem to be a fragment of extremely ancient inherited mental equipment. The use of a common symbolism extends far beyond the use of a common language.

The aetiological significance of sexual life.   The second novelty which emerged after the hypnotic technique had been replaced by free associations was of a clinical nature. It was discovered in the course of the prolonged search for the traumatic experiences from which hysterical symptoms appeared to be derived. The more carefully the search was pursued the more extensive seemed to be the network of aetiologically significant impressions, but the further back, too, did they reach into the patient's puberty or childhood. At the same time they assumed a uniform character and eventually it became inevitable to bow before the evidence and recognize that at the root of the formation of every symptom there were to be found traumatic experiences from early sexual life. Thus a sexual trauma stepped into the place of an ordinary trauma and the latter was seen to owe its aetiological significance to an associative or symbolic connection with the former, which had preceded it. An investigation of cases of common nervousness (falling into the two classes of *neurasthenia* and *anxiety neurosis*) which was simultaneously undertaken led to the conclusion that these disorders could be traced to *contemporary* abuses in the patients' sexual life and could be removed if these were brought to an end. It was thus easy to infer that neuroses in general are an expression of disturbances in sexual life, the so-called *actual-neuroses* being the consequences (by chemical agency) of *contemporary* injuries and the *psycho-neuroses* the consequences (by psychical modification) of *bygone* injuries to a biological function which had hitherto been gravely neglected by science. None of these theses of psycho-analysis has met with such tenacious scepticism or such embittered resistance as this assertion of the preponderating aetiological significance of sexual life in the neuroses. It should, however, be expressly remarked that, in its development up to the present day, psycho-analysis has found no reason to retreat from this opinion.

Infantile sexuality. As a result of its aetiological researches, psycho-analysis found itself in the position of dealing with a subject the very existence of which had scarcely been suspected previously. Science had become accustomed to consider sexual life as beginning with puberty and regarded manifestations of sexuality in children as rare signs of abnormal precocity and degeneracy. But now psycho-analysis revealed a wealth of phenomena, remarkable, yet of regular occurrence, which made it necessary to date back the beginning of the sexual function in children almost to the commencement of extra-uterine existence; and it was asked with astonishment how all this could have come to be overlooked. The first glimpses of sexuality in children had indeed been obtained through the analytic examination of adults and were consequently saddled with all the doubts and sources of error that could be attributed to such a belated retrospect; but subsequently (from 1908 onwards) a beginning was made with the analysis of children themselves and with the unembarrassed observation of their behaviour, and in this way direct confirmation was reached for the whole factual basis of the new view.

Sexuality in children showed a different picture in many respects from that in adults, and, surprisingly enough, it exhibited numerous traces of what, in adults, were condemned as *'perversions'*. It became necessary to enlarge the concept of what was sexual, till it covered more than the impulsion towards the union of the two sexes in the sexual act or towards provoking particular pleasurable sensations in the genitals. But this enlargement was rewarded by the new possibility of grasping infantile, normal and perverse sexual life as a single whole.

The analytic researches carried out by the writer fell, to begin with, into the error of greatly overestimating the importance of *seduction* as a source of sexual manifestations in children and as a root for the formation of neurotic symptoms. This misapprehension was corrected when it became possible to appreciate the extraordinarily large part played in the mental life of neurotics by the activities of *phantasy*, which clearly carried more weight in neurosis than did external reality. Behind these phantasies there came to light the material which allows us to draw the picture which follows of the development of the sexual function.

The development of the libido.   The sexual instinct, the dynamic manifestation of which in mental life we shall call *'libido'*, is made up of component instincts into which it may once more break up and which are only gradually united into well-defined organizations. The sources of these component instincts are the organs of the body and in particular certain specially marked *erotogenic zones;* but contributions are made to libido from every important functional process in the body. At first the individual component instincts strive for satisfaction independently of one another, but in the course of development they become more and more convergent and concentrated. The first (pregenital) stage of organization to be discerned is the *oral* one, in which—in conformity with the suckling's predominant interest— the oral zone plays the leading part. This is followed by the *sadistic-anal* organization, in which the *anal* zone and the component instinct of *sadism* are particularly prominent; at this stage the difference between the sexes is represented by the contrast between active and passive. The third and final stage of organization is that in which the majority of the component instincts converge under the *primacy of the genital zones*. As a rule this development is passed through swiftly and unobtrusively; but some individual portions of the instincts remain behind at the prodromal stages of the process and thus give rise to *fixations* of libido, which are important as constituting predispositions for subsequent irruptions of repressed impulses and which stand in a definite relation to the later development of neuroses and perversions.

The process of finding an object, and the Oedipus complex.   In the first instance the oral component instinct finds satisfaction by attaching itself to the sating of the desire for nourishment; and its object is the mother's breast.   It then detaches itself, becomes independent and at the same time *auto-erotic,* that is, it finds an object in the child's own body.   Others of the component instincts also start by being auto-erotic and are not until later diverted on to an external object.   It is a particularly important fact that the component instincts belonging to the genital zone habitually pass through a period of intense auto-erotic satisfaction.   The component instincts are not all equally serviceable in the final genital organization of libido; some of them (for instance, the anal components) are consequently left aside and suppressed, or undergo complicated transformations.

In the very earliest years of childhood (approximately between the ages of two and five) a convergence of the sexual impulses occurs of which, in the case of boys, the object is the mother.   This choice of an object, in conjunction with a corresponding attitude of rivalry and hostility towards the father, provides the content of what is known as the *Oedipus complex,* which in every human being is of the greatest importance in determining the final shape of his erotic life.   It has been found to be characteristic of a normal individual that he learns to master his Oedipus complex, whereas the neurotic subject remains involved in it.

The diphasic onset of sexual development.   Towards the end of the fifth year this early period of sexual life normally comes to an end. It is succeeded by a period of more or less complete *latency,* during which ethical restraints are built up, to act as defences against the desires of the Oedipus complex.   In the subsequent period of *puberty,* the Oedipus complex is revivified in the unconscious and embarks upon further modifications.   It is only at puberty that the sexual instincts develop to their full intensity; but the direction of that development, as well as all the predispositions for it, have already been determined by the early efflorescence of sexuality during childhood which preceded it.   This diphasic development of the sexual function —in two stages, interrupted by the latency period—appears to be a biological peculiarity of the human species and to contain the determining factor for the origin of neuroses.

The theory of repression.   These theoretical considerations, taken together with the immediate impressions derived from analytic work, lead to a view of the neuroses which may be described in the roughest outline as follows. The neuroses are the expression of conflicts between the ego and such of the sexual impulses as seem to the ego incompatible with its integrity or with its ethical standards. Since these impulses are not *ego-syntonic*, the ego has *repressed* them: that is to say, it has withdrawn its interest from them and has shut them off from becoming conscious as well as from obtaining satisfaction by motor discharge. If in the course of analytic work one attempts to make these repressed impulses conscious, one becomes aware of the repressive forces in the form of *resistance*. But the achievement of repression fails particularly readily in the case of the sexual instincts. Their dammed-up libido finds other ways out from the unconscious: for it *regresses* to earlier phases of development and earlier attitudes towards objects, and, at weak points in the libidinal development where there are infantile fixations, it breaks through into consciousness and obtains discharge. What results is a *symptom* and consequently in its essence a substitutive sexual satisfaction. Nevertheless the symptom cannot entirely escape from the repressive forces of the ego and must therefore submit to modifications and displacements—exactly as happens with dreams—by means of which its characteristic of being a sexual satisfaction becomes unrecognizable. Consequently symptoms are in the nature of compromises between the repressed sexual instincts and the repressing ego instincts; they represent a wish-fulfilment for both partners to the conflict simultaneously, but one which is incomplete for each of them. This is quite strictly true of the symptoms of hysteria, while in the symptoms of obsessional neurosis there is often a stronger emphasis upon the side of the repressing function owing to the erection of reaction-formations, which are assurances against sexual satisfaction.

Transference. If further proof were needed of the truth that the motive forces behind the formation of neurotic symptoms are of a sexual nature, it would be found in the fact that in the course of analytic treatment a special emotional relation is regularly formed between the patient and the physician. This goes far beyond rational limits. It varies between the most affectionate devotion and the most obstinate enmity and derives all of its characteristics from earlier erotic attitudes of the patient's which have become unconscious. This *transference* alike in its positive and in its negative form is used as a weapon by the resistance; but in the hands of the physician it becomes the most powerful therapeutic instrument and it plays a part scarcely to be over-estimated in the dynamics of the process of cure.

The corner-stones of psycho-analytic theory. The assumption that there are unconscious mental processes, the recognition of the theory of resistance and repression, the appreciation of the importance of sexuality and of the Oedipus complex—these constitute the principal subject-matter of psycho-analysis and the foundations of its theory. No one who cannot accept them all should count himself a psycho-analyst.

Heinz L.
Ansbacher

ADLER'S THEORY OF INDIVIDUAL PSYCHOLOGY *

Adler was the first to develop a comprehensive theory of personality, psychological disorders and psychotherapy, which represented an alternative to the views of Freud, even long before Freud had reached the climax of his acclaim, and simultaneously with Freud's own later development.

Alternatives to Freud have in recent years been restated by many who found his system inadequate to the problems to which it pertains. These developments are known as existential psychology and psychiatry, client-centered counseling, humanistic psychology, the "third force" in psychology, phenomenological psychology, social psychiatry, rational-emotive psychotherapy, neo-Freudian trends, ego psychology, and by many other names. In the aspects in which they depart from Freud, they all can be reconciled far more easily with the basic assumptions of Adler than with those of Freud. To know Adler is to be well prepared for all these developments.

It seems that in the development of modern psychological thinking the Western world first had to go through the Freudian stage, even as Adler himself did for a short period. Fourteen years younger than Freud, he was from 1902 to 1911 a prominent member of Freud's circle. But then he was the first to free himself from Freud as countless others have done since, although Freud's influence was stimulating and fructifying. Now that one reads with increasing frequency that we have entered the post-Freudian era, the appreciation of and interest in Adler are proportionately growing.

Freud represented a half-way station, so-to-speak. Revolutionary as

* This paper appeared originally as "Introduction to the Torchbook Edition" of *Problems of Neurosis* by Alfred Adler (1, pp. ix-xxvi) and is reprinted here, with some omissions and slight modifications, by permission of the author and the publisher, Harper and Row, Publishers, Incorporated.

his theories were and difficult as they seem at first, they were actually more conservative and more easy to understand with reference to the scientific and also to some of the popular thinking then prevailing, than was Adler's thinking. Freud was revolutionary for his day in that he listened to every word of his patients, knowing that this would be valuable basic information for solving the puzzle of mental disorder. But he was scientifically conservative in that he firmly believed that the patient's inner psychological world was ultimately determined by objective causes that rested in his past. Freud was difficult in that he created a large new vocabulary designating numerous drives, stages, areas, and mechanisms which he believed to have "discovered," and which he considered responsible for the full range of human behavior. And yet all this was relatively easy to grasp in that it still was similar to old ways of thinking, according to which mental disorders, like physical illnesses, were caused by forces beyond the individual's control.

It was scientifically more revolutionary to proclaim, as did Adler, that the inner psychological world of the individual, which had such far-reaching consequences, was not objectively caused, but was ultimately the individual's own creation, and that the individual's course of life received its direction not from relatively objective drives, but from his highly subjective goals and values. And it was more difficult to accept that the individual could be quite unaware of the goals and values which he himself had created or accepted, than that he was the pawn of an "unconscious" which supposedly controlled his conscious self.

The essential difference between Freud's and Adler's ways of thinking is that in the former the conception of man's psychological functioning is patterned after the older physical sciences, whereas in the latter it is patterned after the biological sciences, the sciences of life. In the former a mechanistic, elementaristic, and deterministic orientation was adequate. But in the latter it is today widely appreciated that for an understanding of what is specific to life, an organismic and holistic view is more fruitful. Such a view reckons not only with objective determiners from the past but declares that a living organism is a functional unity whose parts cooperate for the good of the whole and that therefore its properties are best understood from this standpoint. As Sinnott (16) has repeatedly explained, it is scientifically fruitful to approach problems of biology from a teleological viewpoint.[1]

If the organismic-holistic viewpoint is the more adequate for biology in general, this must be true especially for the science concerned with the highest manifestation of life, human psychology. Adler embraced this viewpoint, which was not so well defined then as it is today. Its

[1] A more detailed description of Adler's organismic position is given in another paper (5).

principle practical significance is that the individual is understood not as completely determined by outside forces but to a considerable extent as self-determined. Such a conception is particularly useful in psychotherapy in that it gives the patient a feeling of freedom and optimism, so important in enabling him to change.

Theory of personality

The essential principles of Adler's psychology, which he named Individual Psychology, may be considered to be the following.

Unity of the individual

The unit to be studied is the individual person and his way of living. All the general similarities one can observe among people, such as drives, emotions, cultural experiences, must be understood as subordinated to the individual's organization, his *style of life*, life-plan. As in Gestalt psychology the organization of the whole figure will determine how the parts will be perceived, so in Individual Psychology, the organization of the whole person will influence all his partial functions. But, beyond Gestalt psychology, Adler conceived the individual as goal-oriented, and all partial functions, including neurotic symptoms, as serving the overall purpose.

One of the important consequences of this understanding is that the Freudian conscious-unconscious antithesis and the notion of intra-personal conflicts are done away with. The unconscious serves the individual's purposes no less than the conscious; it is not a relatively autonomous function which attempts to rule the individual, while he attempts to repress it. "Individual Psychology distinguishes in the conscious and the unconscious, not separate and conflicting entities, but complementary and cooperating parts of one and the same reality" (p. 29).[2] "We cannot oppose 'consciousness' to 'unconsciousness' as if they were two antagonistic halves of an individual's existence. The conscious life becomes unconscious as soon as we fail to understand it—and as soon as we understand an unconscious tendency it has already become conscious" (p. 163).

Not only the psychological but also the organic functions are subordinated to the style of life, although both were originally factors in its formation. "The organic functions are dominated by the style of life. This is notably the case with the lungs, the heart, the stomach, the organs of excretion and the sexual organs. The disturbance of these

---

[2] Because this paper was written as an introduction to *Problems of Neurosis* (1) nearly all references to Adler are from this book. Where only page references are given, they are to this book.

functions expresses the direction which an individual is taking to attain his goal. I have called these disturbances the organ dialect, or organ jargon, since the organs are revealing in their own most expressive language the intention of the individual totality" (p. 156).

"The dialect of the sexual organs is especially expressive" (p. 156). "My questioners often appear to have been misled . . . into believing that the sexual impulse is the central motive. . . . Our experience is that the sexual components cannot even be correctly estimated except in relation to the individual style of life" (p. 46).

"We are far from disputing that every mental and bodily function is necessarily conditioned by inherited material, but what we see in all psychic activity is the *use which is made* of this material to attain a certain goal" (p. 30).

The individual is not divided against himself. He is not the battleground of conflicting forces. What appears as inner conflicts is derived from man's self-determination, including the freedom and necessity to choose between alternatives presented by the situation. It includes the freedom to make mistakes. "Rightly understood, the whole of this mental process—working from below to above, expressing an inferiority but compensating with a superiority—is not ambivalence but a dynamic unity. Only if it is not understood as a whole do we see it as two contradictory and warring entities" (p. 87).

Unitary motivation

As an organism, a unified whole, the individual is not determined by various drives or motives, but there is one dynamic force, of which all others are only partial and subsidiary aspects. This derives from the growth and forward movement of life itself. It is a general forward striving. The recognition of one master motive is common to all organismic psychologies since Adler. Some of the names that have been chosen by recent workers are: self-actualization, self-expansion, self-consistency, competence.

Adler ultimately spoke of striving for perfection, completion, overcoming, or a goal of success. Earlier he spoke of striving to overcome the difficulties of life (p. 32), the upward strivings of the psyche (p. 33), striving for superiority (p. 13), or, most often, a goal of superiority. Superiority may be personal superiority over others, or superiority over general difficulties, in the sense of perfection, completion, or competence. The former is characteristic of mental disorders, the latter of mental health.

Here a problem arises. Adler's theoretical writing started with the concept of organ inferiority and its compensation, and soon afterwards he stressed feelings of inferiority as a dynamic force. In the present volume we find, "The sense of impotence, or the 'feeling of inferiority,' is the root-conception of Individual Psychology" (p. 33). "We soon perceive a greater or lesser degree of the feeling of inferiority in everyone, together with a compensatory striving towards a goal of superiority" (p. 2).

The problem is: Which comes first, the feeling of inferiority or the striving? A theory of motivation which puts inferiority feelings first would include only what Maslow (14) calls deficit motivation. In this respect compensation is actually a parallel construction to drive-reduction: Without the feeling of a deficit, an inferiority, there would be no striving.

Although Adler never became explicit on this issue, he quietly changed the order in his last writings, putting the striving first. "In comparison with unattainable ideal perfection, the individual is continuously filled by an inferiority feeling and motivated by it" (3, p. 117). "In the struggle for perfection, man is always in a state of psychical agitation and feels unsettled before the goal of perfection" (3, p. 116). This is a great improvement of the theory. Not only does it give room for the concept of growth motivation (14), the primacy of the striving also permits one to consider this striving as a human manifestation of the general growth and expansion movement which is characteristic of all of life. Furthermore, it is not possible to verify a universal primary inferiority feeling in the infant. This can be neither observed directly nor ascertained through introspection; it is merely a conjecture, whereas the striving for success or competence can be very readily observed in the infant (18).

In a paper by Adler (2) published during his last year, summarizing the basic assumptions of Individual Psychology, inferiority feeling is not even mentioned. This does not mean that in the psychology of mental disorders strong inferiority feelings with correspondingly low self-esteem do not remain a central factor. It only means that inferiority feelings are no longer considered primary, but the outgrowth of an impeded striving for success.

Self-determination and uniqueness

Since the human individual is capable of considering himself and his situation, and of extending himself into the future, the master motive derives its direction from the over-all goal the individual sets for himself, his conceptualization of superiority or success. Not all of the goal content is conceptualized; to a greater or lesser extent the individual is only dimly aware of where he is heading. To some extent the subject's goal is also the inference or working hypothesis of the psychologist.

While the objective realities have been used in the formulation of the goal, it is in the end subjectively determined by the inventive or creative power of the individual. This is how individual uniqueness becomes most pronounced. Beyond the uniqueness of the constellation of hereditary and environmental factors in each particular case, the goal of superiority which uses these is capable of infinite individual variation.

"No soul develops in freedom. Each one is in mental, emotional and nutritive dependence upon his immediate environment on the earth and in the cosmos, yet so far independent that he must take up these relations consciously: he must answer them as the questions of life" (p. 36). "As a conscious relation between its organism and environment, the child's psyche seems to have an indefinite *causal* power: so that, normal or abnormal, it never reacts with anything like mathematical exactitude. Life, as opposed to dead material, always reacts thus, in a more or less inaccurate—and spontaneous—manner" (p. 34). "The child's individual conception of the future is the dominant causal factor" (p. 90). "In the world of the psyche there is no principle of individual orientation beyond our own beliefs" (p. 62).[3] Our responses to the world will depend on our conception of it, our beliefs and attitudes. Thus Individual Psychology becomes a cognitive and phenomenological psychology.

As already mentioned, what appears as inner conflicts derives from man's freedom to make choices. This freedom offers particular difficulty for the neurotic, because a choice point marks a step forward while the neurotic is afraid of going ahead. Thus where others speak of inner conflicts, Adler speaks of the "hesitating attitude" (p. 3), wasting time (p. 103) in order to gain time.

From the postulate of the importance of beliefs and attitudes in the guidance of behavior and their ultimate determination by the individual's own creative power, follows an optimistic outlook so important for treatment, also mentioned earlier.

Social context

Just as the partial functions cannot be considered out of the context of the individual, so the individual must be considered within his larger ecological context, including particularly human society. An important part of what makes us human, namely language, is a social product, showing how unscientific it would be to study the individual without taking his social context fully into account. Thus Individual Psychology becomes the study of interpersonal transactions.

This is reflected in the following description of the situation developing from a child's feeling dethroned. "It is a common thing for the first child to hasten his own dethronement by fighting against

---

[3] It is for such statements that Ford and Urban (12) designated Adler's Individual Psychology a "subjectivistic system."

it with envy, jealousy and truculence, which lower him in the parental favour" (p. 102).

Even the function of the sense organs was understood by Adler in the social context. "Imperfections in the sense organs limit the means which a child has of sharing in the life of others" (p. 65).

With regard to the most significant problems that man faces— society, occupation, love—they are all of a social nature. "We must realize that every adaptation we have to make in life, from kindergarten to business management, from school chums to marriage, is, directly or indirectly, a social action. From the earliest times, we face new thoughts and events in a manner which is dominantly social or antisocial, it cannot be neutral. Suppose, for instance, that a boy is terrified by illness and death in his environment. He may allay his fears by the determination to be a doctor, and to fight against death. This is obviously a more social idea than that of being a grave-digger, the one who buries the *others*—a reaction which I have also found in a boy in that situation" (p. 33).

Social interest

In the organismic-holistic view, man is not seen in unavoidable conflict with society and its rules. This does not deny the existence of such conflicts, but does deny their unavoidability. The concept of society itself is only an abstraction. In concrete reality there are only individuals and rules that they have made to facilitate the process of living together. Everyone has the capacity of understanding these "rules of the game," of developing them further, and of contributing something which will become a part of "society" which another individual may have to meet. Human nature "includes the possibility of socially affirmative action" (p. 35).

"The high degree of cooperation and social culture which man needs for his very existence demands spontaneous social effort, and the dominant purpose of education is to evoke it. Social feeling is not inborn; but it is an innate potentiality which has to be consciously developed" (p. 31). The German term is *Gemeinschaftsgefühl*, which has also been translated as social interest.[4] It is not an innate altruistic motive, opposed to a selfish motive. This would be a motivational dualism, foreign to a holistic theory. Social interest is rather a cognitive function which must be *consciously* developed

---

[4] *Gemeinschaft* in the composite term *Gemeinschaftsgefühl* is actually not limited to the social aspect. It rather stands for communality or community, a broader concept. *Gemeinschaftsgefühl* has thus rightly been translated also as community feeling, community interest, communal intuition, or sense of solidarity. It is quite possible to have a feeling of communality with life and the universe in general, to identify with the order of the universe. It is this that Adler meant when he said that the mentally healthy individual "feels at home in life . . . at home upon the crust of the earth," as quoted below.

through education.   It may, however, acquire secondary motivational attributes like any developed capacity such as typing or skiing.   Man likes to do what he is capable of doing well.

The concept of social feeling or social interest is today recognized as one of Adler's extremely important contributions.   It is particularly important for a definition of positive mental health which offers such great difficulty to other theories which do not have this concept.

Theory of mental health, neurosis, and psychotherapy

Mental health

While the definition of positive mental health is still an extensively discussed problem, Adler clearly recognized the necessity of formulating a widely serviceable answer.   He generally did not describe mental disturbances as "illness" but showed how they were mistaken ways of living, mistaken life styles.   He designated those with mistaken life styles as "failures."   Thus mental health could never be the mere absence of illness, but was a less faulty way of living.   The aim of his therapeutic efforts was "to replace the great mistakes by small ones. . . . Big mistakes can produce neuroses, but little mistakes a nearly normal person" (p. 62).

Adler phrased his therapeutic aim in this modest fashion because he had no absolute answer to the right way of living.   We still do not have the answer and probably never shall have, as we have no absolute answer to the meaning of life.

In the face of this dilemma, presented by the necessity of a definition of the right way of living on the one hand, and the impossibility of giving an absolute answer, Adler resorted to a pragmatic answer. Adler observed that those who could be called mentally healthy led lives which in the long run were socially more useful in a broad sense than the lives led by those who could be called mentally "sick." Consequently he made social usefulness the criterion of mental health.

"By useful I mean in the interests of mankind generally.   The most sensible estimate of the value of any activity is its helpfulness to all mankind, present and future, a criterion that applies not only to that which subserves the immediate preservation of life, but also to higher activities such as religion, science, and art" (p. 78).   The healthfulness of such striving is determined by the order of the world according to which a self-centered goal is bound to be limited and precarious, whereas a self-transcending useful goal has the greatest validity attainable.

Such usefulness is the outcome of a well developed social feeling or social interest.   "It is almost impossible to exaggerate the value of an increase in social feeling. The mind improves, for intelligence is a communal function. The feeling of worth and value is heightened, giving courage and an optimistic view, and there is a sense of acquiescence in the common advantages and drawbacks of our lot. The individual feels at home in life and feels his existence to be worthwhile just so far as he is useful to others and is overcoming common instead of private feelings of inferiority. Not only the ethical nature, but the right attitude in aesthetics, the best understanding of the beautiful and the ugly will always be founded upon the truest social feeling" (p. 79).

A similar passage reads: "Courage, an optimistic attitude, common sense, and the feeling of being at home upon the crust of the earth, will enable him to face advantages and disadvantages with equal firmness. His goal of superiority will be identified with ideas of serving the human race and of overcoming its difficulties by his creative power" (pp. 47–48). Here Adler characterizes the way of life of the individual "who has been well prepared for social life" (p. 47) through development of his social interest. Such a person will also "solve all love-problems with loyalty to the partner and responsibility to society" (p. 47).

Neurotic style of life

By contrast, the neurotic life style is essentially that of the pampered child. Such a person does not contribute, but rather leans on others and is likely not to take responsibility for his actions but to shift responsibility and blame upon other factors or other people.

"In the investigation of a neurotic style of life we must always suspect an opponent, and note who suffers most because of the patient's condition. Usually this is a member of the family, and sometimes a person of the other sex, though there are cases in which the illness is an attack upon society as a whole. There is always this element of concealed accusation in neurosis, the patient feeling as though he were deprived of his *right*—i.e., of the center of attention—and wanting to fix the responsibility and blame upon someone. By such hidden vengeance and accusation, by excluding social activity whilst fighting against persons and rules, the problem-child and the neurotic find some relief from their dissatisfaction" (p. 81).

The dissatisfaction stems from the fact that such a person is not prepared when he comes to face the general life problems of society, work, and love, all of which require cooperation and social interest for their satisfactory solution. "All neurotic persons who have developed from a pampered prototype expect to be appreciated *before* they will do anything of social value instead of *after* having done it, thus expecting the natural course of things to be reversed in their own favor" (p. 77). Such people want "to take without giving" (p. 95), want "everything for nothing" (p. 94) and "all or nothing" (p. 55). The result often is nothing.

When an impasse is reached, the neurosis breaks out into the open. The patient shows disabling symptoms. These serve to safeguard his self-esteem and to provide excuses for his failure before himself and others. At the same time the symptoms are hidden accusations of others whom he considers not to have done enough for him. "Neurosis invariably gives relief to the subject, not, of course, in the light of objectivity and common sense, but according to his own private logic: it secures some triumph or at least it allays the fear of defeat. Thus neurosis is the weapon of the coward, and the weapon most used by the weak" (p. 80). "The problem of every neurosis is, for the patient, the difficult maintenance of a style of acting, thinking and perceiving which distorts and denies the demands of reality" (p. 1).

This description of the neurotic may seem harsh. But Adler also makes the important categorical statement: "Every neurotic is partly in the right" (p. 24). By this is meant that he has "good" reasons for his behavior—only, they are not sufficient reasons. The neurotic generally suffered from organ inferiorities or was pampered or neglected as a child (pp. 34–37), all three situations being conducive to the development of the pampered, non-contributive style of life, as Adler formulated it in a later publication. "In these three types of children we encounter the three typical accentuations of the feeling of inferiority. They all weaken the social contact, and tend to isolate the individual in an ever-narrowing sphere of interest" (p. 37).

The point is that the individual was misled by such situations toward his mistaken style of life. To understand a case means to arrive at the conclusion: Considering the circumstances of the patient and his original mistaken interpretation, he is acting quite logically, and we would respond the same way given the same premises. Thus we can empathize and sympathize with the neurotic, and also remain hopeful regarding the possibility of change.

Psychotherapy

If mental health is striving for a goal of superiority or success which is one of general benefit, and if mental disorder is a mistaken striving for a goal which has no general validity, one of personal superiority, then the task of psychotherapy becomes a re-orientation of the patient toward a more useful objective for his striving. The patient came to the therapist because he reached an impasse with regard to a specific life situation with which he is presently confronted. "We must make a change in the deeper motive, in the underlying style of life, and then the patient will see all his life-tasks in a new perspective" (p. 19).   The outcome is a cognitive reorganization.[5]

The mistaken goal stems, as we have seen, from an underdeveloped social interest and increased inferiority feelings.   It thus becomes the task of the therapist to encourage the patient and to strengthen his social interest.   This is done by the therapist himself first extending a sincere social interest to the patient.   Thus psychotherapy is at once repudiated as a detached technology, and becomes a sincere interpersonal relationship.

"The patient must be appealed to in a friendly way, coaxed into a receptive frame of mind.   Indeed, the task of the physician or psychologist is to give the patient the experience of contact with a fellow-man, and then to enable him to transfer this awakened social feeling to others.   This method, of winning the patient's good will, and then transferring it to his environment, is strictly analogous to the maternal function.   The social duty of motherhood is to interpret society to the individual, and if the mother fails in this, the duty is likely to devolve much later upon the physician who is heavily handicapped for the task.   The mother has the enormous advantage of the physical and psychic relation; she is the greatest experience of love and fellowship that the child will ever have. . . .   This is the two-fold function of motherhood, to give the child the completest possible experience of human fellowship, and then to widen it into a life-attitude towards others" (pp. 20–21).

"What the Freudians call transference (so far as we can discuss it apart from sexual implication) is merely social feeling" (p. 73).   "We are far from denying that other schools of psychiatry have their successes in dealing with neuroses, but in our experience they do so less by their methods than when they happen to give the patient a good human relation with the physician, or above all, to give him encouragement" (p. 40).

The task of the therapist is to enable the patient "to realize what he is doing, and to transfer his egocentric interest to social life and useful activity" (p. 40).   The cure depends on the patient's understanding his self-centered goal "which has been hitherto a heavily-guarded secret" (pp. 73–74) from his own understanding.

But Adler made the cure not dependent on such insight alone.   He also had a place for therapy without insight, such as milieu therapy, or as we often say today, social therapy.   "It is true, that, in lighter cases, a patient with very varied symptoms may lose them before he himself or the doctor have come to grasp their coherence.   When this happens it is either because of a favorable change in the patient's

[5] Sundberg and Tyler (17) have very appropriately classified Adler with cognitive and value change theorists of psychotherapy among whom they include Adolph Meyer, Albert Ellis, F. C. Thorne, G. A. Kelly, Lakin Phillips, O. H. Mowrer, and the existentialists, particularly Rollo May and V. E. Frankl.

situation or because the doctor, by encouragement or by chance, renews the patient's interest in others" (p. 54).

Concluding comments [6]

Adler was convinced that it was necessary and possible to communicate basic principles of mental health and adjustment convincingly and effectively to the broadest sectors of society. As we have seen, he considered mental disorder not an illness in the usual sense but a mistaken way of living; the whole community could contribute to reducing this mistake, not only the expert and the individual himself.

Working in this direction, Adler created a network of over 30 child guidance clinics in connection with the Vienna public schools, staffed by volunteers who conducted their counseling sessions in front of qualified audiences. He conducted adult-education classes on a large scale. He considered it most important that teachers be alerted to the social principles of mental health. He fully appreciated that he was in many ways restating principles of religious guidance. In all, Adler thus anticipated many trends of what today is called community psychiatry (15).

In accordance with his practical efforts Adler kept his terminology as simple as possible, limited his theorizing to broad outlines of the essentials and showed indefatigably how these apply to individual cases. Today this plain, minimal theory has been found a suitable framework for the new developments in the hospital treatment of mental patients (6, 7). Rudolf Dreikurs, a foremost Adlerian psychiatrist, has written a series of books presenting principles which have proved directly applicable by teachers in their classrooms (9) and by parents and married couples in their homes (8, 10). And in general it has been stated that "Adler's ideas . . . have become the accepted clinical common sense of our time" (19).

But Adler's simplicity in theory has also had positive scientific advantages in that his terms were kept at the lowest possible level of abstraction, close to the operational level (5), a widely accepted scientific requirement. At the same time Adler seems to have identified truly significant concepts of rather general validity. When Farberow and Shneidman (11, pp. 306–313) asked six clinicians of different orientations (Freudian, Jungian, Adlerian, Sullivanian, Kelly, Rogerian) to make Q-sorts for one suicidal patient, the Adlerian Q-sort showed the highest communality with the other five (.74), the Freudian the next to the lowest (.43), and the Jungian the lowest (.39) (13). These results would seem to offer some tentative experimental confirmation for our initial statement that to know Adler is to be well prepared for many current theoretical developments.

[6] This section has been newly written for the present volume.

From his main concern with the wide practical applicability of his work Adler expressed the following conviction about his Individual Psychology with which we may conclude: "There may be more venerable theories of an older academic science. There may be newer, more sophisticated theories. But there is certainly none which could bring greater gain to all people" (14).

References

1. Adler, A. *Problems of neurosis: a book of case histories* (1929). New York: Harper Torchbooks, 1964.

2. Adler, A. The progress of mankind (1937). In K. A. Adler and Danica Deutsch (Eds.), *Essays in Individual Psychology.* New York: Grove Press, 1959. Pp. 3–8.

3. Adler, A. *The Individual Psychology of Alfred Adler: a systematic presentation in selections from his writings.* Edited by H. L. and Rowena R. Ansbacher, New York: Basic Books, 1956; Harper Torchbooks, 1964.

4. Adler, A. *Superiority and social interest: a collection of later writings.* Edited by H. L. and Rowena R. Ansbacher. Evanston, Ill.: Northwestern University Press, 1964.

5. Ansbacher, H. L. The structure of Individual Psychology. In B. B. Wolman and E. Nagel (Eds.), *Scientific psychology.* New York: Basic Books, 1965. Pp. 340–364.

6. Brooks, G. W., Deane, W. N., and Ansbacher, H. L. Rehabilitation of chronic schizophrenic patients for social living. *J. Indiv. Psychol.,* 1960, *16,* 189–196.

7. Deane, W. N., and Ansbacher, H. L. Attendant-patient commonality as a psychotherapeutic factor. *J. Indiv. Psychol.,* 1962, *18,* 157–167.

8. Dreikurs, R. *The challenge of marriage.* New York: Duell, Sloan and Pearce, 1946.

9. Dreikurs, R. *Psychology in the classroom: a manual for teachers.* New York: Harper and Bros., 1957.

10. Dreikurs, R., and Soltz, Vicki. *Children: the challenge.* New York: Duell, Sloan and Pearce, 1964.

11. Farberow, N. L., and Shneidman, E. S. (Eds.) *The cry for help.* New York: McGraw-Hill, 1961.

12. Ford, D. H., and Urban, H. B. *Systems of psychotherapy.* New York: Wiley, 1963.

13. Kelly, G. A. Nonparametric factor analysis of personality theories. *J. Indiv. Psychol.,* 1963, *19,* 115–147.

14. Maslow, A. H. Deficiency motivation and growth motivation (1955). In *Toward a psychology of being.* Princeton, N.J.: Van Nostrand, 1962. Pp. 19–41.

15. Papanek, Helene. Adler's concepts in community psychiatry. *J. Indiv. Psychol.,* 1965, *21,* 117–126.

16. Sinnott, E. W. *Cell and psyche: the biology of purpose* (1950).   New York: Harper Torchbooks, 1961.

17. Sundberg, N. D., and Tyler, Leona E. *Clinical psychology.*   New York: Appleton-Century-Crofts, 1962.

18. White, R. W.   Adler and the future of ego psychology (1957).   In K. A. Adler and Danica Deutsch (Eds.), *Essays in Individual Psychology.*   New York: Grove Press, 1959.   Pp. 437–454.

19. White, R. W.   Is Alfred Adler alive today?   *Contemp. Psychol.*, 1957, 2, 1–4.

Anthony Storr   **C. G. JUNG ***

Jung, who died in June 1961 at the age of eighty-five, was the last survivor of the great trio of European psychiatrists whose names are household words.   Freud, Jung and Adler were all, in their different ways, pioneers; each contributed ideas that have had a powerful influence, not only upon psychiatry, but upon the general conception that twentieth-century man has of his own nature.

Of the three contributions, that of Jung is the least generally appreciated.   Adler, during his lifetime, exerted considerable personal influence.   His ideas were easy to grasp, and expressed in a style so popular that they are liable to be undervalued by the sophisticated.   Freud's work has been widely accepted; and, although his originality and iconoclasm at first made him enemies, he wrote with such admirable clarity that his books have long been familiar to educated people.   But Jung remains unread, and this is not altogether surprising.   For the man who picks up a book on psychology usually does so in the hope of finding some illumination of his personal problems, and if he turns to Adler or Freud he will inevitably find something that applies to himself.   But if he happens to light on Jung he is likely to be nonplussed.   For he may well find that he is confronted by an erudite discussion of the Trinity, or by an excursion into Chinese Yoga, or by a disquisition on medieval alchemy.   What possible relevance can such esoteric subjects have to the day-to-day problems of living for which the average person seeks advice?   It is understandable that

* From Anthony Storr, "C. G. Jung," *The American Scholar*, 1962, *31*, 395–403.   Reprinted by permission of the author and the publisher, *The American Scholar.*   Copyright by the United Chapters of Phi Beta Kappa.

some conclude either that Jung is too deep for them, or else that he is a crank who has deserted science for some crazy mixture of religion and speculative philosophy.

That this is not so it is the purpose of this article to demonstrate. Jung's point of view is, in some ways, unusual, and during the latter part of his life he was chiefly concerned with patients who differed from the common run of psychiatric cases. But the fact that Jung's viewpoint has not won more general appreciation is not because it is intrinsically bizarre, but because he himself had some difficulty in communicating it. As a talker Jung was superb; anyone who has heard him in private conversation or who has read the verbatim record of his seminars must realize that he was a tough, realistic thinker who could not be dismissed as a crank. But his writings are often obscure, and nowhere did he himself make an adequate summary of his ideas, as did Freud, for instance, in his *Outline of Psychoanalysis*. Jung's influence has been both wide and deep; but his ideas have penetrated by a process of diffusion rather than as a result of detailed study of his actual writings. As he himself said: "I have such a hell of a trouble to make people see what I mean."

Jung's work can best be appreciated by way of an outline of the development of his thought. He was the son of a Swiss pastor, brought up in the country, and as a child somewhat isolated, since his sister was nine years younger. Quite early he developed an interest in the past and originally wanted to be an archeologist. But the family did not have the money for him to pursue a purely academic career, so he turned to medicine as a second choice. At the time when Jung qualified as a doctor, psychiatry was a specialty of negligible importance; but Jung embraced it eagerly, since he saw that in the study of the mind he could combine both his interest in natural science and his extensive knowledge of philosophy and the history of ideas. He obtained a post in the Burghölzli mental hospital in Zurich, where he worked from 1900 to 1909.

During this time he produced a great deal of original work, including the studies in word-association in which he introduced the word "complex," and his famous book on *The Psychology of Dementia Præcox*. By the end of 1900 Jung had read Breuer and Freud's *Studies on Hysteria*, and Freud's *The Interpretation of Dreams*. He at once perceived the value of Freud's conceptions and became his enthusiastic advocate. *The Psychology of Dementia Præcox* was the first attempt to apply psychoanalytic ideas to the study of insanity, and one of the first in which it was demonstrated that there was a hidden meaning in the apparently incomprehensible words and gestures of the insane. Jung sent this book to Freud, and the two men first met in 1907 when Jung went to Vienna at Freud's invitation.

There followed a period of some six years of collaboration, during which Jung was Freud's favorite lieutenant. But a certain intransigence, characteristic of genius, precluded Jung from remaining *in statu pupillari;* with the publication in 1913 of his next book, *The Psychology of the Unconscious,* communication with Freud came to an end. There were many reasons for the break. The temperamental gulf between the two men was a wide one, and there was a considerable difference in age. But, in addition to this, their training and experience were quite dissimilar. Freud's interest, in his early days, was centered upon neurosis; his original theories of mental structure were based upon the study of hysteria. He never worked in a mental hospital for more than a brief period and had little experience of psychotic patients. It was natural enough that his views should derive from the study of repressed, infantile patterns and the tangle of early interpersonal relationships, since this is the material that comes to light in the analysis of neurotic patients.

Jung, on the other hand, was fascinated by schizophrenia, and remained so until the end of his life. While accepting Freud's theory of repression as applied to neurosis, he came to the conclusion that it was inadequate to explain the extraordinary depth and richness of the material produced by patients suffering from schizophrenia. Psychotic phantasies, and many dreams of both normal and abnormal people, could not, he concluded, be explained in terms of the vicissitudes of infancy. There must be a deeper region of the unconscious mind which lay below the level of personal repression; this region Jung named the collective unconscious. Because of his interest in the past, Jung already had a considerable knowledge of the myths of primitive people; he was thus able to demonstrate remarkable parallels between the dreams and phantasies of his patients and recurrent patterns of myth from all over the world. The variations on these mythological themes might be infinite but the underlying patterns remained the same; to these patterns and the figures that appeared in them Jung gave the name of archetypes. In *The Psychology of the Unconscious* Jung took the phantasies of a patient who later became psychotic and showed, with a wealth of detailed parallels, that the production of phantasy was governed not only by the personal experiences of childhood, but also by determinants that the individual shared with all mankind, even with peoples who might be remote both geographically and in time from himself. In Jung's view the child was not born into the world with a mind like a sheet of blank paper on which anything could be imprinted. The child was already predisposed to feel and think along the same lines as his ancestors had done since the beginning of time. The unconscious could not be regarded simply as a part of the mind to which unpleasant emotions were banished. It was the very foundation of our being, and the source not only of mental disturbances but also of our deepest hopes and aspirations.

Freud could not accept this view, and the two men parted.   But it is interesting to record the fact that, in one of his last works, Freud reached a similar conclusion about the nature of the unconscious. "Dreams bring to light material which could not originate either from the dreamer's adult life or from his forgotten childhood.   We are obliged to regard it as part of the archaic heritage which a child brings with him into the world, before any experiences of his own, as a result of the experiences of his ancestors."   Jung's concept of the collective unconscious, common to all mankind, was, therefore, not so controversial as it at first appeared: many Freudians accept something of the kind.   The rift between Jung and Freud, like all such rifts, was surely based on personal conflict, not simply on theoretical differences; and it is time that curiosity about this ancient controversy was replaced by an objective appraisal of the great contribution that each man has made to our understanding of the mind.

The conflict with Freud had, however, one positive result.   It set Jung thinking about how it happened that he, Freud and Adler studied the same material and yet produced such different points of view about it.   From his reflections sprang the idea for which he is best known to the general public, the idea of differing psychological types. Jung saw that men approached the study of the mind, and indeed life in general, from different basic preconceptions, of which they were not always aware.   The extravert valued the outer world, the relation to external objects, whereas the introvert gave his chief esteem to the world he discovered within himself.   Both attitudes were necessary for a full comprehension of reality, but men were usually one-sided and tended toward one or the other extreme. Adlerian psychology, with its emphasis on power, was the product of an introvert, for Adler was concerned with exalting the subject at the expense of the object, as if the object were a threat that might overwhelm the subject. Freudian psychology, on the other hand, was an extraverted construction since Freud regarded sexuality as paramount, and it is in the sexual relationship above all others that the object is most highly valued.

Jung's further subdivision of both types into thinking, feeling, sensation and intuition has not been generally accepted; but his original terms "extravert" and "introvert" have become part of everyday speech. For, as he rightly perceived, this particular dichotomy reflects something fundamental in human nature; many other psychologists, including William James, Kretschmer, Eysenck and Melanie Klein, have found a similar classification valuable.   Jung regarded himself as predominantly an introvert, in whom thinking was the best developed function.   His difficulty in communicating his ideas is characteristic of the introverted type who is often, as Jung said of himself, "at variance with the reality of things" and thus may not realize what it is that prevents other people from understanding him. A gross example of this is the misunderstanding that led to the accusation that Jung was antisemitic and a Nazi sympathizer, a slander that has already been refuted by his Jewish pupils and need not detain us here.

The next step in Jung's thought follows naturally as a result of combining his view of the unconscious with his typology. Neurosis, Jung concluded, was due to a one-sided development of consciousness which certainly had its roots in earliest childhood, but which was chiefly manifested in a lack of adaptation to the present situation. The extravert's danger was that he might lose himself in the press of external affairs; the introvert ran the risk of failing to maintain contact with the outer world. The ideal man would be equally well adapted to the reality of both inner and outer worlds; but such perfect adaptation was a goal toward which to aim rather than a reality that was ever completely achieved. It seemed to Jung that there was a reciprocal relationship between conscious and unconscious, and that the unconscious compensated for a one-sided attitude of consciousness. Hence neurotic symptoms were not simply unpleasant relics of the repressions of childhood, but were also abortive attempts on the part of the mind to remedy its own lack of balance. The psyche, in other words, was a self-regulating entity; and dreams, phantasies and other derivations of the unconscious could not be regarded solely as childish wish-fulfillments, but often as revelations of latent potentialities and as pointers toward the future development of the individual.

The idea that the mind is a self-regulating system is valuable in clinical practice. It is, moreover, a conception that accords well with modern ideas in physiology and cybernetics. The body itself is self-regulating; there are within it numerous devices that serve the purpose of keeping the internal environment constant, so that each cell may function at its optimum efficiency. Such devices, for example, regulate the hormonal system, the acid-base equilibrium of the blood, and body temperature. Automation existed within himself before man ever applied it to machines; and the checks and counterchecks that prevent the internal environment of the body from straying too far from an ideal balance are more complex and more subtle than those in any automatic factory.

It is surprising that Jung's theory of the self-regulating psyche has not attracted more attention. Of all his hypotheses it is the easiest to substantiate with clinical evidence; it is in line with physiology and thus scientifically respectable; it is borne out by the experience of everyday life. We are all familiar with the tough writer who at heart is a sentimentalist; with the frail, emotional woman who is actually ruthless; with the office tycoon who, at home, is a dependent child; with the hard-bitten rationalist who suddenly succumbs to the allure of an outlandish creed. Men are all a mixture of opposites; and the more extreme a person's conscious attitude, the more certainly will one find its opposite within. Jung concluded that the aim of man's development was the integration of the personality, which he conceived as a balance between opposites, between inner and outer reality, between reason and emotion, between extraversion and introversion.   The individual who achieved integration was one who had succeeded in reconciling the opposites within himself and making a whole out of the disparate elements of his personality.   It was not possible for a man to attain complete integration, any more than it was possible for an artist to create a perfect work of art; but this appeared to be the goal of human life toward which the unconsciously directed process of development was tending.

In Jung's view this search for integration and wholeness was characteristic of the second half of life; it is in dealing with the problems of older patients that Jung's analytical psychology comes into its own. Freud and his followers tended to assume that a man's development was complete with the achievement of freedom from parental ties and the establishment of sexual maturity: psychoanalysts have generally been reluctant to treat patients of middle age and over.   Jung, however, found that his practice largely consisted of such patients.   They were often people who had achieved both sexual maturity and professional success and who did not fit into the usual categories of neurosis.   Nevertheless, they had come to a point at which they felt "stuck," and at which life seemed arid and without significance.   The study of such people convinced Jung that at about the age of thirty-five or forty a change took place, at least in the people who consulted him.   It was a time at which the individual might find that the pursuits of his youth had palled and that many of the activities that used to give him pleasure were no longer enthralling.   At such a time the study of the products of unconscious phantasy is often particularly rewarding: Jung found that, in some people, a process of development seemed to be taking place that could be followed both in dreams and in the paintings, poems and other works of the imagination that he encouraged his patients to produce.   This sequential development Jung called the individuation process; its study became the chief preoccupation of his own latter years.

Having formulated the idea that there was, in the second half of life, a psychological process of development tending toward the integration of the individual, Jung started to look about for historical parallels.   For he believed that man's essential nature did not alter much in the course of time, and he therefore felt that there must be evidence in the past of men seeking the same integration for which his patients were looking in the present.

He found his parallel in alchemy.   Those who are unfamiliar with Jung's thought have found it hard to understand why he should preoccupy himself with such matters as the alchemist's quest for the philosopher's stone. Alchemy, like astrology, which was also one of Jung's interests, has long been discredited by science. Of what possible interest can it be today?

The explanation of Jung's interest is simple. Alchemy is interesting psychologically just because there is nothing in it scientifically. It is equivalent to the projection tests that psychologists use in the assessment of personality. Like a Rorschach inkblot, alchemy contains nothing objective, and, since it is far removed from external reality, it provides an admirable field for the study of unconscious processes. The alchemists were searching for something that had no existence in the outside world, but that nonetheless seemed to them of extreme importance. Like Jung's patients, they were looking for integration and wholeness: the symbolism in which they described their quest was remarkably similar to the symbolism that Jung found in the dreams and phantasies of his patients.

In essential terms the alchemical quest was a search for salvation, but one that could not be contained within the framework of conventional religion. Jung found that many of his older patients were also attempting to find a meaning in life in a way that could only be described as religious, although most of them could not accept any orthodox creed. If a man were to attain his full stature as an individual it would seem that he must acquire some philosophy of life, some view as to the meaning of his own existence. As Jung himself said: "Man cannot stand a meaningless life."

It was not only in alchemy that Jung found evidence of the individuation process. He made wide-ranging researches into the fields of comparative religion, Chinese philosophy, Yoga and other arcane subjects; in doing so, he incurred the suspicion of scientists who, without understanding what he was doing, felt that he had abandoned science for mysticism. But the truth is that the less a subject is based on external reality, the more fruitful a field is it likely to be for the study of unconscious processes; Jung's later researches follow logically from his original premises.

Jung has been generally recognized as one of the great original minds of the twentieth century. Freud's psychoanalysis and Jung's analytical psychology have sometimes been regarded as incompatible; but in many respects the two approaches are complementary, and it is only the fanatics of either school who cannot see any value in the other's point of view. Freud's contribution to psychology took a generation to establish. It will probably take at least as long for the full impact of Jung's thought to be assimilated. But Jung's influence has been felt in many fields outside psychiatry, and his place in history is already assured. The concept of the collective unconscious, for instance, has been used by the writer J. B. Priestley in his book

Literature and Western Man, by the historian Arnold Toynbee in *A Study of History,* and by the physicist W. Pauli in his work on the astronomer Kepler.   Sir Herbert Read has acknowledged his debt to Jung in his writings on art, and many creative artists have felt that Jung understood their aims in a way that no previous writer on psychology had been able to do.

Although he was the first to demand that the analyst himself be analyzed, Jung was reluctant to have his teaching codified, and for many years he resisted the setting up of an institute to train pupils in his methods.   He believed that his ideas were no more than a preliminary venture into a new field of research and referred to them as a subjective confession.   Science takes a long time to catch up with intuitive genius; so far, there have been only a few experimental investigations based on Jung's later concepts.   But it should be possible to formulate a series of propositions in such a way that his findings can be objectively demonstrated.   A start has already been made in the study of dreams.

Jung maintained that our ignorance of ourselves is profound.   He considered that man's most urgent task today is to deflect his gaze from the further conquest of the material world toward the study of his own nature.   In a world in which opposites are so far divided that they threaten each other with mutual annihilation, we should do well to listen to Jung's counsel.

Merton Gill

THE PRESENT STATE OF
PSYCHOANALYTIC THEORY *

Psychoanalytic theory is often regarded by its critics as a rigid Procrustean system.   In fact, it is continually changing and growing, although its changes are principally those of widening perspectives, modifications, and additions, rather than alterations in basic assumptions.   The past decade has seen a serious effort to make the system of psychoanalytic theory more explicit and internally consistent.   Though many people contributed to this effort, I would single out for special mention the work, singly and together, of Hartmann, Kris, and

* From Merton Gill, "The Present State of Psychoanalytic Theory," *J. abnorm. soc. Psychol.,* 1959, *58,* 1–8.   By permission of the author and the Managing Editor, the American Psychological Association.

Loewenstein (13, 14, 15, 16, 18, 19, 20, 27, 28, 29), of Rapaport (32, 33, 34, 35, 36, 37, 38, 39), and of Edith Jacobson (23, 24). But it would be incorrect to regard these efforts as simply tidying up the theory. Basic assumptions have been questioned and alternative assumptions have been proposed. A recent paper by Jacobson (24), for example, seriously questions the validity and usefulness of such basic psychoanalytic propositions as primary narcissism and primary masochism. Of course, even more fundamental propositions than these—such as the importance of infantile psychosexuality—have been questioned and discarded by some psychoanalysts (31). The main stream of psychoanalysis, however, holds fast to a number of basic assumptions while adding and modifying others. It is this main stream of the psychoanalytic theory that I will discuss here, though there will be occasional reference to the assumptions of the revisions of psychoanalytic theory. I believe that the ferment in the main stream of psychoanalytic theory is a refutation of the charge that it constitutes an orthodoxy. Any discipline has its share of those who clutch to it as to a religion, and these are not always its strongest members. I will discuss psychoanalytic theory, not psychoanalytic practice. The lag between the two is sometimes great and it may be either theory or practice which forges ahead of the other. It has been generally true in psychoanalysis that the theory of technique lags behind both basic theory and practice.

Important changes in psychoanalytic theory

My plan here is to present a number of the basic assumptions of psychoanalytic theory and to indicate what I regard as the important changes in the theory pertaining to each of these assumptions in the last 20 or 25 years.

1   The psychoanalytic theory of motivation

Psychoanalysis always has been and continues to be a theory that centers on motivation in human behavior. Uniquely characteristic of psychoanalysis is the kind of motivation it postulates: drives rooted in the biology of the organism. These drives are sexual—in the broader sense in which the word is employed in psychoanalysis—and aggressive. They are characterized by their urgency, their intimate connection with various kinds of bodily behavior, both in terms of one's own body and the bodies of other people, and by the rather bizarre quality of their mode of function when viewed in the light of ordinary conscious motivation.

Psychoanalysis has not given up this conception of primitive drives, but it has somewhat changed its view of their place in personality functioning and has added to its theory to account for other kinds of motivation as well. Whereas the psychoanalytic theory of motivation was formerly restricted almost entirely to primitive drive, now it includes a complex hierarchy of motivations that implies a progressive taming of drives with advancing development and progressive infusion of the drive representations with cognitive elements reflecting external reality (34). Its view of the dynamic relationships of the various levels of the motivational hierarchy has so changed as to increase the emphasis on derivative motivations—to which it has always paid some attention—though by no means diminishing the emphasis on more primitive motives.

The very term "derivative motivation" implies the earlier psychoanalytic concept of the relationship of various motivational levels. The primitive drives as such were considered to be active even in derivative motivations, which were regarded as reducible to drives at the primitive level. The surgeon was still considered to be expressing his primitive sadistic impulse, the bibliophile to be expressing his anal wishes. The concept which marks a drastic shift from this point of view is that of secondary autonomy (13). Its implications are similar to that of Allport's "functional autonomy" (1) and it conveys the conclusion that derivative motivations develop a semiautonomy, and can be triggered relatively independently into action. There remains much controversy and unclarity, however, as to the roles played in normal behavior by drives pertaining to the different levels of the motivational hierarchy.

Parallel to the recognition of a motivational hierarchy with degrees of autonomy, there have been developed new concepts of the kind of energy pertaining to motivations. The energy of the primitive drives is libidinal or aggressive but as motivations become progressively autonomous their energy becomes progressively more "neutralized." Such neutralization is said to occur by "delibidinization" and "deaggressivization" (15).

The overthrow of primitive reductionism goes even further, however, than merely to assert that derivative motivations develop a relative autonomy. While formerly all behavior was reduced to primitive drive motivation, now behavior is considered to be determined not only by motivational factors but by other (structural) factors too, which enter into the causal determination of behavior as independent variables and hence are not reducible to motivations, whether primitive or derived.

2   The independent variables other than drive

Despite the fact that from the very beginnings of psychoanalysis concepts other than motivational were used both in theoretical and clinical studies, the prevailing intent of the theory was to reduce every behavior to motivational terms. A sharp change has come about in that now independent variables other than motivation are also assumed in the determination of behavior. These independent variables are of two main sorts.

The first are the factors which are conceptualized as primarily autonomous, that is to say, autonomous from drive (13). Whereas secondary autonomy refers to derivatives of drives, primarily autonomous functions arise independently of drives.[1] These latter are also conceptualized as the apparatuses of the ego and include among others perception, thought, memory, concept formation, and discharge thresholds (34). This is not to say that in any actual perceiving, thinking, remembering, or concept formation, drive factors play no role but rather that independent factors not derivable from drives do play a role in each of these events.

It will be noted that this class of independent variables comprises intraorganismic capacities and structures and that some of them would be called cognitive in general psychological theory. That psychoanalytic theory regards these variables as truly independent is attested to by the relationships conceived between the two kinds of variables—drive and ego apparatus. They are considered to reciprocally influence each other (17) and efforts are made to study both how the development of drive is influenced by the ego apparatuses and how the development of the apparatuses is influenced by drive. It should be noted that the ego apparatuses are only a part of the ego, and the important question has been raised in psychoanalytic theory whether other aspects of ego functioning may not also be primarily autonomous in their origin—as for example, a predilection for the use of a particular variety of defense mechanism (15).

The second class of factors entering into the determination of behavior as independent variables are extraorganismic—those derived from the external environment. These may be classified in various ways—the most usual being a tripartite one into the physical environment, the interpersonal environment and the social environment.

Naturally both psychoanalytic theory and clinical studies have always dealt with environmental factors, especially the interpersonal ones. The entire field of the development of object relationships— that is to say, relationships with other people—comes under this heading. It is true, however, that the explicit theoretical accounting for the role of the organized social environment is relatively recent, and it is true even that only relatively recently has the effort begun to encompass object relationships systematically within the psycho-

---

[1] Whether primarily autonomous functions have available primary neutral energy— that is, neutral energy not derived from libidinal or aggressive energy—remains a moot question (16).

analytic theory (27).   I realize that this account may be challenged. I am aware that object relationships have long been extensively dealt with in psychoanalytic writings, but I believe that only recently have efforts been made to find a place in systematic theory for the role played by other people in the development of object relationships.   In fact I think this lag in psychoanalytic theory proper is one of the reasons that Sullivan's theory (41) has been so favorably received. It made an important contribution in its emphasis on interpersonal relationships but this emphasis became so all consuming as to jettison the psychoanalytic theory of motivation, especially of primitive drive. The same may be said for Horney (22) and with the addition of an emphasis on social factors for Fromm (12).

The problem of the relative roles played by and the relationships between intrapsychic, interpersonal, and social factors is, of course, subject to much controversy.   It remains true by and large that the heaviest stress in psychoanalytic theory (insofar as it is to be distinguished from a general psychological theory) will always be on the intrapsychic factors.   The outstanding demonstration that there nevertheless is room for social factors within the framework of the established psychoanalytic theory proper is Erikson's work (3, 4, 5).

3   Maturation in psychoanalytic theory

I will turn now to question whether or not these changes have resulted in any alteration in another one of the basic pillars of psychoanalytic theory, its heavy emphasis on maturational factors in personality development.   Psychoanalysis continues to emphasize inborn maturational sequences, but in addition to such sequences in the development of drives, they are now postulated for the development of the ego as well (15).   Whatever disputes there may be about the accuracy of the familiar oral-anal-phallic-genital sequence, or the unsettled state of the sequence of stages in ego maturation, psychoanalytic theory continues to put much weight on such maturational sequences. It is true, however, that with the "new regard for the environment" (27), learning has come to occupy a more central role in the psychoanalytic theory of development.   There is little agreement in psychoanalytic, just as in general psychological, theory as to the relative roles to be ascribed to learning as against maturation.   A temporary re-emphasis of maturation as against learning has taken place in some areas of psychoanalytic theory as a reaction against the postulation of highly complex very early object relationships—as early as the first months of life—by the school around Klein (26).   Psychoanalysis has no well-defined and explicit learning theory (21).   Yet it seems clear that psychoanalytic theory is incompatible with S-R learning theory and the discussion of its possible relationship to a cognitive or a motivational learning theory like Tolman's (42) is beyond the scope of this paper. It may nevertheless be mentioned, as pointed out by Rapaport (35), that Hartmann's concept of automatization (13) is the psychoanalytic equivalent of habit. Behavior according to this concept is originally learned in a complex motivational context, but may become structuralized, semiautonomous, triggered by external stimuli, and automatized or, in Lewinian (30) terminology, "ossified." The explanation of the development of the motivational life and of interpersonal relationships by maturational rather than learning processes continues to be much more central to psychoanalysis than to general psychology.

4   Psychoanalysis as a genetic theory

From a discussion of maturation it is natural to turn to another pillar of psychoanalytic theory, its emphasis on longitudinal factors—the genetic point of view. Psychoanalytic theory continues to be heavily genetic in its emphasis. While it is, of course, the case that genetic factors are determinative of current behavior only insofar as they have shaped the form of currently active elements of psychic functioning, it is nevertheless true that psychoanalytic theory holds that many behavioral manifestations become understandable only in terms of their genesis. I should mention here two recent major assumptions in psychoanalytic theory that pertain to what we might call general laws of genesis. The first is that while psychoanalytic theory has long held that the phases of ego development occur in close connection with the correlated phases of libidinal development, it is now proposed that the vicissitudes of aggressive drives and of independent factors in the ego must also be taken into account. An example is Hartmann's proposal that "if the defensive reaction against danger from within is modelled after the one to danger from without, it is possible that there too [in the defense mechanisms] the use of—in this case more or less neutralized—aggressive energy is more regular than the use of desexualized libido" (15). The second major suggestion is that primitive id functions may be "taken over" by the ego and form the basis for quite different functions or different uses of the same function. The defensive functions of the ego again offer the most ready examples. As Hartmann (15) says, "introjection . . . probably exists as a form of instinct gratification before it is used in the service of defense. . . . The ego can use, for defense, characteristics of the primary process, as in displacement. . . . Freud [10] has drawn a parallel between the mechanism of isolation and the normal process of attention." A proper understanding of such an altered function would necessarily involve a knowledge of its genesis. The importance of genetic concepts becomes especially obvious in the partial—though to be sure highly modified—return to earlier forms of function in regressive states. In regression there is to a greater or lesser extent a loss of relative autonomy and a reversion of neutralized energy to more aggressive and libidinal forms.

5   Primary and secondary processes in psychoanalysis

An exceedingly important foundation of psychoanalytic theory—regarded by some as Freud's greatest achievement—and one as yet little regarded by general psychology is the description of two modes of functioning of the psychic apparatus: the primary and secondary processes (8). The primary process abides by the pleasure principle, and employs the mechanisms of displacement, condensation, and symbolization. It is a kind of short circuiting of gratification, disregarding the laws of logic and operating with little reference to the nature of external reality. The secondary process is a mode of psychic functioning that abides by the reality principle, by the laws of logic, and takes into account the nature of real external reality. One of the important developments in psychoanalytic theory is that these two modes of psychic functioning are no longer regarded as a dichotomy and as mutually exclusive. They are now conceived as ideal poles of a continuum (28), and an important new concept, proposed by Kris (29), gives account of the fact of the adaptive use of primary process functioning by the ego, namely: "regression in the service of the ego."

It may be worth pointing out here that the shift in the psychoanalytic view of motivation described earlier can from another point of view be described as a shift from emphasis on primary process functioning to secondary process functioning. The mode of operation of primitive drives in the immature organism is largely by primary process mechanisms. In fact it was an unwarranted generalization of this revolutionary discovery that initially led psychoanalysis to subordinate all else to primitive motivational factors. The recognition of derivative motivations and of independent variables other than drives operating in the determination of behavior—more specifically independent variables relating to the nature of the external world—is a shift to the view that much of normal functioning is secondary process functioning.

6   The unconscious in psychoanalysis

Psychoanalysis continues to insist on the overwhelming importance of unconscious processes in psychological life. It must be pointed out, however, that the significance of unconscious factors is closely related to the psychoanalytic theory of motivation, and alteration in the motivational view will have serious repercussions on the theory of the role of the unconscious. If a good deal of normal behavior is ascribed to derivative semiautonomous motivations which can be conscious, by just that much is unconscious motivation shorn of its significance in normal behavior. Yet there has not been any real diminution in psychoanalysis of emphasis on unconscious motivation. In my opinion, this seeming paradox may be at least partially resolved by the view that the semiautonomous motivations are indeed only semiautonomous and that any particular behavior may be viewed in a "nest" of motivational contexts of increasing generality. It is difficult to describe this conception in just a few words, but it argues that a semiautonomous conscious motive operates in a wider context as a means in relation to a less conscious and more primitive motivation, which in turn operates in a wider context as a means in relation to an even more primitive and unconscious motivation. I would like to repeat that the role that a theoretical system is likely to ascribe to unconscious processes will be intimately linked with its view of the motivational structure of personality.

7 The introduction of the structural point of view

I can summarize a number of the important changes I have sketched in psychoanalytic theory by uniting them under the heading: the introduction of the structural point of view. It is often said that the structural point of view was introduced into psychoanalysis in 1923 with the publication of Freud's work *The Ego and the Id* (9). In some ways this statement is true but in others false. It overstates the case in that structural considerations are both implicit and explicit in psychoanalytic theory from the very beginning. The concept *topographic* rather than structural was first used and the topographic divisions were made in the dimension of consciousness—the unconscious, the preconscious, and the conscious. Under the impact of the realization that both that which was repressed and the repressing forces too could be unconscious, Freud (9) was led to hypothesize the structures id and ego, and later the topographic divisions of consciousness, hitherto called "systems," became regarded as only qualities rather than coherent systems (11). As long ago as in the seventh chapter of *The Interpretation of Dreams,* consciousness itself was regarded as a supraordinate apparatus. In present theory, this apparatus is ascribed to the ego, yet this early concept of consciousness remains the most sophisticated psychoanalytic view of its functioning (38). The statement is further false in the sense that the id-ego-superego trichotomy is only a very gross statement of the structural point of view and actually gave names to structures which had, though not systematically, in part been already marked out. Only in the last several decades has the structural point of view been developed in a thorough and systematic manner.

It is not easy to give a clear yet brief picture of this point of view. A full description of a mental process—a metapsychological description—requires its discussion from three points of view, dynamic, economic, and structural.   Of these points of view, the dynamic refers to the interplay of forces, the economic refers to energy considerations and to the restoration of the homeostatic equilibrium, while the structural refers to that aspect of the mental process which characterizes its place in the enduring, stable organization of the mind (39).   In roughest form, a process is characterized structurally as to its position in one of the three mental structures—id, ego, or superego.   Far more subtle dissection of the structure of mind has been carried out as far as ego functioning is concerned.   Structural considerations within one of the three major structures are called intrasystemic (15). The description of the ego, for example, as an organization of semi-autonomous behavioral dispositions is a structural statement.   Early psychoanalytic theory may be characterized as dynamic and economic. If the early psychoanalytic view of motivation had been taken seriously, the most ordinary item of behavior could be conceived as occurring only as a result of the interplay of powerful forces—what Rapaport called "a battle of Titans" (34).   The introduction of the structural point of view makes possible a view of personality functioning which includes its steady, stable, ordinary, organized, enduring patterns of behavior and thinking.

These advances in the structural conception are another way of stating the change in the psychoanalytic view of motivation, of energy pertaining to motivation, and even of the recognition of independent variables other than motivation determining behavior, since we may restate these propositions as: derivative motivations arise from relatively autonomous (structuralized) apparatuses employing neutralized energy; the primary autonomous apparatuses are ego structures.[2]   The ego as a whole is itself conceptualized as relatively autonomous, from the id on the one hand and the environment on the other (37).

Alternative formulations of trends in psychoanalytic theory

I have now stated in brief the major assumptions of and major changes in psychoanalytic theory.   To achieve further clarification I will now describe various other ways in which these same changes have been stated.

One general way of stating the change is that psychoanalysis has moved into the area of ego psychology in comparison with its former

[2] Whether derivative motivations "arise" in a hierarchy from hierarchically ordered means-structures or whether the motivations themselves must be considered structures requires further clarification.

preoccupation with id psychology. Ego psychology includes considerations of the autonomous apparatuses, the hierarchy of motivations which are the systems of disposition to behavior as we find them in the ego, and the extra-organismic variables which enter into the determination of behavior by way of the cognitive functions of the ego.

Another way of stating the change is to say that psychoanalysis is now not only a psychology of the depths, but of the surface too (6). The psychological surface is the ego, and it is the ego which is in contact with the external real world.

Yet another way of saying the same thing is that psychoanalysis has included adaptation among its basic concepts (13), whereas formerly it was preoccupied with intrapsychic processes. Adaptation implies an ego in contact with the real external world and the determination of behavior by variables other than motivational. The same principle has been expressed as the increased attention paid by psychoanalysis to the environment (27). I have made this point in another way in my discussion of the primary and secondary processes. The secondary process abides by the reality principle, which is the principle of adaptation. The most general way to state the change: psychoanalysis is becoming a complete psychological system, embracing all of human psychological functioning (13). While psychoanalysis was principally concerned with psychopathology, large areas of personality functioning remained unaccounted for by its theory. As a total psychological system, psychoanalysis had to complement its motivational considerations with cognitive and adaptive ones. The social structure, for example, which at least in some ways plays a more obvious though perhaps no more prominent role in "normal" than in "neurotic" function begins to loom larger in present day psychoanalytic theory.

Changing relationships with psychology

Now a few comments on the changing relationships between psychoanalysis and academic psychology. I have said that psychoanalysis aspires towards becoming a total psychological system by including cognitive and adaptive considerations as well as motivational. It will be well to stress that in part the stimulus for this move comes from academic psychology, though references in psychoanalytic theory to the contributions of academic psychologists are few and far between. It is obvious, though, that cognitive and adaptive considerations have been the special provinces of academic psychology, and just as psychoanalysis has moved to include cognitive functions and to recognize more explicitly adaptive considerations so has psychology moved to a greater emphasis on motivation. The so-called "new look" (2) in research on perception—that is, cognition—is essentially the study of perception in a motivational framework   There is a good deal of thought in general psychology about the relationship of the cognitive and motivational factors.   For instance, Klein and Krech (25) consider the dichotomy of cognition and motivation misleading and unnecessary and regard all behavior as consisting of unities which involve cognition and motivation indivisibly.   I agree with this point of view and have separated motivation and cognition in this paper only for convenience of exposition.

It must not be presumed, however, that psychoanalysis and psychology are now merging or becoming indistinguishable.   Indeed many people will find it ridiculous that I sound this warning.   Nevertheless, it is worth pointing out that once propositions from these perspectives are stated on a sufficiently high level of abstraction, vital differences begin to be washed away.   This is most strikingly true with regard to the problem of motivation.   On the one hand, both psychoanalysis and psychology stress motivation and both accept the ideas of primary, derived, and relatively autonomous motivations; on the other, the specific picture of the motivational structure of man is vastly different in the two.

Psychoanalysis still adheres to a view of motivation as built on drives rooted in the biology of the organism.   However much derived motivations are recognized, psychoanalytic theory still views behavior as essentially motivated by and occurring in the context of bodily drives.   Drives for security, success, prestige, status, seem, relative to these basic drives, "superficial" to the psychoanalyst.   He thinks rather of castration fear, oedipal wishes, cannibalistic impulses, homosexuality, or a drive to rend and destroy.   It is often said that the analyst's preoccupation with these primitive impulses stems from his almost exclusive concern with disturbed personalities.   But the analyst believes that the normal person, too, is occupied with dealing with such impulses.   The difference between the normal and the neurotic he sees not in the root of the tree of the motivational hierarchy but much closer to its crown.

A word about the libido theory which is tenaciously defended by psychoanalysts because it represents for them the view of motivation described in this paper as classically and specifically psychoanalytic. In some sense this is unfortunate, because as a consequence criticism of the libido theory and demonstration of errors in it are viewed by some groups of analysts as well as by psychologists as an overthrow of the entire psychoanalytic theory of motivation.   I would like to suggest that what is really being defended by analysts is not the libido theory as such but the overwhelming importance of relatively primitive bodily drives in motivating behavior.   Discussions of the libido theory (40) in my opinion would be more fruitful if it were not regarded as equivalent to the more general psychoanalytic theory of motivation. The place of instinctual libidinal impulses in personality functioning does not stand or fall with the libido theory per se.

Psychologists are also beginning to talk more frequently of unconscious processes in human beings. But here, too, the apparent rapprochement should be taken with a grain of salt. It is easy to employ the concept of unconscious processes without taking them seriously, while they are taken very seriously indeed in psychoanalytic theory and practice. Behavior, as described earlier in this paper, is regarded by psychoanalysis as essentially motivated by unconscious processes. To some extent the difference between the psychoanalyst and the psychologist is the molar-molecular problem. The psychologist is ordinarily concerned with small segments of behavior such as can be observed and controlled in the laboratory, and which do not readily show the presence of unconscious forces in the psychoanalyst's sense. The psychoanalyst on the other hand is more concerned with "real life" behavior and major trends and crises. Some integration of the two points of view may be brought about by what I described earlier as the possibility of viewing any particular behavior as occurring in a "nest" of motivational contexts of increasing generality.

There is much work in contemporary clinical psychology which deals with fairly direct derivatives of unconscious processes; for example, in some types of Rorschach responses. But these must not be confused with the unconscious processes themselves; and just as important is the fact that although the psychologist may recognize these as derivatives of unconscious processes, this should not be taken to mean that the person who has produced these responses is thereby brought any closer to an awareness of, or insight into, the contents of his unconscious.

Summary

To summarize briefly: I have described some of the basic assumptions of psychoanalytic theory and the recent changes which have taken place in them under the headings: 1. The motivational theory; 2. the introduction of independent variables other than drives; 3. emphasis on maturation; 4. the genetic emphasis; 5. the primary and secondary processes; 6. the unconscious; and 7. the introduction of the structural point of view. I then indicated that these changes in psychoanalytic theory are often described as psychoanalysis becoming concerned with: (a) ego psychology; (b) the psychology of the surface; (c) increased attention to the environment; and (d) the introduction of cognitive and adaptive considerations. I closed with a few general comments on the relationship of psychoanalysis and psychology.

References

1. Allport, G. *The nature of personality: Selected papers.* Cambridge: Addison-Wesley, 1950.

2. Blake, R., & Ramsey, G. (Ed.) *Perception, an approach to personality.* New York: Ronald Press, 1951.

3. Erikson, E. *Childhood and society.* New York: Norton, 1950.

4. Erikson, E. The dream specimen of psychoanalysis. *J. Amer. psychoanal. Ass.,* 1954, 2, 5–56.

5. Erikson, E. The problem of ego identity. *J. Amer. psychoanal. Ass.,* 1956, 4, 56–121.

6. Frenkel-Brunswik, Else. Psychoanalysis and the unity of science. *Proc. Amer. Acad. Arts Sci.,* 1954, 80, 271–350.

7. Freud, S. *The interpretation of dreams.* Standard Edition, Vols. IV & V. (Originally published 1900) London: Hogarth, 1953.

8. Freud, S. The unconscious. In *The Standard Edition,* Vol. XIV. (Originally published 1915) London: Hogarth, 1957. Pp. 159–208.

9. Freud, S. *The ego and the id.* (Originally published 1923) London: Hogarth, 1947.

10. Freud, S. *The problem of anxiety.* (Originally published 1926) New York: Psychoanalytic Quarterly Press, 1936.

11. Freud, S. *An outline of psychoanalysis.* (Originally published 1938) New York: Norton, 1949.

12. Fromm, E. *Man for himself.* New York: Rinehart, 1947.

13. Hartmann, H. Ego psychology and the problem of adaptation (abridged). (Originally published 1939) In D. Rapaport (Ed.), *Organization and pathology of thought.* New York: Columbia Univer. Press, 1951. Pp. 362–396.

14. Hartmann, H. On rational and irrational action. In G. Roheim (Ed.), *Psychoanalysis and the social sciences.* New York: International Universities Press, 1947. Pp. 359–392.

15. Hartmann, H. Comments on the psychoanalytic theory of the ego. In *The psychoanalytic study of the child,* Vol. V. New York: International Universities Press, 1950. Pp. 74–96.

16. Hartmann, H. Notes on the theory of sublimation. In *The psychoanalytic study of the child,* Vol. X. New York: International Universities Press, 1955. Pp. 9–29.

17. Hartmann, H., Hoffer, W., & Freud, A. Contributions to symposium on the mutual influences in the development of the ego and id. In *The psychoanalytic study of the child,* Vol. VII. New York: International Universities Press, 1952. Pp. 9–50.

18. Hartmann, H., & Kris, E. The genetic approach in psychoanalysis. In *The psychoanalytic study of the child,* Vol. I. New York: International Universities Press, 1945. Pp. 11–29.

19. Hartmann, H., Kris, E., & Loewenstein, R. Comments on the formation of psychic structure. In *The psychoanalytic study of the child,* Vol. II. New York: International Universities Press, 1946. Pp. 11–38.

20. Hartmann, H., Kris, E., & Loewenstein, R. Notes on the theory of aggression. In *The psychoanalytic study of the child,* Vol. III/IV. New York: International Universities Press, 1949. Pp. 9–36.

21. Hilgard, E. *Theories of learning.* New York: Appleton-Century-Crofts, 1956.

22. Horney, Karen. *New ways in psychoanalysis.* New York: Norton, 1939.

23. Jacobson, Edith. The affects and their pleasure-unpleasure qualities in relation to the psychic discharge processes. In R. Loewenstein (Ed.), *Drives, affects, behavior.* New York: International Universities Press, 1953. Pp. 38–66.

24. Jacobson, Edith. The self and the object world. In *The psychoanalytic study of the child,* Vol. IV. New York: International Universities Press, 1954. Pp. 75–127.

25. Klein, G., & Krech, D. The problem of personality and its theory. In D. Krech & G. Klein (Eds.), *Theoretical models and personality theory.* Durham: Duke Univer. Press, 1952. Pp. 2–23.

26. Klein, Melanie. *Contributions to psychoanalysis, 1921–1945.* London: Hogarth, 1948.

27. Kris, E. Notes on the development and on some current problems of psychoanalytic child psychology. In *The psychoanalytic study of the child,* Vol. V. New York: International Universities Press, 1950. Pp. 24–46.

28. Kris, E. On preconscious mental processes. *Psychoanal. Quart.,* 1950, *19,* 540–560.

29. Kris, E. *Psychoanalytic explorations in art.* New York: International Universities Press, 1952.

30. Lewin, K. Intention, will and need. (Originally published 1926) In D. Rapaport (Ed.), *Organization and pathology of thought.* New York: Columbia Univer. Press, 1951. Pp. 95–153.

31. Munroe, Ruth. *Schools of psychoanalytic thought.* New York: Dryden, 1955.

32. Rapaport, D. On the psychoanalytic theory of thinking. *Int. J. Psychoanal.,* 1950, *31,* 161–170.

33. Rapaport, D. The autonomy of the ego. *Bull. Menn. Clin.,* 1951, *15,* 113–123.

34. Rapaport, D. The conceptual model of psychoanalysis. *J. Pers.,* 1951, *20,* 56–81.

35. Rapaport, D. (Ed.) *Organization and pathology of thought.* New York: Columbia Univer. Press, 1951.

36. Rapaport, D. On the psychoanalytic theory of affects. *Int. J. Psychoanal.,* 1953, *34,* 177–198.

37. Rapaport, D. The theory of ego autonomy: A generalization. *Bull. Menn. Clin.,* 1958, *22,* 13–35.

38. Rapaport, D. Cognitive structures. In *Contemporary approaches to cognition*. Cambridge: Harvard Univer. Press, 1957.

39. Rapaport, D. The structure of psychoanalytic theory (a systematizing attempt). In S. Koch (Ed.), *Systematic resources of psychology*, in press.

40. Reider, N. (Reporter) Re-evaluation of the libido theory. *J. Amer. psychoanal. Ass.*, 1955, 3, 299–308.

41. Sullivan, H. *The interpersonal theory of psychiatry*. New York: Norton, 1953.

42. Tolman, E. A psychological model. In T. Parson & E. Shils (Eds.), *Toward a general theory of action*. Cambridge: Harvard Univer. Press, 1955.

Norman J.
Levy

KAREN HORNEY'S CONCEPT OF HUMAN MOTIVATION *

In *Neurosis and Human Growth* (5), Horney describes the neurotic process as a special and unfortunate form of human development which involves a waste of constructive energies. The development is both different in quality from and antithetical to healthy human growth. When conditions are favorable man will put his energies into realizing his own potentialities. Such development will vary naturally with his particular physical endowment, temperament and gifts. With these determinants together with his background and experiences, he will evolve as a person, softer or harder, more cautious or more trusting, more self reliant or less, more contemplative or more outgoing, attempting to actualize his special gifts.

To the extent the growing child is subjected to inner and outer stresses, he will become alienated from that which is real in himself. He will shift the major part of his energies to the task of molding himself by a rigid system of inner dictates into a being of absolute, god-like perfection and will strive to fulfill his idealized image of himself. In this way he aims at satisfying his pride in those qualities he feels he has, could have, or should have.

Unless a child is a mental defective he will learn in some way to cope with others and acquire some skills. Some forces, however,

* From Norman J. Levy, "Karen Horney's Concept of Human Motivation," *Psychologia*, 1960, 3. 113–118. By permission of the author and the Editor, *Psychologia*.

cannot be acquired or even developed by learning. As an illustration Horney (5) points out that an acorn neither has to be nor can be taught to grow, but given a chance it will develop its intrinsic potentialities and become an oak tree. Similarly, man, given a chance to develop his particular human potentialities, will also develop the unique alive forces of his real self (5) that "central force common to all human beings and yet unique in each which is the deep source of growth." By clarifying his feelings, thoughts, wishes and interests and by tapping his resources, he will be more able to express himself and relate to others spontaneously. Thus in time he will find his values and aims in life and grow toward self realization.

In order to develop his given potentialities, a man needs favorable conditions for his growth. He must have an atmosphere of warmth to give him both a feeling of inner security and inner freedom. This will enable him to have and express his own feelings and thoughts. The good will, guidance and encouragement of others are necessary for him to become a mature, fulfilled individual. In addition to love he also needs the strengthening effect of healthy friction with the wishes and wills of others.

When, through a variety of adverse influences, a child is not permitted to grow according to his individual needs and possibilities, he may develop neurotic difficulties. If the people in his environment are too involved in their own neuroses to be able to love the child, or even to conceive of him as the particular individual he is, if their attitudes toward him are determined by their own neurotic needs and responses, they may be dominating, over protective, intimidating, irritable, over-exacting, over-indulgent, erratic, partial to other siblings, hypocritical and indifferent. One single factor is rarely, if ever, the total determinant in development of a neurosis. The whole constellation of interpersonal reactions may exert untoward influences on the child's growth.

A child who does not develop the experience of being part of or of being accepted will experience an insecure, apprehensive feeling called basic anxiety (1), the feeling of being isolated and helpless in a world conceived as potentially hostile. Cramped by the pressure of his basic anxiety the child is prevented from relating to others with the spontaneity of his real feelings. Instead he must deal with them in ways which do not arouse or increase basic anxiety but rather attempt to allay it. Without going into detail, the particular attitudes of the child are determined both by his given temperament and the impact of the environment. Briefly he may try to cling to the most powerful person around him; he may try to rebel and fight against others or he may try to shut them out of his inner life and emotionally withdraw from them. In principle this means he can move toward, against or away from others. The ability to want and to give affection, to comply through cooperation, the ability to fight and the ability to spend time by oneself occasionally are all necessary for good human relations. They do not mutually exclude one another. These moves become extreme and rigid, however, in a child who feels shaky because of his basic anxiety. Affection, for instance, becomes clinging; compliance becomes appeasement. He may be driven to rebel or to retreat into himself, without reference to his real feelings and regardless of the inappropriateness of his attitude in a particular situation. The degree of compulsiveness, blindness and rigidity in his attitudes is in proportion to the intensity of the basic anxiety lurking within him. The child, driven not just in one but in all of these directions, develops fundamentally contradictory attitudes towards others, and the three moves clash in what Horney calls in "Our Inner Conflict", the basic conflict. In time he tries to solve his basic conflict by making one of these moves consistently predominant. His prevailing attitude then becomes one of compliance, or aggressiveness, or aloofness.

This first attempt at solving neurotic conflicts has a determining influence upon the further course of his neurotic development. Changes of personality occur not only toward others but also in relation to himself. According to his main direction, the child also develops certain appropriate needs, sensitivities, inhibitions and the beginnings of moral values. The child who is predominantly compliant, for instance, will not only tend to ingratiate himself with others and to cling to them, but will also try to be unselfish and good. Similarly the predominantly aggressive child valuing strength will emphasize capacity to endure and to fight. This early solution aims chiefly at a unification of relations with others and since the individual is still divided he needs a firmer and more comprehensive integration. The constant need to be on the defensive drains his inner strength and makes large areas of his personality unavailable for constructive uses. Lacking self confidence he is less well equipped for life. Living in a competitive (1) society, and feeling isolated and hostile, he must strive desperately to lift himself above others.

This need to evolve artificial, strategic ways to cope with others has forced him to become alienated from himself and to override his genuine feelings, wishes and thoughts. When safety becomes paramount, innermost feelings and thoughts must recede in importance. Since his feelings and wishes cease to be determining factors, he becomes driven rather than the driver. He no longer knows where he stands, what he stands for or "who" he is. Needing a feeling of identity to become meaningful to himself and to get a feeling of power and significance, gradually and unconsciously he sets to work through his imagination to create in his mind an idealized self-image. By means of this process he endows himself with unlimited powers and exalted faculties and believes he is all things to all people and all things to himself, hero, genius, supreme lover, saint or god.

This personal idealized image is constructed from the materials of his own special experiences, his earlier fantasies and his particular needs as well as his given faculties. Shortcomings or flaws are dismissed or retouched. Compliance and self-effacement become goodness, love, saintliness; aggressiveness and arrogance become strength, leadership, heroism, omnipotence; aloofness and fear of involvement become wisdom, self-sufficiency and independence.

There are a variety of ways a person may deal with his contradictory trends. He may glorify one aspect of his personality while openly denying but secretly admiring the other two trends. He may so isolate them in his mind that they may seem neither contradictory nor conflicting. He may attempt to elevate all of his qualities to positive accomplishments and gifts. In this way he considers his self-minimizing as humility, his domineering tendencies as leadership and his detachments as objectivity. They become compatible aspects of a rich personality and in his mind he becomes the universal man of the Renaissance.

Eventually the individual begins to make efforts to actualize this secretly cherished image. While the healthy course would be a move toward what was real in himself he now starts to abandon it definitely for the idealized self which represents to him what he could be or should be. It becomes the perspective from which he looks at himself, the measuring rod with which he measures himself. The goal of proving his idealized image in action infiltrates his aspirations, his goals, his conduct of life and his relations to others.

In this search for glory there is a need for perfection which he tries to achieve by a complicated system of shoulds and taboos; neurotic ambition, the drive for external success with emphasis on competition; and the need for a vindictive triumph. This need for a vindictive triumph, this need for vindication, is experienced and expressed as the need to rise to prominence and put others to shame or defeat them and to seek revenge for real or imagined humiliations suffered earlier in life.

The drives for glory aim at the absolute in wisdom, infinite virtue or unlimited powers. A well functioning man needs both the vision of possibilities, the perspective of infinitude *and* the realization of limitations, the necessity of the concrete. If his thinking and feeling are primarily focused upon the infinite, he loses his sense for the concrete, for the here and now. Losing his capacity for living in the moment, his thinking may become too abstract. His feelings for others may evaporate into sentimentality for mankind in the abstract. If, on the other hand, he does not see beyond the narrow horizon of the concrete, the finite, he becomes narrow and petty. Both qualities, the capacity to perceive possibilities and to deal with the concrete are necessary for growth.

The more his irrational imagination has taken over, the more he will be disturbed by anything real, definite, concrete or final. He will tend to resent the definiteness of time, the concreteness of money, the finality of death. There are countless ways in which he disregards evidence which he strategically must avoid. Horney (5) quotes one patient as saying: "If it were not for reality, I would be perfectly all right."

The difference, then, between healthy strivings and neurotic drives for glory is one between spontaneity and compulsion, between recognizing and denying limitations, between focussing on the end-product and a feeling for evolution, between seeming to be and being, illusion and truth.

No matter how averse the neurotic may be to checking with reality, no matter how talented he may be, he still is in all essentials like everybody else. Actually he is not god-like and others do not treat him as though he were god-like. Like everyone else he must perform the biologically necessary functions of eating, sleeping, excreting, breathing etc.; a day has 24 hours, others may act as though he were just an ordinary mortal. What does such a person do who is almost constantly faced with puzzling painful discrepancies? As long as he must cling to his personal aggrandizement, he must therefore find the world at fault. Instead of probing his illusions, he presents a claim to the outside world that it should be different. Others should treat him in accordance with his grandiose notions about himself. When they do not cater to his illusions, he considers it unfair. Feeling he deserves a better deal, his wishes and needs become claims. When these claims are not fulfilled he experiences them as unfair frustrations about which he thinks he has a right to feel outraged.

When the neurotic looks at himself he ignores what he actually is but rather sets to work to mold himself into a being of his own creation. How he feels he should be may encompass the utmost of honesty, generosity, considerateness, justice, dignity, courage, unselfishness. He should be the perfect lover, husband and teacher. He should be able to endure everything, should like everybody, should love his parents, his wife, his country, or he should not be attached to anything or anybody, nothing should matter to him, he should never feel hurt and he should always be serene and unruffled. He should always enjoy life or he should be above pleasure and enjoyment. He should know, understand and foresee everything. He should be able to solve every problem of his own or of others in no time. He should be able to overcome every difficulty of his as soon as he sees it. He should never be tired or fall ill. He should always be able to find a job. He should be able to do things at once and without effort which can actually only be done by putting in time and work. Horney (4) calls these inner dictates, the tyranny of the shoulds. These demands on himself, these inner dictates like political tyranny in a police state, operate with complete disregard for the person's own psychic condition—for what he actually can feel or do. A person operating under the yoke of the shoulds feels the strain in terms of disturbed human relations and impaired spontaneity of feelings, wishes, thoughts and beliefs.

When a person recognizes that he cannot measure up to his inner dictates, he ceases to be proud of the human being he actually is and starts to hate and despise himself. Since neurotic pride is false pride, it collapses whenever it is hurt. The typical reactions to hurt pride are shame and humiliation, rage and fear. Any hurt to our pride may provoke vindictive hostility ranging all the way from dislike to hate, from irritability to anger to a blind murderous rage. Fear, anxiety and panic may occur as reactions to anticipated or actual humiliations or they may be repressed contributing to psychotic episodes, depressions, alcoholism, psychosomatic disorders or the need to sit tight on these emotions of anger and fear with a general flattening of emotion.

Neurotic pride while vitally important to the individual renders him extremely vulnerable at the same time. There is an urgent need to save face and to restore pride when it is hurt or to avoid injuries when it is endangered. Some of the measures employed are the impulse to take revenge for what is felt as humiliation, the striving for safety through restricting one's life and the philosophy that it is safer not to try than to try and fail. The neurotic must develop a system of private values to determine what to like and accept in himself, what to glorify and of what to be proud. This system of values by necessity also determines what to reject, to be ashamed of, to despise, to hate. Pride and self-hate are bound together inseparably. The hatred results from awareness of the discrepancy between what a person would be and what he is. Self-hate results in feeling guilty, inferior, cramped and tormented. Surveying self-hate and its ravaging forces we cannot help but see in it a great tragedy. The great tragedy is that in reaching out for the infinite and absolute, a man starts destroying himself. In terms of the devil's pact, the abandoning of the self corresponds to the selling of one's soul. In psychiatric terms we call it the alienation from the self, the remoteness of the neurotic from his own feelings, wishes, beliefs and energies. The alienated person can not feel he is an active determining force in his own life.

What are the consequences of unresolved conflicts? The protective structure gives rise to fears that its equilibrium will be disturbed, fear of insanity, fear of exposure, and of changing anything in oneself. Living with unresolved conflicts involves a devastating waste of energies, indecisiveness, ineffectualness, and inertia, unconscious pretenses—of love, goodness, interest, knowledge, honesty, fairness and suffering, an unconscious arrogance, and inability to take a definite stand, undependability and a lack of responsibility. Although neurotic entanglements invariably generate a measure of hopelessness, people do manage to carry on in one way or another. They may submerge themselves in work; they may resign themselves to living. They may give up all serious or promising pursuits and turn to the periphery of life, devoting themselves to shallow, frivolous pastimes. They may actually drift in an aimless fashion and gradually deteriorate. Finally persons without hope may turn aggressively destructive and live vicariously through others in a sadistic way. Horney (5) describes in great detail the three major attempts at solving these intrapsychic difficulties, the expansive solution or the appeal of mastery, the self effacing solution or the appeal of love; and the resigned solution or the appeal of freedom.

And what are the goals of the doctor and the patient in psychoanalytic therapy? Since symptoms are not the essential constituents but the outgrowths of the neurotic character structure, the focus must be on resolving the intrapsychic and interpersonal conflicts. The work to be done with regard to himself concerns all that is involved in self-realization. It means striving toward a greater spontaneity in experiencing all of one's feelings, wishes and beliefs. In addition to expressing himself freely he will be capable of voluntarily disciplining himself. By enabling him to tap his resources and to use them for constructive ends, he develops the feeling of being an active force in his life. This makes possible taking responsibility for himself, making decisions and taking the consequences for such decisions. As the patient achieves a sense of inner independence, he is able to establish his own hierarchy of values and apply it to actual living. To the extent he approximates wholeheartedness he will be living with less pretense and with more emotional sincerity. With regard to others it means working toward relating himself to them in a spirit of mutuality with his genuine feelings and toward respecting their individuality with their assets, liabilities and distinctive features. With regard to work it means that he will become more able to enjoy the process of the work itself. This aspect of the job rather than end product will become the major source of his satisfaction. He will aim at becoming more productive by realizing and developing his particular talents and capacities.

In a forward moving analysis, as the individual outgrows his neurotic egocentricity he will become more aware of the broader issues involved in his particular life and in the world at large and will come to experience himself as part of a bigger whole. Whether it be in the family, in the community or even in a larger activity he will be willing and able to assume his share of responsibility in it, contributing constructively in whichever way he is capable.   In this way through active participation he not only widens his personal horizon but also achieves the feeling of belonging that comes when a person finds and accepts his place in the world.   None of these goals is wholly attained but they are approached in a successful analysis.

To conclude this presentation of Horney's concepts of human motivation I should like to present her philosophy as expressed in the introduction of her book *Our Inner Conflicts:* My own belief is that man has the capacity as well as the desire to develop his potentialities and become a decent human being, and that these deteriorate if his relationship to others and hence to himself is, and continues to be, disturbed.   I believe that man can change and go on changing as long as he lives.   And this belief has grown with deeper understanding.

References

1. Horney, Karen: *The neurotic personality of our time.*   New York: W. W. Norton and Company, Inc., 1937.

2. Horney, Karen: *New ways in psychoanalysis.*   New York: W. W. Norton and Company, Inc., 1939.

3. Horney, Karen: *Self analysis.*   New York: W. W. Norton and Company, Inc., 1942.

4. Horney, Karen: *Our inner conflicts.*   New York: W. W. Norton and Company, Inc., 1945.

5. Horney, Karen: *Neurosis and human growth.*   New York: W. W. Norton and Company, Inc., 1950.

Patrick Mullahy

SOME ASPECTS OF SULLIVAN'S THEORY OF INTERPERSONAL RELATIONS *

The goals of human behavior

We begin our exposition of Sullivan with some preliminary distinctions and assumptions.   He differentiates "human performances," which include revery processes, such as day dreaming, and thought, into a

* From Patrick Mullahy, *Oedipus: Myth and Complex,* Thomas Nelson and Sons, New York, 1948. Pages 280–301 reprinted by permission of the author and the publisher.

two-part classification.   In more popular language, the purposes, the goals or end states of human behavior are divided into two actually interrelated classes.   These two classes refer to the pursuit of satis-factions and the pursuit of security.   Satisfactions include sleep and rest, food and drink, sexual fulfillment (the satisfaction of lust). Loneliness is also listed as a "middling example."   These satisfac-tions are closely connected with the bodily organization of man. Hence, loneliness is included by Sullivan because, among other things, we have a desire to touch one another and to be physically close.

The class of pursuits pertaining to security refer more directly to man's cultural equipment than to bodily organization.   The concept of security, in Sullivan's sense, is not easy to explain.   Roughly, it refers to the state of well-being, of "good feeling," of euphoria.   All "those movements, actions, speech, thoughts, reveries and so on which pertain more to the culture which has been imbedded in a particular individual than to the organization of his tissues and glands, is apt to belong in this classification of the pursuit of security." [1]

The process of becoming a human being, for Sullivan, is synony-mous with the process of acculturation or socialization.   The need for security arises from the fact that every person undergoes this process of acculturation which begins at birth.   From the very beginning of life in this world, everyone, at first through "empathy," which we dis-cuss below, is made to feel some of the effects of the culture by the attitudes of the significant person or persons who take care of him: mother, nurse, or their surrogates.   The attitudes of those who take care of the child are themselves socially conditioned.   Because of empathy, long before the infant can understand what is happening, he experiences something of the attitudes of the significant people around him.   Later he is deliberately taught what is right and wrong, "good" and "bad."   In this way, the impulses, the biological strivings of the infant are socially "conditioned," that is, moulded, both as to form of expression and fulfillment, according to the culturally ap-proved patterns.   As we shall see, because of the experiences of ap-proval and disapproval from the parents or their surrogates, the achievement of satisfactions according to the culturally "correct" or approved patterns causes a profound feeling of well-being, of good feeling, of security.   When, for certain reasons, the felt needs of a person, the biological strivings, cannot be fulfilled according to cul-turally approved patterns, which he learned in early life, he feels intense and painful uneasiness and discomfort, insecurity, or *anxiety*.

It is not very difficult to see that the distinction between the pursuit of satisfactions and the pursuit of security and their attainment is logi-cal or conceptual.   The two are inextricably bound up together.   But

[1] Harry Stack Sullivan, *Conceptions of Modern Psychiatry*, The William Alanson White Psychiatric Foundation, Washington, D.C., 1947, p. 6.

these two broad classifications are helpful for preliminary discussion. In general terms they explain what one is after in any situation with other persons, whether real or "fantastic" or a blend of both ("eidetic"). Hence, they represent "integrating tendencies." They explain why a situation in which two or more people—"all but one of which may be illusory" (or eidetic)—are involved or "integrated" becomes an interpersonal situation. It is because of these needs that one cannot live and be human except in communal existence with others.

The concept of tension

Because of the great role which anxiety and tension play in Sullivan's theories, we need first to mention some of his ideas about the latter. The achievement of satisfactions causes a decrease of tonus, tension, of the unstriped, involuntary muscles. But the effort at warding off anxiety (insecurity) is accompanied by heightened tonus, often of the striped, skeletal muscles, often of the unstriped, visceral muscles.

The facts seem to indicate that tonic changes in the unstriped, involuntary muscles of the viscera—the internal organs of the body—are, from birth onward, intimately related to the experiencing of desires, needs for satisfaction. Heightened tone of the stomach wall is called out by depletion of our chemical supplies and the occurrence of vigorous contractions in these tense muscles gives rise to the "pangs of hunger." The taking of food—the ingestion of which probably leads to a release of nutritive substance stored in the liver—promptly relieves the excess tone and the contractions quiet down to the churning of the stomach contents. Hunger, in a way of speaking, is from the first influx of food, more a matter of the oral dynamism than of the stomach. In infants, at least, once this dynamism has discharged itself, alertness disappears, vigilance is withdrawn from circumambient reality, and sleep supervenes. Throughout life the pursuit of satisfactions is physiologically provoked by increased tone in some unstriped muscles; and the securing of the satisfactions is a relaxation of this tone, with a tendency towards the diminution of attention, alertness, and vigilance, and an approach to sleep.[2]

In the securing of satisfaction, the striped, skeletal muscles are "of relatively instrumental value" in very early infancy. They are said to do what is necessary—we are not told what that is—and then relax. But as soon as the mother begins to include prohibitions and disapprovals in educating the youngster, things get complicated. He develops a need for security against primarily "noxious emotional states empathized from the personal environment." Here the skeletal muscles take on a new function.

[2] *Op. cit.*, p. 43.

This function is to get rid of empathized discomfort and painful tension of various origins.

The oral dynamism [the respiratory apparatus, the food-taking apparatus, from which the speaking apparatus is evolved] has been the channel for performances needed to appease hunger—and pain and other discomforts. It may be presumed that its function in emitting the cry has been quite automatic. This may not have worked too well, and delayed response to the cry may be one of the first experiences that tend to focus alertness. But in any case, the oral dynamism is not now effective in securing relief from the discomfort set up by empathy; on some occasions, it is simply ineffectual, and on other occasions, its activity is accompanied by increase of the empathized discomfort. This leads gradually to a differentiation of empathized from other discomforts, and to the *inhibition* of the cry as a universal tool. The inhibiting of a complex pattern of behavior is not as simple as was its automatic initiation. Some of the movements are cut off, but the increase of tone in the appropriate muscles may not be inhibited. The experience of empathized hostility or unfriendly prohibition or, as it later comes to be observed, a forbidding gesture becomes colored by and associated with heightened tone in some striped muscles—at first those concerned with the cry.

The course of acculturation, in so far as it pertains to toilet habits, is also a learning to suffer increasing tension in the bladder and rectum, and to resist the automatic relaxation of the sphincter muscles concerned in retaining the urine and feces. Failures in this are often accompanied by empathized discomfort [due to parental disapproval], and success is often the occasion of empathized comfort which is added to the satisfaction from relief of the tension.[3]

Action which avoids or relieves any of these tensions is experienced as continued or enhanced *self-respect* or self-esteem. Thus a person who has become tense at an expression of hostility from someone he is talking to may subsequently, let us say, be made to laugh heartily at some remark or occurrence. When this happens, he suddenly feels a relief from tension; he "feels better" about himself and others. While the effort to ward off anxiety involves an increase of tension, the relief from anxiety is associated with actions which, among other things, decrease muscle tension.

Anxiety is not synonymous with muscle tension, but the latter is a necessary condition for its experience. As we shall see, *anxiety is always related to interpersonal relations*.

The power motive

Even more important and logically more fundamental than the impulses resulting from a feeling of hunger or thirst is the "power motive," the

[3] *Op. cit.*, p. 44. Sullivan has changed his mind about empathizing comfort before the epoch of childhood, feeling that there is no certain evidence of its existence before then. (Personal communication to the writer.)

impulse to obtain and maintain a feeling of ability. To be able to obtain satisfactions and security is to have power in interpersonal relations; not to be able to do so is to be powerless, helpless. According to Sullivan, the development of actions, thoughts, foresights, etc., which are "calculated" to protect one from insecurity, is based on and springs from the disappointments and frustrations of early infancy. When one achieves power or ability in interpersonal relations, one respects oneself and therefore others. While the attitude toward the self is first determined by the attitude of those who take care of the child, his subsequent attitude toward others is determined by the attitude he has toward himself. "If there is a valid and real attitude toward the self, that attitude will manifest as valid and real toward others." [4]

Empathy

There is said to be "a peculiar emotional relationship" between the infant and those who take care of him. Long before he can understand what is happening to him, this "emotional contagion or communion" between him and the significant adult, the mother or nurse, exists. Sullivan surmises its greatest importance is between the ages of six and twenty-seven months. For example if a mother looks with disfavor on her offspring or she suffers a fright around feeding time, there may be great feeding difficulties. This unclear mode of emotional communication is thought to be biological, for certain animals are said to exhibit a similar phenomenon. Since the attitudes of the mother or nurse are socially conditioned, this mode of emotional communication, which does not seem to occur, in Sullivan's view, through ordinary sensory channels, is very important for understanding acculturation. In later years, however, empathy is not much in evidence.

Three modes of experience

All experience occurs in one or more of three "modes"—the prototaxic, parataxic, and syntaxic. As the Greek roots of this horrendous term indicate, the prototaxic mode refers to the first kind of experience the infant has and the order or arrangement in which it occurs. As grownups, we experience things in terms of time and space, of here and "out there," of before and after. We break up our experience, so to speak, into constituent elements for the purposes of getting along in the world. Furthermore, our experience, or at least much of it, is referable to a self who does the experiencing, the self being a center of reference. "I went for a walk in the park at four o'clock." These are examples of every day distinctions we make. Others, of course, are much more subtle and refined.

[4] *Op. cit.*, p. 7.

Now in the beginning, the infant, Sullivan hypothecates, makes no such distinctions for a variety of reasons. Aside from structural and functional limitations, the organism at birth has had, of course, no direct experience with the cultural heritage. We shall avoid saying he has no mind as yet—for we shall not deal here with the problem of the nature of mind nor with the problem of what he inherits from his life in the womb, concerning which apparently not a great deal is known, at least regarding mind.

According to Sullivan's hypothesis all that the infant "knows" are momentary states, the distinction of before and after being a later acquirement. The infant vaguely feels or "prehends" earlier and later states without realizing any serial connection between them. He has no ego in any distinctive sense because the self has not yet developed. For such reasons, he has no awareness of himself as an entity separate from the rest of the world. In other words, his felt experience is all of a piece, undifferentiated, without definite limits. It is as if his experiences were "cosmic." This mode of experience is often marked in certain schizophrenic states.

The terms "parataxic" and "syntaxic" [5] also are etymologically related to the order and arrangement of experience. At the risk of confusion, we shall remind the reader that parataxic (like syntaxic) is a grammatical term as well, which refers to the ranging of clauses or propositions one after another without connectives such as "and," "or," "since," etc., to show the relations between them.

Gradually the infant learns to make some discrimination between himself and the rest of the world. As Sullivan puts it, he no longer reaches out to touch the moon. In other words he gradually learns to make elementary differentiations in his experience.

We learn in infancy that objects which our distance receptors, our eyes and ears, for example, encounter, are of a quite different order of relationship from things which our tactile or our gustatory receptors encounter. That which one has in one's mouth so that one can taste it, while it may be regurgitated to the distress of everyone is still in a very different relationship than is the full moon which one encounters through one's eye but can in no sense manage.[6]

As the infant develops and maturation proceeds, the original undifferentiated wholeness of experience is broken. However, the "parts," the diverse aspects, the various kinds of experience are not related or connected in a logical fashion. They "just happen" together, or they do not, depending on circumstances. In other words, various experiences are felt as concomitant, not recognized as connected in an orderly way. The child cannot yet relate them to one

[5] Or "syntactic."
[6] *Op. cit.*, p. 16.

another or make logical distinctions among them. What is experienced is assumed to be the "natural" way of such occurrences, without reflection and comparison. Since no connections or relations are established, there is no logical movement of "thought" from one idea to the next. The parataxic mode is not a step by step process. Experience is undergone as momentary, unconnected states of being.

The parataxic mode of organizing experience occurs mainly through visual and auditory channels. Dreams are often examples of this mode of experiencing. But it occurs a good deal of the time in waking life. In other words, we do not—and cannot—always organize our experience into a logically connected, related totality, in which the various elements are compared, contrasted, and ordered in a precise fashion. Ordinarily we do not indulge in careful ratiocination as we dress in the morning, proceed to work, and so on. It is not necessary, and in any case there is not enough time.

As the infant learns the rudiments of language, he is said to pass into the "epoch" of childhood. And here we introduce another term, the "autistic." The autistic is a verbal manifestation of the parataxic. But the capacity for verbal communication is just beginning to be manifested, and the tools, vocabulary, grammar, etc., are scarcely formed and learned. Because of the child's limited equipment and experience with the symbol activity and experience of others, his own symbol activity is arbitrary, highly personal, unchecked and untested. Hence his imagination is not curbed to conform to everyday "reality." Autistic symbols, however, are useful in recall and foresight.

Let us take an example of a child who has been given a picture book also containing words, say, to name or describe the pictures. It will have a picture of a cat, and below or above or somewhere on the page there is written what the child eventually learns is c-a-t. Then, too, to complete the example, the animal who runs around the house also is referred to by the same name as that of the colored or black and white pattern in the book. Sullivan comments on the significance of such a frequent phenomenon in our culture as follows:

I am sure no child who can learn has not noticed an enormous discrepancy between this immobile representation in the book which, perhaps, resembles one of the momentary states that kitty has been in on some occasion. I am certain that every child knows that there is something very strange in this printed representation being so closely connected with the same word that seems to cover adequately the troublesome, amusing, and very active pet. Yet, because of unnumbered, sometimes subtle, sometimes crude experiences with the carrier of culture, the parent, the child finally comes to accept as valid and useful a reference to the picture as "kitty" and to the creature as "kitty."

The child thus learns some of the more complicated implications of a symbol in contradistinction to the actuality to which the symbol refers, which is its referent; in other words, the distinction between the symbol and that which is symbolized.   This occurs, however, before verbal formulation is possible.

From the picture book and the spoken word in this culture one progresses to the printed word and finally discovers that the combination of signs, c-a-t, includes "kitty" in some miraculous fashion, and that it always works. There is nothing like consistent experience to impress one with the validity of an idea.   So one comes to a point where printed words, with or without consensually valid meaning, come to be very important in one's growth of acquaintance with the world.

There was first the visually and otherwise impressive pet, which was called "kitty" (an associated vocalization); then came the picture of the kitten; now comes the generic *c a t* which includes, kitty, picture of kitten, a kitten doll, and alley cats seen from the windows.   And all this is learnt so easily that—since no one troubles to point it out—there is no lucid understanding of the sundry types of reality and reference that are being experienced.   Familiarity breeds indifference in this case.   The possibilities for confusion in handling the various kinds of symbols, naturally, remain quite considerable.[7]

The child gradually begins to catch on to patterns of relationships, to the grammatical structure of the language, and to the usual relationships and distinctions obtaining in his society.   There is a more discriminating realization of the other fellow, the responder.   The child now more clearly realizes that, for example, when he cries "dada," the other person responds in a more or less characteristic fashion. And so the child learns to anticipate the responses of others.   These responses become associated with the use of certain words and gestures.   In other words, the characteristic reactions of the other people give meaning to the language, a meaning that is thus implicitly agreed upon.   Of course, the child does not set out systematically to learn the everyday meaning of the language.   He learns by the trial and error method.   Hence, he also learns that not only one's own experience is important, but that of others.   He also learns to use verbal symbols as an economical way to get a lot to happen in a short time, with little use of energy.

Of course, there is a great deal more than this to be said about the learning process, but this sketch may indicate some of the ways by which, according to Sullivan, a child learns to use language with an interpersonal reference.

In any case, the child gradually learns the "consensually validated" meaning of language—in the widest sense of language.   These meanings have been acquired from group activities, interpersonal activities, social experience.   Consensually validated symbol activity involves an appeal to principles which are accepted as true by the

7 *Op. cit.*, p. 16.

hearer. And when this happens, the youngster has acquired or learned the syntaxic mode of experience.

But the learning process is not always consistent—because the significant others are not always consistent in their behavior. Furthermore, as we know, people do not always take the trouble to teach the child the distinctions between various symbols and that to which they refer. The trial and error method by which a good deal of learning necessarily occurs is not ideally suited for acquiring precise distinctions. For such reasons, language thus comes to have a double meaning—a personal meaning and a consensually validated meaning or a blend of both. In this way, among others, people come to maintain a wide margin of misinformation and illusion about others, themselves, and the world.

Tension, when it occurs in connection with needs, such as those of food and sex, is experienced in the syntaxic and parataxic modes. The tension of anxiety, however, is experienced by grown-ups mainly in the parataxic mode.[8]

The meaning of dynamism

Before taking up an exposition of the self dynamism (or self system or, simply, self), we must try to indicate what the term "dynamism" means. It has been defined as "a relatively enduring configuration of energy which manifests itself in characterizable processes in interpersonal relations."[9] In other words dynamism refers to the way energy is organized and channeled in the human organism. Dynamism implies only a relatively enduring capacity to bring about change. It is analogous to any structure or organization of processes which always contains numerous sub-structures.

For Sullivan energy always means physical energy. He rejects the notion of "psychic energy."

The evolution of the self

As everyone knows, certain restraints are put on the young offspring's freedom which are or are considered to be necessary for his socialization, for training him and making him the sort of person considered right and desirable in the society in which he will live and have his being. These restraints, above everything else, bring about the evolution of the self dynamism. In this evolution, other aspects of the

---

[8] Anxiety is always *felt*. Contrary to previous formulations, Sullivan now is convinced it never occurs in the prototaxic mode but that it occurs mainly in the parataxic. (Personal communication to the writer.)

[9] Harry Stack Sullivan, "Introduction to the Study of Interpersonal Relations," *Psychiatry*, vol. 1, p. 123, footnote, 1938.

personality, such as *the selectively inattended* and *disassociated* processes, those which occur outside of self-awareness, are also developed.

We shall begin our exposition of Sullivan's theories concerning the evolution of personality with the "epoch" of infancy.   Infancy refers to the period from birth to the maturation of the capacity for language behavior.   During this period certain of the attitudes of the parent or nurse are said to be conveyed empathically.   Suppose the mother is tired or upset or angry when she is in close contact with the infant, let us say, when she nurses or bathes him.   Something of her attitude is then conveyed to him.   His sense of well-being, his euphoria, is markedly decreased.   The mother who observes or at least senses this gets anxious, which state is then communicated to the infant, further lowering his feeling of well-being, further increasing his insecurity. And so the process goes on.   It is "dynamic."

Euphoria and anxiety are, conceptually, direct opposites, "polar constructs."   In actuality there is no such thing as "pure" euphoria, in which there is no tension and therefore no action, something like an empty state of bliss.   Perhaps the nearest approximation to euphoria in the "ideal" sense is deepest sleep.   Nor is there any actual state of absolute anxiety.   In the state of terror—in which there is a complete but temporary disorganization of personality—the most extreme degree of tension ordinarily observable occurs.   Euphoria and anxiety are inversely related.

It is not difficult to see that a chronically hostile mother will induce an intense and more or less chronic anxiety in the offspring.   Furthermore, such a mother will deprive him of the experience of tenderness —a deprivation which will have fateful consequences for his future well-being and happiness.

One of the characteristics of anxiety is that it interferes with observation and analysis, with the acquisition of information and understanding and with recall and foresight.   It interferes with alertness to the factors in a situation that are relevant to its occurrence.   Therefore it interferes with effective action.

Sooner or later the infant is recognized as educable.   And when this happens, there is said to be a restriction of tender cooperation. The exhibition of tenderness by the parents tends to be modified so that it will be used more on "suitable" occasions.   The mother, for example, begins to train the child in the "proper" toilet habits, those considered proper in the society in which she lives.   She will express or withhold tenderness and approval as the child learns to conform or not to her desires and methods in this matter.   Thus, training involves the expression of tenderness and approval for some acts and disapproval and the withholding of tenderness for others.   In other words, some performances bring tenderness and approval with the consequent increase of euphoria, while others bring disapproval and hence anxiety. These experiences of rewards and punishments come to be regarded as something special. Gradually the child catches on to the fact that they are related to his feelings of euphoria and anxiety. The more or less abrupt supervention of anxiety gradually teaches or forces him to focus awareness on the performances which bring approval and disapproval. He learns, for example, to recall incidents occurring before anxiety. After a while a forbidding gesture will be sufficient to change his behavior. In other words, as his observation improves, his grasp on the patterns of approval and disapproval becomes more refined. He learns that when anxiety is present and something is done which brings tenderness and approval, the painful discomfort is assuaged or banished.

Hence, the child gradually learns to focus attention on behavior which brings approval and disapproval in order to win rewards, tenderness and approval, and escape punishment, disapproval and disapprobation.

In infancy a vague idea of "my" body arises. From the sentience of the body as a basis, there gradually evolve three "personifications" of "me"— "good me," "bad me," and "not-me." The "good me" is an organization of experiences of approval, tenderness, and general good feeling. The "bad me" is an organization of experiences related to increasing anxiety states. The "rudimentary personification" of "not-me" evolves very gradually. The processes labeled "not-me" belong to the most poorly grasped aspects of living and refer to "uncanny" experiences like horror, dread, loathing, awe. What these uncanny experiences are about is not known, but they seem to originate in the experiences of anxiety in infancy, "primitive anxiety." They occur in the parataxic mode. The personification, "not-me," is not constituted by communicative processes and hence not much can be said about it. Nightmares and certain schizophrenic experiences are examples of uncanny experiences of the "not-me."

The "personifications" of "good me" and "bad me" belong to the self system. In other words, to put this crudely, there are times when "I" am "good me" and times when "I" am "bad me." Whether or not the self is predominantly one or the other depends on the course of experience, especially in early life. But the "good me" is essentially desirable, for it is organized on the basis of experiences of security. Hence "I" shall tend to regard "my" self as essentially the "good me"—at least unless my life experience has been extraordinarily unfortunate.

We can now state in general terms the origin, nature, and function of the self dynamism. It has its basis in the need for alertness to approval, tenderness and disapproval. We should like, too, to call attention to its *restrictive* function.

The self-dynamism is built up out of this experience of approbation and disapproval, of reward and punishment. The peculiarity of the self-dynamism is that as it grows it functions, in accordance with its state of development, right from the start. As it develops, it becomes more and more related to a microscope in its function. Since the approbation of the important person is very valuable, since disapprobation denies satisfaction and gives anxiety, the self becomes extremely important. It permits a minute focus on those performances of the child which are the cause of approbation and disapprobation, but, very much like a microscope, it interferes with noticing the rest of the world. When you are staring through your microscope, you don't see much except what comes through that channel. So with the self-dynamism. It has a tendency to focus attention on performances with the significant other person which get approbation or disfavor. And that peculiarity, closely connected with anxiety, persists thenceforth through life. It comes about that the self, that to which we refer when we say 'I,' is the only thing which has alertness, which notices what goes on, and, needless to say, notices what goes on in its own field. The rest of the personality gets along outside awareness. Its impulses, its performances are not noted.[10]

Among the peculiarities of anxiety is the fact that it is always "at 180° to any other tension with which it coincides." [11]   In other words, it directly opposes the tensions of somatic needs and thereby prevents or hinders the satisfaction of somatic needs. An extremely anxious person cannot obtain proper sexual satisfaction or may be prevented from enjoying food by nausea, vomiting, etc. While all other tensions are followed by activities, either overt or covert, which resolve the tensions and satisfy needs, the tension of anxiety, in Sullivan's language, does not result in energy transformations directed to its relief by the removal of the situational factors obviously concerned in its provocation. The tension of fear, on the other hand, is often manifested in activities which remove the situational factors provoking fear, escapes them, neutralizes their importance or defers being afraid until the near future when the real or apparent danger is over.

As one grows, one learns, if only in a dim way, how to avoid most situations which provoke intense anxiety, but the capacity for it remains. And it will manifest itself throughout life. In this respect, the difference between the "normal" person and the "neurotic" is only one of degree.

Because experiences of approbation and disapproval occur long before one can think, long before one can discriminate what occurs, the earliest attitudes, and the most "deep seated" and pervasive, are acquired unthinkingly, with little or no discrimination. Furthermore,

---

[10] *Conceptions of Modern Psychiatry*, pp. 9–10.
[11] Harry Stack Sullivan, "The Meaning of Anxiety in Psychiatry and in Life," *Psychiatry*, vol. 11, no. 1, p. 4, 1948.

the infant, and to a large extent also, the child, is biologically and psychologically helpless. Not only does he depend on the parents for the necessities of life itself, but he has no or only an incipient ability to think and no or insufficient social experience. Hence, in earliest years the attitudes, codes, and behavior of the parents and their surrogates are necessarily accepted without criticism or discrimination. In Sullivan's language he is still pretty much restricted to the parataxic mode of experience. Later, at least to some degree, he will develop the ability to question, compare and relate his experiences.

The "facilitations and deprivations," that which is approved and disapproved by the parents and others close to the child, becomes the source of the material built into the self dynamism. By and large their behavior will be sufficiently consistent to give the self-system a form and direction which it will maintain throughout life. Any experience which promises to threaten the form and direction of the self will provoke anxiety. When this happens, the person will not clearly notice what is happening; its significance will not be realized. And he will usually, without being aware of it, indulge in behavior calculated to nullify the experience or its importance.

Thus, anxiety is the instrumentality by which the self limits and restricts awareness. It functions so as to maintain its own form and direction.

Even when the self is a derogatory and hateful system it will inhibit and misinterpret any disassociated feeling or experience of friendliness towards others; and it will misinterpret any gestures of friendliness from others. The direction and characteristics given to the self in infancy and childhood are maintained year after year, at an extraordinary cost, so that most people in this culture, and presumably in any other, because of inadequate and unfortunate experience in early life, become "inferior caricatures of what they might have been." Not only the family, but various other cultural institutions less directly, all combine, more or less unwittingly, to produce this effect.[12]

Actions, including thinking, phantasy, and emotions and feelings, if they are to occur within self-awareness, must conform to the characteristics of the self. Otherwise they are "disassociated" or "selectively inattended."

The self may be said to be made up of or at least circumscribed by *reflected appraisals*. The child lacks the equipment and experience necessary for a careful and unclouded evaluation of himself. The only guide he has is that of the significant adults who take care of him, and who treat and regard him in accordance with the way in which they have developed from their own life experience. Hence, the child experiences himself and appraises himself in terms of what

[12] Patrick Mullahy, "A Theory of Interpersonal Relations and the Evolution of Personality," *Psychiatry*, vol. 8, no. 2, p. 191, 1945.

the parents and others close to him manifest. By empathy, facial expression, gestures, words, deeds they convey to him the attitudes they hold toward him and their regard or lack of it for him.

These he "naturally" accepts because he is not yet a questioning, evaluating being. If the significant people express a respecting, loving attitude toward him, he acquires a respecting, loving attitude toward himself. If they are derogatory and hateful, then he will acquire a derogatory and hateful attitude toward himself. Throughout life, save perhaps for the intervention of extraordinary circumstances and allowing for some modification through later experience, he will carry the attitude toward himself he learned in early life around with him just as surely as he will carry his skin.

Sullivan suggests, however, that the controlling limiting function of the self is not absolute. Certain impelling needs, such as the need of sexual satisfaction, if thwarted, may prove too powerful even for the self system. Fortunately children retain a capacity for change. A loving teacher may undo somewhat the effects of a destructive parent, but a hateful destructive teacher may limit or slow up the effects of the loving care of tender parents.

To the extent to which limitations and peculiarities of the self interfere with biologically necessary satisfactions and security, then to that extent a person is mentally ill.

The self-dynamism is not synonymous with momentary self-awareness. It is a more or less stable organization or configuration of interpersonal processes, past, present, and of the prospective future. The self has a before and after. Since it merges with other processes occurring outside discriminating awareness, it has "background," it shades imperceptibly into marginal processes of awareness. These marginal processes of awareness may often be noted just before one "drops off" to sleep. Because the self also manifests itself in focal awareness, it has a "foreground."

Selective inattention and disassociation

It does not seem necessary to emphasize the fact that much of human experience and behavior occurs outside self-awareness. Freud formulated phenomena occurring outside self-awareness in terms of the "preconscious" and "unconscious." But for Freud these concepts have "topographical" and other features which are foreign to Sullivan's thought. Hence the latter usually avoids the use of such terms because they are "loaded" with meaning to which he does not subscribe.

The concepts by which he tries to formulate his thoughts on such matters are labeled "selective inattention" and "disassociation." The difference between the two is one of degree, measured by the difficulty of access to discriminating awareness.

The child gradually learns to pay close attention to behavior which is approved and disapproved.   He must in order to maintain security and avoid anxiety   His attention becomes focused on these performances.   This process is analogous to what goes on when, say, a music lover is present at a thrilling concert.   Such a person becomes absorbed in the music, "wrapped up" in it.   His attention will be entirely focused on the performance and enjoyment of it.   To everything else he will pay little heed.   In fact, he will not be conscious of anything else, such as the people around him, the passage of time, and so on.   For the child his security is at issue, which of course is vitally important, and he will pay close attention to what goes on when approval or disapproval is involved.   Certain other experiences either of himself or others will not be so clearly noticed because they entail no particular approval and tenderness or disapproval.   Hence, his attention and inattention become selective.   To some of his experience and behavior he will be inattentive, and this will then not be carefully discriminated.   It will go on outside of discriminated awareness.

Some of these processes can more easily become the object of careful awareness than others.   Thus, a friend may call attention to some of them, point them out, and in this case they then become subject to the person's awareness.   Such processes are said to be selectively inattended.   They can be accepted by the self.

But there are other processes which, when pointed out, do not get careful attention and scrutiny.   In spite of the friend's efforts, they will not be clearly noticed.   On the contrary, the person will not be able to become consciously aware of them.   He will deny their existence, perhaps becoming tense and angry at the efforts of his friend.   Nor will he, usually, be able to recall any experience of them.   Such experiences are said to be disassociated.   The self refuses to grant them awareness.

Motivational systems or dynamisms existing in disassociation are not necessarily "abnormal."   And they may find expression in an interpersonal situation without those who participate becoming consciously aware of what is going on.   In general, disassociated tendencies are expressed in dreams, phantasies and in unnoticed everyday behavior.   In fact, if this were not so, the self system of "normal" people would disintegrate.   In other words, the disassociated tendencies would prove too powerful for the inhibitions of the self, thus causing unbearable anxiety, and the person would "go to pieces."

The meaning of interpersonal

There is a final point to be mentioned.   The term "interpersonal" refers not only to real people existing in space and time but also to "fantastic personifications" or to people who exist physically but who serve rather as "potent representations" of other people once significant in a person's past, say, one's mother or father. In general, any frame of reference, whether constituted by real people, imaginary people existing only in story books, illusory personifications of real people (eidetic persons), or any idea or object given traits or characteristics possessed by human beings, along with one other real person, can serve to make up an interpersonal situation. We can personify and become "integrated" with almost anything, including cultural entities like the government, the church, the school, who "have their being and their manifestation so far as any particular person is concerned in other people who are significant for one reason or another to him. . . ." [13]

C. H. Patterson

THE SELF IN RECENT ROGERIAN THEORY *

The objective of this paper is to sketch the place of the self in the current client-centered approach to personality. While the self is today becoming of central importance in all theories of personality, it constitutes the core of the Rogerian approach which has, in fact, been designated by some writers (e.g., 9, 15) as "self-theory." Perhaps this is because client-centered theory is based upon the observations of individual clients in therapy.

Rogers' formulations

1947. Rogers' earliest formulation was presented in 1947 (17): "The self is a basic factor in the formation of personality and in the determination of behavior." As the perception of self changes, behavior changes. The person's feeling of adequacy is basic to psychological adjustment. The absence of threat is important for the development of an adequate self-concept and is a condition for changes in the self-concept. The self-concept is, by definition, a phenomenological concept: it is the self as seen by the experiencing person.

* From C. H. Patterson, "The Self in Recent Rogerian Theory," J. Indiv. Psychol. 1961, 17, 5–11. By permission of the author and the Editor, Journal of Individual Psychology.
[13] Conceptions of Modern Psychiatry, p. 23.

1951. In 1951 Rogers (18) amplified and extended his discussion of the self in nineteen propositions. The point of view remained perceptual and phenomenological; there is no reality for the individual other than that given by his perceptions. The self is the central concept of personality and behavior. While the basic drive of the organism is the maintenance and enhancement of the organism, the psychological self may take precedence over the physiological organism.

Once the self has developed, experiences are perceived and evaluated in terms of their relevance and significance to the self. Behavior is normally consistent with the self-concept, even at the expense of the organism. However, organic experiences or needs which are unsymbolized (because they are unacceptable) may at times lead to behavior inconsistent with the self-concept ("I was not myself"), or to psychological tension and maladjustment. Experiences which are inconsistent with the self-concept may be perceived as threatening, and may be rejected, denied, or distorted; the self-concept is defended.

Psychological adjustment or integration, on the other hand, exists when the self-concept is congruent with all the experiences of the organism. Under conditions of absence of threat to the self, all experiences—including the organismic—may be examined and assimilated into the self-concept, leading to changes in the self-concept. This occurs in therapy.

1959. The most recent and most detailed of Rogers' theoretical discussions, a more systematic and extended formulation of earlier expressions, appeared in mimeographed form in 1955 and in print in 1959 (19). Self-actualization becomes an important aspect of a general actualizing tendency.

The self-concept is defined as "the organized, consistent conceptual Gestalt composed of characteristics of the 'I' or 'me' and the perceptions of the relationships of the 'I' or 'me' to others and to various aspects of life, together with the value attached to these perceptions" (19, p. 200). The ideal self is introduced into the theory and is defined as "the self-concept which the individual would most like to possess, upon which he places the highest value for himself" (19, p. 200).

Several concepts having to do with regard are included. Rogers postulates a basic, though secondary or learned, need for positive regard from others—that is for warmth, liking, respect, sympathy, and acceptance—and a need for positive self-regard, which is related to or dependent upon positive regard from others.

Unconditional self-regard is a state of general positive self-regard, irrespective of conditions. Positive self-regard may be conditional, however, when the individual "values an experience positively or negatively solely because of . . . conditions of worth which he has taken over from others, not because the experience enhances or fails to enhance his organism" (19, p. 209). In this case the individual is vulnerable to threat and anxiety.

The central ideas in Rogers' theory of the self may be stated as follows:

1   The theory of the self, as part of the general personality theory, is phenomenological. The essence of phenomenology is that "man lives essentially in his own personal and subjective world" (19, p. 191).

2   The self becomes differentiated as part of the actualizing tendency, from the environment, through transactions with the environment—particularly the social environment. The process by which this occurs is not detailed by Rogers, but is presumably along the lines described by the sociologists Cooley (8) and Mead (13).[1]

3   The self-concept is the organization of the perceptions of the self. It is the self-concept, rather than any "real" self, which is of significance in personality and behavior. As Combs and Snygg note, the existence of a "real" self is a philosophical question, since it cannot be observed directly (6, p. 123).

4   The self-concept becomes the most significant determinant of response to the environment. It governs the perceptions or meanings attributed to the environment.

5   Whether learned or inherent, a need for positive regard from others develops or emerges with the self-concept. While Rogers leans toward attributing this need to learning, I would include it as an element of the self-actualizing tendency.

6   A need for positive self-regard, or self-esteem, according to Rogers, likewise is learned through internalization or introjection of experiences of positive regard by others. But, alternatively, it may be an aspect of the self-actualizing tendency.

7   When positive self-regard depends on evaluations by others, discrepancies may develop between the needs of the organism and the needs of the self-concept for positive self-regard. There is thus incongruence between the self and experience, or psychological maladjustment. Maladjustment is the result of attempting to preserve the existing self-concept from the threat of experiences which are inconsistent with it, leading to selective perception and distortion or denial of experience.

This highly condensed summary does not include the vicissitudes of the self through the processes of disorganization, or the processes of reorganization which take place in therapy.

---

[1] Sociology, I think, anticipated psychology in reacting against behaviorism and recognizing the importance of the self. In the middle thirties, as an undergraduate in sociology at the University of Chicago, I was exposed to the writings of Cooley (8) and Mead (13) on the self. This was where I took on the phenomenological approach. Not until several years later were the self and phenomenology introduced, or rather reintroduced, into psychology. I say reintroduced because James (12) had recognized the importance of the self, and was a phenomenologist as well.

While a number of persons have contributed to the theory, including Raimy (16), Snygg and Combs (21), and many others who have been associated with Rogers, there has been no other comparable exposition of the theory nor are there any adequately stated alternatives or variations of it. Rogers' terminology differs in some respects from that used by other client-centered writers, but the basic concepts are similar if not identical. For example, some theorists, including myself (14), have used the term self-esteem to refer to what Rogers designates as positive self-regard.

Comparison with other formulations

"Me" versus "I".   Several theorists (2, 4, 13, 22) have emphasized two aspects of the self, essentially distinguishing between the *self as object,* the "me," and the *self as subject,* the "I." The first is often referred to as the *self-concept,* the second as the *ego,* although, as Hall and Lindzey (9, p. 468) point out, there is no general agreement upon terms. James called the "me" the empirical self and the "I" the pure ego—the sense of personal identity or the judging thought. This personal identity, he suggested, may not exist as a fact, "but it would exist as a *feeling* all the same; the consciousness of it would be there, and the psychologist would still have to analyze that" (12, p. 333). The ego would appear to be self-consciousness. Mead's conceptions of the "I" and the "me" appear to be similar, although his discussion is difficult to follow. The "I" appears to be the awareness of the self as of the moment of action (13, pp. 173–178, 192).

These concepts, while preferable to the idea of the "I" as an executive, which lends itself to reification, are vague and difficult to pin down. At least I am not able to differentiate actually, practically, or operationally between the executive aspects of the self, and the self as an object to the self. The self of Snygg and Combs is both an object and doer. Others, including Allport (1) and Sherif and Cantril (20), also appear to adopt this view. Hilgard (10) suggests that the concept of the self as a doer is an error into which psychologists have been led by the commonsense or lay view that behavior seems to be self-determined.

In Rogers' theory the self-concept, although an important determiner of behavior, is not an executive or doer. There is no need for positing such an executive. The organism is by nature continually active, seeking its goal of actualization, and the self as part of the organism is also seeking actualization through its constant activity. The self-concept thus influences the direction of activity, rather than initiating it and directing it entirely. Thus Rogers avoids the problem of reification and the ambiguousness of the concept of the "I" or the ego as an executive. James' sense of personal identity might be considered a part of the self-concept, and the ego or "I" as the awareness of the self-concept. However, I am not sure that this solution is entirely satisfactory.

Ideal self. In his recent formulation of the concept of the ideal self Rogers indicates that the perception of the ideal self becomes more realistic, and the self becomes more congruent with the ideal self, as an outcome of therapy. This suggests that personality disturbance is characterized by an unrealistic self-ideal, and/or incongruence between the self-concept and the self-ideal. This formulation has been the basis of some research by the client-centered school (e.g., 3). But it is not incorporated in Rogers' statement of the theory. The theory apparently does not recognize conflict between the self-concept and the self-ideal as a source of disturbance, but emphasizes the conflict between the self-concept and organismic experiences as its source. This is in contrast to some other theories in which the self-ideal is a central concept and an important factor in psychological adjustment of maladjustment, e.g., Horney (11).

The self. The notion of the self, or the self-structure, is broader than the self-concept. It includes the self-concept and the ideal self. What else it includes, is not clear. Combs and Snygg speak of the phenomenal self, defined as the "organization of all the ways an individual has of seeing himself" (6, p. 126). The self-concept includes "only those perceptions about self which seem most vital or important to the individual himself" (6, p. 127). How these are to be differentiated is not indicated. Rogers considers the self-concept to be in the person's awareness, whereas the self may include aspects not in awareness.

Problems of operational definition

Rogers made an effort to keep his constructs and concepts so that they can be operationally defined. The phenomenological approach, it seems to me, fosters this effort. One is not concerned about the "real" self, the "real" environment, etc., but with the perceptions of particular individuals. The self-concept and the self-ideal are perceptions which can be studied and objectified by instruments such as the Q-sort, or by tests of the "Who am I" variety. The latter, though ideally suited for use with client-centered theory, have not, however, to my knowledge, been used in connection with this theory.

Rogers points out the problem of operationally defining the organismic experiences which, it is assumed, conflict with the self-concept. The aspects of the self other than the self-concept and the self-ideal, are also not operationally defined. Maybe we do not need these concepts. I see no need for unconscious elements of the self, for example. Aspects of the self which are not in awareness but which can be brought into awareness, can be tapped by instructions such as "Sort these statements in terms of your concept of yourself as a father." The self, insofar as it is behaviorally effective, may consist only of the various self-perceptions—thus resolving the problem posed above about the area of the self apart from the self-concept and the self-ideal. The organismic experiences, on the other hand, as an essential aspect of the theory, must be brought within the realm of measurement. The approach of Chodorkoff (5), using Q-sorts of self-referent items by clinicians as an "objective description" of the total experience of the individual, though operational, may be questioned as to its validity.

There is also the problem, pointed out by Combs and Soper (7), that although the self-concept may be operationally defined as the individual's statements about himself, these statements do not necessarily correspond to his perception of himself. His statements may be inaccurate for a number of reasons, including inability or unwillingness to give an accurate report. Yet there is no other approach to determining the self-concept, since by definition it is the perception of the self by the individual, and no one else can report upon it or describe it.

In general, what is needed is a more formal theoretical statement which would lead to testable hypotheses for research, not only with clients in therapy, but in many other situations, with many other kinds of subjects.

Summary

The aspects of Rogers' theory which relate to his central formulation of the self-concept have been summarized. A comparison with the thinking of others regarding the self attempted to clarify some differences and showed other differences in need of resolution. Some problems of operational definition were briefly discussed.

References

1. Allport, G. W. The ego in contemporary psychology. *Psychol. Rev.*, 1943, 50, 451–468. Also in *Personality and social encounter: selected essays*. Boston: Beacon Press, 1960. Pp. 71–93.

2. Bertocci, P. A. The psychological self, the ego and personality. *Psychol. Rev.*, 1945, 52, 91–99.

3. Butler, J. M., & Haigh, G. V. Changes in the relation between self-concepts and ideal concepts consequent upon client-centered counseling. In C. R. Rogers & R. F. Dymond (Eds.), *Psychotherapy and personality change*. Chicago: Univer. Chicago Press, 1954. Pp. 55–76.

4. Chein, I. The awareness of the self and the structure of the ego. *Psychol. Rev.*, 1944, 51, 504–514.

5. Chodorkoff, B. Self-perception, perceptual defense, and adjustment. *J. abnorm. soc. Psychol.*, 1954, 49, 508–512.

6. Combs, A. W., & Snygg, D. *Individual behavior.* Rev. ed. New York: Harper, 1959.

7. Combs, A. W., & Soper, D. W. The self, its derivative terms, and research. *J. Indiv. Psychol.*, 1957, 13, 134–145. Also in A. E. Kuenzli (Ed.), *The phenomenological problem.* New York: Harper, 1959. Pp. 31–48.

8. Cooley, C. H. *Human nature and the social order.* New York: Scribner's, 1902.

9. Hall, C. S., & Lindzey, G. *Theories of personality.* New York: Wiley, 1957.

10. Hilgard, E. R. Human motives and the concept of the self. *Amer. Psychologist*, 1949, 4, 374–382. Also in H. Brand (Ed.), *The study of personality.* New York: Wiley, 1954. Pp. 347–361.

11. Horney, K. *Neurosis and human growth.* New York: Norton, 1950.

12. James, W. *The principles of psychology.* Vol. 1. New York: Holt, 1890.

13. Mead, G. H. *Mind, self and society.* Chicago: Univer. Chicago Press, 1934.

14. Patterson, C. H. *Counseling and psychotherapy: theory and practice.* New York: Harper, 1959.

15. Pepinsky, H. B., & Pepinsky, P. N. *Counseling: theory and practice.* New York: Ronald, 1954.

16. Raimy, V. C. Self-reference in counseling interviews. *J. consult. Psychol.*, 1948, 12, 153–163. Also in A. E. Kuenzli (Ed.), *The phenomenological problem.* New York: Harper, 1959. Pp. 76–95.

17. Rogers, C. R. Some observations on the organization of personality. *Amer. Psychologist*, 1947, 2, 358–368. Also in A. E. Kuenzli (Ed.), *The phenomenological problem.* New York: Harper, 1959. Pp. 49–75.

18. Rogers, C. R. *Client-centered therapy.* Boston: Houghton Mifflin, 1951.

19. Rogers, C. R. A theory of therapy, personality, and interpersonal relationships, as developed in the client-centered framework. In S. Koch (Ed.), *Psychology: a study of a science.* Vol. 3. New York: McGraw-Hill, 1959. Pp. 184–256.

20. Sherif, M., & Cantril, H. *The psychology of ego-involvements.* New York: Wiley, 1947.

21. Snygg, D., & Combs, A. W. *Individual behavior.* New York: Harper, 1949.

22. Symonds, P. M. *The ego and the self.* New York: Appleton-Century-Crofts, 1951.

D. Bannister

A SUMMARY OF PERSONAL
CONSTRUCT THEORY *

Introduction

Personal Construct Theory, G. A. Kelly (4), appeared *deus ex machina* after a more or less unpublished 15-year incubation period. The theory is based on the assumption that all men may be thought of as "scientists" in the sense that each is concerned with the prediction and control of his environment. Further, each individual develops his own personal repertoire of constructs by means of which he structures (interprets, conceptualises) his world and tries to anticipate events. These constructs may be thought of as the elements of a system by means of which the individual codifies his experience. Thus the psychology of personal constructs is concerned with the ways in which personal construct repertoires can be analysed and described in generalised terms, and with accounting for the ways in which they develop and change.

Implicit in the theory is the notion that an individual does not respond to the "real" situation X (whatever "real" might mean) but to situation X as he sees it. In turn his interpretation of situation X will be a function of his current construing system. Thus the prediction of human behaviour is primarily dependent on the degree to which construct systems can be theoretically and experimentally subsumed.

Theory

Kelly presented the core of his theory in a formal manner as a Fundamental Postulate and eleven elaborative corollaries.

Fundamental postulate

A person's processes are psychologically channelised by the ways in which he anticipates events.

Kelly emphasises in accounting for his selection of terms that "processes" denotes a concept of man as a continuously behaving organism. He is "not an object which is temporarily in a moving state but is himself a form of motion". "Psychologically" does not imply a conception of psychological *events*, but of events which we are conceptualising in a psychological *manner*, just as they can be con-

* From D. Bannister, "Personal Construct Theory: A Summary and Experimental Paradigm," *Acta Psychologia*, 1962, 20, 104–120. Pages 104–110 reprinted by permission of the author and the Editor, *Acta Psychologia*.

ceptualised in a sociological or physiological manner. "Channelised" implies that a person's processes are not formless but structured, the structure both facilitating and restricting a person's range of activities. "Anticipates" emphasises the motivational nature of the theory. "Anticipation is both the push and pull of the psychology of personal constructs". "Events"—here the teleological nature of psychological processes is implied since "events" refers to future reality.

1 Construction corollary

A person anticipates events by construing their replications.

Kelly argues that construing is not to be confounded with verbal formulation since a person's behaviour may be based on many equivalence-difference patterns which are never communicated in symbolic speech. These may include construing patterns arising in infancy before verbal symbols are available and non-verbal (physiological) construing patterns. It is implied that both pre-verbal and physiological patterns would fall within the range of convenience of construct theory but in practice it seems clear that the focus of convenience of the theory is those construing patterns with equivalent verbal formulations.

The basic argument is that the recurrence of events gives rise to perceived similarities and *per se* differences. Thus the developing organism reaches a point at which 'what is predicted is not that tomorrow will be a duplicate of today but that there are replicative aspects of today's events which may be safely predicted'.

The nature of construing as essentially a question of "similarity-contrast" perception is underlined by reference to basic activities such as counting—"counting makes sense if the things are distinguishable from each other and it makes sense only in the respect that they are alike. Before we can count them we must construe their concrete differences from each other, their abstract likenesses to each other and their abstract differences from other things which are not to be counted". This seems to be the import of the adage that 'you can't add cows and horses' (except when they are construed as 'animals').

2 Individuality corollary

Persons differ from each other in their construction of events.

"People can be seen as differing from each other not only because there may have been differences in the events which they have sought to anticipate but also because there are different approaches to the anticipation of the same events". Kelly argues that this viewpoint relieves his system of the need to make the sharp distinction between external and internal events, stimulus and response, organism and environment, which other systems have required. It is this corollary which would lead the construct theorist to look for explanations of differences in individual behaviour in terms of the differing subjective worlds which individuals inhabit.

3   Organisation corollary

Each person characteristically evolves for his convenience in anticipating events a construction system embracing ordinal relationships between constructs.

"Not only do men differ in their constructions of events but they also differ in the ways they *organize* their constructions of events". This organising is aimed at minimizing incompatibilities and inconsistencies.   Thus a single construct may be superordinate to another single construct in either of two senses.   The construct "good-bad" may subsume the construct "intelligent-stupid" by extending the line of cleavage ("good" includes—inter alia—"intelligent" and "bad"—inter alia—"stupid").   Alternatively the construct "good-bad" may be subsumed under the "evaluative" pole of the construct "evaluative-descriptive".   In the latter case there has been abstraction across the cleavage line.   Whole subsystems of constructs may be subordinate or superordinate to each other.

4   Dichotomy corollary

A person's construction system is composed of a finite number of dichotomous constructs.

Kelly's precise definition of a construct ("a construct is a way in which two things are alike and by the same token different from a third") is derived from this corollary.   He argues that at least three elements are required for a construct to be formed, two to supply the replicative aspect which gives rise to the similarity pole and one to supply the non-replicative aspect which is the basis of the contrast pole.   All constructs are assumed to be dichotomous.

Kelly points out that although one pole may be in use in isolation it only exists by virtue of its contrasting pole, even though a specific verbal label may not exist for this contrasting pole.   "Red" is meaningful only by virtue of "non-red" elements which fall within the *range of convenience* of the construct.   "Thus it makes sense to point to a chair and say 'that is not a table', it makes no sense to point to a sunset and say 'that is not a table' ".

Scalar constructs are said to be built out of dichotomous constructs, the scales representing superordinate constructs which are further abstractions of separate scalar values.   Thus "more greyness—less greyness" is a further abstraction of the construct "black-white".

5   Choice corollary

A person chooses for himself that alternative in a dichotomised construct through which he anticipates the greater possibility for extension and definition of his system.

Since the fundamental postulate asserted that the anticipation of events is the dynamic of psychological processes it follows that in choosing between the two poles of any particular construct an individual will necessarily choose the one which favours successful anticipation in the future—the one which best elaborates the anticipatory (construct) system as a whole.

Kelly is careful to point out that the best elaboration may be in terms of definition *or* extension or both. Definition is the name given to the system's becoming more explicit and clear cut in construing elements already subsumed, extension is the name given to the system's becoming more comprehensive so that it may subsume new elements. An example of the difference between the two types of elaboration is the choice which frequently faces scientific research workers—whether to conduct experiments which will increase the predictive accuracy of an explanation over a restricted range of data (its focus of convenience) or seek to apply the explanation to new types of data and widen its *range* of convenience.

6   Range corollary

A construct is convenient for the anticipation of a finite range of events only.

"One may construe tall houses versus short houses, tall people versus short people, tall trees versus short trees but one does not find it convenient to construe tall weather versus short weather, tall light versus short light or tall fear versus short fear. Weather, light and fear are, for most of us at least, clearly outside the range of convenience of the construct "tall-short".

This underlines the fact that for Kelly the two poles of a construct *between them* define the range of convenience of the construct. In traditional logic things are either A or not—A, for Kelly not—A *only* includes those things which are within the range of convenience of the construct A—not A. Elements outside its range of convenience cannot meaningfully be included under not—A, they are simply irrelevant.

7   Experience corollary

A person's construction system varies as he successively construes replications of events.

"The constructions one places upon events are working hypotheses which are about to be put to the test of experience. As one's anticipations or hypotheses are successively revised in the light of the unfolding sequence of events a construction system undergoes a progressive evolution".

In repeating the phrase "replication of events" Kelly is stressing that the themes perceived as replicated are particular to the subject. Thus in learning experiments the subject may fail to construe as replicating elements the reinforcements and non-reinforcements that the experimenter perceives and, indeed, arranges. The subject may perceive entirely different themes as replicated. Thus "when a subject fails to meet the experimenter's expectations it may be inappropriate to say that 'he has not learned'; rather one might say that 'what the subject learned was not what the experimenter expected him to learn' ".

8 Modulation corollary

The variation in a person's construction system is limited by the permeability of the constructs within whose range of convenience the variants lie.

This corollary defines the condition governing the total amount of change possible within a construct system or subsystem. It is assumed that "determination and freedom are two complementary aspects of structure. They cannot exist without each other any more than up can exist without down or right without left. Neither freedom nor determination are absolutes. A thing is free with respect to *something*; it is determined with respect to *something else*". A construct system is free or determined with respect to its permeability. The more permeable the person's *superordinate* constructs, the more likely he is to be able to vary *subordinate* aspects of his construing system (in order to subsume new data) without psychological collapse. The difference between a permeable and an impermeable construct is exemplified by the difference between a theoretical formulation and a hypothetical formulation in science. "A hypothesis is deliberately constructed so as to be relatively impermeable and brittle so that there can be no question about what it embraces and no doubt about its being wholly shattered or left intact at the end of an experiment. A theory is not so inflexibly constructed. It is stated in relatively permeable terms so that it may in the future embrace many things which we have not yet thought of".

9   Fragmentation corollary

A person may successively employ a variety of construction sub-systems which are inferentially incompatible with each other.

The incompatibility of construct subsystems exists only if they are directly compared; reference to superordinate systems utilised by the person will show a collateral line of descent from one subsystem to the other.

Kelly exemplified this with a construing system of an imaginary psychologist who argued that thumb-sucking for 4 hours a day in the child would lead to say self-indulgent behaviour in the adult.   If we ignore the holding of at least two construct subsystems of differing degrees of superordinacy by the psychologist, then we will be driven to conclude that his inference is a *non sequitur*.   He ought to believe that 4 hours thumb-sucking a day in the child will lead to 15 hours thumb-sucking a day in the adult.   (Inferring from the *single* subsystem which says that adults are larger in all ways than children.)   But if we examine the superordinate constructs he is using to construe child and adult behaviour, we will find permeable superordinate constructs (e.g. a construct of "narcissistic tendency") which (however poor their actual predictive value may be) enables the psychologist to maintain two subsystems which are, by *immediate inference,* incompatible. To know a person's low level construing and consequent behaviour today is not to be able to predict his low level construing and consequent behaviour tomorrow unless we know the superordinate construct systems which govern both.

10   Communality corollary

To the extent that one person employs a construction of events which is similar to that employed by another his psychological processes are similar to those of the other person.

This implies that we should anticipate similarities in psychological process between people of similar construct systems (even if they experience different events) rather than expecting similarities in psychological process between people experiencing the same events.

11   Sociality corollary

To the extent that one person construes the construction process of another he may play a role in a social process involving the other person.

In standard usage a role is an ongoing pattern of behaviour that follows from a person's understanding of how the others who are associated with him in his task think.   Thus a driver in traffic is able successfully to play a role (i.e. avoid collision) to the extent that he construes the construction processes (those concerned with driving) of other drivers.

To construe the construction processes of another is not necessarily to use identical constructs. It is to possess constructs which subsume another's within their range of convenience. Thus for a psychotherapist to play a role in the social processes of a neurotic (e.g. cure him) would not involve the psychotherapist in thinking neurotically but it would require him to have constructs which subsume those of the neurotic (e.g. this neurotic is showing "conditioned avoidance responses", "irrational attitudes", or is "orally fixated" and so forth). . . .

Differentiating characteristics of personal construct theory

Bruner (3) fairly described Personal Construct Theory as "a theory of cognition extrapolated into a theory of personality". The theory purports to be self-sufficient and to comprehend all aspects of psychological process within its range of convenience. For Kelly man is "nothing but a bundle of constructs" by which he means (in line with the philosophy of constructive alternativism) that we may usefully (i.e. for predictive purposes) construe man as nothing but a bundle of constructs. The theory is explicitly self-referring in that it is a way of construing which is itself subject to the laws assumed to govern construing. It must similarly comment on other theoretical frameworks as forms of construing. In emphasis the theory differs from current theoretical frameworks in three respects.

1   It stresses that a person's responses are made in terms of the situation as *he* conceptualises it. True, traditional experimental methods in describing the "real" situation (i.e. the situation as the experimenter conceptualises it) and in measuring the subject's response to this situation, allow us to infer the nature of the subject's conceptualisation from the nature of the response. This traditional approach tends to focus on the experimenter's view of the situation to the point where responses which are not meaningful in terms of this view are regarded as without content. The subject *failed* to learn, the subject was *unmotivated,* the subject did *not* perceive a, b or c. Thus the question of what the subject thought he was doing while he was not responding in the prescribed manner may be by-passed. Personal Construct Theory focuses attention on the idea of seeking directly and explicitly to measure the subject's view of his situation as distinct from regarding his evaluation of stimuli as an intervening variable to be inferred from the stimulus-response pattern.

2   The theory explicitly seeks to account for the behaviour of the experimenter and the behaviour of the subject within the one set of parameters. True, Freudian theory is constantly reminding the analyst that his

reactions to his subject are governed by psychodynamic laws just as are the reactions of subject to analyst but in general the psychologist holds himself to be as separate from his subject as the chemist is from his acids and alkalis. Kelly argues that the whole business of formulating and testing generalisations is a form of construing and the psychologist may use the same generalisations regarding tightness-looseness, constellatory and propositional constructs and so on to analyse and comment on his own thinking that he applies to the thinking of his subject.

3   The theory sets out to account for man as a "thinking animal" rather than resting on dynamics such as the "pleasure principle" or the "law of effect". In having, as its model, man as cognitively striving to control his world it makes the phenomenon of thinking central rather than regarding it as a system of defence mechanisms at the behest of unconscious wishes or as a rather complex pattern of learned responses less amenable to study than the reactions of the rat. . . .

References [1]

1. Bannister, D., Conceptual structure in thought-disordered schizophrenics. *J. Ment. Sci.*, 1960, *106*, 445.

2. Barendregt, J. T., *Research in Psychodiagnostics.* Mouton & Co. The Hague: 1961.

3. Bruner, J. S., A cognitive theory of personality. *Contemporary psychology*, 1956, *I*, 12.

4. Kelly, G. A., *The psychology of personal constructs.* Vols. I and II. New York: Norton.

5. Landfield, A. W., Stern, M. and Fjeld, S., Social conceptual processes and change in students undergoing psychotherapy. *Psychological Reports*, 1961, *8.*

6. Levy, L. H., Personal constructs and predictive behaviour. *J. abn. and Soc. Psychol.*, 1956, *53*, 1.

7. ——— and Dugan, R. D., A factorial study of personal constructs. *J. Consult. Psychol.*, 1956, *20*, 1.

8. Osgood, C. E., Suci, G. J. and Tannenbaum, P. H., *The measurement of meaning.* University of Illinois Press, 1957.

[1] Since the paper has been edited, not all references remain in the body of the paper. For reasons of general interest, however, we have chosen to leave the *list* of references intact.

Lawrence A.
Pervin

EXISTENTIALISM, PSYCHOLOGY, AND PSYCHOTHERAPY *

Recently there has been a growing interest in existentialism. While it has already gained some determined adherents and some vehement enemies, the majority of psychologists and social scientists of related disciplines remain confused about the place of existentialism in their particular field of endeavor. The reasons for this are many: the philosophical nature of existentialism, the varying approaches and emphases commonly called existential, the lack of clarity and completeness in the existential approaches. While thus there are many reasons for the evident confusion, very likely the main reason is the lack of familiarity with existential writings, concepts, and approaches. The following attempts to introduce the reader to some of the basic elements of existentialism and to point to its relevance to psychology and psychotherapy.

Fundamental concepts of existentialism

As described by Tillich (1944), "Existence" emerged in the 1840's and was represented in the works of Schelling, Kierkegaard, and Marx. The movement then subsided until the 1880's. A rebirth was experienced in the *"lebensphilosophie"* or Philosophy of Life of Nietzsche. Contemporary philosophy of experienced existence, represented in the works of Heidegger and Jaspers, has resulted from a combination of Nietzsche's Philosophy of Life with Husserl's phenomenology.

While the existential philosophers express a good deal of variability in their views, there is also some common ground or group of common traits which justifies calling them all existential philosophers. Perhaps most important is the concern with Existence—man in a situation. It is out of this particular common concern that common emphases emerge.

One major aspect of the "existential view" is that of the significance of the individual. As described by Tillich: "Where there is an Existentialist point of view there is the problem of the human situation experienced by the individual" (1952, p. 130). Historically, it was the threat of the loss of the individual person which drove the revolutionary existentialists of the nineteenth century to their attack. The attack has led to a particular view of the individual, for he is now

* From Lawrence A. Pervin, "Existentialism, Psychology, and Psychotherapy," *Amer. Psychologist*, 1960, *15*, 305–309. Reprinted by permission of the author and the Managing Editor, the American Psychological Association.

seen as singular, unique, and irreplaceable. The individual is not just a member of the crowd and the herd, he is unrepeatable. For Kierkegaard the only existential problem is to exist as an individual. This view of the individual has, in part, led to the existentialist's concern with death, for it is here as nowhere else that the individual is himself alone and completely irreplaceable.

The attack and the rebellion further revolve around the existential view of the singular and unique individual. For the existentialists man is free. For Kierkegaard freedom is the self. Nietzsche's individual freely affirms. For Jaspers existence is freedom, and for Sartre consciousness is freedom. Compare Tillich's statement: "Man is essentially 'finite freedom'; freedom not in the sense of indeterminacy but in the sense of being able to determine himself through decisions in the center of his Being" (1952, p. 52) with Freud's: "what we call our ego is essentially passive. . . . We are 'lived' by unknown and uncontrollable forces" (1957, p. 214). Freud's deterministic view of man represents a complete opposite to the existential view of man as absolute freedom. This freedom is highly valued, for it is part of that which distinguishes man from other animals and makes him a human being. Part of this is also the ability of man to see himself as a self, to have consciousness, to be reflective, to question his own existence. These are powers and possibilities of man and man alone.

Freedom involves freedom from and freedom to. Both involve freedom of the instincts, and both involve responsibility. Man is responsible for Being—for his own existence, for his freedom and his choices, for the realization of himself. Man is responsible for being himself and so for being authentic. To flee from one's freedom and responsibility is to be inauthentic, to live in despair and "Bad Faith." Life in Nietzsche's Philosophy of Life is "the process in which the power of being actualizes itself" (Tillich, 1952, p. 27). For Tillich, man is "asked to make of himself what he is supposed to become, to fulfill his destiny. In every act of moral self-affirmation man contributes to the fulfillment of his destiny, to the actualization of what he potentially is" (Tillich, 1952, p. 52).

Existentialists are concerned with the meaning of life. Contemporary existential philosophers are particularly concerned with the problem of restoring meaning to life. According to Tillich, twentieth century man has experienced the universal breakdown of meaning, he has "lost a meaningful world and a self which lives in meanings" (1952, p. 139). This concern about the meaning of life and self enters into the existential view of psychopathology and psychotherapy.

As one examines the above points, he realizes that he has seen similar points made by noted men of a variety of disciplines. The ideas of Fromm correspond in a number of ways to those of the existentialists. Fromm (1941) talks of man as wanting to have a sense of personal identity, to become a unique individual. Because he has fewer predetermined courses of behavior than any other animal, man has gained freedom. But, not freedom to develop as an individual. Concern with the problems of existence, freedom, meaning, and the realization of the individual exemplifies Fromm's indebtedness to existential thought. Goldstein's emphasis upon the unique individual and the realization of potentialities are similarly existential in character.

While existentialism is a European creation and the above theorists are of European heritage, the spirit of the existential rebellion and the need for a new view of man have not left our American scholars untouched. The theory of Carl Rogers is phenomenological in character and stresses the individual and self-realization. Also, the psychology of George Kelly corresponds, in part, to the "existential view." There is a concern with the personal meaning of events to the individual. As we shall soon see, Binswanger and the existential psychoanalysts stress the world-design of the individual. Kelly (1955), in a similar way, stresses the understanding of the construct system of the individual—the way he construes the world. Furthermore, Kelly emphasizes the future as a factor in human behavior and that the individual's construction of the past is open to change—he is not bound to the past.

Some theorists openly avow their indebtedness to the existentialists. In others the influence has been more subtle. And, finally, some have independently arrived at similar points of view. In any case, it must be recognized that existentialism has had and does have something to offer. The possibility that psychology can independently arrive at the desired goals should not be the basis for an evaluation of existentialism. If existentialism can aid in the achievement of the desired goals, psychologists cannot afford to remain ignorant of its concepts. On the other hand, uncritical acceptance forebodes a similarly unhealthy situation.

Two existential approaches

The existentialists are concerned with the beings that we are. It seems natural, therefore, that at least some of these philosophers should turn to the problems of normal man, abnormal man, and the process of "making" the latter into the former. In the following, two existential approaches will be briefly discussed: the approach represented in the new volume of *Existence* (May, Angel, & Ellenberger, 1958) and the approach represented in "On Logotherapy and Existential Analysis" (Frankl, 1958). The two are especially noteworthy since the former culminates primarily from work with psychotic patients while the latter culminates almost entirely from work with neurotic patients.

Existential analysis

The existential analysts emphasize the study of the experiencing individual. Events are looked at in terms of their meaning for the individual. He is seen as a Being-in-the-World. The belief is that the individual reveals himself through his world-project or world-design. According to Kuhn, the world-design is that "which is laid by every human upon everything that exists, through which he interprets everything that exists, and from which he gets a context of reference, wherein each person's existence (*Dasein*) is determined" (May *et al.*, 1958, p. 396).

In an attempt to get at the patient's inner universe of experience, the existential analyst studies how the phenomenological coordinates of time, space, causality, and materiality are experienced. Within the time dimension the future is seen as particularly significant. Medard Boss calls man's capacity to transcend the immediate situation the basic and unique characteristic of human existence. The approach to the future is seen as particularly significant because it affects the view of the past and determines those parts which will be influential in the present. The Being of a person is characterized in terms of three modes: *Umwelt*—the biological world; *Mitwelt*—the world of one's fellow men; and *Eigenwelt*—the mode of relationship to oneself. The three are simultaneous modes of Being-in-the-World. Anxiety, hostility, and aggression are normal states and part of Being-in-the-World.

Human psychopathology is seen in a number of ways by the existentialists. According to Tillich, in the neurotic the self which is affirmed is a reduced one and some or many of its potentialities are not admitted to actualization. From Kierkegaard's view the neuroses and psychoses would be accompanied by a loss of self, an inner alienation. Jaspers views the psychotic as one who has lost his own existence and so has lost the existence of reality. In general, existential analysis points to the deviations of the structure of existence as representative of psychopathology.

The process of existential psychotherapy remains somewhat ill-defined. The central aspect of the process appears to be the patient's recognition and experiencing of his own existence. The patient is oriented toward fulfillment of his existence. As regards technique, there is little that is specific. The belief is that a flexible approach is necessary to understand the person-in-his-world. Technique is varied from patient to patient and from one phase of treatment to another: "What will best reveal the existence of this particular patient at this moment in history?"

Logotherapy

The "school" of Victor Frankl has been known under various names: Logotherapy, Existential Analysis, and Medical Ministry. The name Existential Analysis refers to the influences of Kierkegaard, Heidegger, Jaspers, and other existential philosophers. It is neither related to Binswanger's Daseinanalyse nor to Sartre's Existential Psychoanalysis.

Like all existentialists, Frankl is concerned with preserving the unity of being. An interpretation of nature in terms of concentrically layered structures is felt to preserve this unity. For Frankl, man lives in three dimensions: the somatic, the psychic, the spiritual. Furthermore, human existence is characterized by its spirituality, freedom, and responsibility.

Logotherapy focuses upon the search for meaning in human existence. While psychoanalysis emphasizes the will-to-pleasure and individual psychology the will-to-power, existential analysis emphasizes the will-to-meaning. "This will-to-meaning is the most human phenomenon of all since an animal never worries about the meaning of its existence" (Frankl, 1955, p. 9). Ultimate meaning is represented in the individual's unique task in life, which awaits realization in his personality. Meaning is found through actualizing value, through self-realization.

As stated above, man is both responsible and free. Responsibility springs from the singularity and uniqueness of existence. One is responsible to life for the fulfillment of the spiritual and the realization of values. Freedom means freedom in the face of instincts, inherited disposition, and environment. It involves the fundamental possibility of choosing. Man can decide whether he shall be at all—he can choose suicide—and in this way is distinguished from all other kinds of being.

The will-to-meaning can remain frustrated and unfulfilled. This condition is called existential frustration. Existential frustration is not something pathological itself. But, when it does become pathogenic, it is called a noogenic neurosis. This neurosis is rooted in spiritual conflicts and ethical problems.

For Frankl, the neurotic lacks "instinctive sureness" in sensing his task. He blocks the realization of his own potentialities and plays one life task off against the other. The outstanding feature of the neurotic is his escape from freedom and responsibility. It is seen as a mode of existence in which the person blames his destiny, his childhood, and his environment for what he is.

While not all neuroses are noogenic, there is a psychotherapy appropriate to them: "When a neurosis is really noogenic, spiritually rooted, it requires a psychotherapy having a spiritual basis, and that is what I call Logotherapy, in contrast to psychotherapy in the narrower sense of the word" (Frankl, 1958, p. 34).

As a therapy, Logotherapy calls upon the spiritual in man and upon his will-to-meaning. Frankl proposes two mottos for all psychotherapy: "He who knows a Why of living surmounts almost every How" (Nietzsche) and "If we take people as they are, we make them worse. If we treat them as if they were what they ought to be, we help them to become what they are capable of becoming" (Goethe). Logotherapy, then, seeks to help the patients become what they are capable of becoming, to bring out the ultimate possibilities of the patients, to enable them to find meaning in existence.

The two theories and techniques of psychotherapy described here may be characterized as outgrowths of the existential movement. There are a number of criticisms appropriate to their systems. The two systems are deficient in both theory and technique. While Western belief is seen as holding that understanding follows technique, existential psychoanalysis holds that technique follows understanding. For understanding to be of use to psychology as a science it must be lawful understanding and thus available for formulation into theory. But, theory furnishes another problem for existential analysis. Kuhn states: "Existential analysis is not a finished, beautifully rounded theory which allows us to explain some, or all, events that occur in a psyche. Furthermore, we are at present still at the beginning of work in this direction" (1958, p. 397). Frankl similarly states: "We have not systematically delineated a theory of the neuroses" (1955, p. 201).

While each of these approaches is lacking in certain aspects, they do have contributions to make. The emphasis upon actualization of potentialities, the fulfillment of Being, has found its way into a number of psychotherapies. The attention Logotherapy calls to the significance of meaning in a person's life is well worth the attention of all psychotherapists: "The old question still faces us as it has faced humanity for ages past: What is the meaning of life . . . what might be called the moral and spiritual side of life, something that is basic in man" (Nehru, 1958, p. 110). It is probable that the finding of a personal and meaningful task in life can alleviate many neurotic difficulties. Edith Weisskopf-Joelson goes so far as to say: "Helping patients develop effective and socially acceptable defenses against anxiety—such as a supportive system of ethical values—seems a more realistic, even though perhaps a less ambitious goal of therapy than getting to the roots of the disorder" (1955, p. 702). Weisskopf-Joelson further points out the wisdom in de-emphasizing happiness as a goal and the wisdom of a philosophy that accepts suffering.

Frankl's therapy should be an especially useful aid in dealing with situations of unavoidable suffering.

Finally, the two systems have an approach or view to offer. They represent a badly needed "new view" of man—a view of man worthy of attention, study, and emulation. It is a view of man which allows for and emphasizes man's freedom and courage.

Conclusion

Existentialism and existential analysis can be criticized and found lacking on philosophical grounds. They can also be criticized and found lacking on psychological grounds. While I applaud the existentialists for their emphasis upon the unique individual, I find fault with their conclusions from this. Their emphasis has led them to abandon hope of understanding and predicting human behavior in a lawful way. The existentialists see science and objective reality as appealing to the universal person and to no one in their individuality. Since the individual is unique, they insist that he cannot be covered by laws for all men. Frankl states: "A real human person is not subject to rigid prediction. Existence can neither be reduced to a system nor deduced from it" (1955, p. 169). This emphasis is worthy in cautioning us against unrealistic generalizations and abstractions. The individual is free and unique. But, does this mean that he behaves unlawfully and unpredictably? There is something common to all these individuals that we are, and this may be a subject for scientific endeavor. The understanding of patterned and lawful aspects of human behavior is the subject of inquiry for psychology. If in some way all or part of behavior is lawful, then to that extent human behavior can be predicted. While the laws we ultimately arrive at may not lead to a complete understanding and prediction of each and every individual, or any individual, they may represent a considerable advance beyond the present darkness and mystery. The individual and the human must not be forgotten in abstractions, but psychology's attempt at a lawful understanding of human behavior must be pushed to its limit.

But, the realization of the inadequacies of a view should not blind us to the potential contributions. In Europe, under the direction of such men as Buytendijk, van Lennep, and Wellek, existential psychology and the phenomenological method have made some progress. There are continued reports of the growth in popularity of existential psychotherapy. At Harvard, tests derived from existential categories have already been formulated. Existentialism and existential analysis are far from representing a complete system or theory. It would be foolhardy to accept or reject them in their entirety. Perhaps they can be useful to psychology in terms of the approaches and views they offer. The existential view of man, his uniqueness, his freedom, his responsibility, his own frame of reference, and will-to-meaning are worthy of serious attention and investigation. Their emphasis upon that which distinguishes man from other animals, upon normal guilt, hostility, and anxiety, and upon such categories as that of temporality and spatiality are similarly noteworthy. They represent possible suggestions for further study by psychology. If approached in this light, I think that existentialism may have much to offer and psychology considerable to gain!

References

Frankl, V. E. *The doctor and the soul.* New York: Knopf, 1955.

Frankl, V. E. On logotherapy and existential analysis. *Amer. J. Psychoanal.*, 1958, *18*, 28–37.

Freud, S. The ego and the id. In J. Rickman (Ed.), *A general selection from the works of Sigmund Freud.* New York: Doubleday Anchor, 1957.

Fromm, E. *Escape from freedom.* New York: Farrar & Rinehart, 1941.

Kelly, G. A. *The psychology of personal constructs.* New York: Norton, 1955. 2 vols.

May, R., Angel, E., & Ellenberger, H. F. (Eds.) *Existence.* New York: Basic Books, 1958.

Nehru, J. The tragic paradox of our age. *New York Times*, 1958, Sept. 7, Section 8.

Tillich, P. Existential philosophy. *J. Hist. Ideas*, 1944, 5(1), 44–70.

Tillich, P. *Courage to be.* New Haven: Yale Univer. Press, 1952.

Weisskopf-Joelson, Edith. Some comments on a Viennese school of psychiatry. *J. abnorm. soc. Psychol.*, 1955, *51*, 701–703.

Walter
Katkovsky

SOCIAL-LEARNING THEORY AND MALADJUSTMENT

In 1954 Julian B. Rotter published *Social Learning and Clinical Psychology,* which presented a theory of human behavior based on learning concepts and principles. Social-learning theory, the name given this point of view, had been in the process of development for a number of years, and as a result of extensive research and weekly seminar discussions at Ohio State University concerning the logic of its concepts and postulates and the hypothetical deductions that could be drawn from them, the theory evolved as a set of systematic formulations for understanding and predicting complex human behavior. From the start, the aim was to provide the clinical psychologist with a framework for making decisions about psychological assessment and psychotherapy. Also from the start, the theory was regarded as a tentative statement of a group of related hypotheses which require research and exploratory application to clinical problems for its further development. Special attention was given to developing concepts and hypotheses for which reliable and valid measures could be developed so that changes and additions to the theory could be integrated with controlled research.

The purpose of this paper is to present the basic ideas and concepts of social-learning theory and to describe some ways in which these may help the reader understand adjustment problems and personality disturbances. First some of the basic assumptions concerning human beings and the study of their behavior will be considered. This will be followed by a description of the major concepts and basic hypotheses of the theory. The final section will deal with the application of these concepts to adjustment problems.

Basic assumptions

In order to theorize or formulate hypotheses about human behavior, personality theorists typically make a number of assumptions concerning the nature of man and the variables which will have the most influence on behavior. Specific hypotheses are then deduced from these assumptions and subjected to empirical test. To the extent that the deduced hypotheses are supported by scientific data, both the basic assumptions and the specific hypotheses derived from them gain support. The assumptions, then, act as a starting point for the theorist, and while they are never proved or disproved with absolute certainty, their validity is determined by the extent to which the ideas and hypotheses derived from them aid the theorist in achieving his purposes.

Social-learning theory defines its area of interest with an initial postulate which reads, "The unit of investigation for the study of personality is the interaction of the individual and his meaningful environment" (Rotter, 1954, p. 85). This postulate directs our attention to three things: (1) the individual, his behavior and personality, (2) the environment in which his behavior occurs, and (3) the interaction between the individual and his environment. A number of assumptions and ideas are presented by Rotter on each of these topics and these are summarized below.

Assumptions concerning behavior and personality

1   As is customary with all personality theories, social-learning theory uses the term "behavior" in a broad sense to include not only the individual's actions, but also his thoughts, feelings, desires, motives, etc.   Any learned human response is potentially of interest to the social-learning theorist, and what he chooses to study will be determined by the questions he seeks to answer.   Depending on his purpose, he may wish to study a specific skill, such as dancing, or he may wish to investigate affective reactions of pleasure or displeasure in response to a given stimulus, or he may deal with highly complex internal states such as conflict between opposing needs.

2   The study of personality is regarded as the study of learned behavior, i.e., behavior which develops and changes with experience. The social-learning theorist elects to restrict his investigation to learned reactions because he believes these to be most important in understanding complex human interpersonal behavior.   This is not to imply that unlearned behaviors are considered unimportant.   Reflex actions, biological conditions within the organism, maturational changes, and physiological adaptation are regarded as significant in establishing the conditions in which learning first occurs.   However, the social-learning theorist assumes that it is unnecessary and often unprofitable to attempt to trace learned reactions back to inherited, instinctual, or physiological processes.   Instead, he regards the meanings, feelings, and actions which the individual acquires in connection with unlearned behaviors as more significant in explaining his later behavior than the unlearned behaviors *per se*.   For example, in the study of sexual behavior, the values, attitudes, and physical responses learned in prior experiences dealing with sex are likely to predict the nature of an individual's sexual reactions better than an assessment of his physiological or biochemical state.

3   When studying personality, the theorist must decide to what extent he will conceptualize human behavior as having unity or interdependence and to what extent behaviors may be studied as independent and discrete.   Social-learning theory takes the point of view that personality has unity and that the prediction of any specific behavior is enhanced by studying its relation to the individual's past experiences and other behaviors.   The unity of personality results from the influence an individual's experiences have on one another.   New experiences are colored by what has happened to the person in the past, and old learning is changed by new experiences.   Personality unity is also fostered by the fact that different behaviors often lead to the same outcome or consequence for the individual and these then become *functionally related*.   For example, the person who

receives recognition and praise from others for telling jokes as well as for performing well academically will learn to associate these two behaviors with the same outcome. As a consequence, diverse reactions may take on the same meaning to the individual, and while he may behave differently in different situations, the same purpose may motivate his actions.

4   Another point of emphasis on which the personality theorist must take a position is the degree to which human behavior will be viewed as stable and unchanging and the degree to which it will be seen as alterable and varying under changing conditions. Social-learning theory's position is that all learned responses can be modified by new experiences and the emphasis is on flexibility and amenability to change. While it is assumed that as a person grows older, his behavior will become increasingly stable, the possibility of change will depend on his specific past experiences and not on age *per se.* No developmental stage is arbitrarily cited as a cutoff point after which change or new learning can no longer occur. The potential for change is always present.

5   The study of personality tends to emphasize people's characteristic or typical ways of behaving as contrasted with behaviors which are highly specific to a given situation. In social-learning theory, concepts have been developed which pertain both to general characteristics of behavior and to specific acts, although somewhat greater interest is placed on behavioral generality. The generality of behavior can be explained by the fact that different situations may take on essentially the same meaning to the individual because of similar learning experiences in those situations. If a person categorizes both the college classroom and the corner coffee shop as places where he might attract the attention of members of the opposite sex, his behavior in these two different situations is likely to be more similar than if he learns to associate one situation with academic efforts and the other with heterosexual pursuits. While the social-learning theorist is interested in behavioral generality, he also is concerned with circumstances which evoke specific actions and variations in behavior. In addition, the degree of behavioral consistency depends on an individual's unique experiences, and individual differences in the generality or specificity of behavior are regarded as an important topic of study.

Assumptions concerning the environment

1   In accord with field theory, social-learning theory places considerable importance on environmental factors in determining human behavior. The emphasis, however, is on the "meaningful" environment as perceived and interpreted by the individual rather than on

the objective environment. Each person attends selectively to his surroundings at any given time and attaches significance and meaning to the stimuli that confront him. The particular aspects of the environment with which he deals and the meanings he gives them are based on previous learning experiences. The unique learning experiences of a person result in individualistic perceptions and interpretations, and in order to explain the impact of situational conditions on his behavior, one must know the meaning which those conditions have for him. To the extent that social-learning theory stresses the individual's subjective interpretations of his environment, the theory assumes a phenomenological slant and rejects the position that behavior can be explained without inferring a mediational process between a stimulus and the individual's response. At the same time, the social-learning theorist notes that since the members of a given society—or for that matter, all human beings—share many common learning experiences, people's subjective interpretations of the environment have much similarity. Consequently it is unnecessary to rely completely on a subjective or phenomenological frame of reference to explain and predict human behavior.

2   Since a person may attach the same or similar meaning to many stimuli despite objective differences in them, diverse situations may in essence be the same for him and may result in the same ways of behaving. Similarly, stimuli which objectively remain the same may change their meaning for an individual as a function of time or changes which are not readily observable, and his behavior will change accordingly. The specific cues of the environment which assume meaning for the individual, and the fact that some are grouped together as similar and others are distinguished as different, are learned characteristics, and the social-learning theorist regards it as necessary to determine the nature of such past learning in order to explain and predict the behavior of an individual.

3   The theory is called a *social*-learning theory because it postulates that the major ways of behaving are learned in social situations and that other people constitute the most important aspects of the environment. The development of personality is seen as dependent primarily on the child's interactions and relationships with other people. While much of the behavior of an infant is motivated by biological needs (hunger, thirst, physical discomfort, etc.), the learning which occurs in conjunction with these needs promotes new social needs which involve the persons who care for him. Subsequently, the social needs are more significant in determining the individual's behavior than are the biological needs. Similarly, personality problems and ways of coping with them deal chiefly with an individual's relationships with other people; i.e., they involve his social adjustment.

4   In stating that the most important aspects of the environment are social, theorists with a social-learning point of view do not rule out the idea that a person interacts with and reacts to himself. Subjective awareness of personal characteristics or conditions, e.g., hunger, pain, sexual excitement, and emotional reactions, may serve as a stimulus for the individual's actions. In actuality, however, his response is to the meaning he gives these characteristics or conditions, and these are learned in his experiences with other people. A person may also react to himself in terms of a learned social norm as, for example, when he reacts to himself as thin or fat, handsome or ugly, intelligent or unintelligent. Whatever his reaction, it is based on learned meanings and on how he believes others who are important to him evaluate and react to that characteristic.

Assumptions concerning the interaction between personality and environment

1   The method of social-learning theory in investigating personality is historical; i.e., events are studied in sequence, and a particular behavior is related to relevant conditions which precede its appearance. However, it is unnecessary to attempt to trace a person's experiences since birth or early childhood in order to explain a particular behavior or predict its future occurrence. Also, the idea of a single or basic cause is rejected since any behavior can be related to numerous conditions and events in the past as well as in the present. Instead, the theorist or clinician is concerned with describing relevant antecedent conditions, and he recognizes that there are always numerous conditions that can be related to the behavior and that they can always be traced further back in time. The particular antecedents he chooses to emphasize and the scope of his historical analysis will depend on his purpose and on practical considerations, such as time and efficiency.

2   One of the most important assumptions made by social-learning theory is that human behavior has direction or purpose. Behavior is described as *goal-directe*d, i.e. as oriented toward or away from some aspect of the environment. A person may seek to gain a particular outcome or reward or to avoid a particular outcome or punishment. In social-learning theory, both *needs* and *goals* are inferred from the same directional interaction of an individual with his environment. When the description of the direction of the behavior pertains to the person, the term need is used; when attention is placed on the environmental conditions which determine the aim of the behavior, the term goal is used. For example, a child who asks his teacher to explain to him how to solve an arithmetic problem is described as expressing the need for dependence and as seeking in-

strumental help.   Both the need and the goal are inferred from the direction or purpose of the child's behavior.

3   The assumption that behavior has direction is based on the fact that actions are influenced by the consequences which follow them. If the environmental reaction to a person's behavior is favorable to that person, the reaction is described as a *positive reinforcement* and this reinforcement strengthens the probability that the same behavior will occur again.   If the environmental reaction is unfavorable or undesirable to the person, the reaction is a *negative reinforcement* and decreases the probability of that behavior occurring again.   The fact that satisfying end results tend to increase the probable occurrence of behavior which preceded them, and dissatisfying end results tend to decrease the occurrence of preceding behaviors, is often called the *principle of reinforcement* or the *law of effect*.   Many learning theories which employ the law of effect define a positive reinforcement on the basis of the drive reduction of a "tissue need," i.e., in terms of the diminution of a physiological drive such as hunger, thirst, or sex. Social-learning theory, however, regards this definition as too restrictive to explain complex human behavior and defines reinforcement in a broader sense to include "any action, condition or state that affects movement toward a goal" (Rotter, 1954, p. 98).   When an observable event changes the probability of occurrence of a behavior which preceded it, that event constitutes a reinforcement.

4   Reinforcements differ in value.   The greater the satisfaction an individual anticipates receiving from a reinforcement, the greater the value or importance he will place on that reinforcement.   Conversely, a person attaches little value or importance to reinforcements which he expects will bring him minimal satisfaction, and he assigns a minus value to reinforcements likely to be punishing or dissatisfying. The effect of reinforcements on behavior which precede them will depend on their value to the individual; the higher the reinforcement value, the greater the reinforcing effect on the behavior.   Reinforcements increase or decrease in value with new experiences.   When a reinforcement becomes associated with other positive reinforcements, its value will increase, whereas its association with negative reinforcements will result in a decrease in its value.

5   The specific conditions or events which act as reinforcers must be determined empirically through the study of a given group, culture, or individual.   Similarly, the differential values placed on reinforcements are associated with group and individual characteristics and cannot be assumed.   To some extent, members of a group who share common learning experiences are likely to react similarly to certain events and to attach similar values to reinforcements.   When the focus is on the behavior of a single person, however, one must determine the relative values that individual places on different rein-

forcements in order to predict how he will react when a given reinforcement occurs.

6   A final postulate of social-learning theory states, "The occurrence of a behavior of a person is determined not only by the nature
or importance of goals or reinforcements but also by the person's
anticipation or expectancy that these goals will occur" (Rotter, 1954,
p. 102).   The anticipation of future events as a function of one's
actions is called expectancy and is regarded by the social-learning
theorist as an essential variable in explaining and predicting the behavior of human beings.   What a person expects will happen will
depend on his past experiences concerning the consequences or outcomes of specific behaviors.   To the extent that he has been rewarded for acting in a particular way in the past, his expectancy for
receiving positive reinforcement for continuing to act in that way will
be high.   On the other hand, expectancy for being positively reinforced for behaviors which have been ignored or punished in the past
will be low.   New experiences will change an individual's expectancies depending on the degree to which the reinforcements which follow a behavior differ from those which occurred earlier following that
behavior.   If the new experience results in greater reward than in the
past, the expectancy will increase and the probability of the individual's acting in that same way again will increase.   If the reward
is not so great as before, the person's expectancy and the likelihood
of his repeating that behavior will both decrease.   Thus, expectancies are learned and are subject to change based on the continued
interaction between the individual and his meaningful environment.

7   The use of language is a major factor in the interactions between people and is regarded as very significant in the learning and
maintaining of behavior and personality characteristics.   Words,
ideas, and statements direct attention to specific cues and thereby
help to determine the aspects of the environment a person responds
to and the meaning he gives cues.   Or stated differently, language
plays an important part in defining the environment.   Language enables the individual to group varying situations together as similar
and to generalize and apply behavior which has been learned in one
situation to another.   Or conversely, language helps the individual to
discriminate between situations and thereby promotes changes in
expectancies and behavior from one set of conditions to another.   An
additional important function of language is that it reinforces behavior.
In some instances, words acts as symbols of reinforcements and enable the individual to maintain an expectancy that a particular reward
will be received in the future.   An example is the freshman college
student who studies diligently because he expects this will lead to his
receiving a college degree four years later, which in turn will lead to a
rewarding job, a promising future, etc.   In other instances, language

constitutes a reinforcement in its own right. Statements of praise, recognition, and affection from others are valued highly by most persons in our culture and have a profound influence on their behavior.

Concepts

In an attempt to explain and predict the behavior of an individual in any given situation, personality theories implicitly or explicitly ask such questions as, In what ways has he acted in similar situations in the past? What are alternative ways in which he might behave? What are the differential probabilities that he will act in one way or another? These questions are expressed in social-learning theory by the concept *behavior potential,* which refers to the idea that in any given situation, a variety of behaviors might occur and the potential occurrence of each will depend on the individual's past experiences with each. The behavior which most frequently led to positive reinforcement in comparable situations is the behavior with the greatest potential for occurring again. When the theorist is interested in more general personality characteristics rather than in a single behavior, the concept *need potential* is employed. This term refers to the potential occurrence of behaviors which are functionally related, i.e., which are directed toward the same or similar reinforcements. The distinction between the terms behavior potential and need potential is one of generality; the former refers to a single behavior, whereas the latter is more inclusive and may refer to a number of different acts which are associated with one another because in the past they have all led to the same reinforcement. Thus, one might speak of a student's behavior potential for studying. Or one might be concerned more generally with the student's need potential for academic achievement, which would include all behaviors associated with his academic work.

As indicated in the previous section, a second major concept in social-learning theory is *expectancy.* This is defined as "the probability held by the individual that a particular reinforcement will occur as a function of a specific behavior on his part in a specific situation" (Rotter, 1954, p. 107). The definition points to three separate factors as important to the concept. First, reference is made to "a particular reinforcement"; that is, a specific event which has meaning or value to the person serves as the directional force for the behavior in that the purpose is to bring about that event. Second, the definition notes that the expectancy pertains to "a specific behavior." Theoretically a different expectancy will be held for each behavior which in the past has been associated with the reinforcement. The behavior most likely to occur is the one for which the expectancy is highest that it will lead to the reinforcement. Third, attention is drawn to the importance of "a specific situation." The expectancy for a given reinforcement in one situation may be similar to or different from the expectancy that the reinforcement will occur in another situation. To the extent that different situations are perceived as similar, the expectancy concerning a particular behavior will generalize from one situation to another and thus will be the same or similar.

When the concern is with more general characteristics about the anticipation of future events, two additional concepts involving expectancies are used. *Freedom of movement* refers to the mean expectancy held when a variety of functionally related behaviors are considered. We might speak of the freedom of movement (or mean expectancies) for affiliation, achievement, dominance, or love, each of which represents a separate group of reinforcements which are functionally related. At a still higher level of abstraction and generality, we might describe a person's total state of adjustment in terms of this concept. That is, if an individual expects to be able to gain a great deal of success and satisfaction as a result of his behavior, he is described as having high freedom of movement for life's satisfactions, whereas someone with expectancies for failure, frustration, and punishment is described as having low freedom of movement.

Generalized expectancy refers to the influence of experience from similar situations on the expectancy held in a particular situation. The more an individual perceives a situation as similar to situations he has experienced in the past, the more his expectancies in the new situation will be generalized from past happenings. Generalized expectancies may be developed concerning varied aspects of situations. Different generalizations may be made concerning expectancies in situations with men, as compared with women, or in classrooms, as compared with social situations. One type of generalized expectancy to which social-learning theory has given considerable attention is *the belief in internal versus external control of reinforcements* (Rotter, 1966). The occurrence of a reinforcement may be viewed as a function of one's own behavior (internal control) or as a function of external influences over which one has little or no control (external control). An individual's belief in internal control is based on his assessment of his abilities, knowledge, personality characteristics, physical attributes, or any other characteristics he identifies with himself. Beliefs in external control, on the other hand, may be associated with ideas concerning chance, luck, fate, supernatural forces, or ways in which other people may control or influence the events in one's life. Beliefs in internal versus external control appear to be highly relevant to adjustment and maladjustment. An extreme external orientation may prevent the individual from seeing the part he plays in the difficulties he is having and thus may discourage change.

On the other hand, an extreme internal orientation in which an individual erroneously attributes many events to his own actions may be associated with delusions of grandeur, guilt reactions, and self-punitive behavior.

Reinforcement value is defined as the degree of preference for one reinforcement to occur if the possibilities of several reinforcements occurring are equal.   For example, the reinforcement value of attending a baseball game may be higher or lower than the reinforcement value of attending a concert, depending on an individual's preferences and the degree to which he expects one will be more satisfying than the other.   The value of a given reinforcement is a function of the reinforcements it has been associated with in past experiences.   The more an event has led to satisfying consequences in the past, the higher its positive value will be; and conversely, the more it has been associated with unpleasant happenings, the higher its negative value. A more generalized concept of reinforcement value is termed *need value;* this is defined as "the mean preference value of a set of functionally related reinforcements" (Rotter, 1954, p. 189).   Corresponding in level of abstraction with the concepts need potential and freedom of movement, need value pertains to the importance placed on one set of reinforcements, which through experience have become identified with one another, in comparison with another set.

Another concept of social-learning theory which refers to a special instance of reinforcement value is termed *minimal goal.*   It is possible to place the reinforcements which might occur in any given situation on a continuum in terms of their preference value.   Some of these reinforcements will lead to satisfaction and others to dissatisfaction.   Minimal goal is the theoretical dividing point between those reinforcements which are experienced as satisfactions and those which are experienced as dissatisfactions and is defined as "the lowest goal in a continuum of potential reinforcements for some life situation or situations which will be perceived as a satisfaction" (Rotter, 1954, p. 213).   If we consider course grades on the usual continuum from A to F, one student may be satisfied with his performance as long as he receives a D or better, while another may be dissatisfied with any grade less than a B.   The minimal goal of the latter clearly is considerably higher than that of the former.   An individual's minimal goals for affection, affiliation, dominance, or any other need describe the extent to which that need must be reinforced before he feels satisfied.   The higher the minimal goal, the more reinforcement of that need is required before satisfaction is experienced.

The major concepts of social-learning theory may be brought together into two basic formulas.   The first is

$$\text{B.P.}_{x, s1, Ra} = f\ (E_{x, Ra, s1}\ \&\ \text{R.V.}_a)$$

This formula reads, "The potential for behavior x to occur in situation 1 in relation to reinforcement a is a function of the expectancy of the occurrence of reinforcement a following behavior x in situation 1 and the value of reinforcement a" (Rotter, 1954, p. 108). The second formula is

$$N.P. = f \, (F.M. \, \& \, N.V.)$$

This reads, "The potentiality of occurrence of a set of behaviors that lead to the satisfaction of some need (need potential) is a function of the expectancies that these behaviors will lead to these reinforcements (freedom of movement) and the strength or value of these reinforcements (need value)" (Rotter, 1954, p. 110).

The concept of maladjustment

While social-learning theory is concerned with describing and predicting complex social behavior, it makes no effort to specify which behaviors are healthy and adjusted and which are pathological and maladjusted. In contrast with most psychiatric thinking, which points to certain behaviors as symptomatic of mental illness, and with many theories of personality, which equate a particular way of acting with psychological maturity or immaturity, social-learning theory takes the position that a scientific theory cannot designate the kinds of behaviors which are healthy or unhealthy, adjusted or maladjusted. The labeling of a particular act as maladjusted is in effect a value judgment which must be based on an ethical position and not on a scientific theory. The theory may describe some behaviors as more or less effective, efficient, or successful than others. Such judgments, however, can be made only in terms of the purpose or goal of the behavior, which in itself can be evaluated as healthy or pathological only as it conforms to or deviates from a particular ethical value.

By stating that theory does not indicate what is and what is not maladjusted behavior, the social-learning theorist does not imply that such judgments are unimportant. They are important for a least two reasons: first, professional workers in the field of mental health are called upon to make such judgments and to help bring about changes in people consistent with what is regarded as adjusted, desirable, healthy behavior, and second, these judgments reflect the ethical values which predominate in a given culture and the learning problems which members of that culture have concerning those values. On the first point, we are confronted with the question, How can the professional worker decide what behavior constitutes maladjustment and should be altered? The answer given by the social-learning theorist is that he must select an ethical position concerning good and bad, desirable and undesirable behavior as the basis for his discriminations. Ethical positions from which judgments about the desirability of behavior are made are numerous, but can be summarized into two groups, those which evaluate behavior in terms of its appropriateness and contribution to society and those which judge behavior in terms of its effect on the individual's personal feelings of happiness. Rotter has referred to these two major value systems as the *social-centered approach* and the *self-centered approach.* Included under the first are judgments that particular actions are pathological because they deviate from the statistical norm, or from what others consider socially desirable, or from society's definitions of constructive, adaptive, or ideal actions. The second value system regards as maladjusted any behavior which results in unhappiness, suffering, or internal conflict for the individual concerned and as adjusted behavior, acts which contribute to his subjective sense of harmony and well-being. If the factors which determine the individual's personal state of happiness and the reinforcements from other people which follow his behavior stem from the same value system, a social-centered and a self-centered point of view will be consistent and complementary. In most instances the person who contributes to the welfare of others in turn is rewarded, praised, loved, etc., and consequently feels happy and pleased with his behavior. Similarly, society is likely to withhold desired social reinforcements from, or even punish, the person whose actions do not contribute to the welfare of others, and thus to promote his unhappiness. However, where these two points of view differ and a particular behavior is regarded as maladjusted by one of these criteria and not by the other, the professional worker and his client must decide which criteria to follow or emphasize. Whether social-centered or self-centered values are followed, the social-learning theorist stresses the point that the judgment is made on the basis of ethical considerations and not from psychological theory.

What constitutes maladjustment depends chiefly on the values which predominate in a particular culture and represents the failure of members of that culture to learn to behave in accord with those values. Stated in another way, the theory holds that maladjustment represents learning problems in social situations, and the existence and nature of the problem cannot be determined apart from the specific values of the social situation in which it occurs. Thus, social-learning theory adopts a highly relativistic and cultural point of view concerning maladjustment and rejects the idea of absolute criteria which can be applied to behavior outside of a given cultural context. At the same time, this formulation should not be interpreted to mean that maladjustment is equated with social nonconformity. While deviation from social norms increases the probability that an individual will be regarded as maladjusted by others, a specific culture or social situation may welcome and reward nonconformity, deviance, or innovation and consider extreme conformity undesirable and maladjusted.

The learning problems which constitute maladjustment are of two types: the learning of behavior that the culture regards as inappropriate and undesirable and the failure to learn behavior that the culture regards as appropriate, desirable, or necessary. In most clinical cases these two types of learning problems occur together, and part of the clinician's diagnostic task is to distinguish and separate conceptually the maladjusted behaviors which are present and the adjusted behaviors which are not present. Goals of psychotherapy, or other efforts to promote behavior change, usually are concerned with *both* lessening the probability of the occurrence of undesirable actions and increasing the probability of desirable actions, but one or the other may be stressed in any given case. For purposes of exposition and clarification, these two types of maladjustment will be discussed separately.

Maladjusted behavior

Maladjustment, or behavior regarded as undesirable and deviant, covers an extremely wide variety and range of behaviors from the awkward social acts and embarrassment of the shy adolescent to the unintelligible mutterings and hallucinations of the patient in a mental hospital. No effort will be made here to present a comprehensive list or categorization of maladjusted behavior, but it is important to recognize that such behavior can be distinguished, subdivided, and categorized in terms of numerous criteria. One approach is based on the predominant or distinguishing feature of the behavior, and numerous concepts have been developed in the field of abnormal psychology which group together different maladjusted acts under general headings, such as anxiety, depression, addictions, paranoid reactions, antisocial acts, and compulsive behavior. Another way of classifying maladjustment is in terms of the major goal or need satisfaction to which the behavior is directed. Thus, we might speak of maladjusted dependent behavior, hostile-aggressive maladjustment, or maladjusted efforts to obtain love and affection satisfactions. Sometimes deviant responses are classified by the particular area of life or the distinctive social situations in which they occur, as for example, vocational maladjustment, marital problems, sexual difficulties, or problems with authority figures. Other common dimensions for classifying maladjustment are in terms of the extent to which the person is incapacitated by his problems and reactions to them, the degree of distortion of reality involved and whether the difficulties are acute or chronic. The most profitable way of classifying types of maladjustment eventually may be based on differential treatment programs so that the maladjusted responses which can be altered by one form of treatment or intervention will be distinguished from others which can be altered by different forms of intervention.

An important point concerning the classification of deviant behavior is that social-learning theory rejects the logic and meaningfulness of categorizing maladjustment into distinct entities, diseases, personality types, or character structures.   Terms frequently used in the field of mental health, such as schizophrenia, neuroses, psychopathic personality, and compulsive character structure are regarded by the social-learning theorist as overgeneralized categorizations that often include such varied behaviors within a single grouping that they ignore significant differences between individuals classified in the same way. Social-learning theory regards the classification of *behaviors* as potentially more useful in understanding maladjustment than the classification of *persons* into categories that ignore important behavioral differences.   In addition, categorization in terms of personality types and mental illnesses typically involves assumptions about the development and alteration of behavior which are inconsistent with the major thesis of social-learning theory, that personality problems and maladjustments represent problems in social learning.

Next, let us consider hypotheses concerning the development and continuation of maladjusted behavior.   According to reinforcement theory, in order for a behavior to have been learned, it first must have occurred, and second, must have led to a reward which was valued by the individual.   In the case of maladjusted behavior, explaining its initial occurrence poses no great problem to the theorist; it seems a safe assumption that all persons in the course of their psychological development have at various times behaved in ways which deviate from cultural values, possibly as a result of trial-and-error efforts to gain certain satisfactions or possibly by imitating the behavior of real-life or fictional models.   Social-learning theory holds that more important than the fact that some particular kind of deviant behavior occurs is what reinforcements follow that behavior.   If the behavior results in a negative outcome for the individual, the deviant act is less likely to occur again.   If the outcome is positive, the potential occurrence of the behavior has increased because the individual has learned to expect that he will be rewarded for acting in that way.   The theory also states that for a particular behavior potential to remain high, the individual must continue to expect that it will lead to positive reinforcement.   Herein lies one of the major questions concerning maladjustment: If the behavior is negatively sanctioned by the culture and generally leads to some type of discomfort or punishment, how do we explain the fact that its potential remains high?   Should not the individual learn to expect negative consequences rather than rewards for acting in maladjusted ways and therefore become less likely to do so? Apparently this does not happen.   The continuation of the behavior indicates that the individual's expectancy for reward for that behavior remains higher than his expectancy for punishment.   The problem in understanding maladjusted behavior, then, is to explain why a person subjectively expects to gain some type of satisfaction for a behavior which his culture regards as undesirable and which experience should teach him will lead to negative consequences.

To resolve the above problem with respect to any particular kind of maladjustment, the theorist concentrates on three questions: What does the individual expect will occur as a result of the behavior (expectancies)? What are the goals, or need satisfactions, and their strengths, to which the behavior is directed (reinforcement values)? What consequences actually follow the occurrence of the behavior (reinforcements)? To answer these questions, one needs to understand the individual's past learning concerning the maladjusted behavior. This requires an ideographic analysis, the scope and depth of which will vary with the individual case.

A number of general formulations concerning the bases for maladjustment that are meaningful within a social-learning frame of reference serve as a guide in making such an analysis. One of the first hypotheses a clinician is likely to have is that the maladjusted behavior is associated with low freedom of movement for need satisfactions that have a high value to the individual. Because he feels unable to gain desired reinforcements or because he expects failure, punishment, or other negative reinforcements, the person with low freedom of movement is likely to attempt to gain the reinforcements he desires in substitute ways which involve distortions of reality and avoidance behaviors. Rationalizations, projections, fantasies, and other behaviors involving distortions are likely to lead to increased difficulties with the environment and to progressive distortions of reality as the individual continually tries to perceive the world in accord with them and to justify his reactions to himself and others. Avoidance behaviors, which commonly occur when the person expects punishment, may involve direct physical withdrawal and distance from feared situations or various implicit behaviors such as repression and denial. Both direct and implicit forms of avoidance promote further maladjustment by preventing constructive problem solving and by removing the person from the feared situation so that he is unable to develop more effective ways of dealing with it.

Maladjusted behavior is often associated with high need values, i.e., when an individual places too great an importance on a particular need. He then is prone to perceive diverse situations in terms of that one need and to behave in accord with it, possibly at the expense of other needs or of objective reality. For example, the person who continually is concerned with gaining achievement rewards is apt to distort situations, ignore important stimuli not related to achievement, and act in assertive, competitive ways when this type of behavior is inappropriate. Consequently conflict with his environment will be fostered by his preoccupation with achievement. High minimal goals also tend to be associated with frustration, dissatisfaction, and maladjustment because of the increased likelihood that reality will not satisfy the high demands. The conceptualization of a person's needs or goals may also help explain maladjusted behavior when a given act results in the satisfaction of one need, but the frustration of another. Such a situation might occur when competitive leadership behaviors satisfy one's dominance needs, but result in social rejection and frustration of one's affiliation needs. Conflicts between needs foster ambivalence and indecision, which in turn may promote frustration and deviant efforts to gain satisfactions.

A common, but often overlooked, reason for the existence of maladjusted behavior is that the individual's environment directly encourages it. Sometimes the encouragement is rather blatant, as in the case of a highly dependent and fear-ridden child whose fears are continually reinforced by the fact that his parents respond to them with increased protectiveness, attention, and reluctance to allow him to experience potential dangers. Sometimes the encouragement of maladjustment is very subtle and complex and involves the expectancies, needs, and reactions of important persons in the environment who, without realizing it, are more comfortable if deviant behavior occurs than they would be if it did not occur. Many forms of maladjustment also are positively reinforced by the attention, concern, and special privileges they bring.

Frequently the meanings given reinforcements which are associated with maladjustment are so highly idiosyncratic and symbolic that their importance is not clear without detailed information about the individual. An example is where punitive measures taken against a person who has committed a crime, and which appear to be clear negative reinforcements, actually work in reverse and positively reinforce the criminal behavior because they satisfy guilt feelings and a need for punishment which were developed in earlier experiences. Similarly, maladjustment may be based on the person's failure to discriminate between different reinforcements and situations, and his reactions may constitute overgeneralizations of experience. A common problem found in psychotherapy with adults is that they have failed to learn that behavior which was appropriate and reinforced in childhood often represents maladjustment for an adult and they continue to misapply learning from past experiences to present situations. Failure to discriminate between the behavioral demands of different areas of life and different kinds of people also lies behind many maladjusted reactions. Still another factor underlying maladjustment is that it tends to be directed toward the immediate reinforcements which follow a behavior and to ignore the delayed and long-term consequences of that behavior. Maladjusted behavior frequently leads to immediate reinforcements which are positive and satisfying, but which later give way to strong negative reinforcements. The individual's failure to relate the delayed negative consequences to the maladjusted behavior encourages the continuation of that behavior.

The absence of adjusted behaviors

While maladjustment generally is associated with the presence of deviant or undesirable behavior, failure or inability to act in ways which a culture regards as necessary also is regarded as maladjustment. The specific behaviors which a culture expects or demands of its members vary with different situations and are related to many variables pertaining to the individual, such as his age, sex, occupation, and social standing. Membership in special groups within a culture usually carries with it requirements that certain actions be performed, and failure to perform them constitutes maladjustment in those groups. Thus, the criteria of maladjustment based on failure to perform adjusted acts is highly relative. However, the inability or refusal to behave in certain ways is regarded as deviant and maladjusted in most societies for all persons beyond the first few years of life. For example, feeding and clothing oneself, controlling bladder and bowel functions, learning some form of communication with others, and engaging in rational thinking and purposive behavior are required of all but very young children, and deviations are regarded as maladjustment. As an individual matures and reaches adulthood, an increasing number of behaviors are expected of him, the particular nature of which depends upon his sex and socioeconomic class; these include such behaviors as learning skills which will enable him to earn a living, participating in activities appropriate to his sex, and developing the social behaviors necessary for harmonious interaction with others.

Under reinforcement theory, we might expect all persons to learn to behave in ways their culture sanctions and rewards. The initial occurrence of desirable behaviors is likely to be encouraged by the direct teaching of others and by observation and imitation. Furthermore, the continuation of socially sanctioned actions once they occur is promoted by the fact that they lead to positive reinforcements. Why then do some individuals fail to learn to behave in ways which are considered desirable and adjusted. Social-learning theory postulates two reasons: first, the individual's particular environment may deviate from the general culture and not provide the necessary learning conditions, and second, the prior learning of the individual may interfere with or block his learning of behaviors regarded as desirable. Each of these possibilities is discussed below and in both cases, as is true in trying to understand the basis for the presence of maladjusted behavior, the social-learning theorist adopts an ideographic and historical approach.

Inappropriate conditions for learning a behavior may consist of circumstances which prevent or discourage its initial occurrence or may result when the behavior is followed by no reinforcement or a negative reinforcement.   Although most persons in a culture act in a given way, the unique life conditions of a person may prevent him from witnessing or being able to try out a particular act.   Physical ailments during childhood may restrict exploratory behavior and may make it difficult or impossible to behave in a given way.   Parental restrictions may have this same result.   The absence of a same-sex parent from the home also may discourage the initial occurrence of many sex-appropriate behaviors because of the lack of a model to imitate.   Even when culturally appropriate behaviors occur, the person's life situation may not reinforce them or may negatively reinforce them.   The mother who prefers that her child remain close and dependent on her may discourage appropriate independent behavior to such an extent that the child fails to learn essential skills for caring for himself. Frequently conditions discourage the learning of behavior despite deliberate efforts on the part of others to promote that behavior.   To illustrate, a parent may work intensely with his child to teach him to swim, but if the parent's reactions are critical and frightening to the child, they in effect constitute negative reinforcement for that activity and the child may learn that swimming is something he cannot do and should avoid.

Assuming adequate exposure to cultural influences, in most instances when a behavior which society deems desirable or essential for adjustment is not learned, the failure occurs because of interference from prior learning of the individual.   This is especially true with adults; even though one's childhood background may not have provided the conditions for learning the desired behavior, adult experiences are likely to have communicated the nature of the behavior that has not been learned and the potential rewards which follow it. When this is the case, the person knows that he should act in a given way to be in harmony with his culture, but finds himself unable to do so because of other responses he has learned.

Many of the same theoretical ideas which in social learning explain the presence of maladjusted behavior may account for the interference of past experiences on the learning of adjusted responses.   Probably the most common interference occurs from avoidance and withdrawal responses.   As noted before, responses which remove a person from a stimulus or situation in which he expects negative reinforcement prevent him from learning any other response in that situation.   Consequently they block the development of behaviors which are culturally desirable in those situations.   The interference often consists of the learning of taboos which do not apply at a later time, such as the childhood taboo on sexual activity which can block the development of appropriate sexual responses in the adult. Negative reinforcement of curiosity and assertiveness during childhood also often interferes with the occurrence of these characteristics in the adult when they are desired. In such cases, the individual can be described as having learned too well, or overlearned, so that he is unable to change even though conditions have changed.

The failure to develop appropriate and adjusted responses may result from the failure to discriminate correctly between different times, places, and people. If a behavior resulted in a negative reinforcement in the past, but is positively reinforced in the present, the individual who fails to discriminate between past and present will not become aware of the change. Another example consists of failure to note and respond to differences in behaviors which are appropriate in different groups. Responses which are punished when they occur with authority figures may be desired in peer interactions, and the lack of discrimination between the behavioral demands of these two groups of people may impede the learning of appropriate peer responses. Sometimes a person learns not to behave in a particular way, even though that behavior is desirable, because he has concentrated on the immediate reinforcements which are negative and ignored delayed or long-term positive consequences of that behavior. For example, the college student who has failed to learn to devote himself to his studies may be responding only to the negative reinforcement that studying prevents him from engaging in enjoyable social activities and not to the delayed positive reinforcements, such as receiving a good grade on the final exam, graduating successfully, and obtaining a desired position following graduation.

As we have seen, social-learning theory provides a variety of hypotheses concerning maladjustment consistent with its concepts and assumptions. The validity of these hypotheses can be determined only from their value to the practicing clinician in helping maladjusted persons and from the accuracy of the predictions of human behavior which are derived from them. Further elaboration and development of the theory's application to the understanding and prediction of emotional difficulties and maladjustments are likely to result from research and clinical practice which utilizes social-learning theory concepts.

References

Rotter, J. B. *Social learning and clinical psychology.* Englewood Cliffs: Prentice-Hall, 1954.

Rotter, J. B. Generalized expectancies for internal versus external control of reinforcements. *Psychological Monographs,* 1966, *80,* (1, Whole No. 609).

FOUR

SECTION FOUR THE PROCESS OF ADJUSTMENT

The readings in this section present a broad sample of material pertaining to the process of adjustment. They include such subjects as the factors which influence adjustment, the various ways in which the process of adjustment has been conceptualized, and patterns of adjustment which are considered pathological.

A The determinants of adjustment

The first group of readings reports on some of the variables which generally are considered significant in determining adjustment patterns. Whenever the topic of causal factors in behavior is approached, the question of the relative importance of heredity and environment usually is raised. The influences of hereditary and environmental variables on behavior are, however, so complex and interdependent that we cannot meaningfully separate one from the other. While we may note differences among infants at birth, we are unable to determine the extent of the hereditary influence apart from that of the prenatal environment. Infants with the same hereditary potential may differ markedly because of variations, deficiencies, and mishaps in the maternal condition while the child is *in utero*. Because of the difficulty in isolating hereditary factors, most investigators of the determinants of personality focus on environmental factors which lend themselves more readily to research.

The readings which follow on the determinants of adjustment present a representative picture of current thinking and therefore deal chiefly with environmental influences. The first selection provides a discussion of the significance of cultural factors on individual differences in adjustment, mental health, and personality. Leighton and Hughes muster the evidence in support of a number of basic propositions about the relationships between culture and personality. They persuade us that mental health and other related attributes of individuals need to be seen in the context of culture, and that culture does, in fact, have a powerful impact on adjustment.

The second reading alerts us to an important attribute of our own culture which appears to have relevance for determining adjustment— the variable of *social class*. Dividing our culture into groups based on class structure (determined by an index of ecological area of residence, occupation, and education), Hollingshead and Redlich present findings which indicate significant relationships between social class and the incidence of psychiatric disorders. The enthusiasm of the authors for relating social concepts to particular adjustment patterns seems warranted. As they point out, however, it is important to go beyond showing that statistical relationships exist between social class and mental illness; we must seek the specific ways in which social conditions function to influence the adjustment of individuals. The final report by Hollingshead and Redlich on this project, entitled *Social Class and Mental Illness* (Wiley, New York, 1958), suggests that their research constitutes a very fruitful approach to understanding ways in which social factors determine problems and patterns of adjustment.

The final three selections deal with the developing organism and give accounts of events and experiences which are critical for adequate adjustment. All share a belief in the fundamental hypothesis that early experience has important consequences for adult behavior.

Many psychologists have attributed paramount importance to early childhood experiences because they are viewed as providing the foundation for the nature of subsequent adjustment. The first paper describes four training situations in early childhood which are thought to produce long-lasting effects on the personality characteristics of the individual. Dollard and Miller discuss some of the typical problems and reactions of the child concerning feeding, cleanliness, sex, and hostility. They also specify some of the habits which are acquired in the context of experiences with each of these. One example of this would be the child who is repeatedly punished by a parent. He may learn to perceive all authority figures with the fear and anger he felt toward his parent.

The next selection provides us with a summary report from the Harlows on their well-known research on the effects of rearing conditions on behavior. They have been pursuing the consequences on behavior of a number of early life situations in rhesus monkeys and, while the extent to which their findings can be generalized to human beings is open to question, their observations are exciting. Their general finding that the longer and the more complete the social deprivation, the more devastating are the behavioral effects, supports the hypothesis that early experience is an important determinant of later adjustment.

The final selection is by Erikson. It provides us with an extremely well-known and far-reaching conceptualization of *psychosocial* developmental stages. The interest here is broader than the orthodox Freudian analysis of progress through *psychosexual* stages. Erikson sees the individual as passing through eight social stages, each of which is devoted to the establishment of alternative basic attitudes: basic trusts versus basic mistrust, autonomy versus shame and doubt, initiative versus guilt, etc. Continuity is provided for in Erikson's scheme by the assertion that the character of the resolution of basic attitudes at earlier stages has consequences for the kind of resolution at later stages. In this sense, the events occurring at various stages of life are determinants of later behavior.

Alexander H. Leighton and Jane H. Hughes

CULTURES AS CAUSATIVE OF MENTAL DISORDER *

Introduction

A review of the previous papers makes it evident that mental disorder is considered to be the product of multiple factors. The present paper is in harmony with this orientation, and its title, which was assigned to us, should not be interpreted as implying ideas of mono-causal relationship.

The discussion of our topic will be necessarily limited and selective, since talking about culture in its global sense touches on virtually all aspects of human behavior. Some areas such as family relationships and social change have been discussed earlier. Others such as cultural history and philosophy are too vast to be treated adequately in one chapter. We shall attempt, therefore, to present some points from salient literature, and to give impressions derived from several years of research dealing with socio-cultural factors and mental disorder.

Definition of concepts

Culture. As used here "culture" is a label for an abstraction that encompasses the total way of life of a group of human beings.

Many other definitions have been proposed, and several variants are current in the social sciences (25). Leslie White, for example, em-

* From Alexander H. Leighton and Jane H. Hughes, "Cultures as Causative of Mental Disorder," in *Causes of Mental Disorders: A Review of Epidemiological Knowledge, 1959*, Milbank Memorial Fund, New York, 1961. Reprinted by permission of the authors and the publisher.

ploys the word to mean a pattern of history which can be analyzed and understood without reference to the human beings in whom it is expressed (46). Culture in this sense is a determinant force which follows its own laws irrespective of individual psychology and acts upon, rather than interacts with, human personalities. Such a conceptualization provides a way of explaining other phenomena by means of culture as the causal element. We think, however, that despite some possible usefulness in White's "culturology" with regard to understanding the evolutionary path of society as a whole, it is too divorced from human variation to have relevance for the malformations and malfunctionings of personality known as mental disorders.

Other ways of defining culture point to the material artifacts produced by certain societies and to the relationship between patterns of livelihood and environmental resources. Our concept includes all these factors—history, adaptation to physical environment, technology—but its focal point is what Hallowell has termed the "psychological reality" of culture (15). By this emphasis, culture refers primarily to the shared patterns of belief, feeling, and adaptation which people carry in their minds as guides for conduct and the definition of reality. Besides concerning all aspects of human life—social relationships, economics, and religion, for example—culture as a totality contains patterns of interconnections and interdependencies.

Although all societies have a cultural heritage which is transmitted from one generation to the next, the particular style varies from one group to another. Where contrast is marked, it is impossible to speak of different cultures. Thus cultures have been grouped as "Western and non-Western," "hunting and gathering," "agricultural," and "industrial" (17), or as "peasant societies" and "great traditions" (39).

In studying cultural factors which affect mental disorder, modern urbanites are, of course, as much the focus of attention as nonliterate tribal groups. It is a common practice, however, to direct analysis toward situations which offer contrast to what prevails in our own culture with the hope of moving thereby into greater understanding of problems to which we are somewhat blinded by their being too close to us. It is for this reason that the examples to be cited here deal mainly with non-Western cultures, and the literature reviewed is primarily from the field of anthropology and the subfield "culture and personality" in which anthropologists and psychiatrists have collaborated.

Mental disorder.   Coming as it does at the end of the symposium, our definition of mental disorder should need little elaboration. It is in keeping with the symposium's inclusion of all those behaviors, emotions, attitudes, and beliefs usually regarded as in the field of psychiatry. Such breadth of definition means that neuroses are encompassed as well as psychoses, sociopathic disorders as well as psychophysiological disturbances. It also means the inclusion of brain syndromes and mental retardation—conditions not primarily based on psychological experience but subject nonetheless to the influences of culture through practices of breeding, diet, care of the ill, use of drugs and intoxicants, and the training of the defective child.

How cultural factors may be thought to affect psychiatric disorder

As a means of organizing pertinent ideas, what follows will be presented as a series of statements, each one supplying a different way of completing the sentence "Culture may be thought to. . . ."

1   Culture may be thought to determine the pattern of certain specific mental disorders.   Names representing culture-specific disorders are well known in anthropological literature although they are not part of the standard nomenclatures of Western psychiatry.   A list would include "amok" and "lâtah" both found in Malay (2, 43, 48), "imu" among the Ainu of Japan (47), "koro" in China (44), "witiko" among the Ojibwa Indians of the Northeast Woodlands (27), "piblokto" in the eastern Arctic (3), and "arctic hysteria" in Siberia (20).   Each one embodies a constellation of symptoms found primarily in a given culture area, and often there is association between cultural beliefs or practices and the content of the symptoms.

"Witiko," for example, takes the form of a homicidal spree during which the individual may kill and eat members of his own family (7). In what could be called a delusional excitement the patient believes himself possessed by a spirit from his cultural mythology, the Witiko, a hoary cannibalistic monster with a heart of ice.   "Koro" is an anxiety state in which delusions concern withdrawal of the male sexual organs into the abdomen.   It is associated with fear of death in a culture where it is believed that the sexual organs do disappear from corpses.   Among the Eskimos, "piblokto" refers to a temporary derangement during which various bizarre acts are carried out such as dashing out naked into subzero weather or mimicking the sounds of Arctic birds and animals.

"Lâtah," "imu" and "arctic hysteria" are characterized by involuntary imitating, automatic obedience, shuddering, and fright.   It is believed that women are more frequently sufferers from this disability than men.   In some cultures certain people, especially old women, are known for this affliction, and it is considered sport to use gestures or words which will set off a reaction in which the victim goes into unseemly postures, dances to exhaustion, disrobes, and even harms herself or others.

There are accounts of whole groups of individuals becoming afflicted with a kind of mass hysteria, recalling the "dancing crazes" in Europe during the Middle Ages. One report tells of an instance in which a Cossack officer was drilling a group of Siberian natives. Each order he issued was shouted back first by one individual and then gradually by a chorus of all in the ranks. Every man appeared trapped in an exhausting and self-defeating repetition of the orders (and then curses) uttered by the increasingly infuriated officer (8).

A number of explanations have been invoked to account for such disorders. These comprise the ideas that they are:

1   Reactions based on physical disease such as malaria, tuberculosis, or luetic infection, but patterned in expression by cultural elements (43).

2   Reactions to the stress of severe environment, starvation, or long periods of isolation (37).

3   Reactions to the stress and strain of role characteristics in the culture (1).

4   "Hysteria" (6), that is, variations of a syndrome familiar in Western clinics and which is referred to in the American Psychiatric Association nomenclature as "dissociative reaction" (4).

These explanations are not mutually exclusive. Some of the culturally localized syndromes can be considered as neurotic states involving suggestability, and in which the content of symptoms is produced by the experience of growing up in a particular culture and being inculcated with its shared sentiments. Contributing factors may then be the stress of environment or roles. Dynamic mechanisms or noxious agents can also be regarded as components in the origin and course of the disorder.

The idea that these disorders are hysterical should, however, be treated with some caution. This is said partly from our feeling that such a conclusion is deceptively complete and hence may cut off effort toward penetrating to a less superficial level of understanding. There is also the possibility that it expresses a bias of the Western clinician who may have some tendency to consider any seemingly bizarre behavior as hysterical if there is no organic basis and if it cannot be called schizophrenia. This is further encouraged if the person exhibiting such behavior is uneducated from the Western point of view, is "simple" and "child-like"—qualities which are part of the stereotype we hold of "primitives." It would seem wise not to blanket aberrant behaviors found among the people of this or that culture with the term and concepts of "hysteria" (or of schizophrenia for that matter), but rather examine to see if some cases, at least, may not be on a somewhat different basis from what we are accustomed to see in the West. And even when "hysteria" turns out to be a valid label such an approach might, through comparisons and contrasts, increase our knowledge regarding the nature of the condition, not only as it occurs among non-Western peoples, but also among ourselves.

2   Culture may be thought to produce basic personality types, some of which are especially vulnerable to mental disorder.   The concepts of "basic personality type" (21, 22, 33), "modal personality" (16, 19), and "national character" (35, 14) were developed by anthropologists and psychiatrists to account for the fact that certain personality traits and certain inclinations to symptoms of psychiatric significance seemed to be associated with growing up in particular cultures.   Being middle class American, Japanese, Russian—or, as described in Ruth Benedict's classic volume, being Zuñi, Kwakiutl, or Dobu (5)—appears to predispose individuals toward particular kinds of symptoms.   In the employment of these concepts, culture and personality were held to be essentially two aspects of a single phenomenon (42).   This opened the way for studying personality through cultural data rather than through the behavior of individuals.   The early work in this field by Kardiner and Linton had its foundation in exploring ethnographies and the folklore of non-literate tribes.   Through analysis of child-rearing practices, kinship arrangements, socio-structural stresses, and especially religion and myths considered as projections of common, underlying personality attributes, "basic personality types" were postulated for different cultures.

Bàsic personality was thought of as a central core of values and attitudes which culture stamps into each of its members—a common denominator underlying each person's individual elaboration of life experience.   Once a type had been described, it could be assessed from the psychiatric point of view as to its vulnerabilities.   Thus, if at the cultural level—that is, group practices and beliefs—patterns were found that had psychiatric implications it was assumed that individuals in that culture would have these as psychological weaknesses. Whole cultures were described with psychiatric terms heretofore reserved for diagnosing individuals.   If a society exhibited patterns of suspiciousness, hostility, witchcraft fears, and ideas of grandeur as in the potlatching Indian groups of the Northwest coast, there was a tendency to call such cultures "paranoid."

Since a major component of almost every clinical definition of psychiatric disorder is some deviation from the expected behavior and shared sentiments of the group to which the individual belongs, the use of clinical terms for conforming, group-oriented behavior involves a contradiction.   At best, it is the employment of unclear descriptive labels to characterize patterns of behavior manifested by a society.   At worst, the clinical implications of the words are transferred to the group behavior, and dynamic interpretations are made in this framework. Since the behavior of people in accord with and at variance with group patterns implies major differences of psychological process, these usages can be exceedingly misleading. To say that a group is "paranoid," for instance, may be passable though not admirable if by this is meant behavior that is suspicious and hostile. If, however, the word is intended as some kind of explanation based on individual psychology, then many pre-judgments and unsound inferences from individual to group behavior may enter the picture. One runs the risk of anthropomorphizing the group and regarding it as a deviant individual among a number of other anthropomorphized groups. It is one thing to say that functioning at the personality level and functioning at the socio-cultural level display similarities, and that how well they fit together is significant for adequate functioning at each level. It is another thing, however, to go beyond this and use identical terms in referring to these different levels of abstraction. This is especially true when the psychiatric terms invoked to identify and classify cultural patterns are not well standardized even at their source—psychiatry.

Theories concerning basic personality may also be criticized for a tendency to consider cultural factors as overriding variations based on genetic influences affecting temperament (13) and for ignoring the possible effects of endemic disease and other physiological factors. For the most part "basic personality types" have been derived solely from cultural behavior or from the results of projective tests like the Rorschach. Thus far vulnerability to, or resistance against, mental illness has been postulated without concomitant investigation of the actual distribution and patterning of psychiatric disorder in the population.

Our own inclination is toward a less specific functional view of socio-cultural groups and the personalities which compose them. By this is meant the aim of understanding how psychiatric disorder can arise, take shape, and endure, as a result of interaction between individual functioning (personality) and group functioning. Since a discussion of this viewpoint has been previously published by one of us (30), we shall not here elaborate it further.

3   Culture may be thought to produce psychiatric disorders through certain child-rearing practices. This point is closely allied to its predecessor. The difference is that while basic personality types have been formulated from looking at cultures as wholes, the focus here is directly and more exclusively levelled at socialization practices and the early years of life experience. Freudian theory has provided a means of organizing data from different cultures with regard to toilet training, nurturing, control of aggression, weaning, and encouraging independence (11). It has also provided a way of interpreting cultural variations with regard to probable significance for mental disorder

among adults.   Cultures portray remarkable variation in customs such as swaddling, use of a cradle-board, bottle or breast feeding, varying modes of punishment and reward, and permissive or restraining parental attitudes.   This has given impetus to many hypotheses regarding the differential occurrence of psychiatric disorders.

The risk of this approach is to give undue emphasis to one set of factors, and to one period on the life-arc of individuals, to the exclusion of all other factors and periods of personality growth and development.   Few would quarrel with the importance of the early years of life, but to assume that the experiences of infancy determine everything that comes afterward so far as origin, course, and outcome of psychiatric disorder is concerned, is to assume more than the knowledge currently at our disposal warrants.   Different sets of dynamics are relevant to individual functioning at different stages of life. Physiological and psychological changes in maturation and involution are probably of considerable significance in some kinds of mental disorders.   Since our interest is in discovering cultural factors relevant to the whole range of psychiatric illnesses, it is important to recognize that adolescence, maturity, and senescence are viewed and defined as variously in different cultures as is child-rearing.

4   Culture may be thought to affect psychiatric disorders through types of sanction.   It has long been accepted that there is a relationship between some kinds of disorder and the manner in which a patient handles the problem of conformity or nonconformity—the sense of being right or wrong in the eyes of his social audience.   There is considerable variation among cultures regarding how punishment is meted out to those who defy accepted beliefs and standards about what ought and ought not to be done.   Cultures also vary in what is defined as transgression and the kinds of responsibility demanded of members.   Some groups operate on the principle that society at large is the controller of moral conduct; others appear to maintain social control by implanting in individuals the job of self-monitoring conduct. These two types—"other-directed" and "inner-directed" in Reisman's terminology (40)—have usually been called "shame" and "guilt" cultures in anthropological literature.   A critical discussion of this orientation is given by Piers and Singer (38).   It has been thought that distinctive forms of psychopathology may be found in "shame" cultures where the atonement for sin calls for some kind of public demonstration such as a confession, while other kinds of symptomatology may be fostered in "guilt" cultures where expiation is left to the lonely world of conscience.   One can theorize that where the group as a whole is the court to which account must be made, there would be a tendency for psychiatric disorder to take the form of antisocial behavior, aggression of the sociopathic type.   Where individual super-ego is

stressed, there might be an inclination to self-directed punishment and depression. In short, and in overly simple terms, one type of culture can be thought to encourage symptoms which are disturbing to the group, while the other encourages symptoms which are disturbing to the individual who has them.

With regard to the kinds of behavior for which people are punished, it has been noted that some cultures institute negative sanctions only against what is defined as controllable, while others include involuntary behavior as well (23). Among some peoples, menstruation, multiple births or impotence are thought to be defiling to the whole group or at least an affront to cultural expectations. In a personal communication Dr. T. A. Baasher of Khartoum North has told one of us [1] of the Ingassuma tribe in the Sudan where it is believed that the mother of twins has the evil eye. He reported an instance in which such a mother committed suicide by running her head against a rock while the members of her village looked on.

The psychological burden related to the occurrence of certain uncontrollable and not uncommon events and to some kinds of physiological processes, e.g. menstruation, may be of a magnitude that makes it appropriate to say that a given culture has a serious potential for psychiatric disorder. At least it seems clear that sanctions of this nature have a quite different meaning with regard to mental health from those which relate the occurrence of insanity to more or less self-willed acts such as breaking incest taboos among the Navaho (41), or masturbation as found in some of the folk beliefs of our own culture.

5 Culture may be thought to perpetuate psychiatric malfunctioning by rewarding it in certain prestigeful roles. Under the last point attention was focussed only on negative sanctions. We turn now to the positive side—reward—and also more explicitly to the concept of role (32). The relationship between socio-cultural role and mental disorder is complex, and we shall deal with it in two parts: here in terms of roles which may attract individuals who have certain disorder tendencies and in Statement 6, below, in terms of roles which may produce some types of psychiatric disorder through being seats of conflict and stress.

In non-Western cultures the roles of medicine-man and holy-man—shaman or sahu—are examples of social positions for which, it has been thought, personnel are recruited from unstable members of the culture—hysterics and psychotics (24, 9). Taking the shaman as an instance, behaviors connected with the role have been described as indicative of disorder because emotional lability and frenzy characterize the seance, because the shaman has charismatic dominance over the group of individuals for whom the curing ceremony is held,

[1] AHL.

because the shaman believes that he loses his own identity and becomes possessed by an over-world spirit, and because a fit or epileptic-like seizure culminates the performance.

There are, however, some considerations to be taken into account in following this line of thought. Just because the shaman's behavior resembles psychiatric symptoms is not a warrant for assuming that they are in fact psychiatric symptoms. Whatever else it may be, his behavior is part of the role of shaman and hence it may or may not have a relationship to his personality as a whole which would qualify him as mentally ill in Western terms. The settling of this question would require a thorough psychiatric examination of the person. To make a clinical diagnosis on the basis of role behavior alone is scarcely on a firmer basis than making a diagnosis from cultural patterns as noted [earlier].

What in shamanistic behavior may appear hysterical or psychotic to the Western psychiatrist is, to the people concerned, a time-honored ritual through which practitioners heal sick people or divine the future. Hence the "symptoms" of the shaman may in fact be the result of learning and practice. His role embodies a traditional plan for serving particular ends, and it is available in the culture as a model. The patterning of behavior after this model can, of course, vary greatly in its success, from excellent to poor.

It can also be assumed that a variety of personality types will be attracted to the model and role for a variety of reasons, some making a conscious selection while others act in response to both unconscious factors and extraneous circumstances. In the cultures where shamans are found, there is usually much less diversification of roles than is the case in Europe and America. There the business of life may be managed through nearly all the men being hunters, farmers or warriors, with the women in the main being homemakers. The role of shaman, consequently, may be almost the only variant possible and it is thus likely to collect incumbents for a wide variety of reasons, some of a psychiatric nature, some for matters of temperament, some related to superior and creative qualities, and some based on physical abnormality—blindness or loss of a limb—which makes achievement of the more prevailing roles impossible. It seems to us, that while some shamans or medicine-men may be suffering, from psychiatric disorder, this is probably not by any means the case with all.

The concept of role is traceable in part to 'role' as it is known in the theater. This may serve as a reminder that any given role as performed by an actor is not necessarily a direct and simple reflection of his own personality. Very few Ophelias have really been mad, and mad actresses do not necessarily perform Ophelia well. At the same time we do not wish to suggest that, because they may learn their part, most shamans are conscious fakers. On the contrary, it would seem likely that the ability to perform is enhanced by belief in the importance of the part.

In our own culture there are doubtless certain roles which resemble that of shaman in that they not only offer opportunity to mentally healthy personalities but also provide shelter for those with a certain amount of deviance. The artist comes to mind in this connection. Of course, many artists are mentally healthy, but it is possible for the arts to provide an opportunity for an ill person to express himself creatively and thus have a position in the social system. Artists are often accorded leeway—indeed, may acquire prestige—in the expression of psychiatric symptoms which, if evinced by people in other social roles, might be reason for sanctions, or even hospitalization. Places such as the Left Bank, Greenwich Village, and North Beach give a social medium where fairly large numbers of sick people can float. These areas contain not only the genuine artist but shelter many who act like poets and painters without ever becoming highly original or productive. Certain religious groups and colonies have similar sheltering characteristics for malfunctioning personalities.

6   Culture may be thought to produce psychiatric disorders through certain stressful roles. With this statement attention shifts to the effects of roles rather than their patterning and appearance. It is possible to conduct analysis so as to identify roles considered to be psychologically damaging, even to the extent of producing psychiatric disorder. For the most part this approach has been typical of sociology, in contrast to anthropology's focus on child-rearing.

Roles can be considered stressful in a number of ways. One is the problem of ambiguous definition regarding expected behavior. This is especially true of new roles developed in situations of sociocultural change where tradition gives no guidelines for assisting the recently emancipated to adapt and fulfill his new state. The principle is pertinent whether we observe a freed slave, a modern career woman, or a person in the limbo between magical and rational thought.

Roles may also present the person with inherently conflicting standards of behavior; the man who dedicates his life to humanitarian goals may come to feel he can reach a position effective for launching such a program only by being ruthless and competitive. Or a person may have to fill at one time several roles which make contradictory demands on his personality. We see this for example in students who have cast themselves in the role of liberals yet attempt to be loyal offspring to conservative parents.

The relationship between role stresses and a particular kind of psychiatric disorder has been reported by Linton as occurring among the Tanala of Madagascar (34). These people have a condition called "tromba" which occurs mainly among second sons and childless wives.

This is to be understood in the context of a culture in which inheritance and privilege are based on primogeniture and in which marriages are polygamous with the value of women related chiefly to child-bearing. Not only are role stresses and lack of social value involved, but also the mental illness itself gives opportunity for compensating prestige ("secondary gain"). Normally the family gives little attention to people filling such subservient roles as younger sons and wives without children, but for this illness the family group will finance an elaborate curing rite with attention focussed on the tromba-sufferer.

Innumerable other examples could be given of role stresses peculiar to this or that culture, and it seems probable that many of them are associated with some kind of psychiatric disturbance. It is a hard matter to pin down, however, for while individually persuasive cases can be found, research encounters problems of definition and the assembling of statistics adequate for conclusive statements.

7 Culture may be thought to produce psychiatric disturbance through processes of change. It was intimated in the last section that some of the most striking examples of stressful roles pertain to cultural change—that is to say a given role is conflict-laden because of changes in the web of socio-cultural situations with which it is related. Being a wife and mother may take on this character if, in the changing cultural situation, a woman is also expected to hold a job, vote, be educated, and so forth.

Literature on the relationship between mental disorder and social change through immigration, mobility connected with war, acculturation, and detribalization was reviewed in the last paper. It is not, therefore, appropriate to develop it further here except to indicate that culture is not static social organization and that in the world today, any study of culture is of necessity a study of change—changes of various sorts, at various rates, and with varying degrees of integration and conflict. Although there are numerous methodological problems connected with the use of hospital admission rates or projective tests, we feel that with advances in methods of case finding it is in the area of cultural change that some of the most revealing findings will occur that bear on the relationship between culture and mental disorder (31).

8 Culture may be thought to affect psychiatric disorder through the indoctrination of its members with particular kinds of sentiments. There is now considerable literature in the social sciences on the differences between cultural groups in regard to socially shared feelings and ideas about man, nature, and reality (18). For the most part this has been concerned with values or beliefs held by relatively normal individuals. Implications regarding psychiatric disorders

have, however, been pointed up in a number of ways. It seems probable that some cultures equip people with patterns of fear, jealousy, or unrealistic aspiration, which may foster mental illness; other cultures may be based on themes of self-acceptance and a relationship to natural forces which are more conducive to mental health.

Reality-testing in the tradition of Western empiricism is, for instance, a criterion advanced by modern psychiatry as an essential component of sanity and mental health. With such a base for discrimination, it has been suggested by Kroeber that the practice of magic and witchcraft and the adherence to non-objective beliefs characteristic of "primitive" peoples indicates a diffuse and subtle paranoia (24). Few would argue against the value of reality-orientation as a mark of psychiatric health, but, as many have pointed out, the standard cannot be determined exclusively by scientific rationalism. A better criterion is whether or not a person is capable of assessing and acting in response to reality as it is defined by the group in which he grows up. This opens the way for understanding the relationship of religious faith, folk belief, and emotional coloring of attitudes to the development and maintenance of healthy adjustments and maladjustments. From such a perspective have come attempts to employ concepts which emphasize equally the cognitive, affective, and basic-urge (largely instinctual) forces which come into play in human functioning, and in that light to analyze the significance of differences in the cultural patterning of belief. The Eaton and Weil study of mental illness among the religious communities of Hutterites takes this aspect as one of its points for analysis (10). And it is central in the Stirling County Study (30).

9   Culture per se may be thought to produce psychiatric disorder. All human beings are born and develop in cultural contexts which impose regulation of basic human urges. It has been thought that this is both universal and psychologically noxious with repercussions evident throughout the human race. We may all be, in short, like Chinese women with bound feet. Variations, however, are to be found in the degree of impulse-repression. Thus according to this view, simple and "primitive" societies with cultures which permit expression of sex and aggression are, on the whole, a healthier environment than complex, modern civilizations which compress infants into highly artificial patterns of existence. This is the kind of thing Freud had in mind when he spoke of 'civilization and its discontents' (12).

Most social scientists today would not accept such inherent assumptions about the character of "primitive" and "civilized" cultures. The distinction has limited usefulness and then only when the terms are carefully defined. The more we have learned about "primitive" cultures, the more impressed we are with their potential for being both repressive and suppressive. There is much in favor of the general idea that some kinds and degree of psychiatric disorder may be the price paid for being socialized, somewhat as backache and curvature of the spine may be part of the price paid for walking on our hind legs.

10   Culture may be thought to affect the distribution of psychiatric disorders through patterns of breeding.   This statement and its successor—the final point we shall present as a way in which culture may be thought to relate to mental illness—stand on a different basis from all the previous items.   Until now each statement has shared with others the characteristic of assuming that psychological transactions are the main, if not the only intermediary between cultural factors and the emergence and shaping of psychiatric disorder.   This has, in fact, been the principal orientation of those concerned with culture and its bearing on mental disorder.

Culturally-prescribed inbreeding is found in many groups of people, particularly with reference to some non-Western cultures, elite families, and small communities which for one reason or another live in isolation.   If such groups begin with a prevalence of hereditary factors which make for mental retardation, schizophrenia, manic-depressive psychosis or other forms of emotional instability, it is to be expected that these conditions will become accentuated and prevalent in the group.   Laubscher's early work in the field of cross-cultural psychiatry illustrates an attempt to relate the amount of schizophrenia among the Bantu of Africa to the pattern of cross-cousin marriage (29).

The same kinds of factors may be at work at more subtle levels, and in larger groups.   Thus the accumulating evidence in the West that there is greater prevalence of psychiatric disorder in the lower socio-economic ranges, has one explanation in terms of a socio-cultural process which produces a downward drift and interbreeding of people with genetically determined disabilities.

Heredity as a factor in psychiatric disorder suffers both from over-emphasis and neglect.   Heredity as such is considered *the* matter of importance in many centers of psychiatry, particularly in Europe.   But the question of cultural patterns and their shaping of hereditary processes is scarcely considered, at least in any systematic way.   In other psychiatric centers—especially in the United States—and among most social scientists, the whole of heredity is by-passed in favor of psychological factors.   Here culture is apt to be given more emphasis but not in connection with the distribution of genes.

11   Culture may be thought to affect the distribution of psychiatric disorder through patterns which result in poor physical hygiene. Our concern here is the role of physiological factors as the inter-mediary between culture and psychiatric disorder.   Culture and cul-

tural variation can be supposed to influence the distribution of noxious agents and traumata, and also the distribution of compensating factors and capabilities for resistance. In many non-Western cultures, for instance, contacts with the West which have demanded acculturation and abrupt industrialization have been accompanied by the spread of syphilis, tuberculosis, and many other diseases. Directly and indirectly these can foster disorder, although some have more potential in this regard than others. Of equal importance to the introduction of disease through contact, is the lack of native preventive and therapeutic measures.

Diet, based not only on availability of resources but also cultural preferences, may result in vitamin deficiency and malnutrition which in turn can affect the nervous system. There may also be cultural practices about child delivery, or the use of herbs and concoctions which make for brain damage. In some areas drugs have widespread use in native therapy, in recreation, and in religious ceremonies. There may thus be long-term degenerative effects as well as more immediate toxicities.

Concluding notes

Given the impressions sketched above, what conclusions can be drawn with regard to epidemiological studies of psychiatric disorder in different cultures as a means of expanding knowledge of etiology?

One can say to begin with that if the emphasis is on a primary target of inquiry such as genes, damage to the brain, or family relationships, the cultural context will be of some importance even if secondary. It will be one of the sets of factors to be considered in understanding how the damage comes about—whether *via* hereditary, physiological or psychological means—how it is spread and perpetuated and how it may be controlled.

If we take culture-in-relation-to-psychiatric-disorder as the primary matter for attention, then a major gap is apparent: an incomplete descriptive account of the varieties of psychiatric disorder to which human beings are susceptible across the world. The magnitude of this gap becomes apparent as soon as one begins to look into it. We do not even have a reasonably complete account of psychiatric disorders as these occur in a selection of contrasting cultures. Many of the localized types of illness such as those mentioned earlier are actually based on very few observations, some of them carried out years ago by non-psychiatrists. Despite the fact that psychiatric clinics exist in many non-Western societies, problems of nomenclature, variable criteria, and a Procrustean emphasis on Western systems of classification make assessment and comparison very difficult. Beyond this is a void consisting in the unknown numbers of persons who, though disturbed, do not ever come to clinical attention.

The importance of supplying this lack in our knowledge bears first of all on the descriptive aspect of scientific procedure. While we recognize that not everyone would accept systematic description as a basic component of the scientific process, it would be a digression to argue the case in general terms here. Suffice it to say, then, that if one does believe as a principle that this has its place and contribution to make in the study of man (no less so than in the study of other creatures, or of the earth's crust, or of the stars) then the gap is in obvious need of filling. Although it will take years of painstaking work by many observers, it is a necessary foundation on which to base other kinds of study.

Stepping down, however, from the level of general scientific desirability with its implied faith in serendipity, it is possible to point out a number of more specific goals and opportunities. For one thing, description paves the way for assessment of frequency—be this in terms of prevalence or incidence. Such counts will be essential ultimately, both in critical problems of basic research into etiology and in providing information for programs concerned with treatment and prevention.

Description and the use of these descriptions as criteria for counts of frequency (epidemiology), bring with them the need for developing a system of classification that will stand up across cultures. While this may look on the surface like a rather dry and laborious exercise in taxonomy, shafts run out from it into the foundations of psychiatry, and there may be consequences that will profoundly alter many accepted ideas and change significantly the way the field is perceived.

Psychiatry itself, like most of the rest of medicine, is a product of Western culture. As such, it embodies ideas of illness and wellness, of normal and abnormal, of well-functioning and malfunctioning, of adaption and maladaptation which have their roots in our own shared sentiments regarding the character of reality, of what is desirable, and of what ought to be desired. While the range in these matters is considerable in the West itself, cultural studies make it clear that it is not so great as when the whole world is considered. In other words malfunction, one of the major components of a definition of psychiatric disorder, shifts its character from culture to culture.

This problem is not necessarily limited to differences of shared preference and shared belief as supplied by one culture in comparison to another. It may involve not only feeling and knowing but also the process of thinking. The studies of Mertens and his co-workers using psychological tests in the Belgian Congo suggest that natives who have had a European kind of education think like Europeans, while those who do not, retain a framework quite different from the Aristotelian logic which is second nature to most Westerners (36, 28, 45).

The indications of such plasticity and difference should not lead one to hold that the range of psychological variation is limitless and that there are no transcultural consistencies. Even today there is good reason for believing that universals exist. While definition of malfunction and threshold of tolerance may vary from culture to culture, it is almost certain that mental retardation is known in all, as are also symptoms very like schizophrenia and depression. One of the opportunities in cross-cultural studies is to discover and more precisely specify universals and differentiate them from more localized disorders. Such a step would be a major advance in narrowing the field of possible etiological factors requiring investigation and would point to some as being more important than others.

A system of classification, together with its definitions and under-lying concepts, which would stand up across cultures and take into account the variable and less variable factors, would probably result in some rearrangement and reorientation for psychiatry. At the least it would call for assessment of etiological theories against a broader background and it should bring to the fore the notion that the etiology of diagnosis in this or that cultural setting is a matter that has to be understood before there can be understanding of the etiology of disorder.

Psychiatric disorders are not, however, the only relevant area in need of taxonomic consideration. A problem of equal importance is the development of a system of classification for ordering the socio-cultural environment in a manner relevant to our interests in the effect of socio-cultural factors on the origin and pattern of psychiatric disorders. While some consideration has already been given to cross-cultural and trans-cultural classification of psychiatric illness, very little has been given to categorizing cultures and social groups from this point of view. Yet without this there is severe limitation in generalization, in cross-comparison, and in the identification of salient socio-cultural factors.

While it is our opinion that the problems just mentioned are of first-order importance, it is not our intention to assert that they are the only questions worth tackling. Our inclination is rather to feel that the broad context needs to be kept in mind in any specific study and the limitations recognized which will prevail pending development of systematic knowledge in the wider areas. With this reservation, there is much to be said for pushing ahead with particular studies such as those concerned with relating culture, personality, and psychiatric disorder.

It may well be that descriptive studies of psychiatric disorders in non-Western cultures could be combined and articulated with investigations of culture and personality.   For instance a common syndrome in the Western Region of Nigeria is excitement (26).   It apparently shows up in the clinics there with far greater frequency than it does in Europe or North America.   It is also a component of disorders which have other features as well.   One has the impression, moreover, that excitement at a somewhat lower level, though still high by Western standards, is a prominent aspect of many personalities.   It also seems that the culture itself sets a positive value on states of frenzy under certain conditions.   What are the relationships of these behaviors to each other?   Are there also hereditary and physiological factors to be considered?   Is there, for instance, any connection with what appears to be an unusual frequency of malignant hypertension?   What is the part played by cultural change?

The promise in pursuing such questions is not at present in terms of revealing highly specific relationships such as was done by Pasteur in his work with micro-organisms, but rather in assembling evidence as a means of feeling out the more and less probable hypotheses for later, more crucial investigation.   It is largely a matter of finding suitable targets and discovering the right questions to ask of nature— questions which are answerable by the further procedures of science.

What has been observed above with regard to studies of culture, personality and psychiatric disorder, apply also to investigations of roles, child-socialization, and other questions of a similar type.

With all cultural studies, the possible contribution of hereditary and physiological factors should be given consideration.   Their recognition is important, just as is the case with culture when the primary emphasis is on one of these other topics.

In concluding our paper, we should like to return again to a point mentioned earlier.   This is our impression that comparative study of change is one of the most fruitful opportunities for uncovering the nature of socio-cultural factors in relation to psychiatric disorder.   We regard descriptions and analyses of cultures at a given time as prerequisite to this, as fixing-points in terms of which to understand shifts.   If, following a suggestion made earlier, we were to attempt to build a system for classifying cultures in such a manner as to have maximal relevance for mental health and mental illness, we would choose types of socio-cultural change as our starting point.

References

1. Aberle, D. F.: 'Arctic Hysteria' and 'Lâtah' in Mongolia.   *Transactions of the New York Academy of Sciences,* May, 1952, 14, 7: 291–297.

2. Abraham, J. J.: 'Lâtah' and 'Amok.'   *The British Medical Journal,* February 24, 1912: 438–439.

3. Ackerknecht, E. H.: Medicine and Disease Among Eskimos. *Ciba Symposia*, July–August, 1948, 10. 16–921.

4. American Psychiatric Association, Committee on Nomenclature and Statistics: Diagnostic and Statistical Manual [for] Mental Disorders. Washington, D.C., The Association, 1952. 130 pp.

5. Benedict, R.: Patterns of Culture. Boston and New York, Houghton Mifflin, 1934. 290 pp.

6. Brill, A. A.: Piblokto or Hysteria Among Peary's Eskimos. *The Journal of Nervous and Mental Disease*, August, 1913, 40, 514–520.

7. Cooper, J. M.: The Cree Witiko Psychosis. *Primitive Man*, January, 1933, 6: 20–24.

8. Czaplicka, M. A.: Aboriginal Siberia: A Study in Social Anthropology. Oxford, Clarendon Press, 1914. 374 pp.

9. Devereux, G.: Normal and Abnormal: The Key Problem of Psychiatric Anthropology. Chapter 2 *in* Some Uses of Anthropology: Theoretical and Applied. Washington, D.C., The Anthropological Society of Washington, 1956. 120 pp.

10. Eaton, J. W.; Weil, R. J.: Culture and Mental Disorders: A Comparative Study of Hutterites and Other Populations. Glencoe, Illinois, The Free Press, 1955. 254 pp.

11. Erikson, E. H.: Childhood and Society. New Yᴏʀk, W. W. Norton, 1950. 397 pp.

12. Freud, S.: Civilization and Its Discontents. (J. Riviere, Trans.) London, Hogarth, 1930. 144 pp.

13. Gorer, G.: The Concept of National Character. Personality in Nature, Society, and Culture. (C. Kluckhohn; H. A. Murray; D. M. Schneider, Eds.) New York, Knopf, 1953. 701 pp.; 246–259.

14. Gorer, G.; Rickman, J.: The People of Great Russia. New York, Chanticleer Press, 1950. 235 pp.

15. Hallowell, A. I.: Culture and Experience. Philadelphia, University of Pennsylvania Press, 1955. 434 pp.

16. Honigmann, J. J.: Culture and Personality. New York, Harper, 1954. 499 pp.

17. Howells, W. W.: Back of History: The Story of Our Own Origins. New York, Doubleday, 1954. 384 pp.

18. Hughes, J. M.; Hughes, C. C.; Leighton, A. H.: Notes on the Concept of Sentiment. Appendix A *in* Leighton, A. H.: My Name Is Legion. Foundations for a Theory of Man in Relation to Culture. New York, Basic Books, 1959. 452 pp.

19. Inkeles, A.; Levinson, D. J.: National Character: The Study of Modal Personality and Sociocultural Systems. Handbook of Social Psychology (G. Lindzey, Ed.) Cambridge, Addison-Wesley, 1954. 2 vols.; Vol. 2: 977–1020.

20. Jochelson, Waldemar, [V. I.]: . . . The Koryak. (Publications of the Jessup North Pacific Expedition, Vol. 6.) Memoirs of the American Museum of Natural History, Vol. X, Part II. New York, G. E. Stechert, 1908. 842 pp.

21. Kardiner, A.: The Individual and His Society: The Psychodynamics of Primitive Social Organization. New York, Columbia University Press, 1939. 503 pp.

22. Kardiner, A.: The Psychological Frontiers of Society. New York, Columbia University Press, 1945. 475 pp.

23. Kroeber, A. L.: Anthropology: Race, Language, Culture, Psychology, Prehistory. New York, Harcourt, Brace, 1948. 856 pp.

24. Kroeber, A. L.: Psychosis or Social Sanction. The Nature of Culture. Chicago, University of Chicago Press, 1952. 437 pp.; 310–319.

25. Kroeber, A. L.; Kluckhohn, C.: Culture: A Critical Review of Concepts and Definitions. (Papers of the Peabody Museum of American Archaeology and Ethnology, Harvard University. Vol. 47, No. 1.) Cambridge, Massachusetts, The Museum, 1952. 223 pp.

26. Lambo, T. A.: Neuropsychiatric Observations in the Western Region of Nigeria. *British Medical Journal,* December 15, 1956, 2: 1388–1394.

27. Landes, R.: The Abnormal Among the Ojibwa. *The Journal of Abnormal and Social Psychology,* January, 1938, 33: 14–33.

28. Laroche, J. L.: "Recherche sur les aptitudes des écoliers noirs au Congo Belge." [Thèse de doctorat] Louvain, Institut de Psychologie Appliquée, 1958.

29. Laubscher, B. J. F.: Sex, Custom and Psychopathology: A Study of South African Pagan Natives. New York, Humanities Press, 1952. 347 pp.

30. Leighton, A. H.: My Name Is Legion. Foundations for a Theory of Man in Relation to Culture. New York, Basic Books, 1959. 452 pp.

31. Leighton, A. H.: Mental Illness and Acculturation. Medicine and Anthropology (I. Gladston, Ed.) New York, International Universities Press, 1959. 170 pp.

32. Linton, R.: The Study of Man. An Introduction. New York, Appleton-Century, 1936. 503 pp.

33. Linton, R.: The Cultural Background of Personality. New York, Appleton-Century, 1945. 157 pp.

34. Linton, R.: Culture and Mental Disorders. Springfield, Illinois, Thomas, 1956. 139 pp.

35. Mead, M.: National Character. Anthropology Today. An Encyclopedic Inventory. (A. L. Kroeber, Ed.) Chicago, University of Chicago Press, 1953. 966 pp.; 642–667.

36. Mertens de Wilman C., Vers une étude plus systématique des variables psychologiques de l'acculturation. *Revue de psychologie appliquée,* January, 1958, 8: 1–23.

37. Novakovsky, S.: Arctic or Siberian Hysteria as a Reflex of the Geographic Environment. *Ecology,* April, 1924, 5: 113–127.

38. Piers, G.; Singer, M. B.: Shame and Guilt: A Psychoanalytic and a Cultural Study. Springfield, Illinois, Thomas, 1953. 86 pp.

39. Redfield, R.: Peasant Society and Culture: An Anthropological Approach to Civilization. Chicago, University of Chicago Press, 1956. 162 pp.

40. Riesman, D.: The Lonely Crowd: A Study of the Changing American Character. New Haven, Yale University Press, 1950. 386 pp.

41. Spencer, K.: Mythology and Values: An Analysis of Navaho Chantway Myths. Philadelphia, American Folklore Society, 1957. 240 pp.

42. Spiro, M. E.: Culture and Personality: The Natural History of a False Dichotomy. *In* Readings in Child Development. (W. E. Martin; C. B. Stendler, Eds.) New York, Harcourt, Brace, 1954. 513 pp.; 117–141.

43. van Loon, F. H. G.: Amok and Lâtah. *The Journal of Abnormal and Social Psychology*, January–March, 1927, 21: 434–444.

44. Van Wulfften Palthe, P. M.: Psychiatry and Neurology in the Tropics. Chapter 8 *in* A Clinical Textbook of Tropical Medicine. (C. D. de Langen, and A. Lichtenstein, Eds.) Amsterdam, G. Kolff, 1936. 557 pp.

45. Verhaegen, P.: Utilité actuelle des tests pour l'étude psychologique des autochtones congolais. *Revue de psychologie appliquée*, 1956, 6: 139–151.

46. White, L. A.: The Science of Culture: A Study of Man and Civilization. New York, Farrar, Straus, 1949. 444 pp.

47. Wielawski, J.; Winiarz, W.: Imu—A Psychoneurosis Occurring Among Ainus. *Psychoanalytic Review*, 1936, 23: 181–186.

48. Yap, P. M.: The Lâtah Reaction: Its Pathodynamics and Nosological Position. *The Journal of Mental Science*, October, 1952, 98: 515–564.

August B. Hollingshead and
Frederick C. Redlich

SOCIAL CLASS AND
PSYCHIATRIC DISORDERS *

Introduction

The research reported here grew out of the work of a number of men, who, during the last half-century, have demonstrated that the social environment in which individuals live is connected in some way, as yet not fully explained, to the development of mental illness (1). Medical men have approached this problem largely from the viewpoint of epidemiology (2). Sociologists, on the other hand, have analyzed the question either in terms of ecology (3), or of social disorganization (4). Neither psychiatrists nor sociologists have carried on extensive research into the question we are concerned with, namely, interrelations between the class structure and the development of mental ill-

* From August B. Hollingshead and Frederick C. Redlich, "Social Class and Psychiatric Disorders" in *Interrelations between the Social Environment and Psychiatric Disorders*, Milbank Memorial Fund, New York, 1953. Pages 195–207 reprinted by permission of the authors and the publisher.

ness. However, a few sociologists and psychiatrists have written speculative papers in this area (5).

The present research, therefore, was designed to discover whether a relationship does or does not exist between the class system of our society and mental illnesses. Five general hypotheses were formulated to test some dimension of an assumed relationship between the two. These hypotheses were stated positively; they could just as easily have been expressed either negatively or conditionally. They were phrased as follows:

1   The *prevalence* of psychiatric disorders is related significantly to the class structure.

2   The *types* of psychiatric disorders are connected significantly to the class structure.

3   The type of *psychiatric treatment* is associated with an individual's position in the class structure.

4   The *psycho-dynamics* of psychiatric disorders are correlative to an individual's position in the class structure.

5   *Mobility* in the class structure is neurotogenic.

Each hypothesis is linked to the others, and all are subsumed under the general theoretical assumption of a functional relationship between stratification in society and the prevalence of particular types of mental disorders among given social classes or strata in a specified population. Although our research was planned around these hypotheses, we have been forced by the nature of the problem of mental illness to study *diagnosed* prevalence of psychiatric disorders, rather than *true* or *total* prevalence. This point should be kept in mind, when we present some of our preliminary findings.

Methodological procedure

The question of how these hypotheses are being tested leads us to a brief discussion of methodological procedures. In the first place, the research is being done by a team of four psychiatrists,[1] two sociologists,[2] and a clinical psychologist.[3] The data are being assembled in the New Haven urban community, which consists of the city of New Haven and surrounding towns of East Haven, North Haven, West Haven, and Hamden. This community had a population of some 250,000 persons in 1950.[4] The New Haven community was selected because the community's structure has been studied intensively by sociologists over a long period. In addition, it is served by a private

---

[1] Drs. F. C. Redlich, B. H. Roberts, L. Z. Freedman, and Leslie Schaffer.
[2] August B. Hollingshead and J. K. Myers.
[3] Harvey A. Robinson.
[4] The population of each component was as follows: New Haven, 164,443; East Haven, 12,212; North Haven, 9,444; West Haven, 32,010; Hamden, 29,715; and Woodbridge, 2,822.

psychiatric hospital, three psychiatric clinics, and twenty-seven practicing psychiatrists, as well as state and Veterans Administration
facilities.

Four technical operations had to be completed before the hypotheses could be tested. Briefly these operations were: (1) the delineation
of the class structure of the community; (2) selection of a cross-sec-
tional control of the community's population; (3) the determination of
who was receiving psychiatric care; and (4) the stratification of both
the control sample and the psychiatric patients.

August B. Hollingshead and Jerome K. Myers took over the task of
delineating the class system. Fortunately, Maurice R. Davie and his
students had studied the social structure of the New Haven community
in great detail over a long time span (6). Thus, we had a large body
of data we could draw upon to aid us in blocking out the community's
social structure.

Stated categorically, the community's social structure is differentiated *vertically* along racial, ethnic, and religious lines; each of these
vertical cleavages, in turn, is differentiated *horizontally* by a series of
strata or classes. Around the socio-biological axis of race two social
worlds have evolved: A Negro world and a white world. The white
world is divided by ethnic origin and religion into Catholic, Protestant,
and Jewish contingents. Within these divisions there are numerous
ethnic schisms. The Irish hold aloof from the Italians, and the Italians move in different circles from the Poles. The Jews maintain a
religious and social life separate from the gentiles. The *horizontal*
strata that transect each of these vertical divisions are based upon
the social values that are attached to occupation, education, one's
place of residence in the community, and associations.

The vertically differentiating factors of race, religion, and ethnic
origin, when combined with the horizontally differentiating ones of
occupation, education, place of residence, and so on, produce a social
structure that is highly compartmentalized. The integrating factors
in this complex are twofold. First, each stratum of each vertical
division is similar in its cultural characteristics to the corresponding
stratum in the other divisions. Second, the cultural pattern for each
stratum or class was set by the "Old Yankee" core group. This core
group provided a cultural model that has shaped the status system of
each sub-group in the community. In short, the social structure of
the New Haven community is a parallel class structure within the
limits of race, ethnic origin, and religion.

This fact enabled us to stratify the community, for our purposes,
with an *Index of Social Position.*[5] This *Index* utilizes three scaled

[5] A detailed statement of the procedures used to develop and validate this *Index*
will be described in a forthcoming monograph on this research tentatively titled
Psychiatry and Social Class, August B. Hollingshead and Frederick C. Redlich.

factors to determine an individual's class position within the community's stratificational system: (1) ecological area of residence; (2) occupation; and (3) education. Ecological area of residence is scaled into a six point scale; occupation and education are each scaled on a seven point scale. To obtain a social class score on an individual, we must know his address, his occupation, and the number of years of school he has completed. Each of these factors is given a scale score, and the scale score is multiplied by a factor weight determined by a standard regression equation. The factor weights are as follows: Ecological area of residence—5; occupation—8; and education—6. Then the three factor scores are summed. The resultant score is taken as an index of this individual's position in the community's social class system.

This *Index* enabled us to delineate five *main* social class strata within the horizontal dimension of the social structure. These principal strata or classes may be characterized as follows:

Class I   This stratum is composed of wealthy families whose wealth is often inherited and whose heads are leaders in the community's business and professional pursuits. Its members live in those areas of the community generally regarded as the best; the adults are college graduates, usually from famous private institutions, and almost all gentile families are listed in the New Haven *Social Directory*, but few Jewish families are listed. In brief, these people occupy positions of high social prestige.

Class II   Adults in this stratum are almost all college graduates; the males occupy high managerial positions, many are engaged in the lesser ranking professions. These families are well-to-do, but there is no substantial inherited or acquired wealth. Its members live in the "better" residential areas; about one-half of these families belong to lesser ranking private clubs, but only 5 per cent of Class II families are listed in the New Haven *Social Directory*.

Class III   This stratum includes the vast majority of small proprietors, white-collar office and sales workers, and a considerable number of skilled manual workers. Adults are predominantly high school graduates, but a considerable percentage have attended business schools and small colleges for a year or two. They live in "good" residential areas; less than 5 per cent belong to private clubs, but they are not included in the *Social Directory*. Their social life tends to be concentrated in the family, the church, and the lodge.

Class IV   This stratum consists predominately of semi-skilled factory workers. Its adult members have finished the elementary grades, but the older people have not completed high school. However, adults under thirty-five have generally graduated from high school. Its members comprise almost one-half of the community; and their residences are scattered over wide areas. Social life is centered in the family, the neighborhood, the labor union, and public places.

Class V   Occupationally, Class V adults are overwhelmingly semi-skilled factory hands and unskilled laborers. Educationally most adults have not completed the elementary grades. The families are concentrated in the "tenement" and "cold-water flat" areas of New Haven. Only a small minority belong to organized community institutions. Their social life takes place in the family flat, on the street, or in the neighborhood social agencies.

The second major technical operation in this research was the enumeration of psychiatric patients. A Psychiatric Census was taken to learn the number and kinds of psychiatric patients in the community. *The Psychiatric Census was limited to residents of the community who were patients of a psychiatrist or a psychiatric clinic, or were in a psychiatric institution on December 1, 1950.* To make reasonably certain that all patients were included in the enumeration, the research team gathered data from all public and private psychiatric institutions and clinics in Connecticut and nearby states, and all private practitioners in Connecticut and the metropolitan New York area. It received the cooperation of all clinics and institutions, and of all practitioners except a small number in New York City. We are convinced that we have data on at least 98 per cent of all individuals who were receiving psychiatric care on December 1, 1950.

Forty-four pertinent items of information were gathered on each patient by a team composed of a sociologist and a psychiatrist, and placed on a schedule. Sociological data were collected by the sociologists, and psychiatric data by the psychiatrists. The schedule included such psychiatric items as symptomatology and diagnosis; onset of illness and duration; referral to the practitioner and the institution; the nature and intensity of treatment. On the sociological side, we were interested in age, sex, occupation, education, religion, race and/ or ethnicity, family history, marital experiences, and so on.

The third technical research operation was the selection of a control sample from the normal population of the community. The sociologists drew a 5 per cent random sample of households in the community from the 1951 New Haven *City Directory*. This directory covers the entire communal area. The names and addresses in it were compiled in October and November, 1950, a period very close to the date of the Psychiatric Census. Therefore, there were comparability of residence and date of registry between the two population groups. Each household drawn in the sample was interviewed, and data on the age, sex, occupation, education, religion, and income of family members, as well as other items necessary for our purposes were placed on a schedule. This sample is our Control Population.

Our fourth basic operation was the stratification of the psychiatric patients and of the control population with the *Index of Social Position*. As soon as these tasks were completed, the schedules from the Psychiatric Census and the 5 per cent Control Sample were edited and coded, and their data were placed on Hollerith cards.   The analyses of these data are in process.

Selected findings

Before we discuss our findings relative to Hypothesis I, we want to reemphasize that our study is concerned with *diagnosed* or *treated* prevalence rather than *true* or *total* prevalence.   Our Psychiatric Census included only psychiatric cases under treatment, diagnostic study, or care.   It did not include individuals with psychiatric disorders who were not being treated on December 1, 1950, by a psychiatrist.   There are undoubtedly many individuals in the community with psychiatric problems not being treated by psychiatrists who escaped our net.   If we had *true* prevalence figures, many findings from our present study would be more meaningful, perhaps some of our interpretations would be changed, but at present we must limit ourselves to the data we have.   With this caveat in mind, we shall turn to a discussion of our findings relative to our hypotheses.

Hypothesis I. To recapitulate, Hypothesis I, as revised by the nature of the problem, stated: *The diagnosed prevalence of psychiatric disorders is related significantly to an individual's position* in the class structure.   A test of this hypothesis involves a comparison of the normal population with the psychiatric population.   If no significant difference between the distribution of the normal population and the psychiatric patient population by social class is found, Hypothesis I should be abandoned as untenable.   However, if a significant difference is found between the two populations by class, Hypothesis I should be entertained until more conclusive data are assembled. Pertinent data for a limited test of Hypothesis I are presented in Table 1.   The data included in Table 1 show the number of individuals in the normal population and the psychiatric population by class level. What we are concerned with in this test is how these two populations are distributed by class.

When we analysed these population distributions by the use of the chi square method, we found a *very significant* relation between social class and treated prevalence of psychiatric disorders in the New Haven community.   A comparison of the percentage distribution of each population by class readily indicates the direction of the distortion of psychiatric cases.   For example, Class I comprises 3.1 per cent of the community's population, but only 1.0 per cent of the psychiatric cases.   Class V, on the other hand, includes 17.8 per cent of the community's population, but it contributed 36.8 per cent of the psychiatric patients.   The chi square tests show that these differences are far beyond the limits of chance even at the .001 level

Table 1
Distribution of normal and psychiatric population by social class

Social class	Normal population [1]		Psychiatric population	
	No.	Per cent	No.	Per cent
I	358	3.1	19	1.0
II	926	8.1	131	6.7
III	2,500	22.0	260	13.2
IV	5,256	46.0	758	38.6
V	2,037	17.8	723	36.8
Unknown [2]	345	3.0	72	3.7
Total	11,422	100.0	1,936	100.0

$P < .001 \; X^2 = 408.16$

[1] These figures are preliminary, they do not include Yale students, transients, institutionalized persons, and refusals.
[2] The unknown cases were not used in the calculation of X^2. They are (1) individuals drawn from the sample and (2) psychiatric cases whose class level could not be determined because of paucity of data.

of probability. On the basis of our data Hypothesis I clearly should be accepted as tenable.

Hypothesis II. Hypothesis II postulated a significant connection between the *type* of psychiatric disorder and social class. This hypothesis involves a test of the ideas that there may be a functional relationship between an individual's position in the class system and the type of psychiatric disorder that he may present. This hypothesis depends, in part, on the question of diagnosis. Our psychiatrists based their diagnoses on the classificatory system developed by the Veterans Administration (7). For the purposes of this paper, we grouped all cases into two categories: the neuroses and the psychoses. The results of this grouping by social class are given in Table 2.

A study of Table 2 will show that there is a distinct inverse relationship between neuroses and psychoses by social class. The neuroses are concentrated at the higher levels, and the psychoses at the lower end of the class structure. Our team advanced a number of different

Table 2
Distribution of neuroses and psychoses by social class
Based on the Psychiatric Census

Social class	Neuroses		Psychoses	
	No.	Per cent	No.	Per cent
I	10	52.6	9	47.4
II	88	67.2	43	32.8
III	115	44.2	145	55.8
IV	175	23.1	583	76.9
V	61	8.4	662	91.6
Total	449		1,442	

$P < .001 \; X^2 = 296.45$

theories to explain the sharp differences between the neuroses and psychoses by social class. One assumption was that the low percentage of neurotics in the lower classes was a direct reaction to the cost of psychiatric treatment. But as we accumulated data in a series of case studies, for tests of Hypotheses IV and V, we became skeptical of this simple interpretation. Our detailed case records indicate that the social distance between psychiatrist and patient may be more potent than economic considerations in determining the character of psychiatric intervention. This question requires further research.

The high concentration of psychotic patients in the lower strata is probably the product of a very unequal distribution of psychotics in the general population. To test this idea, Hollingshead selected schizophrenics for special study. Because of the severity of this disease the probability is that few schizophrenics are not receiving some kind of psychiatric care. This diagnostic group comprises 44.2 per cent of all patients, and 58.7 per cent of the psychotics, in our study. Ninety-seven point six per cent of these schizophrenic patients had been hospitalized at one time or another, and 94 per cent were hospitalized at the time of our census. When we analyze these patients in terms of their class level we find that there is a highly significant inverse relationship between social class and schizophrenia.

Hollingshead decided to determine, on the basis of our data, what the probability of the prevalence of schizophrenia by social class might be in the general population. To do this he used a proportional index to learn whether or not there were differentials in the distribution of the general population, as represented in our control sample, and the distribution of schizophrenics by social class. If a social class exhibits the same proportion of schizophrenia as it comprises of the general population, the index for that class will be 100. If schizophrenia is disproportionately prevalent in a social class the index will be above 100; on the other hand, if schizophrenia is disproportionately

Table 3
Comparison of the distribution of the normal population with schizophrenics by class, with an index of probable prevalence

Social class	Normal population (5 per cent sample)		Schizophrenics		Index of prevalence
	No.	Per cent	No.	Per cent	
I	358	3.2	6	.7	22
II	926	8.4	23	2.7	33
III	2,500	22.6	83	9.8	43
IV	5,256	47.4	352	41.6	88
V	2,037	18.4	383	45.2	246
Total	11,077	100.0	847	100.0	

low in a social class the index will be below 100. The bias for or against the probability of schizophrenia in a given social class is given in the last column of Table 3.

The fact that the Index of Prevalence in Class Level I is only one-fifth as great as it would be if schizophrenia was proportionately distributed in this class, and that it is two and one-half times as high in Class Level V as we might expect on the basis of proportional distribution, gives further weight to the tenability of Hypothesis II. The fact that the Index of Prevalence is 11.2 times as great in Class V as in Class I is a remarkable finding.

Hypothesis III. Hypothesis III stipulated that the type of psychiatric treatment a patient receives is associated with his position in the class structure. A test of this hypothesis involves a comparison of the different types of therapy being used by psychiatrists on patients in the different social classes. We encountered many forms of therapy, but they were grouped under three main types; psychotherapy, organic therapy, and custodial care. The patient population, from the viewpoint of the principal type of therapy received, was divided roughly into three main types; psychotherapy, organic therapy, and custherapy; 31.7 per cent received organic treatments of one kind or another; and 36.3 per cent received custodial care without treatment. When we analyzed these types of therapy by class a distinctly significant increase occurred in the percentage of cases who received no treatment, other than custodial care, as one moved from the higher to the lower classes. The same finding applies to organic treatment. Psychotherapy, on the other hand, was concentrated in the higher classes. Within the psychotherapy category there were sharp differences between the types of psychotherapy administered to the several classes. For example, psychoanalysis was limited to Class I and II, whereas patients in Class V who received any psychotherapy were treated by group methods in the state hospitals. The number and percentage of patients who received each type of therapy is given in Table 4.

Table 4
Distribution of the principal types of therapy by social class

Social class	Psychotherapy		Organic therapy		No treatment	
	No.	Per cent	No.	Per cent	No.	Per cent
I	14	73.7	2	10.5	3	15.8
II	107	81.7	15	11.4	9	6.9
III	136	52.7	74	28.7	48	18.6
IV	237	31.1	288	37.1	242	31.8
V	115	16.1	234	32.7	367	51.2

$P < .001$ $X^2 = 336.58$

The data of Table 4 shows very definitely that Hypothesis III should be retained.

At the moment we do not have data available for a test of Hypotheses IV and V.   These hypotheses will be put to a test as soon as we complete work on a series of cases now under close study.   Preliminary materials give us the impression that they too will come out positively.

Conclusions and interpretations

This study was designed to throw new light upon the question of how mental illness is related to social environment.   It approached this problem from the perspective of social class to determine if an individual's position in the social system was associated significantly with the development of psychiatric disorders.   It proceeded on the theoretical assumption that if mental illnesses were distributed randomly in the population, then the hypotheses we phrased to test the idea that psychiatric disorders are connected in some functional way to the class system would not be found to be statistically significant.

The data we have assembled demonstrate conclusively that mental illness, as measured by diagnosed prevalence, is not distributed randomly in the population of the New Haven community.   On the contrary, psychiatric difficulties of so serious a nature that they reach the attention of a psychiatrist are distributed in highly significant ways along social class lines.   In addition, types of psychiatric disorders, and the ways patients are treated are strongly associated with social class position.

The objective statistical tests of our hypotheses indicate that there are definite connections between particular types of social environments in which people live, as measured by the social class concept, and the emergence of particular kinds of psychiatric disorders, as measured by psychiatric diagnosis.   They do not tell us: (1) what these connections are; nor (2) do they tell us how they are functionally connected to a particular mental illness in a given individual.   They do indicate, however, that we are proceeding on promising and safe ground.   The next step, we believe, is to turn from the strictly statistical approach to an intensive study of the social environments associated with particular social classes, on the one hand, and of individuals in these environments who do or do not develop mental illnesses, on the other hand.   Currently the research team is engaged in this next step, but we are not ready to make a formal report of our findings.

References

1. For example, *see:* Rosanoff, A. J.: Report of a Survey of Mental Disorders in Nassau County, New York.   New York: National Committee for Mental

Hygiene, 1916; Stern, Ludwig: *Kulturkreis und Form der Geistigen Erk-rankung* (Sammlung Zwanglosen Abshandlungen aus dem Gebiete der Nerven-und-Geitesdrankheiten), X, No. 2, Halle a. S:C. Marhold, 1913, 1–62; Sutherland, J. F.: Geographical Distribution of Lunacy in Scotland. *British Association for Advancement of Science,* Glasgow, Sept. 1901; White, William A.: Geographical Distribution of Insanity in the United States. *Journal of Nervous and Mental Disease,* XXX (1903), 257–279.

2. For example, *see:* Braatoy, Trygve: Is It Probable that the Sociological Situation Is a Factor in Schizophrenia? *Psychiatrica et Neurologica,* XII (1937), 109–138; Gerard, Donald L. and Siegel, Joseph: The Family Background of Schizophrenia. *The Psychiatric Quarterly,* 24 (January, 1950), 47–73; Hyde, Robert W. and Kingsley, Lowell V.: Studies in Medical Sociology, I: The Relation of Mental Disorders to the Community Socio-economic Level. *The New England Journal of Medicine,* 231, No. 16 (October 19, 1944), 543–548; Hyde, Robert W. and Kingsley, Lowell V.: Studies in Medical Sociology; II: The Relation of Mental Disorders to Population Density. *The New England Journal of Medicine,* 231, No. 17 (Oct. 26, 1944), 571–577; Hyde, Robert W. and Chisholm, Roderick M.: Studies in Medical Sociology, III: The Relation of Mental Disorders to Race and Nationality. *The New England Journal of Medicine,* 231, No. 18 (Nov. 2, 1944), No. 3, Malamud, William and Malamud, Irene: A Socio-psychiatric Investigation of Schizophrenia Occurring in the Armed Forces. *Psychosomatic Medicine,* 5 (Oct. 1943), 364–375; Malzberg, B.: Social and Biological Aspects of Mental Disease, Utica, N.Y. State Hospital Press, 1940; Roth, William F. and Luton, Frank H.: The Mental Health Program in Tennessee: Statistical Report of a Psychiatric Survey in a Rural County. *American Journal of Psychiatry,* 99 (March, 1943), 662–675; Ruesch, J. and others, Chronic Disease and Psychological Invalidism.: New York: American Society for Research in Psychosomatic Problems, 1946; Ruesch, J. and others, Duodenal Ulcer—A Socio-psychological Study of Naval Enlisted Personnel and Civilians, Berkeley and Los Angeles: University of California Press, 1948; Ruesch, Jurgen; Jacobson, Annemarie; and Loeb, Martin B.: Acculturation and Illness. *Psychological Monographs: General and Applied,* 62, No. 5, Whole No. 292, 1948 (American Psychological Association, 1515 Massachusetts Ave., N.W., Washington 5, D.C.); Tietze, C.; Lemkau, Paul; and Cooper, M.: A Survey of Statistical Studies on the Prevalence and Incidence of Mental Disorders in Sample Populations. *Public Health Reports,* 1909–27, 58 (Dec. 31, 1943); Tietze, C.; Lemkau, P.; and Cooper, Marcia: Schizophrenia, Manic Depressive Psychosis and Social-Economic Status. *American Journal of Sociology,* XLVII (Sept. 1941), 167–175.

3. Faris, Robert E. L. and Dunham, H. Warren: Mental Disorders in Urban Areas. Chicago: University of Chicago Press, 1939; Dunham, H. Warren: Current Status of Ecological Research in Mental Disorder, *Social Forces,* 25 (March 1947), 321–326; Felix, R. H. and Bowers, R. V.: Mental Hygiene and Socio-environmental Factors. *The Milbank Memorial Fund Quarterly,* XXVI (April 1948), 125–147; Green, H. W.: Persons Admitted to the Cleveland State Hospital, 1928–1937, Cleveland Health Council, 1939.

4. Faris, R. E. L.: Cultural Isolation and the Schizophrenic Personality. *American Journal of Sociology,* XXXIX (Sept. 1934), 159–169; Faris, R. E. L.: Reflections of Social Disorganization in the Behavior of a Schizophrenic Patient. *American Journal of Sociology,* I (Sept. 1944), 134–141.

5. For example, *see:* Davis, Kingsley: Mental Hygiene and the Class Structure. *Psychiatry* (February 1938), 55–56; Parsons, Talcott: Psychoanalysis and the Social Structure. *The Psychoanalytical Quarterly,* XIX, No. 3 (1950), 371–384; Dollard, John and Miller, Neal: Personality and Psychotherapy. New York: McGraw-Hill, 1950; Ruesch, Jurgen: Social Technique, Social Status, and Social Change in Illness. Personality in Nature, New York: Alfred A. Knopf, 1949, 117–130; Warner, W. L.: The Society, the Individual and His Mental Disorders. *American Journal of Psychiatry,* 94, No. 2 (September, 1937), 275–284.

6. Davie, Maurice R.: The Pattern of Urban Growth. Studies in the Science of Society, edited by G. P. Murdock, New Haven, 1937, 133–162; Kennedy, Ruby J. R.: Single or Triple Melting-pot Intermarriage Trends in New Haven, 1870–1940. *American Journal of Sociology,* 39 (January 1944), 331–339; McConnell, John W.: *The Influence of Occupation Upon Social Stratification.* Unpublished Ph.D. thesis, Sterling Memorial Library, Yale University, 1927; Myers, Jerome K.: Assimilation to the Ecological and Social Systems of a Community. *American Sociological Review,* 15 (June 1950), 367–372; Minnis, Myra: The Relationship of Women's Organizations to the Social Structure of a City. Unpublished Ph.D. thesis, Sterling Memorial Library, Yale University, 1951.

7. *Psychiatric Disorders and Reactions,* Veterans Administration, Technical Bulletin 10A–78, Washington, October 1947.

John Dollard and
Neal E. Miller

CRITICAL TRAINING
SITUATIONS IN CHILDHOOD *

The culture, of course, takes a position—a traditional position—on the various needs of the child. It has a design for the feeding situation, for cleanliness training, for sex training, for the treatment of anger responses in the child; and as the society imposes its will through the acts of the parents, the child reacts in its blind emotional way. Each

* From John Dollard and Neal E. Miller, *Personality and Psychotherapy,* McGraw-Hill Book Company, Inc. New York, 1950. Pages 132–154 reprinted by permission of the authors and the publisher.

one of the above-mentioned training situations can produce long-lasting effects on the character and habits of the individual and each is worth a brief discussion. We are by no means sure that these four are all of the dilemmas which can produce acute emotional conflicts, but we do know that each one of them has, in known cases, done so.

I   The feeding situation: Conflicts and attitudes

Much important learning takes place in reference to the hunger drive and the strong responses it excites. During the nursing period the child cannot "comfort" itself. It cannot, so to say, tell itself "It won't be long now," or "Only twenty minutes 'til feeding time." The hunger of the child is an urgent, incessant, and timeless pressure which, obviously, produces the most intense activation. If the child is fed when hungry, it can learn that the one simple thing it can do to get results (*i.e.*, cry) can make a difference in what happens. Learning to cry as a signal for food is one small unit in its control of the world. Such a trait could be the basis of a later tendency to be "up and doing" when in trouble, of a belief that there is always a way out of a painful situation.

Apathy and apprehensiveness.   If the child is not fed when it is crying, but is instead left to "cry itself out," it can, similarly, learn that there is nothing it can do at that time to change the painful circumstances. Such training may also lay the basis for the habit of apathy and not "trying something else" when in trouble. In the second case, when drive is allowed to mount, the child can also learn that being a little bit hungry is followed by being very painfully hungry. When the child is then fed, only its most violent responses are reinforced. In this case the child can learn to fear being very hungry when it is only slightly hungry and to make the frightened response appropriate to severe hunger when only mild hunger exists. It is thus learning to "overreact," to be apprehensive of evil even when the circumstances of life seem calm. This learning occurs through the behavior mechanism of anticipation.

Sociability and "love."   On the other hand, probably the feeding experience can be the occasion for the child to learn to like to be with others; that is, it can establish the basis of sociability. When the hungry infant is fed, some of the wonderful relaxation responses which it experiences can be conditioned to the stimuli of those persons who are caring for the child. Thereafter the mere appearance of the mother can produce a momentary feeling of well-being. The child will learn to stop crying at the sound of her footstep, the rustle of her dress, or the sound of the tap water which is warming its bottle. These experiences have an intense emotional quality which is often attached thereafter to the word "mother" as the source of all beneficence.

Likewise, if the child is properly held, cared for, and played with, the blessed relaxing quality of these experiences also will attach to those who care for it. Since the mother or caretaker stands at the very head of the parade of persons who become "society" for the child, it is quite important that she evoke such benign and positive responses in the child.

Lack of social feeling.   The reverse of all this can also take place if the child is stuffed when it is not hungry. If its food rewards are in various ways cut down and spoiled, it may not care much whether "the others" are there or not. It may tend to be "low in social feeling." If the child is actually punished for crying when it is hungry, as by being slapped, a true hunger-anxiety conflict will be created. Though this may be rare, it does undoubtedly happen, especially when the child is overactive as a result of gastric upset and so is able to provoke anger in the ill-disciplined parent.

One origin of fear of being alone.   The child can learn another dangerous habit in this period. It can learn to fear being alone. Teaching a child to fear being alone is easy to do and is often done inadvertently. Let the child get very hungry when it is alone, let it cry and not be heard or attended to, but let the quantity of stimulation in its body from hunger and from crying continue to rise. When the child is finally fed, these very strong terminal responses are reinforced and can be attached to all the stimuli which were present during the period of its intense hunger. These responses can produce stimuli of drivelike strength. Similarly responses which produce strong drives can be attached to the darkness, to the immobility of objects, to quietness, to absence of parental stimuli. Once the child has inadvertently learned to "fear" darkness and quietness and immobility, it will also learn to escape from the darkness into the light, from the quietness into noise, and from immobility into the presence of others.

This escape may be perceived by the parents as an additional nuisance when they are expecting their hours of relaxation; the child insists on being with them even though "there is nothing wrong with it." They may then take punitive measures, forcing the child back into the dark or the quiet and creating a true conflict between fear of darkness and the newly learned fear of the irate parent. This must indeed be a very common conflict, since fear of quietness and darkness are not innate in children and yet are frequently seen.

If this fear persists into adult life, it can be an element in the character of a person who is compulsively driven to social contacts, who cannot tolerate being alone. Compulsive sociability may also involve a sacrifice in creativeness, since in order to be creative the individual must be able to tolerate a certain amount of loneliness.

Weaning. In the case of weaning also, severe traumatic circumstances may arise. If the child is suddenly changed from one type of food or mode of feeding to another, it may go on a hunger strike which the parents obstinately oppose, saying "It will eat when it gets hungry enough." Indeed it will, but in the meantime it may have learned some of the fears or the apathy already listed. If parents punish the child for its refusal to eat the new food a genuine conflict is created which in turn will have its consequences. There seems hardly anything valuable that an infant can learn by punishment under such circumstances, and parents should take the greatest pains to avoid this.

Colic and recurring hunger. The child with colic is also a sore trial to itself and its parents. One of the simplest circumstances producing "colic" is that the infant has eaten too much and must regurgitate some of the food or the gases which its digestion produces. Once it has been laboriously walked or patted into parting with food or gas it may be hungry again. Unimaginative parents, not understanding that hunger has innocently recurred, will fail to feed the child. If the mother does feed it, the child may overeat again and the cycle of gastric tension, vomiting, and hunger may recur. However, until an infant learns to make its gastric distress anticipatory and thus to check itself while eating, there is no way of avoiding these circumstances. The sequence overeating, gastric distress, vomiting, and recurring hunger seems more likely to occur with children fed on schedule since they will get much hungrier while waiting for the scheduled moment of feeding and are more likely to overeat.

If parents lose their tempers and punish the young child at any phase of this awkward kind of learning to eat just the right amount, severe conflict concerning feeding may ensue. If the infant is punished before it is burped, the result may be that it has anxiety attached to burping and regurgitating, and it is thus condemned to bear gastric tension. If it is punished after regurgitating when it is again hungry, anxiety responses will be attached to hunger stimuli. Under these conditions punishment cannot teach the infant anything that will help it along its road to development. Nevertheless this unavoidable circumstance of colic is one to test the character of the most devoted parents.

The foregoing discussion is by no means a check list of all the things that a child can learn during the first year or so of life. For example, in learning to crawl and walk the child is also learning to fear bumps.

It learns not to poke its head under the table and then suddenly try to stand erect. It is learning a few words and common commands. Those interested in the somatic development of the child can consult Gesell (1940). Various specialists in pediatrics such as Spock (1946) have described the behavior problems that are most frequent among young children in the home.

Secret learning of early years.   What we have attempted to do here is to show that the seemingly innocuous feeding situation can be fraught with important emotional consequences. Outsiders who cannot know what is going on in a home may see no reason to suppose that the infant is learning anything at all. Yet observant insiders may see the child becoming apathetic, apprehensive, learning to fear the dark, on the one hand, or becoming loving, sociable, and confident, on the other. It is this secret learning of the early years which must be made the object of scientific research. We are firmly of the opinion that anything that can be sensed can be scaled and thus that apathy, sociability, and fear can be scientifically treated if we but trouble to study the child in the home—where these habits are being learned.

Early conflicts unlabeled, therefore unconscious.   The young child does not notice or label the experiences which it is having at this time. It cannot give a description of character traits acquired during the first year of life nor yet of its hardships, fears, or deep satisfactions. What was not verbalized at the time cannot well be reported later. An important piece of history is lost and cannot be elicited by questionnaire or interview. Nevertheless, the behavioral record survives. The responses learned occur and may indeed recur in analogous situations throughout life. They are elicited by unlabeled cues and are mutely interwoven into the fabric of conscious life. The fact that different children learn different things during this period undoubtedly accounts for some of the variability between children which is often attributed to innate factors.

2   Cleanliness training can create conflicts

If the child has come safely and trustfully through the early feeding and weaning experience it may learn for the first time in its cleanliness training that the culture patterns lying in wait for it have an ugly, compulsive aspect. No child may avoid this training. The demands of the training system are absolute and do not take account of individual differences in learning ability. The child must master cleanliness training or forfeit its place in the ranks of socially acceptable persons. Freud describes the culture's task as building within the personality of the child the psychic dams of loathing and disgust (Freud, 1930, p. 40) for urine and feces and particularly for the latter. The attempt to construct these inward barriers immediately puts the child in a conflict situation.

Observation of children within the home indicates that children begin with the same naïve interest in their feces and urine that they have in the other parts and products of their bodies.   Development of the ability to grasp and finger objects makes it possible for the young child to handle and play with fecal material.   The morning will arrive in every nursery when the astonished parents will observe their beloved child smearing feces over his person, his hair, and his immediate environment with gurgling abandon.   This may be the first occasion for sharp, punishing exhortations, for angry dousing, for the awakening of anxiety in connection with fecal materials.   On pain of losing the parents' love and so exposing itself to the high drives and tensions which occur when they do not support it, and on further pain of immediate punishment, the child must learn to attach anxiety to all the cues produced by excretory materials—to their sight, smell, and touch.   It must learn to deposit the feces and urine only in a prescribed and secret place and to clean its body.   It must later learn to suppress unnecessary verbal reference to these matters, so that, except for joking references this subject matter is closed out and excluded from social reference for life.

Difficulty of cleanliness learning.   Cleanliness training is difficult because culture must work a reversal of a strong innate connection between a cue and a response.   The swelling bladder or bowel produces a strong drive stimulus which at a certain strength releases the urethral sphincter or touches off the evulsion response in the anus. To meet cultural demands this sequence must be rearranged.   The connection between bowel stimulus and the evulsion response must be weakened.   The child must learn to suppress the evulsion response to the bowel drive-stimulus alone.   It must then insert other responses in the sequence.   At first it must learn to call to the parents.   It must later learn to insert, walking, unbuttoning, and sitting on the toilet chair while it is still suppressing the urgent evulsion response.   Only to a new pattern of cues—the bowel stimulus, the cues of the proper room, the sense of freedom of clothes, the pressure of the toilet seat on the child's thighs—may the evulsion response occur without anxiety.

In short, this response occurs not only to the pressure of the primary drive involved but also to the complex stimulus pattern just named.   If one can once get the child to order the responses correctly, the strong tension reduction produced by defecation will reinforce the responses to the pattern of cues enumerated.   The real problem, therefore, is getting the child to suppress the naïve evulsion response and to insert a considerable series of responses into the sequence before evulsion.

We do not revel in the details of this analysis but offer the detailed analysis because we believe it is impossible to understand the difficulty of the learning involved unless one sees all the new units which must be learned. For instance, buttoning and unbuttoning is a difficult habit for small children to learn and may hold up the perfect learning of the sequence for some time. The child, however, is not really trained until it can carry out the whole sequence by itself.

Learning without verbal aids.   The difficulties which produce conflict in this learning arise chiefly from the fact that the child must accomplish it in a period of life when it has to learn mainly without verbal aids, that is, by trial and error.   Learning cleanliness control by trial and error is a slow and vexing business.   The child must learn to wake up in order to go to the toilet, though sleep seems good.   It must learn to stop its play even when social excitement is strong.   It must learn to discriminate between the different rooms of the house— all this by crude trial and error.   In this case, "trial" means urinating or defecating in an inappropriate place, and "error" means being punished for the act so that anxiety responses are attached to the cues of this place.   In the trial-and-error situation this must be repeated for each inappropriate place—bed, living room, dining room, kitchen, "outside."

The function of this training is to attach anxiety responses to the defecation drive so that they win out over the immediate evulsion response.   These anxiety responses also motivate and cue off the next responses in the series, such as calling to the parents, running to the bathroom, unbuttoning the clothes, and the like.   When accomplished by trial-and-error means, this training necessarily takes considerable time, perhaps several years in all, in which child and parent are under severe pressure.

Strong emotions aroused in cleanliness training.   Learning cleanliness is no mere behavioral routine.   It arouses strong emotions— perhaps as strong as are ever evoked in the child again.   Anger, defiance, stubbornness, and fear all appear in the course of such training. Fear may generalize to the toilet itself and excite avoidance responses in the very place where the child is expected to "go."   Unable to discriminate between the safe and the unsafe place, the child may try "not to defecate at all."   This behavior is perfectly automatic, but it may seem willful to the parents, and they may particularly resent the final loss of control after the protracted attempt to inhibit defecation.   Once hit on, this response would be strongly reinforced and tend to become habitual since the drive reduction after prolonged withholding would be much more intense than after a normal period of withholding. When "losing control," instead of deliberately relaxing, is strongly rewarded, the habit of "losing control" should become anticipatory and thus prolong the problem of cleanliness training. In other words, great strictness at early ages may block rather than advance the child in his cleanliness learning.

Learning to escape from sight of parents.   The child may become, from the parents' standpoint, furtive by the following means: When it is punished for a cleanliness error by the parent, anxiety is attached to the sights and sounds produced by that parent.   In order to escape that anxiety the child may attempt to escape from the parental presence and attempt to keep to a minimum the amount of time it spends near the parent.   This state of affairs has the disadvantage that the child is escaping from one of its natural teachers.   It may learn to speak less well than it might because it simply does not remain near those people who could teach it to speak.   Infliction of punishment may also arouse anger toward the inflicting agent.   The child may attempt struggling with the parents, biting them, or slapping at them and, in turn, be punished for this behavior.   Thus, an anger-anxiety conflict is learned.

Excessive conformity and guilt.   Again, the child may get the impression that it is pursued by an all-seeing, punishing guardian and may try making as few responses as possible—and certainly not innovating any novel responses.   Its conclusion on the basis of punishments received may be that unless a response is known to be correct it should not be risked.   Thus may be laid the characterological basis of the excessively timid, conforming individual.   Similarly, the child may not be able to discriminate between parental loathing for its excreta and loathing for the whole child himself.   If the child learns to adopt these reactions, feelings of unworthiness, insignificance, and hopeless sinfulness will be created—feelings which sometimes so mysteriously reappear in the psychotic manifestations of guilt.

Advantages of verbal aids.   From this discussion it will be clear that the trial-and-error method of early training, with its many punishments, has much more risk attached than training carried on at a time when the child can be verbally aided to hit on the right sequence of responses in a few early trials.   Once the child has acquired the words "living room," "kitchen," "bedroom," and "outside," a single punishment trial, if properly conducted, can attach anxiety to all these cues at the same time and so spare the brutal repetition of punishment. If the child has already learned to call for help when it needs help, it can much more easily learn to call for aid when it needs to defecate. If it has learned to stop various activities to the word "stop," it is much easier to get it to check the evulsion response when this is occurring to its innate stimulus. If certain promises of the parents already have reward value attached to them, the child can be aided to make the right responses by being promised simple rewards. If the child already attaches anxiety to certain instructions of the parents, these instructions can have some of the same effect as repeated, direct punishments.

In this case also the reinforcement of the act of defecation itself will fix the correct series of responses into place. This will happen whether the course of the training has been stormy or smooth. However, in the case of the smooth, verbally aided learning there is much less danger of arousing furious anger or of creating maladaptive habits such as retention of feces and loss of control. Extremely strong anxiety reactions do not occur and feelings of excessive worthlessness are less likely. The end result is the same so far as mere cleanliness training is concerned. The difference lies in the fact that the later, verbally aided method of getting out the response has much less risk of violent side reactions and character distortions.

Freud's Superego.   The foregoing analysis employs the thoughts and sentences of Freud reworked from the standpoint of behavior theory. The course of cleanliness training is unlabeled and unconscious. Any one of us may have been through a stormy period of this kind and yet have no recollection of it. The results may show themselves in our symptoms, our most deeply embedded "character" traits, in our dreams, in our intuitive presuppositions about life, but they will not show themselves in our verbal behavior. The record of this training will be found in no man's autobiography, and yet the fate of the man may be deeply influenced and colored by it.

The first broad strands of what Freud calls the Superego are laid down at this time. Anxiety reactions, never labeled, are attached to stimuli, also unlabeled. When these stimuli recur later the anxiety reactions automatically recur. The resulting effect Freud has called the "Superego" or unconscious conscience. When unconscious guilt reactions are severe, the personality is suffused with terror. It is hard to say whether a morbid conscience is a worse enemy of life than a disease like cancer, but some comparison of this kind is required to emphasize the shock produced in the witness when he sees a psychotic person being tortured by such a conscience. Enough is known now to convince us that we should make the humble-seeming matter of cleanliness training the subject of serious research.

3   Conflicts produced by early sex training

Sex-anxiety conflicts seem frequently to be involved in neuroses arising in civilian life.   The recurrent appearance of sex as a conflict element does not seem to be due to the fact that sex is the strongest of
human drives.   At their highest levels, pain, hunger, and fatigue certainly outrank it.   Many strong secondary drives such as anxiety, ambition, and pride can also be stronger than sex.   Sex seems to be so
frequently implicated because it is the most severely attacked and
inhibited of primary drives.   Even though relatively weaker, sex can
exert a strong pressure which produces great activation in the organism
and great misery if blocked for long periods.   In no other case is the
individual required to wait so many years while patiently bearing the
goading drive.

Source of first sex conflict—the masturbation taboo.   Erection of
the penis can be observed in male infants as a reflexive response to
interrupted feeding or to urethral drive pressure (Halverson, 1938).
At the age of a year the child is able to grasp an object quite perfectly.
The sensitivity of the genital and the ability to prehend make masturbation possible.   It seems likely also that there is some kind of reward associated with masturbating.   On the basis of his observations,
Kinsey *et al.* (1948) believes that small boys acquire the capacity for
orgasm long before they become able to ejaculate; similarly an experiment by Sheffield, Wulff, and Backer (1950) demonstrates that sexual
responses short of ejaculation can serve to reinforce learning in the
albino rat.   It is certainly a fact that, if unchecked, children do learn
to masturbate and that they sometimes obstinately persist even when
quite severe sanctions are applied.

The sight of a child masturbating evokes intense anxiety in the
adults of our culture and they promptly apply sanctions, ranging from
persistently removing or jerking the child's hand away from its genital
to slapping and spanking it.   The result is to set up in the child the
same sex-anxiety conflict which the adults have.   As in other cases,
masturbatory conflicts established in the first years of life are invariably unconscious.   A vague negative feeling, a tendency to withdraw, an unease is established at the act, sight, or thought of masturbatory behavior.   These conflicts differ for different individuals in
many ways and for many reasons.   Some individuals may be caught
in the act more often than others; some may be punished more severely than others; some may have stronger innate sex drive than
others.   Some may have had more time to learn the habit before
being caught and punished and may thus have a stronger appetite for
this behavior than other persons.   Some may, so to say, scare easier
than others because they already have strong anxieties established in

the cleanliness-training situation.   Such anxieties generalize easily from urethral to the genital stimuli.   Often both are called "nasty" and the cue produced by the common verbal response helps to mediate generalization of fear.   In this case it is easy to train the individual out of the masturbatory habit, since the fear does not have to be learned but only generalized to the sex stimuli.

Parents don't notice effects of taboo.   The imposition of a masturbation taboo can have important effects on the child's life.   There may be immediate and direct changes in behavior. . . .   When behavior changes occur it seems quite surprising that parents do not notice them as results of conflict over masturbation.   The fact that they do not so notice is, however, easily explained.   Intimate as their contact is with the child they may yet be very poor observers of cause and effect.   Most of the young child's emerging life is mysterious to parents anyway.   They may further have particular avoidances against noticing matters and connections which arise in the sexual sphere. Likely, they believe themselves to have been sexless in childhood and can do no less than believe the same in respect to their children. Whether correctly evaluated by parents or not, the masturbatory taboo is the first of the important sex taboos, and it sets up a sex-anxiety conflict in each of us.

Sex typing of personality.   The sexual development of the child cannot be understood without understanding the forceful training in sex typing which it receives.   The unspecialized or less specialized human being, the infant, is identified as boy or girl and its relationship with others is defined in terms of sex type.   Sex typing is a strictly conventional arrangement that varies from society to society (Mead, 1949).   Our own society is strongly organized around sex specialization of personality.   This begins with male and female names, clothes, play patterns, toys, and continues throughout life by defining specialized sex roles for man and woman.   The ultimate love object of the child is defined as a member of the opposite sex.   The nascent sexual reactions of the child are directed toward stimuli of the opposite sex.   The child is led to expect eventual sex rewards from persons of the opposite sex.

The taboo on homosexuality.   Training in sex typing has the indirect effect of imposing a vigorous taboo on homosexuality.   Homosexual objects are not presented, are treated by neglect or, if need be, vigorously condemned.   The errors children make while learning sex typing are the source of much amusement to adults.   The little girl declares she is going "to marry mommie" when she grows up or the little boy states he will marry his admired older brother.   Children are carefully corrected and trained into making the appropriate distinctions. Furthermore, it seems probable that parents, already sex-typed, help to develop this turning toward the opposite sex by themselves "favoring" the child of the opposite sex.

Students of sexual abnormalities have suspected that the failure to define sharply the sex type is a factor in producing perverse sex adjustment (Henry, 1948). Thus, if a boy child were ardently desired, the parents might fail to impose sharp feminine sex typing on the girl who actually arrived. Or, in the opposite case, a mother who prefers her son to remain her "baby" may make him effeminate when she should be emphasizing his masculine character. Such inversions of social sex typing cannot directly produce a sexual perversion since sex responses must be attached to same-sex cues before a perverse sex appetite can exist; but they might tend to confuse the child about what its socially expected sex goals were and thus contribute to deviation.

After sex typing has been imposed and well learned, the child is in about this net position: masturbation has been tabooed, and it cannot give itself sex rewards by this means; sex behavior between siblings has been suppressed; on the other hand, a new channel, though a long one, has apparently been opened through the fact of sex typing. The child is vaguely led to expect something rewarding in the general direction of the opposite sex. These two circumstances set up the situation of the Oedipus complex.

How fear is attached to heterosexual approach responses. The anxiety which adolescents, and often adults, show at the prospect of heterosexual contact must be explained. It does not arise by chance. It arises rather in the family situation which is the child's most important early learning situation. The first definition of sexual responses is learned in relation to parents and siblings and only later transferred to others. Freud calls this the Oedipus situation.

We will illustrate from the case of the boy child, where the matter seems to be clear, and rehearse and paraphrase the familiar facts discovered by Freud. The boy child turns to his mother in fact or thought in the hope of getting sex rewards when he can no longer get them by himself. He expects sex rewards partly by generalization (Miller, 1948b; von Felsinger, 1948) of expectation of reward—that is, by analogy to the many rewards the mother has already given him—and partly from the fact that by sex typing he has learned to expect sex rewards from a woman and his mother is the woman at hand. Doubtless some of the anxiety already learned in connection with masturbation generalizes to the sex impulse when it begins to show itself toward family women.

A new source of anxiety appears, however; that is, fear of the father. The five-year-old boy knows his father is the head of the house, the symbolic source of punishments and discipline. He also knows that his father is the husband of his mother and has some unique relationship to her. This rivalry of the father does not exist merely in the boy's mind. It is often made very concrete in the father's behavior. The father may complain that the little boy sleeps in the mother's bed when he is already "too old" for such behavior. The father may object to the fact that the child or children sop up so much of the mother's time and leave so little to him. The father may impose certain restrictions about entering the parents' room which leave the child with a mystery on his hands. Whenever the male child makes emotional demands on the mother, the father may become more critical of him in other and more general respects, saying that the boy talks too much, that he does not work enough, and so forth. If the boy reacts with fear toward his father as a rival, it is because the father, consciously or unconsciously, is acting in a way that seems fearsome and rivalrous. The child is usually unable to discriminate between opposition on ground of sexual leanings and that evoked by its other claims on the mother. The whole thing may be played out as a kind of dumb show. The heterosexual strivings of the boy toward the mother may be behaviorally real and active but not labeled in the boy's mind. On the other hand, the opposition of the father, though active and effective, may be oblique and unconscious.

Often the mother herself rejects the claims of the boy. She has anxiety at any overtly sexual responses from the child, stops fondling him, and may suddenly and inexplicably change from being loving and approving to being horrified, disgusted, and disapproving.

In this case there is less need for the father to be harsh and hostile. But if the mother does not reject and does not clearly show her separate loyalty and adherence to the father, a great burden is placed upon him to maintain his control of his wife. The mother, for example, may use the seeming need of the child as a way of escaping from her husband and from the sexual conflicts which she has in regard to him. She may favor and cozen the son while avoiding her husband, and unconsciously this may seem to the father like a genuine kind of preferment. The father may then react by very actively arousing the boy's fears.

Specific genital anxiety. If the boy's motives are sexual, the increased threat from the father produces anxiety which is directly attached to the sexual motives and interpreted as a sexual threat. This is one way in which castration anxiety may become an important factor in the boy's life even though the father never threatens castration in so many words. The boy has learned that the punishment often fits the crime.

There are other and less ghostly sources of the castration threat. Very often it has been specifically associated with the masturbation taboo—*i.e.*, that if the boy plays with his penis, the penis will be cut off. The threat may appear in the fables of childhood which are told so eagerly. One of the authors as a six-year-old boy was permitted to participate in an after-dark session of older boys. They were telling the tale of how Bill Smith, a prominent citizen of the town, had come home and surprised his wife in bed with her lover. Smith thereupon pulled out a spring-labeled jackknife (demonstration of length and viciousness of same by boy telling the story) and proceeded to unman the lover. Such a story does not remain, however, as a mere "fable." It is taken to heart and has the effect of teaching straight-out castration fear to sex motives.

The castration idea may occur in still another way; that is, as an inference from the lack of penis in the girl. The parents do not explain the different nature of the girl's genital. The uninstructed boy may assume that the girl once had an external genital but has been deprived of it, perhaps as a punishment. There is no doubt that this inference is often made. The authors have repeatedly heard it in those in-family situations where children are first questioning their elders about sexual matters. It is further surprising in the history of adults how often the idea of bodily damage occurs in relation to sex "sins." Castration fear has been shown clinically to be connected with fears of bodily damage, especially in the cases of heart and brain, to aversion to crippled people, and to avoidance of women in their genital aspect. Castration fear is frequently escaped by approaching the bachelor girl (who has no husband or father at her side) or by recourse to women of lower class or racial status (whose normal protectors are not allowed to function).

In any case, and engendered by whatever of these several means or combination of them, the sex conflict takes a new twist when it is worked out within the family. Anxiety which was once attached only to the masturbation impulse is now attached to the heterosexual approach situation. If this anxiety is made very strong it can produce a certain relief in the intensity of the conflict. This is the so-called "resolution" of the Oedipus complex. When anxiety is greatly dominant over approach tendencies, the conflicted individual stays far from his goal and but few of the acquired elements in the sexual appetite are aroused. Thus, that part of the intensity of the conflict which is produced by appetitive sex reactions is missing, and the conflict is therefore lessened. However, this conflict should and does recur when the individual is placed near his goal object and cannot easily escape, as frequently happens in adolescence. Then again the full strength of the sex reactions is pitted against the terror of sexual injury. Marriage evidently seems to some adults a similar situation —that of being held close to a feared goal—and they make the blind escape responses which would be expected.

Heterosexual conflict not labeled. If the prior intimidation of the person has been very great, and if the mother's stand is correct, much less fear need be imposed by the father. If sex appetite is weak rather than strong, there is much less pressure from the child's side and less anxiety need be imposed to counteract it.

All these events are but poorly labeled at the time they occur. The culture is niggardly about giving names to sexual organs, sexual feelings, or the fears attached to them. The child is therefore not able to make a logical case for itself and, so to say, "put it up to the parents." Furthermore, repression sets in in two ways: Children are frequently forbidden to talk to others about their sexual reactions. Such sentences or thoughts as do occur tend to make the conflict keener both by arousing sex appetites and by cueing off the anxiety attached to them. The child is pained when it tries to think about sexual things and relieved when it stops. The result is repression. This repression has one unfortunate consequence for science. When the individual is later interviewed he is not able, promptly and freely, to give account of these matters. The renaming and mental reestablishment of these bygone events can thereafter only be made through the weary work of psychotherapy.

Science is not the only loser. The individual himself has lost his opportunity to use higher mental activities in solving the conflicts involving sex and authority. There are many ways in which the person can be victimized. A sexual perversion may lurk behind the blank surface of repression. The individual may never again be able cheerfully and amiably to accept a measure of authority exerted over him. Acute anxiety may be attached to his heterosexual impulses and when the time comes that society expects, almost requires, that he marry, he may be unable to do so. Even though he is able to get over the line into marriage, he may find the years of his marital life haunted and poisoned by constant, unconscious anxiety. In this case, the individual has automatically generalized to all women the anxiety proper only to the incest situation. He has failed to discriminate, as a free mental life would enable him to do, between the tabooed sexual feelings and objects of childhood and the relative freedom permitted to adults. To every authoritarian figure in his life he generalizes the intense anxiety that he once experienced when attempting to rival his father in the sexual field. Only when higher mental processes are restored can the individual make those discriminations which allow him to proceed freely and constructively with his life as an adult.

4   Anger-anxiety conflicts

At this point we are more interested in the connection between angry emotions and fear than we are in the problem of how angry feelings are aroused in the child.   We assume, however, as before (Dollard *et al.*, 1939) that anger responses are produced by the innumerable and unavoidable frustration situations of child life.   In the frustration situation, new and strong responses are tried out.   Some of these have the effect of inflicting pain on other people.   Society takes a special stand toward such anger responses, generally inhibiting them and allowing them reign only in a few circumstances (self-defense, war, etc.).   Many of these attack, or "put through the act," responses produce strong stimuli, and these we recognize as the emotion of anger. Lift the veil of repression covering the childhood mental life of a neurotic person and you come at once upon the smoking responses of anger.

Patriarchal code on child's anger.   Parents intuitively resent and fear the anger and rage of a child, and they have the strong support of the culture in suppressing its anger.   Direct punishment is probably used much more frequently when the child is angry and aggressive than in any other circumstance.   More or less without regard to what the child is angry about, fear is attached to the stimuli of anger.   The virtuous chastisement of the rebellious child is an age-old feature of our patriarchal culture.   According to the old Connecticut Blue Laws, a father could kill a disobedient son (Blue Laws of Connecticut, 1861, Section 14, p. 69).   Even though this code was never exercised in this extreme in recent times, it shows the complete freedom to punish which was once culturally allowed parents.   As the domestic representative of the patriarch in his absence, the mother is free to punish children "in their own interest."

How fear is attached to anger cues.   We have already noted the situation of early cleanliness training as one tending to produce angry confusion in the small child.   At earliest ages the cultural practice seems to be that of extinguishing anger rather than punishing it; that is, the child is segregated, left to "cry and thresh it out."   However, parents' motivation to teach the child cleanliness training is so strong that they frequently also use punishment, especially in the case of what they interpret as stubborn or defiant behavior.   Anxiety responses therefore become attached not only to the cues produced by the forbidden situation but also to the cues produced by the emotional responses which the child is making at the time.   It is this latter connection which creates the inner mental or emotional conflict.   After this learning has occurred, the first cues produced by angry emotions may set off anxiety responses which "outcompete" the angry emotional responses themselves. The person can thus be made helpless to use his anger even in those situations where culture does permit it. He is viewed as abnormally meek or long-suffering. Robbing a person of his anger completely may be a dangerous thing since some capacity for anger seems to be needed in the affirmative personality.

Other frustrations producing anger. The same state of affairs can prevail and be additionally reinforced as a result of the frustrations occurring in the sex-training situation. If the child is punished for masturbating it may react with the response of anger. The parent may not notice the provocative circumstance but see only that the child has become mysteriously "naughty." Its naughtiness may be punished and the connection between anger and fear be strengthened.

Parental rejection or desertion may likewise produce anger in the child. If the child feels secure only when the parents are present, it may react with fear when the parents leave or when they threaten to leave again. When the parents return, the child may make excessive claims, want unusual favors, "be clingy." To these demanding and possessive gestures on the part of the child the parent may react with unintelligent punishment, thus again teaching the child to fear.

The new tasks involved in growing up impose many frustrations on the child. Giving up long-standing privileges may arouse rage. Being forced to try out new responses, such as putting on its own clothes or tying its own shoe laces, can anger the child. If it screams, lunges, slaps at the parent in these circumstances, punishment is the almost inevitable answer, and the connection between anger and fear is additionally strengthened.

Sibling rivalry. Rivalry between siblings is a constant incitement to anger, and such rivalry occurs in every household, without exception, where there are siblings of younger ages. The occasions for rivalry seem innumerable. Siblings may compete for evidences of parental love. If the parent disappoints a child, that child may "take it out" on the luckier brother or sister. Younger children may anger older ones by being allowed to assume too quickly privileges which the older have long waited and worked for. Older children may tease and torment younger ones in retaliation. Sometimes the younger child is resented merely for existing and for having displaced the older one and alloyed its satisfaction in being the unique child.

The younger children may enjoy privileges which the older have been forced to abandon and thus create some degree of unconscious resentment. Younger children may tyrannize over older ones by too freely playing with or even destroying their toys and precious objects. Parents should intervene and prevent such behavior but often they do not, and the older child revenges himself in roundabout ways. Younger children may resent the privileges enjoyed by the older and attempt to punish older siblings for their greater freedom. These angry displays result in punishment of the one or the other child by the parents—and sometimes of both. The younger children tend to "catch it" more from the older, and the older children more from the parents. Though parents may mitigate these angry relationships between siblings by just rules which are honestly enforced, there seems no way to take all the hostile strain out of such relations.

Mental limitations.   Small children confront an unintelligible world. Many of their frustrations result from this fact. They do not have the mental units to be patient and foresightful. They do not know how to comfort themselves while waiting. They cannot live in the light of a plan which promises to control the future. Since so much is frustrating to them that is later bearable, they are especially prone to anger. They want to know "Why isn't the circus here today?" "Why do I have to wait 'til my birthday to get a present?" "Why does Daddy have to go to work just when it's so much fun to play with him?" Living in the present and being unable to reassure themselves about the future, young children resort to anger at these inevitable frustrations. Adults experience the hostile or destructive behavior of young children as a nuisance, do not understand its inevitability, and frequently punish aggressive responses.

Devious aggression.   If anger must be abandoned as a response in a frustrating situation, other responses will be tried out such as pleading for what one cannot take by force or submitting to frustrations which can only be worsened through opposition. Devious forms of aggression are particularly likely to occur in this case. The individual can be punished for direct anger responses but it is much harder to catch him at roundabout aggression. He may learn to lie in wait and take revenge by hastening and sharpening punishment which his opponent has invoked in some other way. Gossip, deceit, creating dangerous confusion about agreements and life relationships may all be indirect modes of angry reaction.

Anger conflict unlabeled.   As in the case of sex-anxiety conflicts, the anger-anxiety conflict is likely to be poorly labeled. Verbal skills are at a low level when much of this training is going on. Repression of the language describing anger-anxiety conflicts may occur because conflict is thus, momentarily at least, reduced. As a result, the individual cannot, in later life, be selectively angry, showing anger in just those social situations in which it is permitted and rejecting anger where it is not.

The overinhibited person.   Inhibition of anger may occur in two different degrees.   The overt, or some of the overt, responses of direct aggression may be inhibited.   Some such inhibitions must occur if a child is to live in our culture.   The process may, however, go farther and the emotion of anger itself be throttled.   If the response-produced drives of anger evoke intense fear, the individual may be incapable of a normal life.   The victim loses the core of an affirmative personality. He may be unable to compete as is demanded by our society in school or business spheres.   He may be additionally shamed because he cannot bring himself to fight.   He may depend unduly on others, waiting for them to give him what is everyone's right to take.   Such a child cannot be a self-maintaining person because he cannot produce any anger responses at all, let alone those which are "legitimate and proper."

Since many outlets for anger are permitted adults which are not permitted to children, the person who is overtrained to inhibit anger may seem childish in that he is still following the age-graded code of childhood and is unable to embrace the freer standards of adulthood. One of the chief tasks of psychotherapy, in the case of unduly inhibited persons, is to enable them to name and describe their angry feelings so that they may extinguish undue fear and begin to learn a proportionate self-assertiveness.

Frustrated mobility aspirations produce aggression

There is little doubt that adults can be in conflict concerning their mobility strivings and that these conflicts can lead to pathological results in behavior (Ruesch, Loeb, *et al.*, 1946).   The conflict could be described somewhat as follows: In order to be strong and safe, or stronger and safer, the person wants to identify with and possess the symbols of a social group above that of his original family.   In order to make this transition, however, certain prescribed routes must be followed.   The person must have a talent which brings him in touch with and makes him useful to the group into which he wants entry. This talent could be intellectual, could be a facility for making money, could be beauty, could be an exceptionally loving and understanding personality.   If an individual has the wish to change position but does not have such a talent or does not enjoy it to a sufficient degree, he may find it impossible to make the transition.   He may find himself unable to establish the contacts which will enable him to learn the rituals of behavior of the superordinate group.   He may gradually come to know that, though "the promised land" is in sight, he will never enter it.   Meanwhile the group he is trying to leave punishes him for being "different" and the group he tries to enter rejects him as presumptuous.   The realization, conscious or unconscious, that his campaign has failed may serve as a severe frustration and produce varying types of aggressive and compensatory behavior. The resentment of the person who fails of mobility is likely to be severely punished and thus to create an acute anger-fear conflict.

Mobility conflicts which are unconscious.   Except in one circumstance, which we shall come to in a moment, it does not seem likely that conflicts such as the one just described are engendered in early childhood.   The conflict may nevertheless be unconscious.   This unconsciousness of the elements of an adult conflict can arise because the mobile person gets little help from his society in labeling his behavior.   He is not told what he is trying to do, and he has no clear understanding of what the techniques are.   If he hits on the means of mobility, it is, from his point of view, a matter of luck or accident.   He is ordinarily not permitted to think that different social classes exist because the social beliefs which protect the class system forbid this recognition.   Usually the mobile individual sees himself only as rising in some value such as "wealth" or occupation but he does not realize that his real mobility will be founded on a complex set of behavioral adaptations and changes in taste and outlook.   Usually, therefore, the mobile person does not know what is happening to him while it is happening, does not know how he failed if he fails, and does not know until "afterward" how he succeeds if he succeeds. This is a set of conditions which is bound to baffle and to arouse a confusion of angry, rebellious, apathetic, and submissive responses.

Children of a mixed-class marriage.   The one circumstance that we can see under which difference in social class can have an effect on a small child is the case where the child is born of a mixed-class marriage.   If the mother is superordinate, she might in some ways "look down" on the father, apologize for him, and limit his usefulness as a model to her male child.   Such a mother may be unduly "ambitious" for her children, attempting to speed them over the landscape of childhood instead of allowing them to find their natural pace through it.   She may get satisfaction in imposing early cleanliness training because it seems to her like a guarantee of the future precocity of the child.   She may inculcate the sex taboos strongly because she feels that the "goodness" of the child in this respect will keep it out of "bad company" and aid its development in the schools.   She may handle its angry tendencies severely in the hope of making it amenable and yet urge it to highly competitive performance outside the home.   One would predict that this kind of family training would give a special coloring to the circumstances which ordinarily produce conflict in small children (Davis and Havighurst, 1947; Warner, 1949, pp. 70–72).

A child in a class-stable family with parents matched from the class standpoint would not ordinarily discover in the early years of life that there is any group "above" its parents.   During the formative period these parents would play their august roles, majestic in their competence and authority so far as the child could see. It would only be later in life, perhaps first during school days, that the child would learn that there are any people who look down upon it or its parents.   Undoubtedly such knowledge would have some kind of effect on the career of the child, but we cannot say what the possible outcomes might be.   We can be sure, however, that the evaluation put on the self and the family by the surrounding society will be a fact of importance in the developmental history of every child.

References

Blue Laws of Connecticut. Capital Laws. Code of 1650, Section 14, Duane Rulison, Philadelphia, 1861.

Davis, Allison, and Havighurst, Robert, Father of the Man, Houghton Mifflin, Boston, 1947.

Dollard, John, Doob, L. W., Miller, N. E., and Sears, R. R., Frustration and Aggression, Yale University Press, New Haven, 1939.

Freud, Sigmund, Three Contributions to the Theory of Sex, 4th ed., Nervous and Mental Disease Publishing Company, Washington, D.C., 1930.

Gesell, Arnold, The First Five Years of Life, Harper, New York, 1940.

Halverson, H. M., "Infant sucking and tensional behavior," J. gen. Psychol., 53:365–430, 1938.

Henry, G. W., Sex Variants, 1-vol. ed., Hoeber-Harper, New York, 1948.

Kinsey, A. C., Pomeroy, W. B., and Martin, C. E., Sexual Behavior in the Human Male, Saunders, Philadelphia, 1948.

Mead, Margaret, Male and Female, Morrow, New York, 1949.

Miller, N. E., "Theory and experiment relating psychoanalytic displacement to stimulus response generalization," J. abnorm. soc. Psychol., 43:155–178, 1948b.

Ruesch, Jurgen, Loeb, M. B., et al., Chronic Disease and Psychological Invalidism: A Psychosomatic Study, American Society for Research in Psychosomatic Problems, New York, 1946.

Sheffield, F. D., Wulff, J. J., and Backer, Robert, 1950. "Reward Value of Sexual Stimulation without Ejaculation" (in preparation).

Spock, Benjamin, Baby and Child Care, Pocket Books, New York, 1946.

von Felsinger, John, "The Effects of Ovarian Hormones on Learning," Ph.D. dissertation, Yale University, New Haven, 1948.

Warner, W. L., and Associates, Democracy in Jonesville, Harper, New York, 1949.

Harry F. Harlow and
Margaret K. Harlow

THE EFFECT OF REARING
CONDITIONS ON BEHAVIOR *

A wealth of clinical evidence shows that human children who have never had adequate maternal care or who have been separated from adequate maternal care within some critical stage, suffer disturbance and delay or even irreparable damage in terms of subsequent personal-social development. The importance of maternal ministrations in the child's development is further supported by many clinical investigations and by some limited experimental data.

Personality malfunctions that have been attributed to maternal inadequacy include such syndromes as marasmus, hospitalism, infantile autism, feeble-mindedness, inadequate maternal responsiveness, and deviant or depressed heterosexuality. If these disorders are the results of maternal inadequacy, only research with human subjects can establish the conditions and kinds of maternal behavior that produce them. Unfortunately, experiments critical to the resolution of these problems cannot be done with human subjects. We cannot rear babies in illuminated black boxes during the first half-year, year, or two years of their lives. We cannot have mothers rear their children in isolation from other children and from adults for the first two, four, or eight years. We dare not have human children reared with either no mothers or inadequate mothers while providing them with maximal opportunity to interact with age-mates, either identically reared or differentially reared. Yet these are the kinds of experiments which are required if we are to assess the effects of maternal variables unconfounded with other experiential variables on the child's personal-social development.

Most clinical investigations have given primary attention to the effects of maternal privation, defined as absence or inadequacy of maternal responsiveness, or to maternal deprivation, defined as infant separation after the infant has established profound, or at least adequate, maternal attachments. Relatively little attention has been given to the effects of the absence or inadequacy of opportunity for the child to interact with other children and to form adequate affectional patterns with and for them. We know that it is important for the child to form effective infant-mother affectional patterns, but it also is likely that he must form effective child-child affectional patterns if he is to attain normal personal-social, sexual, and paternal patterns. Obviously these affectional systems are not independent. It is pos-

* From Harry F. Harlow and Margaret K. Harlow, "The Effect of Rearing Conditions on Behavior," Bull. Menninger Clinic, 1962, 25, 213–226. Reprinted by permission of the authors and the Editor, Bulletin of the Menninger Clinic.

sible, but by no means a certainty, that at the human level, normal child-child affection requires previous affectional bonds between mother or mother-figure and child. It is certain that the mother plays an important role in the formation of peer affections by providing for and encouraging associations between infants or children, or by preventing or discouraging such associations. Human mothers may also markedly influence the nature and course of child-child relationships.

Psychoanalytic theory, which looks for temporal reduction and temporal primacy, will ascribe primary importance to the earliest causes and conditions whether or not these are of greatest importance. Initial traumas have a false clarity as causative agents since they are not confounded by preceding events, whereas the role of all subsequent events is confounded by the role of these events operating during previous experience. Yet primacy in time need not, and often should not, be equated with primacy in importance.

Effects of total social deprivation on monkeys

Six years ago we took two newborn rhesus monkeys, one male and one female, and subjected them to total social deprivation for the first two years of life. Each was placed in a solid, illuminated cage such that it never saw any other animal—monkey or human—even though it was tested for food responsiveness and learning by remote-control techniques. During isolation these monkeys adapted to solid food slowly and learned with great difficulty, but they were found to have normal weight and good coats when removed—there were no signs of marasmus. At the conclusion of the two years' isolation, they were tested for social responsiveness to each other and to normal monkeys smaller and younger than themselves. They did not respond to each other and either froze or huddled in a corner when abused by the younger animals. Placed together in a cage in a room with many caged monkeys, they showed withdrawal from this new external world, and in the more than two years they lived together, they remained abnormally frightened, showed minimal interaction, and engaged in no sex activities. In follow-up social tests at four years of age with smaller and weaker monkeys, they made no effort to defend themselves except for one brief episode with one of the pair, after which it curled into a ball and passively accepted abuse. The potential for social behaviors in these animals had apparently been obliterated.

We have preliminary, incomplete data on the effects of such total social deprivation confined to a six-month period and are obtaining other data on the effects of such deprivation over a twelve-month period. The results to date indicate severe but not complete withdrawal from external environmental stimulation. Repeated testing in our playroom situation, shown in Figure 1, reveals that one of these

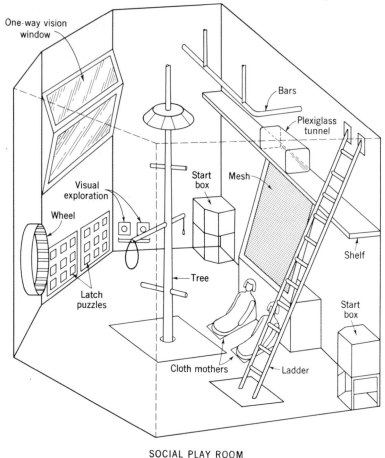

SOCIAL PLAY ROOM

Figure 1

monkeys is almost totally unresponsive socially and the other only occasionally engages in brief, infantile-type social interactions. Normally, the playroom is a highly stimulating situation for monkeys. It is 8 feet high with 36 square feet of floor space, and it contains multiple stationary and mobile toys and tools, flying rings, a rotating wheel, an artificial tree, a wire-mesh climbing ramp, and a high, wide ledge, offering opportunities to explore and play in a three-dimensional world.

We also have data on eight monkeys subjected to total social isolation from other monkeys during the first 80 days of life. Although they neither saw nor contacted nor heard other monkeys, they did see and contact human experimenters, who removed them from their isolation boxes and tested them repeatedly on learning problems after the second week of life. A year later these animals appear to be normally responsive to external environmental stimulation and they are socially responsive to each other when tested in the playroom. This social responsiveness as measured by the appearance of increasingly complex play patterns has become qualitatively normal, but probably it is depressed somewhat quantitatively. Whether there will be subsequent effects on heterosexual and maternal behavior remains for future observation.

If we assume a rough developmental ratio of four to one for monkey to man, the results on these eight monkeys are not completely in accord with human clinical data, which at best are only roughly comparable to our experimental situation. Social isolation up to eight or ten months of age is reported to endanger or impair the personal-social development of human infants. It may be that the stimulation and handling of the monkeys in the learning experiments played a positive role in preparing them for subsequent exposure to a monkey environment, thus minimizing the isolation effects. It is also possible that the human infant is more susceptible than the monkey infant to damage from social isolation.

Effects of early partial social deprivation

We have data on various groups of monkeys raised from the day of their birth without their mothers and without any monkey companionship at least through the first half-year. One group of 56, now ranging in age from five to eight years, was raised in individual bare wire cages where they could see and hear other monkeys, but not touch them. A group of four was similarly housed for up to five years, but had access to a single wire surrogate [1] during the first half-year of life. A third group of over 100 monkeys was raised identically except for access to a cloth surrogate [2] or to both a cloth surrogate and a wire surrogate during at least six months of the first year.[3] Approximately half of these animals have been housed after six months or one year of age with another monkey of like age and like or unlike sex for part or all the time since.

Although there may be differences in the personal-social behaviors of the monkeys comprising these groups, we cannot be sure at the present time, and for this reason we group them together. Many members of all three groups have developed what appear to be abnormal behaviors, including sitting and staring fixedly into space, repetitive stereotyped circling movements about the cage, clasping the

---

[1] A wire surrogate mother is a bare, welded wire cylindrical form surmounted by a wooden head with a crude face and supported semiupright in a wooden frame.

[2] A cloth surrogate differs from the wire surrogate in that the wire cylinder is cushioned with a sheathing of terry cloth.

[3] Harlow, H. F.: The Nature of Love. *Amer. Psychologist*, 1958, *13*, 673–685. Harlow, H. F.: Love in Infant Monkeys. *Sci. Amer.*, 1959, *200*, 68–74.

head in the hands and arms while engaging in rocking, autistic-type movements, and intrapunitive responses of grasping a foot, hand, arm, or leg and chewing or tearing at it with the teeth to the point of injury.

The sex behavior of the six oldest wire-cage-raised monkeys was first measured by Mason [4] in 1960 and compared with that of rhesus monkeys of equal age which had lived in the wild during most of the first year of life. All the wild-raised monkeys, male and female, showed normal sex behavior, characterized in the male by dorsoventral mounting, clasping the legs of the female by the feet, and holding the buttocks by the hands. The females in turn sexually presented themselves by elevating their buttocks and tails, lowering their heads, and frequently looking backward without threatening. No laboratory-raised male or female showed normal sex behavior. Attempted mounting by the male was random in regard to body part, and the most frequent pattern was grasping a side of the female's body and thrusting laterally. The female's patterns were totally disordered and often involved sitting down and staring aimlessly into space. Although none of these animals was sexually mature, heterosexual positioning in both male and female normally develops during the second year.

Attempts to breed the cage-raised monkeys approximately two years later also ended in complete failure. When the oldest wire-cage-raised females were between five and seven years of age and the oldest surrogate-raised females were between three and five years, repeated attempts were made to breed 11 of the wire-cage-raised females and four of the cloth-surrogate-raised females with highly selected males from our breeding colony. The females were placed in the large breeding cages during estrus, and if no fighting ensued within 15 minutes, they were left overnight. Eventually one wire-cage-raised female and three cloth-surrogate females became pregnant. Although observation did not reveal clear-cut differences in the behavior of these two groups, the differences in pregnancy approach significance in spite of—or possibly because of—the greater immaturity of the cloth-surrogate-raised females. Actually, no female, impregnated or not, demonstrated a normal pattern of sexual behavior. Many females tried to avoid the males; some actually threatened the males and would probably have been injured had our males not been carefully screened. When the males approached and positioned the females, the females usually collapsed and fell flat on the floor. Impregnation of the four females was achieved only through the patience, persistence, knowledgeability, and motor skill of the breeding males.

We have subsequently tested many wire-cage- and surrogate-mother-raised males and females with experienced breeding females and experienced breeding males, respectively, in a large 8-foot by 8-foot by

---

[4] Mason, W. A.: The Effects of Social Restriction on the behavior of Rhesus Monkeys: I. Free Social Behavior. *J. Comp. Physiol. Psychol.*, 1960, *53*, 582–589.

8-foot room especially designed for breeding studies. All the males have continued to show the disorganized and inappropriately oriented sexual responsiveness which we have already described, and no male has ever appropriately mounted our experienced and cooperative breeding-stock females, let alone achieved intromission.

With a single exception we have never seen normal, appropriate sexual posturing in our wire-cage- or surrogate-raised females. The females do not approach the males, nor do they groom or present. One cloth-surrogate-raised female was not impregnated throughout six mating sessions, and during this time she began to respond positively and appropriately to the males and eventually developed a normal, full-blown pattern of sexual presentation and sexual posturing during copulation.

Effects of maternal conditions

Direct comparison of the effects of being raised by real monkey mothers and cloth surrogate mothers on subsequent personal-social development has been measured by the use of our playpen test situation. In two playpen situations babies were housed with their real mothers, and in a third setup the babies were housed with cloth mothers. The playpen, whose floor plan is given in Figure 2, consists of large living cages each housing a mother and an infant and adjoining a compartment of the playpen. A small opening in each living cage restrains the mother, but gives the infant continuous access to the adjoining playpen compartment. During two daily test sessions, each an hour in length, the screens between playpen compartments were raised, permitting the infant monkeys to interact as pairs during the first six months and as both pairs and groups of four during the

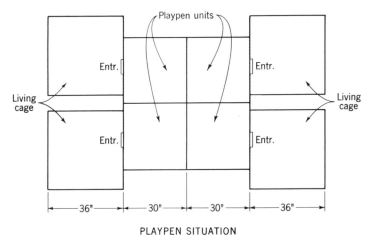

PLAYPEN SITUATION

Figure 2

second six months.   Two experimenters independently observed and recorded the behavior exhibited during test sessions.

The infants raised by real monkey mothers were more socially responsive to each other than were the infants raised by the cloth surrogates.   They showed a wider range of facial expressions, and, probably of paramount importance, they developed simple interactive play patterns earlier than the surrogate-raised monkeys and achieved a level of complex play patterns not achieved by the surrogate-raised monkeys during an 18-month test period.

All the male, mother-raised infants have at one time or another responded sexually toward the mother with pelvic thrusting and in at least two cases by dorsoventral mounting.   In three cases pelvic thrusting to a female was observed before 50 days of age and in a fourth case, before 100 days of age.   Only two (one male and one female) cloth-surrogate-raised monkeys were observed to show pelvic thrusting to the surrogate, and this occurred initially at approximately 100 days of age. Frequency of this sexual play was much higher toward real mothers than toward surrogates.   In both situations maximal frequency occurred at about five months and then declined, apparently being superseded by thrusting directed toward other infants.

Surrogate babies and mothered babies showed no significant differences in first-observed, infant-directed thrusting, but the actual mean score of the surrogate group was lower.   The frequency of sexual play was higher for the real-mothered babies than for the surrogate babies. Finally, seven of eight mother-raised monkeys showed appropriate adult-form sex behaviors during the first 18 months, including ankle clasp by the males, whereas adult-oriented sex behavior was not observed in the cloth-surrogate-raised babies.

There is every reason to believe that normal mothering facilitates the development of heterosexual behavior in rhesus monkeys.   This may be in part the result of direct contacts with the mother growing out of the intimate bonds between mother and child.   One must not, however, underestimate the importance of the role which the real mother apparently plays, indirect though it is, in stimulating the infants to associate with other infants.   This is accomplished from the third month on by discouraging the infant from constant clinging as it matures.   From time to time the mother restrains the infant's approaches or cuffs it if it nips her or pulls her hair.   The chastised infant seeks the companionship of other babies until the storm subsides—the other mothers by this time generally reject all but their own babies—and in the infant-infant interchanges, strong affectional bonds develop along with behaviors, sexual and nonsexual, appropriate to the sexes.

In the present study, as in all ordinary human situations, there is confounding in the roles played by the mother-infant affectional systems and the infant-infant and peer-peer affectional systems in determining later behavior. We expect to resolve this in part by raising two groups of monkey babies with real mothers, but denying them any opportunity to interact with other infants for six months in the one group and 12 months in the other before subjecting them to social testing.

Some information is supplied by another experiment involving eight rhesus babies raised on cloth surrogate mothers, but tested 20 minutes a day in the playroom, which is a more stimulating environment than that afforded by the relatively cramped and bare confines of the play compartments of the playpen situation. These surrogate-mothered babies showed excellent and appropriately timed play behaviors and very early came to assume both sexual and nonsexual behaviors appropriate to males and females. The males threatened, the females did not; the males initiated rough-and-tumble play, but not the females. Males chased males and males chased females, but females practically never chased males and seldom chased females. By a year of age considerable appropriate male and female sex behavior had occurred, and full and complete copulation, other than insemination, was repeatedly observed in the two males and two females on which observations were continued during the second year of life.

It is obvious that we must not underestimate the importance and role of the infant-infant affectional system as a determiner of adolescent and adult adjustments. It is more than possible that this system is essential if the animal is to respond positively to sheer physical contact with a peer, and it is through the operation of this system, probably both in monkey and man, that sexual roles become identified and, usually, acceptable.

The role of the mother in the formation of the adult personality is obviously important, but the exact mechanics are open for experimentation. The most tender and intimate associations occur at a stage in which the monkey infant and human infant can to a considerable extent be molded. Monkey and human mother both have the obligation of gradually dissolving the intense physical bonds which characterize the early mother-child relationship. For the monkey mother it is easy and natural—when the infant becomes mature enough and strong enough to become bothersome, she rejects or punishes it and the baby retreats for a time. Subsequently, she welcomes the baby back. Independence is gradually established. For the human mother, with her more complicated motivational systems and her complex culture, it may be difficult to achieve this gradual separation. The overprotective mother is a well-known clinical extreme in the human problem of weaning the infant and child emotionally. Probably the surrogate monkey mother is a parallel of the overprotective human mother, failing usually to equal the normal mother in rearing socially and sexually adjusted monkeys because, at least in part, she is ever available to provide comfort and security.

She never discourages contact and thereby never encourages independence in her infant and affectional relationships with other infants and children. The normal state of complete dependency necessary in early infancy is prolonged until it hinders normal personal-social development.

As we have already pointed out, four of our laboratory-raised females never had real mothers of their own, one being raised in a bare wire cage and three with cloth surrogates. The first week after the birth of the baby to the wire-cage-raised female, the mother sat fixedly at one side of the cage staring into space, almost unaware of her infant or of human beings, even when they barked at and threatened the baby. There was no sign of maternal responses, and when the infant approached and attempted contact, the mother rebuffed it, often with vigor.

The next two unmothered mothers constantly rebuffed the approaches of their infants, but, in addition, frequently engaged in cruel and unprovoked attacks. They struck and beat their babies, mouthed them roughly, and pushed their faces into the wire-mesh floor. These attacks seemed to be exaggerated in the presence of human beings, and for this reason all formal testing was abandoned for three days for the third unmothered mother because we feared for the life of the infant. The fourth unmothered mother ignored and rejected her infant but did not exhibit excessive cruelty.

In strong contrast to the frailty of the maternal affectional system was the vigor and persistence of the infants' bondage to the mother—time after time, hour after hour, the infants returned, contacted, and clasped the mother in spite of being hit, kicked, and scraped unceremoniously off the mother's body. The physical punishment which these infants took or sought for the privilege of brief contact even to the back or side of the mother's body testified to the fact that, even in infants, attachment to the mother may be prepotent over pain and suffering. One could not help but be reminded of children, removed from indifferent or cruel, indigent, and alcoholic parents, whose primary insistent wish is to return home.

The degree to which monkey data are generalizable to the human being will remain an unsolved dilemma. Nevertheless, we are so struck by the many apparent analogies that we are tempted to say the monkey experiments give us faith in the human clinical observations.

Summary

Infant rhesus monkeys have been reared starting on the first day of life in a variety of situations, including total isolation; partial isolation, either in individual bare wire cages in a colony room for two years or longer, or in individual wire cages with access to one or two mother surrogates for at least the first six months; and in situations with real or surrogate mothers plus contact with other infants for the first year or two of life.

Total isolation for two years resulted in failure to display social or sexual behavior in the next two years, spent in a joint living cage. Results on six months of such isolation are still being gathered and suggest severe, but not complete, social deficits. Only mild effects have been observed thus far in monkeys isolated through the first 80 days of life.

Partial isolation has produced behavioral aberrations in many monkeys and sexual inadequacy in all males and in all but one female. Four females were impregnated, in spite of inadequate posturing, and proved to be completely inadequate mothers.

Infants raised by live mothers were more advanced in social and sexual behavior than infants raised by surrogate mothers in a controlled playpen situation. The mother's role is not entirely clear, however, because in a more stimulating playroom situation, surrogate-mothered babies have shown normal social and sexual behavior.

Over all, it appears that the longer and the more complete the social deprivation, the more devastating are the behavioral effects. Further research is needed to evaluate the relative contributions of live mothers and infant companions to later adjustment.

Erik H. Erikson   **EIGHT AGES OF MAN ***

Basic trust vs basic mistrust

The first demonstration of social trust in the baby is the ease of his feeding, the depth of his sleep, the relaxation of his bowels. The experience of a mutual regulation of his increasingly receptive capacities with the maternal techniques of provision gradually helps him to balance the discomfort caused by the immaturity of homeostasis with which he was born. In his gradually increasing waking hours he finds that more and more adventures of the senses arouse a feeling

* From Erik H. Erikson, "Eight Ages of Man," *International Journal of Psychiatry*, 1966, 2, 281–297. Pages 281–294 reprinted by permission of the author and W. W. Norton & Company, Inc., New York, publisher of *Childhood and Society* where the material first appeared. Copyright 1950, 1963, W. W. Norton & Co., Inc.

of familiarity, of having coincided with a feeling of inner goodness. Forms of comfort, and people associated with them, become as familiar as the gnawing discomfort of the bowels. The infant's first social achievement, then, is his willingness to let the mother out of sight without undue anxiety or rage, because she has become an inner certainty as well as an outer predictability. Such consistency, continuity, and sameness of experience provide a rudimentary sense of ego identity which depends, I think, on the recognition that there is an inner population of remembered and anticipated sensations and images which are firmly correlated with the outer population of familiar and predictable things and people.

What we here call trust coincides with what Therese Benedek has called confidence. If I prefer the word "trust," it is because there is more naïveté and more mutuality in it: an infant can be said to be trusting where it would go too far to say that he has confidence. The general state of trust, furthermore, implies not only that one has learned to rely on the sameness and continuity of the outer providers, but also that one may trust oneself and the capacity of one's own organs to cope with urges; and that one is able to consider oneself trustworthy enough so that the providers will not need to be on guard lest they be nipped.

The constant tasting and testing of the relationship between inside and outside meets its crucial test during the rages of the biting stage, when the teeth cause pain from within and when outer friends either prove of no avail or withdraw from the only action which promises relief: biting. Not that teething itself seems to cause all the dire consequences sometimes ascribed to it. As outlined earlier, the infant now is driven to "grasp" more, but he is apt to find desired presences elusive: nipple and breast, and the mother's focused attention and care. Teething seems to have a prototypal significance and may well be the model for the masochistic tendency to assure cruel comfort by enjoying one's hurt whenever one is unable to prevent a significant loss.

In psychopathology the absence of basic trust can best be studied in infantile schizophrenia, while lifelong underlying weakness of such trust is apparent in adult personalities in whom withdrawal into schizoid and depressive states is habitual. The re-establishment of a state of trust has been found to be the basic requirement for therapy in these cases. For no matter what conditions may have caused a psychotic break, the bizarreness and withdrawal in the behavior of many very sick individuals hides an attempt to recover social mutuality by a testing of the borderlines between senses and physical reality, between words and social meanings.

Psychoanalysis assumes the early process of differentiation between inside and outside to be the origin of projection and introjection which remain some of our deepest and most dangerous defense mechanisms. In introjection we feel and act as if an outer goodness had become an inner certainty. In projection, we experience an inner harm as an outer one: we endow significant people with the evil which actually is in us. These two mechanisms, then, projection and introjection, are assumed to be modeled after whatever goes on in infants when they would like to externalize pain and internalize pleasure, an intent which must yield to the testimony of the maturing senses and ultimately of reason. These mechanisms are, more or less normally, reinstated in acute crises of love, trust, and faith in adulthood and can characterize irrational attitudes toward adversaries and enemies in masses of "mature" individuals.

The firm establishment of enduring patterns for the solution of the nuclear conflict of basic trust versus basic mistrust in mere existence is the first task of the ego, and thus first of all a task for maternal care. But let it be said here that the amount of trust derived from earliest infantile experience does not seem to depend on absolute quantities of food or demonstrations of love, but rather on the quality of the maternal relationship. Mothers create a sense of trust in their children by that kind of administration which in its quality combines sensitive care of the baby's individual needs and a firm sense of personal trustworthiness within the trusted framework of their culture's life style. This forms the basis in the child for a sense of identity which will later combine a sense of being "all right," of being oneself, and of becoming what other people trust one will become. There are, therefore (within certain limits previously defined as the "musts" of child care), few frustrations in either this or the following stages which the growing child cannot endure if the frustration leads to the ever-renewed experience of greater sameness and stronger continuity of development, toward a final integration of the individual life cycle with some meaningful wider belongingness. Parents must not only have certain ways of guiding by prohibition and permission; they must also be able to represent to the child a deep, an almost somatic conviction that there is a meaning to what they are doing. Ultimately, children become neurotic not from frustrations, but from the lack or loss of societal meaning in these frustrations.

But even under the most favorable circumstances, this stage seems to introduce into psychic life (and become prototypical for) a sense of inner division and universal nostalgia for a paradise forfeited. It is against this powerful combination of a sense of having been deprived, of having been divided, and of having been abandoned—that basic trust must maintain itself throughout life.

Each successive stage and crisis has a special relation to one of the basic elements of society, and this for the simple reason that the human life cycle and man's institutions have evolved together. In this chapter we can do little more than mention, after the description of each stage, what basic element of social organization is related to it.   This relation is twofold: man brings to these institutions the remnants of his infantile mentality and his youthful fervor, and he receives from them—as long as they manage to maintain their actuality—a reinforcement of his infantile gains.

The parental faith which supports the trust emerging in the newborn, has throughout history sought its institutional safeguard (and, on occasion, found its greatest enemy) in organized religion.   Trust born of care is, in fact, the touchstone of the *actuality* of a given religion.   All religions have in common the periodical childlike surrender to a Provider or providers who dispense earthly fortune as well as spiritual health; some demonstration of man's smallness by way of reduced posture and humble gesture; the admission in prayer and song of misdeeds, of misthoughts, and of evil intentions; fervent appeal for inner unification by divine guidance; and finally, the insight that individual trust must become a common faith, individual mistrust a commonly formulated evil, while the individual's restoration must become part of the ritual practice of many, and must become a sign of trustworthiness in the community.[1]   We have illustrated how tribes dealing with one segment of nature develop a collective magic which seems to treat the supernatural Providers of foods and fortune as if they were angry and must be appeased by prayer and self-torture. Primitive religions, the most primitive layer in all religions, and the religious layer in each individual, abound with efforts at atonement which try to make up for vague deeds against a maternal matrix and try to restore faith in the goodness of one's strivings and in the kindness of the powers of the universe.

Each society and each age must find the institutionalized form of reverence which derives vitality from its world-image—from predestination to indeterminacy.   The clinician can only observe that many are proud to be without religion whose children cannot afford their being without it.   On the other hand, there are many who seem to derive a vital faith from social action or scientific pursuit.   And again, there are many who profess faith, yet in practice breathe mistrust both of life and man.

Autonomy vs. shame and doubt

In describing the growth and the crises of the human person as a series of alternative basic attitudes such as trust vs. mistrust, we take recourse to the term a "sense of," although, like a "sense of

---

[1] This is the communal and psychosocial side of religion. Its often paradoxical relation to the spirituality of the individual is a matter not to be treated briefly and in passing.

health," or a "sense of being unwell," such "senses" pervade surface and depth, consciousness and the unconscious. They are, then, at the same time, ways of *experiencing* accessible to introspection; ways of *behaving*, observable by others; and unconscious *inner states* determinable by test and analysis. It is important to keep these three dimensions in mind, as we proceed.

Muscular maturation sets the stage for experimentation with two simultaneous sets of social modalities: holding on and letting go. As is the case with all of these modalities, their basic conflicts can lead in the end to either hostile or benign expectations and attitudes. Thus, to hold can become a destructive and cruel retaining or restraining, and it can become a pattern of care: to have and to hold. To let go, too, can turn into an inimical letting loose of destructive forces, or it can become a relaxed "to let pass" and "to let be."

Outer control at this stage, therefore, must be firmly reassuring. The infant must come to feel that the basic faith in existence, which is the lasting treasure saved from the rages of the oral stage, will not be jeopardized by this about-face of his, this sudden violent wish to have a choice, to appropriate demandingly, and to eliminate stubbornly. Firmness must protect him against the potential anarchy of his as yet untrained sense of discrimination, his inability to hold on and to let go with discretion. As his environment encourages him to "stand on his own feet," it must protect him against meaningless and arbitrary experiences of shame and of early doubt.

The latter danger is the one best known to us. For if denied the gradual and well-guided experience of the autonomy of free choice (or if, indeed, weakened by an initial loss of trust) the child will turn against himself all his urge to discriminate and to manipulate. He will overmanipulate himself, he will develop a precocious conscience. Instead of taking possession of things in order to test them by purposeful repetition, he will become obsessed by his own repetitiveness. By such obsessiveness, of course, he then learns to repossess the environment and to gain power by stubborn and minute control, where he could not find large-scale mutual regulation. Such hollow victory is the infantile model for a compulsion neurosis. It is also the infantile source of later attempts in adult life to govern by the letter, rather than by the spirit.

Shame is an emotion insufficiently studied, because in our civilization it is so early and easily absorbed by guilt. Shame supposes that one is completely exposed and conscious of being looked at: in one word, self-conscious. One is visible and not ready to be visible; which is why we dream of shame as a situation in which we are stared at in a condition of incomplete dress, in night attire,, "with one's pants down." Shame is early expressed in an impulse to bury one's face, or to sink, right then and there, into the ground. But this, I think, is essentially rage turned against the self. He who is ashamed would like to force the world not to look at him, not to notice his exposure. He would like to destroy the eyes of the world. Instead he must wish for his own invisibility. This potentiality is abundantly used in the educational method of "shaming" used so exclusively by some primitive peoples. Visual shame precedes auditory guilt, which is a sense of badness to be had all by oneself when nobody watches and when everything is quiet—except the voice of the superego. Such shaming exploits an increasing sense of being small, which can develop only as the child stands up and as his awareness permits him to note the relative measures of size and power.

Too much shaming does not lead to genuine propriety but to a secret determination to try to get away with things, unseen—if, indeed, it does not result in defiant shamelessness. There is an impressive American ballad in which a murderer to be hanged on the gallows before the eyes of the community, instead of feeling duly chastened, begins to berate the onlookers, ending every salvo of defiance with the words, "God damn your eyes." Many a small child, shamed beyond endurance, may be in a chronic mood (although not in possession of either the courage or the words) to express defiance in similar terms. What I mean by this sinister reference is that there is a limit to a child's and an adult's endurance in the face of demands to consider himself, his body, and his wishes as evil and dirty, and to his belief in the infallibility of those who pass such judgment. He may be apt to turn things around, and to consider as evil only the fact that they exist: his chance will come when they are gone, or when he will go from them.

Doubt is the brother of shame. Where shame is dependent on the consciousness of being upright and exposed, doubt, so clinical observation leads me to believe, has much to do with a consciousness of having a front and a back—and especially a "behind." For this reverse area of the body, with its aggressive and libidinal focus in the sphincters and in the buttocks, cannot be seen by the child, and yet it can be dominated by the will of others. The "behind" is the small being's dark continent, an area of the body which can be magically dominated and effectively invaded by those who would attack one's power of autonomy and who would designate as evil those products of the bowels which were felt to be all right when they were being passed. This basic sense of doubt in whatever one has left behind forms a substratum for later and more verbal forms of compulsive doubting; this finds its adult expression in paranoiac fears concerning hidden persecutors and secret persecutions threatening from behind (and from within the behind).

This stage, therefore, becomes decisive for the ratio of love and hate, cooperation and willfulness, freedom of self-expression and its suppression.   From a sense of self-control without loss of self-esteem comes a lasting sense of good will and pride; from a sense of loss of self-control and of foreign overcontrol comes a lasting propensity for doubt and shame.

If, to some reader, the "negative" potentialities of our stages seem overstated throughout, we must remind him that this is not only the result of a preoccupation with clinical data.   Adults, and seemingly mature and unneurotic ones, display a sensitivity concerning a possible shameful "loss of face" and fear of being attacked "from behind" which is not only highly irrational and in contrast to the knowledge available to them, but can be of fateful import if related sentiments influence, for example, interracial and international policies.

We have related basic trust to the institution of religion.   The lasting need of the individual to have his will reaffirmed and delineated within an adult order of things which at the same time reaffirms and delineates the will of others has an institutional safeguard in the *principle of law and order*.   In daily life as well as in the high courts of law—domestic and international—this principle apportions to each his privileges and his limitations, his obligations and his rights.   A sense of rightful dignity and lawful independence on the part of adults around him gives to the child of good will the confident expectation that the kind of autonomy fostered in childhood will not lead to undue doubt or shame in later life.   Thus the sense of autonomy fostered in the child and modified as life progresses, serves (and is served by) the preservation in economic and political life of a sense of justice.

Initiative vs. guilt

There is in every child at every stage a new miracle of vigorous unfolding, which constitutes a new hope and a new responsibility for all. Such is the sense and the pervading quality of initiative.   The criteria for all these senses and qualities are the same: a crisis, more or less beset with fumbling and fear, is resolved, in that the child suddenly seems to "grow together" both in his person and in his body.   He appears "more himself," more loving, relaxed and brighter in his judgment, more activated and activating.   He is in free possession of a surplus of energy which permits him to forget failures quickly and to approach what seems desirable (even if it also seems uncertain and even dangerous) with undiminished and more accurate direction. Initiative adds to autonomy the quality of undertaking, planning and "attacking" a task for the sake of being active and on the move, where before self-will, more often than not, inspired acts of defiance or, at any rate, protested independence.

I know that the very word "initiative" to many has an American, and industrial, connotation.   Yet, initiative is a necessary part of every act, and man needs a sense of initiative for whatever he learns and does, from fruit-gathering to a system of enterprise.

The ambulatory stage and that of infantile genitality add to the inventory of basic social modalities that of "making," first in the sense of "being on the make." There is no simpler, stronger word for it; it suggests pleasure in attack and conquest. In the boy, the emphasis remains on phallic-intrusive modes; in the girl it turns to modes of "catching" in more aggressive forms of snatching or in the milder form of making oneself attractive and endearing.

The danger of this stage is a sense of guilt over the goals contemplated and the acts initiated in one's exuberant enjoyment of new locomotor and mental power: acts of aggressive manipulation and coercion which soon go far beyond the executive capacity of organism and mind and therefore call for an energetic halt on one's contemplated initiative. While autonomy concentrates on keeping potential rivals out, and therefore can lead to jealous rage most often directed against encroachments by younger siblings, initiative brings with it anticipatory rivalry with those who have been there first and may, therefore, occupy with their superior equipment the field toward which one's initiative is directed. Infantile jealousy and rivalry, those often embittered and yet essentially futile attempts at demarcating a sphere of unquestioned privilege, now come to a climax in a final contest for a favored position with the mother; the usual failure leads to resignation, guilt, and anxiety. The child indulges in fantasies of being a giant and a tiger, but in his dreams he runs in terror for dear life. This, then, is the stage of the "castration complex," the intensified fear of finding the (now energetically erotized) genitals harmed as a punishment for the fantasies attached to their excitement.

Infantile sexuality and incest taboo, castration complex and superego all unite here to bring about that specifically human crisis during which the child must turn from an exclusive, pregenital attachment to his parents to the slow process of becoming a parent, a carrier of tradition. Here the most fateful split and transformation in the emotional powerhouse occurs, a split between potential human glory and potential total destruction. For here the child becomes forever divided in himself. The instinct fragments which before had enhanced the growth of his infantile body and mind now become divided into an infantile set which perpetuates the exuberance of growth potentials, and a parental set which supports and increases self-observation, self-guidance, and self-punishment.

The problem, again, is one of mutual regulation. Where the child, now so ready to overmanipulate himself, can gradually develop a sense of moral responsibility, where he can gain some insight into the institutions, functions, and roles which will permit his responsible participation, he will find pleasurable accomplishment in wielding tools and weapons, in manipulating meaningful toys—and in caring for younger children.

Naturally, the parental set is at first infantile in nature: the fact that human conscience remains partially infantile throughout life is the core of human tragedy.   For the superego of the child can be primitive, cruel, and uncompromising, as may be observed in instances where children overcontrol and overconstrict themselves to the point of self-obliteration; where they develop an overobedience more literal than the one the parent has wished to exact; or where they develop deep regressions and lasting resentments because the parents themselves do not seem to live up to the new conscience.   One of the deepest conflicts in life is the hate for a parent who served as the model and the executor of the superego, but who (in some form) was found trying to get away with the very transgressions which the child can no longer tolerate in himself.   The suspiciousness and evasiveness which is thus mixed in with the all-or-nothing quality of the superego, this organ of moral tradition, makes moral (in the sense of moralistic) man a great potential danger to his own ego—and to that of his fellow men.

In adult pathology, the residual conflict over initiative is expressed either in hysterical denial, which causes the repression of the wish or the abrogation of its executive organ by paralysis, inhibition, or impotence; or in overcompensatory showing off, in which the scared individual, so eager to "duck," instead "sticks his neck out."   Then also a plunge into psychosomatic disease is now common.   It is as if the culture had made a man overadvertise himself and so identify with his own advertisement that only disease can offer him escape.

But here, again, we must not think only of individual psychopathology, but of the inner powerhouse of rage which must be submerged at this stage, as some of the fondest hopes and the wildest fantasies are repressed and inhibited.   The resulting self-righteousness—often the principal reward for goodness—can later be most intolerantly turned against others in the form of persistent moralistic surveillance, so that the prohibition rather than the guidance of initiative becomes the dominant endeavor.   On the other hand, even moral man's initiative is apt to burst the boundaries of self-restriction, permitting him to do to others, in his or in other lands, what he would neither do nor tolerate being done in his own home.

In view of the dangerous potentials of man's long childhood, it is well to look back at the blueprint of the life-stages and to the possibilities of guiding the young of the race while they are young.   And here we note that according to the wisdom of the ground plan the child is at no time more ready to learn quickly and avidly, to become bigger in the sense of sharing obligation and performance than during this period of his development.   He is eager and able to make things cooperatively, to combine with other children for the purpose of constructing and planning, and he is willing to profit from teachers and to emulate ideal prototypes. He remains, of course, identified with the parent of the same sex, but for the present he looks for opportunities where work-identification seems to promise a field of initiative without too much infantile conflict or oedipal guilt and a more realistic identification based on a spirit of equality experienced in doing things together. At any rate, the "oedipal" stage results not only in the oppressive establishment of a moral sense restricting the horizon of the permissible; it also sets the direction toward the possible and the tangible which permits the dreams of early childhood to be attached to the goals of an active adult life. Social institutions, therefore, offer children of this age an *economic ethos,* in the form of ideal adults recognizable by their uniforms and their functions, and fascinating enough to replace the heroes of picture book and fairy tale.

Industry vs. inferiority

Thus the inner stage seems all set for "entrance into life," except that life must first be school life, whether school is field or jungle or classroom. The child must forget past hopes and wishes, while his exuberant imagination is tamed and harnessed to the laws of impersonal things—even the three R's. For before the child, psychologically already a rudimentary parent, can become a biological parent, he must begin to be a worker and potential provider. With the oncoming latency period, the normally advanced child forgets, or rather sublimates, the necessity to "make" people by direct attack or to become papa and mama in a hurry: he now learns to win recognition by producing things. He has mastered the ambulatory field and the organ modes. He has experienced a sense of finality regarding the fact that there is no workable future within the womb of his family, and thus becomes ready to apply himself to given skills and tasks, which go far beyond the mere playful expression of his organ modes or the pleasure in the function of his limbs. He develops a sense of industry—that is, he adjusts himself to the inorganic laws of the tool world. He can become an eager and absorbed unit of a productive situation. To bring a productive situation to completion is an aim which gradually supersedes the whims and wishes of play. His ego boundaries include his tools and skills: the work principle teaches him the pleasure of work completion by steady attention and persevering diligence. In all cultures, at this stage, children receive some *systematic instruction,* although it is by no means always in the kind of school which literate people must organize around special teachers who have learned how to teach literacy. In preliterate people and in nonliterate pursuits much is learned from adults who become teachers by dint of gift and inclination rather than by appointment, and perhaps the greatest amount is learned from older children. Thus the *fundamentals of technology* are developed, as the child becomes ready to handle the utensils, the tools, and the weapons used by the big people. Literate people, with more specialized careers, must prepare the child by teaching him things which first of all make him literate, the widest possible basic education for the greatest number of possible careers. The more confusing specialization becomes, however, the more indistinct are the eventual goals of initiative; and the more complicated social reality, the vaguer are the father's and mother's role in it. School seems to be a culture all by itself, with its own goals and limits, its achievements and disappointment.

The child's danger, at this stage, lies in a sense of inadequacy and inferiority. If he despairs of his tools and skills or of his status among his tool partners, he may be discouraged from identification with them and with a section of the tool world. To lose the hope of such "industrial" association may pull him back to the more isolated, less tool-conscious familial rivalry of the oedipal time. The child despairs of his equipment in the tool world and in anatomy, and considers himself doomed to mediocrity or inadequacy. It is at this point that wider society becomes significant in its ways of admitting the child to an understanding of meaningful roles in its technology and economy. Many a child's development is disrupted when family life has failed to prepare him for school life, or when school life fails to sustain the promises of earlier stages.

Regarding the period of a developing sense of industry, I have referred to *outer and inner hindrances* in the use of new capacities but not to aggravations of new human drives, nor to submerged rages resulting from their frustration. This stage differs from the earlier ones in that it is not a swing from an inner upheaval to a new mastery. Freud calls it the latency stage because violent drives are normally dormant. But it is only a lull before the storm of puberty, when. all the earlier drives re-emerge in a new combination, to be brought under the dominance of genitality.

On the other hand, this is socially a most decisive stage: since industry involves doing things beside and with others, a first sense of division of labor and of differential opportunity, that is, a sense of the *technological ethos* of a culture, develops at this time. We have pointed in the last section to the danger threatening individual and society where the schoolchild begins to feel that the color of his skin, the background of his parents, or the fashion of his clothes rather than his wish and his will to learn will decide his worth as an apprentice, and thus his sense of *identity*—to which we must now turn. But there is another more fundamental danger, namely man's restriction of himself and constriction of his horizons to include only his work to which, so the Book says, he has been sentenced after his expulsion from paradise. If he accepts work as his only obligation, and "what works" as his only criterion of worthwhileness, he may become the conformist and thoughtless slave of his technology and of those who are in a position to exploit it.

Identity vs. role confusion

With the establishment of a good initial relationship to the world of skills and tools, and with the advent of puberty, childhood proper comes to an end. Youth begins. But in puberty and adolescence all sameness and continuities relied on earlier are more or less questioned again, because of a rapidity of body growth which equals that of early childhood and because of the new addition of genital maturity. The growing and developing youths, faced with this physiological revolution within them, and with tangible adult tasks ahead of them, are now primarily concerned with what they appear to be in the eyes of others as compared with what they feel they are, and with the question of how to connect the roles and skills cultivated earlier with the occupational prototypes of the day. In their search for a new sense of continuity and sameness, adolescents have to refight many of the battles of earlier years, even though to do so they must artificially appoint perfectly well-meaning people to play the roles of adversaries; and they are ever ready to install lasting idols and ideals as guardians of a final identity.

The integration now taking place in the form of ego identity is, as pointed out, more than the sum of the childhood identifications. It is the accrued experience of the ego's ability to integrate all identifications with the vicissitudes of the libido, with the aptitudes developed out of endowment, and with the opportunities offered in social roles. The sense of ego identity, then, is the accrued confidence that the inner sameness and continuity prepared in the past are matched by the sameness and continuity of one's meaning for others, as evidenced in the tangible promise of a "career."

The danger of this stage is role confusion.[2]   Where this is based on a strong previous doubt as to one's sexual identity, delinquent and outright psychotic episodes are not uncommon. If diagnosed and treated correctly, these incidents do not have the same fatal significance which they have at other ages. In most instances, however, it is the inability to settle on an occupational identity which disturb individual young people. To keep themselves together they temporarily overidentify, to the point of apparent complete loss of identity, with the heroes of cliques and crowds. This initiates the stage of

[2] *See* "The Problem of Ego-Identity," *Journal of the American Psychoanalytic Association*, 4 (1956), 56–121.

"falling in love," which is by no means entirely, or even primarily, a sexual matter—except where the mores demand it. To a considerable extent adolescent love is an attempt to arrive at a definition of one's identity by projecting one's diffused ego image on another and by seeing it thus reflected and gradually clarified. This is why so much of young love is conversation.

Young people can also be remarkably clannish, and cruel in their exclusion of all those who are "different," in skin color or cultural background, in tastes and gifts, and often in such petty aspects of dress and gesture as have been temporarily selected as *the* signs of an in-grouper or out-grouper. It is important to understand (which does not mean condone or participate in) such intolerance as a defense against a sense of identity confusion. For adolescents not only help one another temporarily through much discomfort by forming cliques and by stereotyping themselves, their ideals, and their enemies; they also perversely test each other's capacity to pledge fidelity. The readiness for such testing also explains the appeal which simple and cruel totalitarian doctrines have on the minds of the youth of such countries and classes as have lost or are losing their group identities (feudal, agrarian, tribal, national) and face world-wide industrialization, emancipation, and wider communication.

The adolescent mind is essentially a mind of the *moratorium*, a psychosocial stage between childhood and adulthood, and between the morality learned by the child, and the ethics to be developed by the adult. It is an ideological mind—and, indeed, it is the ideological outlook of a society that speaks most clearly to the adolescent who is eager to be affirmed by his peers, and is ready to be confirmed by rituals, creeds, and programs which at the same time define what is evil, uncanny, and inimical. In searching for the social values which guide identity, one therefore confronts the problems of *ideology* and *aristocracy*, both in their widest possible sense which connotes that within a defined world image and a predestined course of history, the best people will come to rule and rule develops the best in people. In order not to become cynically or apathetically lost, young people must somehow be able to convince themselves that those who succeed in their anticipated adult world thereby shoulder the obligation of being the best.

Intimacy vs. isolation

The strength acquired at any stage is tested by the necessity to transcend it in such a way that the individual can take chances in the next stage with what was most vulnerably precious in the previous one. Thus, the young adult, emerging from the search for and the insistence on identity, is eager and willing to fuse his identity with that of others.　He is ready for intimacy, that is, the capacity to commit himself to concrete affiliations and partnerships and to develop the ethical strength to abide by such commitments, even though they may call for significant sacrifices and compromises.　Body and ego must now be masters of the organ modes and of the nuclear conflicts, in order to be able to face the fear of ego loss in situations which call for self-abandon: in the solidarity of close affiliations, in orgasms and sexual unions, in close friendships and in physical combat, in experiences of inspiration by teachers and of intuition from the recesses of the self.　The avoidance of such experiences because of a fear of ego loss may lead to a deep sense of isolation and consequent self-absorption.

The counterpart of intimacy is distantiation: the readiness to isolate and, if necessary, to destroy those forces and people whose essence seems dangerous to one's own, and whose "territory" seems to encroach on the extent of one's intimate relations.　Prejudices thus developed (and utilized and exploited in politics and in war) are a more mature outgrowth of the blinder repudiations which during the struggle for identity differentiate sharply and cruelly between the familiar and the foreign.　The danger of this stage is that intimate, competitive, and combative relations are experienced with and against the selfsame people.　But as the areas of adult duty are delineated, and as the competitive encounter, and the sexual embrace, are differentiated, they eventually become subject to that *ethical sense* which is the mark of the adult.

Strictly speaking, it is only now that *true genitality* can fully develop; for much of the sex life preceding these commitments is of the identity-searching kind, or is dominated by phallic or vaginal strivings which make of sex-life a kind of genital combat.　On the other hand, genitality is all too often described as a permanent state of reciprocal sexual bliss.　This then, may be the place to complete our discussion of genitality.

For a basic orientation in the matter I shall quote what has come to me as Freud's shortest saying.　It has often been claimed, and bad habits of conversation seem to sustain the claim, that psychoanalysis as a treatment attempts to convince the patient that before God and man he has only one obligation: to have good orgasms, with a fitting "object," and that regularly.　This, of course, is not true. Freud was once asked what he thought a normal person should be able to do well.　The questioner probably expected a complicated answer.　But Freud, in the curt way of his old days, is reported to have said: "Lieben und arbeiten" (to love and to work).　It pays to ponder on this simple formula; it gets deeper as you think about it. For when Freud said "love" he meant *genital* love, and genital *love;* when he said love *and* work, he meant a general work-productiveness which would not preoccupy the individual to the extent that he loses his right or capacity to be a genital and a loving being.   Thus we may ponder, but we cannot improve on "the professor's" formula.

Genitality, then, consists in the unobstructed capacity to develop an orgastic potency so free of pregenital interferences that genital libido (not just the sex products discharged in Kinsey's "outlets") is expressed in heterosexual mutuality, with full sensitivity of both penis and vagina, and with a convulsionlike discharge of tension from the whole body.   This is a rather concrete way of saying something about a process which we really do not understand.   To put it more situationally: the total fact of finding, via the climactic turmoil of the orgasm, a supreme experience of the mutual regulation of two beings in some way takes the edge off the hostilities and potential rages caused by the oppositeness of male and female, of fact and fancy, of love and hate.   Satisfactory sex relations thus make sex less obsessive, overcompensation less necessary, sadistic controls superfluous.

Preoccupied as it was with curative aspects, psychoanalysis often failed to formulate the matter of genitality in a way significant for the processes of society in all classes, nations, and levels of culture.   The kind of mutuality in orgasm which psychoanalysis has in mind is apparently easily obtained in classes and cultures which happen to make a leisurely institution of it.   In more complex societies this mutuality is interfered with by so many factors of health, of tradition, of opportunity, and of temperament, that the proper formulation of sexual health would be rather this: A human being should be potentially able to accomplish mutuality of genital orgasm, but he should also be so constituted as to bear a certain amount of frustration in the matter without undue regression wherever emotional preference or considerations of duty and loyalty call for it.

While psychoanalysis has on occasion gone too far in its emphasis on genitality as a universal cure for society and has thus provided a new addiction and a new commodity for many who wished to so interpret its teachings, it has not always indicated all the goals that genitality actually should and must imply.   In order to be of lasting social significance, the utopia of genitality should include:

1   mutuality of orgasm
2   with a loved partner
3   of the other sex
4   with whom one is able and willing to share a mutual trust
5   and with whom one is able and willing to regulate the cycles of
a   work
b   procreation
c   recreation
6   so as to secure to the offspring, too, all the stages of a satisfactory development.

It is apparent that such utopian accomplishment on a large scale cannot be an individual or, indeed, a therapeutic task. Nor is it a purely sexual matter by any means. It is integral to a culture's style of sexual selection, cooperation, and competition.

The danger of this stage is isolation, that is, the avoidance of contacts which commit to intimacy. In psychopathology, this disturbance can lead to severe "character-problems." On the other hand, there are partnerships which amount to an isolation à deux, protecting both partners from the necessity to face the next critical development—that of generativity.

Generativity vs. stagnation

The term *generativity* encompasses the evolutionary development which has made man the teaching and instituting as well as the learning animal. The fashionable insistence on dramatizing the dependence of children on adults often blinds us to the dependence of the older generation on the younger one. Mature man needs to be needed, and maturity needs guidance as well as encouragement from what has been produced and must be taken care of.

Generativity, then, is primarily the concern in establishing and guiding the next generation, although there are individuals who, through misfortune or because of special and genuine gifts in other directions, do not apply this drive to their own offspring. And indeed, the concept *generativity* is meant to include such more popular synonyms as *productivity* and *creativity*, which, however, cannot replace it.

It has taken psychoanalysis some time to realize that the ability to lose oneself in the meeting of bodies and minds leads to a gradual expansion of ego-interests and to a libidinal investment in that which is being generated. Generativity thus is an essential stage on the psychosexual as well as the psychosocial schedule. Where such enrichment fails altogether, regression to an obsessive need for pseudo intimacy takes place, often with a pervading sense of stagnation and personal impoverishment. Individuals, then, often begin to indulge themselves as if they were their own—or one another's—one and only child; and where conditions favor it, early invalidism, physical or psychological, becomes the vehicle of self-concern. The mere fact of having or even wanting children, however, does not "achieve" generativity. In fact, some young parents suffer, it seems, from the retardation of the ability to develop this stage. The reasons are often to be found in early childhood impressions; in excessive self-love based on a too strenuously self-made personality; and finally (and here we return to the beginnings) in the lack of some faith, some "belief in the species," which would make a child appear to be a welcome trust of the community.

As to the institutions which safeguard and reinforce generativity, one can only say that all institutions codify the ethics of generative succession. Even where philosophical and spiritual tradition suggests the renunciation of the right to procreate or to produce, such early turn to "ultimate concerns," wherever instituted in monastic movements, strives to settle at the same time the matter of its relationship to the Care for the creatures of this world and to the Charity which is felt to transcend it.

Ego integrity vs. despair

Only in him who in some way has taken care of things and people and has adapted himself to the triumphs and disappointments adherent to being, the originator of others or the generator of products and ideas—only in him may gradually ripen the fruit of these seven stages. I know no better word for it than ego integrity. Lacking a clear definition, I shall point to a few constituents of this state of mind. It is the ego's accrued assurance of its proclivity for order and meaning. It is a postnarcissistic love of the human ego—not of the self—as an experience which conveys some world order and spiritual sense, no matter how dearly paid for. It is the acceptance of one's one and only life cycle as something that had to be and that, by necessity, permitted of no substitutions: it thus means a new, a different love of one's parents. It is a comradeship with the ordering ways of distant times and different pursuits, as expressed in the simple products and sayings of such times and pursuits. Although aware of the relativity of all the various life styles which have given meaning to human striving, the possessor of integrity is ready to defend the dignity of his own life style against all physical and economic threats. For he knows that an individual life is the accidental coincidence of but one life cycle with but one segment of history; and that for him all human integrity stands or falls with the one style of integrity of which he partakes. The style of integrity developed by his culture or civilization thus becomes the "patrimony of his soul," the seal of his moral paternity of himself (". . . pero el honor/Es patrimonio del alma": Calderón). In such final consolidation, death loses its sting.

The lack or loss of this accrued ego integration is signified by fear of death: the one and only life cycle is not accepted as the ultimate of life. Despair expresses the feeling that the time is now short, too short for the attempt to start another life and to try out alternate roads to integrity. Disgust hides despair, if often only in the form of "a thousand little disgusts" which do not add up to one big remorse:

mille petis dégôuts de soi, dont le total ne fait pas un remords, mais un gêne obscure" (Rostand).

Each individual, to become a mature adult, must to a sufficient degree develop all the ego qualities mentioned, so that a wise Indian, a true gentleman, and a mature peasant share and recognize in one another the final stage of integrity. But each cultural entity, to develop the particular style of integrity suggested by its historical place, utilizes a particular combination of these conflicts, along with specific provocations and prohibitions of infantile sexuality. Infantile conflicts become creative only if sustained by the firm support of cultural institutions and of the special leader classes representing them. In order to approach or experience integrity, the individual must know how to be a follower of image bearers in religion and in politics, in the economic order and in technology, in aristocratic living and in the arts and sciences. Ego integrity, therefore, implies an emotional integration which permits participation by followership as well as acceptance of the responsibility of leadership.

Webster's Dictionary is kind enough to help us complete this outline in a circular fashion. Trust (the first of our ego values) is here defined as "the assured reliance on another's integrity," the last of our values. I suspect that Webster had business in mind rather than babies, credit rather than faith. But the formulation stands. And it seems possible to further paraphrase the relation of adult integrity and infantile trust by saying that healthy children will not fear life if their elders have integrity enough not to fear death. . . .

B   Dynamics of adjustment

The papers which follow discuss various ways in which the process of adjustment has been conceptualized. While the authors of these papers frequently differ in their theoretical orientations and specific ideas concerning adjustment, they adopt the general view that man's behavior is a dynamic process resulting from the interplay of forces impinging on him. They base their ideas on the assumption that man is a changing, modifiable organism. The personality characteristics and behavior man displays are the result of the continuous interaction of internal and external stimulation. Conflicts and frustrations are viewed as inevitable, and in order to resolve them, man learns or adopts different modes of thinking, believing, and acting. In this group of readings the adjustment process is analyzed, and some of the methods, techniques, and styles of adjustment which are typical in our culture are considered.

In recent years considerable attention has been devoted to the various methods of adjustment or patterns of behavior characteristic of individuals and groups when dealing with conflict and frustration.

Since Freud's description of the "ego defenses," increasing emphasis has been placed on the classification of specific styles of adjusting and the motivations and purposes underlying them. The study of characteristic methods of dealing with conflict and anxiety is especially relevant to an understanding of the adjustment process. On the one hand, defensive techniques enable the individual to maintain a sense of equilibrium and mitigate the anxiety and discomfort he would experience without them. On the other hand, some defensive maneuvers appear to result in negative consequences which in turn give rise to additional stress and anxiety for the individual. It follows then that the relationship between adjustment and defense mechanisms is a complex one depending on numerous factors such as the frequency of the occurrence of a particular method of defense, the situations in which it occurs, and the reactions of others to it. For example, an individual's tendency to retreat into fantasy whenever he encounters frustration may enable him to maintain a sense of composure and balance under adverse conditions. But a frequent or intense withdrawal into fantasy, or its occurrence at inappropriate times, or the intolerance of others for this type of reaction may promote further difficulty for the individual rather than aid him.

The first paper in this section gives a more or less traditional account of the mechanisms of defense. McCall distinguishes between two alternatives in responding to threats to self-esteem. One may cope with threat in a realistic manner or one may engage in defensiveness. The paper consists of an analysis of the latter alternative and describes the variety of ways in which individuals attempt to nullify threat to their self-esteem and integrity. While acknowledging the debt to Freud and his daughter on the part of anyone writing in this area, McCall chooses to describe the mechanisms logically and phenomenologically rather than psychoanalytically. The mechanisms, therefore, are not viewed solely as protective devices against anxiety arising from sexual impulses, but are viewed as arising from *any* threat to self-esteem—"incompetence, stupidity, selfishness, indecisiveness. . . ."

The papers by Karen Horney and Eric Fromm provide us with still other ways of conceptualizing patterns of adjustment to anxiety, frustration, and conflict. Horney adopts the position that conflict is the basis of maladjustment and specifies the importance of conflicts associated with the individual's interactions with others. She refers to a *basic conflict* underlying all maladjustment which involves the individual's ambivalences about the role he wishes to play with others. Where the individual overemphasizes one style of relating to others (for example, a highly aggressive attitude) at the expense of other possible modes of interacting, the basis for increased conflict and friction are present. Adjustment, according to Horney, consists of a harmonious, flexible style of interacting with others; maladjustment consists of rigid interpersonal styles, *moving toward people, moving against people*, and *moving away from people*.

The excerpt from Fromm's book *Man for Himself* describes variations in what the author refers to as the *nonproductive personality*. For Fromm, the healthy individual has developed a sense of identity which enables him to actualize his abilities and potentials so that he is in effect a productive member of society. The nonproductive character orientations, however, are *types* of persons who have not learned to relate to others in ways which enable them to fulfill their basic needs and potentials. Instead these individuals continue to seek adjustment by ineffective styles of behavior which serve to increase the frustrations and conflicts they experience. In addition, it is worth noting that Fromm pays a good deal of attention to the role culture plays in promoting differences in adjustment.

Let us summarize and integrate these three papers by noting that the defense mechanisms of McCall, the rigid interpersonal styles of Horney, and the nonproductive character orientations of Fromm may all be viewed as behavior serving the function of allaying anxiety, distress, loss of esteem, etc.

The next three papers deal with some adjustive responses that have received considerable *research* attention in recent years: *conformity behavior, affiliation*, and *self-disclosure*. Conformity research studies individual differences in yielding to group pressure and the conditions under which persons will yield; the affiliation literature studies factors influencing the need to be with others; and the self-disclosure literature studies factors influencing the extent to which one tells others about himself. While all three of these response patterns may be motivated by a variety of reasons, they may also properly be viewed as ways of coping with fear or anxiety arising from one source or another. One conforms out of fear of "being out of step"; one affiliates, as some research has shown, to cope with induced fear (under conditions of fear people generally prefer being with others than being alone); one inhibits self-disclosure from fear that others may discover that one is somehow lacking (wanting) in some important way.

The Krech, Crutchfield, and Ballachey paper provides a conceptual account of the meaning and nature of conformity together with a description of the experimental procedure for its investigation. It also contains a summary of the findings of a good deal of the conformity research literature. The Sarnoff and Zimbardo paper is a report of an experimental investigation of the hypothesis that fear and affiliation behavior are related (in our terms, that affiliation is an adjustment to fear). The paper is also noteworthy for its effort to study affiliation in response to *fear* in contrast to anxiety on the psychoanalytic distinction that fear is a function of external threat while anxiety derives from repressed material. The Jourard paper proposes a close relationship between self-disclosure and mental health: the mentally healthy person is a discloser, and self-disclosure is a technique for achieving mental health. In addition, it should be noted that disclosure and the inhibition of disclosure may be in the service of anxiety-fear reduction and may be properly viewed as an adjustment pattern.

A feeling of guilt or a sense of sin may act as both a motivator of behavior and an adjustive response. A lively discussion concerning guilt is contained in the papers by Mowrer and Ellis. Mowrer here reiterates a position which he has stated many times—that the psychoanalytic hypothesis that neurosis is a function of inhibiting id impulses is incorrect; neurosis is a function of inhibiting the superego. Sin and unexpiated guilt lead to "hell-on-this-earth." Mowrer reads the record as favoring his belief that guilt, confession, and expiation will be at the center of therapeutic programs in the future. Ellis, on the other hand, in a spirited reply, contends that giving anyone a sense of sin or guilt "is the worst possible way to help him be an emotionally sound and adequately socialized individual."

The final paper deals with creativity, in which there is a great deal of current interest and which may also be viewed as adjustive behavior. Creative behavior may be conceived as serving the same functions of reducing anxiety as the typical mechanisms of defense and the social-psychological variables of affiliation, self-disclosure, and conformity. It may be distinguished from these latter behaviors, however, by the fact that it often leads to socially valued products for which the individual is highly rewarded by his society. Golann's paper is a review of the research literature and contains the results of research on the motivation and personality attributes of creative persons.

Raymond J. McCall

THE DEFENSE MECHANISMS RE-EXAMINED *

The phenomenology of defense mechanisms

. . . No one who writes in this area can be unaware of the fact that we are all standing on Freud's shoulders, and there is good reason to commend Anna Freud as well for her attempt to present systematically

* From Raymond J. McCall, "The Defense Mechanisms Re-examined: A Logical and Phenomenal Analysis," *Catholic Psychological Record*, 1963 *1*, 45–64. Pages 47–64 reprinted by permission of the author and the Editor, *Catholic Psychological Record*.

the Freudian position. But in acknowledging our debts to the Freuds, *père et fille*, we may still be chary of subscribing to Freudian constructs and postulates which are far removed from simple phenomenological description and which constitute a kind of systematic mythology of the libido.   In this mythology is included the highly dubious assumption that the "ego" is entirely the vassal of the "instinctual apparatus" (the "id"), that sexual and destructive impulses, the latter arising from the "death instinct," are the only sources of anxiety, and that the subject of the defense-mechanisms is always this same anxiety.   Because we employ the generic term "defense mechanism" and in most instances the specific terms (such as *rationalization, compensation, displacement, projection*) for particular instances thereof, terms which were coined by Freud or his immediate followers, we perhaps commit ourselves to general concepts like "psychic conflict" and "unconscious motivation" but in no significant degree are we bound to the elaborate theoretical system which Freud and his followers have built up to account for these phenomena, or to specific aspects of this system which are supposedly related directly to "ego defense." We may, for example, accept the notion of hostility as frequently involved in the defense mechanism of *projection* without committing ourselves to the "death instinct" as its ultimate root, or to infantile "spitting out" as its prototype, or to homosexuality as is concomitant (Fenichel, 1945).

Adhering, then, as closely as possible to a phenomenological method, we may begin by describing defense mechanisms as *self-protective maneuvers, pertaining to perception and motivation, mental or psychic, yet largely unconscious, designed to soften or disguise what is unacceptable in or to the self.*   Though not deliberately adopted, defense mechanisms have an apparent utility as disguises of our weaknesses and baser motives.

Not only Freud and the orthodox Freudians, but many others, have seen the defense mechanisms as essentially protection against *anxiety,* particularly of the sort deriving from aberrant sexual impulse. However important this particular kind of defense may be—and we should be careful not to underestimate it—there is little evidence in favor of regarding all defense mechanisms as deriving from it.   We run less risk of over-generalization (or misplaced concreteness), therefore, if we maintain that *whatever* is threatening to our self-esteem is a fitting subject for cognitive-appetitive self-defense.   Perhaps sexually derived anxiety has a special importance and intensity, but it would seem that the defense mechanisms may be evoked by anything that conflicts with our *minimum ideal* of what the self must be.   This might include incompetence, stupidity, selfishness, indecisiveness, or any other self-devaluating experience or circumstance.   It may be that the three interrelated conditions of the self—*anxiety, hostility* and *sexuality*—are peculiarly suited to elicit the *habitual and exaggerated* employment of defenses which seems to characterize the neurotic, but our description and analysis of the defense mechanisms should take cognizance of the fact that they are employed by normal as well as by neurotic and other types of abnormal persons.

On this, as well as on other accounts, defense mechanisms should not be confused with *symptoms* of neurosis or other abnormal conditions.[1]   The mechanisms are purely *endopsychic* or mental (cognitive-appetitive) devices, ways of perceiving and desiring, giving a protectively distorted registration of the self and its world, and connoting a matching wish to have them free of threats to our self-regard. Symptoms, on the other hand, are not limited to the psychic, to ways of thinking and wishing, but attach themselves to our behavior in any of a thousand ways as well as to our thoughts and feelings, and may disturb our physiological as well as our psychological functioning. Thus, *perceiving* your boss as though he were your tyrannical father connotes the defense-mechanism of *displacement,* while developing a severe *phobia* at the prospect of going out of the house on work days (without knowing why) would be a *neurotic symptom,* just as developing high blood pressure after a short time on the job might be designated a *psychosomatic* or *psychophysiologic symptom.*   In many instances the defense mechanism and the symptom may be related as antecedent and consequent, but there is no justification for confusing relatively simple cause with its more heterogeneous and often distant effects.

To say that the defense mechanisms are largely *unconscious* is to stress by implication that they are always in corresponding degree *self-deceptive.*   If, indeed, the individual were not taken in by them they would not serve to defend his self-esteem against the intimation of inadequacy or dereliction.   That unconscious *defense* is less effectively adjustive than conscious *coping* is evident if we consider that, however variously the ideal of self-realization may be construed, the self-directively adjustive life is a *conscious* life; a never-ending task of modifying situations to suit the demands of the self, modifying the latter to suit the requirements of the former, or (most often) effecting some compromise between the two.[2]   From any perspective, this involves insightful awareness in such matters as understanding the limitations of one's own powers and performance; recognizing our social dependence and the need of acquiescing in the reasonable demands of others; acknowledging the irrational and imperfect elements in ourselves (not just in others or in the institutions of our society); ad-

[1] This confusion detracts from much of Anna Freud's analysis in her widely admired book, *The Ego and the Mechanisms of Defense* (1954).

[2] Recall the famous prayer: "O Lord, give me the courage to change what has to be changed, the patience to bear what cannot be changed, and the wisdom to tell the difference between the two."

mitting to oneself at least failure of adaptation when it occurs and the consequent need for self-correction, renewed effort, and variation in our approach. Not only, we should add, are these modes of coping different from defense; they are made difficult or impossible by the subjectively protective set of the defense mechanisms which in effect blinds us to our own real requirements other than those dictated by self-esteem.

It would appear, therefore, that the self which is defended by defense mechanisms is not the insightful, reality-oriented, and socialized self. Rather, it is the infantile self with its islands of self-ignorance, its imperfectly socialized dependency, its delusive over-valuation of itself ("narcissism"), and its defective reality-contact. However important it may be for self-realization that the individual retain his energizing self-regard, it seems that when subjectively oriented defense assumes primacy over objectively oriented coping, we have an immature and intrinsically maladaptive organization, perhaps indeed the very *Anlage* of the neurotic personality structure.

Descriptive analysis of defense mechanisms

Lists of defense mechanisms are variable in length and in the intricacy of the logical and psychological considerations offered in their support. We shall consider an even dozen in what appears to be the most nearly logical order for an understanding of their pertinence to abnormal psychology. They are:

1   Repression
2   Isolation
3   Rationalization
4   Reaction-formation
5   Compensation
6   Defensive devaluation
7   Displacement
8   Projection
9   Withdrawal
10   Identification
11   Undoing
12   Autism

1   Repression.   *The attempted exclusion from awareness of self-devaluating experiences* such as shameful memories and unacceptable motives whether hostile, fearful, sexual, pettily selfish, crude, dishonest, or contemptible.

Repression is said to be the most fundamental of defense mechanisms, since unless the self-devaluating memory or motive is somehow removed from the center of consciousness, it is difficult to see how we can be deceived into using other means to defend against it. All other mechanisms would thus seem to depend upon at least an initial repression. At the same time, the very existence of other mechanisms indicates that repression is not entirely successful in "warding off" the self-depreciating experience. If to rationalize or project or displace a hateful impulse or shortcoming I must be less than perfectly aware of that impulse or shortcoming, by the same token there would be no need for me to rationalize, or project, or displace if through repression I had succeeded in putting the whole matter out of mind. It is for this reason that the term *"attempted* exclusion" has been incorporated in our definition of repression.

The Freudians speak of repression in quasi-topographical terms as a process by which "drives and memories" are "pushed down into the unconscious." Pursuing the metaphor, they hold that such repressed material continues to exist *unchanged* "in the unconscious," but being barred from direct expression, can return only in symbolic or disguised form as "symptoms," "sublimations," or other "derivatives." One possibility, however, which they acknowledge but to which they seem not to have devoted sufficient attention, is that repression may be *from the beginning* less than an all or none affair, and that what they are pleased to call "the return of the repressed" may sometimes signalize only its failure to depart.

There is a tendency, too, for them to regard conscious-unconscious as a simple dichotomy, and to speak of mental states as one *or* the other. It is more in accord, however, both with scientific usage and with everyday experience to think of conscious and unconscious as the opposite ends of a continuum rather than as dichotomous contraries, and to recognize that the departure from and approach to consciousness may be gradual. Of some experiences I may be quite unconscious, as of events taking place prior to my second birthday, and you may be utterly unaware of crassly selfish reasons for wanting to do someone a good turn. Frequently, on the other hand, we are able to bring past events to the margin of consciousness, if not to its center—as psychoanalysis has made very clear—and frequently, too, we dimly sense an element of self-seeking in our more "unselfish" attitudes.

There is thus much in our psychic life that is neither clearly conscious nor entirely unconscious. Perhaps if we imagine clear and focal consciousness as the center of a spiral, and unconsciousness as exemplified by increasing removal from that focal center but having its exact boundaries fluid and unspecified, we shall have a topographical analogy that limps a little less than the one implied by the sharply divided surface and subsurface of the Freudian iceberg. It would seem, at any rate, more descriptively accurate to think of repression as initially incomplete, and of the unconscious as a relative condition, than to assume a total repression into total unconsciousness of a totally unchangeable psychic content that can be re-admitted to awareness only by way of symbolization. Only the Freudian penchant for an over-simplified, two-valued logic and for a mechanical model of the human psyche requires thinking in such rigid categories.

In discussing repression and the unconscious it also seems worthwhile to keep in mind the difference between the psychic *process* of repression, and its *product*, the repressed experience. Even if we assume that the act of repression is totally unconscious, it does not follow that the self-devaluating experience is always rendered totally unconscious, or even rendered unconscious in all its self-devaluating aspects. Though I am not conscious of repressing, I may remain conscious of certain parts of an experience which has self-depreciating implications, and perhaps even vaguely conscious of the self-depreciating elements themselves. It is possible, in short, that at times repression is only partially successful because it is only partial. This does not rule out the possibility that some repressed material may return to awareness in symbolic form, but leaves open the additional possibility that in some instances only part of the original experience is repressed.

2   Isolation.   Isolation may be defined as *the cutting off or blunting of unacceptable aspects of a total experience*. To accept isolation as a mechanism underscores the partial nature of at least some repression, since isolation seems to be nothing but a special kind of partial repression, one indeed whose partial nature is most evident. Thus in the most common manifestation of isolation the individual appears to be in possession of all the facts of a situation but not to recognize them for what they are, or not to register the whole situation in its most obvious implications of a derogatory sort. This is likely to impress the ordinary observer as peculiar or queer as when the mother of a severely retarded child regards her child's behavior as little different from that of other childern despite its gross deficiencies; or when the long-suffering wife of the alcoholic sees her husband's trouble only in his being a little too sociable; or when the notably homely girl fails to appreciate the unmistakable implications of her unattractiveness. This kind of isolation seems to defend against deficiency in ourselves or in those close to us.[3]

We should note, however, that it is not so much the *existence* of the fact which is nullified by the partial repression as is its *motivational relevance* and *emotional implications*, from which its existence is isolated. In another kind of isolation—that found in certain types

---

[3] Allport (1937) especially has noted the manner in which the self tends with maturity to broaden so as to include those closest to us. I am thus not only my physical and isolated self but, in a very real sense, those with whom I "identify."

of obsessional neurosis and concerned with unacceptable impulses in the self—it is again not the fact which is denied to consciousness. In these cases the individual acknowledges the unacceptable desire but cannot recognize its relevance to his own motivational system. ("I love my wife. Why should I feel this crazy impulse to strangle her?") Perhaps, too, the homely girl *knows* that she is homely but fails to see this fact as relevant to her seldom being invited out by eligible males. Such "selective imperception" is very palpably defensive, not denying the experience but separating or isolating it from elements threatening to self-esteem.

3   Rationalization.   Rationalization may be described as *pseudo-explanation of criticizable behavior or attitude which substitutes acceptable (often fancied) motives for its actual motives.* The rationalizer will view his idleness as needed relaxation, his cowardice as caution, his impatiently severe discipline as in the child's best interests.

In the classical view rationalization always involves repression of an unacceptable motive and its return in some disguise which is still close enough to the original to awaken defensive processes. Though it may in many instances be true, this smacks a little of cloak-and-dagger melodrama. Less mysterious and equally worth noting again is the palpable incompleteness or partial failure of the repression. It would seem, indeed, that *the sense of having an unacceptable purpose behind our action must be at least vaguely present in order for there to be any occasion to rationalize,* and this means that what is threatening to self-esteem has not been effectively repressed. Without recourse to the notions of banishment and return incognito, we might assume that in some instances a particular evil inclination has been repressed but that a residual, in the form of a vague or general feeling of guilt or unworthy disposition, abides with us and demands that somehow it be "explained away."

The compulsory character of this demand for explanation is not hard to understand when we recall that from infancy on each of us is expected to be able to account for his conduct according to the standards of "reason" and "common sense" dictated by his culture and sub-cultures. The *fear of disapproval* by others for what is base and unworthy in one's conduct is one of the most powerful motives in human existence, and a plausible basis for that nameless but often unsettling apprehension which we call "anxiety" (McCall, 1962). In this sense there can be no reasonable doubt that rationalization operates as a defense against anxiety, reinforcing our efforts to escape disapproval by concocting allegedly laudable purposes for our behavior.

The task of rationalization is made somewhat easier by the fact that most of our actions are *multiply motivated* ("over-determined" is the

Freudian barbarism), so that there may be "good" as well as "bad" reasons for our behaving as we do. The work of rationalization in this case is to point up, rather than invent, the good reasons for our action when repression has reduced, without quite eliminating, our awareness of the bad.

4   Reaction-formation.   A singularly unhappy term for *defending self-esteem against one's partially repressed and unacceptable dispositions by over-desiring their opposite.* If rationalization is a kind of "refutation by argument" of implied unworthiness, reaction-formation is a "refutation by action." I lay the ghost of suspected meanness by behaving so very, very nobly that no one could possibly doubt the purity of my motives. Least of all, we should add, myself!

Though overworked in certain circles, reaction-formation ("antithetic counteraction" or "counteractive inversion" would be a more precisely descriptive term) is probably important in the genesis of certain moralistic compulsions and attitudes. It is fanciful to suppose that all perfectionism is motivated, as Freud thought, by the repressed desire for the exact opposite: that extreme neatness, for example, is simply "warding off" a powerful disposition to be disgustingly messy, that the ideal of perfect benevolence is motivated by an unacknowledged but uncompromising hostility and a savage cruelty, or that those who are most on the side of the angels are the biggest devils at heart. It is possible, nevertheless, to cite enough examples of "antithetically counteractive" motivation to give plausibility to such exaggerations; and where an individual's ethical attitudes are extreme and inflexible at the same time that he gives evidence of excessive preoccupation with the violation of ethical standards (especially by others), we may reasonably suspect something like reaction-formation to be at work.

To justify suspicion of reaction-formation, however, there should be indications of the persistence in some form (perhaps only symbolic) of the rejected motive while the reaction against it is truly immoderate, a "bending over backwards," a tendency to "protest too much" in action as well as in words, and an obsessive concern with morality and immorality in this particular area. Sexual irregularities may offer a special occasion for reaction-formation since sexual motivation is likely to be at once powerful and devious, yet subject to much restriction and criticism. Certainly those who spend a great deal of time investigating and exposing the sexual depravities of others are thereby afforded an opportunity to wallow in the shocking details thereof themselves. This may offer simultaneously a partial gratification of their own repressed sexual impulses (perhaps voyeuristic or Peeping Tom-like in nature) and the appearance of absolute virtuousness.

The Reverend Davidson in Somerset Maugham's classic "Rain" is close to an ideal embodiment of reaction-formation. His implacable hatred of sexual immorality, his relentless persecution of the loose woman, Sadie Thompson, his consuming joy at her "conversion," the aridity of his own married life, even his dreams of mountains which resemble a woman's breasts, point to the defensive and self-deceptive nature of his own rejection of sex. It is not then from an ideal morality that reaction-formation springs but from a rigid and uninsightful moralistic excess, through which symbolic glimpses of a very different sort of motivation appear. And, of course, it is not merely sexuality that may thus emerge. As Plato said of Antisthenes' contempt for worldly honors and other goods: "His vanity peeps out through the holes in his cloak."

Reaction-formation is not, however, to be confused with hypocritical pretense. The person employs this mechanism indeliberately rather than with full awareness, and there is usually little doubt of the sincerity of his desire for ethical righteousness. It is, in fact, the extremity of this desire which gives him away, making clear the defensive rather than adjustively coping nature of his love of virtue.

5   Compensation.   If what remains threatening to self-esteem in the way of deficiency or dereliction cannot be "explained away" (rationalization) or "acted away" (reaction-formation), it can perhaps be *made up for*. This is the way of *compensation*. Compensation may then be described as a *defense mechanism which enables us to offset unacceptable tendencies or weaknesses by overvaluing and overstressing acceptable motives or strengths*. The interdependence of the two elements, "*over*valuation" and "weakness" is essential to the notion of compensation as a defense mechanism rather than as a mode of coping; and in defensive compensation there is always in all probability some repression, so that the deficiency or aberration is not consciously faced.

Alfred Adler, who invented the term "compensation," saw clearly that every style of life demands the stressing of certain values and the subordination or diminution of others. We have no warrant to speak of compensation as an unrealistic and uninsightful defense, however, unless the valuation of one goal is exaggerated as a means of defending self-esteem against an unacknowledged imperfection. So, to set great store by intellectual accomplishment is not compensation unless it is extreme and designed (unconsciously) to make up for physical or other defects; and strivin gor a successful career may well be nothing but adjustive coping unless it serves as a means of offsetting social unattractiveness or a comparable shortcoming.

Compensation is also to be distinguished from deliberate emphasis upon certain capacities and dispositions where these reflect natural endowment or general group expectation. Thus for the musically talented child in 18th century Germany to devote more of his energies to music than to any other interest, or for the athletically endowed American boy to work in and out of season to perfect his skills in fielding or foul-shooting, is by no accounting necessarily compensatory.

Nor should a direct attack on a weakness, designed to overcome whatever incapacity that weakness may connote, be confused with defensive compensation. The boy with polio who becomes a distance runner, the stutterer who will one day be a great orator, the frail child who develops into a partisan of the vigorous life are manifesting an actively coping rather than a defensive orientation. We should be chary of labeling as compensatory any behavior that does not imply unrealistic over-valuation and unadmitted defect.

A form of supposed compensation said to be common among modern women, due to their inferior status in our society and their resentment of male superiority and privilege, was designated by Adler "masculine protest." Whatever the merits of this notion (which has considerable currency among clinicians working with neurotic women), it too should not be overworked. In his later years Adler gave up the contention that one's entire style of life is determined by the mode of compensation for the sense of inferiority originating in childhood, and he relegated the famous "inferiority complex" to a secondary though still significant place in the development of personality. In any case, it would be a dangerous oversimplification to disregard the constructively adjustive aspect of much feminine striving, and to reduce all the efforts of women to overcome their dependent and subordinate status in our culture to a "masculine protest." Even to conjoin under this heading all instances of aggressive feminism, from the fastidiousness of the D.A.R. to the zealousness of the W.C.T.U., not excluding the manipulative proclivities of women executives, matriarchal dictators, and lady wrestlers, is to dilute the meaning of "masculine protest" to that of an anti-feminine expletive. Even following a more restrained usage, however, it is doubtful that much of what is called "masculine protest" has any bearing on compensation as a defense mechanism.

6   Defensive devaluation.   If we cannot compensate for weaknesses and transgressions, we can divert our own and others' attention from them by concentrating on the faults of others. Though not included in the classical lists of defense-mechanisms, defensive devaluation appears to be an important self-protective maneuver, of a cognitive sort basically, *a focusing upon the weaknesses and aberrations of others as a means of calling attention away from one's own deficiencies*.

Behaviorally, defensive devaluation is likely to be expressed by endless and unwarranted "griping" at the bosses, the "brass," the government, or "people" generally. But the true defensive devaluator does not criticize in the hope of effecting reform but as a defense against his own sense of inadequacy and perhaps guilt.   The presence of repression is indicated by his general insensitivity to faults in himself in the face of an extreme sensitivity to the inconsiderateness, stupidity, and similar faults of others.   He sees the mote of his neighbor's eye but misses the splinter in his own, and with a vengeance.   Yet he does not directly overemphasize his own assets as in compensation, nor does he attribute his own motives to others, as is supposed to take place in *projection*.   Nor does defensive devaluation connote the profound lack of insight, characteristic of reaction-formation and, as we shall see, projection.   It is thus perhaps the "least abnormal" of mechanisms, enabling us to say in effect "I know I have my weaknesses, but what do they amount to when you consider . . . ," followed by a litany of the foibles and iniquities of others, thereby mitigating the threat to self-esteem of our own failings without denying their existence.

7   Displacement.   *Attaching an unacceptable motive and its accompanying affect to an alternative object which can provide partial (usually symbolic) release for the original motive without bringing the latter to awareness.*   Examples are numerous, as in the peculiar joy derived from beating a business rival at golf or bridge, satisfying a prying tendency by taking a job which involves conducting investigations into the lives of others (perhaps that of a psychologist!), carrying over a repressed hatred and fear of one's father to one's relations with his boss or with older authority figures generally.

The Whether displacement plays as enormous a role in human motivation as postulated by Freud is open to considerable doubt, but there is no question that as a defense mechanism it has unusual importance in the genesis of neurotic symptoms and of neurotic "tendencies" found even in the normal person.

The symbolic and defensive nature of displacement is manifested by the presence of intense feeling quite disproportionate to the acknowledged importance of the current circumstance.   When, for example, a man attaches a value to winning at bridge that the card game in itself could not by any reckoning warrant, when he is upset for days over a bad play or at losing to a neighbor, playing and replaying every trick in his mind, planning his strategy for the next game in great and anxious detail, we infer that beating his opponent at bridge is symbolic to him of something larger, that not the game itself but his self-regard is somehow at stake.   So when a man is hatefully resentful of a superior where there is little or nothing in the behavior of the superior to justify this malevolent attitude, we may again look beyond the present situation to some other relation of which it may be symbolic and which, having been repressed, has been denied expression, such as resentment toward a domineering parent, rivalry with an older brother, and the like.

We may note in such cases a *reason to repress* the original motive and feeling. Thus the love and respect which we are supposed to feel, and often actually do feel, toward our parents or siblings, may make attitudes of dislike or resentment unacceptable and self-devaluating. This does not seem to be the case with all symbolic displacements, however, which therefore may not serve any special defensive purpose but take place simply as a result of the inevitable human disposition to symbolize. Thus my transfer of negative feeling from an earlier experience to a present one may be maladaptive without serving to protect self-esteem, as when I react to a new acquaintance on the basis of his (unrecognized) resemblance to an old rival. Though maladaptive, such displacements are unlikely to be productive of neurosis since the aberrant tendency is not reinforced by the continuing need to safeguard self-esteem and may be more readily modified by corrective experience.

In postulating that the defensive symbolism of displacement renders intelligible much peculiar feeling and behavior, and that phobias and compulsions and conversion symptoms often "make sense" in the light of their symbolically defensive purpose, Freud unquestionably contributed more than any other person to our understanding of neurotic and other abnormal phenomena. Freud also seems to have had reason on his side in arguing that sexual motives, because of their intrinsic urgency and the severe disapproval with which their manifestation in the young is likely to be greeted, are specially subject to symbolization and displacement, following inadequate repression.

It is something less than necessary, however, to concur in Freud's speculations regarding the unlimited displaceability of sexual motives and to conclude with him that not only many neurotic symptoms but many entirely normal activities of a higher order such as religious rituals, artistic endeavor, and intellectual interests equally represent symbolic fulfilments of sexual urges. To interpret prayer as satisfying the impulse to masturbate, painting as a displacement of the motive to smear excrement, and intellectual curiosity as a symbolic equivalent of the wish to play Peeping Tom in the parental bedroom, requires a degree of credulity in the magical power of symbolism which is so far fortunately confined to some psychoanalysts and psychotics.

Some instances of apparent displacement involve little or no symbolism and most probably denote a rather obvious kind of "safety-valve" mechanism, as when the business man who has had to contain his ire all day takes it out on his wife and children in the evening; or when we, having put up with a series of frustrations or indignities, "blow up" at some trifling contretemps. These bear only a superficial resemblance to the systematically symbolic and elaborately self-deceptive displacements we find in many neurotics, and should not be considered to exemplify the defense-mechanism in any strict sense. Symbolism as well as self-defense is thus probably, as Freud thought, essential to the kind of displacement which contributes to neurosis.

8   Projection.   Projection is one of the most important mechanisms for the understanding of psychological abnormality, but it is more pertinent to psychosis and the so-called personality pattern disturbances than it is to the relatively minor abnormalities or neuroses. To project is *to defend against unacceptable motives by attributing to others either the motives themselves or the criticism of oneself for having such motives.* The unacceptable is not explained away, counteracted, or made up for (as in rationalization, reaction-formation, and compensation); one gets rid of it projecting it onto others, by regarding it as the creation of others and not of oneself. Projection is instanced by interpreting neutral behavior in another as hostile, while not recognizing the reality and primacy of one's own hostility; by reacting to homosexual or other deviant sexual tendencies in oneself by first over-vigorously denying the possibility of any such tendencies, and thereupon ascribing to others unjust accusations against the self of having such tendencies.   The two examples illustrate what may be distinguished as *primary projection* (direct attribution of our unacceptable motives to another); and *secondary projection* (attribution to others of critical attitudes toward the self for allegedly having unacceptable motives).   What is projected in the latter case is *one's own* self-devaluating attitude which may well be a greater threat to self-esteem than the original (unacceptable) motive.

Since both kinds of projection ascribe to others what is actually our own motivational or attitudinal stance, the use of projection as a defense mechanism presupposes a profound lack of insight and a deep repression of our irrational and censurable dispositions.   To project is thus not just to blame others for our problems; it is to blame others for our own baser motives and consequent self-critical attitudes. It would seem then that projection could be sustained only by a defensively "touchy" and uninsightful view of the self as irreproachable, combined with a basically suspicious and hostile view of others, a singularly unappealing combination but one whose existence is supported by the clinical impression that those with a high quota of hostility and low insight find projection relatively easy.   It is worth noting, too, that when hostile motives are projected the inner need which they connote can still be satisfied by the counter-hostility we feel justified in manifesting after we have projected our original hostility to others.   Projection may thereby be reinforced through rationalization, while a defensively devaluative attitude toward others may prepare the ground for it.

Since friction is an inevitable consequence of social closeness, and insight is achieved with difficulty, while the empathic understanding of others is rare indeed, it is not surprising that some tendencies toward hostile projection—sometimes called "paranoid trends"—are found everywhere. Extensive and elaborate use of projection is, however, rare in normal persons, probably because it involves so much distortion of the self-picture and so many uncritical suppositions regarding the motives of others. The deepening and stabilization of primary projection is characteristic of what is known as paranoid personality disorder, rather than of neurosis; and the elaboration of self-deceptive notions regarding the accusatory attitude of others toward oneself for sexual irregularities and the like (secondary projection) is generally symptomatic of paranoid psychosis. Perhaps the tendency to project is ubiquitous, but it is fortunately subject to limitation and correction where reality contact is good and insight at all present.

9   Withdrawal.   This is a so-called minor mechanism, representing a defensive reaction to weakness or ineptitude which is at the opposite pole to compensation. It should not be confused with the symptomatic behavior of *social withdrawal*, though it may be antecedent thereto. In itself, defensive withdrawal is a purely mental mechanism, an *endopsychic retreat from what is desired but considered unattainable*. Like other defense mechanisms it presupposes the operation of repression, in this case at least to reduce the awareness of failure or incompetence. The complementary function of withdrawal is thus to reduce motivation or desire for the object whose attainment is thought to be beyond reach.

Coping or constructive adjustment demands, of course, that we learn our limitations and cease trying to reach the unattainable. Defensive withdrawal is something else: a subtle self-deception in which we convince (or all but convince) ourselves that we don't care about the loss of something we very much wanted. By relinquishing interest, by saying to myself "I don't care," I defend myself against the highly self-devaluating experience of failure, prospective or retrospective. "I didn't fail," I say in effect, "I just didn't try. And I didn't try because it doesn't really matter to me." What makes withdrawal essentially maladjustive is its prevention of further effort to attain the desired goal or even of the attempt to re-assess the situation. Perhaps what is needed in many cases is not a psychological "leaving the field" but the taking of a new tack, or a hard look at our past efforts in order to discover the reason for their failure. The stabilization of the withdrawal mechanism, however, so lowers the attraction of the goal—at least to consciousness—that re-appraisal and renewed effort are most unlikely to occur. If the habitual "withdrawer," then, "wards off" failure by giving up almost in advance, he effectively "wards off" success as well. Withdrawal-in-advance may thus be the mark of the inept or inadequate personality, while withdrawal after the event may be akin to the rationalization of failure. The fable of the fox and the sour grapes, though often interpreted quite differently, appears to exemplify this kind of withdrawal more than any other defense-mechanism.

10   Identification.   Identification is *defending against the conviction of inadequacy and weakness by viewing oneself as somehow the same as or one with some figure of power or status.* It is probably less dependent on repression than most other mechanisms, though it may involve a diminished awareness of one's separate identity as a creature of weakness. In its original, childish form identification results in a detailed and intense imitation of a parent or other status person. It may be very thoroughgoing because it is a kind of natural extension of the process of learning by imitation, and because it may also involve a normal expression of affection. But behind this extreme imitation there is likely to be the primitive, magical thinking of identification which concludes in effect: "If I am like him in every act, I will take on his attributes of power and competence." Identification in this sense is undoubtedly important for the development of personality in childhood and early adolescence. It is to a great extent by "trying on" the attitudes and manners of acting suggested by others —most often through deeds rather than words—parents to begin with, but also older siblings, teachers, peer group leaders, and various other status figures, that we find for ourselves the style of life that (more or less) fits.

Despite the importance of identification for personality development, the persistence into adulthood of its childlike mode of thinking results in a neurotic immaturity. The individual may have to begin by identifying with a father or other mentor, but as he matures he must alter and adapt the model to the dimensions of circumstance and the substance of his own individuality. The ideal self must come closer to the capacities of the real self and to the possibilities determined by the actual and present life situation. To behave exactly like your father, for example, when your own capacities and temperament are quite different from your father's, and where the surroundings in which you find yourself are also quite different, is certainly maladjustive, however impressive your father's behavior may have been.

If identification does not disappear, it becomes radically altered in the normal adult, acquiring flexibility, becoming more broadly socialized, object-oriented, coping rather than defensive. The normal adult manifests a great deal of what is sometimes loosely called "group identification." He "identifies" with his profession or trade, his family, his country, his political party, his local community, his religion. If his identifications are thereby multiplied, they are also less total and involuntary and have only a limited resemblance to the defense mechanism found in the abnormal and the developmental contrivance employed by the immature.   Adult identifications reflect what Allport has called the objectification and extension of the self: they manifest what through socialization the individual has become (Allport, 1937). Defensive identification, on the other hand, reflects what the individual is *not* but would become, as a means of escape from the self-devaluating reality of his own limitations.

In normal persons, too, identification (whether developmental or adult) seems closely related to affiliation and affection.   The normal child loves and admires the parent with whom he identifies.   The normal man "cathects" his family, his religion, his profession, his school.   There is little affection manifested, however, in what the Freudians aptly call "identification with the aggressor," as when a child imitates to the letter in his actions toward a younger sibling the behavior of a brutal father whom he fears and hates; or when lighter-skinned Negroes exhibit prejudice toward their darker fellows; or when, as has been reported, concentration camp inmates outdo their guards in brutality toward their fellow prisoners, not stopping at murder and torture, and even sewing scraps of Gestapo uniform to their prison garb that they might resemble more closely their tormentors.

11   Undoing.   Undoing is *symbolic restitution for a present impulse or past behavior considered unacceptable.*   Distinction must again be made between restitution as a conscious and deliberate social act, designed to make up at least partially for a wrong done to another, and defensive undoing, a self-deluding kind of magical thinking by which we annul our delinquencies.   The latter, like other defense-mechanisms, is based upon at least partial repression, while social reparation, which the psychoanalysts and others often confuse with undoing, presupposes a consciousness of wrong done and of a connection between the restitutional act and the original transgression. Nor is the thinking involved in the latter necessarily magical.   When we apologize for an insult, for example, we do not ordinarily deceive ourselves or others into thinking that thereby the offending action is undone.   Rather we express a wish, recognized as contrary-to-fact, that we had not committed the injury and we signify an intention not to repeat it.   It is as an expression of present attitude and augury for the future that reparative behavior has social meaning.   So the husband who brings flowers to his wife after he has treated her badly need not suppose that his past action is nullified, but simply that his present behavior gives some indication of his positive feeling toward her, which may serve to offset the earlier evidence of disregard.   It

is only when he is unaware of the relation between the two acts, or when he has displaced both actions to an entirely symbolic and unreal plane, that he gives evidence of employing undoing as a defense-mechanism in the strict sense.

Of course, there is some connection between defensive undoing and social reparation, especially developmentally. For the child who can see no connection between his behavior (which has been ad-judged wrong) and the verbal formula, "I'm sorry," the latter may appear to be simply an incantation which prevents the evil conse-quences to him of the former. With the development of intelligence, however, he should acquire some understanding of the real, as op-posed to the magical, effect of efforts to redress socially harmful actions. It is only when, as an adult, he reverts to a childishly magi-cal use of symbolic restitution that we can regard his behavior as self-deceptively defensive and potentially neurotic.

12   Autism.   A special kind of daydreaming by which *achieve-ment in fantasy substitutes for achievement in fact and defends self-esteem against the sense of inadequacy and failure.* Autism goes farther than isolation and withdrawal since it substitutes a kind of activity for the deficiency or failure. It does not, however, go as far as compensation since the substituted activity is merely fantasy. This fantasy, moreover—and this is significant in differentiating autism as a defense-mechanism from ordinary fantasy—tends to prevent further effort toward real goals by consuming our time and attention in the effortless and empty satisfactions of reverie. Such fantasy neither prepares for nor relaxes from endeavor but substitutes therefor, and since its rewards are as faint as they are easy, it has a natural tendency to proliferate and expand.

James Thurber's short story "The Secret Life of Walter Mitty" re-mains the perfect literary expression of autism as a defense, but the mechanism does not require the elaborately inventive imagination manifested by Thurber's character. The tendency to use fantasy as an unconscious substitute for the motive and effort to achieve and as a means of disengagement from the self-devaluating experience of nonachievement suffices. And if, in this age of wonders, the personal fantasy-making mechanism falters, we have but to turn on the tele-vision set, make for the nearest movie house, or open the pages of any of the many unfunny "comic books" or apocryphal "true story" magazines, to have available a pre-packaged fantasy world in which even the effort of imagination has been minimized.

Where achievement in the direction of self-realization (*coping*) is prevented by reason of age (as in childhood, adolescence, and old age), or by reason of inability to accept the approved goals of one's culture or subculture—consider the man of integrity living in a dictatorship or the creative artist forced to live and work among Philistines—the autistic mechanism may prove a useful buffer against a too harsh reality. Where good adjustment is impossible, as it may be for the best of men in a bad society, or when caught in the web of adverse circumstance, fantasy may mitigate frustration and ward off despair. The self-depreciating but by no means ingenuous query "I can dream, can't I?" summarizes the understandably defensive posture of the normal man blocked by external factors over which he has little control, but not surrendering hope. What differentiates this from the autism found in the abnormal is that the adequate person will prefer coping to fantasy, where coping is possible; the inadequate may not.

Summary

This paper provides a phenomenological analysis of 12 major defense mechanisms. The mechanisms are viewed as self-deceptive psychic strategies for protecting self-esteem against self-devaluating experiences. The debt to Freud is acknowledged, but the analysis is for the most part based on grounds other than the psychosexual.

Defense mechanisms are distinguished sharply from psychopathological symptoms, and while repression is admitted to be fundamental, its partial and unsuccessful nature is also stressed. Departing from classical views, isolation is defined in terms of motivational relevance; rationalization is related to "over-determination"; "antithetic counter-action" is regarded as a more precise term than "reaction-formation"; the coping types of compensation including masculine-protest are distinguished from the defensive variety; a new mechanism, somewhere between compensation and projection and labeled "defensive-devaluation" is introduced; the Freudian overuse of displacement is criticized; distinction is made between primary and secondary projection; the developmental is contrasted both with the mature and the defensive use of identification; undoing is differentiated from realistic social reparation; and the normality of some kinds of autism acknowledged.

References

Allport, G. W. *Personality: A psychological interpretation.* New York: Holt, 1937.

Fenichel, O. *The psychoanalytic theory of neurosis.* New York: Norton, 1945.

Freud, Anna. *The ego and the mechanisms of defense.* London: Hogarth, 1954.

McCall, R. J. Invested Self-expression: Toward a Theory of Human Structural Dynamics. In A. A. Schneiders and P. J. Centi (Eds.), *Selected Papers from the ACPA Meetings of 1960–1961.* New York, Fordham Univer., 1962.

Karen Horney   **THE BASIC CONFLICT ***

Conflicts play an infinitely greater role in neurosis than is commonly assumed. To detect them, however, is no easy matter—partly because they are essentially unconscious, but even more because the neurotic goes to any length to deny their existence. What, then, are the signals that would warrant us to suspect underlying conflicts? In . . . examples cited . . . their presence was indicated by two factors, both fairly obvious. One was the resulting symptoms—fatigue in the first case, stealing in the second. The fact is that every neurotic symptom points to an underlying conflict; that is, every symptom is a more or less direct outgrowth of a conflict. We shall see gradually what unresolved conflicts do to people, how they produce states of anxiety, depression, indecision, inertia, detachment, and so on. An understanding of the causative relation here helps direct our attention from the manifest disturbances to their source—though the exact nature of the source will not be disclosed.

The other signal indicating that conflicts were in operation was inconsistency. In the first example we saw a man convinced of a procedure being wrong and of injustice done him, making no move to protest. In the second a person who highly valued friendship turned to stealing money from a friend. Sometimes the person himself will be aware of such inconsistencies; more often he is blind to them even when they are blatantly obvious to an untrained observer.

Inconsistencies are as definite an indication of the presence of conflicts as a rise in body temperature is of physical disturbance. To cite some common ones: A girl wants above all else to marry, yet shrinks from the advances of any man. A mother oversolicitous of her children frequently forgets their birthdays. A person always generous to others is niggardly about small expenditures for himself. Another who longs for solitude never manages to be alone. One forgiving and tolerant toward most people is oversevere and demanding with himself.

Unlike the symptoms, the inconsistencies often permit of tentative assumptions as to the nature of the underlying conflict. An acute depression, for instance, reveals only the fact that a person is caught in a dilemma. But if an apparently devoted mother forgets her children's birthdays, we might be inclined to think that the mother was more devoted to her ideal of being a good mother than to the children themselves. We might also admit the possibility that her ideal collided with an unconscious sadistic tendency to frustrate them.

Sometimes a conflict will appear on the surface—that is, be consciously experienced as such. This would seem to contradict my assertion that neurotic conflicts are unconscious. But actually what appears is a distortion or modification of the real conflict. Thus a person may be torn by a conscious conflict when, in spite of his evasive techniques, well-functioning otherwise, he finds himself confronted with the necessity of making a major decision. He cannot decide now whether to marry this woman or that one or whether to marry at all, whether to take this or that job, whether to retain or dissolve a partnership. He will then go through the greatest torment, shuttling from one opposite to the other, utterly incapable of arriving at any decision. He may in his distress call upon an analyst, expecting him to clarify the particular issues involved. And he will necessarily be disappointed, because the present conflict is merely the point at which the dynamite of inner frictions finally exploded. The particular problem distressing him now cannot be solved without taking the long and tortuous road of recognizing the conflicts hidden beneath it.

In other instances the inner conflict may be externalized and appear in the person's conscious mind as an incompatibility between himself and his environment. Or, finding that seemingly unfounded fears and inhibitions interfere with his wishes, a person may be aware that the crosscurrents within himself issue from deeper sources.

The more knowledge we gain of a person, the better able we are to recognize the conflicting elements that account for the symptoms, inconsistencies, and surface conflicts—and, we must add, the more confusing becomes the picture, through the number and variety of contradictions. So we are led to ask: Can there be a basic conflict underlying all these particular conflicts and originally responsible for all of them? Can one picture the structure of conflict in terms, say, of an incompatible marriage, where an endless variety of apparently unrelated disagreements and rows over friends, children, finances, mealtimes, servants, all point to some fundamental disharmony in the relationship itself? . . .

Proceeding now to evolve my own position, I see the basic conflict of the neurotic in the fundamentally contradictory attitudes he has acquired toward other persons. Before going into detail, let me call attention to the dramatization of such a contradiction in the story of Dr. Jekyll and Mr. Hyde. We see him on the one hand delicate, sensitive, sympathetic, helpful, and on the other brutal, callous, and egotistical. I do not, of course, mean to imply that neurotic division always adheres to the precise line of this story, but merely to point to a vivid expression of basic incompatibility of attitudes in relation to others.

To approach the problem genetically we must go back to what I have called basic anxiety,[1] meaning by this the feeling a child has of being isolated and helpless in a potentially hostile world. A wide range of adverse factors in the environment can produce this insecurity in a child: direct or indirect domination, indifference, erratic behavior, lack of respect for the child's individual needs, lack of real guidance, disparaging attitudes, too much admiration or the absence of it, lack of reliable warmth, having to take sides in parental disagreements, too much or too little responsibility, overprotection, isolation from other children, injustice, discrimination, unkept promises, hostile atmosphere, and so on and so on.

The only factor to which I should like to draw special attention in this context is the child's sense of lurking hypocrisy in the environment: his feeling that the parents' love, their Christian charity, honesty, generosity, and so on may be only pretense. Part of what the child feels on this score is really hypocrisy; but some of it may be just his reaction to all the contradictions he senses in the parents' behavior. Usually, however, there is a combination of cramping factors. They may be out in the open or quite hidden, so that in analysis one can only gradually recognize these influences on the child's development.

Harassed by these disturbing conditions, the child gropes for ways to keep going, ways to cope with this menacing world. Despite his own weakness and fears he unconsciously shapes his tactics to meet the particular forces operating in his environment. In doing so, he develops not only *ad hoc* strategies but lasting character trends which become part of his personality. I have called these "neurotic trends."

If we want to see how conflicts develop, we must not focus too sharply on the individual trends but rather take a panoramic view of the main directions in which a child can and does move under these circumstances. Though we lose sight for a while of details we shall gain a clearer perspective of the essential moves made to cope with the environment. At first a rather chaotic picture may present itself, but out of it in time three main lines crystallize: a child can move *toward* people, *against* them, or *away from* them.

When moving *toward* people he accepts his own helplessness, and in spite of his estrangement and fears tries to win the affection of others and to lean on them. Only in this way can he feel safe with

[1] Karen Horney, *The Neurotic Personality of Our Time*, W. W. Norton, 1937.

them. If there are dissenting parties in the family, he will attach himself to the most powerful person or group. By complying with them, he gains a feeling of belonging and support which makes him feel less weak and less isolated.

When he moves *against* people he accepts and takes for granted the hostility around him, and determines, consciously or unconsciously, to fight. He implicitly distrusts the feelings and intentions of others toward himself. He rebels in whatever ways are open to him. He wants to be the stronger and defeat them, partly for his own protection, partly for revenge.

When he moves *away from* people he wants neither to belong nor to fight, but keeps apart. He feels he has not much in common with them, they do not understand him anyhow. He builds up a world of his own—with nature, with his dolls, his books, his dreams.

In each of these three attitudes, one of the elements involved in basic anxiety is overemphasized: helplessness in the first, hostility in the second, and isolation in the third. But the fact is that the child cannot make any one of these moves wholeheartedly, because under the conditions in which the attitudes develop, all are bound to be present. What we have seen from our panoramic view is only the predominant move.

That this is so will become evident if we jump ahead now to the fully developed neurosis. We all know adults in whom one of the attitudes we have sketched stands out. But we can see, too, that his other tendencies have not ceased to operate. In a predominantly leaning and complying type we can observe aggressive propensities and some need for detachment. A predominantly hostile person has a compliant strain and needs detachment too. And a detached personality is not without hostility or a desire for affection.

The predominant attitude, however, is the one that most strongly determines actual conduct. It represents those ways and means of coping with others in which the particular person feels most at home. Thus a detached person will as a matter of course use all the unconscious techniques for keeping others at a safe distance because he feels at a loss in any situation that requires close association with them. Moreover, the ascendant attitude is often but not always the one most acceptable to the person's conscious mind.

This does not mean that the less conspicuous attitudes are less powerful. It would often be difficult to say, for instance, whether in an apparently dependent, compliant person the wish to dominate is of inferior intensity to the need for affection; his ways of expressing his aggressive impulses are merely more indirect. That the potency of the submerged tendencies may be very great is evidenced by the many instances in which the attitude accorded predominance is reversed. We can see such reversal in children, but it occurs in later life as well. Strickland in Somerset Maugham's *The Moon and Sixpence* would be a good illustration. Case histories of women often reveal this kind of change. A girl formerly tomboyish, ambitious, rebellious, when she falls in love may turn into a compliant, dependent woman, apparently without ambition. Or, under pressure of crushing experiences, a detached person may become morbidly dependent.

Changes like these, it should be added, throw some light on the frequent question whether later experience counts for nothing, whether we are definitely channeled, conditioned once and for all, by our childhood situation. Looking at neurotic development from the point of view of conflicts enables us to give a more adequate answer than is usually offered. These are the possibilities: If the early situation is not too prohibitive of spontaneous growth, later experiences, particularly in adolescence, can have a molding influence. If, however, the impact of early experiences has been powerful enough to have molded the child to a rigid pattern, no new experience will be able to break through. In part this is because his rigidity does not leave him open to any new experience: his detachment, for instance, may be too great to permit of anyone's coming close to him, or his dependence so deep-rooted that he is forced always to play a subordinate role and invite exploitation. In part it is because he will interpret any new experience in the language of his established pattern: the aggressive type, for instance, meeting with friendliness, will view it either as a manifestation of stupidity or an attempt to exploit him; the new experience will tend only to reinforce the old pattern. When a neurotic does adopt a different attitude it may look as if later experiences had brought about a change in personality. However, the change is not as radical as it appears. Actually what has happened is that combined internal and external pressures have forced him to abandon his predominant attitude in favor of the other extreme—but this change would not have taken place if there had been no conflicts to begin with.

From the point of view of the normal person there is no reason why the three attitudes should be mutually exclusive. One should be capable of giving in to others, of fighting, and of keeping to oneself. The three can complement each other and make for a harmonious whole. If one predominates, it merely indicates an overdevelopment along one line.

But in neurosis there are several reasons why these attitudes are irreconcilable. The neurotic is not flexible; he is driven to comply, to fight, to be aloof, regardless of whether the move is appropriate in the particular circumstance, and he is thrown into a panic if he behaves otherwise. Hence when all three attitudes are present in any strong degree, he is bound to be caught in a severe conflict.

Another factor, and one that considerably widens the scope of the conflict, is that the attitudes do not remain restricted to the area of human relationships but gradually pervade the entire personality, as a malignant tumor pervades the whole organic tissue. They end by encompassing not only the person's relation to others but also his relation to himself and to life in general. If we are not fully aware of this all-embracing character, the temptation is to think of the resulting conflict in categorical terms, like love *versus* hate, compliance *versus* defiance, submissiveness *versus* domination, and so on. That, however, would be as misleading as to distinguish fascism from democracy by focusing on any single opposing feature, such as their difference in approach to religion or power. These are differences certainly, but exclusive emphasis upon them would serve to obscure the point that democracy and fascism are worlds apart and represent two philosophies of life entirely incompatible with each other.

It is not accidental that a conflict that starts with our relation to others in time affects the whole personality. Human relationships are so crucial that they are bound to mold the qualities we develop, the goals we set for ourselves, the values we believe in. All these in turn react upon our relations with others and so are inextricably interwoven.

My contention is that the conflict born of incompatible attitudes constitutes the core of neurosis and therefore deserves to be called *basic*. And let me add that I use the term *core* not merely in the figurative sense of its being significant but to emphasize the fact that it is the dynamic center from which neuroses emanate. This contention is the nucleus of a new theory of neurosis. . . . Broadly considered, the theory may be viewed as an elaboration of my earlier concept that neuroses are an expression of a disturbance in human relationships.

Erich Fromm

THE NONPRODUCTIVE
CHARACTER ORIENTATIONS *

(a) The receptive orientation

In the receptive orientation a person feels "the source of all good" to be outside, and he believes that the only way to get what he wants—

* From Erich Fromm, *Man for Himself*, Rinehart and Company, Inc., New York, 1947. Pages 62–73 reprinted by permission of the author and the publisher.

be it something material, be it affection, love, knowledge, pleasure—
is to receive it from that outside source.   In this orientation the problem of love is almost exclusively that of "being loved" and not that of
loving.   Such people tend to be indiscriminate in the choice of their
love objects, because being loved by anybody is such an overwhelming experience for them that they "fall for" anybody who gives them
love or what looks like love.   They are exceedingly sensitive to any
withdrawal or rebuff they experience on the part of the loved person.
Their orientation is the same in the sphere of thinking: if intelligent,
they make the best listeners, since their orientation is one of receiving, not of producing, ideas; left to themselves, they feel paralyzed.
It is characteristic of these people that their first thought is to find
somebody else to give them needed information rather than to make
even the smallest effort of their own.   If religious, these persons have
a concept of God in which they expect everything from God and nothing
from their own activity.   If not religious, their relationship to persons
or institutions is very much the same; they are always in search of a
"magic helper."   They show a particular kind of loyalty, at the bottom of which is the gratitude for the hand that feeds them and the
fear of ever losing it.   Since they need many hands to feel secure,
they have to be loyal to numerous people.   It is difficult for them
to say "no," and they are easily caught between conflicting loyalties and promises.   Since they cannot say "no," they love to say
"yes" to everything and everybody, and the resulting paralysis
of their critical abilities makes them increasingly dependent on
others.

They are dependent not only on authorities for knowledge and help
but on people in general for any kind of support.   They feel lost when
alone because they feel that they cannot do anything without help.
This helplessness is especially important with regard to those acts
which by their very nature can only be done alone—making decisions
and taking responsibility.   In personal relationships, for instance, they
ask advice from the very person with regard to whom they have to
make a decision.

This receptive type has great fondness for food and drink.   These
persons tend to overcome anxiety and depression by eating or drinking.   The mouth is an especially prominent feature, often the most
expressive one; the lips tend to be open, as if in a state of continuous
expectation of being fed.   In their dreams, being fed is a frequent
symbol of being loved; being starved, an expression of frustration or
disappointment.

By and large, the outlook of people of this receptive orientation is
optimistic and friendly; they have a certain confidence in life and its
gifts, but they become anxious and distraught when their "source of
supply" is threatened.   They often have a genuine warmth and a wish

to help others, but doing things for others also assumes the function of securing their favor.

(b) The exploitative orientation

The exploitative orientation, like the receptive, has as its basic premise the feeling that the source of all good is outside, that whatever one wants to get must be sought there, and that one cannot produce anything oneself. The difference between the two, however, is that the exploitative type does not expect to receive things from others as gifts, but to take them away from others by force or cunning. This orientation extends to all spheres of activity.

In the realm of love and affection these people tend to grab and steal. They feel attracted only to people whom they can take away from somebody else. Attractiveness to them is conditioned by a person's attachment to somebody else; they tend not to fall in love with an unattached person. We find the same attitude with regard to thinking and intellectual pursuits. Such people will tend not to produce ideas but to steal them. This may be done directly in the form of plagiarism or more subtly by repeating in different phraseology the ideas voiced by others and insisting they are new and their own. It is a striking fact that frequently people with great intelligence proceed in this way, although if they relied on their own gifts they might well be able to have ideas of their own. The lack of original ideas or independent production in otherwise gifted people often has its explanation in this character orientation, rather than in any innate lack of originality. The same statement holds true with regard to their orientation to material things. Things which they can take away from others always seems better to them than anything they can produce themselves. They use and exploit anybody and anything from whom or from which they can squeeze-something. Their motto is: "Stolen fruits are sweetest." Because they want to use and exploit people, they "love" those who, explicitly or implicitly, are promising objects of exploitation, and get "fed up" with persons whom they have squeezed out. An extreme example is the kleptomaniac who enjoys things only if he can steal them, although he has the money to buy them.

This orientation seems to be symbolized by the biting mouth which is often a prominent feature in such people. It is not a play upon words to point out that they often make "biting" remarks about others. Their attitude is colored by a mixture of hostility and manipulation. Everyone is an object of exploitation and is judged according to his usefulness. Instead of the confidence and optimism which characterizes the receptive type, one finds here suspicion and cynicism, envy and jealousy. Since they are satisfied only with things they can take away from others, they tend to overrate what others have and underrate what is theirs.

(c) The hoarding orientation

While the receptive and exploitative types are similar inasmuch as both expect to get things from the outside world, the hoarding orientation is essentially different.   This orientation makes people have little faith in anything new they might get from the outside world; their security is based upon hoarding and saving, while spending is felt to be a threat.   They have surrounded themselves, as it were, by a protective wall, and their main aim is to bring as much as possible into this fortified position and to let as little as possible out of it.   Their miserliness refers to money and material things as well as to feelings and thoughts.   Love is essentially a possession; they do not give love but try to get it by possessing the "beloved."   The hoarding person often shows a particular kind of faithfulness toward people and even toward memories.   Their sentimentality makes the past appear as golden; they hold on to it and indulge in the memories of bygone feelings and experiences.   They know everything but are sterile and incapable of productive thinking.

One can recognize these people too by facial expressions and gestures.   Theirs is the tight-lipped mouth; their gestures are characteristic of their withdrawn attitude.   While those of the receptive type are inviting and round, as it were, and the gestures of the exploitative type are aggressive and pointed, those of the hoarding type are angular, as if they wanted to emphasize the frontiers between themselves and the outside world.   Another characteristic element in this attitude is pedantic orderliness.   The hoarder will be orderly with things, thoughts, or feelings, but again, as with memory, his orderliness is sterile and rigid.   He cannot endure things out of place and will automatically rearrange them.   To him the outside world threatens to break into his fortified position; orderliness signifies mastering the world outside by putting it, and keeping it, in its proper place in order to avoid the danger of intrusion.   His compulsive cleanliness is another expression of his need to undo contact with the outside world. Things beyond his own frontiers are felt to be dangerous and "unclean"; he annuls the menacing contact by compulsive washing, similar to a religious washing ritual prescribed after contact with unclean things or people.   Things have to be put not only in their proper place but also into their proper time; obsessive punctuality is characteristic of the hoarding type; it is another form of mastering the outside world. If the outside world is experienced as a threat to one's fortified position, obstinacy is a logical reaction.   A constant "no" is the almost automatic defense against intrusion; sitting tight, the answer to the danger of being pushed.   These people tend to feel that they possess only a fixed quantity of strength, energy, or mental capacity, and that this stock is diminished or exhausted by use and can never be replenished.   They cannot understand the self-replenishing function of all living substance and that activity and the use of one's powers increase strength while stagnation paralyzes; to them, death and destruction have more reality than life and growth.   The act of creation is a miracle of which they hear but in which they do not believe.   Their highest values are order and security; their motto: "There is nothing new under the sun."   In their relationship to others intimacy is a threat; either remoteness or possession of a person means security. The hoarder tends to be suspicious and to have a particular sense of justice which in effect says: "Mine is mine and yours is yours."

(d) The marketing orientation

The marketing orientation developed as a dominant one only in the modern era.   In order to understand its nature one must consider the economic function of the market in modern society as being not only analogous to this character orientation but as the basis and the main condition for its development in modern man.

Barter is one of the oldest economic mechanisms.   The traditional local market, however, is essentially different from the market as it has developed in modern capitalism.   Bartering on a local market offered an opportunity to meet for the purpose of exchanging commodities.   Producers and customers became acquainted; they were relatively small groups; the demand was more or less known, so that the producer could produce for this specific demand.

The modern market [1] is no longer a meeting place but a mechanism characterized by abstract and impersonal demand.   One produces for this market, not for a known circle of customers; its verdict is based on laws of supply and demand; and it determines whether the commodity can be sold and at what price.   No matter what the *use value* of a pair of shoes may be, for instance, if the supply is greater than the demand, some shoes will be sentenced to economic death; they might as well not have been produced at all.   The market day is the "day of judgment" as far as the *exchange value* of commodities is concerned.

The reader may object that this description of the market is oversimplified.   The producer does try to judge the demand in advance, and under monopoly conditions even obtains a certain degree of control over it.   Nevertheless, the regulatory function of the market has

[1] Cf., for the study of history and function of the modern market, K. Polanyi's *The Great Transformation* (New York: Rinehart & Company, 1944).

been, and still is, predominant enough to have a profound influence on the character formation of the urban middle class and, through the latter's social and cultural influence, on the whole population. The market concept of value, the emphasis on exchange value rather than on use value, has led to a similar concept of value with regard to people and particularly to oneself. The character orientation which is rooted in the experience of oneself as a commodity and of one's value as exchange value I call the marketing orientation.

In our time the marketing orientation has been growing rapidly, together with the development of a new market that is a phenomenon of the last decades—the "personality market." Clerks and salesmen, business executives and doctors, lawyers and artists all appear on this market. It is true that their legal status and economic positions are different: some are independent, charging for their services; others are employed, receiving salaries. But all are dependent for their material success on a personal acceptance by those who need their services or who employ them.

The principle of evaluation is the same on both the personality and the commodity market: on the one, personalities are offered for sale; on the other, commodities. Value in both cases is their exchange value, for which use value is a necessary but not a sufficient condition. It is true, our economic system could not function if people were not skilled in the particular work they have to perform and were gifted only with a pleasant personality. Even the best bedside manner and the most beautifully equipped office on Park Avenue would not make a New York doctor successful if he did not have a minimum of medical knowledge and skill. Even the most winning personality would not prevent a secretary from losing her job unless she could type reasonably fast. However, if we ask what the respective weight of skill and personality as a condition for success is, we find that only in exceptional cases is success predominantly the result of skill and of certain other human qualities like honesty, decency, and integrity. Although the proportion between skill and human qualities on the one hand and "personality" on the other hand as prerequisites for success varies, the "personality factor" always plays a decisive role. Success depends largely on how well a person sells himself on the market, how well he gets his personality across, how nice a "package" he is; whether he is "cheerful," "sound," "aggressive," "reliable," "ambitious"; furthermore what his family background is, what clubs he belongs to, and whether he knows the right people. The type of personality required depends to some degree on the special field in which a person works. A stockbroker, a salesman, a secretary, a railroad executive, a college professor, or a hotel manager must each offer different kinds of personality that, regardless of their differences, must fulfill one condition: to be in demand.

The fact that in order to have success it is not sufficient to have the skill and equipment for performing a given task but that one must be able to "put across" one's personality in competition with many others shapes the attitude toward oneself.   If it were enough for the purpose of making a living to rely on what one knows and what one can do, one's self-esteem would be in proportion to one's capacities, that is, to one's use value; but since success depends largely on how one sells one's personality, one experiences oneself as a commodity or rather simultaneously as the seller *and* the commodity to be sold.   A person is not concerned with his life and happiness, but with becoming salable.   This feeling might be compared to that of a commodity, of handbags on a counter, for instance, could they feel and think.   Each handbag would try to make itself as "attractive" as possible in order to attract customers and to look as expensive as possible in order to obtain a higher price than its rivals.   The handbag sold for the highest price would feel elated, since that would mean it was the most "valuable" one; the one which was not sold would feel sad and convinced of its own worthlessness.   This fate might befall a bag which, though excellent in appearance and usefulness, had the bad luck to be out of date because of a change in fashion.

Like the handbag, one has to be in fashion on the personality market, and in order to be in fashion one has to know what kind of personality is most in demand.   This knowledge is transmitted in a general way throughout the whole process of education, from kindergarten to college, and implemented by the family.   The knowledge acquired at this early stage is not sufficient, however; it emphasizes only certain general qualities like adaptability, ambition, sensitivity to the changing expectations of other people.   The more specific picture of the models for sucess one gets elsewhere.   The pictorial magazines, newspapers, and newsreels show the pictures and life stories of the successful in many variations.   Pictorial advertising has a similar function.   The successful executive who is pictured in a tailor's advertisement is the image of how one should look and be, if one is to draw down the "big money" on the contemporary personality market.

The most important means of transmitting the desired personality pattern to the average man is the motion picture.   The young girl tries to emulate the facial expression, coiffure, gestures of a high-priced star as the most promising way to success.   The young man tries to look and be like the model he sees on the screen.   While the average citizen has little contact with the life of the most successful people, his relationship with the motion-picture stars is different.   It is true that he has no real contact with them either, but he can see them on the screen again and again, can write them and receive their auto-graphed pictures.   In contrast to the time when the actor was socially despised but was nevertheless the transmitter of the works of great poets to his audience, our motion-picture stars have no great works or ideas to transmit, but their function is to serve as the link an average person has with the world of the "great." Even if he can not hope to become as successful as they are, he can try to emulate them; they are his saints and because of their success they embody the norms for living.

Since modern man experiences himself both as the seller and as the commodity to be sold on the market, his self-esteem depends on conditions beyond his control. If he is "successful," he is valuable; if he is not, he is worthless. The degree of insecurity which results from this orientation can hardly be overestimated. If one feels that one's own value is not constituted primarily by the human qualities one possesses, but by one's success on a competitive market with ever-changing conditions, one's self-esteem is bound to be shaky and in constant need of confirmation by others. Hence one is driven to strive relentlessly for success, and any setback is a severe threat to one's self-esteem; helplessness, insecurity, and inferiority feelings are the result. If the vicissitudes of the market are the judges of one's value, the sense of dignity and pride is destroyed.

But the problem is not only that of self-evaluation and self-esteem but of one's experience of oneself as an independent entity, of one's *identity with oneself*. . . . the nature and productive individual derives his feeling of identity from the experience of himself as the agent who is one with his powers; this feeling of self can be briefly expressed as meaning *"I am what I do."* In the marketing orientation man encounters his own powers as commodities alienated from him. He is not one with them but they are masked from him because what matters is not his self-realization in the process of using them but his success in the process of selling them. Both his powers and what they create become estranged, something different from himself, something for others to judge and to use; thus his feeling of identity becomes as shaky as his self-esteem; it is constituted by the sum total of roles one can play: *"I am as you desire me."*

David Krech,
R. S. Crutchfield,
and
E. L. Ballachey

THE NATURE OF
CONFORMITY *

Meaning and nature of conformity

The problem of conformity has become one of the foremost concerns of
the editorial writer, the commencement speaker, the social scientist.
Indeed ours has been called the Age of Conformity (to say nothing of
the Age of Anxiety, the Age of Togetherness—all of which designa-
tions are, in fact, psychologically related).   The term "conformity" is
used in many different ways, however, and we should first clarify the
particular meaning that we shall attach to it in the following discussion—a meaning which, for our purposes, differentiates among "conformity," "uniformity," and "conventionality."

That high degrees of *uniformity* in social beliefs, values, and practices may exist is not alone a sufficient criterion of conformity. . . .
There are many reasons why common attitudes and actions are widely
found in a society.   Such uniformity may derive from many sources,
quite unrelated to social pressures toward orthodoxy.   That most people in our society believe the earth is round is scarcely evidence of
conformity.

Nor can demonstrations of sheer *conventionality* be simply equated
with conformity.   Conventional ways of acting represent established
solutions to problems; conventions are well-oiled grooves of social
conduct which are provided ready-made and often followed with minimal conflict.   For a man to wear trousers in our society does not con-
vict him of conformity.   Conventionality and uniformity do, of course,
result partly from conformity.   As we shall later see, the conformist
tends to hold more conventional values.   But the converse does not
necessarily hold.   Highly conventional individuals may often be quite
able to resist conformity pressures.

The essence of *conformity*, in distinction to uniformity and conventionality, is *the yielding to group pressures*.   For there to be conformity there must be *conflict*—conflict between those forces in the
individual which tend to lead him to act, value, and believe in one
way and those pressures emanating from the society or group which
tend to lead him in another way.

The pressures from the group need not be explicit; that is, the group
need not overtly threaten or coerce the individual.   The pressures may

* From David Krech, R. S. Crutchfield, and E. L. Ballachey, *Individual in Society*,
McGraw-Hill Book Company, Inc., New York, 1962. Pages 504–515 reprinted by
permission of the authors and the publisher. Slightly edited.

be implicit; that is, the mere existence of a group judgment or action which the individual perceives to differ from his own may exert pressures on him, pressures arising out of fears of being wrong, of "being out of step" with the group, etc. Thus, when an individual is required to express a judgment in a group on some particular issue, and when his own private conviction on the matter is at noticeable variance with the expressed judgments of all the other group members, he is placed in a conflict situation. There are two main courses of action open to him: he may announce his own deviant judgment, thus remaining *independent* of the group consensus; or he may announce his agreement with the group judgment, thus *conforming*.

The actual conformity response under group pressure may take the form of overt action by the individual. He may, for example, join his fellow villagers in stoning a victim. Or the conformity response may be merely verbal; the individual may *say* something that is in agreement with what the group *says*. Such verbal behavior is, of course, of prime significance in our complex society where most social "action" is actually indirect and symbolic. The greater part of the conformity behavior manifested by the individual in the course of his everyday social life is of this verbal type.

Conformity pressures also often take the form of an *inhibition* or *prevention* of action—whether direct or indirect. The individual may be led by conformity pressures to refuse to take action on an issue, to refuse to express a stand. Under many social circumstances this may be the more insidious and ultimately more deadly form of conformity behavior, in that the individual eventually comes not only to yield on particular opinions but to yield even his right to *express* an opinion.

"Expedient" vs. "true" conforming. Not all acts of conforming are identical in psychological meaning. One significant distinction is between "expedient" conforming (discussed by Kelman (1958) as "compliance"), in which the individual *outwardly* agrees with the group but remains in *inward* disagreement, and "true" conforming, in which the individual *both* inwardly and outwardly is brought to agree with the group. We would expect "expedient" conforming—unlike "true" conforming—to be transitory and unstable, with the individual tending to revert to his unaffected private judgment when the immediate group pressure is removed, e.g., after he leaves the group scene. (One is reminded of the politician who, after losing an election, said bitterly, "Well, I shook hands with ten thousand liars!") And as we shall later see, there is good evidence that these two different types of conforming exist, as well as for the point that there are differences in the personality make-up of persons who are typically one or the other type of conformer.

Counterformity vs. independence.   Just as we must distinguish among types of conforming behavior, so must we distinguish among types of behavior where the group pressure is resisted.   The avoidance of conformity is often talked about under the general rubric of "nonconformity," but unfortunately this term fails to allow for important distinctions.   Not all nonconformity is the same.   One crucial type to distinguish from others is what we may call *counterformity*. This is the case in which the person is actively *opposing* the group, being negativistic, hostile, compulsively dissenting from it.   The counterformist not only resists having his judgments and actions move toward those of the group; his judgments and actions tend to be repelled by the group norms; he seeks to *widen* disagreement between himself and the group.   The counterformist may thus be driven at all costs to repudiate the group's beliefs or actions even when he perceives that the group is right!   One might argue that the cognitions and actions of the counterformist are just as surely and predictably being determined by the group as are those of the conformist. For the counterformist, the group serves as a *negative* reference group.

Distinct both from conformity and counterformity is *independence* of judgment and action, wherein the individual makes up his own mind, being able to "take the group or . . . leave it," as his own good sense would dictate.   The independent person, in short, is neither unduly susceptible to the pressure of the group nor unduly driven by forces of alienation from the group.

Conformity, independence, and counterformity are thus not to be thought of as three points along a single continuum.   Rather they represent three vertices of a triangle.   A proper understanding of the whole problem of conformity must take full account of the important differences among these three forms of reaction to group pressure.

Conformity as "trait of the situation."   Every individual displays a good deal of conformity behavior throughout his social life.   He inevitably finds himself in kinds of situations where conforming is the only "reasonable" or possible form of behavior, and in which virtually everyone conforms.   Here conformity might be thought of as a "trait of the situation."   There are also marked individual differences in general readiness to conform, over a wide variety of situations.   These differences, as we shall later see, reflect conformity as a "trait of the person."

This distinction between conformity as reflecting the conformity-inducing properties of a situation and as reflecting the conforming propensity of a person should be kept well in mind.   Much of the controversy and misunderstanding about the facts and theories of conformity stems from a confusion of these two aspects of conformity.

Experimental measurement and study of conformity

The power of group pressure to induce conformity of judgment in the individual is dramatically revealed in the widely known experiments of Asch (1951, 1952, 1956).   His technique enables the experimenter to place an individual under group pressure that can be systematically manipulated and controlled, and then measure the individual's readiness or tendency to yield to such pressure.

In one of his basic experiments, groups of seven to nine college students were assembled and given the following instructions:

This is a task which involves the discrimination of length of lines.   You see the pair of white cards in front.   On the left is a single line; on the right are three lines differing in length.   They are numbered 1, 2, and 3 in order.   One of the three lines at the right is equal to the standard line at the left—you will decide in each case which is the equal line.   You will state your judgment in terms of the corresponding number.   There will be twelve such comparisons.   As the number of lines is few and the group small, I shall call upon each of you in turn to announce your judgment, which I shall record here on a prepared form.   Please be as accurate as possible.   Suppose we start at the right and proceed to the left.

Actually, all but one of the students were confederates of the experimenter, who had been instructed beforehand to give, unanimously, incorrect responses on certain of the line-judgment trials.   It was so arranged that the one naive subject sat near the end of the row, so that he gave his judgment following most of the group.   The naive subject thus found himself in a situation where the correct answers, on certain critical trials, would be in opposition to those given by a unanimous majority.

The line stimuli were chosen by Asch so that the bogus judgments by the group were grossly different from the correct judgments, the discrepancies ranging from one-quarter of an inch to an inch and three quarters.

Findings with the Asch technique.   In Asch's first experiments, 123 naive subjects were tested on twelve critical judgments.   Of the total number of judgments given, 37 per cent were in error, that is, were in conformity with those of the unanimous majority.   Control subjects, judging alone, made virtually no errors.

Marked individual differences in response to the majority pressure were found, ranging for complete independence of the majority by some individuals to complete yielding on all twelve critical trials by other individuals.

After each session, the naive subject was interviewed.   None of the subjects reported that he had wholly disregarded the judgment of the majority. For most of the subjects, the discrepancy between their judgment and that of the majority created a difficulty which they localized in themselves, that is, they tended to question their own judgment, not that of the majority. Most of the subjects reported that they "longed" to agree with the majority. . . .

Situational factors governing conformity

. . . [A] set of crucial determinants of [conformity] has to do with the nature of the group—its size, composition, unanimity, extremeness of judgment, coercive force. And, finally, it is important to consider the nature of the larger social context within which the group is functioning.

Group size. It would appear reasonable that group pressure is more intense the larger the majority arrayed against the individual. But it is also likely that beyond a certain range of group size, additional members do not add appreciably to the effective pressure. Asch discovered that when the individual was opposed by a single other person, there was very little yielding; with two opposing him there was some yielding; with three or four opposing him the amount of yielding approached a maximal level and was just about as much for these groups as for groups of fifteen or more.

These results do not mean, of course, that a *single* individual cannot effectively influence the judgment of another person. For example, Sherif (1935), in a by now classic experimental study of social norms, showed that when pairs of subjects judged a highly ambiguous stimulus (a visible illusion of movement of a stationary light in a dark-room—*autokinetic movement*), the judgments of each tended to converge toward the other. But in Asch's case we are dealing with highly structured stimuli, where the degree of discrepancy is very great, and here we find the individual better able to resist a single other person.

In some "real life" situations it is quite possible that larger groups *can* produce additional conformity above and beyond that produced by somewhat smaller groups simply because the threat of reprisal to the deviant individual can be made stronger the larger the group.

The main point, however, is that under many circumstances there exists a kind of crucial "threshold of yielding." If the person can resist the growing opposition up to a certain point, then he will not be easily moved regardless of how big the opposition becomes.

Group composition. Aside from sheer size of group there is the important matter of *who* the opposing members are. The members may be equal in status to the individual, or they may be seen by him as superior or as inferior in various attributes. If the attributes are relevant to the issue being judged, it is likely that the effective pressure will be greater or smaller depending upon whether the individual views the others as more competent or less competent than himself. For example, a layman is very likely to conform to the consensus of a group of atomic physicists on the dangers of atomic fallout—even if they are wrong. Conversely, an atomic physicist, contradicted by a group of laymen on this issue, may easily resist the group pressure— even if the laymen are right.

When a group is composed entirely of peers, the conflict engendered by the discrepancy between the individual and the group judgment often tends to be particularly acute. A scientist in a group of scientists when judging a relevant scientific issue may feel highly competent. Yet he is confronted by the fact that his scientific peers *whom he must also regard as highly competent* disagree with him. Thus he may conform. For example, in one of Crutchfield's studies, groups of high-level mathematicians were subjected to the standard group-pressure treatment, including some items involving simple arithmetical logic. Some of these mathematicians—though not many, to be sure —conformed to a false group consensus on some of these items, giving wrong answers that they would never have given under normal circumstances. The fact that the items were very easy did not necessarily help them resist the pressure because *they had to assume that the items must also be easy for the other mathematicians,* all of whom agreed on another answer.

Whether the group is composed of friends or of strangers is also significant for amount of conformity. The relations are complex, however. Among friends an individual may feel emotionally more secure than among strangers and thus feel less threat if he deviates. On the other hand, he may respect the judgments of his friends more highly and thus be more swayed by them; and he may fear the danger of losing their respect if he deviates, whereas among strangers he may not care. However, if he is the single lonely stranger in a group, the rest of whom are friends, and he wishes to be accepted as part of their group, then—being a "marginal man"—he is likely to be under even greater pressure to conform. In short, much depends upon what, for the individual in the given situation, constitutes his immediate and functional reference group. Among the people Crutchfield studied it was regularly observed that persons belonging to ethnic and racial minorities conformed highly when tested in groups where they were the only minority member.

Unanimity of group consensus. Asch has found strong experimental evidence demonstrating the importance of social support for resistance to group pressure. He did this by comparing the amount of yielding in groups which were unanimously arrayed against the single individual with the amount in those groups in which the single individual had the support of *one other person* in the group, a "partner," who agreed with his judgment. Yielding was markedly lower in the latter kind of group. The social implications of this finding may be very great. It suggests, for example, that a dissident opinion, if expressed loudly and clearly, can have a tremendous effect in strengthening the independence of like-minded people. The expression of a dissident opinion may not *change* the majority's belief, but it can *conserve* the minority view.

Extremeness of group consensus. How *large* the individual perceives the discrepancy to be between the group consensus and his own judgment affects the resulting conformity behavior. But . . . the effects are complex; there appears to be no simple relation between amount of yielding and size of discrepancy.

Tuddenham (1961) makes the interesting suggestion that when the distorted group norm lies within the range of judgments acceptable to the individual, its effect is to increase the homogeneity of judgments —a process for which Tuddenham would reserve the term "conformity." In contrast, when the distorted norm lies well outside the range of acceptable judgments, so-called "yielding" occurs in some individuals only, the net effect being a *decrease* in homogeneity among the judgments.

Strength of coercion. The extent of conformity elicited will also depend heavily upon the strength of the coercion exerted by the group. Explicit threats of reprisal for resisting or explicit promises of reward for conforming may have powerful influence. Yet we should not underestimate the coercive power of *implicit* group pressure. Silent reproach or silent contempt from the group, whether really present or merely imagined by the individual, can be a crushing force on him.

How much coercive power the group applies depends upon the significance of the issue being judged to the functioning of the group. On many kinds of issues individual dissent will have little or no effect on achievement of the group's goals; hence the group may tolerate or ignore such dissent. But on other issues central to the group welfare, dissent may be regarded as threatening to the group and the deviant member may be punished [see Schachter (1951), Schachter et al. (1954)].

Larger social context. No single group lives a self-contained life; it is always part of a larger social context—a context of the existing political, sociological, and historical conditions. The amount of conformity induced by group pressure to some extent reflects this larger context.

When the general climate is one of attack on deviancy—for instance, in an era of McCarthyism or of Communist or other forms of totalitarian suppression—then conformity tendencies are likely to be heightened.   Part of this is due to the fact that the individual's face-to-face groups, mirroring the prevailing social orthodoxy, may demand more conformity of him; part of it may be that he realistically recognizes (or thinks he does) that deviancy at this inauspicious time will have serious personal consequences for himself.

It also happens, all too rarely, that a general climate develops which *favors* independence of thought and expression.   Sometimes, too, these climates shift rapidly and the individual may be hard-pressed to accommodate to the prevailing political winds.   When Mao Tse-tung, the Chinese Communist leader, briefly encouraged free dissent a few years ago, proclaiming that "A thousand flowers shall bloom," many unwary Chinese intellectuals, eager for the opportunity to express their deviant ideas, took him at his word—much to their subsequent distress.   And American college students have had their perplexities, too.   It is not so long after the era of McCarthyism, of academic loyalty oaths, and all the other pressures toward safe orthodoxy that students are now being nationally berated for their passivity and overconformity!

References

Asch, S. E.   Effects of group pressure upon the modification and distortion of judgment.   M. H. Guetzkow (Ed.), *Groups, leadership, and men.*   Pittsburgh: Carnegie Press, 1951.

Asch, S. E.   *Social psychology.*   Englewood Cliffs, N.J.: Prentice-Hall, 1952.

Asch, S. E.   Studies of independence and conformity.   A minority of one against an unanimous majority.   *Psychol. Monogr.,* 1956, *70,* No. 9 (Whole No. 416).

Crutchfield, R. S.   Conformity and character.   *Amer. Psychol.,* 1955, *10,* 191–198.

Crutchfield, R. S.   Conformity and creative thinking.   Paper delivered at Symposium on Creative Thinking, U. of Colorado, 1958.

Crutchfield, R. S.   Personal and situational factors in conformity to group pressure.   *Acta Psychologica,* 1959, *15,* 386–388.

Crutchfield, R. S.   The effect on individual conformity of authoritative confirmation or repudiation of group consensus.   Paper delivered at meeting of Eastern Psychol. Assn. Atlantic City, N.J., 1959.

Kelman, H. C.   Compliance, identification and internalization.   *J. Conflict Resolution,* 1958, *2,* 51–60.

Schachter, S.   Deviation, rejection and communication. *J. abnorm. soc. Psychol.*, 1951, *46, 190–207.*

Schachter, S., Nuttin, J., DeMonchaux, C., Maucorps, P. H., Osmer, D., Duijker, H., Rommetveit, R., and Israel, J.   Cross cultural experiments on threat and rejection. *Hum. Relat.*, 1954, *7, 403–439.*

Sherif, M. A.   A study of some social factors in perception. *Arch. Psychol.*, 1935, No. 187.

Tuddenham, R. D.   The influence upon judgment of the apparent discrepancy between self and others. *J. soc. Psychol.*, 1961, *53, 69–79.*

Irving Sarnoff
and
Philip G. Zimbardo

ANXIETY, FEAR, AND SOCIAL AFFILIATION *

In his recent monograph, Schachter (1959) reports that anticipated exposure to a painful external stimulus determines the degree to which persons wish to affiliate with each other: the greater the anticipated pain, the stronger the desire to await the onset of that pain in the company of others in the same predicament.   In attempting to account theoretically for this finding, Schachter mentions such motivational forces as the subjects' needs for reassurance, distraction, escape, and information.   However, among the various possible explanations, Schachter appears to favor one derived from Festinger's (1954) theory of social comparison processes.   Adapting that theory to the phenomena under investigation, Schachter postulates that the arousal of any strong emotion evokes a need for comparison.   Emotions are assumed to be quite unspecific states of affect.   Hence, persons can only evaluate the quality, intensity, and appropriateness of their emotions properly by comparing their own reactions with those of others.   Moreover, novel emotion producing stimuli should induce a greater tendency to affiliate than familiar stimuli.   By definition, a novel stimulus is one that is more difficult to fit into a person's established frame of reference for emotive states.   Accordingly, the individual is more obliged to seek out others in order to define the emotional effects of novel stimuli.

The explication of Schachter's (1959) results in terms of the theory of social comparison processes is appealingly parsimonious.   How-

* From Irving Sarnoff and Philip G. Zimbardo, "Anxiety, Fear, and Social Affiliation," *J. abnorm. soc. Psychol.*, 1961, 62, 356–363.   Reprinted by permission of the authors and the Managing Editor, the American Psychological Association.

ever, it requires the assumption that *all* emotive states have the same effect on affiliative behavior. Thus, Schachter, like many contemporary psychologists, does not deal with the possible conceptual distinctions between fear and anxiety. Yet, it seems to us that, by adopting an alternative assumption about the psychological properties of emotions, to be presented briefly below, it is possible to formulate predictions concerning affiliative responses that could not have been derived from the theory of social comparison processes. Indeed, by employing Freud's (1949a, 1949b) conceptual distinctions between fear and anxiety, we are led to predict a tendency toward social isolation—rather than affiliation—as a consequence of certain conditions of emotional arousal.

The present experiment was, thus, undertaken with two objectives: to assess the empirical validity of conceptual differentiation between fear and anxiety, and to evaluate the extent to which the theory of social comparison processes may be applied to the relationship between all emotions and affiliative behavior. In order to implement these objectives, we have conducted an experimental investigation of the differential effects of fear and anxiety upon social affiliation.

Functional relationship between emotions and motives

The guiding assumption of our experiment holds that all emotions are consciously experienced epiphenomena of motives.[1] When our motives are aroused, we experience subjective reactions to which we learn, over time, to attach commonly agreed upon labels that signify the various emotions.

Motive, on the other hand, is defined as a tension producing stimulus that provokes behavior designed to reduce the tension. Each of our motives (innate or learned) requires the performance of a *different* response for the maximal reduction of its tension.

Fear and anxiety viewed as motives

The motive of fear (which Freud called objective anxiety) is aroused whenever persons are confronted by an external object or event that is inherently dangerous and likely to produce pain. Only one type of overt [2] response can maximally reduce our fear: separation from the threatening aspects of the feared object, accomplished by flight from the object, at one extreme, and conquest, at the other. In the

---

[1] The concept of motivation which we have chosen to employ has been elaborated elsewhere (Sarnoff, 1960a).

[2] Space limitations do not permit a consideration of the two types of covert (ego defensive) responses, denial and identification with the aggressor, which persons may employ in their efforts to cope with external threat. A full discussion of these ego defenses is presented by Sarnoff (1960a).

case of fear, then, one's energies are mobilized toward dealing with the external stimulus; to eliminate, through some mode of escape or attack, the threat that is clearly and objectively present in the stimulus.

If we examine the consequences of anxiety (which Freud termed neurotic anxiety), we see no such correspondence between the internal disturbance of the person and an objectively harmful environmental stimulus.   Instead, anxiety is typically aroused by stimuli which, objectively considered, are *innocuous*.[3]   For example, in the case of the classical phobias, harmless objects possess a special motivational significance for certain people.   These objects activate some motive other than fear, and this other motive, in turn, arouses the consciously perceived motive of anxiety.   Hence, the emotional reaction of the anxious person is inappropriate to the inherent characteristics of the external stimulus.

Regardless of their content, the motives whose arousal evokes anxiety share a common property: they are all *repressed*.   These repressed motives continue unconsciously to press for the reduction of their tensions; and anxiety signals the threat of possible expression of these repressed motives.   Consequently, the person develops a number of additional ego defenses that function to safeguard the initial effects of repression.   If the ego defenses do their work effectively, the motives are kept under repression, the inner danger passes and the individual's anxiety is reduced.

Implications of the motives of anxiety and fear for affiliative behavior

It follows from the foregoing discussion that, when their anxieties are aroused, people are more inclined to become preoccupied with the reassertion of inner self-control than with modes of dealing with the anxiety evoking external object.   Because the anxious person tends to be aware of the element of *inappropriateness* in his feelings, he is loath to communicate his anxieties to others.   To avoid being ridiculed or censured, he conceals anxiety aroused by stimuli which he guesses do not have a similar effect upon others, and which, he feels, ought not so to upset him.   Thus, when anxiety is aroused, a person should tend to seek isolation from others.   On the other hand, when fear is aroused and he is unable to flee from the threatening object, he welcomes the opportunity to affiliate.   Since the usual responses to fear, flight and fight, are restricted in the experimental situation,

[3] In fact, since anxiety arousing stimuli are often related to unconscious libidinal motives, they may be regarded by most people as intrinsically pleasurable, rather than in any way painful.   For example, owing to the manner in which their heterosexual motives have been socialized, some men may tend severely to repress their sexual cravings for women.   Hence, when such men are shown photographs of voluptuous nudes, stimuli which might be quite evocative of pleasurable fantasies among most of their fellows, they are likely to experience anxiety (Sarnoff & Corwin, 1959).

the subject seeks other fear reducing responses.   Therefore, the probability of affiliation increases because it mediates fear reduction through the potentiality for catharsis and distraction as well as the emotional comparison offered by interpersonal contact.

We are led, therefore, to the hypothesis that the motives of fear and anxiety should influence social affiliation behavior differently: the greater the fear aroused, the more the subjects should choose to be together with others while they await actual contact with the fear arousing object.   Conversely, the greater the anxiety elicited, the more the subjects should choose to be alone while they await contact with the anxiety arousing object.

Method

The experiment was presented to the subjects as a physiological in-vestigation of the cutaneous sensitivity of various parts of the body. A 2 × 2 design was used in which two levels of fear and of anxiety were experimentally aroused.   The dependent variable of social affili-ation was measured by having the subjects state whether they pre-ferred to spend an anticipated waiting period alone or in the company of others.

Subjects

The subjects were 72 unpaid, male undergraduate volunteers from six introductory psychology classes in Yale University.   An additional 36 subjects were used to pretest the manipulations and measuring de-vices, and an additional 13 subjects were excluded from the analyses because they did not qualify as acceptable subjects, i.e., were friends, misunderstood the instructions, did not believe the rationale.

Procedure

Background information was collected by an accomplice alleged to be from the counseling program of the Student Health Department.   A questionnaire was designed to obtain background information on the subjects and also their preferred mode of defense mechanism.   The latter data were in response to four Blacky cards.   As in a recent experiment by Sarnoff (1960b), each card was accompanied by three alternatives that were to be rank ordered according to the subjects' reaction to the theme of the card (sibling rivalry, achievement, and two of sucking).   The alternatives reflected predominantly an accept-ance of the motive, projection of the motive upon others, or a reaction formation against the motive.

About one month later, the experimenter was introduced to the psychology classes as a physiological psychologist studying physiological responses to sensory stimuli.   The subjects were subsequently recruited individually, and randomly assigned to the four experimental treatments.   The specious purpose of the experiment and of the conditions of waiting were further established by marking the experimental room "Sensory Physiology Laboratory" and two nearby rooms "Waiting Room A" and "Waiting Room T."   Because of absentees, the size of the groups tested varied from three to five, and was usually composed of four subjects.   In order to avoid the development of superficial friendships during the experiment, and eliminate the possibility that the subjects might react to cues from each other or from the experimenter, the subjects were isolated in adjacent cubicles, no communication was allowed, and the tape-recorded instructions were presented through earphones.

The experimental conditions and instructions common to all subjects will be presented first.   After rolling up their sleeves, removing their watches from their wrists, and gum or cigarettes from their mouths ("They interfere with the recording electrodes"), the subjects were told:

Our experiment falls in the general area of physiological psychology.   As you may know, one branch of physiological psychology is concerned with the reactions of the sense organs to various kinds of stimulation.   Our present experiment deals with the skin [or mouth] as an organ of sensation.   We are interested in studying individual differences in response to particular stimuli applied to it.

There has been a good deal of controversy about the relative sensitivity of the fingertips [lips] as compared to the palms [tongue], and upper surface of the hand [palate].   Our experiment will help to provide data upon which we may be able ultimately to draw a detailed map of the cutaneous sensitivity of the human hand [mouth].

In order to measure your physiological reactions, we are now going to attach some instruments to your arm and finger [corner of your mouth].   These instruments are electrodes which are connected to a machine which records exactly the strength of your response to each stimulus. . . .   Electrode jelly will be applied first to the area to insure that we get a good electrical contact.   (The electrodes were then attached by a female laboratory assistant of middle age.)

In order to provide a reasonable basis for asking the subjects to wait in other rooms (and, thus, for making the choice of affiliation or isolation), the subjects were told that it was necessary to assess their basal rates of responding prior to the application of the actual stimuli. They were led to believe that their individual sensitivities were being recorded while they viewed a series of slides of a typical subject who had participated in the experiment.   They anticipated that a waiting period would come after the slides, and then in the second—and purportedly major—part of the experiment their direct reactions to the actual stimuli would be measured.   Accordingly, they were told:

Now that your basal rates have been recorded on our polygraph recorder, it will take us about 10 minutes while we tally the data and reset our measuring instruments so that they will be geared to your individual basal rates as you are run one at a time through the rest of the experiment.   While we are doing these things, we are going to ask you to wait in other rooms which are available to us.   We will come to get you when it is your turn to go through with the experiment.   Incidentally, we have found that some of our subjects prefer to do their waiting alone, while others prefer to wait together with other subjects.   Therefore, we are going to give you your choice of waiting alone or with others.   In either case, you will be ushered to a comfortable room furnished with adequate reading material.

After indicating their preference of waiting alone or together with others, the subjects also indicated the intensity of this preference on an "open-ended" scale in which 0 represented a very weak preference and 100 a very strong preference.   On this relatively unstructured scale there was as much as 175 points of difference between subjects (from "75-alone" to "100-together").

Presentation of the slides during the experiment served two purposes in addition to the one previously mentioned.   The content of the slides (appropriate to each experimental treatment) served to reinforce the subjects' differential expectations of the nature and severity of the stimulus situation.   Furthermore, the subject seen in the slides became a focal point for measuring the effectiveness of the experimental manipulations.   It was assumed that a direct attempt (by means of a scaled question) to appraise the level of the subjects' fear or anxiety would be likely to: sensitize them to the true purpose of the experiment; yield unreliable results since the subjects might neither be consciously aware of, nor able to verbalize, their anxiety reaction; and evoke resistance since some subjects might not want to admit to being anxious or fearful, calling their masculinity into question.

Therefore, it was necessary to use an indirect, disguised measure to evaluate whether the experimental inductions had actually aroused two levels of both fear and anxiety.   Immediately after the slides had been shown (but before the affiliation choices had been made), the subjects were told:

As you may know, an individual shows his physiological reaction in a variety of behavioral forms.   We are interested in seeing whether it is possible to estimate how ill-at-ease or upset individuals are at the prospect of receiving the stimulation in this experiment.   Recalling the subject whom you just saw in the slides, how upset or ill-at-ease did he seem to you?   Please assign a number anywhere from zero to 100 to indicate your feeling.   (Zero = unconcerned, at ease;   100 = extremely concerned and ill-at-ease.)

Since the subject in the slides was a posed model instructed to remain poker faced throughout, it was assumed that there was no objective difference in his expression. Thus, any systematic difference in ratings between groups should reflect a projection of the subjects' own motives upon this screen.

However, because the content of the slides was not identical for every group but rather "tailored" to each specific treatment, it was possible that the model may have actually looked more fearful in the slides shown to the subjects in the High Fear than in the Low Fear condition. As a control check on this possibility, four additional introductory psychology classes ($N = 108$) served as judges. They were told that the slides were of a typical subject in a recently completed experiment, and their task was to estimate how ill-at-ease and concerned he appeared (on the same scale used by the experimental subjects). Two of the classes saw only the face of the model (the rest of the slide was blacked out) and were told only that he was a subject in a physiological experiment in which stimuli were applied and responses measured. The other two classes saw the entire stimulus field of the slides and were given the same complete description that the experimental subjects received. Since each class of judges rated the slides for all four experimental treatments, the order of presentation was counterbalanced.

After the projective measure of motive arousal and the measure of affiliation, the electrodes were removed and a measure taken of the subjects' reasons for choosing to affiliate or be isolated. This was done with the rationale that a social psychologist had become interested in the fact that some of our subjects preferred to be together while others preferred to be alone, and he had asked us to get some information for him about the reasons underlying this preference.

The questionnaire, designed by Gerard and Rabbie (1960), contained both open-ended and structured questions asking for reasons for the affiliation choice. Finally, the subjects noted whether or not they wished to continue in the experiment. Only one subject (in the High Fear condition) refused to remain for the "stimulation" part of the experiment.

The true purpose, hypothesis, design, and reasons for the various deceptions (and, at a later time, the results) were explained fully to each subject.

High fear

A high level of fear was induced by leading the subjects to anticipate a series of painful electrical shocks. Although they expected to endure each of the shocks for 2 minutes, the subjects were assured that the shocks would not cause damage or injury.

The female assistant (dressed in a white lab coat, as was the experimenter) then attached electrodes to each subject's arm and fingertip and strapped his arm onto a cotton-padded board.   The leads from the electrodes appeared to go to a polygraph recorder, which also was seen in the series of slides of the typical subjects.   Another slide showed an enormous electrical stimulator, and the implication was that it was behind a curtain in the experimental room.   It was called to the subjects' attention that:

The four dials shown in the upper right-hand corner of the stimulator enable us to regulate automatically the frequency, duration, delay, and intensity of the shock you will get.

The other slides portrayed the subject with earphones and electrodes attached (like the subjects themselves), "listening to the instructions," and then "about to receive his first painful shock," administered by the experimenter, who could be seen in the background manipulating the dials on the stimulator.   A final situational factor that may have enhanced the effectiveness of the High Fear manipulation was that the experimental room housed electrical generators which made a continuous buzzing sound, a cue interpreted by the High Fear subjects as the electrical stimulator "warming up," but unnoticed or quickly adapted to by the other subjects.   An unobtrusively posted sign reading "Danger/High Voltage," present only for the High Fear subjects, gave further credence to this notion.

Low fear

In the Low Fear condition the word "shock" was never used, and all cues in the situation associated with shock, fear, or pain were removed; i.e., no white lab coats, arms not strapped to boards, etc.   The expectations of these subjects were guided by instructions stating that our methodology was to apply a 10-second stimulus of very low intensity that would be just sufficient to elicit a measurable physiological response.

In the series of slides viewed by these subjects, the imposing electrical stimulator was replaced by a small innocuous looking apparatus (actually a voltmeter), and the experimenter was seen not in the active role as an agent of pain, but in the passive role of recording data from the polygraph recorder.

High anxiety

Anxiety was manipulated by arousing a motive that was assumed to have been repressed by most of the subjects.   In Freudian terminology, the motive might be called "oral libido," a desire to obtain pleasurable gratification by sucking on objects that are clearly related to infantile nursing experiences.   The female breast is, of course, the prototype of such objects, but others include nipples, baby bottles, and pacifiers.   Thus, to arouse this oral motive and, hence, the anxiety that should follow its arousal, subjects in the High Anxiety condition were led to believe that they would have to suck on a number of objects commonly associated with infantile oral behavior.   They were told that their task would be to suck on these objects for 2 minutes while we recorded their physiological responses from the skin surfaces stimulated by the objects.   In clear view in front of the subjects were the following items: numerous baby bottles, oversized nipples, pacifiers, breast shields (nipples women often wear over their breasts while nursing), and lollipops.

The same variety of stimulus objects was shown arrayed in front of the subject in the slides.   He could be seen, tongue hanging out, lips puckered, about to suck his thumb (as one of the objects of stimulation) or one of the other objects.   Subjects were told that the contact taped to the mouth recorded the direct reaction to the oral stimulation, while the arm contact recorded peripheral reactions.

Low anxiety

The instructions to the Low Anxiety subjects did not mention "suck," nor any stimulation that they would receive from putting the objects in their mouths.   Moreover, they were led to believe that they would keep each object in their mouths for only 10 seconds.   The stimulus objects were not in immediate proximity to the subjects while their electrodes were being attached.   The stimulus objects which they anticipated putting in their mouths were shown in the slides: whistles, balloons, "kazoos," and pipes.   Since these objects do not require sucking (but rather, in general, blowing), the model's tongue was not seen as he prepared to use the stimuli in the slides.

Results

Evidence of the effectiveness of the experimental manipulations

In using the subjects' estimates of the degree to which the model seen in the slides was upset by the prospect of receiving the stimulation in the experiment, it was assumed that the subjects would tend to project their induced level of fear and anxiety.   Table 1, which presents the mean projection scores for each experimental treatment, offers evidence that this assumption was valid and the manipulations effective.

Table 1
Mean projection scores for each experimental treatment

| Motive | Level of arousal | | p value |
	Low	High	
Fear	24	42	$< .01$ ($t = 3.05$)
Anxiety	14	31[a]	$< .01$ ($t = 2.95$)
	ns	ns	

Note.—The larger the score, the greater the degree of projection.
[a] Variance greater than in High Fear group, $p < .10$; SD for High Anxiety $= 24$, for High Fear $= 16$.

The High Arousal subjects perceived the model to be significantly [4] more upset, concerned, and ill-at-ease than did the Low Arousal subjects.

Our theoretical distinction between fear and anxiety, and the way these concepts were operationally defined in this experiment, lead to the prediction that, assuming similarity of past experience, persons facing the same clearly, objectively present threat should react in a relatively homogeneous fashion. This close correspondence between stimulus and response is not assumed to hold for anxiety. We have already noted that a stimulus that produces anxiety for some persons is not an anxiety producing cue for many others. Since the significance of the stimulus depends upon its symbolic and generally idiosyncratic associations, one would expect that a stimulus which elicited anxiety for persons with relevant predispositions (repressed motives) would have less effect on those who had more adequately resolved the conflict over the expression of the same motives. Thus, one way of determining whether our experimental manipulations produced two different motives, fear and anxiety (rather than only two levels of one motive), is to compare the variability in response between treatments.

The heterogeneity of response in the High Anxiety group is, as predicted, greater than in the High Fear and the Low Arousal conditions. The same difference in response variability between the High Anxiety group and all other groups is manifested as well in the dependent variable of social affiliation. The questionnaire data to be presented in a later section offer further support to the distinction between fear and anxiety.

Before presenting the major results, it is necessary to account for two possible sources of artifact in the just reported data on projection. They are: by chance sampling, the High Arousal groups could have contained more subjects who characteristically used projection as a mechanism of defense than the Low Arousal groups; and the subject seen in the High Fear and High Anxiety slides was objectively more

---

[4] All p values reported throughout the paper are based on two-tailed tests of significance.

upset and concerned than he was in the Low Fear and Low Anxiety slides. If either of these alternatives were true, then the projection measure would not be a reflection of differences due to the experimental arousal of levels of fear and anxiety.

The pretest data of the subjects' mode of defense preference on the Blacky Projection test show no initial significant difference between any of the groups in their tendency to use projection.

Among the groups of neutral judges who evaluated all the slides shown in the study, from 68%–98% reported perceiving either no difference in the degree to which the model appeared upset, or a difference opposite to that reported in Table 1. The result holds for both fear and anxiety, and regardless of the order of presentation or amount of the stimulus field seen (model's face only or entire slide). Thus, it appears that the projection measure can be used as an index of the efficacy of the experimental conditions and manipulations.

Effects of fear and anxiety on social affiliation

The results bearing upon the hypothesis of the study are presented in Table 2, where for each condition the mean intensity of desire to affiliate, as well as the number of subjects choosing to affiliate and to be alone, are presented. It is evident that there is a strong positive relationship between fear and the index of affiliative tendency, but a strong negative relationship between anxiety and affiliation, so that as fear increases affiliation also increases, while an increase in anxiety results in a decrease in affiliation. Thus, our prediction of an interaction between kind of motive and level of arousal is clearly supported by the data. While some 95% of the High Fear subjects chose the "together" alternative (with more than 0 intensity), only 46% of the High Anxiety subjects chose to wait together. The marked mean difference between these groups in intensity of choice (51.0–8.0) is significant well beyond the .01 level ($t = 3.63$). The large mean difference in affiliative tendency between the High and Low Fear groups ($p < .07$, $t = 1.96$) represents a replication of Schachter's (1959, p. 18) results. While the mean difference between High and Low Anxiety was even larger than that between the Fear conditions, it only approached significance ($p = .16$, $t = 1.46$) due to the marked heterogeneity of variance of the High Anxiety group.

Reasons given for affiliation choice

The final measure taken was a questionnaire that explored the reasons the subjects gave for choosing to wait together with others or to wait alone. The 11 structured items on the questionnaire each presented a possible motive for affiliation; and each was accompanied by a 70-

Table 2
Relationship of motive to social affiliation

	Mean affiliation strength [a]	Number of subjects choosing	
		Together	Alone or "0-together"
Fear			
Low	34.0	12	3
High	51.0	19	1
Anxiety			
Low	27.0	11	4
High	8.0	10	12

Interaction: (Motive $\times$ Level) $p < .05$, $t = 2.30$, $df = 68$.

[a] The larger the score, the greater the affiliation tendency; isolation intensity score subtracted from affiliation intensity score.

point scale on which the subject indicated how important he thought the motive was in determining his choice. The highly significant interaction between experimental treatment and questions ($p < .001$, $F = 3.74$, $df = 30.570$) on a repeated-measurement analysis of variance justified a search for those questions (motives for affiliation) that differentiated the groups.

Since there were too few subjects choosing the alone condition, the analysis is limited to those wanting to affiliate. The motives for affiliation that were most important for the High Fear subjects and most distinguished them from the Low Fear subjects were (the lower the mean, the greater the importance; 10 = extremely important):

1   I am not sure whether I am reacting in the same way as the others to the prospect of getting shocked and would like to compare my reactions to theirs. [Emotional comparison] High Fear $\bar{x} = 38$, Low Fear $\bar{x} = 54$, $p < .001$.

2   I feel worried about getting shocked and would like to know to what extent the others are worried too. [Extent of comparison] High Fear $\bar{x} = 40$, Low Fear $\bar{x} = 61$, $p < .001$.

3   I want to be distracted in order to take my mind off the prospect of getting shocked. [Distraction] High Fear $\bar{x} = 44$, Low Fear $\bar{x} = 59$, $p < .01$.

4   I am worried about the prospect of getting shocked and felt that talking with someone about it would get it off my chest. [Catharsis] High Fear $\bar{x} = 50$, Low Fear $\bar{x} = 59$, $p < .05$.

The reasons for affiliation given spontaneously to a single open-ended question also reflect the importance of these same considerations. Among High Anxiety subjects choosing to be alone, the major reason given spontaneously and supported by the scaled questions is the desire "to be alone to think about personal affairs and school work."

Curiosity as to "what the others were like" was important, but equally so across all conditions. Of least importance among all subjects are the following motives for affiliation ("oral stimulation" substituted for "shock" for Anxiety groups):

"It would be clearer in my own mind as to how I feel about getting shocked if I could express my reactions to someone else." "I anticipated that the others would offer reassuring comments." "I want to be with others to re-assure myself that I am not the only one who was singled out to be shocked." "I feel that perhaps together we could somehow figure out a way to avoid getting shocked."

There are several large differences between the High Fear and High Anxiety groups; with the former finding the following motives as signif-icantly more important: emotional comparison, extent of comparison, distraction, catharsis, and the physical presence of others ($p < .05$ in each instance). Similarly, an internal analysis of the High Fear group reveals these same motives (especially catharsis and emotional comparison) to be more important for those subjects who chose to affiliate most strongly than for those below the group median in affiliation strength.

Ordinal position and its relation to affiliation

While the reasoning used in the planning of the present study did not include predictions of the effects of ordinal position upon affiliation, data relevant to this question were nevertheless obtained, to check on Schachter's (1959) finding that affiliation tendencies increased with emotional arousal only among first- and only-born children. This finding is duplicated in the present study. First-born children want to affiliate significantly more than later-borns under conditions of high fear, but not when the level of fear is low. While the mean affiliation intensity for the first-born High Fear subjects was 62, it was only 23 for the later-born High Fear subjects ($p = .05$, $t = 2.10$). This same general finding holds for the High Anxiety group, but again the within-group variability does not permit the large mean difference obtained (16 for first-borns and −3 for later-borns) to be statistically significant.

Discussion

Since our basic hypothesis has been supported, our results lend credence to the previously drawn conceptual distinction between fear and anxiety. In view of the fact that our anxiety arousing stimulus was specifically designed to tap only one kind of repressed motive, it of course remains an empirical question whether or not the evocation of other types of presumably repressed motives also leads to social isolation.

In order to predict the consequences of the arousal of a motive, therefore, it is necessary to know which responses are required to reduce its tension. The probability of the social comparison response is, thus, a function of: the kind of motive aroused, the intensity of the motive, the degree of novelty of the emotional experience, the response hierarchy associated with the specific motive, and certain attributes of those with whom the person is to affiliate.

We do not question the assumption that the need for some kind of cognitive-emotional clarity and structure is a basic human motive. However, we feel that the need for self-evaluation is not the *most* salient motive aroused in the experimental situations that Schachter (1959) and we employed. We do not view the cognitive need to structure a vague emotional state as the primary motive in these experiments; we see social comparison not as an end in itself but merely as one of the several responses that are instrumental in reducing the tension associated with the situationally more salient motives of fear and anxiety.

Strict application of the theory of emotional comparison processes to the present experimental situation should lead one to predict greater affiliation tendencies for the High Anxiety subjects than the High Fear subjects, since the Anxiety situation was more unusual than that of Fear, and the emotion aroused was probably more novel and vague. The opposite prediction, supported by the results, demands an approach, such as the one followed here, that specifies the probability of the response alternatives evoked by the dominant motives aroused.

As the emotional experience becomes very novel and unusual, the need for comparison of one's reactions with others should increase, and, hence, intensify affiliation tendencies. The induction of esoteric states of consciousness by "anxiety producing drugs" (being studied presently by Schachter) may be the kind of situation in which emotional comparison theory offers the best explanations and predictions. Under such circumstances, it may be possible to create emotional states that are epiphenomena of motives whose neurophysiological bases had never previously been set into motion. A more natural counterpart of this novel emotional experience occurs the first time a person experiences the emotions associated with the death of a loved one.

The predictive importance of knowing the specific responses appropriate to the motive aroused is clearly illustrated by the following examples. If a person's guilt is aroused, his response to feelings of guilt should be to seek out others only if they could be expected to punish him and, thus, to expiate his guilt, but not to affiliate with individuals perceived as unable to fill this role. Similarly, if repressed homosexual anxieties are aroused, isolation should generally be preferred to affiliation, as with oral anxiety in the present study. However, affiliation tendencies should increase if the subject is allowed to wait with females, but not if he can wait only in the company of males.

While our questionnaire data offer support for the importance of emotional comparison, they also point up the role of other motives such as need for catharsis and distraction. The marked difference in the importance of the reasons given for affiliation between the High Fear and High Anxiety groups is perhaps the most substantial evidence that the experimental manipulations have indeed led to the arousal of two quite different motives.

A final point of interest concerns the data about ordinal position. The finding that first-born children show greater affiliation tendencies than later-born children when either fear or anxiety are aroused supports Schachter's (1959) results. Theoretical and experimental attempts to uncover the dynamics underlying this "static" variable should prove interesting and fruitful.

Summary

This experiment tests the utility of the psychoanalytic distinction between fear and anxiety for making differential predictions about social affiliation. It also assesses the breadth of generalization of Schachter's (1959) empirical finding of a positive relation between emotional arousal and affiliation. Seventy-two subjects were randomly assigned to four experimental treatments in which low and high levels of fear and anxiety were manipulated. The success of these inductions was established by a projective device and questionnaire data. The dependent variable of social affiliation was measured by having the subjects choose to await the anticipated exposure to the stimulus situation either alone or together with others.

The results show that, while the desire to affiliate increases as fear increases (a replication of Schachter's, 1959, results), the opposite is true for anxiety; as anxiety increases the desire to affiliate decreases. Thus, as predicted, our findings lend empirical support to the theoretical distinction between fear and anxiety. At the same time, our results suggest that the theory of social comparison processes may not be adequate to account for the general relationship between emotions and affiliative tendencies.

References

Festinger, L. A theory of social comparison processes. *Hum. Relat.*, 1954, 7, 117–140.

Freud, S. *Inhibitions, symptoms, and anxiety.* (Originally published 1936) London: Hogarth, 1949. (a)

Freud, S. *New introductory lectures on psychoanalysis.* (Originally published 1933) London: Hogarth, 1949. (b)

Gerard, H. B., & Rabbie, J. M. Fear and social comparison. Unpublished manuscript, Bell Telephone Research Laboratories, 1960.

Sarnoff, I. Psychoanalytic theory and social attitudes. *Publ. opin. Quart.,* 1960, *24,* 251–279. (a)

Sarnoff, I. Reaction formation and cynicism. *J. Pers.,* 1960, *28,* 129–143. (b)

Sarnoff, I., & Corwin, S. M. Castration anxiety and the fear of death. *J. Pers.,* 1959, *27,* 374–385.

Schachter, S. *The psychology of affiliation.* Stanford: Stanford Univ. Press, 1959.

Sidney M. Jourard **HEALTHY PERSONALITY AND SELF-DISCLOSURE ***

For a long time, health and well-being have been taken for granted as "givens," and disease has been viewed as the problem for man to solve. Today, however, increasing numbers of scientists have begun to adopt a reverse point of view, regarding disease and trouble as the givens, with specification of positive health and its conditions as the problem to solve. Physical, mental and social health are values representing restrictions on the total variance of being. The scientific problem here consists in arriving at a definition of health, determining its relevant dimensions and then identifying the independent variables of which these are a function.

Scientists, however, are supposed to be hard-boiled, and they insist that phenomena, to be counted "real," must be public. Hence, many behavioral scientists ignore man's self, or soul, since it is essentially a private phenomenon. Others, however, are not so quick to allocate man's self to the limbo of the unimportant, and they insist that we cannot understand man and his lot until we take his self into account.

I probably fall into the camp of those investigators who want to

* From Sidney M. Jourard, "Healthy Personality and Self-Disclosure," *Ment. Hyg. N.Y.,* 1959, *32,* 499–507. Reprinted by permission of the author and the Editor, *Mental Hygiene.*

explore health as a positive problem in its own right, and who, further, take man's self seriously—as a reality to be explained and as a variable which produces consequences for weal or woe. This paper gives me an opportunity to explore the connection between positive health and the disclosure of self. Let me commence with some sociological truisms.

Social systems require their members to play certain roles. Unless the roles are adequately played, the social systems will not produce the results for which they have been organized. This flat statement applies to social systems as simple as that provided by an engaged couple and to those as complex as a total nation among nations. Societies have socialization "factories" and "mills"—families and schools —which serve the function of training people to play the age, sex and occupational roles which they shall be obliged to play throughout their life in the social system. Broadly speaking, if a person plays his roles suitably, he can be regarded as a more or less normal personality. Normal personalities, however, are not healthy personalities (Jourard 1958, 16–18).

Healthy personalities are people who play their roles satisfactorily, and at the same time derive personal satisfaction from role enactment; more, they keep growing and they maintain high-level physical wellness (Dunn 1958). It is probably enough, speaking from the standpoint of a stable social system, for people to be normal personalities. But it is possible to be a normal personality and be absolutely miserable. We would count such a normal personality unhealthy. In fact, normality in some social systems—successful acculturation to them— reliably produces ulcers, paranoia, piles or compulsiveness. We also have to regard as unhealthy personalities those people who have never been able to enact the roles that legitimately can be expected from them.

Counselors, guidance workers and psychotherapists are obliged to treat with both patterns of unhealthy personality—those people who have been unable to learn their roles and those who play their roles quite well but suffer the agonies of boredom, frustration, anxiety or stultification. If our clients are to be helped they must change, and change in valued directions. A change in a valued direction may arbitrarily be called growth. We have yet to give explicit statement to these valued directions for growth, though a beginning has been made (Fromm 1947, Jahoda 1958, Jourard 1958, Maslow 1954, Rogers 1954). We who are professionally concerned with the happiness, growth and well-being of our clients may be regarded as professional lovers, not unlike the Cyprian sisterhood. It would be fascinating to pursue this parallel further, but let it suffice for us to be reminded that we do in fact share membership in the oldest profession in the world. Our branches of this oldest profession probably began at the same time that our sisters' branch began, and all branches will continue to flourish so long as they meet the needs of society.   We are all concerned with promoting personality health in the people who consult with us.

Now what has all this to do with self-disclosure?

To answer this question, let's tune in on an imaginary interview between a client and his counselor.   The client says, "I have never told this to a soul, doctor, but I can't stand my wife, my mother is a nag, my father is a bore, and my boss is an absolutely hateful and despicable tyrant.   I have been carrying on an affair for the last ten years with the lady next door and at the same time I am a deacon in the church."   The counselor says, showing great understanding and empathy, "Mm-humm!"

If we listened for a long enough period of time we would find that the client talks and talks about himself to this highly sympathetic and empathic listener.   At some later time the client may eventually say, "Gosh, you have helped me a lot.   I see what I must do and I will go ahead and do it."

Now this talking about oneself to another person is what I call self-disclosure.   It would appear, without assuming anything, that self-disclosure is a factor in the process of effective counseling or psychotherapy.   Would it be too arbitrary an assumption to propose that people become clients because they have not disclosed themselves in some optimum degree to the people in their life?

An historical digression: Toward the end of the 19th century Joseph Breuer, a Viennese physician, discovered (probably accidentally) that when his hysterical patients talked about themselves, disclosing not only the verbal content of their memoires but also the feelings that they had suppressed at the time of assorted "traumatic" experiences, their hysterical symptoms disappeared.   Somewhere along the line Breuer withdrew from a situation which would have made his name identical with that of Freud in history's hall of fame.   When Breuer permitted his patients "to be," it scared him, one gathers, because some of his female patients disclosed themselves to be quite sexy, and what was probably worse, they felt quite sexy toward him.

Freud, however, did not flinch.   He made the momentous discovery that the neurotic people of his time were struggling like mad to avoid "being," to avoid being known, and in Allport's (1955) terms, to avoid "becoming."   He learned that his patients, when they were given the opportunity to "be"—which free association on a couch is nicely designed to do—they would disclose that they had all manner of horrendous thoughts and feelings which they did not even dare disclose to themselves, much less express in the presence of another person. Freud learned to permit his patients to be, through permitting them to disclose themselves utterly to another human.   He evidently didn't trust anyone enough to be willing to disclose *himself vis à vis,* so he disclosed himself to himself on paper (Freud 1955) and learned the extent to which he himself was self-alienated.

Roles for people in Victorian days were even more restrictive than they are today, and Freud discovered that when people struggled to avoid being and knowing themselves they got sick. They could only become well, and stay relatively well, when they came to know themselves through self-disclosure to another person. This makes me think of George Groddeck's magnificent *Book of the It (Id)* in which, in the guise of letters to a naive young woman, Groddeck shows the contrast between the public self—pretentious role-playing—and the warded off but highly dynamic *id*—which I here very loosely translate as "real self."

Let me at this point draw a distinction between role relationships and interpersonal relationships—a distinction which is often over-looked in the current spate of literature that has to do with human relations. Roles are inescapable. They must be played or else the social system will not work. A role by definition is a repertoire of behavior patterns which must be rattled off in appropriate contexts, and all behavior which is irrelevant to the role must be suppressed. But what we often forget is the fact that it is a person who is playing the role. This person has a self—or, I should say, he *is* a self. All too often the roles that a person plays do not do justice to all of his self. In fact, there may be nowhere that he may just *be* himself. Even more, the person may not *know* his self. He may, in Horney's (1950) terms, be self-alienated.

This fascinating term "self-alienation" means that an individual is estranged from his real self. His real self becomes a stranger, a feared and distrusted stranger. Estrangement—alienation from one's real self—is at the root of the "neurotic personality of our time" so eloquently described by Horney (1936). Fromm (1957) referred to the same phenomenon as a socially patterned defect.

Self-alienation is a sickness which is so widely shared that no one recognizes it. We may take it for granted that all the clients we encounter are self-alienated to a greater or lesser extent. If you ask anyone—a client, a patient, or one of the people here—to answer the question, "Who are you?" the answer will generally be, "I am a psychologist, a guidance worker, teacher or what have you." The respondent will probably tell you the name of the role with which he feels most closely identified. As a matter of fact, the respondent spends a greater part of his life trying to discover who he is, and once he has made some such discovery, he spends the rest of his life trying to play the part. Of course, some of the roles—age, sex, family or occupational roles—may be so restrictive that they fit a person in a manner not too different from the girdle of a 200-pound lady who is struggling to look like Brigitte Bardot. There is Faustian drama all about us in this world of role-playing. Everywhere we see people who have sold their souls—their real self, if you wish—in order to be a psychologist, a guidance worker, a nurse, a physician, a this or a that.

Now I have suggested that no social system can exist unless the members play their roles and play them with precision and elegance. But here is an odd observation, and yet one which you can all corroborate just by thinking back over your own experience. It's possible to be involved in a social group, such as a family or a work setting, for years and years, playing one's roles nicely with the other members—and never getting to know the *persons* who are playing the other roles. Roles can be played personally and impersonally, as we are beginning to discover in nursing. A husband can be married to his wife for fifteen years and never come to know her. He knows her as "the wife." This is the paradox of the "lonely crowd" (Riesman 1950). It is the loneliness which people try to counter with "togetherness." But much of today's "togetherness" is like the "parallel play" of 2-year-old children, or like the professors in Stringfellow Barr's novel (1958) who, when together socially, lecture past one another alternately and sometimes simultaneously. There is no real self-to-self or person-to-person meeting in such transactions.

Now what does it mean to know a person, or, more accurately, a person's self? I don't mean anything mysterious by "self." All I mean is the person's subjective side—what he thinks, feels, believes, wants, worries about, his past and so forth—the kind of thing one could never know unless one were told. We get to know the other person's self when he discloses it to us.

Self-disclosure, letting another person know what you think, feel or want, is the most direct means (though not the only means) by which an individual can make himself known to another person. Personality hygienists place great emphasis upon the importance for mental health of what they call "real self being," "self-realization," "discovering oneself" and so on. An operational analysis of what goes on in counseling and therapy shows that the patients and clients discover themselves through self-disclosure to the counselor. They talk, and to their shock and amazement the counselor listens.

I venture to say that there is probably no experience more horrifying and terrifying than that of self-disclosure to "significant others" whose probable reactions are assumed but not known. Hence the phenomenon of "resistance." This is what makes psychotherapy so difficult to take and so difficult to administer. If there is any skill to be learned in the art of counseling and psychotherapy, it is the art of coping with the terrors which attend self-disclosure, and the art of decoding the language—verbal and non-verbal—in which a person speaks about his inner experience.

Now, what is the connection between self-disclosure and healthy personality? Self-disclosure, or should I say "real" self-disclosure, is both a symptom of personality health (Jourard 1958, 218–21) and at the same time a means of ultimately achieving healthy personality. The discloser of self is an animated "real self be-er." This, of course, takes courage—the "courage to be" (Tillich 1954). I have known people who would rather die than become known, and in fact some did die when it appeared that the chances were great that they would become known. When I say that self-disclosure is a symptom of personality health, what I mean really is that a person who displays many of the other characteristics that betoken healthy personality (Jourard 1958, Maslow 1954) will also display the ability to make himself fully known to at least one other significant human being. When I say that self-disclosure is a means by which one achieves personality health, I mean something like the following: It is not until I *am* my real self and I *act* my real self that my real self is in a position to grow. One's self grows from the consequence of being. People's selves stop growing when they repress them. This growth-arrest in the self is what helps to account for the surprising paradox of finding an infant inside the skin of someone who is playing the role of an adult.

In a fascinating analysis of mental distress, Jurgen Ruesch (1957) describes assorted neurotics, psychotics and psychosomatic patients as persons with selective atrophy and overspecialization in the aspects of communication. I have come to believe that it is not communication *per se* which is fouled up in the mentally ill. Rather, it is a foul-up in the processes of knowing others and of becoming known to others. Neurotic and psychotic symptoms might be viewed as smokescreens interposed between the patient's real self and the gaze of the onlooker. We might call the symptoms devices to avoid becoming known. A new theory of schizophrenia has been proposed by an anonymous former patient (1958) who "was there" and he makes such a point.

Alienation from one's real self not only arrests one's growth as a person; it also tends to make a farce out of one's relationships with people. As the ex-patient mentioned above observed, the crucial break in schizophrenia is with sincerity, not reality (Anonymous, 1958). A self-alienated person—one who does not disclose himself truthfully and fully—can never love another person nor can he be loved by the other person. Effective loving calls for knowledge of the object (Fromm 1957, Jourard 1958). How can I love a person whom I do not know? How can the other person love me if he does not know me?

Hans Selye (1946) proposed and documented the hypothesis that illness as we know it arises in consequence of stress applied to the organism.   Now I rather think that unhealthy personality has a similar root cause, and one which is related to Selye's concept of stress.   It is this: Every maladjusted person is a person who has not made himself known to another human being, and in consequence does not know himself.   Nor can he find himself.   More than that, he struggles actively to avoid becoming known by another human being.   He works at it ceaselessly, 24 hours daily, and it is work!   The fact that resisting becoming known is work offers us a research opening, incidentally (Dittes 1958, Davis and Malmo 1951).   I believe that in the effort to avoid becoming known a person provides for himself a cancerous kind of stress which is subtle and unrecognized but nonetheless effective in producing not only the assorted patterns of unhealthy personality that psychiatry talks about but also the wide array of physical ills that have come to be recognized as the stock in trade of psychosomatic medicine.   Stated another way, I believe that other people come to be stressors to an individual in direct proportion to his degree of self-alienation.

If I am struggling to avoid becoming known by other persons then of course I must construct a false public self (Jourard 1958, 301–302).   The greater the discrepancy between my unexpurgated real self and the version of myself that I present to others, the more dangerous will other people be for me.   If becoming known by another person is a source of danger, then it follows that merely the presence of the other person can serve as a stimulus to evoke anxiety, heightened muscle tension and all the assorted visceral changes which occur when a person is under stress.   A beginning already has been made in demonstrating the tension-evoking powers of the other person through the use of such instruments as are employed in the lie detector, the measurement of muscle tensions with electromyographic apparatus and so on (Davis and Malmo 1958, Dittes 1958).

Students of psychosomatic medicine have been intimating something of what I have just finished saying explicity.   They say (Alexander 1950) that ulcer patients, asthmatic patients, patients suffering from colitis, migraine and the like, are chronic repressors of certain needs and emotions, especially hostility and dependency.   Now when you repress something, you are not only withholding awareness of this something from yourself; you are also withholding it from the scrutiny of the other person.   In fact, the means by which repressions are overcome in the therapeutic situation is through relentless disclosure of self to the therapist.   When a patient is finally able to follow the fundamental rule in psychoanalysis and disclose everything which passes through his mind, he is generally shocked and dismayed to observe the breadth, depth, range and diversity of thoughts, memories and emotions which pass out of his "unconscious" into overt disclosure.   Incidentally, by the time a person is that free to disclose in the presence of another human being, he has doubtless completed much of his therapeutic sequence.

Self-disclosure, then, appears to be one of the means by which a person engages in that elegant activity that we call real-self-being. But is real-self-being synonymous with healthy personality?   Not in and of itself.   I would say that real-self-being is a necessary but not a sufficient condition for healthy personality.   It is in fact possible for a person to be much "nicer" socially when he is not being his real self than when he is his real self.   But an individual's obnoxious and immoral real self can never grow in the direction of greater maturity until the person has become acquainted with it and begins to be it.   Real-self-being produces consequences, which in accordance with well-known principles of behavior (Skinner 1953) produce changes in the real self.   Thus, there can be no real growth of the self without real-self-being.   Full disclosure of the self to at least one other significant human being appears to be one means by which a person discovers not only the breadth and depth of his needs and feelings but also the nature of his own self-affirmed values.   There is no conflict between real-self-being and being an ethical or nice person, because for the average member of our society self-owned ethics are generally acquired during the process of growing up.   All too often, however, the self-owned ethics are buried under authoritarian morals (Fromm 1947).

If self-disclosure is one of the means by which healthy personality is both achieved and maintained, we can also note that such activities as loving, psychotherapy, counseling, teaching and nursing all are impossible of achievement without the disclosure of the client.   It is through self-disclosure that an individual reveals to himself and to the other party just exactly who, what and where he is.   Just as thermometers, sphygmomanometers, etc. disclose information about the real state of the body, self-disclosure reveals the real nature of the soul or self.   Such information is vital in order to conduct intelligent evaluations.   All I mean by evaluation is comparing how a person is with some concept of optimum.   You never really discover how truly sick your psychotherapy patient is until he discloses himself utterly to you.   You cannot help your client in vocational guidance until he has disclosed to you something of the impasse in which he finds himself.   You cannot love your spouse or your child or your friend unless he has permitted you to know him and to know what he needs to move toward greater health and well-being.   Nurses cannot nurse patients in any meaningful way unless they have permitted the patients to disclose their needs, wants, worries, anxieties and doubts. Teachers cannot be very helpful to their students until they have permitted the students to disclose how utterly ignorant and misinformed they are. Teachers cannot even provide helpful information to the students until they have permitted the students to disclose exactly what they are interested in.

I believe we should reserve the term interpersonal relationships to refer to transactions between "I and thou," (Buber 1937), between person and person, not role and role. A truly personal relationship between two people involves disclosure of self, one to the other, in full and spontaneous honesty. The data that we have collected up to the present time (using very primitive data-collecting methods) have showed us some rather interesting phenomena. We found (Jourard and Lasakow 1958), for example. that women consistently are higher self-disclosers than men; they seem to have a greater capacity for establishing person-to-person relationships—interpersonal relationships—than men. This characteristic of women seems to be a socially-patterned phenomenon, which sociologists (Parsons and Bales 1955) refer to as the expressive role of women, in contradistinction to the instrumental role which men universally are obliged to adopt.

Men seem to be much more skilled at impersonal, instrumental role-playing. But public health officials, very concerned about the sex differential in mortality rates, have been wondering what it is about being a man, which makes males die younger than females. Here in Florida, Dr. Sowder, chief of the state health department, has been carrying on a long-term, multifaceted research program which he has termed "Project Fragile Male." Do you suppose that there is any connection whatsoever between the disclosure patterns of men and women and their differential death rates? I have already intimated that withholding self-disclosure seems to impose a certain stress on people. Maybe "being manly," whatever that means, is slow suicide!

I think there is a very general way of stating the relationship between self-disclosure and assorted values such as healthy personality, physical health, group effectiveness, successful marriage, effective teaching, effective nursing, etc. It is this: A person's self is known to be the immediate determiner of his overt behavior. This is a paraphrase of the phenomenological point of view in psychology (Snygg and Combs 1949). Now if we want to understand anything, explain it, control it or predict it, it is helpful if we have available as much pertinent information as we possibly can. Self-disclosure provides a source of information which is relevant. This information has often been overlooked. Where it has not been overlooked it has often been misinterpreted by observers and practitioners through such devices as projection or attribution. It seems to be difficult for people to accept the fact that they do not know the very person whom they are confronting at any given moment. We all seem to assume that we are expert psychologists and that we know the other person, when in fact we have only constructed a more or less autistic concept of him in our mind.

If we are to learn more about man's self, then we must learn more about self-disclosure—its conditions, dimensions and consequences. Beginning evidence (Rogers 1958) shows that actively accepting, empathic, loving, non-punitive responses—in short, love—provides the optimum conditions under which man will disclose, or expose, his naked, quivering self to our gaze. It follows that if we would be helpful (or should I say human?) that we must grow to loving stature and learn, in Buber's terms, to confirm our fellow man in his very being. Probably this presumes that we must first confirm our own being.

References

Alexander, Franz, *Psychosomatic Medicine.* New York, Norton, 1950.

Allport, Gordon, *Becoming: Basic Considerations for a Psychology of Personality.* New Haven, Yale University Press, 1955.

Anonymous, "A New Theory of Schizophrenia,"*Journal of Abnormal Social Psychology,* 57(1958), 226–36.

Barr, Stringfellow, *Purely Academic.* New York, Simon and Schuster, 1958.

Buber, Martin, *I and thou.* New York, Scribners, 1937.

Davis, F. H. and R. B. Malmo, "Electromyographic Recording during Interview," *American Journal of Psychiatry,* 107(1951), 908–16.

Dittes, J. E., "Extinction during Psychotherapy of GSR Accompanying 'Embarrassing' Sexual Statements," *Journal of Abnormal and Social Psychology,* 54 (1957), 187-91.

Dunn, H. L., "Higher-level Wellness for Man and Society," *American Journal Public Health,* 1959 (in press).

Freud, Sigmund, *The Interpretation of Dreams,* New York, Basic Books, 1955.

Fromm, Eric, *Man for Himself.* New York, Rinehart, 1947.

Fromm, Eric, *The Sane Society.* New York, Rinehart, 1957.

Groddeck, G., *The Book of It.* New York and Washington, Nervous and Mental Diseases Publishing Co., 1928.

Horney, Karen, *Neurosis and Human Growth.* New York, Norton, 1950.

Horney, Karen, *The Neurotic Personality of Our Time.* New York, Norton, 1936.

Jahoda, Marie, *Current Concepts of Positive Mental Health.* New York, Basic Books, 1958.

Jourard, S. M., *Healthy Personality: An Approach through the Study of Healthy Personality.* New York, Harper and Brothers, 1958.

Jourard, S. M., and P. Lasakow, "Some Factors in Self-Disclosure," *Journal of Abnormal and Social Psychology,* 56(1958), 91–98.

Maslow, A. H., *Motivation and Personality.* New York, Harper and Brothers, 1954.

Parsons, Talcott and R. F. Bales, *Family, Socialization and Interaction Process.* Glencoe, Ill., Free Press, 1955.

Riesman, David, *The Lonely Crowd.* New Haven, Yale University Press, 1950.

Rogers, Carl R., *The Concept of the Fully-Functioning Person.* (Mimeographed manuscript, privately circulated, 1954.)

Rogers, Carl R., "The Characteristics of a Helping Relationship," *Personnel and Guidance Journal,* September 1958).

Ruesch, Jurgen, *Disturbed Communication.* New York, Norton, 1957.

Selye, Hans, "General Adaptation Syndrome and Diseases of Adaptation," *Journal of Clinical Endocrinology,* 6(1946), 117–28.

Skinner, B. F., *Science and Human Behavior.* New York, Macmillan, 1953.

Snygg, D., and A. W. Combs, *Individual Behavior.* New York, Harper and Brothers, 1949.

O. Hobart Mowrer

SOME CONSTRUCTIVE FEATURES OF THE CONCEPT OF SIN *

In some ways it is perhaps not surprising that we are assembled here today to explore the question of whether real guilt, or sin, is relevant to the problem of psychopathology and psychotherapy.   For half a century now we psychologists, as a profession, have very largely followed the Freudian doctrine that human beings become emotionally disturbed, not because of their having done anything palpably wrong, but because they instead lack insight.   Therefore, as would-be therapists we have set out to oppose the forces of repression and to work for understanding.   And what is this understanding, or insight, which we so highly prize?   It is the discovery that the patient or client has been, in effect, *too* good; that he has within him impulses, especially those of lust and hostility, which he has been quite unnecessarily inhibiting.   And health, we tell him, lies in the direction of recognizing and expressing these impulses.

But there are now widespread and, indeed, ominous signs that this logic and the practical strategies it seems to demand are ill-founded.

* From O. Hobart Mowrer, "Some Constructive Features of the Concept of Sin," *J. counsel. Psychol.*, 1960, 7, 185–188.   Reprinted by permission of the author and the Editor, *Journal of Counseling Psychology.*

The situation is, in fact, so grave that, as our presence here today suggests, we are even willing to consider the possibility that misconduct may, after all, have something to do with the matter and that the doctrine of repression and insight are more misleading than helpful.

I   A considerable predicament

However, as soon as we psychologists get into a discussion of this problem, we find that our confusion is even more fundamental than might at first appear. We find that not only have we disavowed the connection between manifest misconduct and psychopathology; we have, also, very largely abandoned belief in right and wrong, virtue and sin, in general.

On the other occasions when I have seen this issue under debate and anyone has proposed that social deviousness is causal in psychopathology, there is always a chorus of voices who clamor that sin cannot be defined, that it is culturally relative, that it is an unscientific concept, that it is a superstition—and therefore not to be taken seriously, either in psychopathology or in ordinary, everyday experience. And whenever an attempt is made to answer these objections, there are always further objections—often in the form of reductions to absurdity—which involve naivety or sophistry that would ill-become a schoolboy. Historically, in both literate and nonliterate societies, human beings are supposed to have reached the age of discretion by early adolescence; yet here we have the spectacle of grown men and women soberly insisting that, in effect, they cannot tell right from wrong—and that no one else can.

Now I realize how futile it is to try to deal with this kind of attitude in a purely rational or logical way. The subversive doctrine that we can have the benefits of orderly social life without paying for it, through certain restraints and sacrifices, is too alluring to be counteracted by mere reason. The real answer, I believe, lies along different lines. The unassailable, brute fact is that personality disorder is the most pervasive and baffling problem of our time; and if it should turn out that persons so afflicted regularly display (or rather hide) a life of too little, rather than too much, moral restraint and self-discipline, the problem would take on an empirical urgency that would require no fine-spun argument.

Sin used to be—and, in some quarters, still is—defined as whatever one does that puts him in danger of going to Hell. Here was an assumed cause-and-effect relationship that was completely metaphysical and empirically unverifiable; and it is small wonder that it has fallen into disrepute as the scientific outlook and method have steadily gained in acceptance and manifest power. But there is a very tangible and very present Hell-on-this-earth which science has not yet helped us understand very well; so I invite your attention to the neglected but very real possibility that it is this Hell—the Hell of neurosis and psychosis—to which sin and unexpiated guilt lead us and that it is this Hell that gives us one of the most, perhaps the most realistic and basic criteria for defining sin and guilt. If it proves empirically true that certain forms of conduct characteristically lead human beings into emotional instability, what better or firmer basis would one wish for labeling such conduct as destructive, self-defeating, evil, sinful?

II   Common fallacies reviewed

If the Freudian theory of personality disorder were valid, one would expect neurotic and psychotic individuals to have led exemplary, yea saintly lives—to have been just too good for this world. The fact is, of course, that such individuals typically exhibit lives that have been disorderly and dishonest in extreme degree. In fact, this is so regularly the case that one cannot but wonder how so contrary a doctrine as that of Freud ever gained credence. Freud spurned The Wish and exalted Reality. What he regarded as Reality may yet prove to have been the biggest piece of wishfulness of all.

Or, it may be asked, how is it if sin and psychic suffering are correlated that not all who sin fall into neurosis or psychosis? Here the findings of the Kinsey studies are likely to be cited, showing that, for example, many persons have a history of sexual perversity who are later quite normal. In other words, the argument is that since sin and persistent suffering do not always go hand-in-hand, there is perhaps no relationship at all. The answer to this question is surely obvious. Some individuals, alas, simply do not have enough character, or conscience, to be bothered by their sins. These are, of course, the world's psychopaths. Or an individual may have been caught in his sin and punished for it. Or it may have weighed so heavily on his conscience that he himself has confessed it and made appropriate expiation. Or, quite conceivably, in some instances the individual, without either detection or confession, may have set upon a program of service and good works which has also brought him peace and redemption. In other words, there is, surely, no disposition on the part of anyone to hold that sin, as such, necessarily dooms a person to interminable suffering in the form of neurosis or psychosis. The presumption is rather that sin has this effect only where it is acutely felt but not acknowledged and corrected.

Also, it is sometimes contended that individuals, who eventually come to the attention of psychotherapists have, to be sure, been guilty of major errors of conduct; but, it is held, the illness was present first and the misconduct was really just an expression or symptom thereof. If this were true, where then would we draw the line? Is there no such thing as moral responsibility and social accountability at all? Is every mean or vicious thing that you or I, as ordinary individuals do, not sin but rather an expression of "illness"? Who would seriously hold that a society could long endure which consistently subscribed to this flaccid doctrine?

Then there is, of course, the view that, in the final analysis, all psychopathology—or at least its profounder forms—has a constitutional or metabolic basis. One must, I believe, remain open-minded with respect to this possibility—indeed, perhaps even somewhat hopeful with respect to it; for how marvelous it would be if all the world's madness, stupidity, and meanness could be eliminated through biochemistry. But over the years we have seen one approach after another of this kind come into prominence, with much heralding as the long-awaited break-through on the problem of mental disease, only to fade out as manifestly not quite the panacea we had imagined it to be. Some of us may, at this point, even suspect that today the main incentive for keeping the biochemical hypothesis alive is not so much the supporting empirical evidence, which is meager enough, but instead the fact that it at least obliquely justifies the premise that the whole field of mental disorder is the proper and exclusive domain of medicine. Also, and again somewhat obliquely, it excuses the clergy from facing squarely the responsibilities that would devolve upon them if neurosis and psychosis should indeed turn out to be essentially moral disorders.

III   A look at the record—and the future

The conception of personality disturbance which attaches major etiological significance to moral and interpersonal considerations thus faces formidable resistance from many sources; but programs of treatment and prevention which have been predicated on these other views have gotten us nowhere, and there is no clear reason to think they ever will. Therefore, in light of the total situation, I see no alternative but to turn again to the old, painful, but also promising possibility that man is pre-eminently a social creature (or, in theological phrase, a child of God) and that he lives or dies, psychologically and personally, as a function of the openness, community, relatedness, and integrity which by good action he attains and by evil action destroys.

As long as we could believe that the psychoneurotic's basic problem was not evil but a kind of ignorance, it did not seem too formidable a task to give him the requisite enlightenment or insight. But mental hospitals are now full of people who have had this kind of therapy, in one guise or another, and found it wanting; and if we are thus forced to reconsider the other alternative, the therapeutic or redemptive enterprise, however clear it may be in principle, is by no means simple in practice.   If the problem is genuinely one of morality, rather than pseudo-morality, most of us in the secular healing professions of psychology, psychiatry, or social work, find ourselves reduced to the status of laymen, with no special training or competence for dealing with or even approaching the problem in these terms.   We know something, of course, about procedures for getting disturbed persons to talk about themselves, free-associate, "confess"; but the whole aim of this strategy has been insight, not redemption and personal reformation.   And clergymen themselves have so often been told, both by their own leaders and by members of the secular healing professions, that they must recognize their own "limitations" and know when to "refer," that they, too, lack the necessary confidence and resources for dealing with these problems adequately.

Many present-day psychoanalysts will offer no serious objection to the way in which classical Freudian theory and practice have been evaluated in this paper; but they will insist that many advances have been made since Freud's time and that these put the whole problem in a very different light.   If we ask, Precisely what *are* these advances? we are told that they have to do with the new emphasis upon "ego psychology" rather than upon "the unconscious."   But what did Emilian Gutheil (1958) tell us at our convention last year in Washington about ego psychology?   He said that although analysts now recognize the ego as much more important than formerly, they know next to nothing about the conditions for modifying or strengthening it; and the same position has been voiced earlier by Lawrence Kubie (1956), and, in one of his very last papers (1937), even by Freud himself.

Therefore, I do not see how we can avoid the conclusion that at this juncture we are in a real crisis with respect to the whole psychotherapeutic enterprise.   But I do not think we are going to remain in this crisis, confused and impotent, indefinitely.   There is, I believe, growing realism with regard to the situation on the part of both psychologists and psychiatrists, on the one hand, and ministers, rabbis, and priests, on the other; and I am hopeful and even confident that new and better ways of dealing with the situation are in the making.

What, precisely, these ways will be I do not know; but I venture the impression that Alcoholics Anonymous provides our best present intimation of things to come and that the therapeutic programs of the future, whether under religious or secular auspices, will, like AA, take guilt, confession, and expiation seriously and will involve programs of *action* rather than mere groping for "insight."

References

Freud, S. Analysis terminable and interminable. In *Collected papers*, Vol. V. London: The Hogarth Press, 1950.

Kubie, L. S. Some unsolved problems of psychoanalytic psychotherapy. In *Progress in psychotherapy* (Fromm-Reichmann & Moreno, eds.). New York: Grune & Stratton, 1956.

Gutheil, E. Pseudoneurotic symptoms in psychosis. *Amer. Psychol.*, 1958, *13*, 350.

Albert Ellis

THERE IS NO PLACE FOR THE CONCEPT OF SIN IN PSYCHOTHERAPY *

Let me begin my contribution to this Symposium by listing my points of agreement with Hobart Mowrer's lucid and challenging presentation. I heartily agree with Hobart that psychotherapy must largely be concerned with the patient's sense of morality or wrongdoing; that classical Freudianism is mistaken in its implication that giving an individual insight into or understanding of his immoral or antisocial behavior will usually suffice to enable him to change that behavior; that if any Hell exists for human beings it is the Hell of neurosis and psychosis; that man is preeminently a social creature who psychologically maims himself to the degree that he needlessly harms others; that the only basic solution to the problem of emotional disturbance is the correction or cessation of the disturbed person's immoral actions; and that the effective psychotherapist must not only give his patient insight into the origins of his mistaken and self-defeating behavior but must also provide him with a highly active program of working at the eradication of this behavior.

In the main, then, it would appear that I am in close agreement with Hobart Mowrer's concepts of sin and psychotherapy. Paradoxically enough, however, this is not quite true: since I shall now stoutly uphold the thesis that there is no place whatever for the concept of sin in psychotherapy and that to introduce this concept in any manner, shape, or form is highly pernicious and antitherapeutic. I shall con-

* From Albert Ellis, "There Is No Place for the Concept of Sin in Psychotherapy," *J. counsel. Psychol.*, 1960, 7, 188–192. Reprinted by permission of the author and the Editor, *Journal of Counseling Psychology*.

tend, in other words, that no human being should ever be blamed for anything he does; and it is the therapist's main and most important function to help rid his patients of every possible vestige of their blaming themselves, others, or fate and the universe.

Operational definition of sin

My pronounced differences with all those who would advocate making patients more guilty than they are, in order presumably to get them to change their antisocial and self-defeating conduct, can perhaps best be demonstrated by my insistence on a more precise and reasonably operational definition of the terms "sin" and "guilt" that is usually given by those who uphold this concept. In their recent *Comprehensive Dictionary of Psychological and Psychoanalytical Terms*, English and English (1958) give a psychological definition of "sin" as follows: "Conduct that violates what the offender believes to be a supernaturally ordained moral code." They define a "sense of guilt" in this wise: "Realization that one has violated ethical or moral or religious principles, together with a regretful feeling of lessened personal worth on that account." English and English do not give any definition of "blame" but Webster's New World Dictionary defines it as "1. a blaming; accusation; condemnation; censure. 2. responsibility for a fault or wrong."

The beauty of these definitions, if one pays close attention to them, is that they include the two prime requisites for the individual's feeling a sense of sin, or guilt, or self-blame: (a) I have done the wrong thing and am responsible for doing it; and (b) I am a blackguard, a sinner, a no-good-nik, a valueless person, a louse for having done this wrong deed. This, as I have shown my patients for the last several years, and as I have briefly noted in several of my recent papers on rational psychotherapy (Ellis, 1957, 1958, 1959), is the double-headed essence of the feeling of sin, guilt, and self-blame: not merely the fact that the individual has made a mistake, an error, or a wrong move (which we may objectively call "wrongdoing") but the highly insidious, and I am convinced quite erroneous, belief or assumption that he is worthless, no good, valueless as a person for having done wrong.

The problem of morality

I fully accept, then, Hobart Mowrer's implication that there is such a thing as human wrongdoing or immoral behavior. I do not, as a psychologist and a member in good standing of the American Sociological Society and the American Anthropological Association, believe that we can have any absolute, final, or God-given standards of morals or ethics. But I do believe that, as members of a social community, we must have *some* standards of right and wrong. My own feeling is that these standards are best based on what I call long-range or socialized hedonism—that is, the philosophy that one should primarily strive for one's own satisfactions while, at the same time, keeping in mind that one will achieve one's own best good, in most instances, by frequently giving up immediate gratifications for future gains and by being courteous to and considerate of others, so that they will not sabotage one's own ends. I am also, however, ready to accept almost any other rationally planned, majority-approved standard of morality that is not arbitrarily imposed by an authoritarian clique of actual men or assumed gods.

With Mowrer and almost all ethicists and religionists, then, I accept the fact that some standard of morality is necessary as long as humans live in social groups. But I still completely reject the notion that such a standard is only or best sustained by inculcating in individuals a sense of sin or guilt. I hold, on the contrary, that the more sinful and guilty a person tends to feel, the less chance there is that he will be a happy, healthy, or law-abiding citizen.

The problem of all human morality, it must never be forgotten, is not the problem of appeasing some hypothetical deity or punishing the individual for his supposed sins. It is the very simple problem, which a concept of sin and atonement invariably obfuscates, of teaching a person (a) not to commit an antisocial act in the first place and (b) if he does happen to commit it, not to repeat it in the second, third, and ultimate place. This problem, I contend, can only consistently and fully be solved if the potential or actual wrongdoer has the philosophy of life epitomized by the internalized sentences: (a) If I do this act it will be wrong; and (b) Therefore. how do I *not* do this act. Or: (a) This deed I have committed is wrong, erroneous, and mistaken; (b) now how do I *not* commit it again.

The concept of sin breeds sickness

If, most objectively, and without any sense of self-blame, self-censure, or self-guilt, any human being would thoroughly believe in and continually internalize these sentences, I think it would be almost impossible for him to commit or keep committing immoral acts. If, however, he does not have this objective philosophy of wrongdoing, I do not see how it is possible for him to prevent himself from being immoral, on the one hand, or for him to be moral and emotionally healthy on the other hand. For the main alternatives to the objective philosophy of nonblaming morality which I have just outlined are the following:

1 The individual can say to himself: (a) If I do this act it will be wrong; and (b) If I do this wrong act, I will be a sinner, a blackguard. If this is

what the individual says to himself, and firmly believes, he will then perhaps be moral in his behavior, but only at the expense of having severe feelings of worthlessness—of being a sinner. But such feelings of worthlessness, I submit, are the essence of human disturbance. So, at best, we have a moral individual who keeps himself so only by feeling worthless. And since none of us are angels, and all must at some time make mistakes and commit immoral acts, we actually have a moral individual who hates himself. Or we would have, as Mowrer might well put it, if he were more precise about what a sense of sin actually is and what it does to human beings, an individual who is in the Hell of neurosis or psychosis.

2   The self-blaming or guilty individual can say to himself, as I contend that most of the time he does in actual practice, (a) If I do this act it will be wrong; and (b) If I am wrong I will be a sinner. And then, quite logically taking off from this wholly irrational and groundless conclusion, he will obsessively-compulsively keep saying to himself, as I have seen patient after patient say, "Oh, what a terrible sinner, I will be (or already am); Oh, what a terrible person! Oh, how I deserve to be punished." And so on, and so forth. In saying this nonsense, in equating his potential or actual act of wrongdoing with a concomitant feeling of utter worthlessness, this individual will then never be able to focus on the simple question "How do I *not* do this wrong act? or How do I not repeat doing it now that I have done it?" He will, instead, keep focusing senselessly on "What a horrible sinner, what a blackguard I am!" Which means, in most instances, that he will, ironically enough, actually be diverted into doing the wrong act or repeating it if he has already done it. His sense of sin will literally drive him away from not doing wrong and toward doing it. Or, in other words, he will become a compulsive wrongdoer.

3   The self-blaming person or individual with a pronounced sense of sin may say to himself (a) If I do this act it will be wrong; and (b) If I am wrong I am a worthless sinner. Then, being no angel and being impelled, at times, to commit the wrong deed, and being prepared to condemn himself mercilessly (because of his sense of sin) for his deeds, he will either refuse to admit that he has done the wrong thing or admit that he has done it but insist that it is not wrong. That is to say, the wrongdoer who has an acute sense of sin will either repress thoughts about his wrongdoing or psychopathically insist that he is right and the world is wrong.

Any way one looks at the problem of morality, therefore, the individual who sanely starts out by saying (a) It is wrong to do this act and then who insanely continues (b) I am a sinner or a blackguard for doing this act (or for even thinking about doing it) can only be expected to achieve one or more of four very unfortunate results: (1) a deepseated feeling of personal worthlessness; (2) an obsessive-compulsive occupation with and possible performance of the wrong act for which he is blaming himself; (3) denial or repression of the fact that his immoral act was actually committed by him; and (4) psychopathic insistence that the act was committed but was not really wrong.

To make matters infinitely worse, the individual who has a sense of sin, guilt, or self-blame inevitably cannot help blaming others for their potential or actual wrongdoings—in which case he becomes angry or hostile to these others; and he cannot help blaming fate, circumstances, or the universe for wrongly or unjustly frustrating him in the attainment of many of his desires—in which case he becomes self-pitying and angry at the world. In the final analysis, then, blaming, in all its insidious ramifications, is the essence of virtually all emotional disturbance; and, as I tell my patients on many occasions, if I can induce them never, under any circumstances, to blame or punish anyone, including and especially themselves, for anything, it will be virtually impossible for them ever to become seriously upset. This does not mean that no child or adult should ever be objectively or dispassionately penalized for his errors or wrongdoings (as, for example, psychologists often penalize laboratory rats by shocking them when they enter the wrong passage of a maze); but merely that no one should ever be blamefully punished for his mistakes or crimes.

There are several other reasons why, invariably, giving an individual a sense of sin, or of self-worthlessness in connection with his wrongdoing, will not make for either less human immorality or greater happiness or mental health, but I shall only briefly mention them here, since I am quickly running out of space. For one thing, guilt and self-blame induce the individual to bow nauseatingly low to some arbitrary external authority, which in the last analysis is always some hypothetical deity; and such worship renders him proportionately less self-sufficient and self-confident. Secondly, the concept of guilt inevitably leads to the unsupportable sister concept of self-sacrifice for and dependency on others—which is the antithesis of true mental health. Thirdly, guilty individuals tend to focus incessantly on past delinquencies and crimes rather than on present and future constructive behavior. Fourthly, it is psycho-physically impossible for a person to focus adequately on changing his moral actions for the better when he is obsessively focused upon blaming himself for his past and present misdeeds. Fifthly, the states of anxiety created in an individual by his self-blaming tendencies induce concomitant breakdown states in which he cannot think clearly of anything, least of all constructive changes in self.

Because of these most serious disadvantages of giving individuals a serious sense of sin and because any deity-positing religion almost by necessity involves endowing those members who violate its god's laws with a distinct concept of blameworthiness or sin, I am inclined to reverse Voltaire's famous dictum and to say that, from a mental health standpoint, if there were a God it would be necessary to uninvent Him.

Psychotherapy attacks the concept of sin

Although I still agree heartily with Hobart Mowrer that the healthy and happy human being should have a clearcut sense of wrongdoing, and that he should not only try to understand the origin of his antisocial behavior but do something effective to become more morally oriented, I contend that giving anyone a sense of sin, guilt, or self-blame is the worst possible way to help him be an emotionally sound and adequately socialized individual.   As psychotherapists, by all means let us show our patients that (a) they have often acted wrongly, badly, and self-defeatingly by their antisocial actions; but that (b) that is no reason why they should feel sinful or guilty or self-blaming about the actions for which they may well have been responsible.   Instead, we must help these patients temporarily to accept themselves as wrong-doers, acknowledge fully their responsibility for their acts, and then focus intently, in their internalized sentences and their overt activities, on the only real problem at hand—which is: How do I *not* repeat this wrong deed next time?

If, in this thoroughly objective, nonguilty manner, we can teach our patients (as well as the billions of people in the world who, for better or worse, will never become patients) that even though human beings can be held quite accountable or responsible for their misdeeds, no one is ever to blame for anything, human morality, I am sure, will be significantly improved and for the first time in human history civilized people will have a real possibility of achieving sound mental health. The concept of sin is the direct and indirect cause of virtually all neurotic disturbance.   The sooner psychotherapists forthrightly begin to attack it the better their patients will be.

References

Ellis, A.   Outcome of employing three techniques of psychotherapy.   *J. clin. Psychol.*, 1957, *4*, 344–350.

Ellis, A.   Rational psychotherapy.   *J. gen. Psychol.*, 1958, *59*, 35–49.

Ellis, A.   Rationalism and its therapeutic application.   In Ellis, A. (Ed.), *The place of values in the practice of psychotherapy.*   New York: Amer. Academy of Psychotherapists, 1959.

English, H. B., & English, Ava C.   *A comprehensive dictionary of psychological and psychoanalytical terms.*   New York: Longmans, Green, 1958.

Stuart E. Golann

PSYCHOLOGICAL STUDY
OF CREATIVITY *

The purpose of the present paper is to review recent theory and research pertaining to the psychological study of creativity so as to
highlight the issues and emphases reflected in the literature.   Three
issues are apparent: (*a*) What is creativity?—questions of definition
and criteria, (*b*) How does creativity occur?—questions of the process
viewed temporally, and, (*c*) Under what conditions is creativity manifest?—questions of necessary personal and environmental conditions.
A striking feature of the literature on creativity is the diversity of interests, motives, and approaches characteristic of the many investigators.   Creativity has been viewed as a normally distributed trait,
an aptitude trait, an intrapsychic process, and as a style of life.   It
has been described as that which is seen in all children, but few adults.
It has been described as that which leads to innovation in science,
performance in fine arts, or new thoughts.   Creativity has been described as related to, or equatable with, intelligence, productivity, positive mental health, and originality.   It has been described as being
caused by self-actualization and by sublimation and restitution of
destructive impulses.   Clearly there is a need for organization and
integration within the psychological study of creativity.   What are the
many investigators studying?   How are they studying it?   Four contemporary emphases are apparent: products, process, measurement,
and personality.   The organization herein will follow this same order.
The scope of the paper precludes an exhaustive presentation of all
theoretical statements and research reports.   The reader is referred to
an annotated bibliographical volume prepared by Stein and Heinze
(1960).   French and Italian bibliographies (Bédard 1959, 1960) are
also available.

Emphasis on products

The use of products as criteria of creativity is most frequently encountered in investigations in technological or industrial settings.   In
such studies creativity is assumed to be a unitary or multifaceted trait
which is distributed in the population in a manner comparable to
other intellective or personality traits (see Gamble, 1959, p. 292).
Several authors believe that creativity can best be studied through
products.

* From Stuart E. Golann, *"Psychological Study of Creativity,"* Psychol. Bull., 1963, 60,
548–565.   Reprinted by permission of the author and the Managing Editor, the American Psychological Association.

In the "Committee Report on Criteria of Creativity" (Gamble, 1959), it was stated that the products of creative behavior should be the first object of study. After the products are judged "creative" the term can be applied to the behavior which produced them, and also the individuals who performed the behavior can be classed as possessing to some degree the trait of creativity.

Several possible product criteria of creativity were proposed by McPherson (1956) who reviewed the problem of determining "inventive level" of patents. Ghiselin (1958) stated that the approach outlined by McPherson would not provide the true criteria of creativity and distinguished two levels of creativity. A higher level of creativity introduces some new element of meaning or some new order of significance while a lower level gives further development to an established body of meaning by initiating some advance in its use.

While the utility of studying creativity through products remains an issue, Harmon (1958), Taylor (1958), and C. Taylor (1959) have studied relationships between criterion variables and determinants of judges' creativity ratings. Harmon reported correlations of .61 and .76 between judged creativity and number of publications. D. Taylor reported a correlation of .69 between ratings of creativity and ratings of productivity given by supervisors of research personnel. In later reports, Taylor (1960, 1961) argued that distinctions among problem solving, decision making, and creative thinking can best be made in terms of the product. A large number of measures were refined by C. Taylor to yield 56 scores on each of a group of research scientists. Included in the refined measures were supervisor, peer, examiner, and self-evaluations; counts of reports and publications; official records; and membership in professional societies. Factor analysis yielded 27 factors. The finding that among the many correlations four out of any five variables were independent of a given criterion was cited as evidence for the "almost overwhelming complexity of the criterion problem."

Emphasis on process

Creative process and illumination

An alternative to the study of creativity through products is to study the process of creativity. Wallas (1926) described the stages of forming a new thought as follows: preparation, incubation, illumination, and verification. While the four stages could be distinguished from one another, Wallas noted that they do not occur in an uninterrupted problem and solution sequence. Controversy has appeared concerning the distinctness of the stages and the relative importance of conscious or other modes of mental activity.

Dashiell (1931) noted the four stages of the creative process and related inspiration to insight in learning. Recall is dependent on the absence of interfering associations set up by excessive concentration on the recalling. Similarly, Woodworth (1954) stated that incubation implies a theory he prefers not to accept. Illumination, he believed is the result of laying aside a problem, giving the mind a chance to rest and at the same time to get rid of false sets and directions. Relating the recall of a forgotten name to creative insight, Woodworth stated that the sudden recall of a forgotten name after previous futile attempts suggests that an essential factor in illumination is the absence of interferences which block progress during the preliminary stage.

In addition to considering explanations of unconscious processes and the weakening of erroneous sets, Crutchfield (1961) suggested that incubation may permit, perhaps unaware to the individual, new and better cues from the environment and from ideation to develop while one engages in other activities. An experiment cited suggested that the subject's performance on a former task may facilitate insight on a later task even though they report no awareness of the relevant cue present in the preceding task. Instead of the study of distinct stages, Crutchfield recommended a functional analysis which would seek lawful accounts of the manner in which each step of the creative thinking process was functionally determined by prior steps and in turn governed succeeding steps.

Ghiselin (1956) described insight as the crucial action of the mind in creation. He too preferred to consider the creative process as consisting of fewer discrete steps, and stated that no sort of calculation from known grounds will suffice for creative production. Required for creativity is a fresh formulation, rather than copying with variations or elaborations. Although he believed that concepts of unconscious thoughts are imprecise, he did admit the importance of diversion which is conceptualized as being related to what he terms preconfigurative consciousness.

The illumination controversy could be enlarged upon and conceptually updated. However, the guidelines seem clear in regard to the creative process. Crutchfield's paper is helpful in that he attempted to translate the somewhat literary descriptions of the creative process into better conceptualized psychological variables.

Creative process: Systematized,
goal directed, or plastic

For Harmon (1956) the creative process is any process by which something new is produced: an idea or object, a new form or arrangement of old elements. The essential requirement is that the new creation must contribute to the solution of a problem.   The creative process is goal directed.   Harris (1959) saw the creative process as consisting of six steps: (a) realizing the need, (b) gathering information, (c) thinking through, (d) imagining solutions, (e) verifying and (f) putting the ideas to work.   He stated that the difference between the electrified or illuminated minds of some geniuses and the processes in ordinary people is the speed with which they proceed from Step a to Step d (see also Arnold, 1959).

Taking a different view, I. Taylor (1959) stated that the rules of logic and scientific method are a psychological straight jacket for creative thought.   He proposed five levels of creativity which he identified by the analysis of over 100 definitions of creativity.

Expressive creativity is most fundamental, according to Taylor, involving independent expression where skills, originality, and the quality of the product are unimportant.   Spontaneity and freedom are apparent from which later creative talents develop.   Individuals proceed from the expressive to the productive level of creativity when skills are developed to produce finished works.   The product is creative in that a new level of accomplishment is reached by the person though the product may not be stylistically discernible from the work of others. Inventive creativity is operative when ingenuity is displayed.   This level involves flexibility in perceiving new and unusual relationships between previously separate parts.   It does not contribute to new ideas but to new uses of old parts.   Innovative creativity requires strong abstract conceptualizing skill and is seen when basic foundation principles are sufficiently understood so as to allow improvement through modification.   The highest form of creativity is "emergentive creativity," which involves the conception of an entirely new principle at a most fundamental and abstract level.   The core of the creative process in Taylor's view is the ability to mold experiences into new and different organizations, the ability to perceive the environment plastically, and to communicate the resulting unique experiences to others.

Stein (1956) stated that creativity is a process of hypothesis formulation, hypothesis testing, and the communication of results which are the resultant of social transaction.   Individuals affect and are affected by the environment in which they live.   The early childhood family-environment transaction facilitates or inhibits creativity.   An empirical definition of manifest creativity is suggested by Stein (1956):

Creativity is that process which results in a novel work that is accepted as tenable or useful or satisfying by a group at some point in time [p. 172].

Potential creativity is suggested when an individual does not satisfy the requirements of the stated definition, but nevertheless performs on psychological tests like individuals who do manifest creativity.   In an earlier paper Stein (1953) elaborated upon his definition of creativity.

Emphasis on measurement

Factor analytic approach

Since the publication of Chassell's (1916) paper numerous investigators have attempted to devise or adapt tests that would measure creative abilities. Although the types of tests have not changed very much over the past 55 years, the methods of analysis have become more complex. For example, Guilford attempted to define the entire structure of intellect by factor analytic methods. In one of the more recent revisions of his system, he presented a "unified theory of intellect" making use of a cubical model of intellectual abilities in which each dimension represents a mode of variation among the factors (Guilford, 1959a). The lack of psychological knowledge in the area of creativity may be attributable, according to Guilford (1959b) to the inappropriateness of the SR model for the study of higher processes.

Instead, Guilford (1959b) recommended a trait approach for the study of creativity and stated that the most defensible way of discovering dependable trait concepts is factor analysis. He attempted to place his research on creativity within the larger context of the structure of intellect. Noting some 47 known factors of intellect, Guilford suggested that they can be put into a three-way classification according to: the kind of material or content of thought, the varieties of activities or operations performed, and the varieties of resultant products. In this system each primary intellectual ability represents the interaction of a kind of operation applied to a kind of material, yielding a kind of product. Most needed, according to Guilford, was a more thorough understanding of the nature and components of intellect. Accordingly, most of the data reported concern the isolation of a primary factor believed to be of importance for creativity.

The factorial aptitude traits that Guilford currently believes to be related to creativity are described as: ability to see problems, fluency of thinking (the factors of word fluency and ideational fluency), flexibility of thinking (the factors of spontaneous flexibility and adaptive flexibility), originality, redefinition, and elaboration. The types of cognitive abilities Guilford believes to be of importance for creativity are reflected in the measuring devices he has designed or adapted. Very briefly described, his tests require individuals to state defects or deficiencies in common implements or institutions; to produce words containing a specified letter or combination of letters; to produce in a limited time as many synonyms as they can for a stimulus word; to produce phrases or sentences; to name objects with certain properties (for example, objects that are hard, white, and edible); or to give various uses for a common object. Guilford's (1959b) practice of scoring fluency factors is to emphasize sheer quantity—"quality need not be considered so long as responses are appropriate [p. 146]." Other tests employed ask examinees which of a given list of objects could best be adapted to make another object; or to construct a more complex object from one or two simple lines.

Guilford (1959b) presented three ways to measure the trait of originality: counting the number of responses that are judged to be clever, utilizing items calling for remote associations, and weighting the subject's responses in proportion to their infrequency of occurrence in a population of subjects. The first two procedures require a quality criterion.

Much of the research efforts of Guilford and associates has been devoted to the definition of factor traits by isolating patterns of concomitant variation (see Guilford, 1957; Guilford, Kettner, & Christensen, 1954, 1956; Kettner, Guilford, & Christensen, 1959). The studies reviewed herein cluster into two groups: (a) those studies demonstrating a relationship between measures of the factors and criterion variables and (b) those studies suggesting no relationship between measures of the factors and judged creativity.

Correlations of .25 between grades in an astronomy course and performance on a test of expressional fluency, .37 between scores on a test of ideational fluency and a criterion of engineer performance based on pay increases, and .31 between a measure of adaptive flexibility and the pay increase criterion were reported by Guilford (1956). Adaptive flexibility was reported to have consistently shown a relationship to performance in mathematics (average r .33). Three Guilford originality tests (Unusual Uses, Consequences, and Plot Titles) were reported by Barron (1956) to correlate in the range of .30–.36 with 10 judges' ratings of originality. Significant multiple correlations were reported by Chorness (1956) between a composite factor score from the Guilford battery and United States Air Force student-instructor characteristics judged to be demonstrative of creative expression. The best single predictor was a test of controlled associations. Statistically removing the effects of intelligence demonstrated that the creativity tests could be employed as predictors of instructor performance since the factor composite predicted the student instructor grades for the phase of the program studied better than an intelligence index which had previously been relied on.

No significant differences between groups rated as creative or not creative on the factors of redefinition, closure, ideational fluency, associational fluency, spontaneous flexibility, sensitivity to problems, and originality were found by Drevdahl (1956). Similarly, Gerry, De-Veau, and Chorness (1957) reported no significant differences on the

Guilford battery between awarded and nonawarded employees when the groups had been equated for intelligence, job performance, and education.

Surveying several years. of research on creative, effective people, MacKinnon (1961) stated that in all samples studied, the Guilford tests, scored for quantity or quality, did not correlate well with the degree of creativity as judged by experts in the subjects' own fields. Substantiating this, correlations reported by Gough (1961) between criterion ratings of creativity and several of the Guilford tests were: Unusual Uses (quantity −.05, quality .27); Consequences (quantity −.27, quality −.12); Matchsticks (.04); Gestalt Transformations (.27).

Relationship between measured creativity
and measured intelligence

Using an IQ measure (Stanford-Binet, Wechsler Scale for Children, or Henmon-Nelson) and five creativity measures (Word Association, Uses for Things, Hidden Shapes, Fables, and Make-Up Problems), Getzels and Jackson (1959) selected two experimental groups. One group was composed of children who placed in the top 20% on the creativity measures when compared with same-sexed age peers, but below the top 20% in measured IQ. The second group consisted of subjects who placed in the top 20% in IQ, but below the top 20% on the creativity measures. Despite the similarity in mean IQ between the high creative group (IQ = 127) and total population (IQ = 132), and despite the 23-point difference in mean IQ between the two experimental groups in favor of the high intelligence group (IQ = 150), the achievement scores of the two experimental groups on standard subject-matter tests were equally superior to the ahcievement scores of the remainder of the school population. These data are discussed more fully in a recent volume (Getzels & Jackson, 1962).

The main criticisms of the Getzels-Jackson report have centered around the use of a single atypical school. Torrance studied creative thinking in the early school years (see Torrance, 1958, 1959a, 1959b, 1959c, 1959d, 1959e, 1960a, 1960b, 1960c, 1960d; Torrance, Baker, & Bowers, 1959; Torrance & Radig, 1959) and brought together eight partial replications of the Getzels-Jackson study. Two batteries of creativity tests were used; both consisted of modifications of Guilford-type tests with the exception of the Ask and Guess Test developed by Torrance (Torrance & Radig, 1959). The procedure followed by Torrance (1960c) is similar to Getzels and Jackson in that he selected groups who placed in the upper 20% on either the creativity or IQ measures, but not in the upper 20% on the remaining measure.

In six of Torrance's eight groups, there was no significant difference on measured achievement between the high creative and high intelligence groups. In two of the elementary schools (the small town school and the parochial school) there was a significant difference in measured achievement in favor of the high intelligence group. The question is then raised: Under what conditions do "highly creative" pupils achieve as well as "highly intelligent" ones? Additional data reported by Torrance suggests a tendency for the highly creative groups to be better on reading and language skills than on work-study or arithmetic skills.

Meer and Stein (1955) reported a significant relationship between research chemists scores on the Wechsler-Bellevue, Miller Analogies, and supervisors' ratings of creativity. When education was controlled, they concluded that with opportunity held constant, IQ beyond the ninety-fifth percentile is not significant for creative work. Similarly, summarizing several studies, Barron (1961) suggested that a small correlation (about .40) exists between the total ranges of creativity and intelligence. However, beyond an IQ of about 120, measured intelligence is unimportant for creativity. He pointed instead to the importance of motivational and stylistic variables.

Criterion group empirical approach

The Welsh Figure Preference Test (WFPT; Welsh, 1949, 1959a, 1959b) is a different type of psychometric instrument used in the study of creativity. In short, it is a nonlingual test composed of 400 India ink drawings, to each of which the examinee must respond "like" or "don't like." Of primary interest in the present context is an empirical scale derived by contrasting the likes and dislikes of 37 artists and art students with the likes and dislikes of 150 people in general (Barron & Welsh, 1952). This scale has since been revised by Welsh to eliminate any response set and in its present form the Revised Art (RA) scale consists of 30 drawings that artists like more frequently than people do in general, and 30 items that artists dislike more often than people do in general.

Rosen (1955) attempted to use the earlier form of the Art scale (BW) as a predictor of originality and level of ability among artists. He reported a significant difference between artists and art students as contrasted with nonartists, but no evidence that Art scale score increased as a function of level of training of the artist. One art product of each of the students was rated on a 5-point scale of originality by each of the art faculty. The correlation between the Art scale score and the average of the ratings was .40. The correlation between the Art scale score and the grade-point average of the students was .34.

Rank-order correlations of .40 and .35 between scores on the RA scale and creative writing instructor's ratings of originality and creativity of their students were reported by Welsh (1959a). Gough (1961) reported that the BW scale showed the highest single correlation (.41) with criterion judgments of research workers' creativity. Among the many measures which did not correlate well with the criterion judgments were three ability measures, the Allport-Vernon value scales, 56 of the 57 Strong Vocational Inventory scales, Barron's Originality scale, Barron's Preference for Complexity scale, the originality coefficient from Gough's Differential Reaction Schedule, and the six Guilford measures already noted.

Data obtained by MacKinnon (1961) indicated that a group of highly creative architects placed in the same range as artists on the BW scale, while a less creative group obtained lower scores, and a third group not distinguished for its creativity scored lowest.

Emphasis on personality

Personality is another major emphasis within the psychological study of creativity. It can be subdivided into: (a) the study of motivation of creative behavior and (b) the study of personality characteristics or life styles of creative individuals. Regarding motivation, two divergent viewpoints are apparent. One describes creative behavior as an emergent property which matures as the individual attempts to realize his fullest potentials in his interaction with his environment, while the second treats creativity as a byproduct of repressed or unacceptable impulses.

Among the concepts related to the first viewpoint are Allport's (1937) functional autonomy, Goldstein's (1939), Roger's (1954, 1956), and Yacorzynski's (1954) self-actualization; as well as May's (1959) and Schachtel's (1959) motives for creativity. Individuals are described as being creative because it is satisfying to them since they have a need to relate to the world around them so they may experience their selves in action.

Antithetical to these views are the concepts of psychoanalytic authors who have discussed creativity. Freud (1910, 1924, 1948) originally postulated that all cultural achievements are caused by the diversion of libidinal energy. This displacement, producing higher cultural achievements, he called sublimation (Freud, 1930). Several authors have described creativity as motivated by efforts to defend against unacceptable impulses (see Bergler, 1947; Bychowski, 1951) or as motivated by unconscious restitution for destructive urges (see Fairbairn, 1938; Lee, 1947, 1948, 1950; Rickman, 1957; Sharpe, 1930, 1950). Other reductionistic treatments of creativity can be found in the writings of Abraham (1949), Adler (1927), Bellack (1958), Bischler (1937), Brill (1931), Ehrenzweig (1949), Grotjahn (1957), Kohut (1957), Kris (1952), Levey (1940), Rank (1916), and Sachs

(1951). Criticisms of sublimation theory were offered by Bergler (1945), Deri (1939), and Levey (1939).

It is difficult to compare these viewpoints experimentally for several reasons. Creativity has not been defined by either group and it does not seem that they are describing the same types of behaviors. The reductionistic authors most often discuss painting and writing in their attempts to explain creativity. The self-actualizing group seem to describe a much more global style of interacting with one's environment which could lead to products that would be judged as creative. Moreover, such concepts as sublimation and self-actualization are not easily definable or measurable. There are a few experimental studies which have yielded data of varying degrees of consistency or inconsistency with the two views of motivation for creative behavior.

Studies of motivation for creativity

Münsterberg and Mussen (1953) attempted to study several hypotheses derived from psychoanalytic formulations of the creative personality. They interpreted the data as supporting the following hypotheses: (a) more artists than nonartists have intense guilt feelings, (b) more artists are introverted and have a rich inner life, (c) more artists than nonartists are unable or unwilling to comply with their parents. No support was reported for the following hypotheses: (a) nonartists are more likely to show overt aggressive tendencies, (b) appreciation of the product supplies basic narcissistic gratification for the artist, (c) the artist interprets appreciation as evidence that others share his guilt. Evidence was reported supporting the single hypothesis which was not derived from psychoanalytic formulations—that more artists than nonartists show a need for creative self-expression.

Myden (1959) defined a highly creative group by choosing 20 subjects from "the top rank" of diverse fields of the arts. Content and formal analysis of the Rorschach suggested that the creative group did utilize primary process significantly more than the noncreative group. Myden stated that in the creative individual the primary process appeared to be integrated with the secondary process and did not seem to arise from, or increase, anxiety. Regression appeared to be a part of the thinking of creative individuals, rather than symptomatic of loss of ego control. No quantitative difference in anxiety was apparent between the two groups. The creative group was reported to employ significantly less repression than did the noncreative group. Myden believed that this may account for the finding that they show a greater amount of psychosexual ambivalence.

One large difference between the two groups, which is not considered in the psychoanalytic literature, was noted to be a significantly stronger sense of psychological role-in-life characteristic of the creative group.

Myden (1959) described them as "inner-directed and not easily swayed by outside reactions and opinions [p. 156]."

Golann (1961, 1962) proposed a hypothetical construct—the creativity motive—through which he attempted to express the view that creative products are only one segment of creative behavior which becomes manifest when individuals actively interact with their environment so as to experience their fullest perceptual, cognitive, and expressive potentials. He argued that high creativity motive subjects should prefer stimuli and situations which allow for idiosyncratic ways of dealing with them. In an attempt to demonstrate this, and in an attempt towards explanation of positive correlations between the Art scales of the WFPT and judged creativity in painting, writing, and research, it was shown that the 30 RA scale items liked by artists were significantly more ambiguous than the RA items artists did not like. A second study revealed that individuals who scored high on the RA scale, subjects who preferred the ambiguous, evocative figures, indicated preference on a questionnaire for activities and situations which allowed more self-expression and utilization of creative capacity, in contrast to low RA subjects who preferred more routine, structured, and assigned activities.

Personality attributes of creative individuals have been treated through experimental study and theoretical descriptive reports. Maslow's (1959) description of self-actualizing creativeness and Rogers' (1954) discussion of conditions within the individual that are closely associated with a potentially creative act are highly similar. Both authors placed a great deal of importance on openness to experience rather than premature conceptualization, and on an internal locus of evaluation rather than over concern with the opinions of others. The theme of individuals' desire to fully achieve their potentials through their interaction with the environment is prominent in these writings. Similar or related observations have been made by Fromm (1959), Murphy (1947, 1958), and Mooney (1953a, 1953b).

Studies of personality attributes
of creative individuals

The experimental study of personality attributes of creative individuals tends to contrast criterion groups on either self-descriptions, others' descriptions, test performance, life history material, or work habits. The criterion groups have been selected on the basis of either ratings of creativity, performance on Guilford tests, scores on BW or RA of the WFPT, or nomination of individuals of outstanding creativity by a panel of experts in their field.

The relationship between self-description and degree of creativity has been studied by several investigators. Barron (1952) reported that subjects at the lower extreme on the BW scale described themselves as contented, gentle, conservative, unaffected, patient, and peaceable.   In contrast, the high BW subjects characterized themselves as gloomy, loud, unstable, bitter, cool, dissatisfied, pessimistic, emotional, irritable, and pleasure seeking.   Similar results were reported by Barron (1958) in a later study.   Relating self-descriptions to a productivity criterion VanZelst and Kerr (1954) reported that productive scientists described themselves as more original, imaginative, curious, enthusiastic, and impulsive, and as less contented and conventional.   Stein (1956) reported that creative subjects regard themselves as assertive and authoritative, while less creative regard themselves as acquiescent and submissive.   Self-descriptions for highly creative and less creative female mathematicians have been reported by Helson (1961) and by MacKinnon (1961) for groups of architects varying in creativeness.   MacKinnon reported that the highly creative stress their inventiveness, independence, individuality, enthusiasm, determination, and industry while the less creative stress virtue, good character, rationality, and concern for others.   He suggested that the highly creative are able to speak frankly, in a more unusual way about themselves because they are more self-accepting than their less creative colleagues (see also Barron, 1961).

A dimension similar to that apparent in the self-descriptions is reflected in the test performance of subjects varying in creativity.   The values of subjects at the extremes on the BW scale were inferred by Barron (1952) from fine arts preferences.   He reported that low BW subjects approved of good breeding, formality, religion, and authority and rejected the daring, esoteric, or sensual.   In contrast, high BW subjects approved of the modern, experimental, primitive, and sensual while they disliked the aristocratic, traditional, and emotionally controlled.

Barron (1953) equated performance on the BW scale with a bipolar factor of preference for perceiving and dealing with complexity as opposed to preference for simplicity.   Positive relationships reported for preference of complexity included: personal tempo, verbal fluency, impulsiveness, expansiveness, originality, sensuality, sentience, esthetic interest, and femininity in men.   Negative relationships of preference for complexity included: rigidity, constriction, repressive impulse control, political-economic conservatism, subservience to authority, ethnocentrism, and social conformity.   This dimension is discussed more fully in a later report (Barron, 1961).

Studying the relationship between aptitude and nonaptitude factors, Guilford (1957) stated that the intercorrelations were generally low. Subjects who scored higher on ideational fluency were more impulsive, self-confident, ascendent, more appreciative of originality and somewhat less inclined towards neuroticism.   Subjects higher on originality were more interested in esthetic expression, reflective and divergent thinking, more tolerant of ambiguity, and felt less need for orderliness.

Independence as a personality attribute was stressed in several theoretical discussions of creativity. Barron (1953b) reported that subjects who did not yield to the incorrect group consensus in the Asch line judgment situation scored significantly higher on the BW scale than a group of yielders. Barron (1961) also noted that subjects who regularly perform in a creative or original manner on Guilford tests are independent in judgment when put under pressure to conform to a group opinion in conflict with their own.

The suggestion that the real difference between high and low creative individuals might be a function of the lows' defensiveness which inhibits generalization and communication of hypotheses was offered by Stein and Meer (1954). They administered the Rorschach to subjects at exposures ranging from .01 second to full. Their scoring system gave the highest score to a well-integrated response given to a difficult card at the shortest exposure. A biserial correlation of .88 between total weighted score and criterion creativity ratings was reported.

The work style of similarly employed individuals varying in creativity has also been the object of study. Roe (1949) reported that biologists selected for eminence in research were very unaggressive, had little interest in interpersonal relations, were unwilling to go beyond the data presented, and preferred concrete reality to the imaginary. Other data on Rorschach and Thematic Apperception Test performances of groups of eminent scientists are discussed in this and other reports (see Roe, 1946, 1949, 1951, 1952). Bloom (1956) administered projective techniques to outstanding scientists and reported personality and temperamental characteristics similar to those described by Roe. The willingness to work hard seems to be the most general characteristic of the samples studied.

Two research styles were reported by Gough (1961) to correlate with criterion ratings of creativity: the man who is dedicated to research and sees himself as a driving researcher with exceptional mathematical skills; the man with wide interests, analytic in thinking, who prefers research which lends itself to elegant, formal solutions. In a previous paper, Gough (1958) had described eight types of researchers and how these were conceptualized.

Another source of data bearing on creativity and personality is life history material. Roe (1953) reported that social scientists' interaction with their parents involved overprotection while physical and biological scientists developed early a way of life not requiring personal interaction.

A negative relationship between rated creativity and socioeconomic as well as educational status of the parents has been reported by Stein (1956). Creative subjects were more likely to feel that their parents were inconsistent in attitudes towards them.   Less creative subjects were more likely to engage in group activities in childhood while the more creative preferred solitary activities.   Similar trends were reported in extensive biographical studies by Cattell (1959). MacKinnon (1961) reported relationships between life history material and rated creativity which require and warrant further investigation.

Crutchfield (1961) attempted to describe personality attributes which tend to characterize creative individuals in general.   He reported that in cognitive spheres they are more flexible and fluent; their perceptions and cognitions are unique.   In approach to problems they are intuitive, empathic, perceptually open, and prefer complexity.   In emotional-motivational spheres they demonstrate freedom from excessive impulse control, achieve via independence rather than conformity, are individualistic, and have strong, sustained, intrinsic motivation in their field of work.

Studies with children

Few studies have been reported on creativity in children despite the great interest in the creativeness of childhood.   Mattil (1953) attempted to study the relationship between the creative products of children and their adjustment.   The data led Mattil to conclude that elements of adjustment and mental abilities are directly related to creative products.

Limited data on creativity in children is included in a monograph by Adkins and her associates (Adkins, Cobb, Miller, Sanford, Stewart, Aub, Burke, Nathanson, Stuart, & Towne, 1943).   Teacher ratings of creativity in school children are reported to correlate positively with independent measures of the following variables: .81 with need for sentience (pleasures) .65 with intraception (imaginative, subjective, human outlook); .65 with the need to produce, organize, or build things; .63 with the need for understanding; .60 with the need to explain, judge, or interpret; .50 with the need to restrive after failure and to overcome weakness; .50 with the enjoying of thought and emotion for its own sake or preoccupation with inner activities.   Negative correlations reported for the same teacher ratings include: —.79 with sameness (adherence to places, people, and modes of conduct; rigidity of habits); —.57 with the need of acquisition; and —.54 with the need to reject others.

Reid, King, and Wickwire (1959) reported that creative subjects exhibited superior performance on almost all cognitive variables, indicating that cognitive abilities (as measured by general intelligence, aptitude, and achievement instruments) are related to peer nominations of creativity.   While these results can be interpreted as generally consistent with studies on adult populations, the findings that the creative group was significantly higher on *cyclothymia,* while the non-creatives were higher on *schizothymia,* contradicts replicated results with adults who have been described as withdrawn or individualistic and have themselves said they preferred individual pursuits as children.

A recent study by Torrance (1959d), in which he attempted to explore some of the relationships between talkativeness and creative thinking, may help resolve the apparent contradiction. He reported that in the first grade, those children perceived as not speaking out their ideas tend to be more frequently seen as having good ideas, more frequently chosen as friends, higher on a measure of spontaneous flexibility, more intelligent, and higher on a nonverbal measure of creativity. This pattern gradually begins to shift, and by the fourth grade, the highly talkative individuals are more frequently perceived as having good ideas and receive more friendship choices. Thus, highly talkative children tend to earn higher scores on the verbal test of creativity, but not on the nonverbal measure. Torrance's results suggested that a sociometric criterion will select children with well-developed and exercised verbal abilities who are not necessarily more creative than many of their peers. A wide range of issues concerning the development of creativity in children is discussed in a paper by Lowenfeld (1959).

Critical overview

What is creativity? Creativity has been viewed as a normally distributed trait; as such its investigation has proceeded in an attempt to find product criteria from which the presence or absence of the trait in an individual could be inferred. Creativity has been viewed as the outcome of a complex of aptitude traits; as such its investigation has proceeded in an attempt to demonstrate the presence of such traits through factor analysis and to develop measuring instruments. Creativity has been viewed as a process culminating in a new thought or insight; as such its investigation has proceeded by introspective reporting, or investigator observation of the temporal sequence. Creativity has been described as a style of life, the personality in action; as such its investigation has been concerned with personality descriptions and assessment of people believed to be creative and investigation of motives for creativity.

All of the possible emphases within the study of creativity require no justification other than noting that each is capable of making important contributions. It would seem, however, that data reported by Taylor, Smith, and Ghiselin (1959), which indicated a very low degree of association among the many possible product criteria, argue against the likelihood of a product approach providing a comprehensive understanding of creativity.   Crutchfield's (1961) discussion of the creative process should be helpful to those attempting experimental studies.   His explanation of illumination will require careful study in the light of recent reports (see Spielberger, 1962) which suggest that the examiner's awareness of the subject's awareness may be a function of the extent of the postexperimental interview.   Difficulty may arise when investigators, working within one area of emphases, with one explicit or implied definition and set of criteria, lose sight of the inherent limitations of their choices.   The point can perhaps be illustrated by a reconsideration of the relationship between creativity and intelligence.

The studies by Getzels and Jackson (1959) and Torrance (1959e) indicated that measured intellectual ability and measured creative ability are by no means synonymous.   Torrance presented additional data which indicated that in his sample, using only the Wechsler Intelligence Scale for Children, to determine giftedness would have excluded 70% of the children placing in the upper 20% on the creativity measures.   The same ratios obtain using other measures of intelligence.   Meer and Stein (1955), Barron (1961), and MacKinnon (1961) agree essentially that while there is a correlation over the entire ranges of intelligence and creativity, the magnitude of the correlation varies greatly at different levels of intelligence.   Meer and Stein cite the ninety-fifth percentile, Barron an IQ of 120, as the approximate point above which intelligence is unimportant for creativity. The point that needs to be stressed is that these data are in a sense arbitrary: intelligence is not performance on a test; creativity is more than test performance or being judged as creative.   What is needed for the understanding of the relationship between creativity and intelligence is not only data at the correlational level, but conceptual reorganization as well.   Just as the choice of a series of Guilford tests or judgment procedures implies one definition of creativity, the choice of an intelligence test implies one of many possible definitions of intelligence.   I. Taylor (1959), for example, believes intelligence to be an invention of Western culture, which stresses how fast relatively unimportant problems can be solved without making errors.   He feels that another culture might choose to measure intelligence in a way more congruent with a high level of creativity.

For these reasons Guilford has attempted to employ a wide variety of criterion measures, grouped by factor analysis, and study relationships among the factors.

One could, however, select criterion measures on the basis of theoretical constructs and still pay careful attention to the predictive efficacy of the criterion and compare its predictive ability with other possible selection criteria.   This author agrees with Guilford that what is needed is better understanding of the nature of intellect but does not agree that factor analysis presents the best way of defining one's constructs. The factor analytic approach does not solve the problem of how well the measuring instrument is sensitive to variations in the construct its user believes it to measure. It does not seem that factor analysis will, itself, enrich basic understanding of creative phenomena. Required are not only data at a correlational level, but a developmental understanding as well, and also an understanding of different situations where different correlations are obtained between the same criteria.

If the choice is made to select subjects on conceptual rather than factor analytic bases it would seem that the investigator should attempt in some manner to isolate the contribution of a single criterion choice. The point to be made can perhaps best be seen in the work reported by Barron and MacKinnon. Their studies utilized a compound criterion in the selection of subjects: creative, effective individuals. The criteria of creativity in all cases were judgments clearly the most carefully collected, reliable of all those reported, but judgments nonetheless. The reports by Harmon (1958) and D. Taylor (1958) indicated that judges' ratings of creativity seem heavily determined by the productivity of the individual. Note that the self-descriptions of productive scientists reported by VanZelst and Kerr (1954) are very similar to the self-descriptions of creative individuals reported by Gough, Harmon, and MacKinnon. While it is crucial that creative, productive people be studied as such, it must be kept in mind that the portion of the reported findings attributable to creativity cannot be separated from that portion attributable to that which makes for productivity, and that which leads to being seen by judges as creative. It is possible, and perhaps we are now readly to utilize personality and stylistic modes as criterion variables. In such an approach our criterion variables might be tolerance for or seeking of ambiguity, openness to experience, childlike traits, self-actualization or expression, internal frames of evaluation, or independence of judgment, to name but a few theoretically based descriptive concepts which appear again and again in the literature and deserve further investigation. The important questions would then become: how do these cognitive, stylistic, or motivational modes of interacting with one's environment develop? What are the environmental, interpersonal, and intrapersonal conditions that tend to facilitate or discourage them? How in turn are these factors related at different age levels to behavior which is judged to be creative, effective, and productive? In no sense would this approach solve the problem of using judgments. The argument is not that this approach corrects or circumvents most of the problems inherent in other approaches. However, it is my belief that the use of theoretically derived personality factors as criterion variables has, because of its own inherent difficulties, been neglected, yet hold most promise of providing a functional developmental understanding of creativity.

Summary

In this review of the psychological study of creativity there are four emphases; products, process, measurement, and personality. Three main issues concern questions of: definition and criteria, the process viewed temporally, and necessary personal and environmental conditions. The relationship between creativity and intelligence is discussed to illustrate the need for conceptual reorganization as well as correlational data. We should now be able to utilize personality and stylistic modes as criterion variables and to study how these factors are related at different age levels to behavior that is judged to be creative. This approach holds promise for providing a functional, developmental understanding of creativity.

References

Abraham, K. The influence of oral erotism on character formation. In, *Selected papers of Karl Abraham.* (Trans. by D. Bryan & A. Strachey) London: Hogarth Press, 1949. Pp. 393–406.

Adkins, Margaret M., Cobb, Elizabeth A., Miller, R. B., Sanford, R. W., Stewart, Ann H., Aub, J. C., Burke, Bertha, Nathanson, I. T., Stuart, H. C., & Towne, Lois. Physique, personality, and scholarship. *Monogr. Soc. Res. Child Develpm.*, 1943, 8(1, Ser. No. 34).

Adler, A. *The practice and theory of individual psychology.* New York: Harcourt, Brace, 1927.

Allport, G. W. The functional autonomy of motives. *Amer. J. Psychol.*, 1937, 50, 141–156.

Arnold, J. F. Creativity in engineering. In P. Smith (Ed.), *Creativity.* New York: Hastings House, 1959. Pp. 33–46.

Barron, F. Personality style and perceptual choice. *J. Pers.*, 1952, 20, 385–401.

Barron, F. Complexity-simplicity as a personality dimension. *J. abnorm. soc. Psychol.*, 1953, 48, 162–172. (a)

Barron, F. Some personality correlates of independence of judgment. *J. Pers.*, 1953, 21, 287–297. (b)

Barron, F. The disposition towards originality. In C. Taylor (Ed.), *The 1955 University of Utah research conference on the identification of creative scientific talent.* Salt Lake City: Univer. Utah Press, 1956. Pp. 156–170.

Barron, F. The needs for order and for disorder as motives in creative activity. In C. Taylor (Ed.), *The 1957 University of Utah research conference on the identification of creative scientific talent.* Salt Lake City: Univer. Utah Press, 1958. Pp. 119–128.

Barron, F.   Creative vision and expression in writing and painting.   In, *Conference on the creative person.*   Berkeley: University of California, Institute of Personality Assessment and Research, 1961.   Ch. 2.

Barron, F., & Welsh, G. S.   Artistic perception as a possible factor in personality style: Its measurement by a figure preference test.   *J. Psychol.,* 1952, *33,* 199–203.

Bédard, R. J.   *Creativity in the arts, literature, science, and engineering: A bibliography of French contributions.*   (Creativity Research Exchange Bulletin No. 10) Princeton, N.J.: Educational Testing Service, 1959.

Bédard, R. J.   *Creativity in the arts, literature, science, and engineering: A bibliography of Italian contributions.*   (Creativity Research Exchange Bulletin No. 9) Princeton, N.J.: Educational Testing Service, 1960.

Bellack, L.   Creativity: Some random notes to a systematic consideration.   *J. proj. Tech.,* 1958, *22,* 363–380.

Bergler, E.   On a five-layer structure in sublimation.   *Psychoanal. Quart.,* 1945, *14,* 76–97.

Bergler, E.   Psychoanalysis of writers and of literary productivity.   In G. Roheim (Ed.), *Psychoanalysis and the social sciences.*   Vol. 1.   New York: International Universities Press, 1947.   Pp. 247–296.

Bischler, W.   Intelligence and higher mental functions.   *Psychoanal. Quart.,* 1937, *6,* 277–307.

Bloom, B. S.   Report on creativity research at the University of Chicago.   In C. Taylor (Ed.), *The 1955 University of Utah research conference on the identification of creative scientific talent.*   Salt Lake City: University of Utah Press, 1956.   Pp. 182–194.

Brill, A. A.   Poetry as an oral outlet.   *Psychoanal. Rev.,* 1931, *18,* 357–378.

Bychowski, G.   Metapsychology of artistic creation.   *Psychoanal. Quart.,* 1951, *20,* 592–602.

Cattell, R. B.   The personality and motivation of the researcher from measurements of contemporaries and from bibliography.   In C. Taylor (Ed.), *The 1959 University of Utah research conference on the identification of creative scientific talent.*   Salt Lake City: Univer. Utah Press, 1959.   Pp. 77–93.

Chassell, L. M.   Tests for originality.   *J. educ. Psychol.,* 1916, *7,* 317–329.

Chorness, M. H.   An interim report on creativity research.   In C. Taylor (Ed.), *The 1955 University of Utah research conference on the identification of creative scientific talent.*   Salt Lake City: Univer. Utah Press, 1956.   Pp. 132–153.

Crutchfield, R.   The creative process.   In, *Conference on the creative person.*   Berkeley: University of California, Institute of Personality Assessment and Research, 1961.   Ch. 6.

Dashiell, J. F.   *Fundamentals of general psychology.*   New York: Houghton Mifflin, 1931.

Deri, F.   On sublimation.   *Psychoanal. Quart.,* 1939, *8,* 325–334.

Drevdahl, J. E. Factors of importance for creativity. *J. clin. Psychol.*, 1956, *12*, 21–26.

Ehrenzweig, A. The origin of the scientific and heroic urge. *Int. J. Psychoanal.*, 1949, *30*, 108–123.

Fairbairn, W. R. D. Prolegomena to a psychology of art. *Brit. J. Psychol.*, 1938, *28*, 288–303.

Freud, S. *Three contributions to the theory of sex.* New York: Nervous & Mental Disease Publishing Company, 1910.

Freud, S. "Civilized" sexual morality and modern nervousness. (Orig. publ. 1908) In, *Collected papers.* Vol. 2. (Trans. by J. Riviere) London: Hogarth Press, 1924. Pp. 76–99.

Freud, S. *Civilization and its discontents.* (Trans. by J. Riviere) New York: Cope & Smith, 1930.

Freud, S. The relation of the poet to day-dreaming. (Orig. publ. 1908) In, *Collected papers.* Vol. 4. (Trans. by J. Riviere) London: Hogarth Press, 1948. Pp. 173–183.

Fromm, E. The creative attitude. In H. Anderson (Ed.), *Creativity and its cultivation.* New York: Harper, 1959. Pp. 44–54.

Gamble, A. O. Suggestions for future research. In C. Taylor (Ed.), *The 1959 University of Utah research conference on the identification of creative scientific talent.* Salt Lake City: Univer. Utah Press, 1959. Pp. 292–297.

Gerry, R., DeVeau, L., & Chorness, M. *A review of some recent research in the field of creativity and the examination of an experimental creativity workshop.* (Proj. No. 56–24) Lackland Air Force Base, Tex.: Training Analysis and Development Division, 1957.

Getzels, J. W., & Jackson, P. W. The highly intelligent and the highly creative adolescent: A summary of some research findings. In C. Taylor (Ed.), *The 1959 University of Utah research conference on the identification of creative scientific talent.* Salt Lake City: Univer. Utah Press, 1959. Pp. 46–57.

Getzels, J. W., & Jackson, P. W. *Creativity and intelligence: Explorations with gifted children.* New York: Wiley, 1962.

Ghiselin, B. The creative process and its relation to the identification of creative talent. In C. Taylor (Ed.), *The 1955 University of Utah research conference on the identification of creative scientific talent.* Salt Lake City: Univer. Utah Press, 1956. Pp. 195–203.

Ghiselin, B. Ultimate criteria for two levels of creativity. In C. Taylor (Ed.), *The 1957 University of Utah research conference on the identification of creative scientific talent.* Salt Lake City: Univer. Utah Press, 1958. Pp. 141–155.

Golann, S. E. The creativity motive. Unpublished doctoral dissertation, University of North Carolina, 1961.

Golann, S. E. The creativity motive. *J. Pers.*, 1962, *30*, 588–600.

Goldstein, K. *The organism.* New York: American Book, 1939.

Gough, H. G.   Stylistic variations in the self-views and work attitudes of a sample of professional research scientists.   Paper read at Western Psychological Association, Monterey, California, April 1958.

Gough, H. G.   Techniques for identifying the creative research scientist. In, *Conference on the creative person.*   Berkeley: University of California, Institute of Personality Assessment and Research, 1961.   Ch. 3.

Grotjahn, M.   *Beyond laughter.*   New York: McGraw-Hill, 1957.

Guilford, J. P.   The relation of intellectual factors to creative thinking in science.   In C. Taylor (Ed.), *The 1955 University of Utah research conference on the identification of creative scientific talent.*   Salt Lake City: Univer. Utah Press, 1956.   Pp. 69–95.

Guilford, J. P.   Creative abilities in the arts.   *Psychol. Rev.*, 1957, 64, 110–118.

Guilford, J. P.   Intellectual resources and their values as seen by scientists. In C. Taylor (Ed.), *The 1959 University of Utah research conference on the identification of creative scientific talent.*   Salt Lake City: Univer. Utah Press, 1959.   Pp. 128–149.   (a)

Guilford, J. P.   Traits of creativity.   In H. Anderson (Ed.), *Creativity and its cultivation.*   New York: Harper, 1959.   Pp. 142–161.   (b)

Guilford, J. P., Kettner, N. W., & Christensen, P. R.   A factor-analytic study across the domains of reasoning, creativity, and evaluation: I. Hypotheses and description of tests.   *U. Sth. Calif. Psychol. Lab. Rep.*, 1954, No. 11.

Guilford, J. P., Kettner, N. W., & Christensen, P. R.   A factor analytic study across the domains of reasoning, creativity and evaluation: II. Administration of tests and analysis of results.   *U. Sth. Calif. Psychol. Lab. Rep.*, 1956, No. 16.

Hadamard, J.   *An essay on the psychology of invention in the mathematical field.*   Princeton: Princeton Univer. Press, 1945.

Harmon, L. R.   Social and technological determiners of creativity.   In C. Taylor (Ed.), *The 1955 University of Utah research conference on the identification of creative scientific talent.*   Salt Lake City: Univer. Utah Press, 1956.   Pp. 42–52.

Harmon, L. R.   The development of a criterion of scientific competence. In C. Taylor (Ed.), *The 1957 University of Utah conference on the identification of creative scientific talent.*   Salt Lake City: Univer. Utah Press, 1958.   Pp. 82–97.

Harris, R. A.   Creativity in marketing.   In P. Smith (Ed.), *Creativity.* New York: Hastings House, 1959.   Pp. 143–166.

Helson, Ravenna.   Creativity, sex, and mathematics.   In, *Conference on the creative person.*   Berkeley: University of California, Institute of Personality Assessment and Research, 1961.   Ch. 4.

Kettner, N. W., Guilford, J. P., Christensen, P. R.   A factor analytic study across the domains of reasoning, creativity, and evaluation.   *Psychol. Monogr.*, 1959, 73(9, Whole No. 479).

Kohut, H.   Observations on the psychological functions of music.   *J. Amer. Psychoanal. Ass.*, 1957, 5, 389–407.

Kris, E. *Psychoanalytic explorations in art.* New York: International Universities Press, 1952.

Lee, H. B. On the esthetic states of mind. *Psychiatry,* 1947, *10,* 281–306.

Lee, H. B. Spirituality and beauty in artistic experience. *Psychoanal. Quart.,* 1948, *17,* 507–523.

Lee, H. B. The values of order and vitality in art. In G. Roheim (Ed.), *Psychoanalysis and the social sciences.* Vol. 2. New York: International Universities Press, 1950. Pp. 231–274.

Levey, H. B. A critique of the theory of sublimation. *Psychiatry,* 1939, 2, 239–270.

Levey, H. B. A theory concerning free creation in the inventive arts. *Psychiatry,* 1940, 3, 229–293.

Lowenfeld, V. *Educational implications of creativity research in the arts.* (Creativity Research Exchange Bulletin No. 8) Princeton, N.J.: Educational Testing Service, 1959.

MacKinnon, D. W. The study of creativity and creativity in architects. In, *Conference on the creative person.* Berkeley: University of California, Institute of Personality Assessment and Research, 1961. Ch. 1 & 5.

McPherson, J. H. A proposal for establishing ultimate criteria for measuring creative output. In C. Taylor (Ed.), *The 1955 University of Utah research conference on the identification of creative scientific talent.* Salt Lake City: Univer. Utah Press, 1956. Pp. 62–68.

Maslow, A. H. Creativity in self-actualizing people. In H. Anderson (Ed.), *Creativity and its cultivation.* New York: Harper, 1959. Pp. 83–95.

Mattil, E. L. A study to determine the relationship between the creative products of children, aged 11–14, and their adjustments. Unpublished doctoral dissertation, Pennsylvania State University, 1953.

May, R. The nature of creativity. In H. Anderson (Ed.), *Creativity and its cultivation.* New York: Harper, 1959. Pp. 55–68.

Meer, B., & Stein, M. I. Measures of intelligence and creativity. *J. Psychol.,* 1955, *39,* 117–126.

Mooney, R. L. *Classification of items in "A preliminary listing of indices of creative behavior."* Columbus: Ohio State University, Bureau of Educational Research, 1953. (a)

Mooney, R. L. *A preliminary listing of indices of creative behavior.* Columbus: Ohio State University, Bureau of Educational Research, 1953. (b)

Münsterberg, Elizabeth, & Mussen, P. H. The personality structures of art students. *J. Pers.,* 1953, *21,* 457–466.

Murphy, G. *Personality: A biosocial approach to origins and structure.* New York: Harper, 1947.

Murphy, G. *Human potentialities.* New York: Basic Books, 1958.

Myden, W. Interpretation and evaluation of certain personality characteristics involved in creative production. *Percept. mot. Skills,* 1959, *9,* 139–158.

Rank, O., & Sachs, H.   *The significance of psychoanalysis for the mental sciences.*   Washington, D.C.: Nervous & Mental Disease Publishing Company, 1916.

Reid, J. B., King, F. J., & Wickwire, Pat.   Cognitive and other personality characteristics of creative children.   *Psychol. Rep.,* 1959, *5,* 729–737.

Rickman, J.   On the nature of ugliness and the creative impulse.   (Orig. publ. 1940) In W. Clifford & M. Scott (Eds.), *Selected contributions to psychoanalysis.*   London: Hogarth Press, 1957.   Pp. 68–89.

Roe, Anne.   Artists and their work.   *J. Pers.,* 1946, *15,* 1–40.

Roe, Anne.   Psychological examinations of eminent biologists.   *J. consult. Psychol.,* 1949, *13,* 225–246.

Roe, Anne.   A psychological study of eminent biologists.   *Psychol. Monogr.,* 1951, *65*(14, Whole No. 331).

Roe, Anne.   *The making of a scientist.*   New York: Dodd-Mead, 1952.

Roe, Anne.   A psychological study of eminent psychologists and anthropologists and a comparison with biological and physical scientists.   *Psychol. Monogr.,* 1953, *67*(2, Whole No. 352).

Rogers, C. R.   Toward a theory of creativity.   *Etc.,* 1954, *11,* 249–260.

Rogers, C. R.   What it means to become a person.   In C. Moustakas (Ed.), *The self.*   New York: Harper, 1956.   Pp. 195–211.

Rosen, J. C.   The Barron-Welsh art scale as a predictor of originality and level of ability among artists.   *J. appl. Psychol.,* 1955, *39,* 366–367.

Sachs, H.   *The creative unconscious.*   (2nd ed.) Cambridge, Mass.: Science-Art Publishers, 1951.

Schachtel, E. G.   *Metamorphosis.*   New York: Basic Books, 1959.

Sharpe, Ella F.   Certain aspects of sublimation and delusion.   *Int. J. Psychoanal.,* 1930, *11,* 12–23.

Sharpe, Ella F.   Similar and divergent unconscious determinants underlying the sublimations of pure art and pure science.   In M. Brierly (Ed.), *Collected papers on psychoanalysis.*   London: Hogarth Press, 1950.   Pp. 137–154.

Spielberger, C. D.   The role of awareness in verbal conditioning.   *J. Pers.,* 1962, *30,* 73–101.

Stein, M. I.   Creativity and culture.   *J. Psychol.,* 1953, *36,* 311–322.

Stein, M. I.   A transactional approach to creativity.   In C. Taylor (Ed.), *The 1955 University of Utah research conference on the identification of creative scientific talent.*   Salt Lake City: Univer. Utah Press, 1956.   Pp. 171–181.

Stein, M., & Heinze, Shirley.   *Creativity and the individual.*   Glencoe, Ill.: Free Press, 1960.

Stein, M. I., & Meer, B.   Perceptual organization in a study of creativity.   *J. Psychol.,* 1954, *37,* 39–43.

Taylor, C. (Ed.)   *The 1959 University of Utah research conference on the identification of creative scientific talent.*   Salt Lake City: Univer. Utah Press, 1959.

Taylor, C. W., Smith, W. R., & Ghiselin, B. Analysis of multiple criteria of creativity and productivity of scientists. In C. Taylor (Ed.), *The 1959 University of Utah research conference on the identification of creative scientific talent.* Salt Lake City: Univer. Utah Press, 1959. Pp. 5–28.

Taylor, D. W. Variables related to creativity and productivity among men in two research laboratories. In C. Taylor (Ed.), *The 1957 University of Utah research conference on the identification of creative scientific talent.* Salt Lake City: Univ. Utah Press, 1958. Pp. 20–54.

Taylor, D. W. Thinking and creativity. *Ann. N.Y. Acad. Sci.,* 1960, *91,* 108–127.

Taylor, D. W. Environment and creativity. In, *Conference on the creative person.* Berkeley: University of California, Institute of Personality Assessment and Research, 1961. Ch. 8.

Taylor, I. A. The nature of the creative process. In P. Smith (Ed.), *Creativity.* New York: Hastings House, 1959. Pp. 51–82.

Torrance, E. P. *Sex-role identification and creative thinking.* Minneapolis: University of Minnesota, Bureau of Educational Research, 1958.

Torrance, E. P. *Explorations in creative thinking in the early school years: II. An experiment in training and motivation.* Minneapolis: University of Minnesota, Bureau of Educational Research, 1959. (a)

Torrance, E. P. *Explorations in creative thinking in the early school years: V. An experimental study of peer sanctions against highly creative children.* Minneapolis: University of Minnesota, Bureau of Educational Research, 1959. (b)

Torrance, E. P. *Explorations in creative thinking in the early school years: VI. Highly intelligent and highly creative children in a laboratory school.* Minneapolis: University of Minnesota, Bureau of Educational Research, 1959. (c)

Torrance, E. P. *Explorations in creative thinking in the early school years: VII. Talkativeness and creative thinking.* Minneapolis: University of Minnesota, Bureau of Educational Research, 1959. (d)

Torrance, E. P. Explorations in creative thinking in the early school years: A progress report. In C. Taylor (Ed.), *The 1959 University of Utah research conference on the identification of creative scientific talent.* Salt Lake City: Univer. Utah Press, 1959. Pp. 58–71. (e)

Torrance, E. P. *Changing reactions of girls in grades four through six to tasks requiring creative scientific thinking.* Minneapolis: University of Minnesota, Bureau of Educational Research, 1960. (a)

Torrance, E. P. *A collection of ideas for developing the creative thinking abilities through the language arts.* Minneapolis: University of Minnesota, Bureau of Educational Research, 1960. (b)

Torrance, E. P. *Educational achievement of the highly intelligent and the highly creative: Eight partial replications of the Getzels-Jackson study.* Minneapolis: University of Minnesota, Bureau of Educational Research, 1960. (c)

Torrance, E. P.   *Social stress in homogeneous and heterogeneous groups.* Minneapolis: University of Minnesota, Bureau of Educational Research, 1960.   (d)

Torrance, E. P., Baker, F. B., & Bowers, J. E.   *Explorations in creative thinking in the early school years: IV.   Manipulation of objects and inventiveness.*   Minneapolis: University of Minnesota, Bureau of Educational Research, 1959.

Torrance, E. P., & Radig, H. J.   *The Ask and Guess Test: Scoring manual and rationale.*   Minneapolis: University of Minnesota, Bureau of Educational Research, 1959.

VanZelst, R. H., & Kerr, W. A.   Personality self-assessment of scientific and technical personnel.   *J. appl. Psychol.,* 1954, *38,* 145–147.

Wallas, G.   *The art of thought.*   New York: Harcourt, Brace, 1926.

Welsh, G. S.   A projective figure-preference test for diagnosis of psychopathology: I.   A preliminary investigation.   Unpublished doctoral dissertation, University of Minnesota, 1949.

Welsh, G. S.   *Preliminary manual: Welsh Figure Preference Test.*   (Res. ed.) Palo Alto, Calif.: Consulting Psychologists Press, 1959.   (a)

Welsh, G. S.   *Welsh Figure Preference Test.*   (Res. ed.) Palo Alto, Calif.: Consulting Psychologists Press, 1959.   (b)

Woodworth, R. S., & Schlosberg, H.   *Experimental psychology.*   (2nd ed.) New York: Holt, 1954.

Yacorzynski, G. K.   The nature of man.   In F. L. K. Hsu (Ed.), *Aspects of culture and personality.*   New York: Abelard-Schuman, 1954.   Pp. 173–186.

C   Psychopathology

The final group of readings in this section also deals with specific patterns of adjustment but the patterns described here are generally considered pathological or deviant.   The study of the abnormal or pathological is extremely important to an understanding of the adjustment process.   By focusing our attention on the abnormal, we hope to develop methods by which maladjusted behavior can be decreased and adjusted behavior increased.   In addition, those members of our society who behave in ways which seem atypical, ineffective, or disturbed enable us to learn about the conditions likely to lead to adjustment difficulties.

The initial steps in the study of psychopathology are those of distinguishing between the normal and abnormal and classifying the abnormal into distinctive groups.   This procedure is referred to as diagnosis.   However, in order for diagnoses to be useful in helping us prevent and alleviate adjustment difficulties, the specific groupings or classifications should be based on more than the differential descriptions of the ways people behave.   We wish our diagnostic terms to be more than mere labels which sort individuals into groups.   An ideal diagnosis should do the following: (1) provide us with a description of the difficulty; (2) give us an understanding of the factors which led up to it; (3) predict the consequences or future course of the difficulty; and (4) inform us of methods by which we can remedy, control, or alter these consequences.

Our present diagnostic terms hardly approach this ideal. All the problems associated with research methods, terminology, and personality theory make the task difficult. Of particular significance in the area of psychopathology is the designation of meaningful concepts. In no other area of psychological inquiry have the difficulties of developing clear and useful concepts been highlighted so extensively. Numerous investigations have found that the agreements between diagnoses made by different workers are extremely low. Too often the specific diagnosis made by a psychiatrist, psychologist, or social worker depends more on his own theoretical and personal predilections than on the patient's condition. Even when different workers agree, the diagnostic classification provides little or no information about treatment techniques likely to be effective. Methods of treatment which are beneficial for many pathological conditions are not necessarily related to a given diagnosis. Our present diagnostic terms also encourage overgeneralizing from the observations we make and oversimplifying the individual's condition. The tendency to overgeneralize and to assume that one basic factor or entity determines pathological behavior promotes serious limitations in our efforts to deal with these conditions.

Many of the problems associated with our diagnostic efforts can be traced to historical influences. Since early times man has attempted to explain behavior by postulating that one basic, all-influencing force compels us to act in a given way. Whether this force was attributed to a mystical being or to some internal factor, it represented man's attempt to explain everything about himself in one easy sweep, i.e., with one basic idea. As science progressed, the notion was introduced that all psychological characteristics, including feelings, thoughts, and actions, are centered in the brain. Consequently it was thought that psychological disturbances must be caused by disturbances in the brain. This formulation, originally proposed by Hypocrates and expanded in the last century by Kraepelin, undoubtedly represented advanced thinking over the mystical connections drawn between behavior pathology and witchcraft. It should be noted, however, that attributing pathology to brain disturbance continues to involve the belief that one factor—in this case one part of the body— can explain the psychological characteristics of man. In addition, the brain hypothesis attempts to explain psychopathology solely on the basis of anatomy and physiology and in so doing, models itself along the lines of medicine's approach to disease. This approach equates a psychological disturbance with a state of disease and assumes that the disturbance is the result of an anomaly in the structure of the organism which causes a specific pattern of symptoms. Kraepelin attempted to classify pathology by seeking and labeling a unique feature of each condition. His classifications and the disease-entity logic on which they are based constitute the major approach to formal diagnosis today and often lead us to ignore the significance of motives, conflicts, experience, and learning in psychopathology.

Our present diagnostic concepts for psychopathology involve no systematic scheme of classification. Sometimes diagnostic terms represent a summary description of the individual's behavior (*depression, obsessive-compulsive, anxiety neurosis*); sometimes they are differentiated on the basis of a hypothesized cause (*psychosomatic illness, involutional melancholia, alcoholism*); and sometimes a term is used chiefly because it has become linked traditionally with the intensity of disturbance or with one or two predominant characteristics (*schizophrenia, manic-depressive psychosis, epilepsy*). In almost every case our terms fall short of the ideal and can hardly deserve to be called diagnostic concepts. For the most part diagnosticians today use the formal classifications of disorders as rough, summary descriptions of the individual's most apparent difficulty. In actual practice they have found it more fruitful to evaluate the individual patient's condition by considering the particular adjustment problems he is having, his typical approach to them, and the consequences of his actions. In other words, in order to make a useful diagnosis of an individual's adjustment difficulties, one must consider a complex of variables rather than a single aspect which the disease-entity approach suggests.

The first four papers in this section represent notable efforts to bring some order to the literature of behavior pathology by focusing on a variety of characteristics of disturbed behavior. Upon reviewing data both from the clinical observation of disturbed human beings and from the experimental investigation of pathology in animals, Wilson concludes that several major and similar features appear: the presence of intense anxiety, the development of stereotyped and repetitive symptoms, and fixation at an immature level. Wilson feels, therefore, that similar principles govern pathology in several species and that animal research can yield results applicable at the human level.

Another effort to integrate psychopathology is reported in the paper by Lorr, Bishop, and McNair. The authors adopt the view that the diagnosis of the "milder disorders" (nonpsychotic psychiatric patients) should be based largely on interpersonal styles. Support for their position is in the theoretic formulations of Horney, Fromm, Sullivan, and many others. Upon employing a statistical procedure whereby clusters of similar interpersonal behavior patterns may be identified, Lorr *et al.* found the four patient types reported in their paper.

Wittenborn's paper is focused on psychoses rather than on neuroses. In addition, his interest is in providing a description of the full range of psychotic symptomatology rather than a description of interpersonal characteristics alone. The analysis reported in his paper gives us some sense of the classic dimensions along which psychotic individuals vary.

The next paper consists of a report of research by Jenkins, whose intent was to find a basis for diagnostic classification of children based on behavior symptoms. His research identified five symptom clusters. Jenkins extended his study by investigating the relationships between family background and membership in various symptomatic groups.

The final paper in this section deals with the problems of suicide, a topic which has generated a good deal of attention in recent years. Suicidal impulses have come to be recognized as more frequent than supposed earlier, and many communities have organized suicide-prevention bureaus for the purpose of providing help to individuals experiencing suicidal crises. Braaten's paper reports a summary of his research on suicide in a college population and is notable for his effort to introduce discriminations among suicides and suicidal individuals.

The papers in this group by no means cover all forms of psychopathology. Not included are the psychosomatic conditions (*ulcers, hypertension, allergies,* etc.), abnormal conditions related to disorders of the central nervous system (*general paresis, Huntington's chorea, multiple sclerosis,* etc.), pathological states associated with specific deviant behaviors (*drug addiction, alcoholism, sexual deviations,* etc.), and intellectual retardation (*cretinism, mongolism, microcephaly,* etc.). Descriptions of these can be found in any standard text in abnormal psychology.

Ronald S. Wilson   **ON BEHAVIOR PATHOLOGY** *

Investigation of behavior pathology has a long heritage, but perhaps two significant trends can be nominated as having substantially in-

* From Ronald S. Wilson, "On Behavior Pathology," *Psychol. Bull.* 1963, *60,* 130–146. Reprinted by permission of the author and the Managing Editor, the American Psychological Association.

creased our understanding of functional disorders since the turn of the century. On the one hand, the advent of psychoanalysis laid the foundation for a dynamic theory of human pathology, and in a broader sense it recast the traditional conceptions of personality into a more kinetic form. Emotion, conflict, and anxiety received increasing emphasis as basic operators in human behavior, and disturbances in emotional relationships became the focal point for interpreting behavior disorders. The theory was fashioned from data secured in the therapeutic treatment room, but as child psychiatry and clinical psychology developed, the domain of data expanded markedly and broadened the empirical framework on which the theory rested.

The transition from an organic view of pathology to a dynamic functional view was of inestimable significance for treatment and diagnosis. Nevertheless, the concepts introduced to account for pathological phenomena were not always clearly defined or open to verification; and some pointed criticisms were raised about the subjective bias of both patient and analyst that might enter into the interpretation of data.

The second major trend is of somewhat more recent vintage, dating from Pavlov's investigation of conditioned reflexes, and it can be referred to as the experimental investigation of behavior pathology. It is represented by the work of Gantt and Liddell on experimental neurosis, by Masserman's work on conflict, Maier on frustration, and the work of Solomon and his colleagues on traumatic avoidance learning. Although the conceptual schemata differ, these experiments share common properties in terms of the behavior disturbances produced, and within the limits of design differences they generally corroborate one another. As will subsequently become evident, the major features of pathology revealed in these studies also correspond to several important features of human pathology as seen in the clinic. Yet this body of research, which clearly satisfies the criteria of being objective and controlled, has not been embraced by clinicians, mainly because its significance for human pathology is somewhat obscure; and the experimentalists themselves have made only nominal efforts to integrate their results with clinical data.

The purpose of the present essay is to focus upon points of common agreement between the clinical and experimental areas, and to suggest that the same principles apply to both areas. To this end a selected group of clinical studies will be reviewed in an effort to establish some basic parameters that cut across the traditional categories of behavior pathology. Subsequently the experimental literature will be examined for concepts and empirical laws that will anchor our clinical concepts more securely. The final section will touch briefly on the implications of this review for the analysis of behavior pathology.

Clinical studies of human pathology

Kubie on neurosis

In an early paper Kubie (1941) analyzed the characteristics of neurotic behavior in search of a general principle that would unify the commonly recognized symptoms. He proposed the principle of *repetitiveness,* or more particularly, that distortions in the normal process of repetitiveness constituted the core of neurotic behavior. Kubie argued that the organization of the central nervous system provides for sustained impulses through the operation of open and closed circuits; consequently, the psychological development of the organism is rooted in repetition of experience. Motivated by diffuse tension, the infant responds with random efforts which gradually evolve into more economical forms until they finally become specifically goal directed. The acquisition of skills depends upon endless but flexible and spontaneous repetition of motor activity.

While these skills are developed primarily to relieve states of tension, they soon acquire secondary meaning as rewarding activities in their own right. Functions such as walking, talking, manipulating objects, exploring and mastering new situations are practiced time and again because the child is highly gratified by the exercise of these new functions. Great emotional significance attaches to these skills, either of delight and satisfaction in the case of uninterrupted practice, or of tension and rage where such activities are interfered with.

Kubie believes that frustration intervenes most markedly at this point, for the repetitive behavior of the child may stimulate inhibitory controls from his parents. When punishment or threats are applied to curtail such behavior, the child responds with rage and temper tantrums. If the parents vigorously suppress this outlet also, the stage is set for severe conflict.

It is at this point that the shift from normal flexible repetitiveness to rigid neurotic repetitiveness takes place. Successive expressions of the need are no longer modified by reward or punishment, but are cast rigidly as the only possible compromise solution of all the child feels in the conflict situation. Consequently, the repetitive act becomes irresistible to the child, and it displays a rigid intensity that eliminates flexible problem solving behavior.

In a later paper, Kubie (1954) sums up the basic distinction between normal and neurotic behavior:

[Normal] patterns of behavior, no matter how varied they may be, will have one basic characteristic in common, namely that any repetitiveness which that behavior may exhibit with respect to impulse, thought, action or feeling, or any combination of these, will be flexible, modifiable, satiable. . . . [Neurotic behavior] will have precisely opposite characteristics; it will be repetitive, obligatory, insatiable, and stereotyped (pp. 202–203).

Alexander and French (1946) are also persuaded that repetitive behavior is a prominent feature of neurosis. Drawing on extensive therapeutic contacts with neurotic patients, they summarize the basic problem as follows:

In normal development, patterns from the past undergo progressive modification. One learns from experience by correcting earlier patterns in the light of later events. When a problem becomes too disturbing to face, however, this learning process is interrupted and subsequent attempts to solve the problem must, therefore, assume the character of stereotyped repetitions of previous unsuccessful attempts to solve it. A neurosis may be defined as a series of such stereotyped reactions to problems that the patient has never solved in the past and is still unable to solve in the present (p. 76).

Frustration and schizophrenia

In behavior disturbances more severe than neurosis, similar tendencies toward rigid repetition of certain acts, regardless of their consequences, have been noted.

Jenkins (1950, 1952) has proposed that frustration carried beyond the tolerance level of the individual stimulates disorganization, withdrawal, and stereotypy. Drawing on Maier's (1949) experimental work, Jenkins attributes the schizophrenic process to profound frustration that arises chiefly in the area of interpersonal relationships. After repeated rebuffs, the schizophrenic gradually withdraws from emotional contact with other people and dwells more and more in the realm of fantasy. Efforts to establish rewarding relationships are gradually replaced by regressive, stereotyped responses that further aggravate the problem.

Jenkins (1950) finds considerable support for his position in the published clinical literature, much of which assigns a prominent role to early frustrating experiences as a causal factor in schizophrenia. Studies of the schizophrenic's family often disclose an overpowering mother who is described by such adjectives as perfectionistic, dominating, aggressive, overanxious and overprotective—the type of mother who markedly interferes with the child's growth toward independent selfhood. The point is illustrated by a sample of statements chosen more frequently by mothers of male schizophrenics (Mark, 1953).

1   A mother should make it her business to know everything her children are thinking.
2   Children should not annoy parents with their unimportant problems.
3   A watchful mother can keep her child out of all accidents.
4   A devoted mother has no time for social life.
5   Playing with a child too much will spoil him.

6   A mother has to suffer much and say little.

7   Children who take part in sex play become sex criminals when they grow up.

8   Too much affection will make a child a "softee."

Jenkins (1952) reasons that pervasive control measures invade the day-to-day experience of the child throughout a wide range of situations and "make it more than usually difficult for a child to maintain a sense of his individuality, except in the autistic withdrawal of fantasy" (p. 740).   Frustration at this stage interferes with the development of effective coping mechanisms and forces the child into regressive, stereotyped patterns of behavior.

A more phenomenological analysis of schizophrenia is offered by Guntrip (1952), who states that the primary danger for psychological development lies in early object-relationships that are frustrating for the child.   When the mother is cross, impatient, and punitive with her child, or is emotionally detached and unresponsive, the child experiences such behavior as frustrating his most important needs. Consequently the mother becomes a bad object, and "an inner psychic world is set up . . . in which one is tied to bad objects and feeling, therefore, always frustrated, hungry, angry and guilty, and profoundly anxious" (p. 348).

Guntrip argues that a bad object cannot simply be dismissed.   The most primitive reaction to early deprivation is to become pathologically attached to the object, and to continually rehearse these frustrating experiences in fantasy in an effort to make them turn out positively. They never do, though, and the schizophrenic remains fixated at a primitive level of emotional development, intensely preoccupied with problems of nurturance and support.   He senses his own needs as being overwhelming and all-consuming, capable of exhausing the resources of anyone offering a supportive relationship.   By the same token, the schizophrenic is acutely fearful of being rejected or exploited by a potentially gratifying object.   He is therefore repetitively drawn into relationships offering support, but once established, the schizophrenic finds them too threatening to be maintained.   He is terrorized by the pospect of a relationship which he perceives as mutually destructive, and his emotions are so poorly controlled that he is in constant danger of being overwhelmed by tension.

Set aside the mentalistic overtones of Guntrip's argument and it is evident that he is pointing in the same direction as Kubie and Jenkins. Frustration and deprivation in severe degree interfere with the normal course of development, and pathology is reflected in repetitive patterns of behavior and thought, in extreme tension levels, and in a freezing of emotional development, where needs of historical significance continue to plague the individual long beyond the stage they are appropriate.

There is a loose consensus here about the important features of human pathology, a grouping that is amenable to further investigation.   Since the foregoing studies have cast childhood frustration in a principal role, we turn now to a series of reports on behavior pathology in children, to see if disturbances at an early age are expressed in the same way.

Behavior problems in children

Erikson (1940, 1953) has observed that repetitive sequences in a child's play activities are often traceable to conflicts being expressed with the toys.   He suggests that play serves for the anxious child the same function as talking over problems or vicariously rehearsing them does for adults: it provides a limited sphere somewhat removed from the conflict situation in which the central features of the problem can be replayed, examined, and alternatives evaluated.   But even here anxiety may intercede if the play activities too closely parallel the real life conflict.   When the problem is of central significance to the child yet he cannot resolve it, play activities assume a repetitive, intense nature, inevitably leading to some emotional dead end and consequent play disruption.   The problem may be defensively adjusted through unconscious transformations to avoid outright recognition, but its repetitive expression in play testifies to the position of prominence it occupies in the life of the child.

More serious behavior disturbances in children have been investigated by Bettelheim (1950) and by Redl and Wineman (1951, 1952). Bettelheim's children are notable for their withdrawal, their autistic reconstruction of reality, for serious problems with such fundamental processes as eating, elimination, and sleep; and they exhibit a host of repetitive behaviors that are heavily colored with symbolic significance. The prelude to these difficulties is suggested by the social history of the children, where deprivation and rejection are recurrent themes.

Perhaps the most significant change during treatment is the gradual freeing of needs and impulses that heretofore had been drastically inhibited.   In the supportive atmosphere of the treatment center, where no restrictions are placed on regressive behavior, the child may experiment with indulging his primitive needs.   If the problem touches on nourishment and security, as it does for most of these children, regressive behavior with food occupies a prominent role.   Socialized eating habits are dispensed with in favor of manually stuffing the mouth full of food.   Demands to be spoon fed or nursed from a bottle are not uncommon.

Yet the reactivation of these needs brings about a serious anxiety reaction that the child cannot cope with.   It is particularly disruptive because his history is notably deficient of experiences wherein some behavior on his part was successful in relieving tension. Having only a limited repertoire of coping mechanisms, the child is overwhelmed by the strength of his impulses and he fears losing control of himself. As insurance he may institute compulsive rituals to protect himself from anxiety.

Behavior gradually becomes more flexible and reality-oriented as the child avails himself of unrestricted gratification. His emotional reactions are updated to conform to present circumstances, rather than being dominated by past experiences of frustration. He can enlarge his sphere of interests and more importantly, he develops inner controls to initiate and modify behavior in adaptive fashion—a series of coping mechanisms to operate on the environment and regulate impulse expression. Instead of being passively overwhelmed, the child now participates actively in growth experiences that promote a sense of confidence in his ability to manage his life.

The emphasis here upon inner controls recalls the point made by Jenkins and Kubie about the development of mastery skills—how these play a fundamental role in adjustment. Where circumstances combine to interfere with their growth, the child is seriously handicapped in his transactions with the environment and in the management of his impulses. The Pioneers of Redl and Wineman, to whom we turn next, also illustrate the point but with the unique twist of having a few mastery skills, or ego functions, overworked in the service of defense.

The children chosen for treatment by Redl and Wineman (1951, 1952) were highly aggressive and destructive, characterized by serious deficiences in behavior control. These delinquents were unable to handle reasonable amounts of tension without becoming disorganized. Fear, excitement, guilt, recall of past memories—even in minor doses these events sufficed to overwhelm the control system and stimulate violent acting out. The ego functions of appraisal, control, and delay were quickly swamped by unmanageable tension and the child's behavior exhibited regressive, stereotyped characteristics.

But in sharp contrast to their helplessness in coping with internal tension, the Pioneers exhibited a set of shrewdly developed defenses that protected their gratification outlets and insulated them from the implications of their behavior. It is exemplified by the delinquent's attempt to provoke restrictive, punitive action from adults, thereby justifying his belief that he is persecuted and is entitled to express his hatred and aggression against the persecutors. Distrust of adults is strongly rooted in early experiences of frustration and rejection, and techniques to close off interference from that quarter, to minimize potential danger to impulse expression, have been sharpened through a long history of warfare with a hostile environment. Concurrently, self-protective mechanisms develop as an armor against recognizing personal responsibility for the behavior in question. Thus fortified, the delinquent shrewdly gears his behavior to maintain free license and justify his delusional belief that all adults are out to get him. But the defensive nature of these activities is disclosed by their rigid repetitiveness even in the benign atmosphere of the treatment home, and by the appearance of regressive demands for gratification once a positive relationship with an adult is established.

Natural experiment in adult frustration

The discussion thus far has emphasized the effects of frustration during early development. However, the same mechanism is conceived to be operative under conditions of stress at all stages of maturity, although during adulthood the effects on well established behavior patterns may be less marked. In particular, stereotypy of behavior is expected as an outgrowth of extreme tension, as well as a progressive breakdown in the more highly refined behavior controls.

Hinkle and Wolff (1956) have impressively documented this process in their study of Communist indoctrination techniques. Analyzing the prisoner's experience in the hands of the Communist police, Hinkle and Wolff emphasize that he is confronted with a continuous series of frustrations. They compare the indoctrination procedure with experimental studies of frustration and observe that the reaction of the prisoner is basically similar to that of the experimental subject, with the exception that the prisoner's reaction is more all-embracing and devastating. The sequence of behavior following imprisonment runs as follows: purposeful exploratory activity; random exploration, with a general increase in motor activity; excitement, anxiety, hyperactivity; gradual subsidence of activity, with the exception of isolated repetitive acts. Such acts are endlessly repeated although they can never provide a solution. If pressure is continued long enough, the ultimate response is one of total inactivity, accompanied by strong feelings of dejection. The prisoner is unusually receptive to approval or human support (adapted from Hinkle & Wolff, 1956, p. 160).

The prison situation is unique in the degree to which it interferes with the biological and social routines of the prisoner's life. In addition, the prisoner is subjected to repeated interrogations that play upon his emotional weak points and constantly pressure him to compromise his position on an issue he may not clearly understand. Effective use is made of stress, although seldom in the form of outright torture, until the prisoner's resistance eventually decays. Behavior becomes more primitive and psychological withdrawal accompanies the development of stereotyped responses. The entire process may be understood as a reaction to acute and unremitting tension.

Common parameters

This brief survey of clincial research discloses three significant features that seem to cut across all classes of behavior pathology. There is on the one hand a rigid, intense manner of expressing symptomatic behavior, no matter what the content may be. Symptomatic behavior may be understood as a compromise activity that has been crystallized by its success in relieving tension, although it is demonstrably ineffective in securing need satisfaction. As an activity it pursues a stereotyped course and is relatively indifferent to control through reward or punishment. In form and function the symptoms may mirror a behavior pattern of historical significance, now no longer appropriate; they may express a conflict symbolically, or they may include postural and motor adjustments that bear no discernible relationship to the problem at hand.

In the second place, needs and emotions operative at the time of frustration seem to be fixated, and they furnish the individual with residual tensions that are chronologically out of step with his development in other areas. It is obvious that much surplus and subjective meaning attaches to the terms "need" and "emotion"; nevertheless, they are roughly descriptive of an internal state of affairs that exercises pressing control on the individual's behavior. The adult who is described as an oral character still maintains certain interests appropriate to an earlier phase of development, and the gratifications he seeks are thinly disguised holdovers from this period. The steady progression to mature, differentiated forms of emotional expression and impulse control is interrupted, and old problems of historical significance continue to bias all contemporary relationships. The individual cannot escape the past, and his techniques for coping with the environment likewise remain at a primitive, immature level.

The third important feature of behavior pathology is the presence of an intense anxiety reaction, and the manifold changes in behavior produced by anxiety. Due to its compelling drive properties, anxiety forces the individual into response patterns that ward off or alleviate anxiety, regardless of their adaptive value for other purposes. Precision and control give way to disorganization and panic. Flexible, goal directed adjustments are disrupted and behavior is crystallized into a stereotyped pattern. Subjectively, an anxiety reaction is accompanied by feelings of overwhelming dread and terror that are unpleasant in the extreme for the individual. His behavior is then dominated by primitive attempts to terminate the anxiety reaction and to ward off future attacks at all costs. These attempts will generally include internal defensive operations that process threatening thoughts or memories out of awareness, as well as the formation of stereotyped symptoms that forestall anxiety. Where anxiety is severe enough or is chronically sustained, it forces drastic changes in behavior of a pathological nature. From this viewpoint, anxiety appears to be the common denominator that underwrites the major features of behavior pathology.

These clinical phenomena serve as a basic point of reference for interpreting behavior pathology. But we are hindered at this stage by a certain looseness of terminology and concept, a vagueness about the exact nature and operation of these phenomena. The experimental literature on behavior pathology has made substantial inroads in this direction, and a survey of some of these studies may help to clarify the points in question.

Experimental investigations of behavior pathology

The transition from the clinic to the laboratory reveals some abrupt changes in design and procedure, as well as a shift from human to animal subjects. We shall be principally concerned with three overlapping categories of research that offer powerful concepts for interpreting human pathology. They are: frustration, traumatic avoidance learning, and experimental neurosis. While the procedures differ markedly in each case, the results uniformly reveal serious disturbances in behavior. A brief review of these studies may serve to illustrate the basic conditions that give rise to behavior pathology.

Frustration and response fixation

The most extensive work on frustration has been carried out by Maier, whose theory and experiments were reported originally in his 1949 monograph, and the theory has been extended in a more recent publication (Maier, 1956). The basic apparatus Maier uses is the Lashley jumping stand and the problem on which the animal is trained is a discrimination between two visual patterns. Once a discrimination is established, frustration is introduced by locking the two doors randomly, so that neither a position response nor a discriminated pattern response leads to reward more than 50% of the time. Maier's definition of frustration flows directly from this procedure: forcing the animal by means of an air blast or electric shock to respond to a presently insoluble problem.

Under these conditions, the jump latency increases and the animal may interpolate several abortive jumps into his response pattern. The tension under which the animal operates is reflected by the number of seizures experienced on the jumping platform. One response, usually a position response, becomes increasingly stereotyped and is routinely performed on each trial. As the stereotyped response is established, less resistance to jumping is manifest and seizures decrease; apparently it provides an outlet for tension. Once established, the response continues indefinitely. Even when the problem is made soluble again the animal does not break the pattern, although he may give evidence of recognizing what the correct response is. Short of some specialized therapeutic measures, the animal's behavior is remarkably invariant.

Maier (1956) has introduced the concept of frustration threshold to handle these data, suggesting that extreme frustration precipitates a sharp transition to massive and uniquely patterned autonomic reactions that override voluntary control. Maier reasons that tension pitched at a very high level may remove cortical inhibition of primitive neural mechanisms and facilitate gross emotional discharge in the form of seizures, tantrums, and rage. Tension functionally reverses the processes of individuation and specificity in neural control and pushes behavior towards more primitive forms. While Maier has not yet clearly coordinated these superthreshold tensions with the behavioral characteristics of frustration—response stereotypy, abnormal fixations—the evidence is strongly in favor of some mechanism by which internal tension transforms normally variable, goal oriented behavior into an immutable response pattern.

Traumatic avoidance learning

We turn now to a series of studies that have focused explicitly upon the behavior changes effected under acute pain-fear conditions. Using electric shock of just subtetanizing intensity, Solomon and his colleagues e.g., Solomon & Wynne, 1953, 1954) have traced the course of avoidance learning and explored the physiological correlates of massive pain-fear reactions mobilized by shock.

The apparatus is a shuttle box with a gridded floor, separated into two compartments by an adjustable barrier and a drop gate. The dog is placed in one compartment, the conditioned stimulus (CS) is presented, the drop gate removed, and 10 seconds later shock is administered. After a period of intense panic activity, the dog scrambles over the barrier and by so doing terminates both shock and the CS.

The basic datum is the latency of the animal's jump over the barrier, measured from the onset of the CS. The first few trials are escape trials, the animal failing to jump until shocked, but by the fifth trial the average dog has executed an avoidance response within the 10-second interval and therefore is not shocked. By definition the animal is now in the extinction phase, and the experiment is continued indefinitely to assess resistance to extinction.

These animals manifest an abrupt shift from escape to avoidance responses, and of greater significance, the jump latencies gradually *decrease* while the animal is executing successful avoidance responses. As trials cumulate, the animal jumps with increasing rapidity until a stable latency of about 1.6 seconds is reached. It should be emphasized that latencies stabilize long after the last shock is received, i.e., during the extinction phase. Solomon and Wynne (1954) conclude that fear has replaced shock as the drive, and escape from the fear producing CS serves to strengthen and move forward the jumping response.

The persistence of the jumping response is remarkable. Animals carried through 600 or more extinction trials showed no sign of extinction. But during this period when the avoidance response is being precisely executed each time, the overt signs of anxiety rapidly disappear as the dog becomes more and more stereotyped in his jumping activities. A rather casual attitude replaces the acute panic reaction manifested earlier. If, however, the dog is forcibly prevented from jumping by means of a barrier, an intense overt anxiety reaction develops immediately (Solomon, Kamin, & Wynne, 1953).

Solomon and Wynne (1954) advance a carefully reasoned argument to account for their results. Their argument is derived from two-process learning theory, but with two additional principles: anxiety conservation, and partial irreversibility of high intensity pain-fear reactions. These additions form a conceptual base from which protracted resistance to extinction and the apparent loss of overt anxiety can be derived. The theory offers a major inroad to problems of human pathology and will be briefly outlined here.

Anxiety conservation. This principle grows out of observations that animals appear more relaxed as the response latency decreases to some stable value around 1½ seconds. Moreover, if an animal delays appreciably on one trial before jumping, he appears quite upset following the jump and responds very rapidly for the next few trials. On the strength of these observations, Solomon and Wynne suggest that the animal gradually establishes a stable response latency which is short enough to prevent full arousal of the anxiety reaction. When the CS is presented, a finite time lag intercedes before all components of the anxiety reaction are mobilized, and by virtue of a speedy instrumental response the animal terminates the CS and thus prevents full arousal of the anxiety reaction. Solomon and Wynne (1954) carefully evaluate the literature on latency of autonomic functioning and conclude that at least 2 seconds, perhaps longer, must elapse before feedback from the peripheral autonomic nervous system can appreciably affect central motor processes. Moreover, variations in latency exist for the several autonomic responses that constitute the anxiety reaction. Consequently, the intensity and scope of the anxiety reaction activated by the CS is a direct function of the exposure period and many elements of the anxiety reaction are not aroused.

Based on these considerations, the substance of the anxiety conservation principle is:

if nonreinforced exercise of a CS-CR relationship is the necessary condition for extinction, then the extinction of the associational linkage and at least this [the unaroused] portion of the anxiety reaction cannot take place. In one sense, the amplitude of the anxiety reaction is being *conserved* as a relatively intact potentiality, a latent functional entity (p. 359).

Put another way, the animal does not test reality by remaining with the CS long enough to find that it is no longer followed by shock. The instrumental response, established under extraordinary levels of pain-fear, now is sustained by its efficacy in preventing full scale arousal of anxiety. So long as the animal can perform the avoidance response rapidly, he can control anxiety; he has, at the behavioral level, the equivalent of a defense mechanism. But the very act that prevents anxiety also eliminates the conditions that must obtain for extinction to occur, namely, repeated arousal of anxiety within the CS situation but with the original reinforcement absent. So anxiety continues as a latent but nonetheless potent state, supporting all manner of avoidance activities in a situation that has long since ceased to have its former significance.

This treatment is roughly analogous to the clinical interpretation of defensive mechanisms. When some event has been associated with severe anxiety, defense mechanisms are instituted to prevent subsequent arousal of anxiety. Defense mechanisms usually process out internal stimuli (thoughts, impulses), but they may also impose selective distortions upon the perception of external events that are threatening to the individual. Anxiety is thus the motivator of defense mechanisms, and at the same time it is the emotionally distressed state the individual avoids by dint of his defenses. By eliminating or disguising the internal stimuli that have become a signal for anxiety, the defense mechanisms successfully prevent an anxiety attack, just as withdrawal from the CS eliminated signs of anxiety in Solomon's dogs.

Partial irreversibility of intense pain-fear reactions.   While anxiety may be conserved against extinction by a rapidly performed avoidance response, there are instances where the instrumental response either is not or cannot be executed quickly. A barrier may prevent jumping altogether, or on one trial the jump latency may lag below its usual stable value. On such occasions more anxiety should be aroused, and in the absence of pain as the unconditioned stimulus (UCS) the anxiety reaction should be fractionally reduced. Theoretically, a slow and gradual loss in the anxiety reaction would be expected. While extinction may be extended by the principle of anxiety conservation, it should not be permanently postponed.

On the strength of their data and related literature on avoidance learning, Solomon and Wynne (1954) believe that it is empirically possible to produce avoidance responses that will last for thousands of trials. They believe that ordinary extinction procedures will be ineffective for cases of severe trauma; anxiety will never be completely eliminated. They conclude, "Therefore, there must be a point at which the anxiety conservation phase is buttressed in some way; there must be some reason for such resistance to extinction . . ." (p. 361).

The second principle, *partial irreversibility*, constitutes the reason, and it means simply that when an intense pain-fear reaction of wide autonomic scope is classically conditioned to a CS, the stimulus is permanently invested with power to evoke a residual anxiety reaction. Repeated extinction trials may depress the anxiety reaction, but there is a fixed threshold value beyond which normal extinction procedures have no effect. Solomon thinks of partial irreversibility as a neurophysiological phenomenon, reflecting a relatively permanent reorganization within the central nervous system. The change is assumed to represent a decreased threshold of sensitivity, analogous to the partial reorganization of hormonal functioning that Selye (1950) incorporates in his concept of the adaptation syndrome.

With these two principles, Solomon and Wynne are able to interpret behavior that is functionally impervious to extinction. Clinicians have long since suspected that maladaptive behavior must be controlled by some such principles because it persists paradoxically even though causing distress and punishment. Of prime significance here is Solomon's observation that punishment may actually strengthen rather than weaken the instrumental avoidance response. Once the jumping response is firmly established, shocking the animal for performing the response seems to increase anxiety more than it inhibits jumping. This gives rise to the peculiar spectacle of an animal squealing vigorously as the CS is presented, yet inexorably jumping into shock. If our earlier equation of avoidance responses with human defensive activities is valid, it becomes increasingly clear why punishment does not eradicate anxiety-motivated behavior in clinical patients.

Experimental neurosis

Behavior disturbances in animals have occupied a prominent research niche ever since Pavlov produced a "neurosis" in dogs who could no longer discriminate between positive and negative conditioned stimuli. Gantt (1944, 1953) and Liddell (1944, 1953) are among the principal American investigators using the conditioned reflex technique to study behavior disturbances, and their results are of considerable theoretical significance for the problem of anxiety.

Liddell on the vigilance reaction

Liddell has experimented extensively with sheep, goats, and pigs, using a feeble electric current applied to the foreleg to condition leg flexion. A metronome beat is introduced as the CS, and after a number of pairings the CR is firmly established.   Subsequently, a second metronome beat is introduced but this beat is never followed by the UCS. After repeated trials a clear discrimination is established and the animal does not flex the leg to the negative stimulus.   The animal does exhibit a sharp alerting reaction, just as for the positive stimulus, but in the negative instance he remains tense and vigilant although no response is performed.   Paradoxically, the mild current applied following the positive stimulus produces relaxation and an abrupt decrease in tension.

By steadily converging the two metronome beats, the animal is required to make finer and finer discriminations until the threshold is passed.   At this point the animal responds erratically, former discriminations are lost, and behavior disturbances appear.   The animal may attack the apparatus, he may exhibit continuous tantrum behavior, or he may become cataleptic.   Liddell has used several other procedures which are covered in detail in his 1944 article, but in all instances his conclusions are basically the same.

As a prelude to Liddell's basic thesis, we might note that the feeble electric current used here is in distinct contrast to the shock applied in traumatic avoidance learning.   Liddell emphasizes that it is a startle stimulus rather than a pain stimulus; the current is set to be barely perceptible on the moistened fingers of the experimenter. Consequently, disruptions in behavior must be referred to the preliminary training procedures and the internal tension level of the animal, not to the traumatizing nature of the external stimulus.

Liddell (1953) proposes that the vigilance reaction is the emotional foundation out of which experimental neurosis develops.   He documents his thesis by observing that a primordial function of the nervous system is vigilance, watchfulness, and generalized suspiciousness. This primitive sentinel activity is a behavioral equivalent of Cannon's emergency reaction.   It is graded in intensity and reveals itself in qualitatively diverse behaviors, ranging from a startle reaction to panic.   The vigilance reaction constitutes an emotional substrate for behavior, and when raised to disabling intensity it will disrupt prior habits and the flexible adjustments needed to insure adaptive behavior.

Conditioned reflex techniques lay the first stone by introducing the animal to an unfamiliar situation in which he is restrained by straps and has portions of the apparatus attached to his body. A long period of training is required for the animal to submit docilely to the conditioning regimen, during which impulsive behavior is gradually subordinated to habits of remaining alert yet self-contained and quiet while employed in the apparatus. Such restraints inevitably create tension in the animal, revealed by periodic outbursts of tantrum behavior. Measures of respiration, heart rate, and gastrointestinal activity similarly testify to internal arousal at the time the animal appears to be quietly responding to the CS. If training is continued long enough, emotional arousal reaches a disabling intensity and disrupts organic processes as well as overt behavior.

Whatever the neurological basis, behavior disturbances produced by this method seem to be facilitated by an absence of patterned motor activity which would relieve the aroused state of the animal. One might argue that the animal's spontaneous behavior, consisting mainly of efforts to escape, is gradually inhibited because it is ineffective in securing release from the confines of the Pavlov frame. But overt habituation does not signify a decline in emotional arousal. Self-restraint is maintained at some expense, and even a thoroughly trained animal is easily disturbed by events that increase arousal or otherwise depart from the normal training schedule. It appears that the animal can inhibit only a limited amount of tension before more primitive mechanisms in the nervous system effect a gross discharge. As Judson Herrick observed, the mammal is constructed to be active and cannot tolerate restrictions in this sphere indefinitely without pathological consequences.

Gantt on experimental neurosis

For a period of some 12 years, Gantt (1944) intensively studied the behavior disturbances produced in one dog by conditioned reflex techniques. Basically, Gantt used a procedure identical to that of Liddell except salivation was conditioned rather than leg flexion. After the neurosis was established, Gantt made extensive autonomic recordings and systematically altered features of the conditioning situation, always observing whether the animal's symptoms improved or degenerated. His conclusions have been validated with numerous other subjects, but Nick serves as the best focal point for discussion.

Once a discrimination between positive and negative conditioned stimuli had been established, Gantt gradually converged the two stimuli and forced the limits of discrimination. Under these circumstances a widescale emotional reaction developed that might be termed anxiety. The animal was extremely upset during the conditioning session and actively resisted being placed in the apparatus. Autonomic changes appeared that surpassed in intensity the effects produced by such natural trauma as fighting, attack by another animal, or painful insult to the body.   Respiratory difficulties, cardiac acceleration, increased blood sugar, and chronic pollakiuria are representative of the changes at this level.   Coincidentally, these reactions became keyed to the CS; whenever the stimulus was presented a widescale and abrupt acceleration in autonomic processes immediately followed. And these dysfunctions were intractable; once elaborated in the form of a widespread anxiety reaction, they persisted erratically long after the more obvious signs of pathology had disappeared.   At a more molar level, the behavior of the animal fell into a stereotyped format of overt symptoms.   Gantt refers repeatedly to the "marked character, regular manifestation and stereotypy of pattern of the symptom complexes."

It is a matter of some consequence to understand how a situation that does not include pain can produce such an intense, chronic level of anxiety.   Disturbed behavior is intuitively reasonable when considerable amounts of punishment have been absorbed; but what is responsible for breakdown in the artificial world of reflex conditioning, where the most innocuous of stimuli are used?

Gantt and Liddell agree that conditioning in the Pavlov apparatus is essentially emotional in nature, and the nominal CR is but an incidental feature that best serves as an index of the underlying emotional state.   Stable responses testify to reasonable stability and integration in the animal's emotional reaction; unstable and fluctuating CRs are an indicator of widespread autonomic and behavioral disruptions that may develop percipitately.   Even in the traditional salivary conditioning experiments where no instance of behavior disturbance is reported, the emotional undertone is clearly revealed during extinction.   When meat powder is omitted, the animal exhibits increasing agitation following the CS, and at a later stage he may become extremely upset and attack the apparatus.   While the salivary response drops out under these circumstances, a simple report of the number of unreinforced trials to extinction hardly does justice to the complex features of the animal's behavior.[1]

Experimental neurosis capitalizes upon this emotional substrate of behavior; in Liddell's terms, upon the innate vigilance reaction the animal brings to the conditioning situation.   It plays upon processes endogenous to the organism; processes, in fact, that are at the heart of adaptation and survival.   But in this instance the emotional processes are not keyed to the contingencies of the environment.   They are aroused in situations of no biological significance to the animal, and they cumulate because spontaneous escape activity is inhibited.

[1] In quite a different context, O. R. Lindsley (1956) has applied operant conditioning techniques to a psychotic population and he reports that chronic schizophrenics often urinate or defecate during the extinction phase, again suggesting a strong emotional involvement.

So they pervert their normal function, contributing to disintegration rather than adaptation.

An overview

With all their diversity of emphasis and procedure, the experimental studies nevertheless are tied together by certain recurrent themes. Taking the studies as a group, two significant features stand out in all cases of behavior pathology.   On the one hand, the foundation for pathology is laid by a progressive state of emotional arousal that finally reaches disastrous proportions.   Acute anxiety is the common denominator of these studies, and at early stages it is expressed in autonomic fluctuations, in panic reactions, and in behavioral disorganization.   Whether initiated by traumatically painful episodes or elaborated out of the vigilance reaction, anxiety is the basic operator in behavior pathology.

Secondly, the constant feature of the behavioral symptoms is their stereotypy and repetitiveness.   Once established, the symptoms are remarkably intractable to control by external reward or punishment. They may qualify as instrumental avoidance responses or they may simply include primitive response patterns that were incidentally fixated, but in either case the behavior is continued long after the task requirements have changed.

These two characteristics of behavior pathology, anchored as they are in careful experimental work, furnish substantial corroboration for the two similar features noted earlier in the clinical literature.   We seem to be dealing here with principles of sufficient generality and power to produce consistent results even when a wide variety of species and procedures are sampled.   The experimental studies do not provide any evidence on the third feature of clinical pathology, namely, the fixation of emotions and needs during early stages of development, but they were not designed to obtain data of this sort.   Perhaps a group of experiments designed for this purpose, such as those of Hunt and his colleagues (1941, 1947), would produce the type of data desired.

If this be true, if in fact a set of principles can be established that apply to pathology in various species, then it would seem that we are in a more powerful position to isolate the basic conditions that underwrite pathology.   Through animal studies the conditions that aggravate the emotional state of the organism can be explored, and nonverbal methods of therapeutic treatment can be systematically examined.   There are enough striking parallels in symptoms between man and other mammals to suggest that valuable insights might be derived from such studies, insights that could be transposed and beneficially applied at the human level.

This is not to suggest that human pathology is devoid of any distinguishing characteristics. Human pathology has many unique features, to be sure, features that are interwoven with the advanced mental processes available to man. One cannot fail to be impressed with the florid ideation and rich detail of schizophrenic thinking. But if disturbances in behavior are keyed principally to emotional conditioning, perhaps the cognitive processes serve chiefly to express the problem more complexly, to extend through language and ideation the range of relevant experiences that are associated with the pathological state. In this sense the peculiarly symbolic quality that enters into human disturbances may be considered a secondary phenomenon, just as the ability to cast the problem in verbal terms and communicate it to a therapist is. They are adjuncts that testify to man's ability to symbolically represent his experience at several different levels. But the indispensable feature of pathology is the state of anxiety keyed to significant portions of the individual's experience, not the special verbal or mental images through which the experience is elaborated.

Summary

Two separate realms of discourse have contributed heavily to current conceptions of behavior pathology. The clinical realm, influenced largely by the theories of Freud, has offered dynamic interpretations of human disorders that are couched in a framework of drive, conflict, and defense. Its opposite number, experimental psychopathology, has been mainly occupied with animal studies in which behavior disturbances are methodically produced under carefully controlled conditions. There has been a noticeable lack of interchange between the two areas, yet a selective review of the literature suggests that behavior pathology in humans and animals may share some common principles.

In the clinical area there appear to be three general characteristics that apply to the functional behavior disorders. The first of these is the presence of an intense anxiety reaction that disrupts goal directed behavior and mobilizes defensive processes aimed at warding off anxiety. Secondly, behavior relevant to the anxiety provoking situation becomes stereotyped and repetitive, furnishing the individual with a set of symptoms that are remarkably intractable to change. Finally, needs and emotions operative at the point of severe frustration seem to be fixated, and consequently the steady progression to mature forms of emotional expression and impulse control is disrupted. The individual is preoccupied with residual interests that are appropriate to an earlier phase of development, and current experiences are refracted to conform with these themes.

The experimental literature reveals that the presence of acute anxiety and the formation of stereotyped, repetitive symptoms are typical characteristics of this area as well, and these data provide a firm experimental foundation for the two similar characteristics observed in the clinical realm. The experimental studies yield no evidence about the fixation of emotions and needs because they were not designed to obtain data of this sort, but some suggestive results in this direction have been obtained by other experiments on infantile feeding frustration.

In combination, the clinical and experimental research raises the possibility that the same principles control behavior pathology in more than one species. The unique features of human pathology seem to be traceable to the complex cognitive processes through which the problem is expressed, rather than a fundamental difference in how the pathology originates. We would tentatively conclude that the indispensable feature of pathology is a strong anxiety reaction keyed to significant aspects of the individual's experience; and if this be valid, suggest further that animal research on nonverbal techniques of therapy might yield results that could be translated and beneficially applied to the human level.

References

Alexander, F., & French, T. M. *Psychoanalytic therapy.* New York: Ronald, 1946.

Bettelheim, B. *Love is not enough.* Glencoe, Ill.: Free Press, 1950.

Erikson, E. H. Studies in the interpretation of play: I. Clinical observation of play disruption in young children. *Genet. Psychol. Monogr.,* 1950, 22(4), 557–671.

Erikson, E. H. Growth and crises of the "healthy personality." In C. Kluckhohn, H. A. Murray, and D. M. Schneider (Eds.), *Personality in nature, society and culture.* (2nd ed.) New York: Knopf, 1953. Pp. 185–225.

Gantt, W. H. *Experimental basis for neurotic behavior.* New York: Hoeber, 1944.

Gantt, W. H. Principles of nervous breakdown: Schizokinesis and autokinesis. *Ann. N.Y. Acad. Sci.,* 1953, 56, 143–163.

Guntrip, H. A study of Fairbairn's theory of schizoid reactions. *Brit. J. med. Psychol.,* 1952, 25, 86–103. (Reprinted in C. F. Reed, I. E. Alexander, and S. S. Tomkins [Eds.], *Psychopathology.* Cambridge: Harvard Univer. Press, 1953. Pp. 344–369.)

Hinkle, L. E., Jr., & Wolff, H. G. Communist interrogation and indoctrination of "enemies of the states." *Arch. Neurol. Psychiat.,* 1956, 76, 115–174.

Hunt, J. McV. The effects of infant feeding-frustration upon adult hoarding behavior. *J. abnorm. soc. Psychol.*, 1941, *36*, 336–360.

Hunt, J. McV., Schlosberg, H., Solomon, R. L., & Stellar, E. Studies of the effects of infantile experience on adult behavior in rats: I. Effects of infantile feeding-frustration on adult hoarding. *J. comp. physiol. Psychol.*, 1947, *40*, 291–304.

Jenkins, R. L. Nature of the schizophrenic process. *Arch. Neurol. Psychiat.*, 1950, *64*, 243–262.

Jenkins, R. L. The schizophrenic sequence: Withdrawal, disorganization, psychotic reorganization. *Amer. J. Orthopsychiat.*, 1952, *22*, 738–748.

Kubie, L. S. The repetitive core of neurosis. *Psychoanal. Quart.*, 1941, *10*, 23–43.

Kubie, L. S. The fundamental nature of the distinction between normality and neurosis. *Psychoanal. Quart.*, 1954, *23*, 167–204.

Liddell, H. S. Conditioned reflex method and experimental neurosis. In J. McV. Hunt (Ed.), *Personality and the behavior disorders.* New York: Ronald, 1944. Pp. 389–412.

Liddell, H. S. A comparative approach to the dynamics of experimental neuroses. *Ann. N.Y. Acad. Sci.*, 1953, *56*, 164–170.

Lindsley, O. R. Operant conditioning methods applied to research in child behavior. *J. abnorm. soc. Psychol.*, 1953, *48*, 185–189.

Maier, N. R. F. *Frustration: The study of behavior without a goal.* New York: McGraw-Hill, 1949.

Maier, N. R. F. Frustration theory: Restatement and extension. *Psychol. Rev.*, 1956, *63*, 370–388.

Mark, J. C. The attitudes of the mothers of male schizophrenics toward child behavior. *J. abnorm. soc. Psychol.*, 1953, *48*, 185–189.

Redl, F., & Wineman, D. *Children who hate.* Glencoe, Ill.: Free Press, 1951.

Redl, F., & Wineman, D. *Controls from within.* Glencoe, Ill.: Free Press, 1952.

Selye, H. *The physiology and pathology of exposure to stress.* Montreal: Acta, 1950.

Solomon, R. L., Kamin, L. J., & Wynne, L. C. Traumatic avoidance learning: The outcomes of several extinction procedures with dogs. *J. abnorm. soc. Psychol.*, 1953, *48*, 291–302.

Solomon, R. L., & Wynne, L. C. Traumatic avoidance learning: Acquisition in normal dogs. *Psychol. Monogr.*, 1953, 67(4, Whole No. 354).

Solomon, R. L., & Wynne, L. C. Traumatic avoidance learning: The principles of anxiety conservation and partial irreversibility. *Psychol. Rev.*, 1954, 61, 353–384.

Maurice Lorr,
Patricia F. Bishop, and
Douglas M. McNair

INTERPERSONAL TYPES AMONG PSYCHIATRIC PATIENTS *

Recent literature has emphasized the role of faulty interpersonal behaviors in the psychoneurotic and personality disorders. Indeed to Horney (1945), Fromm (1947), and Sullivan (1947), the milder behavior disorders represent mainly problems in relating to people. A similar view has been taken by Leary (1957) and his colleagues Coffey, Freedman, Ossori, and LaForge. They have sought to develop a scheme for multilevel interpersonal diagnosis. Conventional psychiatric diagnoses, on the other hand, are described mainly in terms of patient symptoms and complaints. The psychoneurotic disorders are defined principally by symptoms in *Mental Disorders* (APA, 1952). However, interpersonal characteristics receive somewhat greater emphasis in definition of the personality disorders.

The view taken here is that diagnoses of the milder disorders should be based primarily on characteristic interpersonal behavior patterns. Associated neurotic symptoms and complaints should be regarded as secondary to maladaptive patterns of interpersonal adjustment. The present study was undertaken to explore the use of currently observable interpersonal behavior as the primary criterion of classification. Specifically the study aims were (*a*) to isolate the major classes of homogeneous interpersonal profiles within a sample of nonpsychotic psychiatric patients, (*b*) to determine the constancy of the classes isolated across three subsamples, and (*c*) to identify any systematic differences between the classes isolated with respect to background characteristics.

* From Maurice Lorr, Patricia F. Bishop, and Douglas M. McNair, "Interpersonal Types among Psychiatric Patients," *J. abnorm. Psychol.*, 1965, 70, 468–472. Reprinted by permission of the authors and the Managing Editor, the American Psychological Association.

Method

Rating instrument

The basic measuring device was the Interpersonal Behavior Inventory (IBI-3). The development of the IBI, its standardization, factor structure and reliability, and a theory of the organization of its 15 categories are presented elsewhere (Lorr & McNair, 1963, 1965). The inventory consists of 160 statements descriptive of manifest interpersonal behaviors. The format permits the rater to indicate how often the person rated exhibits the behavior in question: not at all, occasionally, fairly often, or quite often. A category score is the sum of 7 to 11 unit-weighted items defining each factor. The interpersonal categories are labeled as follows: Dominance, Recognition, Hostility, Mistrust, Detachment, Inhibition, Abasiveness, Submissiveness, Succorance, Deference, Agreeableness, Nurturance, Affection, Sociability, and Exhibition. Table 1 presents illustrative examples of each of the categories.

Sample

The patient sample consisted of 212 men and 313 women being seen in individual psychotherapy at least once a week for a minimum of 3 months. The therapists were instructed to rate a sample of their case load as diverse as possible with respect to interpersonal behavior, occupation, and social class. All rated were to be nonpsychotic. Actually the typical patient had received 95 therapy interviews. Approximately 92% were high-school graduates and 68% had received some college training. The average patient was 33 years old; 72% were married. Approximately 48% were diagnosed psychoneurotic, 37% were labeled personality disorders, and 16% were categorized otherwise.

The therapists' sample consisted of 104 psychologists and 12 psychiatrists. Most were members of the Clinical Division of the American Psychological Association and a majority had been certified by ABEPP. The cases each reported were being seen in private practice, and in university, community, and state outpatient clinics. Therapists were paid a modest fee for each patient rated. While no claim is made for representativeness, the therapists included did come from all parts of the country and were uniformly well qualified.

Typing process

To establish a common scale, the raw factor scores were converted into standard scores with a mean of five and a standard deviation of one.

Thus each individual was represented by 15 derived standard scores. The index of similarity used was the correlation coefficient. A correlation coefficient reflects primarily similarity in the shapes of two profiles. However, in the process to be described, it is always possible to bring in level as well, after profiles alike in shape have been grouped. In contrast, a distance measure (D), advocated by some, has no unique meaning. It may reflect a large difference between two profiles on one score, or dimension, or the sum of small differences on all dimensions. The D measure also fails to take the direction of differences into account; it fails to differentiate between profiles with opposite slopes.

The typing process begins by listing with each coded profile, the code numbers of all other profiles that correlate with it .55 or higher. At this value a coefficient is significant at the 5% level and two profiles are defined as "similar." The profile with the longest associated list is selected as a pivot. To the pivot is added the profile with the highest average correlation with all members in the pivot list. To the first pair is added the profile that correlates highest on the average with both. Other profiles are added to the group of profiles by the same procedure until none correlates on the average above .55 with other group members. Next, any profile in the residual matrix that correlates above .40 (on the average) with the first group or type is deleted. The second type is then evolved from the residual matrix by the first listing with each profile all other profiles that correlate .55 or better with it. The pivot and the members of the second cluster are selected in the manner previously described. Again profiles correlating about .40 with the second group are deleted from the matrix. All later types are formed by the same selection procedure described. The final step involves computing the mean correlation between each member of a given type with all members of all the other types, each type being taken separately. If the profile correlates (on the average) above .40 with another type it is removed. Any type with less than four members is dropped.

Each type is then characterized by its mean profile and by the highest and lowest score on each of the categories defining it. Members of a type are those individuals whose standard scores lie within each and every bound set by the highest and lowest scores. Thus defined the classes of homogeneous profiles or types are mutually exclusive.

The typing process described has been programmed for data processing equipment and can handle as many as 150 variables at one time. Because only 150 cases could be processed at one time 3 subsamples each were selected after the entire sample had been randomized. Randomization was necessary because the inventories received did not come from all sources at equal rates.

Table 1
Statements exemplifying the fifteen interpersonal categories of IBI-3

Category	Statements
Dominance	Bosses his friends and associates around.
	Takes charge of things when he's with people.
Recognition	Seizes opportunities to rival and surpass others.
	Strives for symbols of status and superiority to others.
Hostility	Ridicules, belittles or depreciates others.
	Uses a sarcastic or biting type of humor.
Mistrust	Mistrusts the intentions of others toward him.
	Expresses suspicion when someone is especially nice to him.
Detachment	Acts business-like and impersonal with co-workers.
	Keeps aloof from his neighbors.
Inhibition	Shows discomfort and nervousness when people watch him at work or at play.
	Shows signs of self-consciousness with strangers.
Abasiveness	Blames himself when interpersonal friction with others occurs.
	Apologizes for not having done better when he completes a task.
Submissiveness	Gives in rather than fight for his rights in a conflict.
	Lets his friends or spouse push him around.
Succorance	Asks others to look after his interests.
	Asks for help on jobs he could handle himself.
Deference	Carries out orders of his superiors with zest.
	Takes the role of helper or supporter of authority figures.
Agreeableness	Contributes positively as a member of some group or team.
	Relates to and treats people as equals.
Nurturance	Listens sympathetically to others talk about their troubles.
	Puts aside his own work or pleasure if someone asks for help.
Affection	Shows a real liking and affection for people.
	Acts close and personal with people.
Sociability	Invites friends and acquaintances to his home.
	Drops in to visit friends just to socialize.
Exhibition	Draws attention to himself in a group by telling jokes and anecdotes.
	Acts the clown or amuses others at a party.

Results

The analysis yielded four patient types in two of the subsamples and five in the third. Because the fifth type in the last subsample consisted of only four members and remained unconfirmed, it will not be discussed. The average correlations within and between types are given in Table 2. It is clear that the positive between-group correlations are all low, none being higher than .13. The within-group

Table 2
Average correlations within and between
clusters for sets 1, 2, and 3

Relation	Set 1	Set 2	Set 3
1 versus 1	65	68	71
1 versus 2	−32	−52	−14
1 versus 3	01	−15	03
1 versus 4	−64	07	−64
2 versus 2	72	68	66
2 versus 3	−59	−08	−64
2 versus 4	13	−01	09
3 versus 3	65	65	66
3 versus 4	17	−59	01
4 versus 4	68	63	67

correlations are relatively high indicating adequate similarity between members.

Table 3 presents evidence of the degree of constancy in patient type from one subsample to the next. The coefficient of congruency (Harman, 1960) was employed as a measure of the degree of similarity between the mean profiles of the four types. The subsample types are coded by subsample and type. For example, type 1.1 is the first type found in the first subsample. If a coefficient of .75 indicates adequate similarity and a coefficient of .90 marked similarity then all of the types have clear matches in each of the subsamples.

Each type will be described in terms of those elements of its profile that average at least one standard deviation above the overall mean for the entire patient sample. By this criterion (see Table 4), Type I is primarily an inhibited, submissive, and abasive group. The type may be further characterized by the absence of Dominance, Competitiveness, and Hostility. As will be seen shortly this type is most likely to be labeled neurotic and to be accepted for psychotherapy. Type II is characterized by Agreeableness, Nurturance, Affection, and Sociability. As might be anticipated, Hostility, Mistrust, and tendencies toward Detachment are very low. Leary (1957) describes a similar patient group whom he characterizes as sweet, bland, conventional, and hysteric.

Type III is defined primarily by high Hostility, Mistrust, and Detachment from others. Agreeableness, Nurturance, Love, and Sociability are rated low. It seems likely that Type III would ordinarily be designated Schizoid. The last replicated type (IV) is predominantly exhibitionistic, dominant, competitive, and hostile. Naturally such patients score low on Inhibition, Submissiveness, and Abasiveness.

Type differences

The types were compared with respect to age, marital status, and highest grade completed. The only significant difference between

Table 3
Congruencies between mean cluster profiles

Type	Sub-sample	Type I			Type II			Type III			Type IV		
		1.1	2.4	3.2	1.2	2.1	3.4	1.3	2.2	3.1	1.4	2.3	3.3
I	1.1												
	2.4	90											
	3.2	94	88										
II	1.2	-41	-46	-45									
	2.1	11	01	13	78								
	3.4	18	13	19	77	97							
III	1.3	03	04	05	-93	-86	-92						
	2.2	01	01	13	-80	-72	-88	90					
	3.1	-14	-25	-17	-68	-80	-90	91	92				
IV	1.4	-91	-82	-94	20	-39	-44	21	09	39			
	2.3	-94	-89	-98	48	-10	-15	-10	-17	15	92		
	3.3	-92	-86	-93	57	-02	-05	-21	-28	06	87	97	

Note.—Decimals have been omitted.

445

Table 4
Mean standard scores on fifteen
interpersonal categories of IBI-3

Category	Type			
	I	II	III	IV
Dominance	3.89	5.13	4.91	6.61
Recognition	3.97	4.84	5.19	6.34
Hostility	3.91	4.12	6.06	6.13
Mistrust	4.49	3.88	6.08	5.51
Detachment	5.68	4.09	6.10	4.14
Inhibition	5.98	4.10	5.69	3.93
Submissiveness	6.17	4.79	4.44	3.91
Succorance	5.25	4.27	4.96	4.85
Abasement	6.02	4.61	4.44	4.02
Deference	5.31	5.62	4.11	4.74
Agreeableness	5.99	6.44	3.82	4.66
Nurturance	5.11	6.20	3.92	4.83
Affection	4.87	6.24	3.88	5.09
Sociability	4.34	5.85	3.97	6.03
Exhibition	4.15	4.69	4.75	6.59

the types was with respect to age; Type II members were older as a group. The mean age of the types ranged from 32 to 36. The percentage married ranged from 59 to 79. The percentage with some college education ranged from 62 to 74. Thus background variables appeared not to relate closely to the patient types.

Table 5 presents the therapist's diagnostic impressions grouped by major disorder. A chi-square test indicated differences among the cells significant at $p < .01$. Type I members (self-effacing and submissive) compared to other types tend to be diagnosed as psychoneurotic or personality pattern disorders. Diagnosis appears not to differentiate Type I from Type III (withdrawn, hostile, suspicious). Type II members (agreeable, helpful, responsible, friendly) tend to be labeled psychoneurotic or to be left undiagnosed. Personality pattern diagnoses (Schizoid or Paranoid Personality) are less frequent for Type II than for the others. Type IV members (dominant, competitive, exhibitionistic) compared to other classes, are more frequently diagnosed personality trait disturbances, that is, Passive-Aggressive, Aggressive, or Compulsive.

Further insight into the character of the types can be gained from their occupations. Type I members tend to be housewives. Type II members tend to come from any of the white-collar occupations and are least frequently housewives. On the other hand, Type III members (withdrawn, suspicious) tend to come from unskilled and semiskilled blue-collar occupations. Type IV members, consistent with their aggressive and competitive interpersonal profiles, tend to be in administration, management or in one of the professions.

Table 5
Type member distribution by occupation in percentages

Occupation	Type			
	I	II	III	IV
Administration	2	9	8	13
Teaching	8	12	12	5
Professional	12	17	10	21
White collar	18	23	21	8
Manual worker	6	7	14	8
Housewife	43	21	25	33
Student or unemployed	10	12	8	13

Table 6
Patient diagnosis by type

Disorder	Type			
	I	II	III	IV
Psychoneurotic	26	25	22	10
Personality pattern	11	2	11	5
Personality trait	9	6	12	19
Other	3	10	3	5
Total	49	43	48	39

Discussion

Some comparison of present findings with those from a prior study (McNair & Lorr, 1965) seems warranted. In the initial study a sample of 450 veterans in outpatient psychotherapy were described by their therapists ($N = 259$) on an earlier rating form called IBI-2. The inventory measured 11 rather than 15 dimensions of interpersonal behavior. A type analysis essentially the same as described here was employed. However, the criterion for separation of types was less exacting. Of the eight patient types isolated in the earlier analysis, three appear to have a good match among the types reported here. The McNair-Lorr Type B (dominant, hostile, mistrustful) appear to be very similar to Type IV. A Type C (nurturant, affiliative, sociable) resembles Type II, while Type D (hostile, detached, mistrustful) seems a close match to Type III. Finally a Type F (passive, abasive, nurturant) partially resembles Type I. The evidence, although qualitative in nature, tends to lend support to the viability of the types reported here.

An important applied question relates to decision rules for assigning cases to one of the four types with the fewest number of misclassifications. A solution to this problem was not pursued because of the exploratory nature of the study. The clustering process classified between 48% and 49% of the 150 members of each sample to one of the types. These results suggest that rules could be established to assign a high proportion of all cases without excessive error.

The interpersonal behavior factors of nonpsychotic but disturbed individuals have been shown to be essentially no different from those of normals (Lorr & McNair, 1965). Interpersonal tendencies in the individual needing psychiatric help are principally more extreme or accentuated. Why then is the characteristic interpersonal behavior profile more important diagnostically than the symptom grouping? One answer is that interpersonal variables are more crucial and relevant therapeutically. Therapists find such variables are more predictive of expected patient behavior in group or individual treatment. Also the ability of the individual to form a relationship and the nature of the relationship may be anticipated better with such knowledge (Leary & Coffey, 1955).

Characteristic interpersonal "styles" or ways of relating to peers, authority figures and to subordinates are relatively enduring characteristics. Interpersonal style in turn influences, and is influenced by, preferred defense mechanisms for resolving inner conflict. Accordingly it is plausible to hypothesize that the submissive-abasive-inhibited type tends to turn against himself, while the detached-hostile-suspicious type turns against others and withdraws. Perhaps the friendly-agreeable-helpful type tends to use denial and repression. In the dominant-competitive-exhibitionistic individual we may find use of acting out or displacement.

In conclusion, it can be said that the method of typing yields meaningful, mutually exclusive and replicable outpatient types. Relationships between the types and conventional psychiatric diagnosis are not very strong. However, as the criteria of classification are quite different in the two systems of classification, close correspondence should not be expected. On the whole, when one considers the exploratory nature of the study, the approach and the findings show promise for a useful and fruitful system of patient classification.

Summary

The aims of the study were to isolate some of the main interpersonal behavior types within a sample of nonpsychotic psychiatric patients in psychotherapy, to determine the constancy of the isolated types across the 3 subsamples of 150 cases, and to identify any systematic differences among them. Each patient was described by his therapist on the 15 factors of the Interpersonal Behavior Inventory. The 4 replicated types were (a) inhibited, submissive, abasive; (b) agreeable, nurturant, sociable; (c) hostile, mistrustful, detached; (d) dominant, competitive, exhibitionistic. Some diagnostic and occupational differences were found.

References

American Psychiatric Association. *Diagnostic and statistical manual for mental disorders.* Washington, D.C.: Mental Hospital Service, 1952.

Fromm, E. *Escape from freedom.* New York: Rinehart, 1947.

Harman, H. H. *Modern factor analysis.* Chicago: Univer. Chicago Press, 1960.

Horney, Karen. *Our inner conflicts.* New York: Norton, 1945.

Leary, T. *Interpersonal diagnosis of personality.* New York: Ronald Press, 1957.

Leary, T., & Coffey, H. S. Interpersonal diagnosis: Some problems of methodology and validation. *Journal of Abnormal and Social Psychology,* 1955, 50, 110–124.

Lorr, M., & McNair, D. M. An interpersonal behavior circle. *Journal of Abnormal and Social Psychology,* 1963, 67, 68–75.

Lorr, M., & McNair, D. M. Expansion of the interpersonal behavior circle. *Journal of Personality and Social Psychology,* 1965, 2.

McNair, D. M., & Lorr, M. Differential typing of psychiatric outpatients. *The Psychological Record,* 1965, 15, 33–41.

Sullivan, H. S. *Conceptions of modern psychiatry.* Washington, D.C.: William Alanson White Psychiatric Foundation, 1947.

J. R. Wittenborn

DISTINCTIONS WITHIN PSYCHOTIC DIMENSIONS *

Introduction

This report describes symptomatic distinctions within general psychotic dimensions and is based on a factor analysis by the method of principal components. In a recent report the writer described major psychotic dimensions shown by centroid analyses (5). The patients, all males, were at the Lyons, New Jersey, Veterans Administration Hospital and all but 21 bore a diagnosis of some form of schizophrenia. The diagnoses for 12 of the 150 patients involved organic considerations, and only nine patients had some other kind of diagnosis, such as severe neurosis or depression. Since the pur-

* From J. R. Wittenborn, "Distinctions within Psychotic Dimensions: A Principal Components Analysis," *J. nerv. ment. Dis.,* 1963, *137,* 543–547. Reprinted by permission of the author and the publisher. Copyright 1963, The Williams and Wilkins Company, Baltimore, Md. 21202, U.S.A.

pose of the study had been to survey the dimensions of chronic psy·
chosis with the employment of a new comprehensive set of symptom
rating scales designed specifically for rating distinctions among
chronic patients, the Lyons sample was considered to be an appropriate one.   The results of the analysis were congruent with the earlier
investigations of the writer (4, 6), as well as with the reports of other
investigators (1–3).

In the study of the dimensions of psychosis among chronic patients,
the factors were extracted by the centroid method.   This method has
been generally used for such analyses by most investigators, including the writer.   From a purely quantitative standpoint, however, the
method of principal components for extracting factors is more efficient
than the centroid method in the sense that a greater portion of the
common variance of each of the variables may be expressed in terms
of factors.   When a large number of variables is employed, this advantage of the principal component method could be appreciable.

Thus, although the centroid method was desirable from the standpoint of reconciling the descriptive implications of the new set of symptom rating scales with other less comprehensive sets of scales which
had been analyzed by the centroid method, there were two reasons
for providing an analysis by the method of principal components:

1   In general, the method of principal components could be expected to
be more informative than the centroid method of analysis because a greater
portion of the common factor variance would be involved.
2   A scrutiny of the intercorrelations among the variables contributing
to certain of the rotated centroid factors published in the "Dimensions of
Psychosis" (5), particularly Factors B and D, suggested a possibility of
systematic clustering of symptom rating scales within the sets of scales
comprising the centroid factors.   It was hoped that a more efficient analysis
by the method of principal components might reveal the nature of these apparent intra-factor clusters.

Accordingly, the intercorrelated symptom ratings scales, based on
the Lyons sample and analyzed by the centroid method for the purpose of the "Dimensions of Psychosis" report, were re-analyzed by the
method of principal components.[1]

The principal component analysis
with an orthogonal rotation

The principal component analysis of the intercorrelations was conducted by an application of a well-tested program for large electronic

[1] The ratings, which were provided by grant funds, were conducted with unusual
care under the joint supervision of the writer and Dr. Herman Efron, of the Veterans
Administration Hospital, Lyons, New Jersey.   The principal component analysis and
a modification of a varimax rotation procedure were conducted by Dr. David Saunders.

computing machines. The amount of common factor variance represented by the successive factors dropped sharply after Factor XXII, and no further appreciable diminution in the contribution of the successive factors occurred.

These 22 factors were submitted to a series of orthogonal rotations sufficient to establish convergence according to the criteria of simple structure. Virtually all of the factors are subject to clinically acceptable interpretation and provide descriptive distinctions which were not found in the centroid analysis.[2]

Factor B in the earlier centroid analysis was a bi-polar factor. One of the poles was described as indicative of a general *Depressive Retardation*. (This is not to be confused with retarded depression; it is possible that some other label, such as *General Retardation,* would have been a better choice.) In the present principal component solution, Factors I, II, III and VIII all comprise symptom rating scales which were a part of the retarded pole of Factor B in the original centroid solution. The possible interest of the factors which the present analysis distinguishes within Factor B can best be judged by an examination of their content.

Specifically, *Factor I* describes a constellation of symptoms of *intellectual impairment*. The rating scales it comprises refer to such symptoms as little recent memory, general memory faults, inability to identify self, can't identify other persons, poor comprehension, inability to concentrate.

Factor II describes an obstructive, disruptive pattern of behavior and involves such symptoms as being resistant and oppositional, actively resisting attendants, disrupting routines and failing to complete tasks.

Factor III is a factor of *social withdrawal* and involves such symptoms as stays in one spot, not participating, avoiding people, being unaware of other patients, not helping other patients, speaking rarely and not talking with other patients.

Factor VIII describes a quality of *affective flatness* and includes such symptoms as lack of insight into his present situation, little affective involvement, avoiding talk of relatives, appearing to be unaware of the feelings of others and not attempting to be helpful.

The distinctions suggested by these symptomatic clusterings have an obvious clinical plausibility, the practical value of which must be determined by the particular interests of the reader.

[2] A copy of the complete intercorrelation table has been deposited as Document number 7064 with the ADI Auxiliary Publications Project, Photoduplication Service, Library of Congress, Washington 25, D.C. A copy of the rotated factor matrix has been deposited as Document number 7574. A copy of the intercorrelation table may be secured by citing the Document number and by remitting $3.75 for photoprints, or $2.00 for 35 mm microfilm. The cost of a copy of the rotated factor matrix is $2.50 for photoprints and $1.75 for microfilm. Advance payment is required. Make checks or money orders payable to: Chief, Photoduplication Service, Library of Congress.

Factors VII, XI, and XII were, with a few exceptions in Factor VII, part of the original Factor D, *Psychotic Belligerence.* Their appearance further attests to the possibility that distinctions which may be implicit in a centroid analysis can become quite explicit in a principal component analysis.

Factor VII is an *attention-demanding* factor. It includes such behavior as demanding to see high-level personnel, engaging in plans which are wholly unrealistic, demanding help, showing an interest in other people's problems, being generally attention demanding and being generally nosy.

Factor XI describes *spontaneous assaultiveness* and includes such items as initiating physical assaults, attacking without provocation and great variation in rate of speech.

Factor XII describes a *manic excitement,* including abrupt changes in mood, exaggerated affect, singing and talking loudly, great variation in rate of speech, and profane or obscene speech.

Some of the symptom rating scales comprising Factor VII were included in the manic pole of centroid Factor B; others were important in centroid Factor D. It is interesting to note the various ways in which new factors emerge in the principal component analysis. Factor VII is generated by a combination of items from centroid Factors B and D, while Factor I in the principal component analysis is determined by scales which not only had important correlations with Factor B, but actually determined Factor E (Intellectual Impairment) in the centroid analysis.

Some of the factors which are revealed in the principal component analysis are quite similar in their content and implications to factors established by the centroid analysis, *e.g.,* Factors V, VI, X, XIV, XVII, and XX are identified with centroid factors C, A, I, J, F and K respectively and are described in the following paragraphs.

Factor V describes *delusions of persecution* and involves feeling persecuted, having ideas of influence, believing that he is hated by everybody, delusional misinterpretations and uncontrollable obsessions.

Factor VI indicates a verbal aspect of *schizophrenic excitement* which includes speaking to hallucinations, delusional thoughts, shouting and mumbling, being generally unintelligible, stilted speech and using words that were not relevant to a recognizable idea. This factor excludes the compulsive, restless, motoric features which were a part of the centroid Factor A.

Factor X implies *homosexual motivation* and involves such symptoms as direct sexual approaches to other patients, insists on controlling patients, delusions that sexual arrangements have been made, a tendency to be nosy, and a tendency to overreact to friendly overtures.

Factor XIV describes *compulsive behavior* and includes such symptoms as continuous compulsive acts, can't resist compulsive acts, failure and blocking, and constant movement.

Factor XVII suggests *hysterical conversions* and includes psychosomatic symptoms, physical claims without an organic basis, and a tendency to use physical symptoms for secondary gains.

Factor XX describes a quality of *anxiety* which is somewhat similar to the phobic factor (Factor XVIII).   Factor XX includes fear of committing an abhorred act and delusions of guilt.

There are other factors indicated in the principal component analysis which have a clinical plausibility but which do not bear a simple clear-cut relationship with any one of the centroid factors.

Factor IV is a factor of *incontinence* and comprises symptoms of incontinence and of discarding clothing.

Factor IX describes a quality of concern in interpersonal relationships which is difficult to interpret.   It includes fear of being misunderstood and interest in other patients' problems.   These symptoms were a part of the manic pole of centroid Factor B.

Factor XIII describes a *motoric passivity* characterized by the symptoms of submissiveness and slowed motions.

Factor XV suggests a quality of *silliness* and includes such symptoms as inappropriate laughter, rapid change of ideas, and behavior without any function.   This factor, like Factor XII, may be a part of a familiar manic constellation.

Factor XVI, ideas of grandeur, involves the symptoms of ideas of grandeur and of great variation in speech.   Like Factors XV and XII, it suggests a manic quality.

Factor XVIII describes an anxious, *phobic* reaction which includes such symptoms as phobias, fear of impending doom, and hopelessness.

Factor XIX is a factor of *resistance,* somewhat similar in its implications to Factor II and includes such symptoms as lying or stealing indiscriminately, refusing to eat and repudiating earlier insights.   It should be noted that the scales determining Factor XIX were important in the centroid Factor G, and the scales determining Factor II were relatively high for Factor G but did not reach .40.   Thus, it would appear that Factors II and XIX drew appreciable portions of their variance from centroid Factor G which was described as a *Hebephrenic Negativism.*

Factor XXI implies a *greediness* and comprises the symptoms of stuffing self gluttonously and lying and stealing indiscriminately.

Factor XXII implies a *suicidal* quality and includes a record of having attempted suicide and claims of an inability to sleep.   Suicidal attempts were a part of Factor F, the *Hysteria* factor in the centroid analysis.

The principal component analysis makes explicit numerous possible distinctions which remained obscured in the centroid analysis. With few exceptions this elaboration of principal component factors emerged from centroid factors in the general form of subordinate-supraordinate relationships and may be summarized in the outline below. In this outline the main headings are the centroid factors identified by the capital letters use din the initial report. The subheadings are the principal component factors identified by the Roman numerals employed in the preceding discussion. Those principal component factors which may be related to more than one centroid factor are marked by an asterisk while those which bear an unclear relation to a centroid factor are preceded by a question mark.

A. Schizophrenic Excitement:
      VI. Verbal Schizophrenic Excitement
B. (Bi-polar)
   Depressive Retardation:
      I. Intellectual Impairment *
      II. Obstructive, Disruptive *
      III. Social Withdrawal
      VIII. Affective Flatness
   Manic State:
      XII. Manic Excitement *
      VII. Attention Demanding *
      ?XVI. Ideas of Grandeur
      ?IX. Not interpreted
      ?XV. Silliness
C. Paranoid Schizophrenia:
      V. Delusions of Persecution
D. Psychotic Belligerence:
      VII. Attention Demanding *
      IX. Spontaneous Assaultiveness
      XII. Manic Excitement *
E. Intellectual Impairment:
      I. Intellectual Impairment *
F. Conversion Hysteria:
      XVII. Hysterical Conversions
      ?XXII. Suicidal
G. Hebephrenic Negativism:
      II. Obstructive, Disruptive *
      ?XIX. Resistance
      ?IV. Incontinence
H. Not interpreted
I. Homosexual Dominance:
      X. Homosexual Motivation
      ?XXI. Greediness
J. Phobic Compulsive:
      XIV. Compulsive Behavior
K. Anxiety:
      XX. Anxiety

Not Anticipated by Centroid Analysis:
    ?XIII. Motoric Passivity
    ?XVIII. Phobic

Discussion

Since the same data are involved in both studies, it is obvious that the method of principal components breaks down some of the factors which are produced by the centroid method. Such fractionation of the broader factors provided by the centroid method is advantageous in the sense that it draws distinctions to our attention. Nevertheless, such fractionation unaccompanied by a centroid analysis or some other method for showing the general picture could be disadvantageous because the fine distinctions do not indicate the existence or the nature of the broadly general dimensions of mental illness. It is possible that the broad picture provided by the centroid analysis confers a more useful general understanding of the realm of behavior under consideration than the complexly fragmented minor factors resulting from a principal component analysis. This question can be better answered by criteria which are pertinent to the investigator's purpose in undertaking the analysis than by mathematical criteria which disregard the nature of the behavioral problem that led the investigator to a factor analytic approach to the formulation of effective constructs.

It is possible that principal component factors rotated obliquely could result in a comprehensive view which would include both the broad understanding provided by the centroid solution and the distinctions found in the orthogonal principal component analysis. Specifically, it is possible that principal component factors, when rotated obliquely, could retain their useful identity and that the intercorrelations among the oblique factors could reveal the broad trends provided by the centroid solution; the intercorrelations among the factor axes could be submitted to a second-order analysis, and the second-order factors might provide the desired general picture. This possibility is being explored and will be described in a forthcoming report.

Summary

A set of symptom rating scales designed to reveal distinctions among chronic mental hospital patients had been applied earlier (5) to a sample of 150 chronic male patients at the Veterans Administration Hospital at Lyons, New Jersey. These 98 rating scales were intercorrelated and submitted to a centroid analysis described in the earlier report. The centroid analysis generated 12 factors which confirmed the implications of earlier studies. Upon scrutiny, some of these 12 factors appeared to be both symptomatically and statistically heterogeneous, suggesting that possible distinctions were obscured by some of the broadly general centroid factors.

The present report describes a principal component analysis of the intercorrelated symptom rating scales which had provided the basis for the earlier centroid analysis. Since the principal component analysis is more efficient than the centroid analysis from the standpoint of involving a maximal amount of the common factor variance, it was hoped that the principal component analysis would provide distinctions which were not provided by the centroid analysis. This expectation was fulfilled; the principal component analysis yielded 22 factors which, with one or two exceptions, were judged to have a clinical plausibility and to have provided worthwhile clarifying distinctions concerning the patterning of symptomatic manifestations in chronic male patients.

References

1. Degan, J. W. Dimensions of a functional psychosis. *Psychometr. Monogr.*, No. 6, 1952.

2. Lorr, M., O'Connor, J. P. and Stafford, J. W. Confirmation of nine psychotic symptom patterns. J. Clin. Psychol., *13:* 252–257, 1957.

3. Moore, T. V. The essential psychoses and their fundamental syndromes. Stud. Psychol. Psychiat., *3:* 1–128, 1933.

4. Wittenborn, J. R. Symptom patterns in a group of mental hospital patients. J. Consult. Psychol., *15:* 290–302, 1951.

5. Wittenborn, J. R. The dimensions of psychosis. J. Nerv. Ment. Dis., *134:* 117–128, 1962.

6. Wittenborn, J. R. and Holzberg, J. D. The generality of psychiatric syndromes. J. Consult. Psychol., *15:* 372–380, 1951.

Richard L. Jenkins **PSYCHIATRIC SYNDROMES IN CHILDREN ***

The development of high-speed computers does not offer any substitute for thinking, but once data have been assembled, it does facilitate routine comparisons which otherwise would not be possible. Our diagnostic understanding evolved largely from the slow process of case comparisons. In the field of child psychiatry, in which our diagnostic understanding leaves so much to be desired, it seems appropriate that

* From Richard L. Jenkins, "Psychiatric Syndromes in Children and their Relationship to Family Background," *Amer. J. Orthopsychiat.* 1966, 36, 450–457. Reprinted by permission of the author and the Editor, *American Journal of Orthopsychiatry.*

computer techniques should be employed to facilitate such comparisons and the resulting development of understanding.

The basis for this study is 500 cases on which IBM cards were carefully prepared by a former associate, Dr. Lester Hewitt, some years ago at the Michigan Child Guidance Institute. Each card represents a case examined at the Institute, and the case records were unusually complete. On each card each of 90 symptoms was checked if it was noted in the case record.

This material was the basis for two articles in this Journal (1, 2) and a monograph (3) which contrasted the three most prominent syndromes. The findings of the study have been confirmed (4, 5, 6).

The present study is a reexamination of this material by computer techniques which were not available at the time of the original study. Its purpose was to determine what background factors might be associated with any clusters so determined. From this material the existence of five clusters of symptoms was established by computer.[1] The symptoms most characteristic of each of these clusters were used to assign the cluster membership of cases. The first two groups are illustrated in Table 1.

Table 1 lists six symptoms selected as most characteristic of what I shall call the shy-seclusive group. Sixty-one cases in the 500 had at least three of these symptoms and also had more symptoms characteristic of this group than of any other group. Of these 61 cases, 21 per cent were girls. The interquartile age range, which contains at least half of the cases, was 9 to 14.

---

[1] The procedure was to take the 500 cards in four groups of 125 cards each. (This division into smaller groups was occasioned by the finite memory of our computer.) Each card in a group was compared successively with every other card in the group. Let us suppose that card one and card two had five entries in common, and card one had a total of ten and card two a total of fifteen entries. Then card one shared 50 per cent of its entries with card two, and card two shared 33.3 per cent of its entries with card one. These two values were summed to provide a convenient index (.833) of the resemblance between card one and card two. (An average of these two values would accomplish the same thing but presented no advantage.) If card one and card three shared two entries and card three had sixteen entries in all, then card one shared 20 per cent of its entries with card three, and card three shared 12.5 per cent of its entries with card one. The resemblance between card one and card three is represented by sum of these values, .325. Thus, card one resembles card two more than it resembles card three.

All possible comparisons were made in this way within each group of 125 cards. Each card was then placed with the card it resembled most. This process formed clusters and these were our initial clusters.

The fact that a card was placed with the card it resembled most did not insure that it was in the cluster it resembled most. Proceeding from initial groupings, the average value of the resemblance of each card to all the other cards in each cluster was calculated. Those cards with a greater average resemblance to the cards of another cluster than to the cards of their own cluster were reassigned to the cluster they resembled most closely. Then the process of calculating average resemblances was repeated and reassignments were made again until the groups stabilized. Some clusters disappeared in this process.

At this point, a card was made out for each cluster. If an item were present in 50 per cent or more of the members of a cluster, it was considered characteristic of that cluster and punched on the cluster card. The cluster cards were then treated in a matrix just as the original cards had been treated. The result was five clusters of clusters or "superclusters."

Table 1
Two inhibited groups
Each child showed at least 3 of the traits listed

Shy-seclusive group	Overanxious-neurotic group
Seclusive	Sleep disturbances
Shyness, timidity	Fears
Absence of close friendships	Cries easily
Apathy, underactivity	Fantastic thinking (overimaginative)
Depressed or discouraged attitude	Marked inferiority feeling
Sensitiveness	Nervousness
N = 61 21 per cent girls	N = 43 37 per cent girls
Typical age 9–14	Typical age 9–12

Table 1 also lists the symptoms characteristic of the overanxious-neurotic group.   There were 43 cases with three or more of these symptoms and in which the symptoms falling in this group were more numerous than the symptoms falling in any other group.   These 43 cases were 37 per cent girls, the highest percentage of girls appearing in any of our groups.   The interquartile age range was 9 to 12.

As might be expected, there was some overlap between these two groups.   Both these groups were classified as inhibited.   The next three groups to be described were classified as aggressive.

Table 2 lists the characteristic symptoms of a hyperactive group characterized by poor concentration.   Seventy-six cases, 16 per cent girls, had at least three of these symptoms, and more of these than of the symptoms of any other group.   This is our youngest group, with an interquartile age range of 9 to 11 years.   Of the aggressive groups, this is the one with the most in common with the overanxious-neurotic children.   These are immature, poorly organized children.

Table 2 next presents an older group which I call the undomesticated children.   This group tends to overlap with the hyperactive group but presents a more serious picture.   There are 58 children in

Table 2
Three aggressive groups
Each child showed at least 3 of the traits listed

Hyperactive-distractible group	Undomesticated group	Socialized delinquent group
Hyperactive	Negativistic	Furtive stealing
Lack of concentration	Defiance of authority	Cooperative stealing
Mischievousness	Vengefulness	Running away from home overnight
Inability to get along with other children	Sullenness	Habitual truancy from school
Overdependent	Malicious mischief	Association with undesirable companions
Bashfulness	Temper outbursts	Petty stealing
N = 76 16 per cent girls	N = 58 24 per cent girls	N = 53 9 per cent girls
Typical age 9–11	Typical age 11–14	Typical age 12–15

this group, 24 per cent girls.   The interquartile age range is 11 to 14. The extreme of this group is the antisocial or psychopathic personality.

Our last and oldest group, consisting of the socialized delinquents, is also included in Table 2.   The interquartile age range is 12 to 15 years.   There are 53 cases, of which only 9 per cent are girls.   The extreme of this group is the dyssocial reaction.   By contrast with the undomesticated group, these individuals are not basically unsocialized.   Rather they are more or less socialized with the narrow but exacting limits of a predatory and fighting group.   They depend on each other.

We regard the discovery of five groups as significant in disclosing or confirming the existence of five differentiable core types of behavioral deviations.   Too much significance should not be ascribed to the *size* of the groups obtained, as it is possible to vary the size by narrowing or widening the definition.   For example our hyperactive-distractible group is our largest group.   It is possible to define this group so narrowly and extremely as to restrict it largely to brain-damaged children who can be diagnosed chronic brain syndrome, or to define it so broadly (as we do) that it includes many functionally immature children.

If now we compare our two groups of inhibited children, the shy-seclusive group and the overanxious group with the three groups of aggressive children, the hyperactive children, the undomesticated children and the socialized delinquents, certain statistically significant [2] contrasts are evident.   The inhibited children are prone to worrying and to daydreaming.   They are often submissive, often have finicky food habits and often show a speech defect.   I suspect that this last is true because having a speech defect intends to inhibit a child rather than because either of these symptom groups tends to produce a speech defect.

The aggressive children, on the other hand, differ from the inhibited children in that they are prone to stay out late at night and to be deceptive.   They often use profane or obscene language, are sometimes cruel and often project blame on others.

The inhibited children seldom dislike their schoolteachers, and disturbing behavior in school is rare.   The aggressive children often dislike their schoolteachers, and disturbing behavior in school is frequent.

A further significant difference is that the aggressive children are disposed to have a particular talent for or interest in sports, while the inhibited children are prone to have a particular talent for or interest in art.   The inhibited children are prone to lack physical coordination or dexterity.   It does not seem surprising that a child lacking physical

---

[2] A difference which would be expected to occur on a chance basis less than once in 20 times was accepted as significant.   Calculations were based on a chi-square with P $<$ .05 for a two-tailed distribution.

Table 3

Inhibited children	Aggressive children
	Typical traits
Worrying	Staying out late at night
Daydreaming	Deceptive (lying, cheating, crafty, sly)
Often submissive	Often obscene and profane language
Often finicky food habits	Sometimes cruel
Often speech defect	Often projects blame
	School adjustment
Seldom dislike teacher	Often dislike teacher
Disturbing behavior rare	Disturbing behavior frequent
	Specific talents or interests
Art	Sports
	Special deficiencies
Lack of physical coordination or dexterity	
	Mother person
Natural mother	Often substitute mother
Rarely openly hostile	Often openly hostile
Child does not feel rejected by mother	Child sometimes feels rejected by mother
	Father person
Natural father	Often substitute father
	Guilt feeling
Adequate	Often inadequate

coordination and dexterity is less likely to be interested in sports or to be aggressive.

When we look for elements of family background which distinguish these groups and are presumably related to these differences, we find the inhibited children nearly always with both natural parents, the aggressive children less likely to be with both natural parents. The mother person of the inhibited child was rarely openly hostile toward the child, and in none of our cases was the child recorded as feeling rejected by the mother person. In the case of the aggressive children, the mother person was often openly hostile, and in each group of aggressive children we not infrequently find the entry that the child sometimes feels rejected by the mother. The association strongly indicates that change of parent figures (which is often interpreted by the child as rejection) and maternal hostility stimulate hostile, rebellious, aggressive responses in the child. The last entry indicates also that these experiences often are related to an inadequate development of conscience and of guilt feeling. The overdeveloped conscience of the inhibited child may present a problem, but typically it is less disturbing or threatening to others, than the underdeveloped conscience of the aggressive child.

If we compare our two groups of inhibited children, we find most of the overanxious children hyperactive, while this symptom is much less prominent in the shy-exclusive group.   This fact relates to the overlap of the overanxious group and the hyperactive group of aggressive children.

A majority of our overanxious-neurotic group have a history of prolonged, serious or repeated illness.   These children frequently come from educated middle-class homes as is indicated by the fact that more than a quarter of the fathers have had some college training.

It is the characteristics of the mother persons, however, which most clearly distinguish these groups.   Nearly half of the overanxious-neurotic children have mothers who were described as neurotic because of extreme nervousness, compulsions or evident emotional complexes. A close and sometimes morbid bond between the natural mother and the child is common enough so that, as compared with the shy-seclusive children, it is much more frequently recorded that the overanxious child prefers the natural mother to the other parent.

Chronic illness, serious crippling or physical impairment occur in a quarter of the mothers of the shy-seclusive children, and one in six was considered mentally inadequate.   Neither one of these two comparisons reaches the conventionally accepted .05 level of significance. Neither one of these contrasts, however, would occur on a chance basis as often as once in ten times, and because of their consistency and the fact that they seem to make sense, we have included them.

The overanxious-neurotic child appears more frequently in more educated families (which are prone to set higher standards) and with neurotic mothers, who are themselves anxious, and the more discouraged shy-seclusive child more frequently has an ill, handicapped or inadequate mother.

Table 4

	Shy-seclusive children	Over-anxious-neurotic children
Hyperactive (restless)	16%	65%
History of prolonged, serious or repeated illness	31%	54%
Father: some college training	8%	26%
Mother person neurotic (extreme nervousness, compulsions, etc.)	23%	44%
Mother person preferred by child over other parent(s)	2%	12%
Mother person: chronic illness, serious crippling or physical impairment *	25%	12%
Mother person mentally inadequate *	15%	5%

* Reaches only 0.1 level of probability with a two-tailed distribution. (All other contrasts are beyond the .05 level.)

Table 5

	Hyperactive group	Undomesticated group	Socialized delinquent group
Nervousness	49%	38%	13%
Quarrelsomeness	54%	55%	9%
Rudeness to person in authority	38%	48%	17%
Staying out late nights	15%	29%	47%
Gang activities	1%	12%	19%

Table 5 gives us a comparison of some symptom entries in our three aggressive groups of children. Nervousness, which was one of the symptoms used in defining the overanxious-neurotic group, is recorded in nearly half of our hyperactive group, in nearly two-fifths of our undomesticated group and in only about an eighth of the socialized delinquent group. This underlines the closeness of our hyperactive group to our overanxious group. Quarrelsomeness and rudeness toward persons in authority are high in the hyperactive group and particularly in the undomesticated group, and are much less frequent among the socialized delinquents who are, in their own way, more socialized. On the other hand, staying out late at night and gang activities are relatively infrequent in the younger hyperactive group, and most frequent among the socialized delinquents.

Table 6 indicates that the backgrounds of the undomesticated children characteristically include an unstable mother unable to relate herself to responsibility, and either a pregnancy unwanted by the mother or maternal rejection occurring after birth but while the child is still in infancy. Frequently, the child is openly hostile to the natural mother, and rarely does he prefer the natural mother to the other parent or parents. Lack of sufficient maternal love and acceptance early in life is a significant factor in this reaction.

Table 7 indicates that the socialized delinquent is, as we might expect, selectively a product of the uneducated family, the large family with the working mother whose children are unsupervised, the unkempt irregular household. If a mother has eight or more children and is working, to take the extreme, it is difficult to see how she could supervise the children's activities.

Table 6

	Hyperactive group	Undomesticated group	Socialized delinquent group
Unstable mother unable to relate self to responsibility	13%	38%	15%
Maternal rejection in infancy	37%	55%	25%
Child openly hostile to natural mother	7%	24%	17%
Child prefers natural mother to other parent(s)	15%	2%	8%

Table 7

	Hyperactive group	Undomesticated group	Socialized delinquent group
Mother completed high school	25%	16%	2%
Father had some college training	16%	10%	6%
Working mother	12%	17%	32%
Eight or more children in the home	0%	5%	21%
Unkempt dwelling interior	12%	19%	32%
Irregularity of meals, work, retiring	10%	12%	38%
Lack of supervision of children's activities	24%	21%	42%

The socialized delinquent is a product not of maternal rejection but of neglect (which may be unavoidable lack of supervision) and a bad neighborhood. In this group, paternal deficiencies are much more prominent than maternal deficiencies. In more than half of our cases the natural father is not regularly at home. In nearly a quarter of the cases he is dead, and in more than two-fifths of our cases the present father person is described in the record as alcoholic. Here the problem is not one of the child's primary socialization. This was accomplished in the home and particularly by the mother early in his life. Here the problem is one of the direction, training and control particularly of the preadolescent and the adolescent boy and the lack of an adequate masculine pattern for identification. Under these circumstances, he may find his emotional security and identification with the delinquent gang. I do not believe that this represents psychopathology so much as social pathology.

Summary

In summary, a purely symptomatic grouping of 500 child guidance clinic cases brings out five symptomatic clusters. The shy-seclusive children and the overanxious-neurotic children are inhibited groups. The hyperactive children, the undomesticated children and the socialized delinquents are aggressive groups.

These symptomatic groups are very significantly related to background factors which may be presumed to have substantial etiological importance.

Anxiety in children is accentuated by illness and by maternal anx-

Table 8

	Hyperactive group	Undomesticated group	Socialized delinquent group
Natural father not regularly in home	34%	38%	53%
Father dead	7%	10%	23%
Alcoholic father person	16%	19%	42%

iety. Hostility is generated by hostile treatment and the feeling of being rejected. The hyperactive syndrome appears to be relatively more age-limited than the others, and under favorable conditions children probably more often outgrow it spontaneously than is the case with the other symptom groups. Maternal rejection early in life and the child's reaction to it appear to be a central factor in the development of the undomesticated child, who is hostile, defiant and vengeful. The socialized delinquent, on the other hand, is typically the product of a combination of poverty, parental neglect, the lack of an adequate father figure, and the delinquent associates of the bad neighborhood. Since his delinquency is typically adaptive, it represents social pathology rather than psychiatric pathology.

References

1. Jenkins, R. L., and L. Hewitt. 1944. Types of personality encountered in child guidance clinics. Amer. J. Orthopsychiat. 14: 84–94.

2. Jenkins, R. L. 1957. Motivation and frustration in delinquency. Amer. J. Orthopsychiat. 17: 528–537.

3. Hewitt, L., and R. L. Jenkins. 1946. Fundamental patterns of maladjustment: The Dynamics of Their Origin. State of Illinois.

4. Lewis, H. 1954. Deprived Children. Oxford University Press, London.

5. Saksida, S. 1959. Motivation mechanisms and frustration stereotypes. Amer. J. Orthopsychiat. 29: 599–611.

6. Jenkins, R. L. 1964. Diagnoses, dynamics and treatment in child psychiatry. Psychiatric Research Report, American Psychiatric Association. 18: 91–120.

Leif J. Braaten

SOME REFLECTIONS ON SUICIDAL TENDENCIES AMONG COLLEGE STUDENTS *

Most college students do not have to resolve major emotional conflicts. They admittedly must work hard to learn, both academically and socially, but they need no professional assistance from the mental health clinician.

* From Leif J. Braaten, "Some Reflections on Suicidal Tendencies among College Students," *Ment. Hyg.*, N.Y., 1963, 47, 562–568. Reprinted by permission of the author and the Editor, *Mental Hygiene*.

However, about 10 per cent of all college students experience serious emotional problems while passing through this phase of late adolescence.   Of particular importance is one such subgroup consisting of both male and female students with suicidal tendencies.

The purpose of this paper is to present and discuss some selected research findings regarding suicidal tendencies among college students.   A more technical and comprehensive report is already in press in the *Psychiatric Quarterly* (1).

This paper deals with such topics as the conceptualization of suicidal subgroups, the incidence of suicidal tendencies, a comparison of suicidal and nonsuicidal patients, psychodynamics, management and treatment.   A longer case illustration, with the necessary disguise to protect the patient's identity, will also be included.

Some fundamental issues

The writer will state the issues in the form of questions and then discuss some tentative answers.

The conceptualization of suicidal subgroups

What is the most adequate conceptualization of suicidal subgroups?

The classical studies did not distinguish between different subgroups of individuals with suicidal tendencies.   Until recently, researchers were only interested in such questions as the incidence of completed suicide in different countries.   Attempts were made to explain the incidence in terms of such concepts as Durkheim's *anomie,* the condition which exists in a social group whose members feel cast loose from their moorings, purposeless, normless, lonely and alienated.

In the opinion of this writer, suicide research took a great step forward when Farberow and Shneidman (3) started to distinguish sharply between threatened, attempted, and completed suicide.   They found some evidence which appeared to justify the assertion that individuals belonging to such suicidal subgroups show significant psychological differences.   For example, it looked as if individuals threatening suicide were emotionally "sicker" than those who made bona fide suicide attempts.

The writer has been puzzled by these results for some time, and he has tried partially to replicate their procedures to see if their results could be corroborated.

Two points are worth making.   First, it should be considered a possible methodological artifact that the "attempts" are less sick than the "threats."   At least in this college setting we typically give the "attempts" psychological tests *after* their drastic act.   Most often the student's first contact with the Mental Health Division takes place when the student is brought to the clinic or infirmary after the suicide attempt.

The generally lower profiles of psychopathology for the "attempts" as compared with the "threats" may be due to the fact that some of the needs of the potential suicide have been satisfied through his desperate behavior. It is referred to the need for self-punishment, the expression of hostility toward some significant other, and the need of the disturbed person that his cry for help be heard by somebody.

The second point is that it is somewhat dangerous that so much is being made of the finding that suicidal subgroups are so different. One sometimes obtains the impression that if you are a "threat," you will probably not change into an "attempt" or a "completed suicide." Therefore, rather than give the indication that we are dealing with discrete categories of suicidal patients, this writer feels that it is a more accurate conceptualization to think in terms of a *continuum of suicidal concern*. This formulation reflects the clinical observation that a patient may change, sometimes very rapidly, from one point on the continuum to another.

In our own study of suicidal tendencies among college students we found the following points necessary to describe adequately such a continuum: the "intellectualizers," the "threats," the "attempts," and the "completed suicides." The *intellectualizers* showed occasional suicidal thoughts or impulses, but rather on an intellectual level, and they could not be tied down to specific events, moods and methods.

The *threats* exhibited rather frequent and intensive suicidal inclinations; precipitating events and possible methods of suicide were contemplated; their mood was usually fairly congruent with the suicidal impulse. Minor acts of self-mutilation, such as superficial cuts of the wrist, still did not exclude them from this category.

The *attempts* were characterized by having actually carried out bona fide suicide attempts, that is, acts appearing to be directed toward destroying the whole of the individual's physical organism, as distinguished from minor acts of self-mutilation, more plainly psychological self-destruction, and completed suicide. Finally, the *completed suicides* were individuals who carried out suicide attempts, with death as a consequence.

As compared with Farberow and Shneidman (3), the only additional category that we isolated was the "intellectualizers." A minimal criterion for this category was that the student had underlined "thoughts of suicide" on the Mooney Problem Check List.

As a *control comparison group* we used other mental health patients from our regular patient population not falling in either of the suicidal subgroups. Because of the lack of "completed suicides" among our mental health patients at Cornell, all our results deal with suicidal tendencies *not* ending with self-inflicted death. Yet in line with our basic conceptualization of a continuum of suicidal concern we believe that our results may shed some light on the general topic of suicidal tendencies, suicide included.

The incidence of suicidal tendencies

What is the incidence of suicidal tendencies?   Whereas there are many studies reporting the incidence of completed suicide, few studies are available reporting the incidence of suicidal tendencies. Therefore, it may be of some interest to report that among the student patients visiting the Mental Health Division of Cornell University the incidence of suicidal tendencies was 11 per cent of our total case load. Sixty-eight per cent of these suicidal patients showed only intellectualized concern, while 27 per cent threatened suicide, and 5 per cent actually made bona fide suicide attempts.

Temby (6) at Harvard has recently reported that their rate of completed suicides is approximately 1.5 persons for every 10,000 students per year.   If we were to assume that the incidence of completed suicides would be roughly the same for the college age, our data would indicate that for every actual suicide there are at least 50 students who have more or less serious suicidal tendencies which do not end in tragic death.

Some of these depressed and unhappy youngsters are probably saved each year through the preventive and therapeutic efforts of the Mental Health Division of the Student Medical Clinic.   A few suicidal patients are so emotionally disturbed that they are granted a medical leave of absence to be given intensive psychotherapy outside the college setting.   But the great majority of suicidal students are successfully treated while they still go to school.

Suicidal and nonsuicidal patients compared

What significant differences were found between the various subgroups in this study?   In terms of objective personality tests, could the "intellectualizers," the "threats," the "attempts," and the "controls" be clearly distinguished from each other?   The tests used were the Minnesota Multiphasic Personality Inventory (the MMPI) and the Mooney Problem Check List (the Mooney).

The most striking result was as follows: Suicidal patients, both males and females, for all subgroups considered together, showed, on the average, significantly more psychopathology than nonsuicidal patients as objectively measured by both the MMPI and the Mooney.   In other words, a suicidal patient is definitely "sicker" than a patient without suicidal tendencies.

When we compared the suicidal patients with the nonsuicidal patients, we found that the suicidal patients were significantly more depressed, more schizoid and more obsessive-compulsive when measured by the MMPI.   Therefore, when a clinician deals with a patient displaying such syndromes, he should be alerted to the possibility of associated suicidal tendencies.

Dahlstrom and Welsh (2) reviewed several studies which had used the MMPI and concluded that ". . . a suicidal impulse may stem from several different personality processes. A recurrent pattern in all these findings is the elevation on depression and psychasthenia, reflecting a combination of feelings of unworthiness, lack of hope for the future, and a self-blaming and deprecating tendency of major proportions. A second pattern appears to be based upon intense frustration and anger, appearing in elevations on scales 4/ psychopathic deviation/, 6/ paranoia/, and occasionally 8/ schizophrenia/."

As you can see, our findings partly confirm their conclusions in that suicidal tendencies among our subjects are associated with high peaks on the Depression and Psychasthenia scales. At the college level, however, suicidal tendencies are not only occasionally correlated with a spike on the Schizophrenia scale; rather, this is the rule. While our suicidal patients showed high peaks on the Psychopathic Deviation and Paranoia scales, these differences were not statistically significant when the suicidal patients were compared with the control group.

The one category on the Mooney which showed a statistically significant difference between the suicidal and the nonsuicidal patients was the so-called "personal psychological problems." In other words, the most common denominator for the suicidal group was emotional problems within the self—intrapsychic conflicts.

It will be recalled that Farberow and Shneidman (3) had found that the "threats" appeared to be "sicker" than the "attempts." The general trend of our findings supports their result. Our "attempts" generally scored lower than both the "intellectualizers" and the "threats." However, on neither the MMPI nor the Mooney were any of these subgroup differences statistically significant for either sex. In our study the definite and impressive difference was found between suicidal and nonsuicidal patients, *not* between the different suicidal sub-groups.

The psychodynamics of the suicidal patient

What are the typical psychodynamics of the suicidal patient? Our answer to this question is based upon our objective test results from the MMPI and the Mooney, item analyses of the significant scales of these tests, and an intensive perusal of the clinical folders for the "attempts." Although the following description of the suicidal patient is most valid for the "attempts," it is our impression that it applies to suicidal patients in general.

The suicidal patient in college is an angry, excessively dependent and very unhappy individual. His anger often assumes the proportions of rage or intense hostility. "Acting out" to get his way is a favorite mechanism. He is often excessively competitive and ambitious both in his work and interpersonal relations. His dependence upon others often becomes nearly unbearable during crises in love attachments and impending academic failure. By assuming that the significant other—a parent, a girl friend, or a parent substitute—is as dependent upon him as he is, the suicidal patient would expect that anything bad that happened to him would also be experienced with sadness and despair by the other person. It is as if he were planning to say: "Now that I have killed myself, you'll be sorry."

Most often the suicidal person would appear very unhappy and depressed. But occasionally the underlying depression would be covered up by motor agitation, that is extreme motor restlessness and confusion, during which the patient, being extremely accident prone, runs off aimlessly. In both sexes there were fears about masculinity-femininity, and, especially in men, more outspoken homosexual worries. Such intensive inner conflicts often interfered with study efficiency, and the tension continued to build up.

The suicidal patient hated himself as well as others. He often displayed a more generalized self-destructive trend, both psychologically and physically. In several cases we observed what Farberow and Shneidman have called a "death trend." Such patients had encountered serious illness or death in the family or among close friends, suicides or suicide attempts, and tragic accidents.

In their most recent book, *The Cry for Help* (4), Farberow and Shneidman listed these significant suicidal psychodynamics: dependency, aggression and hostility, guilt, and anxiety. It is interesting to note both the similarities and the differences between our findings and theirs. We certainly agree that the suicidal patient is basically hostile and dependent. Whereas they emphasize anxiety, we would rather stress depression. Also the factor of guilt did not seem to be too preponderant at the college level.

A case illustration

So far we have presented and discussed some results which are scientific generalizations. It may be of interest to the reader to have a somewhat detailed case description which will illustrate some of our findings.

This patient was admitted to the Cornell Infirmary after he cut himself somewhat seriously with a razor blade. He was in the last part of his senior year in college. He had felt extremely depressed after a quarrel with his girl friend and had cut through the skin several times on his left wrist and forearm. During the self-destructive act he had called the girl on the telephone, read a despondent poem, expressed bitterness and irritation at everybody, and appeared to his girl friend to become weaker from bleeding as he was talking to her. The girl friend notified the campus patrol, and they brought the patient to the Cornell Infirmary.

From things learned later we were able to reconstruct his psychological situation. Many pressures were operating upon him at the time. His parents were going through divorce proceedings after years of an unhappy marriage. Both parents tried to enlist the patient's support against the other spouse. After four years in college he was coming close to the challenge of starting a career. These new responsibilities obviously scared him. His prospective in-laws did not seem to like him. Also, it is true that he was sexually confused. He worried about his manhood.

In spite of a serious, bona fide attempt at suicide we decided to keep him in college, if a good doctor-patient relationship could be established. This was a calculated risk, but it was agreed to by all interested parties, including the family. As things developed, it was found that he was not an easy patient to treat. At times he tried to be overly logical and minimize the significance of the whole episode. At other times he might express regret that he had not succeeded in his suicide attempt.

He was sometimes resentful of everybody, his therapist included. He had a rifle and disliked our taking this away from him. He consented grudgingly not to drink alcoholic beverages as a condition for staying in college. During interviews he often appeared tense; and he smoked incessantly. Behind this tough, somewhat belligerent facade he appeared scared, and he leaned heavily upon the therapeutic relationship. He was demanding. Part of the therapy consisted in helping him to see that within certain reasonable limits he could indeed be understood and accepted as a suffering fellow human being.

During one interview he said: "I have threatened to kill myself many times in the past, and finally I knew that I had to go through with it." This confession is a serious reminder to the clinician as well as the layman that somebody who threatens suicide may indeed one day feel desperate enough to try it. Three weeks after his first suicide attempt he tried again, and this time he cut himself more seriously, although not in a truly dangerous way. He was again picked up by the campus patrol and, when he became unmanageable and tried to run away, was put in jail overnight. After the second episode, the patient reluctantly accepted an enforced medical leave of absence.

The patient was seen by three members of our staff, and one clinician saw him for 15 therapy interviews. And yet, we were not able to help him fully control his powerful self-destructive urge. After he left, he entered long-term intensive psychotherapy in his home city. Because he was a good student with a respectable record he was awarded his degree even though he did not finish up all his courses. We heard two years later that he had married the girl whom he met in college.

The management and treatment of suicidal patients

Are there any unique features to the management and treatment of suicidal patients?

One question which sometimes arises is: Should he be hospitalized? This is not an easy question to answer. As therapists, we are basically working under the assumption that we can and should trust our patients. We believe that the strength of the therapeutic relationship will be enough to keep the suicidal patient from any drastic action. But the case illustration you have just read shows that this assumption is not always justified.

In a community there may be several reasons for occasionally resorting to hospitalization: the danger of a serious suicide attempt seems to be imminent; other people close to the patient become extremely anxious; the doctor cannot stand his own anxiety about a possible suicide.

This writer believes that even with a seriously depressed patient all these reasons may be made explicit to him. Having spent 4½ years in a medical setting at Cornell the writer has both learned to feel freer to use the infirmary for hospitalization and also to tolerate more anxiety about serious self-damaging tendencies in some patients.

And, in the final analysis, a therapist must accept that his patients are free and responsible individuals. In addition to showing the suicidal patient acceptance and empathic understanding the therapist must make his patient feel that if he really wants to kill himself nobody can stop him. More than anything the therapist must work through his own feelings about suicide and death and thus give his patients a chance to explore and feel and verbalize accurately whatever comes to mind about this morbid topic.

In this connection we may have something to learn from Victor Frankl's therapeutic approach as described in his book *From Death-Camp to Existentialism* (5). He sometimes found it helpful to formulate the following existential null hypothesis: "Why is it that you have *not* yet committed suicide?" Sometimes the patient's spontaneous answers to this question can give him a fresh perspective on being alive rather than dead. If he rejects the alternative of self-inflicted death, then he must necessarily affirm something. Thus his life will assume new meaning.

Some conclusions and perspectives

What are some of the more significant conclusions and perspectives about the topic of suicidal tendencies?

1   Suicidal tendencies, as defined in this paper, are much more common than generally assumed. For every completed suicide among college stu-

dents there are 50 with suicidal tendencies not ending with self-inflicted death.

2   We need to do some more thinking about the best way to conceptualize suicidal tendencies.   More studies are needed to determine whether we are really dealing with discrete categories, such as "intellectualizers," "threats," "attempts," and "completed suicides" or whether it is more accurate to talk about a continuum of suicidal concern.

3   At the college level the suicidal patient is significantly more depressed, more obsessive-compulsive, and more schizoid than a control comparison patient.   Among persons in their late adolescence suicidal tendencies seem to have a special affinity to the schizoid personality or borderline schizophrenia.

4   The one most interesting psychodynamic formula which emerged from this study is to look at depression as "pushed-back anger."   The patient is so afraid of the intensity of his anger that he does not dare to express it.   The depressive reaction is partly a defense against this anger. A major task in the therapy of the suicidal person is to help him release this pent-up anger so that such feelings may be fully experienced, verbalized, and communicated within the safety of the doctor-patient relationship.

5   The suicidal patient represents to the therapist a real challenge to work through his own feelings about suicide and death.   Only then can the therapist become a truly helpful participant to his patient in rejecting death and affirming life.   This writer has learned increasingly to have respect for the life-affirming forces within all of us, including patients who appear to be seriously suicidal.

6   Although we are beginning to learn a great deal about the suicidal person, we still have a long way to go in our preventive work.   We must increase our efforts so that the potential suicide can be spotted reliably and referred for professional help.   This task involves the delicate assignment to educate the layman about indicators of suicide without scaring him unduly.

References

1. Braaten, L. J. and C. D. Darling, "Suicidal Tendencies Among College Students," *Psychiatric Quarterly,* 36(October, 1962), 665–92.

2. Dahlstrom, W. C. and G. S. Welsh, *An MMPI Handbook: A Guide to Use in Clinical Practice and Research* (Minneapolis: University of Minnesota Press, 1960).

3. Farberow, N. L. and E. S. Shneidman, "A Study of Attempted, Threatened and Completed Suicide." *Journal of Abnormal Social Psychology,* 50(March, 1955), 230.

4. Farberow, N. L. and E. S. Shneidman, eds., *The Cry for Help* (New York: McGraw-Hill Book Company, 1961).

5. Frankl, V. E., *From Death-Camp to Existentialism* (Boston: Beacon Press, 1959).

6. Temby, W. D., "Suicide," in Blaine, G. B., Jr. and C. C. McArthur, eds., *Emotional Problems of the Student* (New York: Appleton-Century-Crofts, Inc., 1961), 133–52.

FIVE

SECTION FIVE   PSYCHOTHERAPY

The basic goal in the treatment of adjustment difficulties is the alteration of the patient's behavior.   The behavior to be changed may involve both the overt actions of the individual, such as his manner of
interacting with others, and internal characteristics, such as the individuals self-perception or conflicting attitudes and motives.   Numerous methods of effecting changes in behavior are employed in the
treatment of adjustment problems.   Some of these are chemotherapy
(tranquilizing drugs, sedatives, stimulants, etc.), physical therapy
(sports, physical exercise, etc.), psychosurgery (lobotomies and various
other surgical operations on the brain), and electroshock therapy.
The interest here is in the use of psychological approaches to the
treatment of adjustment problems and these are called psychotherapy.
Because of the wide variety of techniques which are based on the
application of psychological principles and which are referred to as
psychotherapy, it is extremely difficult to define the term in more than
a broad fashion.   In general, psychotherapy refers to a controlled
interaction between a person seeking psychological assistance and
another person who is professionally trained to provide it.   The goal is
to bring about a more effective adjustment on the part of the individual seeking aid.   Usually psychotherapy is associated with talking,
since most of the interaction between the persons involved is of a verbal nature.   Some psychotherapeutic techniques, however, stress a
planned program of physical activity in the context of which the interaction between patient and therapist takes place.

Psychotherapies may be classified in numerous ways.   Sometimes
the types of therapy are identified on the basis of the theoretical ideas
underlying them (*psychoanalytic therapy, client-centered therapy,
Adlerian therapy*); sometimes by the particular groups of people or
type of problem for which the approach was designed (*child-guidance
therapy, marriage counseling*); sometimes by the methods employed
(*play therapy, dance therapy*); and sometimes by the goal which the
therapy establishes (*supportive therapy, reconstructive therapy*).
The readings which follow present a sample of the various therapeutic
approaches in common use.   In addition they illustrate the thinking

underlying the three major theoretical approaches which have influenced psychotherapy most: *psychoanalysis, phenomenological theory* or *client-centered therapy,* and *learning theory.*

The first paper by Arnold Allen presents a case study using *psychoanalytic techniques* of a young man experiencing a number of personality difficulties and poor adjustment, including stealing, marital problems, passivity, inefficiency, and inner rage over frustrations of his strong dependence and acceptance needs. The interaction between patient and psychoanalyst illustrates several of the procedures which distinguish psychoanalysis from other forms of psychotherapy. A brief statement of some of these procedures may help the reader identify significant features of the interaction. The most distinctive feature is the use of *free association;* i.e., the patient is requested to state everything that occurs to him and to avoid asserting conscious control over his thoughts. To the extent that the patient is able to do this without censoring his thoughts or imposing logic on them, his feelings, desires, fears, and impulses which are usually suppressed are likely to be revealed to both him and to the analyst. Often in the psychoanalytic session the content of the patient's free association deals with important events in his life or with his feelings while lying on the couch in the psychoanalyst's office. In addition, the patient's dreams frequently are used as a starting point for free association and, as seen in the case presented, serve as a rich source of material for examining the patient's repressed feelings and desires. The patient usually is unable to see the relevance of his free association and dreams to his problems on his own, since awareness of his repressions is extremely threatening, and, in fact, he is apt to resist and defend against understanding. It is only through the psychoanalyst's interest, support, and objectivity that the patient gradually becomes less resistant and willing to accept things about himself which he previously censored from awareness. The primary method which the psychoanalyst uses to help the patient gain insight is *interpretation.* In effect, interpretation refers to the analyst's giving words to the patient which expresses feelings which are not totally conscious, thereby facilitating the patient's awareness of them. In this way the psychoanalyst attempts to make unconscious material conscious. However, awareness per se is not likely to alter the patient's behavior or remove his problems. The feelings, desires, or conflicts which have been causing the emotional difficulties must be considered again and again in connection with many different experiences and areas of life before the patient is able to alter his way of behaving. This is a slow process which is called the *working through stage* and which accounts for a large part of the extensive period, usually years, which Freudian psychoanalysis requires.

As stated in the papers by Freud and Dollard and Miller in previous sections of this book, psychoanalysis postulates that emotional problems are associated primarily with childhood experiences, and consequently much of the psychoanalytic discussion (the patient's free association and the analyst's interpretations) pertain to the patient's childhood.   The case presented by Allen clearly illustrates the psychoanalyst's emphasis on family experiences and relationships during childhood.   The analyst endeavors to learn as much as he can about the patient's early experiences from his spontaneous verbalizations, but in addition, he anticipates that gradually the patient will begin to perceive and respond to him (the analyst) as he perceived and responded to significant people and events in his early life.   This projection on the part of the patient to the analyst is referred to as *the transference* and constitutes another distinctive feature of the psychoanalytic treatment process.   The analyst endeavors to remain an interested, but neutral figure in the relationship with the patient and, in so doing, provides the patient with a stimulus on which to project many of his needs, fears, and desires experienced in early life. His projections enable the analyst to observe directly the patient's perceptions of and reactions to past experiences, and through his interpretations of them, the therapist helps his patient better understand the part they play in his emotional disturbance and gain greater control over them.   In Allen's paper, the patient's reactions to the analyst —his fluctuating dependence and competitiveness, his unwarranted feelings of being rejected, and his presentation of a gift to the analyst —are interpreted as transference reactions which were used to help the patient become aware of painful desires and impulses which unconsciously were motivating his maladjusted behavior.

The article by Carl Rogers which follows describes the characteristics which constitute the essential features of the *client-centered* approach to psychotherapy.   Rogers's purpose in counseling is to promote development and growth in his client, since he regards the troubles, emotional conflicts, and maladjustments of persons who seek professional assistance as the result of a block in personal development.   His focus is on the personal relationship between the individual seeking help and the professional worker, and he believes that the attitudinal characteristics which the latter brings to the relationship are most important in determining whether or not the meetings will be effective in helping the client.   In his paper he discusses the attitudes which he believes the counselor must experience and communicate to the client in order to promote the client's growth.   The most important of these he calls *congruence* by which he means the genuineness of the counselor in revealing his real feelings to the client.   Unless the counselor enters the relationship with a willingness to examine his feelings about and reactions to the client and to communicate these honestly and sincerely to him, Rogers believes the therapeutic interaction will not be a meaningful one. *Empathy* is the second necessary condition of the therapeutic relationship. It is important that the counselor experience "an accurate empathic understanding of his client's personal world" and communicate this to his client. The third characteristic cited by Rogers is that the counselor experience *positive regard* for his client in an unconditional way. The counselor's attitude of warmth, regard, and acceptance should be based on his respect for the client as a separate individual with potential for growth.

Especially interesting in the client-centered approach to psychotherapy, and one of its distinctive features, is the lack of importance given to professional knowledge, training, and the theoretical orientation of the therapist. Whereas the psychoanalyst regards as crucial to successful treatment the therapist's ability to conceptualize the patient's conflicts and dynamics and to deal effectively with the transference situation, Rogers regards as more important the therapist's positive attitude toward the client and his candor and sincerity in communicating his feelings and thoughts in the therapeutic relationship. Another group of psychotherapists, the existentialists, have taken an even stronger position than Rogers concerning the idea that the therapist's theories, techniques, and efforts to achieve specific goals are not important to therapeutic progress; and in fact, most existential psychotherapists regard the therapist's concern with what he should do as likely to lead to unnatural and contrived behavior which will interfere with effective psychotherapy. Instead they regard the essence of the therapeutic interaction as the openness, spontaneity, and sincerity of the participants with each other. Only by renouncing preconceived ideas and methods in dealing with his patients can the therapist bring to the meeting freedom and flexibility of thought and thereby promote similar qualities in his patient. The theoretical rationale for existential psychotherapy is described in Pervin's article in the personality theory section of this book.

The paper by Rachman presents another approach to psychotherapy, *behavior therapy*, which contrasts sharply with the ideas and practices of the client-centered and existential groups. Many psychologists have become increasingly interested in integrating the practice of psychotherapy with knowledge gained from experimental research for the purpose of developing precise and systematic techniques for treating maladjustments and emotional difficulties. These efforts have been associated primarily with learning theories and laboratory research on the learning process conducted with both human beings and animals. The goal of behavior therapy is to eliminate or develop specific responses which are associated with the patient's maladjustment, and a variety of methods for accomplishing this have been developed. Rachman describes several of these and presents illustrations of their application to specific cases.

During the past ten years the popularity of behavior therapy has increased markedly and the literature today abounds with papers reporting on the efficacy of different techniques with specific kinds of cases and discussions concerning the theoretical ideas and assumptions associated with this approach. Undoubtedly the attractiveness of behavior therapy to many psychotherapists is that it encourages the use of specific methods which can be described in a precise way, and it likewise conceptualizes the goals of the treatment concretely and specifically. Many psychotherapists today believe that behavior therapy constitutes the direction in which all psychotherapy will move in the future because of the precision it promises in treating disorders. The greater the precision of treatment methods, the easier it is to conduct research on the methods and to teach the practices to new therapists. At the same time, it is important to realize that many of the practices, assumptions, and ideas about people which are associated with behavior therapy differ markedly, and often contradict, more traditional approaches to psychotherapy, such as those of psychoanalysis and client-centered therapy. For example, the behavior therapist attaches little value to self-understanding and insight which are considered so crucial in psychoanalysis, and he regards the therapeutic relationship which Rogers emphasizes as secondary to technique in the treatment process. Just as there are strong advocates of behavior therapy, many therapists are critical of this approach and question the validity of the behavior therapists' claims. In his paper, Rachman cites some of these criticisms and discusses data pertinent to them. He concludes that large-scale research is warranted on behavior therapy to further substantiate the effectiveness and advantages which this approach appears to offer.

The final two papers in this section describe specialized methods of psychotherapy. In contrast with the preceding articles which pertain to a dyadic arrangement, i.e., meetings of one patient and one therapist, both Burgental and Ackerman deal with group psychotherapy. The practice of group therapy in which one therapist interacts with a number of patients at the same time initially became popular because of the limited number of therapists available and the costliness of individual therapy. Through evaluations of groups procedures, however, their many special advantages over dyadic therapy were recognized. These advantages include the experiences the group situation provides the individual in social interaction, the opportunity to compare one's own problems with those of others, the development of supportive and constructive relationships, etc. Bugental notes that a variety of disparate procedures are included under the heading of group therapy and he proposes a schema for classifying groups based on their purposes and activities. He describes five different kinds of groups and indicates how the behavior of the group members and the therapist in each differ. He also evaluates the value of each type of group in bringing about particular therapeutic experiences for its members.

Ackerman reports on family psychotherapy, which is a type of group therapy distinguished by the fact that the group members belong to the same family. This procedure has been used with increasing frequency in recent years, especially in family agencies where the problems of a child or other family member are clearly associated with unhealthy conditions in the home or in the family interactions. The rationale for family psychotherapy is based on the idea that maladjustments and emotional problems have their origin in the family relationship. By dealing with the total family group rather than with a single patient, the therapist has the opportunity to observe and react to the family as a unit. He can witness how the problems of a single family member are fostered by the behavior of the other members and the subtle influences each individual has on the others. In addition, the fact that the therapist is working with people who make up the environment of one another provides him with a double-barreled method of bringing about change. He can help each member better understand the part he is playing in the disturbance of the family or one of its members and thus promote his changing. As the individual family members alter their actions in the family setting, the environment of the other family members is changed and this may facilitate further growth and progress in all concerned.

The selections presented on psychotherapy offer only a limited number of the large variety of ideas and practices which currently are being used to help emotionally disturbed persons. At present, more than at any other time, questions, innovations, and experimentation are characteristic of the field of psychotherapy. Investigations of the effectiveness of treatment have suggested that many different kinds of practices have proved equally successful in helping people, but that all practices have an appreciable number of failures. Consequently, despite the differences of opinion, psychotherapists of all schools are in the process of studying their ideas and procedures and searching for new methods with the hope of expanding their success in helping persons overcome emotional and adjustment problems.

Arnold Allen

PSYCHOANALYTIC TREATMENT OF A PATIENT UTILIZING STEALING AS A DEFENSE *

Clinical material

. . .

My interest in the subject of stealing was first stimulated by a patient in psychoanalysis in whom stealing was not the primary problem. When first seen, the patient, a professional man, was twenty-seven years old. Even in his first interview he repeatedly made interpretations about himself and his wife that suggested that his intellectualization and his ambivalence about accepting the role of a patient would present difficulties in his analysis. His stated reasons for seeking analysis were that he was 'functioning at only ten per cent of capacity' and 'did not produce without pressure'. For three years he had had all the data needed with which to finish his Ph.D. thesis but had done nothing with it. He realized that without his degree he could not obtain a good professional position. He felt his negligence about completing his thesis was due in part to his fear of producing an inadequate paper; also, he could remain in a passive, dependent role if he did not obtain a good position. This difficulty began during college and increased as the years went by. He managed by maneuvering people with 'diplomacy, charming personality, and even temper', which, of course, was the way he related to me.

Other complaints were difficulties with his wife, with constant arguments and mutual provocation, and with his parents, particularly his mother; he could not decide whether to assume the masculine role of husband and father or to remain 'mother's boy'.

The patient was the older of two children; his sister was nine years younger. He denied any particular feeling about her birth but he had regularly showered her with gifts, many of which he had stolen. He felt that his mother, an aggressive, ambitious, controlling woman, had castrated his father, always nagging at him to be more of a man and depreciating him. She early turned to the patient to make up for disappointments in her husband, but at the same time she infantilized him and blocked his efforts at growth and masculinity. The weak, passive father was uncompetitive and content to work in a factory. The patient never felt close to him and joined his mother in deriding him. Nevertheless he was sorry for him because of all the mortification he suffered at the hands of his wife. The stage was set early

* From Arnold Allen, "Stealing as a Defense," *Psychoanal. Quart.*, 1965, 34, 572–583. Pages 576–583 reprinted by permission of the author and the Editor, *Psychoanalytic Quarterly*.

for the patient's problems in identification: strength and femininity were embodied in the mother, weakness and masculinity in the father. Even more confusing his mother incited him to fierce competition in school; indeed he won many awards in the early grades with compositions written for him by his mother. Despite the constant push to achieve, his mother kept him a baby. She took milk to him at school until he was nine or ten years old and one summer, confined him to the house lest he be exposed to poliomyelitis.

His life was spent as an only child in this setting until the age of nine, when his sister was born. With his peers he felt he did not fit in; he thought of himself as a sissy and was never sure of his role. Faced with the threat of mother's disapproval, he always 'did well' at school.

In his marriage he overtly assumed a passive and nonaggressive role while covertly he seethed with rage at the least slight or deprivation. His choice of a wife seemed to have been determined largely by her being weak, not especially feminine, and not threatening to him as a sexual partner. Prior to his marriage he had had no sexual contacts and his relations with women had been casual and shallow, he playing a passive role in the relationships. His parents objected strongly to his marriage. When he was twenty-four years old, they finally agreed but then became involved in constant discord with his wife. During these arguments the patient would stand by passively, wishing to act somehow but not daring, and secretly rather enjoying his central position.

A dream on the night before his first analytic hour gave some indication of things to come.

I was in a laboratory conducting an experiment. A girl entered and we went out together. I was apprehensive because I was not supposed to be away, but later I returned and nobody was any the wiser.

This dream apparently represented his need to isolate himself from the analysis and indicated also the first entry into the analytic situation of the defense of reversal, of protecting himself against a dependent striving by an aggressive act.

Stealing, which to this patient had no connection with seeking analysis and was not a major problem, had begun following the birth of his sister. He would steal trifles and toys from five-and-ten-cent stores, giving some to his sister and keeping some himself. This stealing appeared to fulfil a variety of functions. First, in the face of intense dependent strivings stirred by his displacement by the younger sister, it served as a denial: 'I don't want what she is getting; on the contrary I enjoy having this rival around so much that I even want to give her things myself'. Thus he both identified with her and denied the identification at the same time. (Anna Freud describes this as an altruistic identification.) At another level he was defending against the anxiety stirred by his strong wish to be given things. By aggressively taking, he was saying in a sense: 'It's not true that I am weak; as a matter of fact I am quite strong, like mother' (identification with the aggressor). Not to be overlooked of course was the dependent gratification in his providing for himself something of which he felt deprived.

The stealing served still another function: after it was discovered by mother, she would punish him. He would then be filled with remorse but relieved of his guilt and temporarily close again to mother of whom he felt deprived. The act thus entailed all of the motivations described in the earlier literature on stealing: dependent id gratification, gratification of superego demands, rivalry with the envied object, and revenge or spite. At the same time it revealed the defensive aspect of the stealing; it protected him from the anxiety mobilized by his dependent strivings.

In later years he took more and more pride in his ability to 'get away with things', considering this a real accomplishment and a demonstration of strength. His petty thievery continued throughout life, even in his current job where he pilfered from the laboratory. He rationalized 'there is so much, it will never be missed', and he used the stolen items to avoid buying things for various home projects, feeling that only a 'weak sucker' would fail to take advantage of the situation. Except for cookies he stole while baby-sitting with his sister, the objects stolen never had particular symbolic significance. It is noteworthy that the stealing was more apt to occur when he felt deprived or humiliated in some way. His great pleasure was to find 'bargains' and 'put one over' on the seller. Humiliation was a recurrent theme in this man's analysis.

The analytic relationship mirrored the situations just described. It was marked by a constant seesaw between overwhelming dependency and his reactive competitiveness, always flavored with dishonesty— getting something for nothing or shirking the work involved—, followed by mounting anxiety. He would then return to passive dependency, feeling small, weak, and humiliated. His greatest fear was of being humiliated by being considered weak and inadequate, which was gradually related to a fear of facing and exposing his intense passive-dependent feminine wishes. Any confrontation with his dependent needs called forth shame and humiliation. The role of patient was for him a humiliation, to keep an appointment on time was a sign of weakness. He had repeatedly to affirm his strength by keeping another person waiting, and this was acted out early in his analysis. A good grade in school was for him not the result of effort but evidence of his having 'put something over', which then was a source of pride. To work on this thesis and acknowledge his wish and need for a Ph.D. was to admit to weakness. The strong thing to do, he felt, was to make it appear he had no need for the degree. Guilt connected with aggressive acts was manifest only when he was caught and faced with disapproval. The recognition of his strong need for approval again led to feelings of weakness and humiliation. His stealing abated as he came to recognize its aggressive defensive nature, and as he made me the forbidding superego to whom he would have to confess and from whom he would meet disapproval. In time he came to think of the stealing itself as a weakness rather than a strength; in other words, it became ego alien.

After the analysis had been in progress for nearly two years, he reported an interesting, hitherto unmentioned matter: when he went to his own refrigerator to take out food (as he often did when he felt frustrated or rejected), he had the feeling that he was stealing, and he would look around to see if he were being watched. This material confirmed the idea of the defensive nature of his stealing. In the face of a feeling of rejection or frustration, his wish to receive was directly expressed in a wish to eat. Yet the feeling of smallness and shame stirred by the awareness of a dependent need, and the resultant anxiety, were defended against by the fantasy that he was stealing; that is, aggressively grabbing rather than expressing a passive need. It was as if he had a fleeting unconscious fantasy of being fed at the moment before he decided to 'steal' from his own refrigerator. His ego seemed to prefer facing superego anxiety rather than anxiety stirred by infantile id needs.

An illuminating incident occurred in the patient's third year of analysis which illustrated some of the behavior described earlier. One day he arrived a half hour early and asked that I be informed of his presence. He was told that I would see him when I had completed the session with the patient now in my office, who he was aware was a young woman who had begun her analysis some time after he began treatment. As he sat in the waiting room he became increasingly angry. He explained his behavior by the following reasoning: I would like to know he was there so that I could start earlier with him and thus go home earlier. (He had repeatedly denied the fact that another patient followed him.) He saw the previous patient leave and I called him in ten minutes earlier than usual. As soon as he got into my office he expressed strong disapproval of my secretary for failing to inform me of his presence. Ignoring that he had seen my patient leave, he believed that he had waited fifteen or twenty minutes for me after her departure. When I confronted him with the fact that not over two or three minutes had elapsed between her leaving and his coming in, he was amazed. Analysis revealed his wishful fantasy that I be interrupted while with my previous patient, that I discharge her and immediately take him in so that he would not have to wait. Associations led to his feeling 'left out' as though he did not exist, repeating his childhood feeling when mother was preoccupied with his little sister. He became aware of the intensity of his own dependent needs and that his early arrival was not for my benefit but for his. His response to this was a feeling of shame, weakness, and humiliation. In the next hour he offered me as a gift a pipe he had just acquired—'a terrific bargain'. A friend had smuggled it into the country. This chain of events is a clear-cut illustration of strong defensiveness mobilized by his awareness of dependent strivings in his relationship with me, followed by an aggressive pseudomasculine act.

Among other such sequences was a dream of stealing which followed an argument with his wife that ended in her refusal to speak to him and his feeling 'out in the cold'. Another dream was of an act of sabotage which came after a humiliating recognition of dependency, stirred by my not giving him a 'special reception' upon his return from a vacation.

Psychic operations similar to this have been observed in at least two other patients who were seen in brief psychotherapy. Basic intense, unresolved dependency strivings were seen in both. One, a potentially successful business man of great ability, repeatedly failed in what could have been very profitable business ventures when, in the fact of possible realistically motivated dependency on other men, he felt compelled to steal, with consequent disastrous results. He identified himself with his father, who took more pride in wealth acquired by theft and subterfuge than in legitimately earned money. Another patient, a physician, damaged his practice by losing patients because he kept no records. The reason for this was to avoid paying income taxes—the evasion of which did more to bolster his faltering concept of himself as a man than could a more adequate income easily achievable by realistic and legitimate means. A colleague has told me of a patient who had great difficulty in accepting his dependency which he attempted to handle by stealing something immediately before coming to each therapeutic hour.

Summary

As suggested by Alexander, Fenichel, and others, there is little doubt that my analytic patient's stealing represented an expression of infantile oral receptive attitudes, a spite reaction, a superego bribe, and a way of re-establishing a lost relationship. However, I should like to emphasize the concept, introduced by Alexander, elaborated by Menaker, and supported by Waelder, that many functions can be served by a single act. In certain cases, particularly where there is a strong need to reject underlying dependent strivings, stealing primarily represents an ego defense against anxiety. As in Menaker's boys, the psychopathological family setting, with weak father and phallically perceived mother, was clearly illustrated in my patient. The attempts to solve the bisexual gratification, the fluctuation between masculine and feminine roles, and confusion about them, were also clearly seen. Further he illustrated the type of superego defect which results from inability to identify successfully with the father and from fixation on the pregenital level. His passive homosexual attitude to the father, his failure to identify with him but his wish to be loved by him, and the attempt to identify with a phallic mother were also demonstrated. The most striking finding, however, was the reversal of a desire to be given into active taking, and the use of symptomatic stealing as a defense against passive pregenital wishes for immediate gratification. Rather than the ego's operating passively as a mere tool for instinctual and superego expression, all of this implies definite defensive ego action.

References [1]

1. Abraham, Karl: *Selected Papers.* London: The Hogarth Press, Ltd., 1942.

2. Alexander, Franz and Healy, William: *Roots of Crime.* New York and London: Alfred A. Knopf, 1935.

3. Fenichel, Otto: *The Collected Papers, First Series.* New York: W. W. Norton & Co., Inc., 1953.

4. Freud, Anna: *The Ego and the Mechanisms of Defense.* New York: International Universities Press, Inc., 1946.

5. Glover, Edward: *Selected Papers on Psychoanalysis, Vol. II.* New York: International Universities Press, Inc., 1960.

6. Kirkpatrick, M. and Tiebout, H.: *Psychiatric Factors in Stealing.* Amer. J. Orthopsychiatry, II, 1932, p. 114.

7. Menaker, Esther: *Contribution to the Study of the Neurotic Stealing Symptom.* Amer. J. Orthopsychiatry, IX, 1939, pp. 368–376.

8. Rado, Sandor: *Fear of Castration in Women.* This quarterly, II, 1933, pp. 425–475.

9. Socarides, Charles W.: *Pathological Stealing as a Reparative Move of the Ego.* Psa. Review, XLI, 1954.

10. Waelder, Robert: *The Principle of Multiple Function: Observations on Over-Determination.* This quarterly, V, 1936, pp. 45–62.

11. Zulliger, Hans: *Eine Diebin aus fehlgeleiteter Gewissenreaktion.* Psyche (Heidelberg), VIII/IX, 1954, pp. 545–558.

[1] Since the paper has been edited, not all references remain in the body of the paper. For reasons of general interest, however, we have chosen to leave the *list* of references intact.

Carl R. Rogers

THE INTERPERSONAL RELATIONSHIP IN CLIENT-CENTERED THERAPY *

I would like to share with you in this paper a conclusion, a conviction, which has grown out of years of experience in dealing with individuals, a conclusion which finds some confirmation in a steadily growing body of empirical evidence. It is simply that in a wide variety of professional work involving relationships with people—whether as a psychotherapist, teacher, religious worker, guidance counselor, social worker, clinical psychologist—it is the *quality* of the interpersonal encounter with the client which is the most significant element in determining effectiveness.

Let me spell out a little more fully the basis of this statement in my personal experience. I have been primarily a counselor and psychotherapist. In the course of my professional life I have worked with troubled college students, with adults in difficulty, with "normal" individuals such as business executives, and more recently with hospitalized psychotic persons. I have endeavored to make use of the learnings from my therapeutic experience in my interactions with classes and seminars, in the training of teachers, in the administration of staff groups, in the clinical supervision of psychologists, psychiatrists, and guidance workers as they work with their clients or patients. Some of these relationships are long-continued and intensive, as in individual psychotherapy. Some are brief, as in experiences with workshop participants or in contacts with students who come for practical advice. They cover a wide range of depth. Gradually I have come to the conclusion that one learning which applies to all of these experiences is that it is the quality of the personal relationship which matters most. With some of these individuals I am in touch only briefly, with others I have the opportunity of knowing them intimately, but in either case the quality of the personal encounter is probably, in the long run, the element which determines the extent to which this is an experience which releases or promotes development and growth. I believe the quality of my encounter is more important in the long run than is my scholarly knowledge, my professional training, my counseling orientation, the techniques I use in the interview. In keeping with this line of thought, I suspect that for a guidance worker also the relationship he forms with each student—brief or continuing—is more important than his knowledge of tests and measurements, the adequacy of his record

* From Carl R. Rogers, "The Interpersonal Relationship: The Core of Guidance," *Harvard Educ. Rev.*, 1962, 32, 416–429. Pages 416–424 reprinted by permission of the author and the Editor, *Harvard Educational Review*.

keeping, the theories he holds, the accuracy with which he is able to predict academic success, or the school in which he received his training.

In recent years I have thought a great deal about this issue. I have tried to observe counselors and therapists whose orientations are very different from mine, in order to understand the basis of their effectiveness as well as my own. I have listened to recorded interviews from many different sources. Gradually I have developed some theoretical formulations (4, 5), some hypotheses as to the basis of effectiveness in relationships. As I have asked myself how individuals sharply different in personality, orientation and procedure can all be effective in a helping relationship, can each be successful in facilitating constructive change or development, I have concluded that it is because they bring to the helping relationship certain attitudinal ingredients. It is these that I hypothesize as making for effectiveness, whether we are speaking of a guidance counselor, a clinical psychologist, or a psychiatrist.

What are these attitudinal or experiential elements in the counselor which make a relationship a growth-promoting climate? I would like to describe them as carefully and accurately as I can, though I am well aware that words rarely capture or communicate the qualities of a personal encounter.

Congruence

In the first place, I hypothesize that personal growth is facilitated when the counselor is what he *is*, when in the relationship with his client he is genuine and without "front" or facade, openly being the feelings and attitudes which at that moment are flowing in him. We have used the term "congruence" to try to describe this condition. By this we mean that the feelings the counselor is experiencing are available to him, available to his awareness, that he is able to live these feelings, be them in the relationship, and able to communicate them if appropriate. It means that he comes into a direct personal encounter with his client, meeting him on a person-to-person basis. It means that he is *being* himself, not denying himself. No one fully achieves this condition, yet the more the therapist is able to listen acceptantly to what is going on within himself, and the more he is able to *be* the complexity of his feelings without fear, the higher the degree of his congruence.

I think that we readily sense this quality in our everyday life. We could each of us name persons whom we know who always seem to be operating from behind a front, who are playing a role, who tend to say things they do not feel. They are exhibiting incongruence. We do not reveal ourselves too deeply to such people. On the other hand each of us knows individuals whom we somehow trust, because we sense that they are being what they *are*, that we are dealing with the person himself, and not with a polite or professional facade. This is the quality of which we are speaking, and it is hypothesized that the more genuine and congruent the therapist in the relationship, the more probability there is that change in personality in the client will occur.

I have received much clinical confirmation for this hypothesis in recent years in our work with randomly selected hospitalized schizophrenic patients. The individual therapists in our research program who seem to be most successful in dealing with these unmotivated, poorly educated, resistant, chronically hospitalized individuals, are those who are first of all real, who react in a genuine, human way as persons, and who exhibit their genuineness in the relationship.

But is it always helpful to be genuine? What about negative feelings? What about the times when the counselor's real feeling toward his client is one of annoyance, or boredom, or dislike? My tentative answer is that even with such feelings as these, which we all have from time to time, it is preferable for the counselor to be real than to put up a facade of interest and concern and liking which he does not feel.

But it is not a simple thing to achieve such reality. I am not saying that it is helpful to blurt out impulsively every passing feeling and accusation under the comfortable impression that one is being genuine. Being real involves the difficult task of being acquainted with the flow of experiencing going on within oneself, a flow marked especially by complexity and continuous change. So if I sense that I am feeling bored by my contacts with this student, and this feeling persists, I think I owe it to him and to our relationship to share this feeling with him. But here again I will want to be constantly in touch with what is going on in me. If I am, I will recognize that it is *my* feeling of being bored which I am expressing, and not some supposed fact about him as a boring person. If I voice it as my *own* reaction, it has the potentiality of leading to a deeper relationship. But this feeling exists in the context of a complex and changing flow, and this needs to be communicated too. I would like to share with him my distress at feeling bored, and the discomfort I feel in expressing this aspect of me. As I share these attitudes I find that my feeling of boredom arises from my sense of remoteness from him, and that I would like to be more in touch with him. And even as I try to express these feelings, they change. I am certainly not bored as I try to communicate myself to him in this way, and I am far from bored as I wait with eagerness and perhaps a bit of apprehension for his response. I also feel a new sensitivity to him, now that I have shared this feeling which has been a barrier between us. So I am very much more able to hear the surprise or perhaps the hurt in his voice as he now finds *him*self speaking more genuinely because I have dared to be real with him.   I have let myself be a person—real, imperfect—in my relationship with him.

I have tried to describe this first element at some length because I regard it as highly important, perhaps the most crucial of the conditions I will describe, and because it is neither easy to grasp nor to achieve.   Gendlin (2) has done an excellent job of explaining the significance of the concept of experiencing and its relationship to counseling and therapy, and his presentation may supplement what I have tried to say.

I hope it is clear that I am talking about a realness in the counselor which is deep and true, not superficial.   I have sometimes thought that the word transparency helps to describe this element of personal congruence.   If everything going on in me which is relevant to the relationship can be seen by my client, if he can see "clear through me," and if I am *willing* for this realness to show through in the relationship, then I can be almost certain that this will be a meaningful encounter in which we both learn and develop.

I have sometimes wondered if this is the only quality which matters in a counseling relationship.   The evidence seems to show that other qualities also make a profound difference and are perhaps easier to achieve.   So I am going to describe these others.   But I would stress that if, in a given moment of relationship, they are not genuinely a part of the experience of the counselor, then it is, I believe, better to be genuinely what one is, than to pretend to be feeling these other qualities.

Empathy

The second essential condition in the relationship, as I see it, is that the counselor is experiencing an accurate empathic understanding of his client's private world, and is able to communicate some of the significant fragments of that understanding.   To sense the client's inner world of private personal meanings as if it were your own, but without ever losing the "as if" quality, this is empathy, and this seems essential to a growth-promoting relationship.   To sense his confusion or his timidity or his anger or his feeling of being treated unfairly as if it were your own, yet without your own uncertainty or fear or anger or suspicion getting bound up in it, this is the condition I am endeavoring to describe.   When the client's world is clear to the counselor and he can move about it in freely, then he can both communicate his understanding of what is vaguely known to the client, and he can also voice meanings in the client's experience of which the client is scarcely aware.   It is this kind of highly sensitive empathy which seems important in making it possible for a person to get close to himself and to learn, to change and develop.

I suspect that each of us has discovered that this kind of understanding is extremely rare. We neither receive it nor offer it with any great frequency. Instead we offer another type of understanding which is very different, such as "I understand what is wrong with you" or "I understand what makes you act that way." These are the types of understanding which we usually offer and receive—an evaluative understanding from the outside. It is not surprising that we shy away from true understanding. If I am truly open to the way life is experienced by another person—if I can take his world into mine—then I run the risk of seeing life in his way, of being changed myself, and we all resist change. So we tend to view this other person's world only in our terms, not in his. We analyze and evaluate it. We do not understand it. But when someone understands how it feels and seems to be me, without wanting to analyze me or judge me, then I can blossom and grow in that climate. I am sure I am not alone in that feeling. I believe that when the counselor can grasp the moment-to-moment experiencing occurring in the inner world of the client, as the client sees it and feels it, without losing the separateness of his own identity in this empathic process, then change is likely to occur.

Though the accuracy of such understanding is highly important, the communication of intent to understand is also helpful. Even in dealing with the confused or inarticulate or bizarre individual, if he perceives that I am *trying* to understand his meanings, this is helpful. It communicates the value I place on him as an individual. It gets across the fact that I perceive his feelings and meanings as being *worth* understanding.

None of us steadily achieves such a complete empathy as I have been trying to describe, any more than we achieve complete congruence, but there is no doubt that individuals can develop along this line. Suitable training experiences have been utilized in the training of counselors, and also in the "sensitivity training" of industrial management personnel. Such experiences enable the person to listen more sensitively, to receive more of the subtle meanings the other person is expressing in words, gesture, and posture, to resonate more deeply and freely within himself to the significance of those expressions.[1]

---

[1] I hope the above account of an empathic attitude will make it abundantly clear that I am not advocating a wooden technique of pseudo-understanding in which the counselor "reflects back what the client has just said." I have been more than a little horrified at the interpretation of my approach which has sometimes crept into the teaching and training of counselors.

Positive regard

Now the third condition. I hypothesize that growth and change are more likely to occur the more that the counselor is experiencing a warm, positive, acceptant attitude toward what *is* in the client. It means that he prizes his client, as a person, with somewhat the same quality of feeling that a parent feels for his child, prizing him as a person regardless of his particular behavior at the moment. It means that he cares for his client in a non-possessive way, as a person with potentialities. It involves an open willingness for the client to be whatever feelings are real in him at the moment—hostility or tenderness, rebellion or submissiveness, assurance or self-depreciation. It means a kind of love for the client as he is, providing we understand the word love as equivalent to the theologian's term "agape," and not in its usual romantic and possessive meanings. What I am describing is a feeling which is not paternalistic, nor sentimental, nor superficially social and agreeable. It respects the other person as a separate individual, and does not possess him. It is a kind of liking which has strength, and which is not demanding. We have termed it positive regard.

Unconditionality of regard

There is one aspect of this attitude of which I am somewhat less sure. I advance tentatively the hypothesis that the relationship will be more effective the more the positive regard is unconditional. By this I mean that the counselor prizes the client in a total, rather than a conditional way. He does not accept certain feelings in the client and disapprove others. He feels an *unconditional* positive regard for this person. This is an outgoing, positive feeling without reservations and without evaluations. It means *not* making judgments. I believe that when this nonevaluative prizing is present in the encounter between the counselor and his client, constructive change and development in the client is more likely to occur.

Certainly one does not need to be a professional to experience this attitude. The best of parents show this in abundance, while others do not. A friend of mine, a therapist in private practice on the east coast, illustrates this very well in a letter in which he tells me what he is learning about parents. He says:

I am beginning to feel that the key to the human being is the attitudes with which the parents have regarded him. If the child was lucky enough to have parents who have felt proud of him, wanted him, wanted him just as he was, exactly as he was, this child grows into adulthood with self-confidence, self-esteem; he goes forth in life feeling sure of himself, strong, able to lick what confronts him. Franklin Delano Roosevelt is an example . . . "my friends . . . ." He couldn't imagine anyone thinking otherwise. He had two adoring parents. He was like the pampered dog who runs up at you, frisking his tail, eager to love you, for this dog has never known rejection or harshness. Even if you should kick him, he'll come right back to you, his tail friskier than ever, thinking you're playing a game with him and wanting more. This animal cannot imagine anyone disapproving or disliking him. Just as unconditional regard and love was poured into him, he has it now to give out. If a child is lucky enough to grow up in this unconditionally accepting atmosphere, he emerges as strong and sure and he can approach life and its vicissitudes with courage and confidence, with zest and joy of expectation.

But the parents who like their children—if. They would like them if they were changed, altered, different; if they were smarter or if they were better, or if, if, if. The offspring of these parents have trouble because they never had the feeling of acceptance. These parents don't really like these children; they would like them if they were like someone else. When you come down to the basic fundamental, the parent feels: "I don't like *this* child, this child before me." They don't say that. I am beginning to believe that it would be better for all concerned if parents did. It wouldn't leave such horrible ravages on these unaccepted children. It's never done that crudely. "If you were a nice boy and did this, that and the other thing, then we would all love you."

I am coming to believe that children brought up by parents who would like them "if" are never quite right. They grow up assuming that their parents are right and that they are wrong; that somehow or other they are at fault; and even worse, very frequently they feel they are stupid, inadequate, inferior.

This is an excellent contrast between an unconditional positive regard and a conditional regard. I believe it holds as true for counselors as for parents.

The client's perception

Thus far all my hypotheses regarding the possibility of constructive growth have rested upon the experiencing of these elements by the counselor. There is, however, one condition which must exist in the client. Unless the attitudes I have been describing have been to some degree communicated to the client, and perceived by him, they do not exist in his perceptual world and thus cannot be effective. Consequently it is necessary to add one more condition to the equation which I have been building up regarding personal growth through counseling. It is that when the client perceives, to a minimal degree, the genuineness of the counselor and the acceptance and empathy which the counselor experiences for him, then development in personality and change in behavior are predicted.

This has implications for me as a counselor. I need to be sensitive, not only to what is going on in me, and sensitive to the flow of feelings in my client. I must also be sensitive to the way he is receiving my communications. I have learned, especially in working with more disturbed persons, that empathy can be perceived as lack of involvement; that an unconditional regard on my part can be perceived as indifference; that warmth can be perceived as a threatening closeness, that real feelings of mine can be perceived as false. I would like to behave in ways, and communicate in ways which have clarity for this specific person, so that what I am experiencing in relationship to him would be perceived unambiguously by him. Like the other conditions I have proposed the principle is easy to grasp; the achievement of it is difficult and complex.

The essential hypothesis

Let me restate very briefly the essentially simple but somewhat radical hypothesis I have set forth. I have said that constructive personality growth and change comes about only when the client perceives and experiences a certain psychological climate in the relationship. The conditions which constitute this climate do not consist of knowledge, intellectual training, orientation in some school of thought, or techniques. They are feelings or attitudes which must be experienced by the counselor and perceived by the client if they are to be effective. Those I have singled out as being essential are: a realness, genuineness, or congruence in the therapist; a sensitive, empathic understanding of the client's feelings and personal meanings; a warm, acceptant prizing of the client; and an unconditionality in this positive regard.

Some limitations

. . .

I regard it as entirely possible that there are other conditions which I have not described, which are also essential. Recently I had occasion to listen to some recorded interviews by a young counselor of elementary school children. She was very warm and positive in her attitude toward her clients, yet she was definitely ineffective. She seemed to be responding warmly only to the superficial aspects of each child and so the contacts were chatty, social and friendly, but it was clear she was not reaching the real person of the child. Yet in a number of ways she rated reasonably high on each of the conditions I have described. So perhaps there are still elements missing which I have not captured in my formulation.

I am also aware of the possibility that different kinds of helping relationships may be effective with different kinds of people. Some of our therapists working with schizophrenics are effective when they appear to be highly conditional, when they do *not* accept some of the bizarre behavior of the psychotic. This can be interpreted in two ways. Perhaps a conditional set is more helpful with these individuals. Or perhaps—and this seems to me to fit the facts better—these psychotic individuals perceive a conditional attitude as meaning that the therapist *really* cares, where an unconditional attitude may be interpreted as apathetic noncaring. In any event, I do want to make it clear that what I have given are beginning formulations which surely will be modified and corrected from further learnings.

The philosophy which is implicit

It is evident that the kind of attitudes I have described are not likely to be experienced by a counselor unless he holds a philosophy regarding people in which such attitudes are congenial. The attitudes pictured make no sense except in a context of great respect for the person and his potentialities. Unless the primary element in the counselor's value system is the worth of the individual, he is not apt to find himself experiencing a real caring, or a desire to understand, and perhaps he will not respect himself enough to be real. Certainly the professional person who holds the view that individuals are essentially objects to be manipulated for the welfare of the state, or the good of the educational institution, or "for their own good," or to satisfy his own need for power and control, would not experience the attitudinal elements I have described as constituting growth-promoting relationships. So these conditions are congenial and natural in certain philosophical contexts but not in others. . . .

Conclusion

Let me conclude with a series of statements which for me follow logically one upon the other.

The purpose of most of the helping professions, including guidance counseling, is to enhance the personal development, the psychological growth toward a socialized maturity, of its clients.

The effectiveness of any member of the profession is most adequately measured in terms of the degree to which, in his work with his clients, he achieves this goal.

Our knowledge of the elements which bring about constructive change in personal growth is in its infant stages.

Such factual knowledge as we currently possess indicates that a primary change-producing influence is the degree to which the client experiences certain qualities in his relationship with his counselor.

In a variety of clients—normal, maladjusted, and psychotic—with many different counselors and therapists, and studying the relationship from the vantage point of the client, the therapist, or the uninvolved observer, certain qualities in the relationship are quite uniformly found to be associated with personal growth and change.

These elements are not constituted of technical knowledge or ideological sophistication. They are personal human qualities—something the counselor *experiences*, not something he *knows*. Constructive personal growth is associated with the counselor's realness, with his genuine and unconditional liking for his client, with his sensitive understanding of his client's private world, and with his ability to communicate these qualities in himself to his client.

These findings have some far-reaching implications for the theory and practice of guidance counseling and psychotherapy, and for the training of workers in these fields.

References [1]

1. Barrett-Lennard, G. T.   Dimensions of therapist response as causal factors in therapeutic change.   *Psychol. Monogr.*   (In press)

2. Gendlin, E. T.   Experiencing: A variable in the process of therapeutic change.   *Am. Jour. Psychother.*   *15*, 1961, 233–245.

3. Halkides, G.   An experimental study of four conditions necessary for therapeutic change.   Unpublished doctoral dissertation, University of Chicago, 1958.

4. Rogers, C. R.   The necessary and sufficient conditions of therapeutic personality change.   *Jour. Cons. Psych., 21*, 1957, 95–103.

5. ———.   A theory of therapy, personality, and interpersonal relationships as developed in the client-centered framework.   In S. Koch (ed.)   *Psychology: A Study of a Science, Vol. III.*   New York: McGraw-Hill, 1959, 184–256.

6. Wisconsin Psychiatric Institute: Research Reports (unpublished)

   a. Spotts, J. E.   The perception of positive regard by relatively successful and relatively unsuccessful clients.

   b. Truax, C. B.   Comparison between high conditions therapy, low conditions therapy, and control conditions in the outcome measure of change in anxiety levels.

   c. ———.   Constructive personality change in schizophrenic patients receiving high-conditions therapy, low-conditions therapy, and no-therapy.

   d. ———.   Effects of therapists and effects of patients upon the amount of accurate empathy occurring in the psychotherapeutic interaction.

   e. ———.   Effects of therapists and effects of patients upon the level of problem expression and experiencing occurring in the therapeutic interaction.

[1] Since the paper has been edited, not all references remain in the body of the paper. For reasons of general interest, however, we have chosen to leave the *list* of references intact.

f. ————. The relationship between the patient's perception of the level of therapeutic conditions offered in psychotherapy and constructive personality change.

g. ————, Liccione, J., and Rosenberg, M. Psychological test evaluations of personality change in high conditions therapy, low conditions therapy, and control patients.

h. van der Veen, F. The effects of the therapist and the patient on each other's therapeutic behavior early in therapy: A study of the beginning interviews of three patients with each of five therapists.

i. ————. Perceived therapist conditions and degree of disturbance: A comparison of conditions perceived by hospitalized schizophrenic patients and counseling center clients.

j. Wargo, D. G. The Barron Ego Strength and LH4 Scales as predictors and indicators of change in psychotherapy.

S. Rachman

INTRODUCTION TO BEHAVIOUR THERAPY *

Behaviour Therapy is a term used to describe a number of new psychotherapeutic methods which have been developed in recent years. Although the actual procedures vary from aversion conditioning to desensitization they all have a common theoretical basis (Wolpe, 1958; Eysenck, 1960 a, b; Jones, 1960; Metzner, 1961).

Behaviour therapy derives its impetus from experimental psychology and is essentially an attempt to apply the findings and methods of this discipline to disorders of human behaviour. The area of experimental psychology which has the most immediate and obvious value for psychotherapy is the study of learning processes. The early experience of behaviour therapy seems to vindicate these attempts and one can draw further encouragement from the very extensive information about learning processes which has yet to be tapped by therapists. The literature of experimental psychology provides a firm foundation for the development of scientific methods of psychotherapy.

A brief account of the rationale of behaviour therapy may be stated as follows. The position adapted by behaviour therapists is that neu-

* From Stanley Rachman, "Introduction to Behaviour Therapy," *Behav. Res. Ther.*, 1963, *1*, 3–15. Reprinted by permission of the author and the Editor, *Behaviour Research and Therapy*.

rotic behaviour is acquired.   If neurotic behaviour is regarded as being acquired, then it must follow that such behaviour will be subject to the established laws of learning.   Current knowledge about the learning process concerns not only the acquisition of new habit patterns, but also how habits are eliminated.   The elimination of learned responses occurs either by a process of extinction, or by inhibition.

Wolpe (1961) has defined neurotic behaviour as "any persistent habit of unadaptive behaviour acquired by learning in a physiologically normal organism."   Anxiety is "usually the central constituent of this behaviour, being invariably present in the causal situation."   Similarly, Eysenck (1960a) postulates that "neurotic symptoms are learned patterns of behaviour which for some reason or another are unadaptive."   It should be noted however, that neurotic symptoms may under certain circumstances result "not only from the learning of an unadaptive response, but from the failure to learn an adaptive response", (Eysenck, 1960a; Jones, 1960).   A common example of this type is enuresis.   The re-learning and unlearning techniques which have been used therapeutically include:

1   Desensitization based on relaxation (Wolpe, 1954, 1958 and 1961; Bond and Hutchison, 1960; Lazarus, 1963; Rachman, 1959; Hussain, 1963; Clarke, 1963; Walton, 1960 and 1963; Meyer, 1958).
2   Operant conditioning (Ayllon, 1960 and 1963; Lindsley, 1956 and 1961; King *et al.*, 1960; Brady and Lind, 1961; Ferster and de Myer, 1961).
3   Aversion conditioning—chemical or electrical (Wolpe, 1958; Blakemore *et al.*, 1963; Freund, 1960; Raymond, 1956; Franks, 1960; Max, 1935).
4   Training in assertive behaviour (Salter, 1950; Wolpe, 1958; Lazarus, 1963).
5   Use of sexual responses (Wolpe, 1958; Lazarus, 1963).
6   Use of feeding responses (Jones, 1924a, b; Lazarus, 1960).
7   Extinction based on negative practice (Yates, 1960; Jones, 1960; Williams, 1959).
8   Anxiety-relief responses (Wolpe, 1958).
9   Avoidance learning (Lovibond, 1963; Jones, 1960).

Behaviour therapy has been successfully used in the treatment of a wide range of neurotic conditions including: *Phobias* (e.g. Wolpe, 1958; Lazarus, 1963; Meyer, 1958; Eysenck, 1960), *hysteria* (e.g. Brady and Lind, 1961; Sylvester and Liversedge, 1960; Wolpe, 1958), *enuresis* (e.g. Jones, 1960; Mowrer 1939; Lovibond, 1963), *sexual disorders* (e.g. Blakemore *et al.*, 1963; Rachman, 1961), *tics* (e.g. Yates, 1958; Walton, 1961; Barrett, 1962), *tension states* (e.g. Wolpe, 1958; Eysenck, 1960), *children's disorders* (e.g. Rachman, 1963). Recently, some limited improvements have been obtained even in psychotic illnesses (e.g. Cowden and Ford, 1962; King *et al.*, 1960; Ayllon, 1963.)

Origins

Modern psychology is dominated by what are known as "theories of learning". The two theories of learning which are of direct relevance to psychotherapy are those of Hull (reinforcement theory) and Skinner (operant conditioning). These theories are in a sense, modern versions of Behaviourism. Some of the most significant improvements are the insistence on quantitative studies, increasingly flexible methods and theorizing, and in the case of Hull, the use of the hypothetico-deductive method. In the past thirty years, psychologists have acquired a considerable amount of quantitative information concerning various human processes, particularly in the field of learning. The word 'learning' it should be noted is used in an extremely broad manner and includes any aspect of behaviour which is 'acquired' by experience. This excludes changes in behaviour which result from maturation or by direct intervention in the functioning of the nervous system.

Behaviour therapy has developed partly as a consequence of these advances in psychology and partly as a reaction to psycho-analysis and its derivatives (e.g. Wolpe and Rachman (1960) and Rachman and Costello (1961)). The need for a new approach to psychotherapy is emphasized by the disappointing results obtained with prevailing techniques (Eysenck, 1960c; Levitt, 1957; Bailey, 1956). Since 1948 systematic attempts have been made to apply the facts, theories, and methods of learning theory to the practice of psycho-therapy.

Before dealing with these more recent developments, two earlier investigations should be mentioned. The first is the case of Albert reported by Watson and Rayner (1920). They provided a classical demonstration of the development of a phobia in a young child. Having first ascertained that it was a neutral object, they presented an 11 month old boy, Albert, with a white rat to play with. Whenever he reached for the animal the experimenters made a loud noise behind the boy. After only five trials Albert began showing signs of fear in the presence of the white rat. This fear then generalized to similar stimuli such as furry objects, cotton wool, white rabbits. These phobic reactions were still present when Albert was tested 4 months later. The process involved in this demonstration provides a striking illustration of the way in which phobias can develop. The implications of this work are discussed in detail elsewhere (Wolpe and Rachman, 1960). It is sufficient for present purposes to note that this demonstration provided the first model of a human neurosis.

The second investigation of importance was that reported by Mary Cover Jones in 1924:

A 3 year-old boy, Peter, showed fear of white rats, rabbits, fur, cotton wool and other similar objects. Jones treated Peter by de-conditioning methods.

It was decided to start on the rabbit phobia as this seemed to be a focus of Peter's fears.

Peter was gradually introduced to contacts with a rabbit during his daily play period. He was placed in a play group with 3 fearless children and the rabbit was brought into the room for short periods each day. Peter's toleration of the rabbit was gradually improved. The progressive steps observed in the process included: "rabbit in cage 12 feet away tolerated . . . in cage 4 feet away tolerated . . . close by in cage tolerated . . . free in room tolerated . . . eventually, fondling rabbit affectionately." Another measure employed by Jones involved the use of feeding responses. "Through the presence of the pleasant stimulus (food) whenever the rabbit was shown, the fear was eliminated gradually in favour of a positive response."

Using these techniques Jones overcame not only Peter's fear of rabbits but all his associated fears. The follow-up of this case showed no resurgence of the phobia.

The next important advance in behaviour therapy occurred in 1948. On the basis of the evidence accumulated on experimental neuroses in animals (dating back to Pavlov's work) and on his own experiments, Wolpe (1954, 1958 and 1962a) constructed a systematic theory of neurosis and psychotherapy. Merging the experimental evidence [1] with Hull's theory of learning, Wolpe elaborated the principle of reciprocal inhibition as the main basis of psychotherapeutic effects. Wolpe provided evidence that neurotic behaviour is acquired in anxiety-generating situations and that anxiety is always prominent in these conditions. Successful treatment of a neurosis, therefore, would depend on the reciprocal inhibition of neurotic anxiety responses, i.e. the suppression of the anxiety responses as a consequence of the simultaneous evocation of other responses which are physiologically antagonistic to anxiety. If a response which is incompatible with anxiety can be made to occur in the presence of anxiety-producing stimuli it will weaken the bond between these stimuli and the anxiety responses. Whereas most psychotherapists report cured or improved cases in the vicinity of 60 per cent, Wolpe claims a 90 per cent level of cures or 'marked improvements' with his methods. Wolpe compared his results with those obtained by other methods and by applying the x^2 test for significance, showed that it is highly improbable that his higher proportion of successes can be accounted for by chance.

Wolpe developed several therapeutic techniques on the basis of learning theory and the most prominent of these is 'systematic desensitization'. This method will be described and then illustrated by case histories.

An inquiry is first conducted in order to ascertain which stimulus situations provoke anxiety in the patient. The patient is told that he

[1] Papers dealing with the background evidence include those of Gantt (1944), Liddell (1944), Lazovik and Lang (1960), Metzner (1961), Bandura (1961), Eysenck (1960b, c), Bachrach (1961), and Broadhurst (1960).

can add to or modify this list at any time. The stimuli are then categorized by the therapist and the patient is asked to rank the stimuli in order, from the most to the least disturbing. This ranked list of noxious stimulus conditions is referred to as the hierarchy. In the first case discussed below for example, one would refer to the 'ambulance hierarchy' and the 'hospital hierarchy'. Hierarchies can contain from 5 to 25 items. The hospital hierarchy mentioned above consisted of the following stimulus situations; a hospital in the distance, a hospital ten corners away, walking past the hospital, standing outside the gates, walking in the grounds, standing outside the foyer, in the foyer, walking in the corridors, standing in a small ward of 4 beds, in a larger ward and in a surgical ward with a few bandaged people in bed. The construction of the relevant hierarchies generally takes 1–3 interviews and the patient is concurrently given practice in hypnotic and relaxation procedures. Hypnosis is not an essential requirement, and in these cases where the patient refuses to be hypnotized or requires prolonged practice the procedure can be omitted and deep non-hypnotic relaxation employed instead.

When the hierarchies have been worked out, the subject is told which stimuli are to be presented in each session and is advised to signal with his hand if a stimulus presentation disturbs him unduly. This is an important instruction and should on no account be omitted, for the arousing of anxiety during the session can be damaging. In our experience it has been found that with most patients it is possible by observing his facial expressions, bodily tension, respiration and so forth, to perceive such disturbances before the patient actually signals. When such disturbances occur the therapist immediately 'withdraws' the stimulus and calms the patient. No session should be concluded when a disturbance occurs, but before rousing the patient the therapist should continue and present a further 'easy' stimulus which has already been successfully overcome. The reason for this is to be found in the commonly observed fact that the last item of any learning series is well retained. Anxiety which occurs at the end of a session is likely to require a longer period before dissipating.

When the preliminary instructions have been given, the patient is relaxed (hypnotically or otherwise) and then told to visualize the various stimuli, e.g. 'Picture a hospital in the distance. . . Now stop picturing that and go on relaxing.' Each stimulus is visualized for 5–10 seconds and 2–4 different items are presented each session. Each item is generally presented twice. When the requisite number of stimuli have been presented the patient is slowly roused and then asked for a report on his reactions. If the items were visualized vividly and without undue disturbance, the therapist then proceeds to the next items in the following session. The items lowest in the hierarchy (i.e. the least disturbing ones) are introduced first and the therapist proceeds slowly up the list depending on the progress achieved and the patient's reactions. In this way, it is possible for the patient to eventually picture formerly noxious stimuli without any anxiety whatever. This ability to imagine the noxious stimulus with tranquility then transfers to the real-life situation (see below).

Illustrative cases

Case 1

A 14-year-old boy was referred for treatment of a phobia. He had suffered from a fear of ambulances and hospitals for a period of 4 years. He stated that he was frightened by the sight of ambulances and avoided them wherever and however possible, e.g. by planning his journeys in advance and changing direction when an ambulance was sighted. He reported having fainted on several occasions when an ambulance was nearby. He was also scared of hospitals and nursing homes and refused to visit these institutions. His social and scholastic adjustments were both satisfactory and systematic desensitization was commenced after an initial period of training in relaxation. Separate hierarchies of noxious situations were constructed for the ambulance and hospital phobias. The ambulance-hierarchy ranged from easy (non-disturbing) stimuli such as a parked ambulance in the distance and a derelict ambulance in a scrap-yard, to difficult ones like sitting in an ambulance (a) next to the driver or (b) in the back. In the hospital-hierarchy the first easy situation was a distant hospital which could be barely seen and the final one, a surgical ward. Three days after the third desensitization session the subject walked past a parked ambulance with its rear doors open and experienced no anxiety. Two further situations of a similar nature occurred during the course of therapy and neither of these evoked fear. After 10 interviews he was much improved and was able to visit the hospital and approach ambulances without difficulty. After a 3-month period there has been no recurrence of the earlier fears.

Case 2

A married woman of 34 was referred for treatment of an anxiety neurosis of 5 years' duration. She had received intermittent treatment during this period, including a brief spell of psycho-analysis, without apparent success. Two weeks before her first interview she had been advised to consider the possibility of undergoing a leucotomy.

She complained of attacks of fear with sweating, trembling and severe headaches. A wide variety of situations appeared to provoke these attacks, which tended to occur most severely and frequently in the late afternoon and in dull, overcast weather. The anxiety-producing situations included walking in the street, being outdoors in the afternoon, shopping, telephoning, crowds of people and places of public amenity. She also reported an inability to cope in social situations and disturbing feelings of inadequacy and inferiority. Her sexual activity had been disrupted in recent months as the anxiety had increased and was unsatisfactory. She had been taking 2–3 tranquillizing tablets per day for a short period with slight, variable results.

Application of the Thematic Apperception Test and the Willoughby neurotic-tendency inventory revealed neurotic trends such as guilt, hypersensitivity and a marked lack of confidence (the Willoughby score was extremely high, 87, indicating severe neurotic disturbance).

The patient was instructed in the use of assertive responses and deep (non-hypnotic) relaxation. The first anxiety hierarchy dealt with was that of dull weather. Starting from 'a bright sunny day' it was possible for the subject to visualize 'damp overcast weather' without anxiety after 21 desensitization sessions, and 10 days after the completion of this hierarchy she was able to report that, "The weather is much better, it doesn't even bother me to look at the weather when I wake up in the morning" (previously depressing). In addition to this improvement, she was also able to go out for short periods during the afternoon. The following hierarchies were then dealt with: telephoning, shopping, having guests at the house, walking in the street, going to places of public entertainment, sitting in the garden in the afternoon.

Two weeks after the completion of the last hierarchy, the patient was given the Willoughby test again. Her score had dropped 40 points to the slightly inflated score of 47. She also reported increased sexual responsiveness, a slight improvement in interpersonal relationships and increased self-confidence. The patient commenced a refresher course in stenography with the intention of obtaining employment. She had not worked for 7 years. She voluntarily reduced her dose of tranquillizers to one a day and dispensed with them completely 1 week later.

At this stage the patient's husband fell seriously ill and she was able to support him emotionally despite the considerable effort involved. As her husband's health improved, she suffered a minor relapse for 2 weeks and then returned to her improved state spontaneously.

After 8 months of treatment, comprising 65 interviews devoted largely to systematic desensitization, this patient was 'much improved' in terms of Knight's criteria (symptom improvement, increased productivity, improved sexual relations, improved interpersonal relations, increased stress tolerance).

During the course of therapy, part of the reason for the development of the anxiety state in this patient was unearthed. When she was 17 years old she had become involved in a love affair with a married man 12 years her senior. This affair had been conducted in an extremely secretive manner for 4 years, during which time she had suffered from recurrent guilt feelings and shame, so much so, that on one occasion she had attempted suicide by throwing herself into a river. It was her custom to meet her lover after work in the later afternoon. The dull weather can be accounted for, as this affair took place in London.

Case 3

Bond and Hutchison (1960) obtained marked improvement in a patient with a severe and long-standing case of exhibitionism by using the reciprocal inhibition technique. The patient was a 25-year-old married man of average intelligence. His first exposure occurred at age 13 following sex play with a younger girl. His exhibitionism continued throughout adolescence and had reached "bizarre proportions" by the time he reached adulthood. The attacks of exhibitionism were preceded by tension, dread and sexual excitement. Attacks were often provoked by the perception of attractive young women.

The antecedent tension was constant and the patient often exposed several times a day. He had been convicted for indecent exposure on 11 occasions and had as a result spent a considerable amount of time in detention. The severity of his condition is best illustrated by the author's account. "A frequent practice was to hide completely nude in a small wooded area in the centre of the town where he then lived and spring out and expose himself to the first woman who passed." Various types of therapy had failed to relieve his condition.

It was decided to attempt Wolpe's desensitization procedure and the patient was accordingly trained to relax. A hierarchy of exposure-provoking stimuli was constructed and the patient gradually desensitized over a period of 30 sessions. By the eighth interview the patient evidenced distinct improvements. He was less tense, less prone to expose himself and able to venture out unaccompanied. As the desensitizing therapy continued, further evidences of progress appeared. His exhibitionist urges declined in frequency and strength, his sexual fantasies diminished and he reported an improvement in his sexual relations with his wife.

Therapy had to be discontinued after 29 sessions but the patient reported in succeeding months that he was much improved. He then exposed himself in a feeble and uncharacteristic manner in a store. The patient was returned for treatment on a weekly basis and 2 months later no relapse had occurred.

A full description of these and other methods developed by Wolpe (1958) is given in his book "Psychotherapy by Reciprocal Inhibition."

He also describes the treatment of a wide range of cases, including anxiety states, phobias, compulsions and sexual disorders. Additional case material is provided in "Behaviour Therapy and the Neuroses" edited by Eysenck (1960b). This text also contains several important papers on theory and methodology.

Inhibition and extinction.   Neurotic behaviour has been defined as "persistent unadaptive learned behaviour in which anxiety is almost always prominent and which is acquired in anxiety-generating situations." Behaviour which is learned can also be 'un-learned'. The processes by which responses are ordinarily diminished in magnitude and frequency of occurrence are 'extinction' and 'inhibition'.

Similarly neurotic behaviour is open to modification and elimination by the process of inhibition and extinction. The numerous types of psychological inhibition which have been observed or postulated include proactive, retroactive, external, reciprocal, reactive and conditioned inhibition. For several reasons, mainly of a practical nature, conditioned inhibition has received the greatest amount of attention in psychotherapy. Conditioned inhibition is generated when stimuli are associated with the cessation of a response in the presence of reactive inhibition (a negative drive tending to cause cessation of activity). Conditioned inhibition is acquired in the same way as positive behaviour patterns are learnt. It increases progressively as a function of the number of rewarded or reinforced trials and like all habit patterns is relatively permanent. It does not dissipate spontaneously even over long periods of time. Because of these characteristics, conditioned inhibition has been widely employed by psychotherapists in their attempts to eradicate neurotic behaviour.

Wolpe's technique of psychotherapy is an attempt to produce a conditioned inhibition of neurotic behaviour by the repeated simultaneous presentation of incompatible response tendencies (reciprocal inhibition). In this way, the tendency to respond anxiously to the noxious stimulus (e.g. blood) is superseded by the stronger and incompatible relaxation response. Repeated doses of this reciprocal inhibition (which is by itself temporary in effect) in the consulting room will steadily build up a permanent 'conditioned' inhibition of the neurotic behaviour.

For every behaviour pattern there is another type of behaviour which is incompatible with the first. The task of the therapist is to find an acceptable response pattern which is antagonistic to the neurotic activity of the patient and to substitute this adaptive behaviour for the non-adaptive, neurotic behaviour. Wolpe has proposed relaxation or feeding or avoidance or sexual or assertive responses as possible substitutes for neurotic behaviour, according to the requirements of the case.

Operant conditioning.   The work of Skinner on operant conditioning has recently been applied to problems of psychotherapy.   Although Skinner's theoretical views differ from those of Hull, the practical application of his work to psychotherapy involves a similar rationale.   Behaviour disturbances are regarded as problems in the
acquisition and retention of complex responses.   Consequently,
these disturbances are open to manipulation and modification by the
recognized processes of learning.   Skinner (1953, 1959) argues that
the use of appropriate learning techniques should enable the therapist
to shape human behaviour in the desired direction of improved mental
health.   Operant conditioning has been the subject of intensive
research and the information which has been collected can be
fruitfully applied to the training and re-training of maladjusted behaviour.

From the therapeutic point of view, the four most significant concepts are reinforcement, intermittent reinforcement, selective reinforcement and successive approximation.   In operant conditioning,
the strengthening of the response (reinforcement) is dependent on the
response itself.   Reinforcement cannot follow unless the response
appears.   It is the response which causes the reward to arrive and
this reinforces (strengthens) the responses.   This process is of course
different from that described by Pavlov (classical conditioning).   It will
be noticed that the subject in an operant conditioning situation, plays
an active role in the learning process whereas the subject's part in
classical conditioning is a relatively passive one.

Considerable research has been devoted to the analysis of rewards
(reinforcers) in the operant conditioning situation.   A highly significant
finding is that if reinforcers are presented irregularly (in time or sequence) they are more effective.   This intermittent reinforcement produces stronger responses than can be obtained by rewards presented
on a regular basis.   Apart from its value for the therapist, this observation is useful in the analysis of many aspects of human behaviour
(Ferster, 1958).   For example, it helps to account for the often surprising effects of inconsistent parental care on the behaviour of children.

Experimental work has led to the development of the technique
known as selective reinforcement.   The use of this method enables
one to simultaneously strengthen a desirable response and extinguish
an undesirable one.   Briefly, this method involves rewarding the appearance of the selected response and withholding rewards when the
undesired response appears.   In this way, the person's behaviour can
be shaped in the desired direction.   The skilful use of this method
coupled with 'successive approximation' brings a wide variety of
human behaviour into the range of therapeutic manipulation.   'Successive approximation' refers to the gradual and graduated building up

of a new response on the basis of the person's existing repertoire of responses. By careful planning it is possible to build up the person's simple responses (such as pressing a lever) into complex patterns of socially co-operative behaviour. This process is illustrated by the work of King *et al.* (1957, 1960) on schizophrenic patients.

To date, most of the research on operant conditioning has been concerned with the development of new techniques and the refinement of existing ones. Some examples from case material will, however, illustrate the therapeutic possibilities of operant conditioning.

Case 4

Brady and Lind (1961) were able to cure a patient suffering from hysterical blindness with this method. The patient had lost his sight after being involved in an accident. No organic basis for this loss of vision could be found and he received various types of psychotherapy without success. Two years after the onset of the illness he was treated by a conditioning technique. He was conditioned to respond to the presence of a light in the following way. The patient was informed that he would be rewarded with tokens when he pressed a small lever. These tokens could be exchanged at the hospital canteen for various articles. The light was switched on at irregular intervals and when a lever-pressing response followed the presentation of the light, the patient was given a token. He gradually learnt to respond to the light. This conditioned response was accompanied by vague visual sensations until he eventually reported that he could see the light. After regaining this visual ability he progressed further and full vision was restored.

Numerous studies of the behaviour of psychotic patients raise the possibility of obtaining limited improvements in these cases by the methods of operant conditioning. King, Armitage and Tilton (1960) conditioned 12 schizophrenic patients to operate a lever using food, cigarettes and other items as rewards or reinforcers. When the patients reached a stable rate of responding, they were conditioned to more complex tasks involving verbal behaviour and even social co-operation. By comparison with 3 matched groups comprising 12 schizophrenics each, the conditioned group showed the greatest overall improvement. The patients in the conditioned group improved in "level of verbalization, motivation to leave the ward, more interest in occupational therapy, decreased enuresis."

Other investigations of psychotic patients include those of Lindsley (1956, 1960) and Ayllon and Michael (1959, 1963). Some promising work on the treatment of children has also been reported by Baer (1962) and Bijou and Orlando (1961) among others.

It would be unwise to offer dogmatic assertions until more research work has been conducted but the following assessments are proposed on the basis of the available information. Firstly, operant conditioning methods are likely to prove of particular value in the treatment of what may be called deficit behaviour disorders. This would encompass disorders which arise out of a failure to develop adequate behaviour, such as aphemia, alexia, anorexia and so forth. It could also be used in developing psychological functions which are only partially or improperly operative. Secondly, operant conditioning is likely to prove extremely valuable in the treatment of children's disorders. Many of these disorders are of the deficit variety discussed above and in addition, the technique itself seems to be admirably suited for use with children (Rachman, 1963). It is simple, the control of rewards is easier with children and it can be conducted with a minimum reliance on language.

Some theoretical considerations

An objection which is frequently presented by critics of behaviour therapy is the concept of 'basic causes'. They argue that this therapy deals only with symptoms and leaves the basic cause or causes of the neurosis untouched; that this 'superficial approach' to the treatment of neurotic behaviour is destined to bring about only temporary alleviation of symptoms (at best) and may well aggravate the patient's condition. They claim that it is only when the 'inner forces of the psyche' have been restored to harmony by free association, transference and interpretation that the person is normal again. The major objections may be summarized as follows: Behaviour therapy (a) is superficial, (b) is symptom-orientated, (c) ignores the deep inner causes of the neuroses, (d) can effect only temporary improvements and (e) smothers certain symptoms only to provoke new ones.

Behaviour therapy is not superficial if this implies either that such treatment is 'not complete' or that it can be applied with success only in certain minor types of behaviour disorders. There is considerable clinical and experimental evidence which shows, on the contrary, that such therapy is both complete and capable of being applied in many types of disorder, including those which are regarded as 'deep-seated', e.g. phobic states and anxiety neuroses of long-standing. Examples of therapeutic successes with enuretics, hysterics, stutterers, drug-addicts, homosexuals, phobic states, alcoholics and tension-states, have been reported in which the 'superficial approach' has provided complete or near-complete recovery. In many of the cases referred to here, the improvement has been obtained without either therapist or patient knowing what the 'basic cause' of the illness was. A particularly striking example of such a case is provided by Wolpe (1958);

A 37 year-old miner was seen in a state of intense anxiety.   He had a very marked tremor and a total amnesia for the previous 4 days.   He said that his wife, on whom he was greatly dependent, had cunningly got him to agree to "temporary divorce" 6 months before and was now going to marry a friend of his.   No attempt was made at this juncture to recall the lost memories.   The patient was made to realize how ineffectual his previous attitudes had been and how he had been deceived.   As a result he angrily "had it out" with his wife and a few others.   The anxiety rapidly decreased and he soon felt sufficiently motivated to organize his whole life differently. At his fifth interview (10 days after treatment began) he said that he felt "a hundred per cent" and was full of plans for the future.   Yet he had still recalled nothing whatever of the forgotten 4 days.   The patient later recalled the lost memories under hypnosis.   No important consequences ensued.   A few months later he married another woman and was apparently very well adjusted generally.

Other examples are provided by Lazarus and Rachman (1957), Lovibond (1963) and Salter (1950).

Can this evidence be taken to mean that a knowledge of the causative factors is unnecessary?   The answer to this problem would appear to be a qualified affirmative.   In some instances it seems unlikely that improvement in the patient's condition can be effected without such knowledge.   On the other hand it would appear from the numerous therapeutic failures reported by analysts and other therapists, that in certain cases insight and interpretation do not assist.   A very obvious example of such a state of affairs can be observed in the treatment of psychopathy.   An appraisal of the data leads us to the conclusion that while a knowledge of the causative process and genesis of the individual neurosis can be of considerable value in therapy, improvement can nevertheless be obtained in many cases without such knowledge.

Too great a concern with 'underlying causes' may under certain circumstances even impede therapeutic progress.   The case of the miner treated by Wolpe and quoted above is one such instance.   The 'forward-looking approach' as opposed to the historical technique has much to recommend it.   It is quite conceivable that a patient with some pressing, immediate problem (e.g. pending divorce) may receive a severe and unnecessary jolt from the apparent lack of concern of the non-directive therapist.

With regard to the observation that objective psychotherapy is symptom-orientated, this is generally true.   The treatment of the symptom or symptoms is quite logically one of the first considerations of the psychotherapist.   In numerous cases there is little else that is required as 'the deep inner causes', if they exist, cease to be relevant (Mowrer, 1950).   The five cases reported by Lazarus and Rachman (1957) all bear this contention out.   In Case 1 above, the precise reason or reasons for the ambulance-phobia developing in this 14 year-old boy were never discovered. The fear was inhibited and extinguished by systematic desensitization and this removal of the symptom was sufficient.

Does behaviour therapy effect only temporary improvement? There is some evidence that improvements obtained by these techniques are long-lasting or permanent, but it must be admitted that the design of research work in the field of therapy, both objective and psychoanalytic, has been inadequate in this respect.

Behaviour therapy has also been criticized on the grounds that it merely smothers the neurotic symptoms. Because the 'basic causes' of the maladaptive behaviour have not been treated, it is said that new symptoms will necessarily arise to replace the extinguished behaviour patterns. For example, training an enuretic to relieve himself in the lavatory or teaching a stutterer to speak fluently will merely result in the patient 'adopting' some new deviant response. While such 'transfer' of symptoms can occur, its frequency has probably been unduly exaggerated (Wolpe, 1958; Yates, 1958). In those cases where transferred symptoms arise the therapeutic procedure is quite uncomplicated. The therapist after having desensitized the patient to the original noxious stimulus situations, if confronted with a so-called 'substitute-symptom' would proceed to desensitize this new symptom in turn. When this treatment has been successfully completed, the probability of recurrence is slight. It will be agreed that all neurotic symptoms in the patient have some degree of interdependence and that the weakening or extinction of any one symptom is likely to affect all the others in like manner. The symptom which is treated first is usually the most resistant. Behaviour patterns treated subsequently are more easily modified. If a new symptom arises it can be expected to be of rather weaker strength and hence readily amenable to inhibition or extinction. This symptom-substitution phenomenon and its treatment has been described by Lazarus and Rachman (1957). One of their cases, a married woman of 29, had developed a phobic reaction to dogs as the result of a traumatic incident 5 years earlier. After 3 years of psychoanalysis, her fear of dogs had disappeared but instead she had developed a chronic anxiety state with numerous, varied phobias (symptom-substitution). After 6 weeks of intensive psychotherapy (28 sessions) she was much improved, but her dog-phobia returned. After a further 28 sessions devoted mainly to the inhibition of this phobia, she was discharged as 'much improved'. A year later she was still healthy and the extinction of the dog-phobia had been maintained. This case-history illustrates the treatment of symptom-substitution by objective psychotherapy and also the development of a substitute symptom under psycho-analysis.

Reservations about the improvements obtained with behaviour therapy are sometimes based on the claim that the effective mechanism is not the re-learning process but rather, some aspect of the patient-therapist relationship, for example transference, insight, derepression. Such introductions are unnecessary and in a neat demonstration Wolpe (1962b) was able to isolate the effective agent in the treatment of a woman with a traffic phobia. The therapeutic sessions were restricted to conditioning practice only and it was shown that the time and amount of the patient's improvements were directly related to the conditioning sessions. Furthermore, a change of therapist failed to disturb the direct relationship between conditioning treatment and actual improvements.

Prospect

Behaviour therapy has now developed to the point where large scale field trials with adequate controls can be carried out. The evaluation studies which are presently available can at best be regarded as highly suggestive and encouraging. Wolpe (1958) has reported that nearly 90 per cent of 210 patients had either been much improved or apparently recovered after a median number of 23 interviews. Lazarus (1963) states that 78 per cent of the 408 patients who consulted him derived marked benefit. Of these 408 patients, Lazarus classified 126 as suffering from severe disturbances and in this sub-group the improvement rate was 62 per cent. Hussain (1963) reported that 95 per cent of his 105 patients were much improved by behaviour therapy which generally lasted less than three months. In addition to these reports on the effects of behaviour therapy with large groups of patients, there are numerous accounts of successes claimed with small numbers of patients (e.g. Eysenck, 1960). On the other hand, a small retrospective survey conducted by Cooper (1962) suggested that some phobic cases treated by behaviour therapy tended to relapse. Clearly, the effectiveness of behaviour therapy needs to be determined by strict, highly controlled experiments.

As the recent developments in operant conditioning procedures demonstrate, there are many more therapeutic procedures which can be derived from experimental psychology. It is to be hoped that new clinical methods will continue to increase the scope and effectiveness of behaviour therapy. The high rate of spontaneous remissions in neurotic illnesses constitutes a problem of considerable theoretical and practical importance (Eysenck, 1962) and research in this area would also be most valuable.

Conclusions

Behaviour therapy offers substantial advantages as a method of treating disorders of behaviour. It has developed out of established psychological theories and has a large body of experimental evidence on which to proceed. The therapeutic process and its outcome are both open to quantification. It permits precision and a systematic planning of the treatment required in individual cases. Behaviour therapy has now reached the point where large-scale field tests are possible and indeed, necessary.

References

Ayllon, T. (1960) Some behavioural problems associated with eating in chronic schizophrenic patients. Read at an APA meeting, Chicago.

Ayllon, T. (1963) Intensive treatment of psychotic behaviour by stimulus satiation and food reinforcement. *Behav. Res. Ther. 1,* 53–61.

Ayllon, T. and Michael, J. (1959) The psychiatric nurse as a behavioural engineer. *J. exp. Anal. Behav. 2,* 323–334.

Bachrach, A. L. (1962) *Experimental Foundations of Clinical Psychology.* Basic Books, New York.

Baer, D. M. (1962) Laboratory control of thumbsucking in three young children by withdrawal and representation of positive reinforcement. *J. exp. Anal. Behav.* In press.

Bailey, P. B. (1956) The great psychiatric revolution. *Amer. J. Psychiat. 113,* 147–168.

Bandura, A. (1961) Psychotherapy as a learning process. *Psychol. Bull. 58,* 144–159.

Barrett, B. H. (1961) Reduction in rate of multiple tics by free-operant conditioning methods. Unpublished paper.

Blakemore, C. *et al.* (1963) Application of faradic aversion conditioning in a case of transvestism. *Behav. Res. Ther. 1,* 29–34.

Bond, J. and Hutchison, H. C. (1960) Application of reciprocal inhibition therapy to exhibitionism. *Canad. med. Ass. J. 83,* 123–128.

Brady, J. and Lind, D. L. (1961) Experimental analysis of hysterical blindness. *Arch. Gen. Psychiat. 4,* 331–339.

Broadhurst, P. (1960) Abnormal animal behaviour, in *Handbook of Abnormal Psychology.* Ed. H. J. Eysenck. Pitmans, London.

Clarke, D. F. (1963) Treatment of a monosymptomatic phobia by systematic desensitization. *Behav. Res. Ther. 1,* 63–68.

Cooper, J. E. (1961) Some aspects of the use of behaviour therapy in psychiatry. Dissertation, University of London.

Cowden, R. and Ford, L. (1962) Systematic desensitization with phobic schizophrenics. *Amer. J. Psychiat. 119,* 241–245.

Eysenck, H. J. (1960a) Personality and behaviour therapy. *Proc. royal Soc. Med. 53,* 504–508.

Eysenck, H. J. (1960b) *Behaviour Therapy and the Neuroses.* Pergamon Press, Oxford.

Eysenck, H. J. (1960c) *Handbook of Abnormal Psychology*. Pitmans, London.

Eysenck, H. J. (1962) Spontaneous remission. *Amer. J. Psychiat.* In press.

Ferster, C. B. (1958) Reinforcement and punishment in the control of human behaviour in social agencies. *Psychiat. Res. Rep. Amer. psychiat. Ass. 10*, 101–118.

Ferster, C. B. and de Myer, M. (1961) The development of performances in autistic children in an automatically controlled environment. *J. chron. Dis. 13*, 312–345.

Franks, C. (1958) Alcohol, alcoholism and conditioning. *J. Ment. Sci. 104*, 14–33.

Freund, K. (1960) Problems in the treatment of homosexuality, in *Behaviour Therapy and the Neuroses*. Ed. H. J. Eysenck. Pergamon Press, Oxford.

Gantt, W. H. (1944) Experimental basis for neurotic behaviour. *Psychosom. Med. Monog. Suppl. 3*, Nos. 3 and 4.

Hussain, A. (1962) Unpublished paper.

Jones, H. G. (1960a) The behavioural treatment of enuresis nocturna, in *Behaviour Therapy and the Neuroses*. Ed. H. J. Eysenck. Pergamon Press, Oxford.

Jones, M. C. (1924a) The elimination of children's fears. *J. exp. Psychol. 7*, 383–400.

Jones, M. C. (1924b) A laboratory study of fear: The case of Peter. *Pedagog. Sem. 31*, 308–315.

King, G. F., Armitage, S. and Tilton, J. (1960) A therapeutic approach to schizophrenics of extreme pathology. *J. abn. (soc.) Psychol. 61*, 276–286.

King, G. F., Merrell, D., Lovinger, E. and Denny, M. (1957) Operant motor behavior in acute schizophrenics. *J. Personality 25*, 317–326.

Lazarus, A. (1960) The elimination of children's phobias by deconditioning, in *Behaviour Therapy and the Neuroses*. Ed. H. J. Eysenck. Pergamon Press, Oxford.

Lazarus, A. (1963) The results of behaviour therapy in 126 cases of severe neuroses. *Behav. Res. Ther. 1*, 69–79.

Lazarus, A. and Abramovitz, A. (1962) The use of "emotive imagery" in the treatment of children's phobias. *J. ment. Sci.* In press.

Lazarus, A. and Rachman, S. (1960) The use of systematic desensitization psychotherapy, in *Behaviour Therapy and Neuroses*. Ed. H. J. Eysenck. Pergamon Press, Oxford.

Lazovik, A. D. and Lang, P. J. (1960) A laboratory demonstration of systematic desensitization psychotherapy. *J. Psychol. Stud. 11*, 238–242.

Levitt, E. E. (1957) The results of psychotherapy with children. *J. cons. Psychol. 21*, 189–196.

Liddell, H. S. (1944) Conditioned reflex method and experimental neurosis, in *Personality and the Behaviour Disorders.* Ed. J. McV. Hunt. Ronald, New York.

Lindsley, O. R. (1956) Operant conditioning methods applied to research in chronic schizophrenia. *Psychiat. Res. Rep. Amer. psychiat. Ass. 5,* 118–139.

Lindsley, O. R. (1960) Characteristics of the behaviour of chronic psychotics as revealed by free-operant conditioning methods. *Dis. nerv. Syst. 21,* 66–78.

Lovibond, S. H. (1961) *Conditioning and Enuresis.* Thesis, University of Adelaide.

Lovibond, S. (1963) The mechanism of conditioning treatment of enuresis. *Behav. Res. Ther. 1,* 17–21.

Max, L. (1935) Breaking a homosexual fixation by the conditioned reflex technique. *Psychol. Bull. 32,* 734.

Metzner, R. (1961) Learning theory and the therapy of the neuroses. *Brit. J. Psychol.* Monogr. Suppl. 33.

Meyer, V. (1957) The treatment of two phobic patients on the basis of learning theory. *J. abn. (soc.) Psychol. 55,* 261–265.

Mowrer, O. H. and Mowrer, W. (1938) Enuresis: A method for its study and treatment. *Amer. J. Orthopsychiat. 8,* 436–459.

Orlando, R. and Bijou, S. W. (1960) Single and multiple schedules of reinforcement in developmentally retarded children. *J. exper. anal. Behav. 3,* 339–348.

Rachman, S. (1959) Treatment of anxiety and phobic reactions by desensitization. *J. abn. (soc.) Psychol. 102,* 421–427.

Rachman, S. (1961) Sexual disorders and behaviour therapy. *Amer. J. Psychiat. 46,* 57–70.

Rachman, S. (1962) Child psychology and learning theory. *J. child Psychol. Psychiat. 3,* 149–163.

Rachman, S. and Costello, C. G. (1961) The aetiology and treatment of children's phobias: A review. *Amer. J. Psychiat. 118,* 97–105.

Raymond, M. J. (1956) Case of fetishism treated by aversion therapy. *Brit. Med. J. 2,* 854–856.

Salter, A. (1950) *Conditioned Reflex Therapy.* Creative Age Press, New York.

Skinner, B. F. (1953) *Science and Human Behaviour.* Macmillan, New York.

Skinner, B. F. (1959) *Cumulative Record.* Appleton-Century-Crofts, New York.

Sylvester, J. and Liversedge, L. A. (1960) Conditioning and the occupational cramps, in *Behaviour Therapy and the Neuroses.* Ed. H. J. Eysenck. Pergamon Press, Oxford.

Walton, D. (1961) Experimental psychology and the treatment of a tiqueur. *J. child Psychol. Psychiat. 2,* 148–155.

Walton, D. (1963) The interaction effects of drive, reactive and conditioned inhibition. *Behav. Res. Ther. 1,* 35–43.

Watson, J. B. and Rayner, R. (1920) Conditioned emotional reactions. *J. exp. Psychol. 3,* 1–14.

Williams, C. D. (1959) The elimination of tantrum behaviour by extinction procedures. *J. abn. (soc.) Psychol. 59,* 269–270.

Wolpe, J. (1958) *Psychotherapy by reciprocal inhibition.* Stanford University Press, Stanford.

Wolpe, J. (1961) The systematic desensitization treatment of neuroses. *J. nerv. ment. Dis. 132,* 189–203.

Wolpe, J. and Rachman, S. (1960) Psychoanalytic evidence: A critique based on Freud's case of Little Hans. *J. nerv. ment. Dis. 131,* 135–143.

Wolpe, J. (1962a) Experimental foundations of some new psychotherapeutic methods, in *Experimental Foundations of Clinical Psychology.* Ed. A. J. Bachrach. Basic Books, New York.

Wolpe, J. (1962b) Isolation of a conditioning procedure as the crucial psychotherapeutic factor: A case study. *J. nerv. ment. Dis. 134,* 316–329.

Yates, A. J. (1958) The application of learning theory to the treatment of tics. *J. abn. (soc.) Psychol. 56,* 175–182.

J. F. T. Bugental

FIVE PARADIGMS FOR GROUP PSYCHOTHERAPY *

The literature of group psychotherapy is apt to prove frustrating to the informed and conscientious reader because of the evident range of phenomena which are lumped together under the single name "group therapy" (1, 2, 3, 4, 5, 6, 7, 8, 9). To be sure, such adjectives as "analytic," "intensive," or "activity" are sometimes used to try to denote more specifically what a particular author is discussing; nevertheless, no assurance is available that two different writers, both nominally dealing with, say, "intensive group therapy," have indeed the same sort of program in mind. It is manifest that this situation makes it difficult for the student, the teacher, and the professional journeyman.

It is the purpose of this paper to describe five paradigms for group therapy. In addition to the aid to clearer communication which it is

* From J. F. T. Bugental, "Five Paradigms for Group Psychotherapy," *Psychol. Rep.,* 1962, *10,* 607–610. Reprinted by permission of the author and the Editor, *Psychological Reports.*

hoped this may provide, it is likely that it will enable group therapists to exercise greater precision in conducting their work and greater flexibility in adapting it to the needs of their patients. An adequate taxonomy is an essential of a disciplined procedure.

Let us imagine five different groups among which we may draw contrasts. For our purposes we will focus only on what goes on in the groups. We will be trying to get five different answers to the question, "What does a therapy group do?" Let us recognize at the outset that we will overdraw each of these portraits of the groups in order to highlight contrasts. Here are thumbnail descriptions of the five. *Process-centered group:* First we may think of a group that is close to the so-called "group dynamics" or "training" groups though in one way or another such procedures are used also in therapy. *Activity-projects group:* Some groups center their activity around projects of various kinds which are used for instigating activities thought to be therapeutic. *Interpersonal discussion group:* This group concerns itself primarily with expressing and seeking to understand the actual relations among the members of the group itself. *Expressive-projective group:* In this form, emphasis is placed on catharsis through projections upon ambiguous materials and activities. *Analytic group:* This approach seeks to examine the reinstatement of early emotional conditioning in the transferences among the patients and upon the therapist. Having these first, hasty pictures of the five models, let us next contrast them in terms of characteristics of their functioning, recognizing the while that we are overemphasizing differences in order to understand the phenomena more readily.

Typical activities. What does each group do when it is functioning most nearly as the therapist thinks productive?

The *process* group reviews and looks for underlying implications in an immediately preceding discussion segment. Thus it may look at the sorts of member behaviors that facilitated and blocked understanding, at the patterns of relative frequency of participation, or at competition for group leadership.

The *projects* group may watch a film on different forms of parental discipline and then share memories of the punishments and rewards they received from their own parents or that they mete out to their children. They may each respond to a projective question (such as naming three impossibilities) and then compare the kinds of responses they have given. They may role play a problem in giving sex education to a teen-ager and then compare the ideas, memories, and concerns stimulated.

The *interpersonal discussion* group members share their emotional responses to an interchange which has just occurred among some of the group. They try to bring out candidly the impacts experienced in terms of anger, competition, affection, empathy, and so on, and then seek to understand these in terms of other aspects of their own personalities with which they are becoming familiar.

The *expressive* group uses a variety of media to stimulate and reveal feelings, impulses, fantasies, and unconscious material generally: thus they may all work on a composite drawing with crayons or finger paints, each following the dictates of his own impulses and then reacting to the contributions of the others. They may exchange roles and play out their perceptions of each other. Their participation is encouraged to be freer and will be more characterized by shouting, cursing, weeping, grimacing, etc.

The *analytic* group gives subjective associations to a dream of one of its members; notes and interprets slips of speech or metaphors, and seeks to make explicit the projection of familial identities upon each other and upon the therapists.

Next let us look at *typical therapist functions* in each of these types of groups. The lists are not exhaustive and there is much overlap, but we will try to pick out a few of the most important and most distinguishing.

The *process* group therapist must set an example as a sensitive listener and perceptive reporter. He teaches the importance of the implicit and helps the group get over its content-boundness. He frequently will provide observation schedules and will coach members in their uses.

The *projects* group therapist will supply the projects around which the group centers and guide the group in using them. He may give lecturettes to illuminate aspects with which the group needs help or to encourage greater involvement and to demonstrate the universality of certain experiences.

The *discussion* group therapist tends to be much less active, limiting his interventions more to those of helping the group maintain a here-and-now focus, of encouraging greater candor in interpersonal exchanges, and of pointing out commonalities and differences among reactions.

The *expressive* group therapist will be a resource to his group for media upon which to project. He will interpret resistances to free expression, enforce limits to the acting out, and support patients who verge on being overwhelmed, either from within themselves or from the group.

The *analytic* group therapist tends to be more passive than most of the others as he provides a screen upon which transferences may be projected. However, from time to time, he will interpret resistances or transferences, particularly pointing out the parataxic distortions which may be involved.

Next let us examine the *patient's* role in each of these models.

The *process* group tends to maintain a here-and-now, group-centered, rational orientation in which the patient seeks to increase his interpersonal sensitivities. He is rewarded by the group for subtlety of perception and for manifest changes in his skills in dealing with others.

The *projects* group is more apt to use an historical perspective with a consequently greater attention to the individual than to the group as a group. Availability of memories is encouraged, and there is an emphasis on manifest reasonableness and pertinence.

The *discussion* group maintains an orientation to what is going on now in the group but focuses particularly on relationships. Logic is valued but not to the exclusion of feelings, which the group usually insists must also be expressed. The patient who can sense emotional parallels and contrasts with others' experiences especially gains group approval.

The *expressive* group similarly maintains a here-and-now emphasis but with more attention to the individual as such. Depth and even exoticness of production is prized, and affective coherence far outweighs logical consistency. The patient who most plumbs his emotions and most clearly overthrows super-ego censorship is apt to be most rewarded.

The *analytic* group tends to have a much stronger individual focus and to seek historical materials. The patient is alerted to symbolic meanings in the contributions, and the ability to share dreams and readily associate to them is valued. Similarly a moderate degree of regression in explicitly relating to the therapist as a parent and the other patients as siblings frequently is encouraged.

Although each of these models of group therapy has its proponents, no present evidence exists to demonstrate that one is more universally effective than another. Rather it seems highly probable that each has its values. We will close our descriptions of these five paradigms with some preliminary and highly tentative speculations about the possible functional values of each. It is hoped that in the future, clinical reports and research investigations will provide sounder bases for selecting one form or another in a particular treatment situation.

The *process* group seems to be useful in providing not-too-threatening introductions to behavioral uniformities among superficially different people, to the significance of the implicit and preconscious, and to the values and satisfactions of sharing and interacting with others. As such it can provide a kind of training in socialization and human interaction.

The *projects* group moves more toward a focus on the inner life of the individual as it extends the "introductions" to the psychological world mentioned for the previous group. It may bring about a shallow dipping into the unconscious with the recovery of some less stringently repressed materials. It can aid in achieving insights into one's own processes through demonstrating the uses of introspection, the pertinence of historical material, and the inevitability of ambivalence toward emotionally important figures. In common with all group therapy forms, it offers the reassurance of demonstrations of the universality of certain emotional experiences.

The *discussion* group moves into the inner life more truly than either of the preceding two models. The unconscious is more frequently tapped although still not to the deepest levels. The patient may perceive how he "sets up" the interactions which have long been punishing to him, may become more aware of his distortions of perception, and may discover how much of his behavior has been compulsive rather than truly elective. Similarly—and especially when the patients have individual sessions also—discussion group patients can be introduced to awareness of the functions of symbols and to the reality of transference.

The *expressive* group is particularly suited to freeing overly repressed creative and emotional resources, and, through the catharsis which it encourages, to providing probes to the characterological roots of neurosis (although the method does not provide for a real "working through" of these in most instances). The patient also is apt to be made aware of the more infantile elements underlying his conscious life.

The *analytic* group, through its focus on transferences and symbolic material, is most likely to provide the climate necessary to genuine "working through" of unconscious material. In this group the deep, or truly familial, parataxes may be stimulated repeatedly, leading to the establishment of the transference neurosis and its eventual resolution.

Summary. And so we have set forth five paradigms of therapy groups. For each we have tried to suggest the usual nature of group activity, the roles of therapists and patients, and finally we have advanced some notions about the possible functional values of a successful group experience in each. There is much more that might be said. We have not dealt with such crucially important questions as patient selection, therapist preparation, frequency of meetings, and so on. However, if we have made a first step toward developing a nomenclature which will improve our communications with each other about group therapy, we will have accomplished our purpose.

References

1. Bach, G. R. *Intensive group therapy*. New York: Ronald, 1954.
2. Corsini, R. J. *Methods of group therapy*. New York: McGraw-Hill, 1957.

3. Hinkley, R. G., & Hermann, L. *Group treatment in psychotherapy.* Minneapolis: Univer. of Minnesota Press, 1951.

4. Klapman, J. W. *Group psychotherapy: theory and practice.* (2nd ed.) New York: Grune & Stratton, 1959.

5. Powdermaker, F. B., & Frank, J. D. *Group psychotherapy.* Cambridge: Harvard Univer. Press, 1953.

6. Slavson, S. R. *An introduction to group therapy.* New York: Commonwealth Fund, 1943.

7. Slavson, S. R. Group psychotherapies. In J. L. McCary, & D. E. Sheer (Eds.), *Six approaches to psychotherapy.* New York: Dryden, 1955. Pp. 127–178.

8. Spotnitz, H. Group therapy. In G. Bychowski, & J. L. Despert (Eds.), *Specialized techniques in psychotherapy.* New York: Basic Books, 1952. Pp. 85–102.

9. Ziferstein, I., & Grotjahn, M. Psychoanalysis and group psychotherapy. In F. Fromm-Reichmann, & J. L. Moreno (Eds.), *Progress in psychotherapy: 1956.* New York: Grune & Stratton, 1956. Pp. 248–255.

Nathan W. Ackerman   **FAMILY PSYCHOTHERAPY—
THEORY AND PRACTICE ***

Within the past 15 years, family therapy has emerged as a new dimension in the art and science of mental healing.   It bids fair to become the very core of a newly developing pattern of community mental health services.

In the evolution of family treatment, several distinct, though overlapping, emphases have appeared: (1) Reeducation of the family through guidance; (2) Reorganization through a change in the patterns of family communication; (3) Resolution of pathogenic conflict and induction of change and growth by means of a dynamic, depth-approach to the affective currents of family life.   It is the last of these that will be considered here.

Family psychotherapy is defined as a special method of treatment of emotional disorders, based on dynamically oriented interviews with the whole family.   It is the therapy of a natural living unit, embracing all these persons who share the identity of family and whose behavior

* From Nathan W. Ackerman, "Family Psychotherapy—Theory and Practice," *Amer. J. Psychother.*, 1966, *20*, 405–414.   Reprinted by permission of the author and the Editor, *American Journal of Psychotherapy.*

is influenced by a circular interchange of emotion. Grandparents, extended kin, or other individuals who are significant participants in the stream of family life may be included. The family is viewed as a behavioral system with emergent properties different from a mere summation of the characteristics of its members. The behavior of any one member may be interpreted in four ways: as a symptom of the psychopathology of the family unit; as a stabilizer of the family; as healer of family disorder, and as the epitome of the growth potential of the group. Treatment focuses on the relations between the psychosocial functioning of the family group and the emotional functioning of its members.

The ideal of family therapy is not merely to remove symptoms but to nourish a new way of life. Its goals are to remove emotional distress and disablement and promote the level of health and growth, both in the family group and its members by relieving pathogenic conflict and anxiety; by raising the level of complementation of emotional needs; by strengthening the immunity of the family against critical upsets; by enhancing the harmony and balance of family functions; by strengthening the individual member against destructive forces, both within him and surrounding him in the family environment; and by influencing the orientation of family identity and values toward health and growth.

Historically viewed, perspectives of psychotherapy have moved from the symptoms and conflicts of the individual to the total functioning of personality; to the relations of personality and role adaptation, and finally to the human relations patterns of family and community. Thus, the clinician is irresistibly drawn, as if by a magnet, from a limited concern with the separate individual to the live, dynamic properties of the network of family and community.

The family approach to therapy is propelled into being by a number of confluent forces: (1) The radical transformation of family life induced by social change; (2) The recognition of the principle of contagion of emotional disturbance, the intimate connections between social and mental disorder; the recognition that the family phenomenon is not peripheral but of the very essence of psychiatric illness; (3) The greater appreciation of the limitations of conventional procedures of diagnosis and treatment that are limited to the individual patient; (4) New developments in the behavioral sciences, in ego psychology, small group dynamics, social psychology, anthropology, and communication; with these, changes in the theory of behavior and of causation of emotional illness; (5) The changed role of the psychotherapist in the modern community.

Family psychotherapy, as a distinct method, needs to be seen in historical perspective in relation to psychoanalysis, group therapy, and child therapy. In its classic model, psychoanalytic therapy depends on an environmental condition characterized by a modicum of stability, dependability, and predictability. It is within such a life situation that analyst and patient can, in effect, treat the environment as a constant, bypass it and concentrate on the task of analyzing transference manifestations of childhood conflicts. When, by contrast, the group environment becomes characterized by eruptive, unforeseeable change, and is realistically threatening, then the optimal condition required for the pursuit of the therapeutic progress is no longer present. There can be then only two choices: to reject the environment and to substitute a hopefully better one, or to change the environment by including it in an expanded system of therapeutic intervention.

The issue is clear. The group environment of our time, family and community, is changing at an unprecedented rate of speed; it is unstable, difficult to know and predict. It provides inadequate and erratic support for the emotional needs and growth of the individual. Only too often the individual is captive to his environment. He is the emotional prisoner of the disordered patterns of his group. He can neither leave his environment nor substitute a better one.

Under conditions of radical social change and realistic danger, the psychoanalyst's special task becomes increasingly handicapped. When the environment becomes unstable, the individual armors himself to carry the fight to the environment. He externalizes his conflict and his way of coping with it. In this setting there is often a selective reinforcement of such defenses as projection, denial, and substitution of aggression for anxiety, magic thinking and the omnipotent urge to reshape the world to suit the self. All too frequently, the individual unable to contain his conflict, acts it out irrationally in a shared way with other members of his group. From these considerations, we come to an inescapable conclusion. The sphere of psychic healing must be expanded to embrace the sources of pathogenic influence within the group environment as well as within the individual.

The evolution of group psychotherapy did three things: (1) It focused attention on fundamental interdependence of the individual and the group, and on the phenomena of social role adaptation; (2) It sharpened our understanding of specific deficiencies in existing theories of personality, and broadened our conception of the causation of disordered behavior; (3) It modified our view of the responsibility of the psychotherapist in the modern community.

From still another point of view, the advancing borders of knowledge of child psychiatry, child development, and child psychotherapy, challenged by the concepts of social science, acted as a catalytic force in stirring reevaluation of the principles and practices of psychiatry. Disorders of the marital and parental partnership likewise hindered progress of the child. In child guidance, there was an established tradition of separate treatment of the child by a psychiatrist, the mother by a social worker. The tail seemed to wag the dog. The family was turned upside down. The family was viewed as extension of the child rather than the child as extension of the family. The mother felt accused and guilty; a wave of witch-hunting for rejecting mothers pervaded the climate of child guidance. Therapists took the side of the child against mother and family; therapists were missionaries dedicated to the rescue of hurt children. In a semi-jocular vein, child therapists were labeled "mother-killers." All that was human and good was attributed to the child, the source of evil was the mother. The value distortion is now clear: to save the child, we must also save parents and family. Separate treatment of family members seemed frequently to have the effect of drawing the members apart rather than bringing them closer together. It is by no means rare that one encounters troubled families in which three or four or even all members of the group are undergoing treatment with several therapists. This brings critical complications in the regulation of the emotional life of the family unit.

The artificiality and complications of the custom of separate treatment started a new chain of thought and action, the diagnosis and psychotherapy of the whole family.

In this historical setting, family study and treatment, though relatively new, offers considerable promise. It gives us expanded understanding of the relation between inner and outer experience, past and present, individual and group in the precipitation, course, and outcome of illness. Family therapy lends explicit emphasis to the principle of emotional contagion in family relationships, to the transmission of pathogenic conflict and coping from one generation to the next. It provides a framework for the correlation of the events of family and individual development at each stage of the life cycle. It opens a path to the conceptualization of the relations between family group defense of its continuity, identity and functions and individual defense against anxiety. It clarifies, within the context of family interaction, the meaning of the secondary gain of illness. It illuminates the phenomenon of multiple interacting disturbances among the members of the same family group. It sheds further light on the homeodynamics of family growth and behavior, and on the learning and growth processes of personality within the matrix of family development.

The tasks of diagnosis and treatment are interwoven, interdependent, parallel activities. Diagnosis qualifies the choice of therapeutic goals and the specificity of the techniques of family psychotherapy. Yet, at the same time, the dynamically oriented exploratory interview with the whole family is the pathway to diagnosis.

Regardless of which family member is labeled the "sick one," the whole family is invited to come in and talk it over. Therapeutic interviews with the family group may be conducted both in the office and at home.   Home visits are of great value but insufficiently used.

At the outset, the family is troubled, perplexed, frightened.   The members know something is deeply wrong, but they do not know how or why nor do they know what to do about it.   By tradition, the family pushes one member forward as the sick, disabled one.   Yet, in actuality, several, and sometimes all, members are disturbed although in different ways and at different depths.   What the psychiatrist faces is a cluster of interrelated illness processes, not a "single patient."

In many families, regardless of the symptom picture, there is no urge for psychiatric referral as long as family role relationships are held in tolerable balance.   The timing of the demand for professional help strongly coincides with the immediate dramatic impact of decompensation of the previous state of balance, which then brings in its wake a distressing family conflict.   Critical upsets of the emotional equilibrium of the family group thus become a significant health phenomenon.

In the family interview, what one parent conceals, the other reveals. What the parents together hide, the child blurts out.   What one member expresses in a twisted, prejudiced way is corrected by another. When certain anxiety filled material is touched upon, the family may engage in a silent pact to avoid such areas.   Sooner or later, such denials are broken through.   Family life, by its very nature, is inimical to the guarding of secrets.   Such secrets exist but they are difficult to preserve.   Sooner or later, "the cat comes out of the bag."   It is the clinician's responsibility to distinguish valid secrets from false pathogenic ones.   He respects the former while supporting the family in dissolving the latter.

Family therapy may begin on the surface, it need not stay there; a competent therapist can achieve access to any emotional depth he may require in meeting the problems of a particular family.   The challenge of reaching, as and when needed, selected components of the depth experience of the family, rests, in the ultimate, on therapeutic talent, clarity, know-how, appropriateness of goals, and confidence in action.

A family has a body, a mind, and a spirit; it has a heart; it throbs with the pulse of life; it has both depth and surface; it has an inner face and an outer face.   It builds a facade, a mask.   If we strip the mask we can glimpse the inner being; we enter the conflict experience of the family in depth.   Family therapy begins promptly with the first face-to-face contact.   The therapist makes instantaneous observations of the personalities of family members, their adaptation to family roles.   How do they enter?   Who sits next to whom?   Who away from whom?   Who speaks?   Who listens?   Who smiles?   Who frowns? At a typical session, the family arrives in a state of pent-up pain, fright, thwarted need, and anger.   The therapist gets a quick sense of the emotional climate.   He observes the quality of appeal that the members project to one another and to himself.   Are they coercive? Do they simply give up, and in a mood of resigned apathy cease to ask and expect anything?   He notes the existing confusion, mistrust, and hostile fragmentation of family bonds.

It is the therapist's responsibility to stir interaction among members; to catalyze and enhance a live and meaningful emotional interchange.   He must establish a useful atmosphere of rapport, a touching quality of contact.   As the family members come in touch with the therapist, they come into better touch with themselves.

The clinician integrates his knowledge and use of self in a special way.   He is participant-observer.   He is active, open, fluid, forthright. He moves directly into the stream of family conflict to energize and influence the interactional processes; he withdraws to objectify his experience, to survey and assess significant events, and then moves back in again.   Weighing and balancing the sick and healthy emotional forces, he supports health and counteracts sickness by shifting his function at various stages of the family process.

His responsibilities are multiple and complex.   They require a flexible, open, and undefensive use of self.   Depending on the shifting foci of conflict and anxiety, one or another member joins with and separates from particular elements of the therapist's identity.   These partial joinings and separations reflect elements of both transference fantasy and realism.   The processes of transference, countertransference, and reality must be differently conceptualized in the matrix of family interaction.   They may be interpreted as a fluid, changing balance between clinging to the old, and receptivity to the new in family experience.   The potentials of effective reality testing in this special setting are much enhanced.

In the over-all picture, the therapist feels his way toward the idiosyncratic language of the family—how the members talk, what they choose to talk about, most importantly what they tacitly avoid.   He makes rapid note of what is felt and communicated below the level of words in body stance, facial expressions, inarticulate gestures, and postural avoidances.   He evaluates the outer face of the family, its protective mask.   He perceives and assesses the deeper currents of emotion that parents fear and inhibit; the fright, the suspicion, the despair, the urge for vengeance.   He identifies these sources of anxiety which freeze the reaching out of the members, the asking for closeness and understanding, one with the other, and with the therapist.   He defines for himself the level of coping struggle that characterizes the particular family.   He assays the interplay between preferred defense operations of the family group and individual defenses against anxiety.

In a continual process of communion with self, he brings to his awareness the emotions stirred in him by the deep streams of feeling moving among the family members and toward himself.   He uses his disciplined insights into his personal emotions as a diagnostic yard-stick for what is being experienced by the family.   In so doing, he develops a series of clinical hunches which he progressively tests as he builds his diagnostic image of the family group.   This embraces the balance of family functioning, the patterns of complementarity, conflict, and coping, the interplay of the family and individual defense and, finally, the struggle with conflicting representations of family identity, values, and patterns of action.   In a selective manner, se-quence by sequence, the therapist penetrates the family façade, the patterns of complicity, denials, and disguise of deeper currents of feelings of conflict and fear.

Acting as catalyst, the therapist provokes increasingly candid dis-closures of dormant interpersonal conflicts; he lifts intrapersonal con-flict to the level of interpersonal process.   In due course, he can trace significant connections between family disorder and the intrapsychic anxiety of individual members.   Often one part of the family armors itself, prejudicially attacks and sacrifices another part.   When needed, the therapist intervenes to neutralize these sick patterns of attack.   By counteracting scapegoating as a specific defense against anxiety, the therapist retransposes the underlying conflict to its place of origin in the family group; that is, the conflict may be moved back to its primary source.   In this phase of therapy, it has become possible to identify a cluster of interrelated roles, that of persecutor, victim, peacemaker, or healer of family conflict.

In intervening on the interplay between family group defense and individual defenses, the therapist makes free use of the device of con-frontation.   By a variety of interventions, he penetrates and under-mines the pathogenic patterns of coping and defense.   He calls at-tention to the inefficiency, inappropriateness, and harmfulness of certain sickness-inducing defenses, and fosters the substitution of healthier ones.   This has special relevance for the task of cutting into the vicious cycle of blame and punishment which represents nothing less than an unconscious collusion to prevent change.

To stir movement, the therapist pierces pathogenic operations by a device I call "tickling the defenses."   This is a tactic of catching the family members by surprise, exposing dramatic discrepancies between their self-justifying rationalizations and their subverbal attitudes.   He challenges empty clichés and static or pat formulae for the problems of family living.   He halts fruitless bickering over routine, superficial, or unimportant matters.

Watchful for each clue, he reaches out for more honest and mean-ingful means of communication.   In the service of this effort, he may make effective use of "body talk."   He confronts the members forthrightly with the meaning of certain nonverbal forms of communication as revealed in mood, expression, posture, gesture, and movement. To counteract the tendency to substitute empty verbalisms for genuine emotional interchange, he catalyzes in the members the urge to explore the dramatic contradictions between these verbal utterances and body expressions.

Through his calm, firm presence, he functions as a controller of interpersonal danger, steering between the extremes of intolerable closeness and the risk of eruptions of explosive rage, which might lead to panic and disorganization. He executes other functions: he offers security, emotional support, acceptance, understanding, affirmation of worth, and direct satisfaction of valid emotional needs. He catalyzes the interchange among family members toward cooperation in the quest for solutions to conflict or toward finding more appropriate compromises. Along this path, he activates a shift in the allegiances of family members toward improved complementarity of needs.

As a real parent figure, the therapist offers emotional support on a selective basis, now to one part of the family, now to another; so he may, in all honesty, and with considerable effectiveness, support a weaker member of a group against the attack of a stronger. In the long view, the genuineness of the therapist's concern, his fairness, and the manner in which he continually shifts from one part of the family to another, minimizes any destructive rivalry.

At still another level, the family therapist provides support through a kind of substitute gratification, that is, by supplying the family with elements of emotional imagery of self and others in which the family has before been lacking. In this sense, reality testing, fortified by the therapist's activity, begins at the outset. In the spontaneous give and take among the family members, each has an opportunity to experience the self and other with a lessened sense of danger. Each takes a second look at every other, and at the therapist, and readapts toward a more realistic image of family relationships.

Then there is the question of the clash of competing identities and values. This is expressed in an ongoing contest of needs, identity, and value representations between parental partners which, in turn, can be traced to the links of identity and values of each parent with his family of origin. In this clash, the offspring are forced to take sides and thus the family is split into contesting factions. In such family warfare, each faction competes with every other to push change toward what they want the family to be and do for its members. In this struggle, the family therapist serves as educator to the problems of family living. He epitomizes in his own being a range of models of family health. He shakes up pre-existing alignments and splits and opens ways to new designs of family living. He stirs the family members to find constructive solutions or compromises of conflict, to discover new ways of intimacy, sharing, and identification, to support difference as well as union. Crucial to this, he energizes and enriches the processes of critical reassessment of family identity, goals, and values, especially those that pertain to the maintenance of indispensable family functions.

By the merging of these many functions, as activator or common challenger, common supporter, interpreter, reintegrator, the therapist shakes up pre-existing pathogenic relationship alignments and equilibria, and opens the way to discovery of healthier family bonds.

Summary

The therapist's functions may be itemized as follows:

1   The therapist establishes a useful rapport, empathy, and communication among the family members and between them and himself.

2   He uses this rapport to catalyze the expression of major conflicts and ways of coping. He clarifies conflict by dissolving barriers, defensive disguises, confusions, and misunderstandings. By stages, he attempts to bring to the members a clearer and more accurate understanding as to what is really wrong.

3   He counteracts inappropriate denials, displacements and rationalizations of conflict.

4   He transforms dormant, concealed interpersonal conflicts into open, interactional expression.

5   He lifts intrapersonal conflict to the level of interpersonal exchange.

6   He neutralizes processes of prejudicial scapegoating that fortify one part of the family while victimizing another part.

7   He fulfills, in part, the role of a real parent figure, a controller of danger, a source of emotional support, and a supplier of elements which the family needs but lacks. His emotional nurturing of the family is a kind of substitutive therapy.

8   He penetrates and undermines resistances, and reduces the intensity of shared conflict, guilt, and fear, using both confrontation and interpretation, but relying mainly on the former.

9   He serves as a personal instrument of reality testing for the family.

10   He serves as the educator and personifier of useful models of family health.

The future of family psychotherapy is hinted at in its unique potentials and revolutionary implications. It has a fascination uniquely its own. The therapist hits home, both literally and figuratively. Family therapy may not only unfold as a method in its own right, but may also serve to correct and improve some of the older methods. That this is so is borne out by the conviction of many psychotherapists who have had training in family therapy. "Once a therapist engages in family therapy, he ain't never the same again." Not only does he discover the value of family therapy; he also becomes a more effective psychoanalytic therapist.

Family therapy is a therapy in *vivo* not in *vitro*. It is a natural, not an artificial level of entry into human distress. It encompasses the interdependent, interpenetrating relations of individual and group. It does not pit individual against family or family against individual. It does not heal one part of the family at the expense of another; it supports both. It offers a new and different image of mental illness. It is a profoundly honest way of intervening in human problems. It highlights the importance of contagion of anxiety in family interchange. It provides a natural setting for the continual clash between dream and reality; it offers an effective channel for the living-out of the pain and disillusionment deriving from this clash. It deals with disparities of depth and surface; inner and outer being; the interplay of intra- and interpersonal conflict, and the relations, mutually supporting or oppositional, between family group defense and individual defense. It confronts the interplay of multiple disturbances among family members. It offers an effective means for penetrating the vicious cycle of blame and punishment for things past. It provides an emotional matrix for enhancing mutual understanding, respect, and esteem.

Contrary to Freud's view of therapy, it does not merely take something away, a pathogenic feeling or idea, it adds something new and better to take the place of sick experience. It illuminates the homeodynamic principle of adaptation to change; the matrix for learning and growth in the family. It fosters healthy rather than pathologic healing of family disorders. It does not merely patch-up a damaged individual; it makes room for improved relationship patterns, a new way of life. It relates a valid ethic to the goals of family living.

For the interested therapist, family psychotherapy, however unstandardized it is in its presently evolving form, nevertheless, is full of challenge; full of surprises, and highly rewarding. A science of family behavior, a system of family diagnosis and psychotherapy, hold the promise of becoming a useful and significant addition to our armamentarium of mental health practices.

SIX

SECTION SIX   CURRENT ISSUES

Throughout this volume problems relating to methodology, theory, and application have been presented and discussed. For the most part these issues have meaning and significance chiefly for persons studying psychology. However, many of the problems associated with the study of adjustment have far-reaching import and should attract the interest and concern of a wider audience. The final section of this book is devoted to issues which are of significance to the general community, layman as well as scientist, and raises a number of questions about the relationships between psychological knowledge and various philosophical and practical questions.

The first paper deals with a major problem which confronts scientists in their study of human behavior. As we said in the first section of this book, psychologists ideally would like to apply experimental methods to the investigation of adjustment problems because of the control and precision that can be introduced in experimental studies. However, the manipulation of conditions required by experimental design is extremely difficult both because of the complexity of human behavior and the ethical considerations involved in imposing undesirable conditions on subjects. In recent years scientists interested in how people react to different kinds of situations have used considerable ingenuity in developing experimental techniques which simulate the real-life conditions they wish to study. Under this approach, it often is necessary that subjects not be informed of the true purpose of the experiment since this knowledge may make the experimental conditions artificial and distort the subjects' reactions. The practice of using human subjects in research without informing them of the purpose of the study or falsifying the purpose to them has been criticized as deceptive and unethical. Kelman discusses this issue and offers several suggestions to scientists for working out a balance between their need to introduce disguised experimental conditions in order to study important questions about human behavior and the need for considerate treatment of subjects who participate in psychological research.

The issue of deception in psychological research is important not only to scientists, but also to the general public, and especially to persons who are called upon or volunteer to take part in such research. Therefore, it seems important that we consider not only what the scientist might do to lessen the problems associated with deception, but what subjects might do. As Kelman points out, if the subject's anticipation of deception results in his acting suspiciously and unnaturally, the conditions which the experimenter hoped to create may have been violated and the experiment will be of questionable value. Assuming that the subjects are motivated to be of assistance to the experimenter, they should be as interested in guarding against this as the experimenter. We suggest that if a subject feels highly anxious or suspicious about an experiment and fears that he may act unnaturally, he should let this be known to the experimenter and decide with him whether his continued participation is desirable. His dropping out of the experiment may be beneficial both to him and to the experimenter. In addition, a subject who suspects deception in an experiment should endeavor to trust the experimenter and reserve acting on his suspicions until after the project is completed, at which time he might question the experimenter further about the purpose of the project. Since the cooperation of human subjects is needed in research if we are to learn more about personality and adjustment problems, it clearly would impede scientific progress if subjects were to approach research with the belief, which Kelman describes, that "psychologists always lie" and were to try to outwit the experimenter by acting deviously. In suggesting that subjects who volunteer for psychological research have a responsibility to act as naturally as possible and to trust the experimenter, we do not minimize the obligation of the experimenter to make every effort to avoid deception and to be totally aware of ethical considerations in submitting his subjects to experimental conditions.

While the paper by Kelman refers to a problem psychologists encounter in obtaining scientific information, the next four papers pertain to problems in the application of scientific knowledge. Gaylin discusses difficulties in the application of information about mental health to criminal law. On the one hand, psychiatry and other professions dealing with mental-health problems are called upon to assist the courts in making decisions about criminal activities and accused offenders. On the other hand, there appear to be basic differences in the purposes and ideas concerning human behavior taken by law officials and persons in the mental-health field. Gaylin describes a number of these differences, including the point that the courts assume that man's actions are self-determined and involve free will, while the student of mental health adopts a deterministic explanation of human behavior. Similarly, the psychiatrist or psychologist is interested in understanding the circumstances which compelled the individual to behave as he did rather than in assessing personal responsibility for the act.   Undoubtedly most persons would agree that it is desirable for the courts to utilize the knowledge of human behavior provided by social scientists.   Gaylin, however, argues that the contribution of the social scientist to criminal law should concern methods of punishment rather than attempts to define criminal behavior.   He advocates divorcing psychological concepts concerning purposes and motivation from legal definitions of crime and defining crime solely in terms of the act committed.   This suggestion would lead to a number of changes in legal procedures and decisions such as elimination of a defense plea on grounds of insanity.   Gaylin points out that the social scientist can make a significant contribution to answering questions about the effectiveness and appropriateness of punishment and rehabilitation methods and argues that the scientist's influence should be greater than it is at present in establishing penal practices.

Another problem in the application of scientific knowledge about mental health has become increasingly apparent with the current emphasis on poverty.   That is, mental-health facilities and programs in this country appear to be culture-bound, with primary interest being given to the middle class.   It has often been noted that the majority of both the members and the patients of the mental-health professions represent middle-class backgrounds, but only in recent years has there been a growing realization that the concepts, theories, and methods of treating adjustment problems have been based on the values and life styles of the middle class.   Schneiderman summarizes some of the studies which indicate that the availability and effectiveness of professional services for adjustment and emotional problems are seriously limited for impoverished and disadvantaged persons. The concentration of efforts at the present time to help the poor is stimulating new ideas and procedures for providing professional services to this group.

The article by Auerback discusses a different kind of problem in applying knowledge about mental health—the direct hostility and resistance on the part of many persons to mental-health activities and programs.   In describing a number of anti-mental-health groups and the techniques used for discrediting mental-health activities, Auerback notes that the practices of these groups have interfered seriously with the advancement of mental-health programs in some communities. He suggests that workers in this field must be alert to the sensationalistic appeals which these groups make to the public and must attempt to counter their attacks by informing the public and public officials of the contributions which the mental-health professions are making and can make to society.

The final paper on current issues by Lawrence Kubie deals with the prevention of emotional and adjustment disturbances and describes many of the problems and difficulties associated with preventive efforts. He notes that before large-scale preventive work can be undertaken, the following are needed: a better understanding of childhood development and the factors which provoke psychological disturbances; an increase in the number of professional workers devoted to helping persons who display early stages of maladjustment; the development of new educational techniques; and the reexamination of many cultural institutions which appear to play a part in promoting adjustment and emotional difficulties. Kubie points out that a variety of characteristics of our culture, including practices associated with education, religion, industry, and government, appear to exploit and intensify psychopathology. His enumeration of the myriad ways in which society encourages and supports emotional problems makes us aware of the complexity of prophylactic efforts. In effect Kubie reminds us that the prevention of emotional disturbances requires an ambitious and courageous attack on many social processes and institutions, and the scope of the task invites the question which he raises, Is prevention possible?

Herbert C. Kelman

DECEPTION IN SOCIAL RESEARCH *

In order to advance the understanding of human behavior, psychologists regularly use human beings as subjects in a wide variety of experiments. In many of these experiments, the subject is kept in the dark or misinformed about the true purpose of the experiment. Sometimes the deception exposes him to embarrassing, disturbing, or potentially harmful experiences that he had not bargained for.

There is generally a good reason for the use of deception. Many of the phenomena that the psychologist wishes to study would be altered if the subject knew the purpose of the experiment—if he knew, for example, what psychological processes the experimenter is trying to

* From Herbert C. Kelman, "Deception in Social Research," *Trans-Action,* 1966, July-August, 20–24. Reprinted by permission of the author and the Managing Editor, *Trans-Action,* a publication of the Community Leadership Project, Washington University, St. Louis, Mo.

activate and what reactions he is hoping to observe.   And yet the use of deception, even when it is done for a scientifically valid reason, poses ethical questions.

These questions are fairly obvious when the deception has potentially harmful consequences for the subject; they are more subtle, but nonetheless important, even in experiments where there is little danger of harmful effects.   The issue is: How can we strike a proper balance between the interests of science and the considerate treatment of people who make themselves available as the raw material of research?

The problem of deception has taken on increasingly serious proportions in recent years as its use has become almost a standard feature in psychological experiments.   Deception has been turned into a game, often played with great skill and virtuosity.   A considerable amount of creativity and ingenuity by social psychologists is given to the development of increasingly elaborate deception situations.

For example, the potentially harmful effects of deception are dramatized in some recent studies of obedience.   One volunteer was "smiling and confident" when he entered the laboratory.   "Within 20 minutes," the experimenter reported, "he was reduced to a twitching, stuttering wreck, who was rapidly approaching a point of nervous collapse."   What caused him to become a "wreck" was an experiment in which subjects were led to believe that they were participating in a learning study.   They were instructed to administer increasingly severe shocks to another person, who after a while began to protest vehemently.   In fact, of course, the "victim" was an accomplice of the experimenter and did not receive any real shocks.   But in some cases, the experimenter instructed the subject to continue to "shock" the "victim" up to the maximum level, which the subject believed to be extremely painful when the victim writhed in pain and pounded his head against the wall.

Not surprisingly, both obedient and defiant (those who refused to administer shocks) subjects exhibited a great deal of stress.   And there is surely good reason to believe that at least some of the obedient subjects came away from this experience with lowered self-esteem, realizing that they yielded to authority to the point of inflicting extreme pain on a fellow human being.   The fact that, in the experimenter's words, they had "an opportunity to learn something of importance about themselves, and more generally, about the conditions of human action" is beside the point.

If this were a lesson *from life,* it would constitute an instructive confrontation and provide a valuable insight.   But do researchers, for purposes of experimentation, have the right to provide such potentially disturbing insights to subjects who do not know that this is what they volunteered for?

And yet, this same research illustrates the complexity of the issues raised by the use of deception. These studies of obedience have produced significant and challenging findings which have posed some basic questions about human behavior and social life. Without deception, this line of investigation could probably not have been pursued.

A generation of deceivers

It is easy to view the situation with alarm, but it is much more difficult to formulate an unambiguous position on this problem. As a working experimental social psychologist, I know that there are good reasons for using deception in many experiments. There are many significant problems, like the study of obedience, that probably cannot be investigated without the use of deception—at least, given the present level of development of our experimental techniques. Thus, researchers are always confronted with a conflict of values. If they regard the acquisition of scientific knowledge about human behavior as a positive value, and if an experiment using deception constitutes a significant contribution to such knowledge which could not be achieved by other means, then it is difficult to rule out the experiment unequivocally. The question is not simply whether or not to use deception, but whether the amount and type of deception are justified by the significance of the study and the unavailability of alternative procedures.

What concerns me most, then, is not so much that deception is used, but that it is used without question. I sometimes feel that a whole generation of psychologists now in training will not know there is any other way of doing experiments. Too often deception is used, not as a last resort, but as a matter of course. The attitude seems to be: If you can deceive, why tell the truth?

What are some of the major problems posed by the use of this dangerously doubled-edged tool? There are three areas to consider:

the ethical implications;
the real effectiveness of deception;
the implications for the future of psycho-social research in our society.

Ethical implications.   Ethical problems of a rather obvious nature arise in those experiments in which deception has potentially harmful consequences for the subject. For example, a brilliant experiment was recently designed to observe the effects of threat on group solidarity and the need for strong leadership. In this study (one of the very rare examples of an experiment conducted in a natural setting) independent food merchants in a number of Dutch towns were brought together for group meetings and informed that a large organization would soon open a chain of supermarkets in the Netherlands. In a "high threat" condition, the subjects were told that their towns would probably be selected as sites for such markets, which would cause a considerable drop in their business. On the advice of the executives of the shopkeepers' organizations who had helped to arrange the group meetings, the investigators never revealed, even after the experiment was over, that the supermarket threat was a fiction.

I have been worried about those Dutch merchants ever since I first heard about this study. Did some of them go out of business in anticipation of the heavy competition? Do some of them have an anxiety reaction every time they see a bulldozer? Chances are that they soon forgot about this threat (unless, of course, supermarkets actually did move into town) and that it became just one of the many little moments of anxiety that occur in every shopkeeper's life. But do investigators have the right to add to life's little anxieties and to risk the possibility of more extensive anxiety purely for the purposes of such experiments?

Two other recent studies provide further example of potentially harmful effects arising from the use of deception. In one set of studies, male college students were led to believe that they had been homosexually aroused by photographs of men. In the other study, subjects of both sexes were given disturbing information about their levels of masculinity or femininity, presumably based on an elaborate series of psychological tests they had taken. In all of these studies, the deception was explained to the subjects at the end of the experiment. One wonders, however, whether this explanation removes the possibility of harmful effects. For many persons in this age group, sexual identity is a live and sensitive issue, and the self-doubts generated by this laboratory experience could linger.

What about the less obvious cases, in which there is little danger of harmful effects? Serious ethical issues are also raised by such deception per se, and the kind of use of human beings that it implies. In other inter-human relationships, most psychologists would never think of doing the things that they do to their subjects—exposing them to lies and tricks, deliberately misleading them, and making promises or giving assurances that they intend to disregard. They would view such behavior as a violation of the respect to which all fellow humans are entitled. Yet they seem to forget that the experimenter-subject relationship—whatever else it is—is a *real* inter-human relationship, in which the experimenter has a responsibility towards the subject as another human being whose dignity he must respect. The difference between the experimenter's behavior in everyday life and his behavior in the laboratory is so marked that one wonders why there has been so little concern with this problem.

The broader ethical problem of the very use of deception becomes even more important when we view it in the present-day historical context. We are living in an age of mass societies, in which the transformation of man into an object, to be manipulated at will, occurs on a mass scale, in a systematic way, and under the aegis of specialized institutions deliberately assigned to this task. In institutionalizing the use of deception in psychological experiments we are contributing to a historical trend that threatens the values most of us cherish.

Methodological implications. I have increasing doubts about the effectiveness of deception as a method for social research.

A basic assumption in the use of deception is that a subject's awareness of what the experimenter is really trying to find out would affect the subject's behavior in such a way that the experimenter could not draw valid conclusions from it. For example, if the experimenter is interested in studying the effects of failure on conformity, he must create a situation in which subjects actually feel that they have failed, and in which they can be kept unaware of his interest in observing conformity. In short, it is important to keep the subjects naive about the purposes of the experiment so that they can respond spontaneously.

How long, however, will it be possible to find naive subjects? Among college students it is already very difficult. They may not know the exact purposes of the particular experiment in which they are participating, but many of them know that it is *not* what the experimenter says it is. As one subject pithily put it, "Psychologists always lie!"

There are, of course, other sources of human subjects that have not been tapped, but even here it is only a matter of time until word about psychological experiments gets around and sophistication increases. Whether or not a subject knows the true purpose of the experiment, if he does not believe what the experimenter tells him, then he is likely to make an effort to figure out the purpose of the experiment and to act accordingly. This may lead him to do what he thinks the experimenter wants him to do. Conversely, if he resents the experimenter's attempt to deceive him, he may try to throw a monkey wrench into the works. Whichever course the subject uses, however, he is operating in terms of his own conception of the nature of the situation, rather than in terms of the conception that the experimenter is trying to induce. In short, the experimenter can no longer assume that the conditions that he is trying to create are the ones that actually define the situation for the subject. Thus, the use of deception, while it is designed to give the experimenter control over the subject's perceptions and motivations, may actually produce an unspecified mixture of intended and unintended stimuli that make it difficult to know just what the subject is responding to. Therefore, is there any future in the use of deception?

Implications for the future.   My third main concern about the use of deception is that, from a long-range point of view, there is obviously something self-defeating about it.   As experiments of this kind continue, potential subjects become more and more sophisticated, and scientists become less and less able to meet the conditions that their experimental procedures require.   Moreover, potential subjects become increasingly distrustful, and future   relations between subjects and experimenters upon which successful research depends are likely to be undermined.   Thus, we are confronted with the anomalous circumstance that, the more this research is carried on, the more difficult and questionable it becomes.

The use of deception also involves a contradiction between experimental procedures and the long-range aims of scientists and teachers. In order to be able to carry out experiments, they are concerned with maintaining the naiveté of the population from which they draw subjects.   This perfectly understandable desire to keep procedures secret goes counter to the traditional desire of the scientist and teacher to inform and enlighten the public.   For the long run, it even suggests the possible emergence of a special class, in possession of secret knowledge—a possibility that is clearly antagonistic to the principle of open communication to which scientists and intellectuals are so fervently committed.

Enrichment through experiment

If my concerns about the use of deception are justified—and I think that they are—what are some of the ways they can be dealt with?   I would like to suggest two basic remedies:

exploring ways of counteracting and minimizing the negative effects of deception;
giving careful attention to the devolopment of new experimental techniques that can dispense with the use of deception altogether.

In those experiments in which deception could have harmful effects, there is an obvious requirement to build protections into every phase of the process.   Subjects must be selected in a way that will exclude individuals who are especially vulnerable; the potentially harmful manipulation (such as the induction of stress) must be kept at a moderate level of intensity; the experimenter must be sensitive to danger signals in the reactions of his subjects and be prepared to deal with crises when they arise; and, at the conclusion of the session, the experimenter must take time, not only to reassure the subject, but also to help him work through his feelings about the experience to whatever degree may be required.

In general, a good principle to follow is that a subject ought not to leave the laboratory with greater anxiety or lower self-esteem than he came with. I would go beyond it to argue that the subject should in some positive way be enriched by the experience—he should come away from it with the feeling that he has learned something, understood something, or grown in some way. And this adds special importance to the kind of feedback—about what was really being done —that is given to the subject at the end of the experimental session.

This post-experimental feedback is also the primary way of counteracting negative effects in those experiments in which the issue is deception as such, rather than possible threats to the subject's well-being. If the subject is deceived, then he must be given a full and detailed explanation of what has been done and of the reasons for doing it. It is not enough to give the subject perfunctory feedback. These explanations should be meaningful and instructive for the subject and helpful in rebuilding his relationship with the experimenter. I feel very strongly that, to accomplish these purposes, the experimenter must keep the feedback itself inviolate and under no circumstance give the subject false feedback, or pretend to be giving him feedback while in fact introducing another experimental manipulation.

The case for cooperation

My second suggestion is that scientists invest some of the creativity and ingenuity now being devoted to the construction of elaborate deceptions to the search for alternative experimental techniques that do not rely on the use of deception. They would be based on the principle of eliciting the subject's positive motivations to contribute to the experimental enterprise. They would draw on the subject's active participation and involvement in the proceedings and encourage him to cooperate in making the experiment a success by conscientiously taking the roles and carrying out the tasks that the experimenter assigns to him. In short, the kind of techniques I have in mind would be designed to involve the subject as an active participant in a joint effort with the experimenter.

Perhaps the most promising sources of alternative experimental approaches are procedures using some sort of role-playing—that is, procedures in which the experimenter asks the subject to act as though he were in a certain situation rather than actually creating that situation experimentally as a "real" one. I have been impressed, for example, with the role-playing that I have observed in the Inter-Nation Simulation, a laboratory procedure in which the subjects take the roles of decision-makers of various nations. This situation seems to create a high level of emotional involvement and to elicit motivations that have a real-life quality to them. (See "The Study of Man," 1966, March/April *Trans-action*.)

In general, the results of role-playing experiments have been very encouraging. Despite the fact that they know it is all make-believe, subjects usually react realistically to the experimental stimuli, and these reactions follow an orderly pattern.

There are other types of procedure, in addition to role-playing, that are worth exploring. For example, it may be possible to conduct more experiments in a natural nonlaboratory setting in which, with the full cooperation of the subjects, specific experimental variations are introduced. The advantages of dealing with motivations at a real-life level of intensity might well outweigh the disadvantages of subjects' knowing the general purpose of the experiment. A much simpler alternative, also worth exploring, would be for experimenters to inform the subjects at the beginning of a laboratory experiment that they will not receive full information about what is going on, but ask them to suspend judgment until the experiment is over.

Whatever alternative approaches are tried, there is no doubt that they will have their own problems and complexities. Procedures effective for some purposes may be quite ineffective for others, and it may well turn out that for certain kinds of problems there is no adequate substitute for the use of deception. But there *are* alternative procedures that, for many purposes, may be as effective or even more effective than procedures built on deception.

These approaches often involve a radically changed set of assumptions about the role of the subject in the experiment: *the subject's motivation to cooperate is utilized rather than by-passed.* These new procedures may even call for increasing the sophistication of potential subjects, rather than maintaining their naiveté.

Willard M. Gaylin   **PSYCHIATRY AND THE LAW: PARTNERS IN CRIME ***

When the general population braced itself for the Dallas Dionysia that was referred to by the innocent as the "Trial of Jack Ruby," at least one segment of the population that had long since lost its innocence knew that it, too, would be on trial—I mean American psychiatry.

* From Willard M. Gaylin, "Psychiatry and the Law: Partners in Crime," *Columbia Univer. Forum*, 1965, *8*, 23–27. Reprinted by permission of the author and the Editor, *Columbia University Forum*.

Criminal activity is the *bête noire* of the modern psychiatrist. It is the kind of human behavior about which he is most ignorant, and perversely, about which he is called upon to give the most certain opinions—in testimony under oath. The conditions that bind the relationship of psychiatry and the law today are such that confusion and contradiction are guaranteed.

For years the M'Naghten rules have been the basis throughout most of the United States for establishing a defense on the ground of insanity. As defined by the English judiciary in 1843, the rules required proof "that at the time of the committing of the act, the party accused was laboring under such a defect of reason, from disease of mind, as not to know the nature and quality of the act he was doing, or if he did know it, that he did not know he was doing what was wrong."

In the early days of modern psychiatry this was an adequate, although stringent, application of medical knowledge to the law, for "disease of the mind" was traditionally divided into psychosis and neurosis, with the psychoses being roughly equivalent to the common use of the term "insane." Definitions in criminal law, however, require precision, not rough equivalence, and the M'Naghten rules achieved precision at the cost of defining insanity at its extreme. But as medical understanding of mental processes increased, the terms "insanity" and "psychosis" became progressively less congruent. The borderline between psychosis and neurosis became more difficult to define. Prepsychotic conditions were recognized. Motivation, perception, and their influences on behavior were seen as more subtle and complex, and the term insanity was dropped from the medical vernacular. Insanity is now a legal term exclusively; it has no medical meaning. The typical psychiatrist today, when asked if in his opinion a defendant is legally insane, experiences the same frustration he might feel if asked whether a specific action was a function of black bile or phlegm.

But the "test of right or wrong" is not only archaic. Medically speaking, it is unjust. More suitable as a gauge of feeble-mindedness than of insanity, it arbitrarily endows one form of mental impairment with an immunity denied to other forms equally debilitating, controlling, and restricting. Like other unrealistically rigid laws, the M'Naghten rules have constantly invited evasion and encouraged sophistry. ("Temporary insanity" is a legal defense in only a few states, but what in the world is it? More disturbing, what irrational act could not be so considered?)

As the deficiencies of the M'Naghten rules became more apparent, pressure mounted—partly as a result of the tradition of humanizing the treatment of the criminal, and partly as a result of scientific progress—to redefine the insanity defense in a way more in line with

current psychiatric concepts.   Therefore, when in 1954 Judge David
Bazelon handed down his opinion for the United States Court of Appeals in the now famous Durham case, it was not surprising that most
progressive social thinkers considered it a major advance.   Aware of
the deficiencies of the prevailing tests for insanity (in Washington,
D. C., the jurisdiction of the Durham case, the "irresistible impulse"
test had been added in 1929), Judge Bazelon proposed a new, far
broader, test: that "an accused is not criminally responsible if his
unlawful act was the product of mental disease or mental defect."

Whereas the M'Naghten rules stingily denied clemency to many of
the "psychologically innocent," it at least defined the *type* of defect
involved (a defect of "reason") and the severity of the defect (so "as
not to know the nature and quality of the act").   To absolve the accused from criminal responsibility, the Durham rule would merely
require that the unlawful act be "the product of mental disease."
This broadens the insanity test with a vengeance, and if nothing else,
has the potential to introduce more psychiatric concepts into criminal law than we may care for.   I can best illustrate what I mean by
noting briefly three categories of mental illness in the current psychiatric lexicon.

Let us begin with the few conditions almost universally accepted
by psychiatrists as mental disease; in addition to the classical phobias
and obsessions, this category would now certainly include alcoholism,
drug addiction, and sexual deviation.   Most thoughtful people, lawyers and psychiatrists included, now hold that the excessive drinking
of alcohol, the taking of heroin, the homosexual act are *per se*, symptoms of disease to be treated by a physician rather than crimes to be
punished by law.   Nevertheless the latter two are still crimes in
more than half the states.   The liberalizing influence of the Durham
rule could indeed be useful to help correct this situation, but the logic
implicit in it extends a good deal further.   Society could not afford
to exempt from criminal responsibility *all* actions that could be .de-
scribed psychiatrically as "the product" of these conditions.   Would
we grant immunity to the addict who steals to "feed his habit," while
we hold liable the pauper who steals to feed his hunger?

A much more difficult group consists of the psychosomatic disorders—such as mucous colitis, tension headache, and neuroderma-
titis.   No one is going to be jailed for scratching—his own skin at
least—but who is to say what an itch can drive a man to do.   Theoretically, at least, any action of a person at the end of patience over,
say, migraine headache, might be exempt from liability, if innocence
depended only on establishing a causal relationship between a criminal act and a mental disorder.   As *reductio ad absurdum,* consider
the case of an accused criminal whose lawyer, citing the Durham ruling, enters a plea of not guilty because the crime was "the product

of" acute heartburn (listed as an example of mental disorder 006-580 *Psychophysiological gastrointestinal reaction,* in the American Psychiatric Association's Diagnostic Manual). A novel defense, indeed; yet it would seem to satisfy the logic of the Durham ruling.

Finally, there is a third category that defies all definition, those mental illnesses called character or personality disorders. In modern psychiatry these diseases are distinguished from classical neurosis, in which certain kinds of behavior patterns, often isolated, represent anxiety and the defenses against it. With the character disorder, since it is the very nature of the developed personality that is viewed as disturbed, *all* behavior would be considered by the psychiatrist to be "the product of" mental illness. Indeed, the concept of the character disorder leads to sheer legal irrationality, for it is the fact that a person indulges in antisocial behavior that *defines* him as being sick.

This third category of mental illness at least has been recognized for the legal anomaly it is in the Model Penal Code of the American Law Institute. The section dealing with criminal responsibility states: "The terms 'mental illness or defect' do not include an abnormality manifested only by repeated criminal or otherwise antisocial behavior." The Model Penal Code, which was approved in 1962 by the Institute, is just what its title suggests, a model which it is hoped will serve as a guide for states wishing to reform their criminal law; as such it represents a consensus of some of the best legal minds in the country. The Code's suggested article for the insanity test is as follows: "A person is not responsible for criminal conduct if at the time of such conduct as a result of mental disease or defect he lacks substantial capacity either to appreciate the criminality (wrongfulness) of his conduct or to conform his conduct to the requirements of the law."

With the exception noted above, this is essentially a combination of the M'Naghten rules and the Durham ruling, and although certainly more humane than the former, logically no improvement over the latter from the psychiatrist's point of view. Indeed, Judge Bazelon himself put the problem well in his learned opinion in the Durham case: "In attempting to define insanity in terms of any particular symptom, the courts have assumed an impossible task." As a psychiatrist I can say that defining insanity itself is equally impossible. No, the problem is not, I think, one of finding a definable test for mental illness, but of finding *any* test.

For strangely, psychiatrists as a group have never been able to define mental illness. Professional opinions range from the assumption that all human beings suffer from mental illness in varying degrees to the opposite extreme, that there is no such thing, that "mental illness is a myth." I do not mean that there are no objective criteria in the field of psychiatry. The case is quite the reverse. Present a patient to a group of psychiatrists and they will agree to an amazing extent about the nature of the illness, severity of impairment, areas of malfunctioning, prognosis, and indicated therapy. Indeed, a common reaction of the doctor-in-training is surprise that his first patient talks and acts as though he had read the textbook.

But when the psychiatrist attempts to abstract from clinical data general concepts of mental functioning—concepts of responsibility or of the essence of mental health that might be useful to the law—he is on his least-sure footing. Even in those areas of mental malfunctioning about which there is the most agreement, psychiatry will not serve the law well. For fundamental to the psychiatric view of man are principles antagonistic to the social view of man upon which criminal law is founded.

Before psychoanalysis, psychiatry was a descriptive science without a psychology—without any explanation of mental mechanisms in health or disease. Modern psychiatry now uses general psychological principles borrowed from psychoanalysis. Although many psychiatrists reject psychoanalysis as a treatment technique and dismiss some of its developmental concepts, two axioms of psychoanalytic theory are so widely accepted that they are now represented in almost every psychiatric frame of reference. The first axiom: every individual act of behavior is the resultant of a multitude of emotional forces and counterforces; this is the "psychodynamic" principle. The second: these forces and counterforces are shaped by past experience; this is the principle of psychic causality.

Taken together, these two principles dictate a way of viewing any act of behavior. Suppose three men are threatened by a man with a gun. One flees; one stands paralyzed with fear; one attacks. The stimulus for all three is the same. But the stimulus is only one factor in determining the resultant behavior. Acting on the complex machinery of the human being, it triggers associations, perceptions, and response patterns already "programmed in" by previous experience. This view of behavior rejects the possibility of an isolated or chance act, and whether we like it or not, places psychiatry in the camp of determinism. All acts—healthy, sick, or not-sure-which—share one property: *they are predetermined.*

Many psychiatrists in fact do not like it, and are personally unhappy with determinism; they "believe in" free will. But professionally—and it is in his capacity as a professional expert that the psychiatrist testifies before the law—we have not been able to incorporate "chance" as a relevant phenomenon into the theory of psychiatry. Deterministic it remains and antithetical to the social concept underlying criminal law, which must assume free will, or choice in action. It really is not important which concept is "true"—or if either is true.

For certain purposes either assumption may be useful, or necessary; but to assume both at the same time is logically impossible. Whenever a psychiatrist testifies in an insanity defense, he is doing so not under the M'Naghten or Durham rules, but under the rule of the impossible.

This logical impasse has a further unfortunate consequence for the relationship of psychiatry and the law. The social view of behavior is in essence moralistic: an action is approved or disapproved, right or wrong, acceptable or nonacceptable. A person is guilty or innocent as more or less clearly defined in advance by law. But psychiatrically speaking nothing is wrong—only sick. If an act is not a choice, but merely the inevitable product of series of past experiences, a man can be no more guilty of a crime than he is guilty of an abscess.

I do not mean that psychiatrists are amoral or that they preach amorality. On the contrary, it is the psychiatrist's job to help a person adjust to his environment—and our social environment operates under ethical and moral systems. (The degree to which values and judgments enter treatment is an entirely different *brouhaha* now raging in psychiatry.) What I do mean is that guilt and innocence, as used in criminal law, are not functional concepts in psychiatry. To the typical psychiatrist, guilt is an emotion—and innocence an age.

The remarkable Dr. Karl Menninger was reported to have said, on being invited to examine Mr. Jack Ruby, that he would be delighted to do so after the verdict was in. The implications of this statement are far-reaching. It says that the psychiatrist does not belong in the court of law.

As long as there has been law there has been, however primitive, a concept of justice. And long before psychiatry existed, our ideas of justice dictated that behavior be evaluated in terms of the intention giving rise to it. "Thou shalt not kill" became "Thou shalt not kill" *except;* except in defense of life, ideals, country, home, property, bomb shelter; except in propagation of the faith, a political system, an economic principle, a prejudice. (Indeed, so strong is the humanistic tradition that even God's Commandment can change: in the new Jewish translation of The Holy Scriptures (Exodus 20:13), He legalistically cautions "Thou shalt not *murder.*")

In the beginning it must have seemed easy to enhance the effectiveness of justice by introducing into the law considerations of intention and personal responsibility. A century ago the jurist and social scientist were united in their ignorance of the mechanisms of human behavior. But, at the turn of the century a revolution occurred. Psychology produced its first creative genius; as Copernicus shook the heavens, Freud shook man, and nothing since has looked the same.

The explosion that transformed psychology from a nosological discipline to a dynamic, though primitive, science not only illuminated human behavior as never before, but necessarily began to shift our view of the laws governing that behavior.

The reason for introducing psychological considerations into the criminal law in the first place was to secure justice, and so, as understanding advanced, the test for insanity has been progressively exposed as grossly inequitable. The answer has seemed, to many people, to be to revise criminal law in the light of the new knowledge of human motivation. This, in fact, has been the trend to the present. Although the Durham test has been widely rejected by state courts, the Maine Legislature adopted a test of insanity based upon it in 1961. And early this spring when the New York State Commission on Revision of the Penal Law and Criminal Code recommended an insanity test much less liberal than that adopted by the American Law Institute, *The New York Times* summed up the attitude of many in doubting that "the Commission went far enough in broadening the definition of criminal insanity."

Greater understanding of the implications of Freudian psychology, however, is now beginning to reveal the futility of using psychology to leaven the law. In the psychiatrist's view, if guilt is based on free choice, then no man is guilty, for behavior is predetermined. If guilt is based on intention, then every man is guilty, for every action is intended—if not consciously, then unconsciously, and the borders between the two are amorphous. The criminal law as it now stands is using false and, perhaps worse for legal purposes, indefinable psychological concepts.

What can be done about this? The solution, I think, might be to move precisely opposite to the current trend. Instead of introducing more psychological concepts into the law, we should remove as many as possible. Indeed in many instances this is already done; most of civil law and many minor crimes are defined without reference to intent. One can be guilty of a parking violation irrespective of one's good intentions about putting an extra dime in the meter. By deleting references to purpose and intent, we might eventually come to define all crimes in terms of acts alone: as behavior, not motive. An impossible goal? Perhaps, but impossible goals often indicate rewarding directions.

Even if motivation were eliminated, the result need not be injustice, for in fact the law cannot—and should not—be separated from the new vision of man provided by the behavioral sciences. The criminal code is a two-pronged system. It is concerned not merely with codifying the rules of permissible behavior, but also with the fate of those who violate them. It defines crime and determines punishment. And if the psychiatrist is misplaced in court when attempting to aid a jury decide about the former, he is in his proper role when advising about the latter. It is probably in such a way—not by redefining criminal acts, but by reconsidering punishment—that we could best revise our concept of justice in terms of modern knowledge of behavior.

What is the purpose of punishment? If society merely wishes vengeance, any imposition of pain will serve. But if our aim is larger, then a whole group of questions should be raised which the psychiatrist can help in answering. If punishment is required, which among many is the most effective? Does punishment discourage recidivism? Does the typical criminal require discouragement? Will one man's punishment deter another man's attempt? All of these questions are susceptible to investigation. Some have already been answered—and ignored, awaiting proper education of the society. If we propose, as we often say, not punishment but rehabilitation; or if, more ambitiously, we wish to discover the cause of crime and the environmental forces that encourage or discourage it, the psychiatrist, in conjunction with the other behavioral scientists, can help.

When the social scientist applies himself to this arm of the penal problem, he is in his rightful role—dealing with the familiar concepts of perception, behavior, and learning. He could not guarantee all the answers but he would no longer have to struggle with the guaranteed failure of trying to define crimes psychologically. To the extent he can supply answers, these could form the basis for decisions about what would be done with a given lawbreaker. Punishment would no longer be written into law, but could consist of whatever measures seemed most appropriate and effective, given the conditions of transgression. A sentence could be anything from bed rest to death, if the morality of the society could tolerate either extreme.

Under such circumstances, at least, current psychiatric concepts could enter the law without first evicting logic. To let the law be absolute would not be unjust as long as the dispensation of the criminal is guided by the knowledge of behavioral science. If we could do so we might at long last let the "punishment" fit the "criminal," not the crime—and the very meaning of the word "criminal" might change.

Leonard Schneiderman   **SOCIAL CLASS, DIAGNOSIS
                               AND TREATMENT ***

There is evidence in our health and welfare enterprise that the lowest
social class—the impoverished people who live in the economic cellar
of the community—are the least adequately served; that to an alarm-
ing extent the impoverished are considered as poor service risks in
programs presumably set up to meet their needs; that the poor are
not competing successfully with their middle-class or working-class
neighbors for the attention of social workers and other professional
helpers; that money raised in the name of the poor does not often
reach them in the form of effective services.

Richard Cloward has described a "general disengagement from the
poor by private social agencies" (1). Citing the study on "Patterns
in the Use of Family Service Agencies" recently completed by the
Family Service Association of America, he points out that the income
distribution of clients served during the study period in 1960–61 was
roughly parallel to that of the general population. Only 7 per cent
of Family Service cases were receiving public financial aid. Agency
clients were better educated than the general population and much
better educated than the estimated average for the lowest class of
impoverished persons. (The average FSAA client had education
slightly in excess of high school graduation.)

Using information on income, education and occupation to classify
the clients by social class, the Family Service study reports a disproportionate number of low-class families terminated after one interview.
A client from a low-class status had only three chances in ten of
continuing service while a middle-class client had six chances in
ten to obtain a continuing service. Further, the study showed clearly
that termination of service initiated by social worker as opposed to
termination initiated by client increased sharply as social class declined (1).

Evidence for the Cloward statement concerning the general disengagement from services to the poor is not confined to private social
agencies. Indeed similar findings are reported by him from public,
tax-supported agencies where the commitment to equity in service is
not only morally but legally binding. At the Institute of Juvenile Research in Chicago, for example, persons classified at the high social
class level constituted something less than 30 per cent of all intake,
but just under 50 per cent of all continuing service cases. Persons

* From Leonard Schneiderman, "Social Class, Diagnosis and Treatment," *Amer. J.
Orthopsychiat.*, 1965, *35*, 99–105. Reprinted by permission of the author and the
Editor, *American Journal of Orthopsychiatry*.

at the lowest social class level represented something under 40 per cent of all intake, but only 25 per cent of the ongoing treatment load (1).

The significance of social class to diagnostic and treatment decisions made in psychiatric settings also is documented in the Hollingshead and Redlich study (2). These investigators found that social class position was more highly correlated with acceptance and rejection for treatment, with the choice of the specific treatment offered, and with the duration of treatment, than was the clinical diagnosis. Lowest-class patients were more likely to receive an organic therapy, such as electric or insulin shock and chemotherapy than were middle- and upper-class patients with same clinical disorder. The "talking" therapies, which may be regarded as the treatment of choice for certain disorders, were relatively less frequent among the lowest class.

Obviously, no policy exists in any social agency to deliberately discriminate against the poor. Treatment decisions are based upon careful case study and diagnosis. If we are to understand and to explain case disposition and treatment decisions made, we must look at diagnosis and the diagnostic criteria employed. How do the chronically impoverished appear in this diagnostic process? What behaviors, characteristic of the impoverished, have been defined in social science research?

1 The lower lower class are thought to have little interest in education and to believe that money is to be spent and not saved (3).

2 The lower lower class have a bad reputation among those who are socially above them. This evaluation includes beliefs that they are lazy, shiftless and won't work; that they are incompetent and unwilling or unable to save their money for a rainy day and, therefore, are often dependent on private or public agencies for relief. They are sometimes said "to live like animals" because it is believed that their sexual mores are not exacting and that premarital intercourse, post-marital infidelity, and high rates of illegitimacy (sometimes publicly mixed with incest) characterize their personal and family lives (4).

3 The lower lower class is looked down upon by the high classes who believe that they have no respect for the law or for themselves; that they enjoy their shacks and huts and love their dirty, smoky dives and taverns; that whole families, including children, in-laws, mistresses and all live in one shack; that this is the crime class that produces the delinquency and sexual promiscuity that fills the papers; that their interests lie in sex and its perversion; that the girls are always pregnant; that incestual relations occur frequently; that they are not inspired by education and that only a few are able to make any attainment along this line; that this group lives for a Saturday of drinking and fighting; that they are of low character and have a criminal record (5).

4 Lower lower class persons are thought to desire money, possessions,

education and favorable prestige but to not know how to achieve them. They give the impression of resignation in a community that despises them for their lack of aspiration and poverty. In Elmtown, Hollingshead found that two out of three parents did not complete elementary school and only a small fraction completed a year or more of high school. The husband-wife relationship in the lower lower class tended to be unstable with more than half of the families broken by death, desertion, separation or divorce. Quarrels and vicious fights between husband and wife followed by desertion and divorce were not unusual. Marriage occurred in the middle of the teens for girls and the late teens or early twenties for boys. It was estimated that one-fifth to one-fourth of all births in this class were illegitimate. Adolescent boys of the lower lower class usually began sex activity while in their early or middle teens. Members of the lower lower class took almost no part in organized community activity. Time and punctuality seemed to be of little value, and employers claimed that such persons came to work at irregular times, left when they felt like it, and took off with little or no excuse. Leisure was spent in loafing around the neighborhood, at home or in various designated places of meeting. Family members usually went their separate ways in search of diversion. Social life consisted of informal visiting of neighbors, gossip, petty gambling, attending motion picture theatres, drinking at home or in taverns and festive Sunday gatherings of relatives. Men associated with men, and women with women except for sexual activity (5).

5   The lower lower class are thought to have distinctive patterns of speech, dress, marriage and family life. The father often is viewed as an unstable, undependable or absent family member. Women may have a succession of temporary mates. When the weather permits, a great deal of time is spent on the streets, in yards and on front steps or leaning out of windows (6).

6   The poor generally are seen as unmotivated for service and lacking awareness of their problems and the way in which professional help can be utilized (1).

7   The poor seem to hold "unrealistic expectations" and to make "inappropriate requests" for service. They are unable to understand differences in agency policy and program (1).

8   The poor tend to relate problems to external causes and to outside forces and pressures, in the face of which they feel relatively helpless (1). They "project"! (If one persists in identifying a problem outside the self, one cannot be helped by a service which presumes that between the client and the clinician there exists the necessary raw material for change.)

9   The poor use different rules for ordering speech and thought. The poor, uneducated man describes the personal and material world narrowly, through his own eyes, as it enters and leaves his field of perception. He is likely to locate himself clearly in time and space and give all descriptions in the first person with himself at the center. Persons and events tend to be viewed primarily in terms of the self with little capacity to perceive the self objectively as an interacting part of a total situation or to view that situation from a reference point different from one's own (7).

10   The poor and uneducated are likely to be insensitive to difference in

background experience between themselves and the listener and to consequently use first names, personal pronouns without clear referents. Their point of departure is always personal. The context in which they speak is clear to them but not to the listener. The integrating theme or organizing idea is often difficult to define, and this vagueness results in apparently dissociated comments which may leave the listener wondering what is going on. This produces many questions in an effort to achieve organization. Such constant questioning can and does distort response, sidetrack communication, shatter rapport in the sense that the question represents a repeated statement of no understanding by the listener (7).

The literature of social science is full of other characteristics which might be mentioned. The central issue before us is how we are to evaluate such observation. If we plug these observations into a theoretical system based primarily upon psychoanalytic theory we easily may come up with evidence of psychopathology and a picture which differs radically from our image of an "ideal client." When behaviors such as apparent projection, substitution of activity for anxiety, magic thinking, isolation and acting out are prominent; we easily may conclude that the client has one or another kind of character disorder and that he represents a poor or limited treatment risk.

Have we discriminated against any social class in making such a diagnostic appraisal?

There is substantial evidence to indicate that clinical judgment is heavily infused with middle-class bias; that diagnostic criteria have their source as much in cultural tradition as in science; that such behavior as planning ahead or being deliberate is drawn largely from middle-class society's accumulation of folk wisdom about problem solving. For the chronically impoverished client, consideration of the long range results of his action may be irrelevant and even incapacitating.

A different assessment of the same data is possible—an assessment which views these characteristics of the poor not as indicative of psychopathology or maladjustment or weakness or disorganization but rather of success in adapting to a reality so completely impoverished in resources and opportunities, so qualitatively different from that of their middle-class neighbors, as to necessitate special adaptive patterns for sheer survival. William Haase, for example, found that essentially identical Rorschach inkblot test records were interpreted differently depending on the social class of the patient. The low-income patients more often were classified as psychotic or as having serious character disorders. Their middle-class equivalents were merely labeled neurotic, or dismissed as normal. Hasse points out that since the poor have less opportunity and greater hardships than the middle-class, similar test records may indicate greater, not lesser, mental health. These are not isolated findings (8).

Obviously, the two positions lead to quite different consequences for professional practitioners who feel committed to serve the poor. It may make a difference, after all, in our assessment of client capacity and of our ability to help if we view client social functioning as characterized by weak and inadequate adaptive and problem-solving capacity or as characterized by effective adaptive capacity and problem solving in a completely degrading and inhuman situation.   It may make a difference if we assess client capacity against middle-class standards of adequacy or against the requirements for daily survival in poverty.   Behavior is, after all, not a function of a person alone but of a person in a particular situation.   The capacity of the chronically impoverished client to learn a middle-class life style as a result of intensive therapy may, indeed, be limited or nonexistent.   If it is the intent of our diagnostic procedures to assess this capacity, then they are indeed correct in registering pessimism about client treatability.   There are grounds for serious doubt, however, that this is the appropriate question to be put by our diagnostic procedures; to question whether such recruitment into a middle-class life style is, in fact, the legitimate goal of therapy for such a client.   One would expect rather that the legitimate goal for health and welfare services with such a client is the enhancement of his social functioning within the limits and requirements of his reality.   This, of course, does not mean that the goal of such service is simply to adjust people to reality.   There are some realities to which no one ought to be permanently well adjusted.   Reality, its demands and expectations, resources and opportunities and how they may be enhanced is, however, a good place to begin.

One practical consequence of primary reliance upon theory drawn from psychoanalytic concepts to evaluate such behavior is our tendency to perceive impoverished recipients of service as individual case units without seeing that such impoverished families are also representatives of a community of persons sharing many common life problems and problem-solving methods.   A case unit perception as opposed to a group or community perception has tended to emphasize the unique features of each case rather than the common lot, the shared life style of a large and growing community of persons who live in the economic cellar of the community.   I believe that our inclination to do this reflects the inclination of society, and in part of the professions, to see dependency primarily as a matter of individual responsibility and blame.   No matter how the matter is rationalized in social, psychological and physical terms there is a clear suggestion of individual maladjustment, individual pathology, individual deficiency, individual blame and responsibility in this approach.

An altered view of such families, a perception of them as a community of persons rather than as case units alone, still would permit a personalized approach to individuals. It has the virtue, however, of offering a conceptualization within which it is possible to use the additional dimension of the group, of client to client and community to client relationships in order to bring about change and social improvement. A community or group view of those who are impoverished makes it possible to enlist the latent power in group formation itself to expand the well-being of its members.

A case unit approach tends to view the problem as largely the responsibility of each family. A group or community approach conceptualizes the problems in such a way as to make possible a deliberate approach to facilitating the emergence of indigenous leadership from the group. It seems clear that the poor are without significant voice in the community's social and political affairs and that they are without a sufficient sense of their own power, their own size, the commonality of their experience. A community or group view of the recipients of public financial aid, for example, offers the potentiality that this group can generate from its own members, its own leadership, its own voice and its own participation in community affairs. Such recipients are, after all, citizen-recipients of public aid. There is need to tap the group's own capacity for self-help and self-improvement. Our present perception of these recipients as individual case-units presents an overwhelmingly complex series of individual maladjustments and individual problems standing in need of evermore intense service from evermore professionally trained practitioners. The numbers are overwhelming, the cost staggering, the prospect of intensive individualized service unlikely. It makes sense that in addition to the individualized approach which has proven value, a method of intervention be conceptualized which enlists the group's own capacity for self-help and self-improvement.

There is some evidence that the impoverished do share a common life style or culture which is internally consistent and distinctive from that dominant in the general community (9). There also is evidence that the professions which serve the impoverished are engaged in an intercultural enterprise and that problems in communication and joint goal-setting are to be expected as an inevitable consequence of beginning from different first assumptions about life and its major themes and organizing values. The points of significant differentiation of this culture of poverty from that dominant in the general community include: (1) an inclination to subject oneself to, or to live in harmony with, what is seen as natural or given in life, as opposed to the mastery of man over the forces of his social and physical world which has so characterized American life; (2) an inclination to focus in activity on a relatively free expression of what is conceived as given in human personality, stressing a spontaneous, non-developmental conception of activity in contrast with the doing, accomplishing, go-getting attitudes so valued in American life; (3) a tendency to emphasize the present time over the requirements of either past or future in contrast to the typical American concern for future planning. This concern is supported by the conviction that the future will be better than the present. The conviction gives reality to man's future and represents a resource to be exploited with those reservoirs of time, energy, hope and optimism left over from the daily battles for survival.

It has been suggested that the distinctiveness of this life style has important survival value under the actual conditions of life for the impoverished (10). Resistance to the influence of middle-class professionals is in such a context a sign of health, an effort to protect personal integrity by people who may sense a future no different from the present or past and who feel their life style, and hence their survival, to be threatened by helpers who would invite them to adopt a completely irrelevant, nonfunctional middle-class life style.

To start where the client is means, in the case of the impoverished, to start with the impoverished nature of goods, services and opportunities which exist in his reality. In this reality middle-class attitudes may be nonfunctional.

All studies of poverty in the United States indicate that the impoverished are desperately in need of professional services—services which are directed primarily toward the preservation of those ego strengths and capacities which are functional and useful in social life as it must be lived; services directed toward the generation and enrichment of opportunities, the creation of new resources in the environment of the impoverished which they can take hold of and use for the enhancement of their own functioning and that of their families.

Summary

There is evidence that our health and welfare enterprise is bound by social class and culture; that it is presently aimed at a middle-class clientele; that its almost universal failure to successfully engage and influence the social welfare problems of the impoverished is as much a tribute to the inadequacy of its conceptual and knowledge base as to the complexity of problems confronted. As students of human behavior, as professionals living and working in a political democracy committed to service based on need alone, it is essential that we move away from the Ptolemaic assumption of the universality of our own middle-class values. It is essential to move to the Copernican world of differential life styles and value systems of persons at different social class levels.

References

1. Cloward, R. 1963. Social Class and Private Social Agencies. Proceedings of the Annual Meeting of the Council on Social Work Education.

2. Hollingshead, A. and F. Redlich. 1958. Social Class and Mental Illness. John Wiley and Sons, Inc.

3. Warner, W. L. and P. S. Lunt. 1941. The Social Life of a Modern Community, Yale University Press.

4. Warner, W. L., M. Meeker and K. Eells. 1960. Social Class in America, Harper Torchback Edition.

5. Hollingshead, A. B. 1949. Elmtown's Youth: The Impact of Social Class on Adolescents. John Wiley and Sons, Inc.

6. Miller, W. B. *The Culture of the Roxbury Community,* Mimeographed Speech, Philadelphia, 1957. This reference and those given in footnotes #3–#6 are quoted from: Roberts, R. E. T., *The Urban Lower Class In The United States of America,* Prepared for Training Center, National Federation of Settlements and Neighborhood Centers, Chicago, August, 1963.

7. Schatzman, R. and A. Strauss. Social class and modes of communication, Amer. Jour. Sociol. January, 1955.

8. Riessman, F. New models for treatment of low income groups. Transaction. January, 1964.

9. Schneiderman, L. A study of the value-orientation preferences of chronic relief recipients. Social Work. July, 1964.

10. Schneiderman, L., *op. cit.* also W. F. Klein and W. B. Miller. 1953. Society, Democracy and the Group. Woman's Press. Implications of Urban Lower-Class Culture for Social Work. Social Service Review. September, 1959.

Alfred Auerback

THE ANTI-MENTAL HEALTH MOVEMENT *

Mental disorders have been disturbing occurrences to mankind since earliest recorded history. They have been considered evidence of demons possessing the individual, of punishment by angry gods, even of holiness on rare occasions. The most common social reactions have been hostility, rejection, or withdrawal and, in the not-too-

* From Alfred Auerback, "The Anti-Mental Health Movement," *Amer. J. Psychiat.,* 1963, *120,* 105–111. Reprinted by permission of the author and the Editor, *American Journal of Psychiatry.*

distant past, physical punishment or incarceration for the afflicted individual. Mankind nearly always has looked with fear on the mentally ill individual, a feeling that has associated itself with mental healers down through the ages. This antagonism was compounded by Freud's stressing the sexual components of human behavior. While psychoanalysis has won increasing acceptance, hostility still remains towards many of its concepts, along with some doubt as to its therapeutic effectiveness.

Psychiatry, too, though a branch of medical science, still has not won complete acceptance (1). Whenever criticism has been expressed it has been accepted on the basis that psychiatry is still an inexact science, that we do not yet know the causes of mental illness and that our tools for combatting it are, in large degree, empirical. Yet despite some public and professional criticism, psychiatry and mental health activities generally have been accepted as legitimate undertakings which are continually seeking to perfect themselves.

The last few years have seen major progress in the better understanding of psychiatric needs. This is reflected in the Joint Commission on Mental Illness and Health Report, *Action for Mental Health,* the recommendations of the Governors' Conference of November 1961, and the first Mental Health Congress under the sponsorship of the American Medical Association in Oct., 1962. In Feb., 1963, President Kennedy indicated his personal interest in better care and treatment of the mentally ill and mentally retarded, in his request of Congress for extensive appropriations in this field. Leading to these developments have been the open door policy in mental hospitals, initiation of community mental health services in many states and more intensive use of varied therapeutic methods for hospitalized patients which have brought new horizons in the mental health field.

In recent years a new form of attack has been mounted against the mental health movement that is reminiscent of the Salem witch-hunting days. In contrast to legitimate criticism of deficiencies or methodology, it imputes deliberately evil intent to the mental health program in general and to those engaged in the field. Directly, but most often by innuendo, it accuses mental health associations and psychiatric groups of being subversive, even conspiratorial. The constant refrain is that the entire mental health program is a subversive racket and anti-American or communistic in nature, established by agents of the Kremlin to subvert and take over the United States. The groups making these charges, while containing a few well-meaning persons, seem to be in large measure made up of rabble-rousing individuals who have been involved in various "right-wing" activities over the years. Being well financed and vociferous, they manage to create public turmoil far out of proportion to their actual numbers. They have become effective pressure groups both at the local level and before state legislative bodies, where they have sown seeds of dissension and confusion. At times this has effectively blocked proposed mental health programs or brought about reduced appropriations for new or existing programs.

California survey.　　In Sept., 1961, a study of anti-mental health trends in California was made by a small group representing medical and educational organizations concerned with this problem. An analysis was made of 166 samples of attack on psychiatry or on the mental health movement gathered from 38 different communities in California. The major sources were:

Letters to the editor	—46
News stories and articles	—41
Leaflets and brochures	—21
Newspaper editorials	—17
Newspaper columns	—12

Sampling these items revealed a wide range of targets, including the California Department of Mental Hygiene, the Short Doyle Act, mental health associations, the World Health Organization of the United Nations, commitment procedures in California, psychological testing in the schools, and attacks upon psychiatrists, psychologists and social workers in general. A common thread running through all of them was the charge that these agencies, groups, and individuals were subversive and conspiratorial. Repeatedly it was implied that the mental health program was part of a communist conspiracy or that it was set up for the oppression of anti-communists. The theme was that prayer and time were all that was needed to alleviate the human misery and social problems created by mental illness. Typical statements found in these publications were:

"Mental hygiene is a subtle and diabolical plan of the enemy to transform a free and intelligent people into a cringing horde of zombies." "Mental health programs are part of a communist plot to control the people's minds." "Do we want to become a regimented nation, brain-washed and brain-fed through a powerful army of psychiatrists?"

These attacks are irresponsible, offering no constructive suggestions. They do not even evidence concern for the problem of psychiatric illness or for those afflicted. They use mental illness and the mentally ill as scapegoats for purposes which have no relation to mental illness. The issues are never discussed. They are deliberately dodged by attributing "evil motives" to mental health work in general and to those engaged in it. Running throughout are implications that psychiatric clinics are designed solely to probe into people's minds for subversive purposes; that psychological testing in schools is designed to teach children immorality and disrespect for their country. Never are these charges documented; always, they are by innuendo. At times, the "big lie" technique is used, the repeated out-and-out misstatement.

Development of anti-mental health trends.   The anti-mental health movement is an outcropping of the opposition to all scientific progress, particularly in the field of public health.   Nearly every major advance in this field during the past century has been violently opposed. Pasteurization of milk, chlorination of water and immunization against smallpox, diphtheria and other infectious diseases have evoked strong opposition whenever these measures were introduced.   There are still pockets of opposition to smallpox vaccination and to Salk vaccine. Antagonism to fluoridation of water has mounted in recent years to the point where 14,000 communities are deprived of this caries preventive (2).   Similarly, there has been clamor against the use of animals in laboratory experiments ("vivisection").   The first significant public denunciation against the mental health movement occurred in 1955. It came from a group of some 100 housewives in Burbank, Calif., who called themselves the American Public Relations Forum, Inc.   They were studying legislative bills with the announced purpose of exposing subversion and pounced on a proposed community mental health services bill.   When the bill was defeated this group claimed credit for a "victory for Americanism."   Re-introduction of the California Community Mental Health Services bill in 1957 again brought this group into the fray, but despite its vociferous opposition, the bill passed the legislature.   During its stormy legislative course it was exposed to repeated claims that it was communistically inspired. Despite the fact that the bill was drafted by the California Medical Association, many physicians in that state still oppose it on those baseless charges six years after its passage.

In 1956 the 84th Congress appointed a subcommittee to hold hearings in connection with HR6376, a bill providing for the hospitalization and care of the mentally ill of Alaska.   During the hearings a motley crew harangued in opposition to the bill.   A clever phrase, "Siberia, U.S.A." was coined at this time by a Mrs. Burkeland of Van Nuys, Calif. During the hearings it was worked into such statements as: "This legislation will place any resident of the United States at the mercy of any person with whom they might have a disagreement, causing a charge of 'mental illness' to be placed against them with immediate deportation to 'Siberia, U.S.A.'"   And again: "It is entirely within the realm of possibility that we may be establishing in Alaska our own version of the Siberian slave camps run by the Russian government" (3).   Soon, "Siberia, U.S.A." was being printed all over the country in right wing publications, including those of well-known rabble rousers and of groups with high sounding American names, seemingly dedicated to the perpetuation of American freedom. During the congressional hearings, several witnesses switched from "patriotism" to bigotry. They indicated that the mental health movement was a Jewish plot. One witness testified that 100% of all psychiatric therapy was Jewish and that about 80% of the psychiatrists in the United States were Jewish.

The importance of these congressional hearings to the anti-mental health forces lies in the fact that the verbatim text of the hearings was printed by the United States Government Printing Office, and in some cases later read into the Congressional Record. As a result, the wild statements made at that time have been repeated across the country countless times citing the Congressional Record and thereby implying governmental approval.

Interestingly, whenever mental health work is being attacked the phrases used are identical to those first appearing in the period of 1955–1958. Years after Alaska has built its mental hospital the phrase "Siberia, U.S.A." is still in use. Words like "communist-inspired," "anti-religious" and "conspiracy" are still frequent, but no new labels have evolved. No matter where the opposition has appeared the language is the same while documentation or substantiation remain nil. In many cases merely calling the mental health field "subversive" has proved sufficient.

Although the American Medical Association, the American Psychiatric Association and the National Association for Mental Health supported the Alaska Mental Health Bill, one nationwide group of physicians, the Association of American Physicians and Surgeons (AAPS) opposed it. In circularizing its ten thousand physician members the AAPS repeatedly mentioned the bill's "horrendous provisions." Interestingly, the association's congressional adviser quit in disgust when it refused to retract its stand (4). Over the years, many physicians exposed to this propaganda have continued to repeat the hackneyed clichés and frequently have led the attack on local or state mental health activities. Often this thinking has colored the deliberations of state and county medical societies, a fact substantiated by a recent national study of anti-mental health trends made by the writer. In ten or more states physicians or physicians' wives have played prominent roles in these attacks, at times succeeding in winning official or unofficial support of the medical societies. Perhaps the most striking example of this occurred in the San Fernando Valley near Los Angeles, where a professional propagandist, after attacking "The Mental Health Racket," was given a letter of commendation by the district medical society. Only after forceful argument by outraged members including the psychiatrists was this commendation revoked. This near miss led to publication of a booklet, *The Doctors*

Speak Up (5), in which psychiatrists of the San Fernando area exposed and refuted the false statements and misrepresentations of the propagandist.

On August 15, 1958, an article entitled "Mental Health—a Marxist Weapon" first appeared in the *Economic Council Letter 437*. According to this right-wing publication, mental health was an inaccurate label for what was really a skillful attempt by communist propagandists to bring about Marxist conformity to the Marxist ideology. According to this publication, "nonconformists" would be in actual peril of being judged insane. The contents of the article have been reproduced in countless other "anti-communist" publications and have been repeated *ad infinitum* and *ad nauseam*.

At about the same time there appeared a booklet entitled *"Brainwashing—A Synthesis of a Russian Textbook on Psychopolitics,"* its 64 pages purporting to hold the text of a talk given by Beria, former head of the Soviet Secret Police, to American students attending classes in "psychopolitics" at Lenin University (6). It contained some of the most bald-faced lies ever directed against the psychiatric profession. The book has had a tremendous circulation and has been cited at great length. Quotes crop up in publications of the Daughters of the American Revolution and in various other brochures such as "Lifelines," "Common Sense," "Freedom Builders of America," "Freedom Forum," *etc.* In each it is stated unequivocally that under the "false name of 'mental health' " a communist master plan is being put into operation in hundreds of American cities and that mental health groups are being used to further the goal of communist conquest of the mind. A sampling of this treatise on "brainwashing" must be quoted to indicate the source of phraseology now in frequent use:

Psychopolitics is a branch of geopolitics concerned with mental healing. It is used to produce chaos in the fields of mental healing. It is designed to have every doctor and psychiatrist act as an unwitting agent of the communist doctrine. Through it you achieve dominion over the minds and bodies of the nation. Institutions for the insane provide the means of holding a million persons without any civil rights or any hope of freedom. By use of electric shock or brain surgery you can keep these people so they will never again draw a sane breath. By making readily available drugs of all kinds, by giving the teenager alcohol, by praising his wildness, by stimulating him with sex literature, the psychopolitical operator (psychiatrist) can create the necessary attitudes of chaos, idleness and worthlessness in the teenager. The psychiatrist has no interest in cures, hence the greater the number of insane in hospital, the greater the number of people under his domination and the greater will become the size of his hospitals. Exercises in sexual attack on patients can be practiced by the psychiatrist to demonstrate the inability of the patient to withstand him while indoctrinating the lust for further sexual activities on the part of the patient. If a psychiatric ward could be established in every general hospital in every city in the nation, it is certain that at one time or another leading citizens of the nation could come under the ministrations of the psychopolitical operator. The attraction of the field of mental healing to many people is that it provides unlimited sexual opportunities and the possibility of complete dominion over the minds and bodies of patients, the possibility of complete lawlessness without detection.

While these statements are ludicrous, the fact remains that millions of Americans are being exposed to them over and over again. In addition to thousands of pamphlets and brochures repeating them there are many radio and television stations across the United States which routinely broadcast this philosophy, although in a more subtle manner. The attack on mental health is coupled with attacks on our educational system, churches, minority groups, and governmental institutions amongst others. It must be recognized that this is part of a well organized and well financed campaign against our democratic institutions carried out by groups and individuals making resounding statements about their "patriotism" and "Americanism."

Psychiatrists, generally, assume that educated people pay no attention to such remarks. Regrettably, this is not the case. In the Feb., 1962 issue of *Reader's Digest* (7), with a circulation of 14 million copies, an article entitled "The Tragedy of Sane People Who Get 'Put Away'" indicated that thousands of sane men and women are being "railroaded" into mental hospitals every year. The article further stated: "Only when all men are secure from unjust imprisonment can each of us feel truly free." It considered state hospitals terribly bad places and to be hospitalized in one was comparable to being put in prison. It is too early to measure the damage done by this article but its repercussions will be with us for years.

While the effects of the anti-mental health movement have been felt in Western and Southern states and its influence is spreading across the United States, it has had a profound impact in the southern part of California. In at least a dozen communities mental health activities have been attacked by these groups, in some cases successfully eliminating entire mental health programs. The stand taken by the attacking group or individuals is a rehash of the statements made in connection with the Alaska Mental Health bill or the booklet on psychopolitics. It is somewhat dismaying to find psychiatrists being vilified by other physicians as amoral, fools, knaves, quacks and traitors, to list but a few epithets. Repeatedly these physicians have stated that psychiatric treatment is of little or no benefit, that it undermines moral principles, that psychiatrists are unmindful of individual rights and are violating the Hippocratic oath and medical ethics by conducting worthless or harmful treatments.

When the local press has joined the fray against mental health programs in combination with one or more vociferous physicians, free public discussion of the issues has been impossible. Mental health associations have come under such violent fire that leading citizens have resigned from them as the result of intimidation or the fear of being labelled "pro-communist." Many others have been persuaded by the "big lie" that the model Draft Act is a measure to railroad political dissenters into mental hospitals, although in reality it is a recommended model prepared by federal agencies to provide quick help to the mentally ill through commitment procedures protecting their constitutional rights. As a result, states now attempting to pass mental health legislation invariably meet accusations of "railroading" as well as the demand that every mentally ill person should have a trial by jury before being hospitalized. An interesting derivative of this anti-mental health movement is to be seen in the Community Mental Health Act passed in Utah in 1961 (8):

It shall be a felony to give psychiatric treatment, non-vocational mental health counselling, case finding testing, psychoanalysis, drugs, shock treatment, lobotomy, or surgery to any individual for the purpose of changing his concept of, belief about, or faith in God.

The plan of attack against mental health associations is reviewed in *The Facts . . . a Reply to Anti-Mental Health Critics* (9) published by the National Association for Mental Health in 1962. About the same time the S K & F *Psychiatric Reporter* published an article "Is Mental Health a Communist Plot?" (10). The appearance of such publications would indicate that the increasing virulence of the anti-mental health group no longer permits ignoring them as nonsensical or misguided individuals.

National survey. During January 1963, the writer communicated with the officers of the District Branches of the American Psychiatric Association requesting information about anti-mental health tendencies in their states. In addition, inquiries went to many state mental health associations. An interesting pattern developed. In most states the psychiatric society either knew of no anti-mental health trends or was aware of only isolated instances. Shortly thereafter, there might be a follow-up letter in which it was reported, with considerable surprise, that anti-mental health activities *were* under way in that state! Psychiatrists generally do not move in circles where this opposition operates, whereas mental health associations functioning closer to the community do come in contact with it.

Some states have serious problems arising as consequences of this trend. In the State of Washington, anti-mental health forces precipitated a legislative probe of the state hospital system. At least one legislator who strongly supported the state mental health program was defeated for reelection on this issue and other sympathetic legislators have been threatened with similar political fates. In South Carolina a medical society study of *Action for Mental Health* declared (11)

The field of mental health will likely become within the next 10 to 15 years an enormous federal health empire probably under the direction of the Department of Health, Education and Welfare, which will centrally regulate all the mental health activities in the nation both at a state and community level. Furthermore, by its own statement of intentions, the Joint Commission would place this vast program dealing with one of our greatest health problems largely in the hands of non-medical people. That it would become primarily a political empire seems inescapable.

A graphic expression of anti-mental health trends is reflected in Texas. In this state, a number of well-intentioned, overpatriotic organizations, convinced that anything related to mental health is subversive, have conducted a running campaign against all mental health activities. Organized telephone campaigns and even full page advertisements in the papers attacking mental health work have occurred. As elsewhere, the anti-mental health organizations do not deal openly with the issues but use techniques of harassment and hasty withdrawal when confronted by a challenge to discuss their charges. They avoid libel by verbal inference rather than in written context.

Personality traits. There is no doubt that some of the individuals involved in this trend have paranoid personalities but this does not necessarily encompass the heterogenous group. To understand these individuals the best references are the discussions of ethnocentrism in *The Authoritarian Personality* (12) and the article, "Psychodynamics of Group Opposition to Health Programs" (13). The ethnocentric individual feels threatened by groups to which he does not have a sense of belonging. Where he cannot identify, he must oppose. He believes the "in" groups to which he belongs are superior to the "out" groups, which he considers threatening and power-seeking. The ethnocentrists are nationalistic in thinking, strongly opposed to internationalism in every form. Favoring an authoritarian ideology, they are opposed to any philosophy that stimulates critical evaluation or scientific inquiry. As a consequence psychiatry, which directs the individual to study his own motivations and to look critically both at himself and at his environment, is antithetical to the orientation of ethnocentrism.

Marmor and his associates point out that the same group of people are involved over and over again in opposition to widely diverse health programs. The same individuals and organizations that are active in the fight against water fluoridation can be found in the ranks of those opposing mental health measures and compulsory vaccination. To such individuals, purity is equated with security and health with wholeness. They are equally concerned with pure foods, pure morals and pure races. They are excessively preoccupied with fears of sexual attack, bodily poisoning or ideational contamination. Safety lies in what is old and familiar; the new and unfamiliar are threatening. New habits, new foods, new drugs or new ideas are all viewed with suspicion and apprehension.

Since anti-mental health activities stem from many sources there is no simple solution in terms of coping with them. Much of the strong emotional attitude expressed by anti-mental health partisans reflects their own unconscious anxieties. It also reflects a large degree of conscious opportunism on the part of various self-seeking and self-serving individuals and groups. One of them summarized their philosophy as follows (4):

When you are espousing a right-wing cause you are apt to attract a fairly sizable lunatic fringe which has to be dealt with kindly if for no other reason than to keep them from going over to the enemy. This is just simple realism. There isn't any use denying it, a great many people who are on our side aren't there because of any sound and sincere belief in our principles, but rather because they conceive our side of the argument to be the one that is to their personal and often pecuniary advantage. Nonetheless, when you are in a war you have to take what allies you can find.

The fanaticism of the anti-mental health believer "prevents an appeal to his reason or moral sense. He fears compromise and cannot be persuaded to qualify the certitude and righteousness of his holy cause" (14).

Discussion

Considering these facts, what can psychiatrists, psychiatric organizations and mental health groups do to combat this spreading trend across the country? Most important is the need for all groups and individuals with any interest or concern in the mental health field to recognize the nature and the extent of this problem. Indications are that in the coming years these attacks will increase rather than diminish in proportion to the tensions of domestic politics and the international situation. Direct attack on these groups or individuals after the fact is fruitless; then it can be only a defensive response because of the insidious nature of their activities. Mental health groups, whether state mental health department, mental health association or psychiatric association, must *anticipate* these situations and be prepared to respond immediately. Too often, they are unprepared, inept and too late.

The psychiatric group in the San Fernando Valley of California when attacked prepared a brochure exposing the nature and techniques of the opposition. The Southern California Psychiatric Society also has prepared a memorandum which is being sent to physicians and other interested groups and individuals in Southern California. This is a fact sheet about psychiatry listing anti-mental health statements with rebuttals (16). Material of this nature should be sent *beforehand* to members of legislative bodies, newspaper editors and columnists and other influential policy-making members of the community.

When newspapers or magazines print material of an anti-mental health nature a letter to the editor with a dispassionate rebuttal should be sent. Those publications expressing support for the mental health movement should be sent letters of commendation. The issues at stake no longer permit psychiatrists to remain uninvolved.

Psychiatrists generally have avoided the hurly-burly of political activity and involvement, particularly in medical matters. Consequently when they turn to organized medicine for help most other physicians are loathe to join in the battle. Psychiatrists must become more active participants in their county and state medical societies, in their committees and in their work.

Only by becoming more personally involved in community activities can psychiatrists win a feeling of acceptance by the community. For many people the old stereotypes of the psychiatrist still persist. This atmosphere of uncertainty and suspicion regarding psychiatry provides a potential spawning ground for members of the anti-mental health group. Unless psychiatrists and mental health groups can present themselves and their goals to the public and its governing officials in more clearly defined terms, they pose no obstacles to those who seek to present their biased and bigoted ideas.

Summary
Anti-mental health trends are manifestations of an ideological struggle under way in the United States in recent years. "Right-wing" groups in the name of "patriotism" have been attacking various aspects of our democratic process. Psychiatry and the mental health movement, for historical, sociological and emotional reasons, have been under increasing attack, a trend that will continue. Organizations and individuals connected with mental health activities must anticipate this development and plan to meet it.

Bibliography

1. Miller, M. H., and Halleck, S. L.: Am. J. Psychiat., *119:* 705, 1963.
2. Flemming, Arthur S.: New Med. Mat., *3:* 37, 1961.
3. Washington: U. S. Govt. Printing Office, 1956.
4. Smith, A. Robert: Reporter Magazine: 27, June 28, 1956.
5. The Doctors Speak Up. Los Angeles: Valley M. H. Assoc., 1961.
6. Anonymous: Brainwashing. Box 116, Englewood, Colo.
7. Maisel, Albert Q.: Reader's Digest: 97, Feb. 1962.
8. Salt Lake City, Utah: State Printing Office, 1961.
9. New York: National Ass. for Mental Health, 1962.
10. S K & F Psychiatric Reporter: 5, Sept.–Oct., 1962.
11. Report to Charleston County Medical Society (South Carolina), 1962.
12. Adorno, T. W., *et al.:* The Authoritarian Personality. New York: Harper, 1950.
13. Marmor, Judd, *et al.:* Am. J. Orthopsychiat., *30:* 331, 1960.
14. Hoffer, Eric: The True Believer. New York: Harper, 1958.
15. Los Angeles: Southern Calif. Psychiat. Soc., 1962.

Lawrence S. Kubie

IS PREVENTIVE PSYCHIATRY POSSIBLE? *

There are no easy answers to any of the difficult questions with which preventive psychiatry confronts us; but questions to which we have no answers can nonetheless be useful. It is valuable to recognize the presence of an illness long before we can diagnose its precise nature, much less cure or prevent it. Physicians are reconciled to this fact. Even laymen accept this in medicine, yet tend to be resentful of it in social issues, or in such medico-social problems as the present topic.

Preventive psychiatry derives its vision, its data, and some of its techniques and strategy from the study of mental illness and from the therapists' attempts to interrupt and reverse the causal chains producing psychological illness. The larger goal of preventive psychiatry is a human nature released from the rigidity that limits our freedom to change, destroys our capacity for happiness even under

* From Lawrence S. Kubie, "Is Preventive Psychiatry Possible?" *Daedalus,* 1959, 88, 646–668. Reprinted by permission of the author, the Editor, *Daedalus* and the American Academy of Arts and Sciences. Edited.

favorable circumstances, and distorts our creative potential in science, in art, music, and literature, in scholarship in general, and in politics and economics. Indeed, this is the most difficult problem in human culture: to learn how to bring ourselves up freed from the tyranny of stereotyped, rigid, unlearning, unconscious psychological mechanisms.

The implementation of any such vision will demand several things:

a A more precise knowledge of the psychological development of the human infant, leading to the discovery of new techniques for guiding, modifying, and controlling that development. This implies the introduction of measures to prevent the neurotic process *before* its onset.

b The application of methods to correct and reverse the neurotic process in its early stages. This will require the training of many more individuals in the diagnosis of potential illness before frank illness has crystallized, and in its treatment in its larval stages. This is no "minor" psychiatry, comparable to "minor" surgery. It is "major" psychiatry, precisely because it concerns itself with subtle early deviations from the normal, rather than those more obvious, late disturbances which bring most patients to the psychiatrist's consulting room or to the psychiatric hospital (12, 15). Furthermore, these early manifestations occur largely in nonmedical situations; and their recognition and treatment must take place where they are found. To meet this challenge will require an increase in the number of behavioral scientists educated, certified, and licensed as qualified psycho-diagnosticians and psychotherapists, without requiring that they be physicians. The medical profession alone cannot meet this need because there will never be enough medical specialists for this task. This is the bottleneck which must be broken.

c The development of new educational techniques to help reunite psychological processes which had become dissociated, instead of increasing repressive dissociations, as occurs in education as we have known it (10, 13, 14).

d Finally, preventive psychiatry will demand a critical re-examination of the influence all cultural institutions exercise on the evolution of the neurotic process. Among the factors to be studied are: the structure of the modern family; the impact of longevity and of over-all increases in the population and in population density; the changing age distribution and regional and occupation distribution of the population; the mixed constellation of therapeutic and noxious influences emanating from the several religions as presently organized and practiced; the effects on the neurotic process of various movements within the visual arts, music, and literature; the exploitation, reinforcement, and rewarding of the neurotic component in human nature by every type of economic system man has devised; and the many psycho-noxious influences that emanate from every political influence known. Even this incomplete list makes it obvious that merely to conduct an objective inquiry into these problems will arouse the opposition of every vested interest in our complacent society (17, 19).

When Henry Adams returned to Boston after a long absence, he remarked on his surprise at finding that the Unitarians who dominated the Boston culture of that day seemed to believe they had solved every great philosophical conundrum that had ever convulsed the human spirit (1). Were he to revisit America today, he would be moved to make a parallel comment about our illusions as to the perfection of our political, economic, educational, artistic, literary, and religious systems, each of which interacts in its own way with the ubiquitous but masked neurotic ingredients in so-called "normal" human nature.

Neurosis and repetition

In another connection (5) I have pointed out that a neurotic potential exists in every child, not so defective as to be incapable of learning symbolic thinking, feeling, and action. This potential becomes entangled in the neurotic process when under stress any dissociative repression occurs, i.e., when the link is severed between memory traces of events and their appropriate affects, or when the link becomes distorted or repressed between the symbolic representatives of inner or outer experience and that which the symbol originally stood for. The neurotic process is manifested primarily in personality disturbances. Under special and critical conditions of decompensation, the neurotic state precipitates out of the neurotic process as a constellation of symptoms.

Clearly, prevention must concern itself with the neurotic potential and the neurotic process. It cannot hope to achieve any material reduction in the toll of neuroses if it waits for the imminent occurrence of the neurotic state—the final and most easily recognized, but in a sense the least important, step in the series.

Every moment of behavior is produced by a constellation of concurrent forces. Whenever this constellation is of such a nature that it predetermines the automatic repetition of any pattern of action, thought, or feeling, the result is neurosis. This is our most precise and concise definition of what we mean by "neurotic" as distinct from "normal"; it is an obligatory repetitiveness, predetermined by the pattern of the forces that produce the act (8, 9, 11).

Yet repetitiveness is necessary to life. From the first moment, we breathe and suck, not once but repeatedly. Every bodily need makes itself felt many times. Every gesture, thought, and feeling, and their communication, are repeated. Therefore, repetition is an essential attribute of behavior. Furthermore, data from modern neurophysiology indicate that the organization of the brain is such that its processes tend to continue and to recur unless some active process arises to divert them. It is "easier" for the brain to go on doing the same thing than to change.

This is normal as long as the inherent tendency to repeat alters in response to the changing demands of body chemistry as signaled from the body to the brain through its internal afferent signaling system, both conscious and preconscious. Normal repetitiveness must also be free to alter in response to signals reaching us from outside the body (signals we see and hear and apprehend through all modalities of sensation) and to the signals called symbols.

Organic injuries to the brain can render it nonresponsive to both external and internal signals, thus producing organically determined repetitiveness. Such injuries can be structural, through direct injury or infection, or they can be chemical, through fever, intoxication, and drugs. But the frozen repetitiveness resulting from organic damage is not the object of our concern.

In the neuroses, the capacity to change in response to changing external or internal stimuli is impaired without the interposition of any of these organic variables which can impose automatic repetition on behavior (8). Even with a normal nervous system and a normal biochemistry of the whole body, an obligatory repetitiveness can be imposed on human conduct by psychological variables alone. As already stated, this occurs whenever behavior is dominated by symbolic processes whose roots and relationships are unconscious. Again, neither conscious nor unconscious symbolic processes ever operate alone, but always act concurrently, though with a varied distribution of influence. Moreover, they always exert their influence on thought, feeling, and behavior largely through the continuous central stream of preconscious processing. Where conscious processes exercise the dominant influence on preconscious processing, the resulting behavior is continuously adaptive and responsive to experience, past, present, and future. Consequently, the resulting behavior can be altered by rewards and punishments, by argument, exhortation, and reason. It can respond to success and failure. It can achieve satiation. It can alter after testing the usefulness and the effectiveness of effort. In short, it can learn, since it is flexibly responsive to signals both from the outer world and from the body. Where conscious processes dominate, any repetitions which occur are normal expressions of voluntary choice or of the recurrent tidal needs of body chemistry, or else they are part of the learning process.

On the other hand, where the preconscious processes that mediate behavior are under the preponderant influence of unconscious purposes and conflicts, any pattern will become stereotyped, inflexible, and insatiable, uninfluenced by any appeal to feeling or to reason, incapable of learning from experience and of assembling data creatively into new combinations. Whenever unconscious influences dominate, it becomes impossible for preconscious functions to create anything new. They are restricted to restating the old in a variety of more or less interchangeble symbolic languages. This, of course, is precisely what occurs in much of the neurotogenically overdetermined "modern" modes of art and literature (18). Unconscious psychological processes impose this rigid stereotype on preconscious processing precisely because the symbols representing them are distorted and dislocated from their roots. Since we communicate by means of symbols, wherever such a distortion of the symbolic process occurs we become walled off from the corrective, guiding, feed-back influences of internal or external realities.

This is where psychogenic psychological illness starts. No isolated or transient episode—whether a moment of rage, terror, elation, or depression, or a quick explosion of odd or inappropriate behavior—constitutes an illness. Only if the response becomes an emotional position to which the individual returns like an automaton, only if the individual begins to show fear, rage, depression, or anxiety in an insistent or repetitive manner irrespective of the stimulus, only if any triggered pattern becomes automatic, stereotyped, and repetitive, can we say that certain mechanisms have taken over to predetermine the automatic and obligatory repetitiveness which is the core of that which is neurotic in human nature (5, 7, 9, 11).

From this point of view, the neurotic ingredient in human nature results from the enslavement of behavior by psychological processes inaccessible to our own conscious self-inspection and control. This is the unhappy consequence of the dichotomy of symbolic processes into two systems, in one of which the roots and ramifications are predominantly conscious, whereas in the other they are predominantly unconscious. It is this dichotomy which must be one of the primary targets of preventive psychiatry.

The early manifestations of neurotic repetitiveness are seen in the repetitive play of infancy, or in the familiar wailing, thumb-sucking, rocking, head-bumping, toy-dropping, and night terrors, or in the regurgitation, retention, breath-holding, etc., which characterize some of the transitory neurotic episodes of infancy. We are so accustomed to these events that until recently they were dismissed as unimportant. Yet such transient examples of obligatory repetitions of behavior and feeling are warning signals. Each represents an inner disturbance which will remain active unless it is fully resolved. Otherwise, a constellation of symptomatic acts may disappear, but it will be replaced by another.

These buried and unconscious processes become time bombs with slow fuses. Their masked effects are cumulative, coalescing in the end to form the neuroses and ultimately the psychoses of adult life. These residues may be explosive charges which can be touched off by appropriate trigger stimuli into frank neurotic and psychotic states, or they may exercise a continuously deforming influence on the quality of an entire personality, on the quality of his creations, and on the patterns of his living.

Since they are first laid down in fragmentary fashion during infancy and early childhood, it is at this early age that we must search for the key to prevention, learning how to limit the dissociations that can occur between the symbolic process and what it attempts to represent. After such a split has occurred, it must be detected at once and a resynthesis achieved before cumulative injury occurs to the developing personality of the infant and child. But there are important differences between limiting, checking, or preventing fission when it threatens, on the one hand, and a therapeutic re-fusion after the initial fission has occurred, on the other. If the effort is made early enough, both fall within the field of preventive psychiatry. But if fusion is undertaken only after many secondary consequences of the initial fission have already accumulated, then the process of therapeutic fusion requires those heroic investments of time and effort which constitute psychotherapy and psychoanalysis as we know them today.

Prevention and the human family

The family is a protective environment arising around one or more adults on whom the infant, the toddler, or the child depends, to whom he becomes attached, with whom he identifies, whose images he builds into himself, and who become the objects of intense rivalry, love, fear, hate, and envy. Only a small part of this struggle is experienced on a fully conscious level. Most of it goes on preconsciously; even a great deal of that part of the struggle which receives symbolic representation is subjected to dissociative (i.e., repressive) processes, so that it is represented in partial and distorted fashion by symbols of whose true nature we may be unaware.

Consequently, although the family is necessary for human life, it is at the same time the soil in which the neurotic process takes root. It is out of the tense interpersonal and growth struggles of the nursery years in the family that illness and feuds arise. It is an area for basic research to determine how the family as a necessary institution can be modified so as to yield a larger crop of health and a smaller crop of illness.

There has been a small beginning in this direction. In fact, there is a cultural revolution even in the implications of such a change of phrase as this: whereas former generations said, "What did I do to deserve a brat like that?" the present generation says, "What did I *do?*" This is a valid and moving expression of humility and search.

Although at times it goes too far and involves us in fantasies of parental omniscience, omnipotence, and guilt, it represents a trend in a healthier direction, and the overswing will soon be corrected.

Yet to ask this question is one thing. To define what we could have done to prevent illness is another, involving considerations of education, of religion, of social structure, of population growth and density, of sex and age distribution within the population, of economic influences, of family size and units. The family is not an isolated or static entity. In every conceivable aspect the family as a breeding ground of health and of illness is changing rapidly in an intricate network of cultural processes which are also changing. All we can say now about the effects of these changes is that we do not yet know enough to guide them in a preventive direction (4, 19).

We know that love is essential, yet that alone is not enough: we see many children with severe neuroses coming even out of loving families. We know that faith is not enough—many neuroses arise among the devout. We know that doubt and skepticism are not enough, because they too afford no protection against the neurotic process. Similarly, we can say of simplicity or education, wealth and comfort, poverty and deprivation, ease or suffering, overwork or underwork, that none of these serves a preventive function. If any one factor plays a crucial determining role, it would seem to be the openness with which experience is shared among the generations, since it is the level of awareness on which experience is lived through and on which memory and feeling reverberate which determines whether or not it will give rise to obligatory and repetitive patterns of neurotic distortion. Here the child needs help from the adult world, in thinking and speaking out what is painful to recall and put into words, in place of silent acquiescence in unhealthy pseudo-forgetting.

The conspiracy of silence

Early analytic insights engendered naïve hopes that merely to allow a child to act out his spontaneous impulses would protect him from the cumulative neurotogenic effects of repression. It soon became clear that this was not so, but that on the contrary in the child who acts out his primitive, destructive, lustful, insatiable, and unattainable needs, the very violence of the impulses of which his behavior is a partial expression engenders deep terror and guilt, with spontaneous repressive repercussions. On the other hand, where timid adults shroud the critical inner experiences of childhood in silence, the neurotogenic effects of these experiences are intensified. Indeed, this is precisely where the conspiracy of silence enters into the evolving neurotic processes of youth. The conspiracy of silence, therefore, may perhaps be looked upon as a central target for research into prevention. There is still no general appreciation of how subtle and complex is this conspiracy, how insidiously it irradiates every aspect of child life, how difficult it is to correct, and how much basic research must be done before anybody can hope to offer better alternatives. As usual, it is easier to recognize that something is wrong than to correct it. Nevertheless, its recognition is an essential prerequisite to future prevention.

The conspiracy of silence establishes the basic pattern of that type of fragmentation and dissociation called repression. It implies in the first place a silent acquiescence in a child's confusions. Moreover, these confusions actually tend to be greater for the bright child who acquires words early than for the verbal laggard, because the linguistically precocious child picks up many verbal symbols whose meanings to him are obscure and overlapping. Yet instead of being helpfully and quietly corrected, his verbal precocity is hailed and his confusion is thereby increased. Every bright child harbors countless confused thoughts and confused fantasies, many of which he himself does not even apprehend clearly enough to express in words, unless he is helped to do so by the adult world. If the world does not deliberately bring them out into the open by helping the child to become articulate about his confusions, spoken or unspoken, the child mistakes adult silence for agreement, and they remain uncorrected until at length they are repressed. Furthermore, what the adult world does not talk about becomes itself taboo, just as those parts of the body which the adult covers automatically become taboo.

There are many subtle irradiations from this taboo of silence. Consider the words "private," "privacy," "private parts"—the nameless parts which are special and peculiar to "me" and which "I" must never acknowledge, explore, think about, name, or compare. The mere impulse to inquire and to find out about them is in itself a sinful proof of an inner evil of heart and mind. This feeling spreads to include all body functions. Something happens to the baby's image of himself when the potty ceases to be a proud, happy, social function, but is moved from its dais in the center of the nursery floor and shut away behind closed doors in a room that resembles an operating room in its aspirations to cleanliness. Under the euphemism of modesty, shame is born—shame about the body, its apertures, its products, its smells. The toilet becomes a room to which we refer only by guarded, nice-nelly euphemisms—"the john," the *lavatory* (to stress cleansing instead of excreting), the *little* boy's room or *little* girl's room, as if it becomes slightly less filthy when dedicated to the child's excretory rites.

Moreover, the concept of the privacy of dirt comes to include the family. For each small child there are things he does, talks of, smells, and experiences, but only in "my family." This means to him that only *my* family is dirty, dirtier than the rest of the world. One wonders how much of social snobbery, how much of the cult of the untouchable, is at least in part a compensatory reaction to the child's feeling that "my family is dirty," a thought so painful that it usually is repressed (3).

Nor are these wordless taboos restricted to sex or to bodily things in general. They are operative also in regard to death, disappearance, desertion, and pain. In television, movies, and comics we expose our children to vicarious participation in primitive, gory, and sadistic brutalities, and with all the artful simulation of the sight and color and sound of blood and death and agonizing tortures. Everything but the smell of death is reproduced; and if this becomes sufficiently profitable, Madison Avenue and Hollywood will add that too. We immerse children in a facsimile blood bath—but we are much too nice to talk to children about such things. Consequently each child buries his mixed responses to all this deep in his angry, frightened, and suffering heart. He cannot share it: therefore he cannot clarify it with anyone. Instead, so as to leave our own comfort undisturbed, we pretend that what the child does not ask about has no effect on him. This is the measure of the immaturity and moral complicity of the adult world. If we talked about it, we then would have to do something about it. This would bring us face to face with the entrenched interests of Hollywood and the advertising sponsors of crime television.

In sum, by our silence we create a hierarchy of evil for the child. There are things he can touch and put in his mouth. These are clean. They are not dangerous. Next are the things he can touch but cannot put in his mouth. These are the first degree of danger and dirt. Next are the things he cannot touch but can look at— though perhaps a bit askance. These are the second degree of dirt. Then there are the things he must not even look at, followed in quick succession by the things that must not be talked about, the nameless things about which he must not think or feel.

What the child cannot feel, or talk about, or name, or even think about, automatically becomes repressed. The nameless loses its link to any conscious symbol, and it can be represented only by distorted, masking, dissociated symbols. This is the essential step in the process of repression because it isolates objects, acts, impulses, events, and inner conflicts from those verbal symbols by means of which we are enabled to think, to communicate, and to inquire. This makes correction impossible. Furthermore, although the conspiracy of silence severs or distorts the links between the symbol and its roots, the emotions *are there still.* Yet because they too focus around the unnamable, the wordless, the unthinkable, the untouchable, they also become detached from anything the child can think about and correct. They become free-floating emotions, balloons floating in the air of the child's psychic life. This is what the conspiracy of silence does to the evolving verbal, symbolic, and affective life of childhood.

It is not the trauma of experience or the stress of inner conflicts among irreconcilable impulses that determines sickness or health—this depends on the psychological level on which the reverberations of trauma and the stress of inner struggle are lived out, and this level in turn derives mainly from the adult conspiracy of silence. To all this, of course, the adult adds still further confusion by never bringing his own mistakes out in the open, thus making sure that neither he nor his children nor his children's children will ever learn from past errors, our only potential source of wisdom.

The moment one begins even to contemplate an attack on this multiform and subtly pervasive conspiracy of silence, he finds himself up against taboos that have been strongly entrenched, sometimes for centuries, not only in each individual's separate feelings, but also in laws, traditions, rituals, religious taboos and pronouncements, and above all in our family life, the universal breeding ground for neurotogenic unconscious conflicts. The details of this conspiracy, its form and impact, vary from culture to culture, but no culture is free of it. Nor have our cultural anthropologists or social psychologists made objective comparisons of cultures, specifically in terms of the variations to be found in the conspiracy of silence, the variations in the repressive mechanisms it imposes, and the consequent variations in the forms of the neurotic processes which evolve.

Prevention and education

If we wish to make education an ally of psychological health, we will have to weigh the effects of every ingredient in the conventional educational scene and in the customary educational techniques on the activity of neurotogenic forces (10, 14, 18). We must develop methods to counteract the tendency to fragment experience into unrelated parts, to dissociate thinking, feeling, and action from one another, to bury one fragment and then to represent it in distorted form by means of symbols which are dissociated from their origins. Since creative preconscious processes become imprisoned in the dichotomy between conscious and repressed symbolic processes, any control of dissociation and repression will profoundly influence emotional maturation, intellectual development, and above all the free play of creative imagination.

Such efforts would begin in the nursery school and kindergarten, since here the child first acquires his capacity for symbolic thinking, for feeling and communicating through gesture, mimicry, and sound, even before he learns to use the more highly developed symbolic functions of speech, reading, and elementary arithmetic. To free a child in this way will also free his acquisition of the basic tools. The three R's, as well as the plastic, rhythmical, and musical arts, will benefit. Thus the prevention of neurotogenic processes at their sources would enhance the efficacy of our entire educational system.

From the toddler years to the top levels of postgraduate education, we need school techniques by which dissociation and repression among the various ingredients of psychological function would be limited or reversed as quickly as they start, so that thinking, feeling, and acting would develop as well-synthesized and unitary expressions of an evolving personality, instead of as erratic outcroppings from fragmented and dissociated functions.

Let me repeat that to limit fission is not identical with psychotherapy, which aims at reuniting components which have already been split. In psychological matters, as in physics, the process of fission can release destructive energy, and again as in physics the process of fusion may be accompanied by dramatic explosive discharges. There is no reason to believe, however, that this would be true of procedures by which the primary fission itself was limited or prevented. Therefore, although we have learned our basic principles from the treatment of the neuroses and psychoses, the implications of early psychotherapy are not identical with, and should not be confused with, psychotherapy.

Interactions between social processes and the secondary and tertiary consequences of the neurotic process

Resistance to change is deeply entrenched in all institutions, and the history of all preventive medicine is marked by opposition. An unsparing effort toward the preventive use of psychiatric knowledge and techniques would challenge every human institution. In the face of this challenge, education, religion, industry, and government will have to manifest a humility and honesty to which they are not accustomed.

In addition, it is in the essential nature of that which is neurotic to stay put. Self-examination that might lead to change is therefore opposed with fear, with the anger born of fear, with tenacity and desperation. Everything sick in human nature manifests this obstinate reluctance to change. Individually, this is evidenced by our patients. Socially, it is shown by our defense of cultural institutions that have repeatedly demonstrated their impotence or their actual pathogenicity. Therefore it is not surprising that the ubiquitous yet masked neurotic process struggles to go on being and doing, just as in the past.

We have no evidence that social forces per se are responsible for the ubiquitous neurotic potential, or that they generate the neurotic process that derives from it (5, 9, 11). We do know that they help to shape it, and that in every known culture man is surrounded by social forces that interact in complex ways with both the neurotic process and the fully developed neurotic state (17). The present inquiry will be clearer, therefore, if it distinguishes among these social forces: (a) those that conceivably generate neuroses (an uncertain and debatable claim); (b) those that exploit and prey upon neurotic trends extant in human nature; (c) those that intensify such trends by actively rewarding them; (d) special vested interests that oppose change; (e) deeper individual biases, both conscious and unconscious in origin, that oppose any change even for the better.

By implication this position challenges many frequent assumptions about the ease with which the neurotic process can be averted or limited. I want to underscore this. There can be no doubt that the cultural organization of any society influences both the neurotic process and the price its citizens pay for their neuroses. This, however, is far from claiming that cultural differences can either initiate or prevent the neurotic process. Yet it is always tempting to blame neuroses on aspects of life which for other reasons may be undesirable. Thus we find people who in the same breath say that neuroses are due to poverty and that they are due to wealth, that they are due to overwork and to leisure, to sleeping too much or too little, to ignorance or to excessive education, to superstition or to supersophistication. Others blame neuroses on a lack of love or on excessive loving, on neglect or on overprotection. Neuroses are blamed on the simplicity, barrenness, and isolation of country life; or on the complexity, congestion, and pace of urban existence. Primitivism is blamed, or the rarefied and precious atmosphere of a highly cultivated society. Some blame neuroses on doubt and cynical skepticism, others on credulity or an overcompliant and passive acceptance of religious faith. Thus we find neuroses blamed with splendid impartiality on religion and on skepticism, on puritanism or on license. There was a period not long past when neuroses were blamed on close family ties. This is implicit in certain novels of Louis Couperus, Henry James, G. B. Stern, Louis Golding, Wasserman, and Thomas Mann. In all this fiction we find the masked manifestations of secret accumulations of inexpressible patricidal, matricidal, fratricidal, and incestuous rivalries and tensions within close-knit family units. Conveniently forgetting all this, however, people today place the emphasis on domestic turbulence, family disruption, and the loosening of family ties. Superficial observers blame the breakdown or attenuation of family life, rather than viewing these as important manifestations of the ubiquitous neurotic process.

In this connection we should consider the statistics of the situation, if only as a warning against the kind of fallacy which is so easily substituted for thinking. I have in mind two basic facts: (a) that nearly 20 per cent more of the total population are married today than seventy years ago (18); and (b) that in 1890 families were disrupted and reshuffled by early deaths at a greater rate than occurred through divorce in 1940 (4). During the half-century between these dates the rising divorce rate did not keep up with the falling death rate. One would not hold that the impact of reshuffling because of divorce and the impact of reshuffling because of early deaths are necessarily the same. Certainly, when the reshuffling is because of early deaths it presumably follows a shorter period of family tension, since people may die before intrafamilial tensions have had time to reach explosive states. But which does the major damage to the progeny: the divorce, or the prolonged intrafamilial stress which precedes divorce and which is made possible by longevity? To such questions no one has any right to answer either *ex cathedra* or out of preconceptions, since no one yet has objectively, carefully, and without passion or prejudice explored the influence of these complex psychosocial phenomena.

Let me illustrate other ways in which our thinking has been hobbled. We have assumed that parents are necessarily the best people to bring up their own children. Yet in earlier days when large families with many children and many adults lived under the same wide roof, responsibility for child-rearing was spread thin among the adults. Every child then had an adult ally to whom he could turn when needed, whether against his age peers or against any oppression by the adult group. Few children were "brought up," as today, solely by their inexperienced parents. The child does not have such an ally any more, unless arranged for him outside the family group. Instead, today's family is built like a pyramid, with all the intrafamilial rivalries, tensions, jealousies, angers, hatreds, loves, and needs focused on the untrained, vulnerable, insecure, young, inexperienced, and incompetent parental apex of this pyramid, about whose incompetence our vaunted educational system does nothing. It is, to say the least, foolhardy to take it for granted that this is a healthy way to bring up children. The issue merits objective investigation.

Longevity (an amazing achievement of modern medicine) puts on human ties still other strains never before experienced. For the average man his earning span has not increased, but, if anything, has diminished, while the number of older and younger dependents he must carry has increased. Moreover, the family (like most individual communities) is no longer a producing unit but only a consuming unit. This increases the rivalries and decreases the loyalties, the cooperative spirit, within the family, just as it does in the community. In this and other ways the family has become a source of economic and emotional insecurity instead of a source of strength. The center of security has thus shifted from the individual's effort to earn his own way to a sharing of risk through group insurance, social security, group health, union pension plans, etc. Consequently some remote impersonal agency (i.e., the government, the management, the union, the voluntary mutual insurance group) has taken over what was once a function of the parents, the clan, or the family. What are the effects on human development of replacing individual risk by group risk? What do all such changes do to the human spirit, and to the secondary and tertiary consequences of what is neurotic in all human nature?

Many other profound changes are at work in the family today. The shrinking size of the family unit creates new problems. The increase in population causes more people to live in smaller space. It is harder to smile politely every morning across an apartment-house hall at the neighbor who opens his door as you do yours than to greet such a neighbor once a month when you visit him five miles down the road. When he is that far away you do not have to pretend so often that you always feel like smiling at him. Congestion can reach a saturation point, a threshold beyond which the human spirit cannot breathe. This consideration, however, is singularly unimportant to real estate operators. The more human beings who can be crowded onto the point of an urban pin, the more money can be made, no matter what the cost to the human spirit.

Or take the profound change in the leverage of direct human responsibility for one another. This change results directly from the fact that in his life at home, at work, at play, and in government man has become increasingly detached from his fellows, increasingly faceless. Even on the battlefield, you shoot an enemy you cannot see and are shot by an enemy who cannot see you. In the labor union as in the industrial plant, working life is depersonalized by magnitude. The home itself has become impersonalized, a place for sitting side by side, facing, not one another, but a ground-glass screen to watch imaginary catastrophes happening to someone else. All this creates a gap in what used to be the close-linked chain of human responsibility, a gap filled destructively by the impersonal monolithic structures of labor and industry, religion, states, "entertainment," and gangs—and monoliths are built on the destructive organization of rivalry, envy, acquisitiveness, hate, or fear.

Organized religion is deliberately included in this listing, since so much of the churches' strength rests on the organization, not of loving and individual responsibility, but of mass hating. We are rapidly moving into an era of choice between faith and the sword, forgetting that the right to believe as conscience dictates must include the right to question and doubt also as conscience dictates. Too often religion displays a strange fusion of hucksterism and evangelism, as in the substitution of the shopping list for the manger in our modern degradation of the Christmas festival.

In the meantime, as the entertainment industry and the advertisers take over, ours becomes a spectator culture. The increasing perfection with which the techniques of entertainment simulate reality increases our passivity. It requires a lesser effort of imagination to watch a television show that it once did to read a nickel novel. Nor is this transformation of our culture into a spectator culture attributable to the entertainment industries alone: the art dealers, picture galleries, couturiers, and decorators are all likewise involved.

Finally, we must consider our economy, increasingly gambling its success or failure on consumption by the installment plan. Has anyone since Veblen asked what would happen to such an economy if what is neurotic in human nature were by sudden magic to be eliminated? What would happen to the fashion cults, the beauty cults, the food and drink and tobacco cults with their exploitation of orality, the excretory cult, the cleanliness cults, the size cults, the height cults, the strip-tease cults? Consider the exploitation of hypochondriasis through the drug houses and even our more elite publishing houses. Take also the endless whetting of consumer cravings, the exploitation of the "gimmies" of childhood by transmuting them into the "gimmies" of adult life. Consider the ministering to neurotic needs through size and power: the knight of old has been replaced by Casper Milquetoast in General Motors armor, complete with chromium, unneeded size, unused seating capacity, and a pointless, illegal, and unusable capacity for speed. Or consider the search for happiness anywhere else than where one is, and how the travel industry abets it by vacations on the installment plan.

To repeat, what would happen to our economy if we got well? And what does the exploitation of neurosis by so many forces in our culture do to the neurotic process itself? Is this a culture that breeds health? Is this a culture we can afford to be complacent about? Or have we allowed the enormous creative potential of private enterprise to be enslaved by greed to the neurotic process in industry, exactly as the creative process in art, literature, music, even science, has become the slave of neurosis?

Lest you think I am singling out our culture, our economy, for attack, I repeat that I do not believe that human ingenuity has yet devised any economic system that does not exploit, intensify, and reward much that is neurotic (potentially even psychotic) in human nature.   If the profit-driven economies exploit subtle manifestations of neurotic self-indulgence and short-term needs, so do totalitarian systems, whether Fascist or Communist, exploit power needs and power fantasies in a still more primitive fashion, rewarding the sadistic lusts and the paranoid components of human nature.   As Freud once pointed out, man is still frail enough to need competition for money and for conspicuous display as a buffering device with which to protect himself and his fellows from more brutal forms of the struggle for power.

The paradox here is that primitive cultural, political, and economic forms are inevitably transmuted into more sophisticated forms.   But, because of the persistent influences of the masked neurotic forces in human nature, sophistication leads to its own weakening and self-destruction, so that the cycle returns to the primitive again.   This is perhaps the most vicious cycle in the history of culture, and the one to which least attention is paid: namely, how the initial idealism of a totalitarian economy leads from the struggle for naked power, through perceptible transitions, back to the struggle for the glutting of personal yearnings.   This in turn brings in the neurotic weakening of a profit-motive economy, and thence, through "The Degradation of the Democratic Dogma" (2), to self-destruction, and back once more to the primitive forms of power struggle.   The world would be a safer place if on both sides of the Iron Curtain men would turn their attention to the ways in which each system sows the seeds of its own neurotic destruction.   For these seeds of destruction can be eliminated only if we recognize and attack the subtle, pervasive influence of the concealed neurotic processes in so-called normal men and women, who, in their confused and immature and inept ways make up all human society, whether East or West.

Summary

1   Preventive medicine has always encountered obstacles that are rooted in socially entrenched prejudices.   Preventive psychiatry must overcome obstructive forces even more tenacious than those now vanquished in other fields of medicine.   These forces are built into social institutions, but have their deeper roots in the tendency of the neurotic process itself to resist change.

2   This manifests the basic fact that the neurotic process is interwoven with our growth processes and our highest intellectual and cultural aspirations, giving rise to a tendency to defend this all-pervasive aspect of the neurotic process as something to be prized, rather than disowned as something alien.   Consequently the attitudes of the individual and of society toward the neurotic process differ materially from their attitudes toward other forms of illness.

3   We must attempt to prevent psychiatric disorders on three levels.

a   The organization of society in part determines the price we pay for our neuroses.   Therefore certain elements of our social organization should be altered so as to alter the cost of the neurotic process, both to the individual and to society.   In this connection, every phase of group living influences the fate of the neurotic process—economic differences, population density, longevity, housing, the organization of work and play, educational and religious processes, political and economic processes, the changing structure of the family, etc.   Consequently, to limit the disastrous secondary and tertiary consequences of the neurotic process demands an objective consideration of every aspect of human society.

b   Preventive psychiatry also depends on the earliest possible application of psychodiagnostic and psychotherapeutic methods.   The adult neurosis and indeed the adult psychosis are in large measure the cumulative secondary consequences of the unresolved neurotic process of infancy.   Therefore the early introduction of therapy constitutes one of the primary techniques of prevention in an effort to resolve the neurotic process so early and so completely that no residues remain to produce cumulative distortions in the maturing personality.

Our ability to do this depends first upon the sharpening and refining of our techniques of early psychodiagnosis, and second upon the training of a large number of experts competent to make early and precise psychodiagnoses and to give psychotherapy in situations not ordinarily reached by the psychiatrist.   The training of a new profession, that of a doctorate in medical psychology, must therefore be an integral part of any all-out effort toward preventive psychiatry.

c   The ultimate objective of preventive psychiatry, however, goes even deeper: it aims to limit or reverse the first steps in the neurotic process as these arise in infancy and childhood.   To attain this goal will require much basic research to enable us to recognize those first deviations from the path of normal development which occur in childhood and which subsequently and in varying degrees influence every human life.

In our present stage of knowledge we can recognize several ingredients that require preventive manipulations: (a) a control of those experiences which impose on the infant persisting central emotional positions; (b) a control of those conditioning experiences which link these central emotional positions to trigger mechanisms; (c) a control of the processes of identification by which the developing personality makes destructive and conflicting identifications with destructive and conflicting persons; (d) finally and most important, there must be a significant measure of control of the processes of repression which produce a dichotomy in the symbolic process itself, i.e., the fateful dichotomy into conscious and unconscious components.

None of these goals is easy to achieve; but the recognition of their importance is a step forward.   In coming years the course of preventive psychiatry will depend in part on the development of techniques aimed at these objectives.

4   A further complication is introduced by the fact that in some ways the most important part of the story of the neurosis deals not with an illness from which the patient himself experiences pain, but rather with concealed illness, which has a destructive effect on the lives of those

around the patient and on society as a whole while leaving the patient relatively comfortable, at least until the neurotic process catches up with him in later years. . . .

Yet precisely because these most universal of all manifestations of the neurotic process also cause the patient the least immediate suffering, they are the most difficult to bring into therapy or under control.

5   Psychotherapy (the attempt "to heal a man through the influence of his own mind," as Austen F. Riggs defined it) is part of the age-old struggle for freedom, especially the freedom to change.   In contrast, psychonoxious processes enslave the human spirit. . . .

The most searching test of the creative value of any ingredient in our culture is whether it increases man's capacity to change or entrenches his resistance to change.   This might well become our ultimate criterion of "greatness," in whatever cultural field (18). . . .

6   There are complex technical issues and tough practical obstacles impeding the elimination of the roots of the neurotic process. . . . The idea that we "outgrow" these difficulties without help, or that a happy home and an intact family are enough, or that better high schools, or more formal education, or love alone is enough; the muddled notion that believing is more creative than doubting, faith more powerful in advancing human culture than skepticism, the accepting spirit healthier than the challenging spirit—all these oversimplifications have been tried, and all have failed. As we face both the critical problems of the inner world and the devastating problems of the outer world, one asks whether we dare lull ourselves any longer with these ancient quarter-truths. . . .

Let us now return to the question we asked at the beginning: is preventive psychiatry possible?

Unquestionably it is possible to alter materially the secondary consequences of the neurotic process, that is, to interrupt those social forces whose consequences reactivate the original process so that it builds up to greater tragedy.   It is possible to ameliorate the secondary and tertiary manifestations of the neurotic process by changes in the shape of our society.   Note that this is "possible"—"probable" is another matter.   The least maneuver toward this goal requires an unsparing, critical re-examination of every element in our culture.   If this is to be more than an empty intellectual exercise, it implies a willingness to experiment with changes in those elements in our social structure that reward, exploit, and thus intensify the neurotic process. Yet men live by their affiliation with institutions, and in turn the institutions themselves live by these various cultural stereotypes.   It would be naïve, therefore, to imagine that changes can come easily in the face of strongly entrenched vested interests.

To pinpoint these as specific challenges for basic research on the techniques of prevention is an advance.   But to turn the theoretically "possible" into an ongoing process toward a well-defined goal requires instruments we do not yet possess.   In school, we need instruments of education based on self-knowledge in depth (10). In the home, we require new techniques of child-rearing which will no longer reinforce the neurotic process as our homes do today. Our children need skilled adult allies outside the family circle, such as those who once graced every large household but who disappeared as the family unit shrank to its present sharply pyramidal structure. To this end the community needs prepayment plans for intensive education in the basic principles of child care and in the psychopathology of family living, plus periodic psychotherapy for parents and children (6).

To develop such new devices will require many pilot tests, along lines elsewhere described in detail but never yet subjected to adequate experimental investigation. Though we have no ready panaceas, we can diagnose much that is wrong. This is worth doing, but only if it initiates uncompromising efforts to find better ways and better substitutes for many of our self-adulating institutions.

References

1. Henry Adams, *The Education of Henry Adams* (Washington, D.C., privately printed, 1907), p. 453.

2. ————, *The Degradation of the Democratic Dogma* (New York, The Macmillan Company, 1919), p. 317.

3. Lawrence S. Kubie, "The Fantasy of Dirt," *Psychoanalytical Quarterly*, 1937, 6: 388–425.

4. ————, "Husband-Wife," in M. M. Hughes, ed., *The People in Your Life* (New York, Alfred A. Knopf, Inc., 1951), p. 278.

5. ————, "The Neurotic Potential, the Neurotic Process, and the Neurotic State," *U. S. Armed Forces Medical Journal*, January 1951, 2: 1–12.

6. ————, "A Research Project in Community Mental Hygiene: A Fantasy," *Mental Hygiene*, 1952, 36: 220–226.

7. ————, "Neurosis and Psychosis," *Journal of the American Psychoanalytic Association*, 1953, 1: 59–86.

8. ————, "Some Implications for Psychoanalysis of Modern Concepts of the Organization of the Brain," *Psychoanalytical Quarterly*, 1953, 22: 21–68.

9. ————, "The Concept of Normality and Neurosis," in M. Heiman, ed., *Psychoanalysis and Social Work* (New York, International Universities Press, Inc., 1953), p. 346.

10. ————, "The Forgotten Man of Education," *Harvard Alumni Bulletin*, 1954, 56: 349–353.

11. ————, "The Fundamental Nature of the Distinction Between Normality and Neurosis," *Psychoanalytical Quarterly*, 1954, 23: 167–204.

12. ————, "The Pros and Cons of a New Profession," *Texas Reports on Biology and Medicine*, 1954, 12: 692–737.

13. ————, "The Impact of Behavioral Medicine on Pre-Professional Education for the Future Student," Conference on Pre-Professional Education for

Medicine, 18-19 October 1956 (New York, State University of New York, Downstate Medical Center, College of Medicine), p. 106.

14. ———, "Education and the Process of Maturation," in *Today's Children Are Tomorrow's World*, Fifth Annual Conference, February 1957 (New York, Associates of the Bank Street College of Education), p. 68.

15. ———, "The Need for a New Subdiscipline in the Medical Profession" (read before the Strecker Society, Philadelphia, 10 December 1956), *Archives of Neurology and Psychiatry*, 1957, 78: 283–293.

16. ———, "Freud's Legacy to Human Freedom" (read in part before the Rudolf Virchow Medical Society, 7 May 1956), *Proceedings of the Rudolf Virchow Medical Society*, 1956, *15:* 34–48; reprinted in *Perspectives in Biology and Medicine*, 1957, *1:* 105–118.

17. ———, "Social Forces and the Neurotic Process," in Alexander H. Leighton, ed., *Explorations in Social Psychiatry* (New York, Basic Books, Inc., 1957), p. 452.

18. ———, "Neurotic Distortion of the Creative Process" (Porter Lectures, series 22; Lawrence, University of Kansas Press, 1958), p. 151.

19. ———, *The Disintegrating Impact of "Modern" Life on the Family in America; and Its Explosive Repercussions* (in press).